Dedicated to my ever smiling son, Kayshaun

Thanks

First, I need to give thanks to my lifeline Jesus Christ. Without Him I am nothing.

To all those who have prayed...you have kept me encouraged and shining bright.

To my amazing friends, and people who have inspired me along my way, thank you for being on this journey with me, it has been a blessing.

Thank you to the creative community programs that believed in me and nurtured me.

Thank you Kaykay for saving my life and giving me a reason to smile everyday.

God bless everyone, stay in peace and fight for freedom.

Content Warning

This book contains graphic language, descriptions of rape, sexual assault, suicidal ideation and trauma. Some may find the content in this book sensitive or triggering. Please take care of yourself while reading my story. If you need to talk to someone you can connect to the services below:

http://www.stopvaw.org/
http://www.vawlearningnetwork.ca/
http://www.wavaw.ca/

Women Against Violence Against Women
1-877-392-7583

Canada Suicide Crisis Number
1-833-456-4566 available 24/7

Ontario: Assaulted Women's Helpline:
1-866-863-0511

Contents

Use the legend below to understand how to read different parts of this memoir.

Legend

(shaded box)	Facebook Conversations/Messages
(outlined box)	Facebook Post/Status
To Kate: Dear, friend	Emails

Preface

One of the most admirable human qualities, in my opinion, is resilience.

Especially, resilience in the face of the most difficult experiences. Cola personifies this. When faced with what could possibly be the worst pain a parent can experience, losing a child, Cola accepted the challenge of piecing together what life could look like after such tremendous loss.

To watch her now, more than just surviving but thriving, is to see motivation at the highest level.

Overcoming adversity is one of life's biggest and most important tests of character. Being the poetry in motion that she is, Cola provides a shining example of what life looks like after facing the most debilitating odds.

This book represents what true optimism and resilience looks like. We can all learn from the experiences she so selflessly shares with us. Thank you Cola!

Solitair

Solitair
Canadian rapper and producer, Toronto, Ontario
@solitairmusic

Part One

Love is Cold

The one who does not love has not become acquainted with God [does not and never did know Him], for God is love. [He is the originator of love, and it is an enduring attribute of His nature.]
1 JOHN 4:8

CHAPTER ONE

Cola

All the men of my council hate me; Those I love have turned against me.
-Job 19 :19

Do you know what it feels like to be raped? I do. Do you know how it feels to think a man is really interested in you, only to be tricked? I do. I was a thick chick. A Christian girl. The daughter of a Pastor, but I had very low self-esteem. I think I was a bit too sheltered as a child. Wasn't allowed to take part in certain types of things because of my parents' beliefs. School dances were not a place my parents let me go. I began lying in grade seven so that I could feel like I belonged. I wanted to belong. I was a thick chick; and in my class of skinny girls, I didn't feel like I fit in at all. None of the guys would look my way and I blamed myself. My weight. At 12 years old I started starving myself to look thinner. Nothing seemed to work. I wasn't getting the attention that I wanted.

"Be careful what you wish for" ... is a saying I should have paid more attention to. May 2003, I was in grade eight and I was 14 at the time. A group of guys noticed me. A group of guys raped me. They took my virginity and left me with scars. I've lived this long to be able to share my story. This is Cola's story. This is me.

Fumes were everywhere. The fumes from the different hair sprays were giving me a headache as I sat and waited for my aunt to start my hair. The salon was noisy - tv playing, loud chatter from the barbershop, hair dryers going off. It was overwhelming. We had been waiting for hours; since we were family it meant we got our hair done after all other appointments. I should be used to it by now but today I just couldn't take it. I was forced to leave the shop in search of fresh air to clear my head. Outside the sun shined and the air was so refreshing. I walked to the convenience store-two stores down from the shop and passed a group of men standing around. One man looked at me and smiled, I smiled back and then disappeared into the store to buy a patty. As soon as I left that convenience store he tried to strike up a conversation with me.

Although my mother often said not to talk to strangers, I was flattered by his interest and figured it was harmless. A little chat was completely innocent, right? He asked me my name, my age I said"14", where I lived and said, "You're beautiful, you don't look your age". I was wearing a denim skirt with a split in the front, a purple vest with a white shirt underneath. I didn't think nothing of my outfit, but his comment made me feel kinda special. He smiled, things felt less awkward. He seemed cool, charming and actually interested. Told me his name was Kwams, he was 18 and lived in the area. The shop was boring, my head was hurting, and I was enjoying the fresh air. He asked if I wanted to go for a walk to the park up the street. *Sure, why not?* As I began to walk another guy walked up beside me. *Wait, who's this guy? Where's Kwams?* I recognized this new guy from the group.

"Hey, I'm Ben, I know you were jus talking to my friend Kwams, but I'd really like to chill with you instead if that's cool. You have such a cute face and you look good." "Thank you" *He's tall, cute, light skin...* "Ok I just gotta let my aunty know that I'm going for a walk." I walked back to the shop to let her know then left with Ben. We managed to keep a conversation going as we walked up the street to the park. Age, relationship status, name - but my head was hurting too much to focus on the details of the conversation. All I heard was he's single and all he heard was that I was a pastor's daughter. The fresh air was good for me, for the first time that day I felt my headache slowly lifting. He said, "Most pastor's daughters are freaks". I replied, "Maybe so, but that ain't me." I was a virgin. I hadn't done anything sexual. We finally came to a stop at a more secluded area of the park, closer to my aunt's shop. He asked for my number. I gave it. Then he started to tease me about being such an innocent Christian girl. "You need to live a lil girl, what do you do for fun, just church? You need to experience some fun for a change".

I wasn't sure what he meant so I asked "What kinda fun?" He says, "Have you ever given brains before?" "No, what's that?". "I can show you, do you wanna try it?" "No". "Why not? You don't know what it is, just try it...please?" "I wanna leave now" "I'll bring you back once you do what I asked you to do. Just try it, I know you'll like it". "Can we leave please?" "Just try it once...once and I'll bring you back I promise." So, I began. *Girl jus run. I don't even know where I am.* Don't got no clue why I didn't just run away. I stayed. He tried to coach me through it. *This feels so wrong. I don't like this.* Frustrated, I stopped. We was in a public place and people were coming our way. *My saving grace! How could you have done something like that? That was so awful, I never wanna do that again!* I wasn't even clear that I was giving oral sex. Probably from the lack of sex education I received. All I know is I needed to get back to my family.

We left the park and headed back towards the shop, just like he said. No harm done, right? I checked in with my aunt and then we left again. This time we walked to a deserted spot where he led me down a set of stairs. *Why did you leave again? This don't feel right.* Don't know what made me think that I should leave again. *Maybe he wants to talk more privately or maybe he wants to kiss you without people looking. He likes you. He called you beautiful and if it gets to be too much just tell him you wanna leave and he'll bring you back, just like before.*

He had me sit on the steps, then said he'd be back. *Peaceful. I wish my head would stop spinning.* Next thing I know there was a different man coming down the steps. I stood up to get a better look at him. He was caramel complexion, short, bald and wore sunglasses. Before I fully registered what exactly was going on his rough hands were all over me. *Where the hell did he come from? Who is he?* I didn't know who he was or where the hell he came from, but he handled me so roughly. He snatched up my skirt and pulled my g string to the side. *Ouch!* I heard it rip, but he kept going. I was so confused, but I managed to say who are you? Stop! He didn't say a word. *Seriously, where the hell did he come from?* Where's Ben? He pushed me against the wall and all I felt was the toughness of the concrete as my knees scratched against it. *Ouch!* I can't see anything with my face pushed against the hard surface. He had one hand on my back and one on my waist as he pulled me from the wall and pushed me into a bent over position. Instinctively my hand reaches out to the wall in front of me to brace my fall. *Why is this happening?* He seems to pause for a moment, I feel his dick against my ass, then... *Ahhh! Owww.* My thoughts are interrupted by the pain that followed. *Ahhhh, what is that?* He inserts it and begins to thrust with all his might. *Stop, please! This hurts, stop please,* I yelped in pain. I slipped and twisted my body while trying to stand to my feet. He pushed me back down, pulled me closer and thrust harder and harder. Each thrust left me even more nauseated. I couldn't take anymore. *I'm gonna be sick. Please just make it stop!* It felt like forever, but he finally stopped. I stood in the same spot shocked. I didn't even look to see if he left. *My bum hurts. My clothes are torn. What do I do?*

Before I could even muster up the strength to move, I heard another person come down the steps. I was already on the ground in pain when he unzipped his pants, took my head and put his dick inside my mouth. He held my head in place until he was done. I started choking when this warm liquid entered my mouth. *Ew!* I kept pushing my head around trying to get rid of it. I was finally able to spit it out once he moved his dick. By the time I looked up he was gone. My mind was drawing blanks on what to even do. No sooner after him was another man. Then another. Then another. One by one they all came for a piece of me. Maybe six, maybe more. Time stood still. *You need to leave.* I wanted to but instead I sat in the dirty corner hurt, busted up, bruised, unable to move. I was alone in this pit. My mouth and ass hurt. They hadn't entered me vaginally, but they penetrated my soul, leaving me at the bottom of some filthy stairs like nasty discarded garbage. I laid there confused and light headed. My mind betrayed me. It was off in fairytale land while my body lived the nightmare. *You need to leave.* My body wouldn't move. Somehow, I felt like I was watchin it all happen from a distance. *Get up!! Get up before the next one comes. C'mon get up!* Instead I sat there in a daze.

Next I know, Kwams appeared, he helped me get up and gently led me to sit with him on the stairs. *Finally, a familiar face.* He held my hand, lifted my head up and said "You're so beautiful" *I don't feel good.* "What if I asked you to be my girl?" I had no words. He started kissing my neck and my body melted back into the concrete. It didn't even feel rough anymore. The steps were cold but inviting and I saw the blue sky before my eyes closed. Once I opened my eyes I saw a group of men stood above me at the top of the stairs... To be honest, I didn't even flinch, I was frozen. They were watching.

I closed my eyes again as he moved from sitting next to me to gettin on top of me. *Is that his dick?* My lower body was losing feeling. This was a different kind of hurt. Unfamiliar. Tears fell as he pushed it in further. I felt numb an yet still felt his depth. I wasn't sure, but I heard "How do you like it baby, do you want me to stop?" I whispered yes! He continued. I closed my eyes again an the tears continued to pour. More and more my tears, they wouldn't stop. Somehow, I found the strength to say "stop!" louder than before. He continued. With everything I had left I begged. "Stop. Please just stop. I don't want to do this. Just stop. Please!" He let up. *Thank God.* I was sore. Everything was sore. He left. He said nothing to me. I heard his feet walking up the stairs. Once they were out of earshot I opened my eyes and noticed it was now dark. *Shoot, it's night time? How long have I been out here? Get up girl! Get up! You can do it. Get up!* I rolled onto my stomach and used the steps to brace my arms as I attempted to stand up.

I stumbled up the... the stairs while holding on the... the wall until both my feet had reached the top step. *Which wa-* ... Before I could look around or even fix my clothes two dark skinned men approached me. I move to the side and my way is blocked. One of them spoke and said, "I heard you can help us out, we wanna get our dicks sucked." I reply, "I need to get back to the barbershop, which way do

I go?" All I knew was that I was somewhere in Rexdale. I saw a grey building beside me, everything else was trees and grass. I didn't even get a chance to say anything else, they pulled me backwards, I pushed forward, in the end they won. They pulled me back down the steps. As I'm going down the stairs I see a group of men crowding the top of the steps. They stood in line with their backs facing us. *I'm trapped.* Again, they ask "Now will you give us brains?" "No" I purse my lips together and tried to clench my teeth. They pushed me over and one pushed his dick up against my lips. As I moved, he moved with me. The other guy took his dick and started slapping me with it. The other one joined. While they grabbed my hair and held my head straight they continued to slap my face with their dicks. *Ouch!* "Just do it and we'll let you go" *I just want this to be over.* They held my head until they both ejaculated. As soon as it was done, the men at the top of the stairs moved aside, unblocking the only exit. *I guess I can go now.* I can't explain the amount of hate I felt for myself. It was such a walk of shame up from the bottom of the stairs. I thought I'd never get to the top. I was met with many different faces as they crowded me. I was like food in a pig pen. Creepy photographers stealing the last piece of innocence and dignity I had left. Some of the men had asked for my number and refused to leave until they had it. I was left stunned and immobilized by their actions as they walked away, leaving me alone. *It's over.*

I looked around for anything familiar, but there was nothing - just the back of the building and those disgusting stairs. The darkness was eerily silent... My thoughts cut through any type of peace I tried to establish. *What now?* In the distance I saw a street light, so I walked towards it. Once there, I looked both ways and saw a main road to the left. As I walked away from the street light, I noticed two cars in a parking lot at the front of this building surrounded by groups of men. *Lord please don't tell me all of those guys were with me. No! No! Can't be. Think! Think! Dammit why can't you remember.* I stood frozen in fear as one of the men walked towards me. *Run. Run. Why won't you move? The* closer he got, the more numb my body felt. I coulda fainted if I wasn't so worried that I might not even wake up. *Girl it's Kwams.* "Hey baby you good?" *Say something.* I could feel my heart in my chest, no words came out. "Do you remember how old I told you I was?" "18" I said. "No, I'm 24" *What? Omg, I'm fourteen. Ew that's so gross. Fix your face.* "I would love to make you my girl and take you out, can I get your number" "It's long distance" "That's ok, I don't mind...jus for you." *Shit.*

Physically I was present but absent in mind. My mind deserted me and fled to another place. Somewhere where I could deny everything that was happening. I did say no. I tried to say no. There were so many of them; the nightmare never stopped. If only I knew where I was or how to get back to the shop. What the hell do I do now?

I gave him my number and asked him "How do I get back?" He pointed across the street and walked away. I could hear the cars screeching away but I kept my head in the direction of the plaza across the street. *The whole time I was merely steps away.* I was relieved to be free but scared to go back. *What do I say? This is so embarrassing. I don't even wanna face her.* It seemed to take forever to cross the street as I dreaded facing my aunt. There was a chubby man at the corner smoking and eyeing me. He smiled as I passed him and whispered, "Can I get your number too?" *Why would he ask me that? What does he know? Ew he's so old though.* "No" I replied as I kept walking. I barely made it in the door before my aunt let loose. She was so angry. I was so scared. *Say something.* I had no immediate explanation. "You've been missing for 3 hours, where have you been, I was about to call the cops." "I went for a walk" "FOR THREE HOURS?" I gave no other explanation.

From the looks and smiles I was getting from the men who worked in the shop, it would seem as if they knew. *Why didn't they help me?* As I sat quietly in the chair one of the men who sat directly across from me had signaled for me to open my legs to give him a glimpse. One of the other barbers tried to sneak and ask for my phone number. He whispered, "I'd been watching you for a while and I want to take you out." The only one who knew nothing was my aunt and me? I played my best role yet; I pretended that I wasn't bothered by anything. *Take this to your grave. Say nothing. No turning back now.*

It should come as no surprise that I was banned from my aunt's shop since my disappearing act. My parents questioned the heck outta me, but I never snitched. *They can never find out. What would they say?* I was terrified of my parents finding out what happened. Their questions were the least of my worries, I had to figure out a way to act as normal as possible since I couldn't sit properly. I was so sore. I had flashbacks as I saw the bruises, but the pain kept me from remembering most of what happened. When I showered, I was disgusted. I was scared to scrub my own body. *How do I look at myself and not hate what I see? You should've done more to get away. I hate you.* I cried when I slept and smiled when I awoke. *Just act normal. It's over.*

Two weeks after the incident, my life changed. My phone rang, and it was Kwams. "What's this I hear about you snitching and telling the cops you were raped?" He sounded angry. *Shit, I didn't say anything.* "No, I don't know anything about cops, I'm not going to say anything." "Betta not cause nobody raped you" Click. *Omg who said something, where did he hear this? This can't be happening. No, no, no, no, no.* He had me shook. Within a few days, my parents called me into their room. I had barely woken up and there were a bunch of questions coming from every direction. "What happened that day?" "What day?" "That day you went missing for three hours" I was frozen in step. "Nothing" I tried to return to my room and said "I gotta get ready for school" "You're not going to school until we know what happened" My father said. "Please I just want to go to school" I began to cry. *Please make it go away.* But it didn't. Both my parents walked me down the stairs, I was forced to sit around the kitchen table while my parents explained what they heard. Apparently one of my aunt's clients overheard two men braggin about having sex and gettin brains from some chick from Oshawa. So, my aunt told my grandmother who then told my parents. They speculated that I was raped but wanted to know the truth from me. *I would rather die of shame than confess anything.* I sat and cried in silence. *I just want to be at school. I can't believe this is happening. Just leave it alone. Please.* I felt the sting from the belt that whipped across my arms. *Ahh.* I couldn't hear my own voice. My mouth was opened, and the cries were lost in translation as my ears adjusted to the anger of my father's voice: "Tell me what happened. Let's go Nicola" "Daaadddyy" "No, tell me what happened." I said nothing. I hung my head in shame. I felt the sting of the belt once more. "Let's go, tell me what happened" I couldn't stop crying. In this moment, even my own thoughts abandoned me.

I wanted to crawl into a hole and die. If the earth swallowed me up I would not have been mad. *God Please.* I couldn't stop crying as my parents had me get dressed. My body hurt in so many places it was insane. I found myself at the police station waiting to speak to an officer. A female officer walked in. She spent some time asking me what happened, but I still couldn't talk. If anything, I was more scared now than before. I cried harder. The tears wouldn't stop. I could barely look at the officer, I kept my head in my hands. To break the silence the officer said "You know the age of consent is 14, right? If you don't tell us what happened there is nothing we can do for you." *Age of consent?* The officer informed me that the age of consent was the age where I could decide whether to have sex or not and no one would get charged. *So, if I say I did it, then I can go home. I don't wanna deal with any of this.* "I wasn't raped. I did this all by myself." *Could this get any worse?* With my confession, the cop walked out of the room. I overheard her say to my parents "There's nothing we can do if she doesn't want to talk." With that, we left. *Home time?*

I was then brought to the hospital where we waited hours to get checked out by a doctor. I felt like a zombie. My mind was clouded and I was going through the motions. Even though my mother was next to me, her angry voice was distant, it sounded far away. I couldn't recognize all the words but her tone said it all. I was terrified, yet Mother was so angry. Once I put the gown on, the reality of everything really hit. *This is happening. You can't get away.* I was aware of everything, including my body. *I don't want them to see me.* Being partially naked felt so demeaning. *I don't wanna be here. Why do I have to do this now?* My mind wanted to dream but I was forced to stay present in order to get the STD check. Before I could think, I blurted out "I don't want to be here." My mother responded, "When you decide to make adult decisions then you need to live with the consequences". *Well that was rude.* I was crushed but sucked it up. The nurse called me into a separate room and I was grateful I could leave my mom behind. "How long ago did this incident take place?" the nurse asked as she prepared to do the physical exam. "A couple weeks ago." I replied. I think she could sense I wanted to leave. It was clear my mom was angry and forced me to be here. I answered the nurse's questions without any enthusiasm. "Was a condom used?" "Yes" I lied. I wasn't sure. I remember there were condoms, but I don't know if they were used at all or if they were used every time. "Well ok if there was a condom used then you don't need to take this test" the nurse said. "Ok well thanks, bye." Once the nurse left the room I threw on my clothes and rushed out. As I walked up to my mother I hear her ask "What did she say." I responded "Nothing". Finally, we were able to go home. As we drove home I overheard my mother say to my father "Is there a group home we can send her to?" *I guess she doesn't want me no more. Guess I'm too much of an embarrassment for her.* What does this make me now? A disobedient child. A.... a.... a whore? *I wish she understood what was going on. I wish I understood what was going on.*

Poetic Interlude

Born into a family of two
A little girl struggles an wonders what to do
Cause see her folks be workin hard
Tryna get that money right
While she ends up all alone night after night
They don't see the pain an anguish they cause.
Too busy preachin the gospel an followin bible laws
Picked on an tease this little girl can't understand
Why God would allow her to be placed on this cruel land
full of hatred and trouble.
This girl was double in size
And no one realize the sadness in her eyes
Her parents were too busy for love so she found it
somewhere else
A group of guys all different size came and ripped open her
thighs and took somethin she'll never get back
Thought it was love but it wasn't
Love couldn't be so cold
But how would she know
She was only 14 years old
Never had the courage to stand up an be bold
An tell the truth
It was rape
Like blinds hidden behind a drape
The secret of this encounter would remain taped up and
silence
Silently her tears fell wondering why she never said a thing
Her experience was for her knowledge only
But when the truth came out it only left her lonely
Her mother never understood and wanted to send her
away
But her father seemed to love her enough to let her stay
love what a funny word to be said
Cause this so called love
makes me wish I were dead.

CHAPTER TWO

Repercussion

Dear friends, let us continue to love one another, for love comes from God. Anyone who loves is a child of God and knows God. But anyone who does not love does not know God, for God is love.
1 John 4:7-8

Have you ever had a friend who you thought you could trust and tell your secrets to? I did. *You said you wouldn't say nun. You can trust her, she's your best friend.* Aaliyah was the first person to know my secret. In the girl's bathroom at school. She didn't have much to say or even know what to say, but it felt ok telling her. She didn't look at me weird and she still wanted to be friends. It made me feel like maybe other people would understand the truth. Maybe I wasn't an outcast. Maybe I should just tell the truth. I made her promise not to say anything and she didn't. We never really spoke about it again, instead we talked about our upcoming grade eight graduation. My parents trusted me when I'd visit Aaliyah's house, sometimes Aaliyah and I would go over to Nia's and the three of us would hang out there. We all lived in the same small town, so I was close, but it would still take me about 30 mins to walk to their homes. Both Aaliyah and I were French immersion students while Nia was an English student. We had different classes but still hung out during breaks. I had a huge crush on Nia's older brother Curtis, who also went to the same school. I think he thought I was some young groupie and didn't really take me serious so I aimed to just be his friend. *Better than nothing. Kinda like in the movie Love and Basketball.* Nia and I were cool, the more I hung out there, the more I got to meet the rest of her family, including her step sister and brother. When she would invite me over to chill, I gladly accepted and always hoped there was a chance I would get to see Curtis. As we spent more time hanging and gettin to know each other we became close. Close enough that I felt safe to tell him my story. *Aaliyah understood, maybe he'll get it too.*

One day Curtis had asked if he could come over and since I was home alone I figured why not? *This could be cool. He ain't neva been ova here.* When Curtis showed up, he was with a couple of other guys. Despite not knowing them all, I didn't wanna look lame so I let them in. They had barely made it in my house when one of the guys said he wanted a tour of my house. He was tall, thick, had really big arms and a beard to match. I gave them all a quick tour, but the tall thick one was the only one to follow me upstairs. Once he entered my room he closed the door. While blocking the door he said, "I heard you give brains, can I get some?" "Naw" I refused. The more he asked the more I refused. I stood in front of him at the door trying to pull him away so that I could leave. When I wasn't bargaining to leave my room, I was staring out the window watching to see if my parents were back from Bible study. *Please come back.* They didn't. I was nervous about gettin caught yet I wished that they could save me. *Punishment or entrapment.*

I felt hands on my body as he picked me up and threw me on my bed. He was done playing around. He held me down by my chest and said "You ain't leaving your room until I get something out of this" The luxury of refusals had passed. *What can I do?* I attempted to give him brains but it felt so wrong. *I can't do this.* I felt so out of place. Frustrated by me he finally left. From my room I heard the front door close. I walked downstairs to find no one around. *Ok at least that's over.* Overwhelmed and hungry I walked to my fridge to get something to eat. As I opened the fridge door, I saw syrup poured all over everything. Curtis and his friends had taken my bottle of syrup and made sure it was on every fruit, drawer and container in my fridge. I bawled as I hurried to clean the mess before my parents came home. *I deserved it, right?*

To add to my nightmare, Curtis and his friends seemed more than happy to spread the word of what they assumed had happened. When I walked down the street I would hear snickering and laughter. *Why they keep laughin?* I confronted one of the girls and she says, "You're the town hoe and everybody knows it". *Ughhh I hate them.*

Despite my hate for Curtis, I didn't let it change my friendship with his sister. Whenever I was at her house I spent most time hanging in her room until I got to know her step brother Samuel. Samuel would visit on weekends. He was dark skinned and a lil thick. He was no Shemar Moore. Definitely not but he seemed cool. We would all hang out, but Samuel was relentless in cracking jokes about me and Nia. It was harmless at first, then it seemed as if he was going out of his way to make me feel horrible. My self-esteem took a beating when he was around cause he would pick on my weight. Besides name calling he would ruin my things. One day he took a bat and beat the lights on my bike because he said my bike was ugly. Another time he put a stick in my bike wheel as I rode away. It was always something with him. Just to get a reaction outta me.

One day everything changed and Samuel stopped making fun of me. He...he stopped making fun of my weight. Now my thick body and sexy curves intrigued him. My big lips and brown eyes turned him on. He looked at me differently, he touched me in a different way. He was nice to me. *Finally, ...guess he's growing up.* When he asked me to be his girlfriend I was surprised. *Really? Me? He really sees me like that?* It was cool because there weren't any guys at my school who I liked and who liked me back. The only thing was that we wanted to keep things on the DL (down low) to avoid awkward moments. I liked feeling that a man really truly was capable of caring about me, even if I was thick. *This was some messed up thinking. This man made fun of you and now you ready to be his girl and jus ignore everything.* I just wanted to belong and feel important to someone. Anyone.

Keeping things on the DL was challenging for me cause when it was just us, he was really caring. Very touchy feely, always trying to kiss me. *Aw!* Around the rest of people, we had to pretend there was no interest. Yet there was still something thrilling about dating in secret. I was cool with him touching me and kissing me, then he wanted to have sex with me and I tried to want it as well. He never forced me, he took his time. As he kissed me he would whisper in my ear "You're so beautiful, I love spending time with you." I slowly allowed myself to enjoy him. *Girl this is your man, relax, open up, he don't bite...only sometimes but you like it.* The rapes didn't turn me off from sex, it just made me afraid to trust. Sex took on a different meaning for me. It wasn't emotional, it was jus something to do. Sex went from something scary and painful to exciting and pleasurable. Things between us was great until he asked me about the rape. *What? How'd he know about that?* I never spoke about the rape with him. The only person in their family that knew was Curtis, not even Nia knew. *So that's why he started liking me? Because he knew I wasn't a virgin? He knew this whole time? Shit! I feel like such a fool.* Just when I was starting to trust him. I had been sold out from one brother to another.

It was more apparent now that Samuel's interest in me wasn't anything special. He just wanted to get a piece of me like he heard others had. People I thought were my friends... my man.... were all just fakes. *Fuck em.* Fake ass people who pretended to my face, who tried to fool me. They all set me up, but it's my fault cause I'm the one who fell for it all. But that would never happen again. *Never. Friends fade but family is forever.* Through everything your family always has your back, a lie? Definitely a lie.

While I had hoped for a peaceful summer, the reality was far from it. As my parents were still trying to cope with the disgrace, the rest of my family did their best to alienate me - except one. My grandma, my great grandma, my aunty from the shop and her two kids, and my other aunt and her four kids, and her boyfriend all lived at my grandma's house. I begged my parents to let me stay home when they visited my grandma's house so I wouldn't be forced to endure the embarrassment, yet they weren't interested in sparing me from the horrors of my family. Maybe they didn't know how bad it was. When I would visit, I sat alone in the living room and would hear my cousins outside the door making comments... "What does it feel like to suck a buddy?" "Who does that?" "That's nasty" "What a hoe". When I was home they would text my phone, they would call me, email me, leave comments on social media. It was nonstop. "You're a two-cent hoe" "Dirty Bitch" Fat Bitch" "Gross" "Slut" "Ugly" "Dick Sucker". My family, my cousins; I guess blood relations don't matter. After sifting through the comments for a bit I decided to sit outside. I isolated myself so that I didn't have to be the family joke. At the time, the only person who could stand me, besides my grandma, was my aunt's boyfriend. He would sit on the porch outside with me and talk. I felt human again. I felt like someone saw through the pain and was able to treat me like a normal person. When it seemed like my fake friends and family gave up on me, aside from my best friend Aaliyah, he was someone to talk to. He seemed to understand me at first. Told me not to let it get to me. To ignore it. It would blow over. It was the only moment of peace I got and when my cousins came to the door he would tell them to leave me alone. In a way he protected me. He was older and much wiser. When we would talk about the rape, I felt like he was implying something I was missing. While we sat outside one day, as his friends were cleaning a car he told me his friend was interested in me. His friend was at least in his late 30's and he asked what I thought about his friend liking me and if I'd be interested as well. I felt uncomfortable, so I went inside. I wish I could say it ended there. Apparently, a pretty young thick thing like me drives some old men crazy.

Poetic Interlude

They say stick and stones
But their words won't leave me alone
Penetrating deeper than the dicks that violated me
Bitch
Shaming me into silence
Whore
I cry invisible bloody tears
Dick sucker
Dear diary
Disgusting
Am I really such a horrible person?
Fat slut
If so, why am I here?
Gross
My beauty is no more
Ugly
More than once I didnt think I would make it
Two cent hoe
Is there a future for me?
Is there someone who will save me?
What about all those fairy tales I used to hear about?
Are they all fake?
I need a happy ending
And quickly
Times fading
They all hate me
I can't breathe
Less than human is how they treat me
Can you see me?
Until you care to save me
I'll be here under water
I won't bother holding my breath

CHAPTER THREE

The Aftermath

Return, O LORD, rescue my soul; Save me because of Your [unfailing] steadfast love and mercy.
-Psalm 6:4,

So, I kinda just threw y'all into the mix of things without proper introduction. My name is Nicola Jovita Audriana Bennett. Each name has a meaning that defines who I am as an individual. Nicola means victory of the people. Jovita means joy. Audriana is a combination of two common names, Audrey which means noble strength and Anna which means full of grace. Then there is my last name Bennett which means little blessed one. This is me. And I am a phat chick. P.H.A.T. Pretty Hot and Tempting. I stand at an incredible 5'3 and I currently weigh 268 pounds. I know 268 sounds like a big girl, right? I have curves and a bum that'll make many girls jealous for years to come. I have pretty dark brown eyes that I should be proud of, but I wear colored contacts simply to attract attention. I was so consumed with other people's thoughts about me that I never took the time to deal with my own issues. I even used different online quizzes to tell me bout myself. For the most part they were usually wrong but this quiz "What type of lady are you" really caught my interest. It said:

> "I am lovely and caring. I help others and I spread out a lot of sympathy. My weakness is that I forget about myself, and my own needs. All my time is held back for my family and friends. I am always there for people in trouble. Ready for an emergency. I make a lot of sacrifices just to be a good human being. But every woman has her needs, her longing and her destiny. I must not lose myself in the work of caring for other people's souls. I have my own problems in my life."

This made so much sense to me. I often give a lot of myself and rarely stick up for myself. At this moment, it felt like all people did was trample on my soul, but I didn't want that to make me cold-hearted; so, I needed to find a balance between prioritizing my needs while still helping others. These quizzes allowed me to grow in so many different ways cause it created an understanding of my own strengths and weaknesses. I was obsessed with online quizzes, perhaps like many teens.

Lemme take y'all back to my childhood before the rape, back when life was great. I was born to two loving CHRISTIAN parents. Now I stress Christian parents because growing up with Christian parents seemed different than growing up with non-Christian parents. I had a lot of rules to follow, more rules than my friends, most times I didn't even understand the reason a lot of those rules were put in place.

So, March 3rd, 1989 this six pounds and three ounce beautiful baby girl was born. Three years later...muh lil sista was born. Gosh!!! Even though my sister and I were three years apart, swear sey yu culd neva tell. As we grew muh lil sista and I had the same curfew and the same rules applied to the both of us. By the time I hit my pre-teens, not much had even changed. No phone calls after nine and I had to be in the house. Understandable that my parents both worked nights and needed undisturbed sleep before work, but it seemed excessive. So, I got smarter. I knew that on certain days my parents both left the house around 10:30 pm. I would act like I was sleeping until I heard the front door close, or I would set an alarm to wake up for that time. Either way all of this was jus so I could talk to my friends. Some nights I stayed up till 1 or even 2 in the morning and still managed to wake up for school and play everything like it was all cool. *Ha! Pretty slick eh!*

Now to clarify things a lil, having Christian parents wasn't bad at all. I gained knowledge about God and learned about protection from the destructiveness of the devil. To be honest it really depends on what type of Christian parents a child is raised with. See...I, I was the daughter of a pastor, the assistant pastor of the church we attended. Growing up in church and being the daughter of a pastor meant that there was a certain image to be upheld and anything that strayed from that image was highly looked down upon. Being a pastor's daughter meant I had to play the role of the good little girl who always obeyed. It was made clear that people would always be judging so we had to conduct ourselves in the highest manner. I was the child who sang in choirs, who represented the church when we went to church fundraiser rallies. Since we belonged to the Church of God organization we had different churches in our district that would send representatives to sing while the host would try and collect money for each item. Sometimes it was loads of fun, and other times it would run your pockets broke. Since I was the little golden child with straight A's in school who could sing, I was chosen as the child to represent my church.

I loved it at first because I got to sing with my mom. My parents were so busy in the life of ministry that it felt like I barely got to see them. They were doing great work in church while also working full time. Their dedication to us allowed my sister and I to be involved in a lot of different recreational activities. Church and singing were the only things I had in common with my mom. Unfortunately, after a few years the church split and instead of being really involved, we now just attended and my chances to sing with my mom were over. We were all never really the same.

Self-Reflection

Being a Christian in my family meant: no ungodly music, no piercings, no tattoos, no school dances, nothing that God would be upset with. I learnt that my body was a temple unto God and having tattoos and piercings would be displeasing to Him. Some might say "It's natural, my parents never let me do any of those either and they weren't even Christian, so what's the problem?" My parents never really ever gave me a good explanation of why I wasn't allowed to do certain things. I just knew that it had something to do with displeasing God. Ever not be allowed to participate in Halloween or miss certain events because there was a program planned at church? I wasn't allowed to go anywhere, to explore anything, and my parents were either at work during the night or sleeping during the day or doing work for church. I felt as if I wasn't as important as work or church. Like really truly I'm not tryna make my parents out to be these bad parents because they're not, they're actually pretty great; they worked hard to be able to provide an incredible life for us. We did so many different activities such as piano lessons, roller skating, ice skating, art classes, and swimming lessons. Just about everything imaginable to keep us busy. I understood it must have taken a toll on them to do this sometimes three, four times a week only to get minimal sleep but there wasn't any real time for us to spend together. The older I grew, the less time we spent as a family and it hurt, deeper than I ever would have imagined. Watching tv would upset me when I saw tv family relationships. I felt like we were a wannabe family. We wanted to be tight, but we were so far from it, it wasn't even funny. My parents were not the easiest people to talk to. I always felt like I would be judged or that they just didn't make much of an effort to understand me. So, I kept my distance. Any problems I had, I dealt with it on my own. I learned to hide my feelings for as long as I possibly could. I learned to just deal with life, because more times even if my parents could understand, there was never any time.

I always dreamt that when I had a child I would try more to be involved with him. I would be his best friend, but still remain his mother. I would spend the extra time to show him how much I really cared. If anything ever happened I wanted my child to trust me and not be afraid to talk to me. I would never judge or push him away. He would be my child. My baby. My best friend. I always wanted a son. Don't know why but when I have my first child I would want him to be a boy. This sounded so easy, but I knew nothing about raising a child; I just knew what it was like to be one.

Throughout my childhood, besides dealing with the fact that I was a lil bit chubbier than everyone else in my class, I was teased not only by classmates but also by family. By grade six we had moved further east and it sucked even more because even though I was at a new school, the problems were still the same - I was still teased about my weight. The only good thing was meeting Aaliyah. I moved from a classroom that had a few black kids to a classroom with only one mixed girl. We became friends because it made sense, but it grew into so much more. We both loved to sing together and we both came from Christian homes. Aaliyah was the greatest friend I could ever have. Real talks. Wallah.

I had this theory that if I was real nice to everybody then they would look past my weight. It worked somewhat but I couldn't shake the thought people were always judging me. Laughing at me. I didn't eat at lunch time so that they couldn't make fun of what I ate, then at dinner time I ate a good meal. This continued until my teacher threatened to tell my parents. I tried to be good at sports so that my classmates wouldn't think I was too fat or too lazy to run. I never lost any real weight though. Guys I had a crush on were not interested in me. I was a thick black girl in an all-white school. I had two strikes against me. It hurt. I would sneak into the school dances in hopes that some guy would come and dance with me. It never happened, and I always cried. All of my other classmates got to dance with boys, even Aaliyah but she was tall and beautiful with "nicely tanned skin". I just wanted that same kind of affection too, but it never came. It leads me to believe that the obvious was true, despite how nice I was my weight and race were getting in the way. But what else was I supposed to do? I needed something to fill a void.

CHAPTER FOUR

Grade 9

They have repaid me evil for good, And hatred for my love.
-Psalm 109 :5

He touched me. I didn't even realize at first what was happening. A bump here and there. He brushed past me a couple times. What was I to think? That's my aunty's boyfriend. Uncle. In the kitchen, he would come up behind me and he would slap my ass. He would whisper in passing "You're so beautiful, I like how thick you are." He mostly touched me if no one else was around. A few times he was brave and would brush past me with someone in the kitchen or he would stand behind me when I looked in the fridge and pretended he was looking too. I had no one to tell but then it got so bad that I had to finally tell Aaliyah and this guy I was chillin with at the time. They both urged me to say something, but I felt trapped. The quieter I stayed the bolder he got. I was waiting to use the upstairs bathroom in my grandma's house and as soon as he opened the door and saw me, he pulled me into the bathroom with him. I couldn't make a sound because my family was all there, and he told me to keep quiet. *It must be something that I'm doing to make him want me.* He pushed me down on the counter with one hand while his next hand was up my skirt. He fingered me. I kept moving around trying to push his hand away without making noise. It seemed that the harder I pushed the harder he pushed back. He never took his eyes off me once. He smiled at my reaction. I was in such an awkward position as he played in my pussy. I thought for sure he was gonna rape me. Maybe he would have, but I heard footsteps and he let go. I jumped down and I hit him. "Leave me alone. Do not touch me." He gave me the creepiest smile as he waved his fingers at me. I wanted to say something but how? To who? Who would believe me? He knew it too cause he would tell me "No one would believe you" *Your family already sees you as a whore. Just be more aware when he's around.*

Even when I was aware of his presence around me, it didn't matter. He didn't care. During another visit to my grandma's house I took a nap on the couch only to awake and see my breast cupped in his hand with his tongue on my nipple. *What the fuck?* I freaked. My great grandma was in the house, so he did his best to keep me quiet. He dragged me from the living room all the way up to the bedroom where he unzipped his pants and offered me fifty bucks to suck his dick. *This is not ok. What can I do? This is not ok.* I felt so alienated. *Why the fuck me?* I refused the money. He said, "One day I'm gonna come for you and take you to a hotel." *Omg no. No. Please, no.* He said "I wanna give you more money but your aunty handles the bills and she would know if more money was missing" *I didn't want your dirty money anyway.* I tried to beg my parents to stay home but they didn't trust to leave me alone. Whenever I went down to my aunt's house I tried everything to never be caught alone. When he touched me, I would hit back or move. He would walk past me and whisper in my ear "Mean". He caught me alone one time and said, "Why are you being so mean to me?" *Mean? What the fuck nigga, you expect me to be nice? You crazy right?* This was a 45 year old man. The more I rejected him, the more he smiled, the more he pushed, the more he demanded. He put $10 in my bra one time. I hid it from my parents. I didn't want it but then thought I could use it as evidence against him. The damn thought of that money from him disgusted me, so I spent it just to get rid of it. *How do I make it stop?*

I did my best to manage that situation, but my mind was focused on starting high school. Brand new year, brand new school, brand new people. I found my people when I started high school, Aaliyah and I weren't the only black kids anymore. I got a whole new friend group, different grades but we understood each other. We hung out all the time. There was always someone from the group to chill with, it was a big group, ten people or so.

For once in my life I finally felt like I fit in. There were actually people who shared the same interests as me. After all those years of attending school with majority white kids, high school was a major change. I mean don't get me wrong, I'm not saying that I can't go to school with white kids or nun, but we always got into fights over rap vs. rock, or I always had some white kid tryna imitate being "black". They would say "wassup my wigger". So infuriating. I'm proud to be black, and I didn't need some white kids tormenting me about it. I'm sure they were genuinely curious, but every time February would come around I always had to deal with constant questions such as, since there is BET (Black Entertainment Television), why isn't there a WET (White Entertainment Television)? My response was usually the same, "Are you kidding me? *Y'all get every other station and channel, why can't my people have one station out of many for ourselves?"* These conversations usually ended up in a losing battle, mainly cause they outnumbered me. A million white kids and just me. So, you can imagine how ecstatic I was when I entered high school and saw the group of black people standing in front of the school. February was the best month because of the black history assembly. As a group we got to showcase our talent with dances, raps, monologues, anything creative to pay homage to our ancestors. Ain't nun more exciting. It was cute to see the guys practicing their dances in the hallway. I was still learning everyone's name, but I recognized one of the dancers from my bus.

He was this fiiiinnneee brotha but unfortunately, he had a girl. Somehow a rumor got spread that I thought I could take him from his girl. I dunno who made that up. By the time fourth period came around, while I was walking down the hallway this white girl was getting all up in my face wanting to know why I was sayin I would take her man. *Who said I wanted your man like that? This chic is scary.* Lucky for me a black girl came outta nowhere to sort things out calmly. T*hank God she had my back. I've never had to fight and am not in the mood to start.* I later found out her name was Nicola too. From that day on I stuck to that girl like glue. It's always weird to meet someone with the same name as you. She was a couple years older but also hung out with the crew, so I had seen her before but never talked to her.

Nicola was also bilingual. We didn't have classes together but could swap stories about teachers. We bonded. I felt more comfortable hanging out with the older kids cause my classmates were kids and I didn't feel like a kid. Definitely didn't see anyone my type at my high school, so I started talking to guys online which is how I met my first boyfriend.

The internet. It could be your best friend or worst enemy. Connect you with someone halfway across the world who you may never meet, or it lets you chat with your sister in the next room. People could create fantasies of who they really were or who they wished to be. It was an opportunity for lies. Deception. Betrayal. Imagination. A clean slate. I was the girl that sat at a computer creating profiles while tryna hide the image of the hoe that so many people around me believed I was. Curtis and Samuel really ruined things for me. *Hate them soo much.* I no longer felt safe with the people around me. So, I put my trust into those who knew nothing about me. I was running away from real life. I believed that because I was on the internet nobody could find my past. I was so consumed with the thoughts of what other people thought about me, mainly men, that I made myself believe that staying on the internet was way better than meeting people in person so that they couldn't judge me. I was tired of being judged. I was tired of never being good enough and I really just wanted someone to give me a real fair chance. That's when I was introduced to Blackplanet.

Memba blackplanet? Blackplanet was here before tdot wire and tinder, blackplanet was the black version of MySpace, and it was here first. Back then almost every race had their own type of page. Laugh out loud, there was a Latino site, an Asian site. Talk about segregation. I member taking slack from a lot of the white kids I went to school with. They was feeling like me having a blackplanet page was dumb because they felt as if they wouldn't be welcomed on such a site. This is the kinda shit I grew up with. Oh racism! Whatever, I kept it anyways. Back then I was like a computer whiz, I knew almost everything about computers. I spent hours perfecting my web page, finding hidden links and everything.

I had to put up a profile pic but I hated taking pictures. I realize now that I should have been grateful for the body I had. I was between a size 13-15 but I was beautiful, and I was still pretty healthy and pretty active. I posted a few full body pictures, showing off the curves, but mostly posted pictures of my lips. I received a huge response which led to several friendships. I spent hours on the computer trying to get to know them. I usually had three men I was talking to at one time. Talk about a juggling act. I loved the attention. They were closer to my age and allowed me to feel normal. Talking to them kept me distracted, helped me block out the emotions from the shitty situation I was in. I felt safe because they couldn't get to me unless I wanted them to. *This is the safest way.*

I met my first real boyfriend Kwasi from blackplanet. We talked on the computer for about six months before we ever met in person. He was going through a lot and so was I. It was so easy to talk to him about every and anything. He just understood me. It was crazy how much time I spent on the phone with him, the only thing that kept us apart was the distance. I was so excited to meet him though. The next time my family planned a trip to Toronto, we planned to meet. I had a cell phone, but he had no phone, so we planned ahead to meet in front of Stitches at Scarborough town center. I had only seen a couple of photos of him on the computer, but he had seen plenty of mine. *He should be able to pick me out of a crowd.* Even still we had to plan what each other would wear. He was going to wear black pants and a yellow shirt, and I was going to wear blue jeans and a white sweater. The excitement was overwhelming. I really liked him. I got to Stitches anxiously hoping to see if he was already there, but he was nowhere in sight. I waited. And waited. It felt like forever, but was only 30 minutes. Kwasi never showed. Finally, I went down to the lower level to meet my parents since they were ready to leave. As we made our way through the mall to the exit I passed a tall guy wearing black pants and a yellow t-shirt. Our eyes locked and I just knew...it was him. *He came!!!!* I told my parents I wanted to check out something in a store before we left. He said that once he saw me he knew right away it was me. Our spirits connected. We hid in a hallway and hugged. *Finally!* We made out right there in the hallway not even bothering with what people around us were doing. That day brought us so much closer. I felt safe with him, safe enough to invite him over to my house.

The first time I invited Kwasi over I was nervous. *Shit, what's my parents gonna say? We don't ever talk about boys.* I invited a classmate over to ease the tension. He was supposed to come in the afternoon, but because of the distance and weather it took him longer than I had expected for him to reach my area. He was about 2 hours away from my house by Go bus. By time he got to the bus stop it was late, but I brought my friend with me to go meet him. On our way back to my house, I saw my mom pulling up in a van beside us to offer us a ride the rest of the way home. *Thanks mom.* Once at the house we decided to stay in the basement to watch a movie. My friend had a curfew and left jus as soon as we got back. *Damn there goes my alibi.* My dad's office was in the basement so while we watched the movie he would periodically stand behind us while pretending to "read" a book. *You're not slick papa.* Feeling the awkwardness, Kwasi tried to converse with my father, the assistant pastor. "Do you like sports?". "No". Conversation done. *So awkward. Kill me now.* I tried to ease the tension to allow Kwasi to feel comfortable. We sat in separate chairs so every chance I got, I would move closer, or steal a kiss. He was nervous as shit but to me it was hilarious. Especially since I knew my dad was trying to catch me doing something. It was a game to me. I wasn't even tryna do nun but chill. My mother was a next story. She would call me upstairs, then whisper loudly "Nick, when is your friend leaving? I need to go to bed and I can't sleep while he's still here." "Mom just go to your bed, dad is already downstairs" Within minutes of talking to my mom, my dad came at me with the same question. *I guess they want him to leave? I get that it's late, but he hasn't even been here long.* It was after ten, and the last Go bus in my area had already stopped running. Now my challenge was convincing my father to drive Kwasi to the train station. It wasn't easy, but my father finally agreed. It was one of the most embarrassing nights I've ever had to sit through. Both my parents were far from great behaviour. It wasn't the words they said but their actions. My mom gave off an ice-cold vibe. *Why can't she jus be nice? Why they gotta embarrass me? I swear I'm never bringing another man home for them to meet.* Inviting Kwasi over was the dumbest thing I had ever done.

Poetic Interlude

I've never had the courage to speak cause I know with every truth I would be met with bullets
I was never protected like I am now
I wear the armour of God
It turns bullets into ashes
Darkness into light
I no longer have to fight
He does it for me
My father in heaven has been hurting every time I've cried at the injustice
How do you build trust
When you are an object of lust of an uncle
I had nowhere to hide
When I felt his fingers inside
The stench of his breath has shamed me
It's like a replay of a song for far too long
The minute I decided to talk about it amidst fear I broke free
But freedom often comes at a price
Life has not been playing nice
I see people tryna take shots at me
Let me say this in general
If a person changes in behaviour
If you have ever heard whispers of problems but never said a word
You are a part of the problem
When you call a person a liar or a hoe
You are re victimizing them
Forcing them to relive, Re feel
A moment that they pray to God was never real
I choose to love any accuser still cause at least they've never had to feel
Never had to deal
Or experience the homicide of my adolescence
If you've ever had the courage to live past death
I see you , I love you
Maybe you're asking how to go on

Start by changing the tune of the song
Pray, Ask specifically for peace amidst the storm in your mind
Stay strong , Write it out
For no one but you to see
Cause ignoring it doesn't mean it didn't happen
Own it
Don't let anyone shame you
God's love covers you ten fold
This is how you build life after death
This is how you build from the bottom up
This is how you build in love

CHAPTER FIVE

Kwasi

Sustain me with raisin cakes, Refresh me with apples, Because I am sick with love.
-Songs of Solomon 2:5

People say that the truth will set you free. I'm not sure if I believe that 100% because for me dealing with the truth that I'd been raped, used and dashed, left me in a state of devastation. I had too many unanswered questions. I had lots of emotions all at once. Not to mention how many times I tried to block out my aunt's boyfriend. I was having nightmares. After the embarrassing failed meet and greet with Kwasi, I had to have a sit down with my parents. They gave me a hard time about how late he showed up to the house and how late he stayed. Then I endured countless interrogating questions about who he was and where I knew him from. *Geez, ok! Can we stop with the questions now?* Few days later, my mom still hadn't let it go. "So, he's African?" "Yep" "Just be careful of Africans" she said. "Where does he live?". "He lives in Toronto" I replied. "And he came all the way from Toronto down here just to see you?" *Wow gee mom thanks.* "Yes, he did" The tone in her voice implied, "Why would some guy come all the way from Toronto just to come hang out with you? Toronto was at least 40 minutes to an hour away by driving and by bus it was at least 3 hours away. Apparently, according to her I wasn't worthy of that dedication. *That felt pretty shitty.*

He accepted me. Even though I told him about being molested and about being raped he still wanted to see me. I thought that was special, and mother pretty much just crushed all my positive thinking. We just couldn't get along. My mind kept replaying her asking to send me to a group home. Not to mention that she often said things without thinking. I felt insecure about my weight around her. As a nurse she always had stories of patients who were overweight and heavy to lift or who came in with complications due to weight. She would say "Try not to get that size." *I'll do my best.* I borrowed my sister's shirt one day and when my mother saw me in it, despite the fact that it fit, she said, "Make sure you don't stretch out her clothes" *But I'm not stretching it out though.* I felt like shit. Straight up. I never knew what to say back so I often said nothing. I did everything to stay away from home, even involved myself in school as much as I could. When I was at home, I either locked myself in my room while on the phone or I was in the basement on the computer. I lived in isolation. I saw my family only when I had to. It wasn't hard because I went to school during the day, I saw them for dinner and then they were off for work.

Kwasi lived with a single mother who worked a lot, meaning he was often left alone too. He moved around a lot so there was never anything really stable in his life, except for when he was with me. In order to hang out together without drama, I would invite him over when my parents left for work. *Since he can't come when they're home, he'll come later.* I had everything down to a science. My mom worked various times, always leaving between 7:30 pm and 11 pm and returning by 8:30 am. It was my father's timing that I had to be more cautious of. My father would leave around 11:20 pm meaning Kwasi would have to aim to be at my house for 11:30 pm, right as my dad left. If he came early he would hide in the backyard and wait by the back door. A few times I would turn off the house alarm and sneak him into my room. My dad snored loudly, and it would mask the sound of the alarm. Even when he was awake and left for work he would rarely ever check my room. In the morning, we would have to be awake by 6 am to ensure Kwasi was able to leave and be long gone before my parents came home so I could put the alarm back on.

He was the first man I was "with" since the rape. We waited to have sex. My virginity was already gone so there was nothing really special about having sex, but at least I had a choice and it was with someone I really cared about. My first time with him hurt. Apparently, I was still pretty tight and he had to work his way in there. It didn't take long before we were having sex two, three times a night, and he came to my house as often as he could. We were always careful to clean up all the mess and not to leave any evidence of anything. I really enjoyed spending time with him because every night after we had sex he always slept next to me, held me and made me feel comfortable. The first time he looked at me and said "I love you" I couldn't stop smiling. *He loves you!!! Girl...he loves you.* Not just once, but many times he said he loved me. I loved him too. My first love. I never knew what love was, but he made me feel different. I meant something to him; I could call him anytime and he was there. Always.

I would do anything to spend time with him. One time I thought my father was going to work, but he wasn't and Kwasi was already on his way down. When he arrived at my house I turned off the alarm system and snuck him in through my back door. We waited in the basement until I thought my dad had left but I never heard the alarm go off to indicate that he left. I guess he stayed home sick. I snuck him up to my room regardless, I wasn't afraid to get caught. *I love being around him.*

We had sex anywhere and everywhere. My favorite song at the time was 112 - Anywhere, I connected with it and me and him made it "our song." I was adventurous. Even a little freaky. The thrill of it all made life less boring. I never thought about anything else but being happy. When I was with Kwasi everything seemed right. But after all the fun, I wanted more. I wanted him to come chill, watch movies, go out on dates.

"Hey, what if next time you come, we just chill, no sex?" "Why would we do that?" he answered. *Hmm ouch, sooo you mean you can't come if we don't fuck? That's all I am to you?* "It's a long bus ride down there to jus chill" "So yu don't wanna see me if we ain't having sex? Is that all you want from me?" "No, but c'mon, why do we gotta change how things are?" Such a small conversation turned into a bigger argument. *He really don't think it's worth it to come down if there's no sex. Wow. ok. Fuck him too then.* It was clear that sex was the only thing that kept him coming to me. I mean, I know I was good, but damn, I was pretty sure I was good at being his girlfriend too. *There's otha things I can do besides laying on my back.* That one fight ended our relationship. *I thought he loved me. Nope, he loved my pussy.* I didn't know how to deal. I was hurt but I missed him and our conversations terribly. *My first love. My first heartbreak.*

CHAPTER SIX

Addicted

Because lawlessness is increased, the love of most people will grow cold.
Matthew 24 :12

I love watching Law and Order S.V.U. I think I wanna be a lawyer. Help people, make a difference and seek justice. Each SVU case was different and allowed me to interject myself into a new reality, new possibilities. My obsession with a show about rape victims and justice helped me escape my own life. Perhaps watching other people find justice allowed me to reconcile my own guilt. I never sought justice, never knew how. At least the women in the show had Olivia to protect and believe in them.

I've formed my own opinions about some of the after effects of rape victims from watchin TV, especially SVU. I learned that some rape victims live on and are able to overcome their trouble, some suffer from post-traumatic stress, some become withdrawn and lose trust. Then there are women who aren't capable of fully dealing with the rapes, blame themselves, then use sex to numb the pain. The rape took away their respect, their self-worth, their confidence. These sexual experiences give them a false sense of control. Afraid another man will hurt them, it's easier for them to say yes than to say no and be violated again. It's all a mind game we play on ourselves

I was desperately searching for love. My fantasy of a normal life was shattered when Kwasi and I broke up. At least with him I could pretend the rapes didn't change me, but they did. I was in denial about my ability to control my emotions and my body. I thought I still had control. I tell myself *Ok, so he didn't want me for more than sex, that's fine. It's ok, plenty of fish in the sea, someone else will want me. I'm not that damaged. I am in control. I choose who I have sex with and when I have sex.*

I never kept count of the amount of men I had sex

with. Instead of an emotional eater, I was an emotional beater. Sex was the new way I coped with my anger and my pain. I felt strong, happy. It was exhilarating and intoxicating. I smiled, I laughed, then I cried. A roller coaster of feelings, starting really great, having an amazing climax, but finishing too fast. As quickly as it was over, I found a new ride – a new partner. Always chasing the next high. Slowly dying inside but unable to adjust to anything else. I hated being sad, but even more than that, I hated being alone.

I thought I was running the game, but the game was getting the best of me. I wasn't hurting anyone else but myself, but I was blinded by my pain. I was unable to take a step back and watch how my life was being destroyed. I don't even remember how everything got so bad. Damn. With each man that I met and talked to, I always held out hope that he would love and take care of me, just like the fairy tale I always saw on TV.

I decided that I'm not the type of girl that travels for sex. If they wanted it they had to come get it. Only hoes travel. I didn't like how weak hoes acted. If a man calls up a girl and tells her to reach his house and she goes, she's passive, a hoe, lets guys walk all over her. I didn't allow men to degrade me by the way they spoke. I didn't stand for name calling, acting like they owned me or being told what to do. If a man were to say jump, I'd say "Naw I'm good." If a man wanted pussy, he needed to say please. I hated being disrespected. I wouldn't sleep with a man who was in a relationship. Men had already stolen enough from me, they had no choice but to respect me. Anything less was unacceptable. This was my way to gain control in my life that felt so outta control.

I went on my first double date with Aaliyah, a guy she met at church, and his friend - Paul. We went to a movie and after the movies we drove to some park just to chill out for a bit. It was awkward. I got Paul's number and told him that I would call him. Give it about a week or so, Paul was at my house. It took him all about two minutes before he was done. *What a damn waste of my good stuff.* He dipped right after and we haven't spoken since. Aaliyah on the other hand kept seeing her guy. He seemed like a decent guy from the few times we met. That notion of him disappeared as soon as he tried to convince me to hook up behind my girls back. Now that's my girl, I love her with my whole life, so y'all know I ain't do nun, cause I ain't a trifling G. She had previously mentioned how she felt when he had compared my thickness with her skinniness. I tried to indirectly tell her, but I didn't want her to get mad at me. Luckily her relationship never lasted very long with him. *Paul probably told him the pussy tight. Nigga please!* No lie!

I've always had one man I talked to and a bunch of men that wanted to have sex with me, but I was still empty inside. It was easy to meet guys on the internet. I was young and sex motivated. The more men I had sex with the more I felt empty. I had sex outside, I had sex in newly developed houses, in the forest, in empty buildings, in cars, in the shower, anywhere really. Kwasi and I used to shower together but I always showered in the dark cause I never wanted him to see my body, I was embarrassed. I lived in the dark. Nightcrawler. It was best when I was hidden. This body of mine was not pretty in the light. The light exposed too much so I always had sex with a t-shirt on, never skin to skin. I used protection when it was convenient. If it wasn't convenient, I would pop the morning after pill. I used to pop that thang like M&M's. I lived a double life. I went to church every Sunday, I sang in the choir, hell, I was the choir. I went to school and kept up with good marks. No one saw me self-destructing. I appeared to be the perfect Christian daughter living the perfect Christian life. I would lie and tell my parents I was going rollerblading and leave the house in pants, but underneath was the shortest skirt and I was on my way to an all ages party. I was reckless, I danced recklessly, bent over, whining to the ground, while my friends pulled my skirt down for me. The reggae beats exploded in my heart allowing me to let loose and be free. I got to hang out with my friends, smile, laugh, an jus enjoy music. It only lasted for the night. With my parents being so strict, I barely got to hang out with friends outside of school. Lying seemed to be the only way I could enjoy these good moments. From what I had heard in church, I understood that God didn't approve of my lifestyle, but how else was I supposed to cope?

Society seems to think that Christian families have no problems, but I was drowning and no one could tell. One Wednesday while my parents were at church I invited a new man over. I anticipated that they would be gone longer, but I was caught off guard when they came home early. I hid him in my closet while I spent time with my parents to avoid raising suspicion. I was nervous. *Ooo he gon be mad.* He was in the closet for three hours before my parents left for work. I had to keep a straight face. He was anxious, he wanted to come out, he had never had to hide in a closet. I was just tryna balance the situation as best as I could. Once they left, I let him out of the closet. It was on. He came out so happy and full of adrenaline. Best sex of my life. *Pain is love, right?* I wasn't able to walk for a week. It was the first time I had ever been eaten out and the feeling was great. He focused on me, aimed to please. It was different, better.

We continued to talk but things changed 3 weeks later. I was getting death threats from some chick who identified herself as his girl. I had no clue he had a girl. She said she was coming after me. I was pissed he didn't tell me he had a girl and that she had my number. *He gave her my number? Pathetic ass.* In my mind we were dating, but that was exactly it - it was in my mind only – not his. I was frustrated. So, I did what 15 year olds do. MSN revenge. I had his password, I changed his msn name to say, "I have aids and I love to have sex with little girls". I thought it was funny at the time, it wasn't. I was pissed. I wanted to hurt him back. It turns out he had his pastor and his whole family on his msn. It caused more problems for him than I thought. He never spoke to me again.

My life became a game. I tried to see how many men I could talk to at once. Suzette was my only friend that I talked to about sex and men, and that's alllllll we talked about. No matta what I did she always gave me my props. I always played the victim and got bare sympathy from them. Once I had them I left them. Rotating through men like shoes. Treatin them like objects, I started to take on that persona of how men treated me. Like a piece of ass. This girl and I spent hours on the phone talking to men. Playing prank calls, everything and anything we could do to pass our time. We were bad for each other. When we were together we caused bare trouble.

I met the next one, Maxwell, on blackplanet like usual. He was cute, he talked a good talk, he was dangerous for me. Every time I met a new man, he always took the place of the last man. I told them my sad story of being raped and tried to gain their sympathy. Joke is I never wanted sympathy. I wanted more than anything to believe I was strong and I was in control, but when it came to men I really just wanted one to love me and fix all the pain I was going through. Up until I met Maxwell, every other man was someone I talked to, I had sex with, and it was over. I just loved sex. It gave me a high that I couldn't get otherwise. Maxwell was different. He was always there when I needed him. See how those words keep coming up. I was a needy girl. Maxwell was the first man to really have a mental impact on me. Shit changed. He started playing games with my head. I coulda sworn that Maxwell loved me. I used to take the bus to see him all the time. I remember one time I just couldn't handle things at home. I don't member the argument with my parents, but I remember that I ran away from home. I skipped school and I ran to his house. I stayed and cried all day. He consoled me. Let me know I was safe. Safety. Comfort. A shoulder to cry on. That's all I really wanted. The love that I neglected to get. The day my virginity was stolen, they stole my ability to accept love. Quite simply I was incapable of believing that I was capable of feeling love or being loved. No one wanted me. No one wanted to love me. I was fat. Maxwell was all I had. See the thing about running away from home is that it should have been planned more carefully. Like an idiot I called my parents to check in and I used a calling card which allowed them to trace back the number. *Who in their right mind runs away from home and then calls to let their parents know that they were ok?* Within the hour my dad came to pick me up from the closest mall. I was back at school by the next day. Damn.

CHAPTER SEVEN

Maxwell

with all humility [forsaking self-righteousness], and gentleness [maintaining self-control], with patience, bearing with one another in [unselfish] *love*.

-Ephesians 4:2

My relationship with Maxwell was...confusing as hell. He was really tall, lighter skinned than me, and beautiful. His big brown eyes were so warm, and his smile so inviting. He was so in tune to his emotions, which to me was the most attractive thing about him at the time. He wrote poetry and wasn't afraid to let me know how he felt about me. We developed a beautiful friendship and instantly connected. We spent time getting to know each other on the phone. We would spend hours talking. I ran to him every time my parents and I had an argument. He would make it better. He was very emotional. *Yes!...But maybe he was a bit too emotional.* He was always telling me he loved me, like every other sentence.

I took a family studies class in high school and I learned that women go through many stages of development while trying to figure out their identity. One main fact that stuck out to me is that women tend to use the relationships that they form with the people around them to figure themselves out. Meaning that based on friendships and romantic relationships, some women are capable of figuring out who they are and what they are all about. Maxwell was perfect for me. He understood everything about me. He knew my thoughts, knew how to care for me, knew how to make me smile, especially during my darkest days, but he was no good for me. He was dangerous and mentally unstable at times. He had me right where he wanted me. There were times he used to say things like "I know how to break you. With just my words, I know how to make you happy and how to hurt you." He was right. It felt like mind control. I listened to his every word. At times I was really happy with Maxwell, and there were times when I was also very sad and withdrawn. I won't lie, what Maxwell and I had was very special, but relationships are not meant to break each other down. When we were together we were so good together, but when we were apart, it was hard. Too much even. I had trust issues. The feelings that I got when we weren't together became unhealthy. I felt so alone when he wasn't around and so good when he was. Even though we were on the phone or texting, I was alone. Another rollercoaster.

Our sexual relationship was something very intimate to us because we were such an emotional couple. He was the first man to "make love" to me. He made me feel special. He held me and caressed me. He kissed me and squeezed me. He was real good at giving brains - that's for sure. The most stunning thing about making love to Maxwell was that when he was done, he stayed with me. Never left my side until I was ready to let go. And when I cried, he wiped my tears. It was a beautiful moment and it was one of the happier moments in our lives. Everything should have and would have been perfect. But just like I was needy, he was needy too. I was dealing with so many things at that moment that I couldn't handle being with someone who needed so much from me. He had this muscle problem and was in pain all the time. I always tried to make it better. Nothing I did was ever good enough. The pain made him hopeless and he was depressed. I was soon headed in that same direction. He had a lot of drama and trauma in his life, which I understood, but since both of us were going through things, neither one was able to help uplift the other person. We pretty much just drowned and dragged our relationship through the mud. When he got into one of his depressed modes, I couldn't ever get through to him. He didn't allow me to. It really frustrated me. Do you know how hard it was to watch the man that I cared deeply for in pain? Knowing there was nothing he was willing to let me do. He was unable to truly love me because he never really let go of the pain from his past. We were just unable to work things out between us. So, we went our separate ways and we never looked back. It was for the best, but I was hurt.

CHAPTER EIGHT

Kendrick

Hatred stirs up strife, But love covers and overwhelms all transgressions [forgiving and overlooking another's faults].
Proverbs 10:12

This next gentleman...actually, he's not a gentleman at all...he's a player...a thug...what my girls and I call...a waste man. In my eyes a waste man is a man who can't do anything for himself, or for me. A waste man is a man that doesn't try to succeed in life and is only concerned with making quick an easy money instead of tryna work hard. That brings me to my relationship with Kendrick - a waste man. He was tall, he wasn't the sexiest looker in the world but hey, who am I to judge. The significance of talking to Kendrick was that he was completely opposite from Maxwell. I went from one extreme to the next, from emotional to completely detached. The swift transition wasn't good. Black planet had every kinda guy.

Kendrick was a guy that was into illegal things. Drug dealings...coke selling...weed smoking...break and entering type of man. It started with phone conversations, but they were barely even conversations at all. I was only 15 but loved having deep conversations about school, church, things on TV, people and social behaviors. But we never had anything really to talk about. I would try to talk but he just wouldn't have anything to say. We would often jus sit on the phone in silence. It would seem more like we were tryna force something that didn't even really exist. Living far from each other, we saw each other only once in person during our whole relationship. A few months felt like a long time as a teen.

He had this "I'm so hard" stance about him. It was virtually impossible to speak about our feelings for one another. He often deflected my questions. Never wanting to be vulnerable. It would seem to me like this was a thing that many men I knew had to deal with. I guess it's cause growing up boys are taught not to cry, in return they internalize these emotions and it creates these false personas of "hard detached men". Numb to the world and solidified by society and culture. I wish more men understood the value of being vulnerable, even a little bit, without losing who they were. The rare times when Kendrick was vulnerable it was nice. It was almost like he felt he needed to protect himself from everyone around him because of how hard life was for him. It felt good when I was able to get through to him. In return he did offer a sense of protection that I needed.

With Kendrick it was nothing but drama. We were always fighting, I was always upset or paranoid that he was cheating on me because he often had so many other girls that he would talk to. Being with a "thug man" was definitely a challenge. Kendrick was always in an out of trouble with the law. The man couldn't stay out of trouble even if I paid him. Our relationship didn't last very long cause before I knew it he was on his way to jail. Before he went he said, "Will you wait for me to get out?" I seriously considered it, but...*fuck that I'm 15, what am I doing waiting for a man to get outta jail? Was that my concern? I didn't tell him to go get himself in trouble. Why should it be my responsibility to hold him down for over a year while he in jail?* He was always running from something and I couldn't afford to run with him.

CHAPTER NINE

Church Girl

If you [really] love Me, you will keep and obey My commandments.
-John 14 :15,

Church life is everythin my family stands for. Youth groups, church rally's, concerts. I lived the whole thing. But I was cracking under pressure. I was resistant because as far as I could see it, church was taking my daddy away. Anything that really needed to be done at church my dad was the one to do it. If there was a need at church, family was put on hold. No matta what. I felt like my dad has missed out a lot on my growing up jus cause he was always so busy with church. He failed to see the troubles at home cause he was helping everyone else. It's safe to say that I was struggling as a Christian. Doing my best to seem natural and upkeep the image, but it wasn't easy. Especially when this new guy started to come to church.

He had this look in his eyes that jus seemed to melt my heart. He was bout 5'6, dark skinned, with a sexy Jamaican accent - he was hella cute with a fyne allure about him. Charming panty wetta type personality. He was much older than me and we never saw each other outside of church but when Sunday came around I made sure I looked good. I sat a couple of rows in front of him to make sure he saw my good side. Usually sitting close enough to pass notes through our Bibles, but not so close that it looked suspicious. Our church ain't big at all so if anyone paid a bit too much attention to us they woulda been able to see what was flourishing between us. Hormones got the best of us one Sunday, being at church meant getting creative. He signaled for me to follow him downstairs, so I let him go first, then waited before I proceeded. He was in the single stall men's bathroom waiting for me. All I felt was his lips on my neck and his hands on my ass. He was grabbing me in so many places. He sat on the toilet seat and I sat on top of him, both grinding to the beats of our bodies. He's a great kisser, the thrill and excitement had my heart pounding. If we heard a noise we paused temporarily then went right back to it. I could see the enjoyment on his face and I wanted him to do me right there, but there wasn't enough time. We finally stopped when there was a knock at the door. We quickly jumped up and rearranged our clothes and I cracked the door to check if the way was clear. We left. In the next room his step mom had asked me if I had seen him, I simply said no and ran back upstairs.

We spoke often on the phone and he even gave me a promise ring to show me that he'd never leave me. It woulda been quite special if it weren't for the fact that we would only ever see each other at church. I was well infatuated with this man. It was a tragic lil love story we lived. When we actually came together our emotions ran so high, we missed each other dearly the times we were apart. Finally, people at church started catching on, making it harder for us to sneak around, and one day, he just never came back. An my secret love was over. I never heard from him again. He made me feel so special. Sigh.

The most important thing I learned from church was that God loved me regardless. He continued to bless me despite my faults. He was always looking down on me. Things I wanted to blame God for I couldn't because only I was truly responsible for my own actions. I tried my best to get right with God, but grade 10 jus got the best of me. *Lord forgive me!*

Self-Reflection

I had a lingo I used with my friends that described my attraction to the men I dated. Mother freaking Beautiful, FYNE, Cyan Gwan/Cute, Ugly, then Ross Ugly.

The ross ugly man was the man that you wouldn't be caught dead walking beside for fear of dying from embarrassment. These men could be sloppy, or look busted, smell bad, are dirty or whatever it was; he'd be the type of man that would stop you straight in your tracks an made you say hell no!

Then you have your typical ugly man. Now he's the

type that you'll be seen in public with. Maybe not standing right right next to you, but he's at least somewhere in the vicinity. Now this would be the man who kinda makes you wonder, cause no doubt he's ugly, but he wouldn't make you wanna run and hide and he would have an incredibly sweet personality.

Moving on to the cyan gwan/cute, this was the type of man who had great potential. He had his lil moments where you thought he was so adorable. This man would be walking material. You wouldn't walk faster or slower than him cause he would be just that cute and he would make you smile.

Hmmm hmm hmmm now for the FYNE men. These were the men that you love walking beside cause it made all otha girls jealous of you. Always hatin on the girl with that FYNE man. Eyeing him down like he's some piece of meat. Or an extra scoop of ice cream with your already fabulous cake. The Fyne man pffi is your one way ticket to instant hateration. Plain and simple.

When a man is mother freakin beautiful, he jus takes your breath away. Your nerves are all messed up, your stomach all jittery, you have absolutely no clue what to say to him but all you would wanna do would be to get close enough to touch him. You would sing praises finding that voice you neva thought you had. When you slept he would enter your dreams. He was like a beautiful refreshing glass of something good. And all you would wanna do was drink it alllllll up. If you dat girl he walking with, jus know your life would be in danger. The amount of women who'd wanna take you out jus to get to him was crazy.

My ratings were all superficial though, cause it only gave an account for physical appearance, which may not even mean anything cause I'm sure some women would prefer a ross ugly man if the FYNE ass man was beatin them or if the mother freakin beautiful man was cheatin on them. Which I've seen all too often. Appearance was one piece to the puzzle. Straight up. What was in their mind? What was feeding their soul? What was feeding mine?

CHAPTER TEN

Telephone Game

Do not love the world [of sin that opposes God and His precepts], nor the things that are in the world. If anyone loves the world, the love of the Father is not in him.
-1 John 2 :15

He was cute, super tall, definitely a cyan gwan situation. He loved to ball so I call him Dribbles. 6'3 to 5'3, tall and skinny to short and thick. It looked weird as hell but I ain't care. The only problem was that he was in my grandma's hood so the chances of my family knowing him were hella high, so I should have assumed. We talked for a few months before deciding to meet and since I was basically on house arrest, sneaking out of my grandma's house to meet him was gonna be a challenge. Not impossible though. My family was concerned about me embarrassing them more than I already had which meant anywhere I went, I had a chaperone. I felt dehumanized. Not even caged animals were watched as closely as I was.

I was allowed to follow my cousin to the mall one day and used that as my way to meet Dribbles. It was cool seeing him. He was just as cute as his pictures, and even taller than I thought. It was safe to say we were comfortable "dating" after we met in person once. Our relationship was mostly over the phone cause that's the only thing I had that wasn't monitored.

After a couple months of talking, Dribbles decided to introduce me by phone to his friends. That was a huge mistake cause anytime we spoke after that his friends always wanted to say hi. There were three specific guys he had introduced me to and each one said the same thing, "You have a sexy voice, I wanna get to know you betta". My man was Dribbles so his friends needed to step off but instead of telling them to beat it, he gave one of his friends

Brian my number and told him he was free to call me whenever. *Why would he do that? If I'm his girl why would he tell them it's ok to talk to me? What about me? Don't I get a say in who I can and want to talk to? Or I don't mean anything to him and he don't even care? Why did he give my number and not even ask me if it was ok? He wanna play games, I'll show him games. I'm not a stupid ball he can pass back and forth.* Since he wanted his friends to talk to me then I played right along with it. I let his friends come on to me, soaked it all up and flirted right back. So what? He didn't seem to care. Not very mature on my part but hey...I was young and hurt. So, I had Brian calling me, then somehow a nex guy named Shayne started calling me too. Now I was talking to two of Dribbles' friends. At first I was jus annoyed with Dribbles, but these guys seemed pretty decent, so we developed a friendship, kinda. I would spend time talking to each of them separately for hours sometimes. They spoke about relationships an wanting to travel to come see me, I still made it clear that I was still interested in Dribbles even if it seemed like he clearly passed me off. Dribbles and I were still talking often. If he was jealous he didn't show it which messed me up even more. *Why doesn't he just tell em to step off? Does he even like me?*

To complicate the matter, it turns out I actually knew one of his otha friends from a previous encounter. Months before I had even started talking to Dribbles his friend Derek had chopped me while walking through the mall. We spoke a couple times after, but it never amounted to anything serious. Derek was part of this crew, he was Dribbles friend and Brian's cousin.

One night I was on the phone with Brian and he decided that he and Derek wanted to drive down to my house to chill. By now we were all friends, so why not? I shouldn't have been chillin wit my man's friends, but he did this to himself. Before I let him play me and continue to pass me off Imma show him I ain't the one to play with. They showed up at my house...without Dribbles.

I had no clue what Brian looked like cause I had never met him or seen his pic, but I felt safe enough cause I knew his cousin. When they arrived, I was absolutely flabbergasted. Brian was ross ugly and smelt like he aint shower in a minute. He was like really fat, but it was not so much the weight that bothered me, but the fact that he jus smelt so bad. He was one hot ross ugly mess. Which sucked, cause Brian was the one who was feeling me the most, but I was repulsed by the smell. Instead of hanging out with Brian like he wanted, I hung out with his cousin. At first we were jus playing music and chillin, nun crazy but every time Brian tried to get me alone in a room I made excuses. Derek on the otha hand I was very attracted to and him me. He reminded me how he met me first and that we had unfinished business. *What about Dribbles?* Derek said if Dribbles really wanted me, he wouldn't have handed out my number and let them come see me without him. *That's tru. He playing me. Technically I did meet Derek first.* We moved to the next room, alone, forgetting about everything else around us as we indulged into what was meant to be. Quick but good, his sex matched his appearance. They left soon after and yet again Brian tried to get me alone, but I wasn't the type to double dip in the same night.

Bout maybe two weeks later, I get the infamous telephone call that my family loves to do. It's literally a game of telephone. One person receives a message, and they pass it along to the rest of the family until it gets back to my parents. They never attempt to find the truth in the situation, they just pass along what they hear and expect it to all work itself out. Since I was the slut of the family it must have all been true, right? From what I heard, I had not only slept with Brian but I also sucked his dick. Someone pass a basin cause even repeating it makes me wanna throw up. Like why? It's one thing to lie and say I had sex, but to say I put my lips on that piece of dick that hasn't seen daylight in a while...that's jus hectic.

Sooooo Brian was on some shit and now my whole family was on some shit saying I was dirty cause I slept with him and sucked his dick. They asked me how I even found his dick to suck and how it taste since he don't bathe. I was white like a ghost. *What you mean I slept with him?*

Derek, his cousin ye, but not Brian. Brian musta really been in his feelings to pull a lie like that out his ass. Apparently both Brian and Dribbles were telling my cousins at school that I fucked Brian. First off, Dribbles didn't even ask me if it was true and second, as a friend, how does Brian run back to his own bredrin, look him in the face and say, "Man I slept with your girl and she sucked my dick". Like are you good fam, who says that? There was no mention of me sleeping with Derek though. Obviously since Brian had been to my house, he was able to describe what my place looked like, which gave his story validation. Apparently Dribbles was tryna put me through a test. *I already knew that, I'm not stupid. Your test backfired though.*

What hurt the most was that he didn't even ask me. He jus heard Brian and ran to my family to embarrass and get back at me. It was one thing for my family to call me names, but they harassed me RELENTLESSLY. I would get phone calls from them calling me names: bitch, hoe, gross, fat, ugly, anything and everything before they hung up. Sometimes they wouldn't even say anything, they would jus call my phone and have it ringing, ringing, ringing. I couldn't even answer my cell phone anymore. Then there were emails calling me a disgusting two cent whore. Then it was text messages, then it was messages on my social media wall for everyone to see. It went on for weeks. They wouldn't stop. They just wouldn't stop. If I called to speak to my grandma they hung up the phone on me. I was no longer allowed back at my grandma's house. I could no longer talk to her. It was the worst thing ever. They treated me worse now than when they heard about the gang rape. They said I had nothing to strive for in life cause I had already disgraced the family and they forgave me. But now, they couldn't risk having a hoe like me around. I cried till I couldn't cry no more. No one intervened. None of the adults, I was alone, this was the first time I really jus wanted to die. *What's the point? All of this over some stupid lie. I might as well die, at least they don't have to feel so embarrassed by me.*

I hated Dribbles jus as much as I wanted to die. *Stupid ass mutherfucka. He shoulda asked me. I woulda told him.*

He didn't have to run to them first, especially cause I told him how they were. No one believed me. I was being crucified. Worst of all I had to face my parents. I can't even remember their emotions, but I know they were angry, livid. Even though I told them it wasn't true, they didn't believe me. I didn't have anybody on my side. Bitterness became my poison of choice. *Fuck family. I don't have one. If I catch that nigga Dribbles on the street imma kill him. Imma pour bleach down his throat and all ova his clothes.* I kept fantasizing about death. How it would feel, how peaceful it would be. How beautiful it was. *This pain is too much. This shit is too difficult. I'm tellin the truth an nobody cares. I don't even matter. I'm not even here. I'm invisible. Why should I keep going? I'm just an object, discarded. They'd probably be happy that I was dead.*

Thoughts of suicide felt more an more real. It was on me, I was plagued by it, it was in me, it was about to become me. Death was at my door, it was calling me, I was making deals with the darkness, but something had me log online in the darkest night when I met this guy named Ahmed. He spent the whole night tryna talk me outta killin myself and to let go of harming Dribbles. He wouldn't let me sleep until I promised I wouldn't do it. Till I promised I wouldn't feed into the dark. Slowly, he became my best friend. No matta what he always messaged me to make sure I was good. He was Jamaican, Egyptian and Somali and he was damn FYNE. He was one of the flyest men I knew, and I cherished his friendship cause he saw me at my darkest and loved me back to health. He saw me in my purest form and he wasn't scared. I know it was a God moment cause I was so ready to go. I wanted him to stay forever, I wanted to be with him, I wanted him to keep me going cause without him I wasn't sure I knew how to keep living. Then one day jus like the other men, he disappeared without a trace and I was left alone again. I was tired of people leavin. *What's wrong with me?* No more miss nice Cola. Fuck men. If I don't get invested they can't hurt me. I felt a shift coming too but it was winter entering my heart.

CHAPTER ELEVEN

Live, Love, Cry

Do everything in love..
1 Corinthians 16:14

I'm cold blooded. Limited feelings. I got so damn annoying fussing and obsessing about my weight that I sabotaged everything before anything could get started. I was convinced I needed to protect myself, so I would lay out all my insecurities from early on and let them decide whether or not they wanted to stay. Men online were easier to talk to in a sense cause we all had less to lose and I could control the interactions. Did they want a freaky girl? A smart girl? A bold girl? A church girl? I was everything at any time to anybody. A chameleon with no emotions. Did they want a friendship or just to fuck? Either they spoke up or kept it moving. I had no time to waste. It did more harm than good cause it seemed to scare them away. It was a vicious cycle. I scared them away because I thought they couldn't handle me, and once they left I told myself that was exactly why I didn't trust people. I thought this man was too good looking for me...so I started chatting with his friend. He didn't like that, but I didn't care, plus I had more in common with his friend. We were able to have meaningful conversations about life and everything around us. At first we didn't exchange pictures. At the time it didn't seem as important as being able to connect through our writing. Writing was an important outlet for me and it felt nice to have met someone who shared the same type of passion. He was really into writing poetry too. We would write together, share our deepest secrets, laugh, cry, smile. It was a breath of relief to be connected with him and he even edited my essays for class when I needed the additional help.

Our friendship grew slowly. We spoke briefly about relationships but given our past, we never wanted to rush anything. We were in that awkward stage of "talking" more than friends but not yet dating. We eventually decided to meet but first we wanted to exchange pictures. I had tried to convince myself that looks didn't matter if the person had a great personality, but that was a lie. Looks were somewhat important and unfortunately when I saw his picture I was immediately turned off. *Poor ting.* I couldn't bring myself to tell him I wasn't attracted to him. I really didn't have a reason to be so shallow because I was no prize possession myself, but I allowed his looks to come between our incredible connection. Feeling guilty I started pulling back until eventually things kinda jus hung on by a thread for us. Then I did the unthinkable.

Kwasi an I kept in touch since we broke up and decided to hang out one night for ol time's sake. When he showed up I was in the middle of a conversation with poetry dude. Instead of waiting until I got off the phone, Kwasi started kissing and rubbin on me. It was such a turn on. I should have come off the phone, but I didn't. Kwasi came right in between my thighs, penetrating me and forcing me to let out a silent whisper. He continued as I held in my moans and tried my best to pay attention to the conversation. I was fully havin sex an I didn't even put the phone on mute. I laughed. I smiled hard. It was the most intense sex ever. It was beautiful and yet I felt horrible about my actions. My mind wandered as I exhaled, but just as I was turning my attention back to the conversation Kwasi tells me that the condom broke. *Shit.*

Without explanation, I hung up on poetry dude. Fun was over. Kwasi and I panicked as he grabbed paper to try and wipe his cum outta me. Distraught, I left Kwasi downstairs to clean up while I laid down in my bed and cried my heart out. When he was done cleaning, he came and laid with me and held me the whole night. He apologized while he rubbed my back an told me everything was gonna be cool. Kid or not, we were gonna be ok. When he left the next morning, I prayed and prayed and prayed. "God please don't make me get pregnant, if you do this for me I'll never have sex again." I'm sure God musta been looking down like "Dis chick, really?" Even if God granted my wish, there was nothing He could have done to save me from what happened the next morning.

CHAPTER TWELVE

Cost

A time to love and a time to hate; A time for war and a time for peace.
-Ecclesiastes 3:8

Eva seen your pops cry? It aint a great moment in time to see ya pops crying knowing it was because of you. Like there was nothing I could say because the evidence was right on my face. Couldn't even pull a shaggy an say it wasn't me...like I was just done for. And you know my daddy never said nun much to me. The shock that I was having sex and having it in their house was a lot to handle. Hell, the first thing I thought of was fighting Kwasi for leaving the damn condom in the garbage. *This fool actually left the condom in the empty garbage.* We never been caught before cause he was always so careful, but this time, man this time we was both trippin and when you aint on top of ya game there's bound to be mistakes. When my father was finally able to regain his composure, he asked the dreaded question "Who did you have sex with?" *Hmm excuse me? What was that? Who did I what?* So uncomfortable. I told them it was Kwasi. Ooooo he was immediately banned from my house. Didn't really matta anyway I had bigger things to deal with, like the fear of getting pregnant.

Kwasi and I were no longer on them dealin tips, hadn't been for a while cause of distance so this was just a random sex ting. I was in the middle of my grade ten year and I definitely was not ready for no baby. Not to mention everything my family would say. To get pregnant is one thing, but to get pregnant by an African man? Both his mom and my parents woulda had a problem with that. I wasn't ready to be causing any more division between my family. At this point I pretty much wanted to try and avoid fights at all cost.

CHAPTER THIRTEEN

No air

The LORD keeps all who love Him, But all the wicked He will destroy.
-Psalm 145 :20

I've realized one thing, be as honest as possible and always put on a good show.

I met this man on msn and he seemed pretty cool. We talked often, first primarily by msn, then we moved to the telephone. I joked about life in Oshawa, my fears of being raped again and my fear of getting hurt in relationships. Discussing my rape with him was hard and confusing. He questioned the hell outta me. His questions made me question my memory. I felt like a victim all over again and that I had to once again prove myself. He asked me how it happened, where it happened, and if I knew them. *What was with all the questions? Was he one of the guys? Was he there? Did he hear about me?* His questions and responses felt like he was trying to justify their actions as if he knew. He fucked with my memory. *Was I wrong? Well I did walk off with one of the guys. Maybe I deserved this. Maybe I was sending mixed signals.* I said to him "Were you there? I can't remember the details, but it doesn't mean I'm lying" It was trippy cause I mean he was from Rexdale, and I was raped in Rexdale, maybe he heard whispers. He said no, he was just trying to see the situation from all angles. *Bullshit.*

There was no need for us to keep talking after that, but I woke up to the ringing of my house phone one night. It was late, and he was calling because he wanted to come over. Mind you, we had never met so I knew it wasn't a good idea. He ignored me. I hung up and went back to bed. *This nigga crazy if he think imma let him come see me at this time. Thank God he don't know where I live.* He kept calling. It was such unusual behaviour. The phone wouldn't stop ringing. For fear of waking up my sister, and out of complete annoyance, I answered the phone. He laughed like it was a game. Said he wasn't going to stop calling my phone. He said, "I jus drove to Oshawa, so you need to gimme the directions to your house." I hung up and he called back. He kept calling. There was no way I was gettin any sleep. *Ok jus deal with him, let him chill for a bit then he can go home. If he keeps calling he gon wake up your sister and you ain't gonna get no rest. If he think we bout to fuck he got a next thing coming.* I put on jeans, pants, two shirts and a sweater. I made sure I didn't have anything on that was suggestive in any way. My t-shirt was long as hell and there was a big ugly teddy bear on the front. He arrived with his friend. *This man had some nerve.* We headed to the basement far from my sister to watch a movie. Initially we sat on opposite couches, but he ended up right next to me.

He was short and really thick....not my type at all. To top it off he was dark, just not attractive...period. Compared to him I was small. Pretty sure he coulda lifted me with one finger with barely any effort. I was trying to make small talk, but I was too tired. As he inched towards me, I moved over but then he got on top of me. He pinned me down with his weight while he grabbed at my pants. I tried to push him away while holding onto my pants, no such luck. He pulled my jeans off with ease and didn't even try to take off my panties. His friend that he brought sat beside me and egged him on like his own personal cheerleader. He fully saw me struggling; but the harder I struggled the louder and more energy that went into cheering this man on. With his weight on my chest I could only take short breaths. I was struggling to breathe. I tried to scream with the lil air that I was getting. Hopeless. I kicked. I pushed. I slapped. I unno. I tried everything I could, and the more I tried the more weight he pushed on me and the closer he got to thrusting his dick inside me. I could feel his breath. His friend kept saying "Dig it in deep". "Don't stop". I kept yellin, but no one came. It didn't stop. Finally, he stabbed his dick inside me, ripped open my thighs and pushed deeper and deeper. I pounded on his chest. Tears fell, but I never gave up kicking with whatever energy I could muster up. I kept repeating "Stop", hardly able to say it because I could barely breathe. Nothing. He jus kept on stabbing me until he was satisfied. He only stopped when he was done. Lucky for me he bussed quick, yet it felt like it lasted a lifetime.

"You need to get the fuck outta my house" He eased up enough for me catch a deep enough breath. "Well, my friend drove me out here so can you let him hit it too?" *Excuse me? What the fuck do I look like?* He had the nerve to ask me to service his friend, like I'm some 24 hour gas station. "YOU RAPED ME" that only pissed him off. "I ain't fucking rape nobody". "You said stop and I stopped". By now we had made it to my front door, so I stood with the door knob in hand and gestured for them to get out. He turns to me, hugged me, kissed me, then said "Nobody was raped, I'll hit you up soon." The man actually tried to act like everythin between us was cool.

If depression didn't set in before it was clearly renting space in my life now.

CHAPTER FOURTEEN

Exchange

But I know you and recognize that you do not have the love of God in yourselves.
-John 5:42

After being alienated from my supposed family and the pregnancy scare, I never did get pregnant from that incident, *phew thank God*. After being raped for the second time I was done with sex. Sex was the last thing on my mind. It was the last thing I wanted to do. Months went by of life uninterrupted. I got back into church, even got back into singing on stage and doing my hardest to please God. The only thing was, I never realized how much I depended on sex to help ease my pain. My ignorance was unhealthy.

Old habits die hard, my "Sex" days may have been behind me, but my black planet days were far from over. I met this Kendrick on BP - different person same name. This one is far different. He changed my whole life.

He was thick like me, had swag like me, seemed to like me, but he tried to keep me a secret. I thought we met for the first time on BP but he said he saw me before at church, not the one where my father attended. Apparently, he had already known me through my godmother's church. He had seen me on various occasions when I attended the church to perform at Christmas dinners. By the time I realized that he was a member from my godmother's church, it was too late. Had I known he was from that church, I wouldn't have even started messin with him in the first place. I learned to keep personal and family separate. With Kendrick I declared my celibacy right from the beginning, so he knew what he was in for. I was on the right path now and needed to stay focused. *You could talk to a boy without sex, right?* Since we spent the first few months only talking on the phone it was easier to be celibate.

In the summer of 2005 my family wanted to join a

student exchange program, so we had a girl from Spain come to stay with us for the month of July. What a crazy time that was. She came expecting a white family with a pool and we were a black family with a smaller house. I pretty much counted down the days till her departure, to say the least. It was weird having another person in the house. At first she was so withdrawn but by the time she was set to leave we had become somewhat cordial, so we decided to throw her a party. I used it to my advantage to invite other friends over, including Kendrick. Before my bbq we had never hung out in person, so I was thrilled to know he was making an effort to come from Rexdale jus to see me, only problem was, he never actually showed up until it was done.

He wanted a "tour" of my house, so I left my friends downstairs while we headed upstairs. We began kissing and huggin, he stops and asks, "Would you give head?" "No sorry, I don't do that kinda stuff" He let up. Few minutes lata we was kissin again. This time I stop him an ask "Like what are we?" "What do you want me to be?" "My man" He continues to kiss my body as he replies "I'm already your man, and since I'm your man, you should wanna please me" I hesitated. *Sure, I'd wanna please you but I was successfully celibate for a couple months. I can't mess this up, God would not be pleased.* A knock at the door reminded me I wasn't alone in the house. *Shit ye, my friends.* "Just a minute" "We're gonna take off ok?" "Ok, comin" I got up to see them out and lock the door. I returned to Kendrick upstairs, but the atmosphere seemed off. He was annoyed that I wouldn't give him head, so I gave in. *I hate giving head. It feels so demeaning. There's other ways to please a man.* I gave up after a few minutes.

We went back to kissing and he kept tryna put his dick in and I kept pushing him away. "Please baby, just let me feel it" He placed his dick inside me. He gave me like two to three jukes and whispers "Do you like it?" "No, please stop" He stopped but I could tell he was cheesed. "I need to take a shower; can I get a towel?" After his shower he left and stopped talking to me. In one night, I went from relationship status, back to single. Another piece of me gone. The date was August 1st 2005.

CHAPTER FIFTEEN

A Visit

Therefore I urge you to reinstate him in your affections and reaffirm your love for him.
-2 Corinthians 2:8

Pissed about Kendrick and feeling all alone, I tried to rekindle my lost love with Maxwell. I was excited to know he wanted to see me as well, so I go an visit him sometime late August. I really wanted things to work out between us, even if he was an overly emotional guy. After spending about two hours to travel to Yorkdale mall, it was finally great to see him. He picked me up and we took the bus back to his house.

We were cracking bare jokes, felt like old times. He would not stop laughin at the lack of my braiding skills. He couldn't even catch his breath, he fell off the damn bed laughin so hard. Once he finally regained composure from laughing at me, we decided it was best to leave it alone and just lay back and chill. We ended up napping, I was so tired from the long ass commute. I don't even think I was at his house for even two hours when he got a call from his cousin and he had to leave.

I hoped he would at least take me back to Yorkdale mall because I had no clue where I was... Nope! He told me to find my way then he left me alone. I had no idea what bus to take and this was before google maps on your phone and had no way to navigate. Needless to say, I made it home safe and it took me way longer than 3 hours, but that was the last day I talked to Maxwell. I was pissed he left me to fend for myself. Period. Point blank. Once again a man disappointed me.

Poetic interlude

You neva took the chance to get to know me
Neva took the time to understand the beauty
Your physical attraction
And your dicks reaction to me
Blind sided you
An almost had me in a trance
Trance feeling so high
Wantin to do a victory dance
Thinkin after all the hurt an pain
I'd finally found the one
But mr one yu were da wrong one for me
Lettin sex guide my way
Only led me astray
Thinkin sex is equivalent to love
Dumbin down my feelings
Cause yu said you ain't ready for love
An yu aint sure what yu want
But like a fool I waited
Hanging on yur every word
Even as yu ignored me an stored me away
For what yu consider to be a rainy day
Yu neva took the chance to get to know me
Neva did yu see potential in me
Neva did yu see the wifey in me
Somebody to love n care n hold yu down
No matta how much yu made me cry
I stayed layin around
But like they say what goes around comes around
and I used to love you, I used to love them
But they neva took the chance to get to know me
Goodbye to past relationships
I'm embracin my new future to be
It's a beautiful thing when I let go and focus on me

CHAPTER SIXTEEN

Grade 11

No one has seen God at any time. But if we *love* one another [with unselfish concern], God abides in us, and His *love* [the *love* that is His essence abides in us and] is completed and perfected in us.
1 JOHN 4:12

September brought on a new school year, a new school and an ending to an interesting summer. Back to the single life of course, but in a different reality. I spent two years making friends and fitting in with the black people in town, but because the school was overcrowded they decided to ship the French speaking students to a different school. I hated that they could just up and move me like that. I worked hard to fit in and be a part of the black history celebrations and what not, now it was gone. There was only a handful of black people at my new school. Since I had some experience planning events, and since I was at a new school, it felt like a blank slate and I thought it would be great to implement a black history month tradition. I initially figured I would have some difficulty, but I could never have imagined the amount of trouble and politics I would have to go through just to have one simple yet very important assembly. To begin, when I originally proposed the idea of a black history assembly, I was turned down for no particular reason. So, I used the power of my friends and connections within the school and drew up a petition and signed up teachers just to convince the new principal that having a black history assembly was an important part of high school education.

Once I got the approval, I thought my issues with such a bureaucratic school system would be complete; yet again I was hit with mind boggling information that the principal wanted me to name the assembly that would be taking place during February a DIVERSITY assembly. The nerve of this man, he couldn't even comprehend why I was so annoyed and angered by the request. Now I'm not one to comment on somebody's race, but I found it quite peculiar that my white principal had the bright idea to ask me to rename the black history assembly to a diversity assembly in the interest of including "all minorities". His ignorance was beyond belief especially since the assembly was set to take place during only the most historical month. Regardless I drew up another petition and had the name reinstated cause that principal was trippin on some next level ting, and I'm not fond of people taking advantage of the less powerful, especially not in a school setting. Until now it still blows my mind how someone who holds the power and control over a school isn't forced to take classes on sensitivity to cultural diversity. Word. Now that I got those two things out of the way, it was time to plan the actual assembly and what I had in mind was sure to ruffle some skins. I wanted to have black dancers from Toronto come in to perform since the population of black people was so low, we didn't even have enough people to put on a decent assembly. Nevertheless, I was determined to get over the ignorant comments and more red tape. Apparently having too many black people in an area all at once in Bowmanville was cause for major concern, so yes they did try and shut down the majority of my ideas, but one thing white people hate more than having too many blacks in one area...is looking racist, uncomfortable and uncompromising. Being a new school meant that my reputation was clean and as long as my white teachers were ok with the decisions that I was making, how could anyone else go against it?

This racism thing at school got old pretty damn fast. I had placed myself on the school council to try and make a difference, but I guess I was just too hood for them. It was a battle just to get my ideas in, lucky for me I met this really cool Arabic chick named Farrah. She was my in between, she was able to be hood and diplomatic. She grew up with majority of the white kids and gained quite a bit of popularity. In order to compromise, we ended up having a school dance entitled spring bling hoedown, dats right

SPRING BLING HOEDOWN. For this dance, Farrah and I were able to convince the ignorant counsel to get a black DJ, but honestly I had never seen such a big police presence at school that night. Normally there would be two cops guarding the door. This time we had about six to ten cops guarding the doors, walking the halls and checking tickets. The next day I had some white girl on my student council mention how some big black guys kept grabbing her all night...only to see pictures from that night that clearly show that same girl posing up and smiling and DANCING with the same "scary black dudes".

I was so over the whole high school thing at this point. I mean, really? I hated my school, hated my town, and couldn't wait to leave. The racism was so hard to ignore and cope with. It was constant from every direction, and of course I was expected to look the other way or to try to be more understanding or risk looking like the angry black girl. Fuck it was annoying. There's only so many times a person can hear "How come there's no such thing as WET but you guys get a BET." I damn near lost my mind and I punched the idiot for being dumb enough to ask that question. I cried. School was so stupid, and I still wasn't convinced of why my parents had to raise us so far from civilization where black people run free.

The only positive I saw about being at this new school was the fact that they had a weight room with all brand-new equipment. Golden opportunity to get fit and prove that just because I was thicker didn't mean I hated exercise. Yeah the images on TV were really annoying considering that every time there was someone thick or big on TV they'd always play the part of someone who was on some kinda diet, loud or loved food. Exercise was my way of breaking this stereotype.

I do have to say that I have an issue with schools forcing this whole p.e thing on every student. Not everyone was ok with running laps around a gym and doing painful burpees in front of everyone else for their judgments. At least I now had a choice, and I chose weight training. Something about lifting was intriguing to me. Weight training allowed me to challenge myself and compete with the other guys in my class. I prided myself on the ability to lift as much if not more than the guys. I'd laugh as all the girls struggled and complained about the heavy equipment. I was doing really well, better than most people gave me credit for and as a bonus I was losing a good amount of weight. For once in my life I felt really accomplished. Clothes were loose and I was looking super cute. Not to mention I was eating healthy food.

By December I was rejoicing at the positive changes my body was making except for one small issue - my belly. I felt cursed, why my stomach had chosen to forsaken me and not follow suit with the rest of my body and just lay flat instead of protruding was beyond me. I couldn't understand, I was losing weight everywhere except my stomach which felt unusually hard. Other than that, I felt amazing. After months I started to feel discouraged, and then the rumors started that I was probably pregnant. I have no clue who came up with that crazy idea, but it aggravated me, especially since it wasn't even true.

I was so occupied with school and the assembly I didn't even stop to think of the last time I even saw my period, but there was no time to deal with those fears. I was busy rehearsing for the assembly. I was in charge of choreographing the dance and making sure it all went smoothly. Damn looking back I wish I had gotten some of those performances on video. Classics! Once the assembly rolled around in February it had become increasingly difficult to hide the fact that my limbs had lost weight, but my belly was still the same.

By the time March had come around and the assembly was over, I had a little more free time on my hands. March was my birthday month. I could no longer deny that my stomach was round. *Shit, what if I'm pregnant. I'm 16.* I couldn't remember my last period. I don't remember being taught in school that if you don't see your period seek help cause you might be pregnant. I remember being taught that some girls experience irregular periods. *Maybe that's what it is. I mean, I don't have any pregnancy symptoms.*

I like to solve my own issues before they become other people's problems. *Ok let me think this through, the last time I had sex was end of July, or wait was it end of August. Did I get my period in August? I saw Kendrick end of July, but we didn't even do much. I mean he barely put it in, definitely didn't cum. No way I can get pregnant off of that. But then when I saw Maxwell at the end of August, he ditched me after a few hours. We didn't even get a chance to do anything, did we?. Shit I can't remember that was too long ago. I can't even remember what I ate last night, I was busy. Just relax. It's hard to relax though. My mom said she'd kick me out of the house if I ever got pregnant. Iight lemme ask my girls for their opinion.* Now... maybe... my not so big problem was a huge problem, and otha people problem. I emailed my friends to tell them that I thought there was a chance that I was pregnant. They gave a pretty supportive response. They said it would all work itself out and that if I really needed, I could probably stay with them for a bit. That was a relief, cause I knew that if I was really truly pregnant there was no way that I'd be able to stay in my cozy gospel home. I often felt very numb. I would daydream about running away. Finding a hospital and giving birth on my own and how life was now going to be since I had failed everyone. I basically became the disgraceful failure that they said I was. A baby, at 16? And the pastor's daughter. Wow I reallllllly fucked up. I prayed to God everyday hoping that I wasn't pregnant but with each day that passed, that prayer seemed less likely to come true. It was too late for any abortion, too late to plan, too late to keep my secrets hidden. I had just gotten life together, just started to love myself, just started to breathe. If I am pregnant though, I want it to be a boy. I'd love to have a son I can dress and take to the barber. How do I check if I'm pregnant without suspicion?

I knew nothing about pregnancy. I felt like I was being let down by TV and society. I mean I never developed any real symptoms, and the fatigue and increased appetite that I had experienced seemed perfectly logical since I was in the weight room for an hour every day and my body was going through several changes.

Outside of very mild symptoms, I never experienced any serious issues; no nausea, no headaches, nothing. I still thought I was normal. Besides missing my period and symptoms...the TV didn't teach me anything about being pregnant and Sex Ed... useless.

Rather than deal with my situation I continued to ignore it. I mean, why not? What could possibly go wrong if I ignored my situation for a bit longer, long enough to enjoy my birthday and still have a home to return to. See 17 was close to 18 and at 18 there was not really any reason why my parents have to keep me if I'm not cooperating at home. Except for the fact that I was doing everything really well, I was gettin good grades, still in church, nothing changed. Just my belly and my status went from single to single mother.

One of my classmates and I had birthdays just days apart and we decided to celebrate both of them by going to a Juelz Santana concert. I was never allowed to go to any concerts that weren't Christian, but I really wanted to experience life and a concert outside of church walls. I went there looking fly as hell. I didn't realize the concert was so late at night or that it was a standing only event. It was so different then the concerts I went to at church. We had the option to sit when we got tired, and those concerts ended at the same time this one was beginning. This concert didn't even start till it was past my bedtime. Everything seemed pretty chill, nice vibes, I enjoyed the opening act. My friend and I decided to freshen up in the bathroom before the main act came on. As I'm touching up my hair and makeup, a girl came to me and asked how many months I was. I stood with a look of horror as I responded that I wasn't even pregnant. It felt like she had just exposed my biggest secret to my friend. The look on the girls face was even more horrified than mine as she apologized a million times. It was so awkward. Made me feel uneasy and embarrassed. By the time we left the bathroom, it was time for Juelz to take the stage. I learned that people turn into real groupies at these types of concerts. I saw bare men rushing to the stage. As they rushed, my friend and I got pulled and pushed with them.

While being pushed, some guy punched me in my stomach trying to get to the stage. I was trampled upon, my feet hurt, my clothes torn, my weave was sticking in different directions and my stomach was burning, I was extremely nauseous. Everythin hurt a lot but I made it. This was not the birthday I had imagined. Not even close. I just wanted to go home.

CHAPTER SEVENTEEN

Rumors & Truths

Better is a dinner of vegetables and herbs where love is present
Than a fattened ox served with hatred.
-Proverbs 15 :17

People at school were talking about me being pregnant, the girl at the concert thought I was, and now I had church people saying the same damn thing. It was like everyone could now see what I kept trying so hard to keep hidden. Despite the rumors, one thing I really wanted to do was water baptism. I really felt as though I had overcome many demons and wanted to dedicate my life to God and publicly show that I was trying to make my life better, despite all the circumstances. I lost weight, I was active in church and school, I was no longer haunted by the trauma of the rapes. I was a in a good space and wanted that to continue. It felt like it took forever to even get to this point and I had worked so hard.

Today was the big day. I awoke super stoked about my baptism. I had invited a ton of people to be witnesses. Minutes after my eyes opened, my parents called me to their room. "Is there any chance that you could be pregnant?" It was like being hit with a ton of heavy, heavy bricks. My response to them was, "I don't know". Words escaped my mouth, and my father cried harder than I've ever seen. My answer was the wrong one. I was met with two emotions that day, pain and anger. The pain came from my dad and my mother was angry.

My parent's reactions were fueled by two separate sources. For my father he felt that he failed his household. He was so involved with church that he was missing out on important things at home. He also felt that because of this failure, he was inadequate as a pastor and should resign his position until he was able to create a healthy balance. My mom seemed to be all about image. Her main message to me that day was how embarrassing it was for her, that her peers and members of the church would now look down on her. Especially because she was a nurse, she felt like she should have seen the signs long before it got this far. I felt as though I was just another disappointment for my mom, and in that moment I believed she wished she had sent me to the group home when she had the chance back when all this trouble, embarrassment and disgrace commenced.

Emotions aside, we all still had to put on a happy face and get ready for church. On our drive to church my dad let me know that there was a chance that I wouldn't be allowed to get baptized that day based on the decision of the church board. Even the possibility of being pregnant could disqualify me from being baptized.

Ever wanted something so bad only to have it ripped out right before your eyes? I can't express the emotion that I felt that day, I was hurting bad. I had told so many people about the baptism however my issue wasn't with the fact that so many people knew, it was with the fact that despite everything, I had overcome it all and realized that God still loved me. He accepted me. This was supposed to be a clean start for me.

I stepped into the office with all the members vividly upset as I explained that there was a possibility that I may be pregnant. The pastor looked at me and said that I wasn't allowed to get baptized because it would send the wrong message. I was so confused cause I couldn't understand what message I was sending, God was supposed to love me too. ME! If not even God accepted me as a pregnant teen than who would? So many emotions filled my body as I cried and pleaded and begged my dad and the church committee. I repeated the words over and over "I want to get baptized".

All of sudden my date with God and a new start was hanging on by a thread and I had no control. I waited for their decision and cried in silence. They decided it would be pending an answer from the doctors to confirm whether I really was pregnant. At that point, nothing mattered to me. The only thing I wanted was taken away with the dictation of one person. After taking all the pre-baptism classes I was forced to sit and watch my sister get baptized while I explained to everyone I invited that I was possibly pregnant and therefore banned from taking part. I was crushed, jealous, angry, I cried silently as I stared aimlessly at the stage, the baptism couldn't have felt any longer. It took forever. I could feel the awkward stares and fake sympathetic words from people who didn't know what to say.

Bright and early the next morning my mom was on the phone with my doctor setting up the appointment. Great news, he was able to squeeze me in that day. The visit seemed to go interestingly well since I lied to the doctor. He asked me when my last period was and to save myself the embarrassment of saying I don't know, I told him that my period was regular. The first test we did, the one where I pee on a stick, came back positive. Then to be 100% certain, my doctor sent me for a blood test. That also came back pregnant and stunned just about everyone, I was sent to do an ultrasound to determine how far along I was. I had no clue there woulda been so much testing involved. It was overwhelming. If I complained, my mom would say that it was my fault for getting myself into the situation and she had no sympathy for me. Most questions I had, was either answered by my doctor or google. During the ultrasound appointment I was asked about prenatal care. I didn't even know that existed. "I go to the gym and I eat healthy, that's all the care I've been doing." I could feel the judgments coming from the ultrasound tech. It was like I could feel her saying, "This kid has no clue about life." She tried to keep a smile as she informed me that I was roughly 8 months pregnant. She says, "Of course I can't be sure since you can't tell me when your last period was, but my estimation is that he will be born sometime in May" Then she says, "It's a boy". I thanked her, cleaned myself up then left. I was tired, confused, but happy. *A boy? Really? That's what I was hoping for eventually when I had kids.* I loved boys. The reality was, he was coming, now...not later.

Within a few days of the ultrasound, I had more tests done and more results revealed. I was positive for Chlamydia. Chlamydia? Sounds familiar, I think I had learned about that in school. Great, the one time that class seemed to be helpful. I knew what it was but what I didn't know was who, what, where, and when...I knew the why...I had sex, duh! I had no clue how long I even had this thing. It could have been from a number of incidents. I lied to the nurse after the gang rape, so she never ended up doing any test on me. Having an STD took a different toll on me mentally, especially once I read the effects it could have on the baby. I prayed harder for a healthy baby than I had prayed for anything else in my whole life.

Telling my friends and teachers that I was pregnant wasn't easy, although they were very supportive. I had developed a great report with my teachers and they had grown fond of me. My parents had a hard time getting used to it and my so-called extended family didn't seem surprised at all since they already thought I was a hoe; I basically progressed to the next stage of hoeism. In a short time I had everyone find out before I even had the chance to process what was happening.

Ok, so the ultrasound lady said 8 months, due in May. Lemme count backwards, what month is 8 months ago? Feb, Jan, December, ...November...k, end of July, that means Kendrick. But that was only pre-cum how can anyone get pregnant off that? It was barely anything. Are you kidding me? The proof is in the belly I guess, cause I am pregnant. I am pregnant. I am 16 and pregnant. How the hell do I tell him? The last time I even talked to him was the end of August. I told him my period was late, but he said not to worry about it if my period was usually irregular, which it was. Oh man, I haven't had to think about this for a long time. He probably hasn't given any thought to it either. My periods are irregular, only this time it never came back. What the hell. He's not gonna believe me. It's ok, I'll just do this without him. He doesn't even need to know. Who the hell gets pregnant from pre-cum anyway. It's been too long in between. Yeah, that's what I'll do.

The worst part of everyone finding out was when my dad asked me who the father was, I refused to give him the name and he refused to let the situation go. He grabbed the phone off the wall and held it out as he repeatedly asked me in a stern voice for the number. He left me no option, I was scared. Scared for myself and also for Kendrick. Can you imagine how surprised he must have been when he got a call from my father. I tried to tell my dad that I would tell Kendrick, but he wasn't ok with that either. My dad wanted to be the one to tell Kendrick, he wanted to make sure that he knew the situation. My dad didn't trust that I would actually tell Kendrick myself. He was right, I was so ashamed.

The last time that I spoke to Kendrick was the summer of 2005. Even though my father called him and told him I was pregnant, I knew in my heart that Kendrick wasn't gonna do anything. Besides the fact that all this news was very overwhelming and sudden, he didn't strike me as the mature type. Needless to say, the conversation didn't go too well, there was a lot of anger and yelling. I know that I am to blame for his shock and denial. 8 months was a long time to keep something this major hidden. He didn't seem to understand how I could have gotten pregnant and why we were botherin him about it. Understand I did not blame Kendrick for his skepticism. The logic seemed simple for me, but Kendrick said, "I was just another hoe tryna trap an innocent man." He didn't give a shit about the life of the seed growing inside me. He said he wanted a DNA test, "Sure, once the baby is born." I wasn't surprised by his reaction, this was the whole reason I didn't see a point in telling him.

Poetic Interlude

Take me as I am,
Or jus let me be me
Why judge me
If yu don't really know me
Don't kno where I've come from
Don't even kno how I got to where I'm at
Only God can judge me
Only God can tell me right from wrong
Do yu kno my heart bleeds?

Or when the first cut was?
I wish ppl would take the time to get to know the real me
This me is all I can be
Yet I'm constantly cut down by words
The same words I love
Are the same words that cut me
I am never good enough
Don't matta how much I try
Who cares how much I cry
Secretly it hurts
I would never show emotion
Cause emotions show my weaknesses
I am not weak
But I truly seek
A love that never dies
Sweet love that won't break my heart
Or make me cry
There's only one man that could provide such a love
The only man that's been carryin me through all my rough times
Doesn't live on earth but far far above
Been through my ups an downs
An knows the real me
Not jus from one meeting while sippin on tea
This man took the time to know the ins an outs
I've abused his love
I am my worst critic
There's no way he could possibly love a sinner like me
So why bother?
I told myself yur below him
He's got thousands of ppl to love
So he could never have the time it flies as fast as a dove
Feel like I'm caught in between lives
The sinning life I've lived an the christian life I want
standing outside looking in
won't you please let me in?
or is my big pregnant belly
too much of a sin?

CHAPTER EIGHTEEN

March

Consider how I love Your precepts; Revive me and give me life, O LORD, according to Your lovingkindness.
-Psalm 119 :159

The month of March seemed like it could never end. Though it did lend many lessons to me, as I became so much more aware of my body and the changes. I felt my son's head drop during this month which created this enormous pressure. It felt like I had to constantly run to the bathroom. Unaware of my son before, during this 3rd trimester he was choosing to be a lot more active. Wow those words, MY son...never thought I'd be saying those words so young. Damn. But ye, my son was kicking and moving around a lot more than any other time, so even if I wanted to...there would be no denying him anymore. *What about school? Do I go? Do I drop out? I'm on a really good path to finishing with a high average this year. What do I do about my son? Or his health? There's so much I missed out on and he needs as much care as possible now.* I was given a list of vitamins and prenatal care that I was now responsible for. The health practitioners looked at me as if I was careless even though this was all new to me. I can't drop out, and I can't ignore the baby, so I'll just have to do both, strive for excellence and hope for the best.

I didn't expect any free rides just because I was pregnant. People kept telling me "Once you get pregnant, your life is over" I hated that. I feel as though life could only be over if I allowed it to be over. Life was just...different, and possibly more fulfilling. I made arrangements with my teachers that I would continue my work from home once my son was born, but I would return to class for any exams.

It felt awkward being the pregnant girl in high school once everyone found out. It wasn't all bad though, people were really excited for me and even helped me pick baby names. We played around with different names like Jahlil, I only wanted to name my child something with a powerful meaning. I believe that the name of a person was a testament to who they would become in the world and I needed my child to have a name that would truly represent the gifts that he could eventually bring to the world. My girl Farrah gave him one of his middle names and of course he took my last name. There was no way I was gonna give my child the last name of a man who could care less; his or not.

Opposite to school, things at home weren't as great, my parents, mainly my mother, were having trouble adjusting to the fact that I was pregnant. I mean I get it, I was young, it was a horrible image, blah blah blah; there was no way to change the past, so we needed to get past it, my mother just wasn't ready to. My mother was having difficulty with even the smallest adjustments. I started feeling like her anger and embarrassment was starting to boil over and affect my life as well. Please tell me how someone wakes up mad and yelling? I don't get it, it was as if she drank angerade mixed with a bowl of yelling puffs. My mother was the hardest on me out of everyone. I remember her saying that she thought the reason I didn't say anything to her about the pregnancy was because I knew I'd have to find somewhere else to live. The fact that she vocalized what I already thought meant for me that I was almost vindicated and justified for not saying anything.

But what about the baby? Was it justification that he didn't get to receive any prenatal care or regular checkups? It was almost like the mental awareness of the pregnancy symptoms started once everything was confirmed. I would crave McDonald's cheeseburgers with honey, pizza and pitas...none of which were at close proximity to my house. It would take me at least 20 mins to walk to any of those restaurants. My determination surpassed the walking distance. Plus, this walk was great to clear my head from everything happening with my family.

Things were confusing with my family, hot and cold, loving and hurting. Getting pregnant seemed to "erase" all the "bad" I had done. Being the first of all my cousins to get pregnant there was general interest in the baby. I had trouble making sense out of the fact that this family who cut me down with words and said I was a disgrace was acting like nothing happened. I was still hurt by the words and the treatment, but it was as if they expected me to get over it and move on. Well I couldn't. I didn't want to see them. I wasn't ready to forgive them. As for my aunt's boyfriend, he finally gave up trying. It had been ongoing for almost two years. I got even more bold with avoiding him. I wouldn't even stay in the same room as him. As soon as he entered a room, I left. I would stare him down whenever I saw him. I wanted him to feel as uncomfortable as he made me feel. I guess it was noticeable because he eventually just backed off. I was older now and flat out refused to go to that house, so my mother stopped making me.

The pregnancy forced me to deal with a few issues that weighed heavily on me. I wrote a letter to my parents acknowledging and apologizing for all the trouble I had caused. Then I found the courage to tell them it was a gang rape when I had previously stayed silent out a fear. The last truth came out when my parents asked me if my aunt's boyfriend used to touch me. This time I told them exactly what had been happening.

I think they already suspected something. My grandma had heard rumors and I guess my behavior was noticeably changing. My other family members didn't believe a word that I said. They thought I was talking shit. I heard one of them say "If you were really raped, why wouldn't you say anything? You just didn't want people to figure out the truth that you're a hoe". My aunt said that when she asked him if he had ever touched me he seemed "shocked" and said "I don't know why she would say things like that because it's not true. I've always been nice to her." I heard rumors how he had done the same thing to another girl in the neighborhood...but that's it, they were just rumors and they did nothing to help with my own predicament.

Even though I couldn't depend on my family, at least my friends did their best to create enjoyable moments for me. Just because my friends were happy didn't mean their parents were. I was now branded as the bad friend, the irresponsible misfit that would corrupt their children. Of the friends that were allowed to be around me - mostly white at the time, they had thrown me a baby shower. I had people who went out of their way to get me baby food, clothes, and diapers. It was a cozy, successful event at my friend's house. Impressed upon me was the importance of community instead of isolation. This was a lesson in culture for me. White vs Black. Understanding vs intolerant behaviour. It hurt that none of my family or parents showed up or supported me during the shower.

Even some of the elders of my church seemed to take my pregnancy a lot easier than my family did. They planned their own celebration and showered me with various gifts. It was a moment of joy in a turbulent time. But how do I keep going when I'm pulled in so many different directions?

CHAPTER NINETEEN

Romeo

> "May he kiss me with the kisses of his mouth!" [Solomon arrives, she turns to him, saying,]
> "For your love is better than wine.
> "The aroma of your oils is fragrant and pleasing;
> Your name is perfume poured out;
> Therefore the maidens love you.
> "Draw me away with you and let us run together!
> Let the king bring me into his chambers."
> -Songs of Solomon 1:2-4,

March 14th, 2006. Even though I was dealing with the pregnancy and all the stuff with my family and friends, at least I knew I could rely on MSN. It was the next big thing after black planet. I remember seeing the pop up of someone signing in online with an email address that looked familiar, so I said hey, and an instant conversation was struck when he responded hey back. We started chatting and soon got into deeper topics like family before realizing that we didn't actually know each other. I fully thought he was my girl's man who I would periodically hit up and he thought that I was one of his ex-ting's that set him up to trap him. I didn't think guys actually got paranoid of that situation but here we were, two strangers talking as if we knew each other. I had to convince him I didn't know any of his ting's and from the fact that he didn't recognize me I knew right away he wasn't who I thought he was.

Now before anyone gets any bright ideas and wonders why I was talking to my girl's man...we were friends and had polite conversation. Both men had similar emails with different number combinations.

Anyway, once we got over that, and we were confident it wasn't a setup, the conversation was golden. We had so many things in common it was almost scary. For example: fav color, blue; favorite candy: fuzzy peaches; favorite vegetable: broccoli. Ha! Yes, these all came up in conversation. Favorite movie: *Love & Basketball*, but then again who didn't have that movie on the top of the fav list back then? We spoke for hours about everything, I felt unusually comfortable with him. I couldn't explain it, but it felt like I had known him for years. He just understood me on all levels without me having to over explain myself. We had gotten to a point where I felt like I shouldn't keep my pregnancy a secret. It felt like I was falling too deep too quickly, and I didn't want him to get caught up only to realize I was pregnant. I didn't want to lie. I dreaded telling him cause I half expected him to run away and get offline. The conversation was too good, and I wasn't ready for him to leave yet. "I have something to tell you" I typed it out and waited anxiously for him to type back. Surprisingly when I told him my situation he replied "Ok". Since he seemed to take it so well I also said, "And I have Chlamydia". Once again, I expected him to log off. He said "Ok, I have something to tell you too. I have a son." In the end I guess it kinda worked out for us, we both had one son. It was kind of a weird thing having so much in common with someone who I had never met, granted he could have been lying but I wanted to see where this was going.

We were talking every day but then he signed on and began asking who I was. I was confused until he clarified that who I was actually talking to was his twin sister, Raquel. Apparently Romeo was the type of guy who didn't ever use the computer, but from when we started talking he had moved the shared computer into his room. His sister said it was completely out of character but when he explained how he had met someone she had to see for herself. She told me Romeo hated typing. I never would have guessed since we typed for hours at a time. We spent so much time telling stories that we didn't even think about sharing photos. By the time the conversation of pics came up, we decided it wasn't even necessary. We wanted a chance to get to know each other without the physical element.

Since I was now aware of his dislike for typing, we decided to exchange numbers and start talking on the phone. His voice was hmm, deep and sexy! Just the way I loved it. I tried to picture what he looked like. I knew from conversation he was at least 6 feet, black, muscular...He just sounded delicious. His voice had a way of soothing me and in return I made sure my voice left him hungry for more. Soft, seductive and smiling. It was my specialty.

We both had our own family issues but found comfort in each other. The tension at my home varied each day. The arguments with my mom were constant, and my sister would forever bother me by flicking my stomach just to make my child kick me, and every time she flicked he kicked. It angered me. I didn't have a good relationship with my mom or my sister which added to my daily frustration. It became harder to cope and I spent more time locked in my room with the comfort of my phone, my baby and my man. He was always there for me any time of the day or night, I felt safe talking to him. Back when phone calls were only free after 6 he still called during the day when I needed him.

Tuesday March 21st, 2006 - A week after we met online, he says "Do you wanna be my girl?". I couldn't have been happier. It was early, yes, but we both knew we wanted to be in each other's lives. Not sure if it was classified as "dating" since we hadn't met but it felt very real to us. It felt like we were just reconnecting. It became the beginning to a beautifully dangerous relationship. A roller coaster of emotions that would sail to many highs and lows during the next couple of months.

CHAPTER TWENTY

God's Helper

"O my love, you are altogether beautiful and fair. There is no flaw nor blemish in you!
-Songs of Solomon 4 :7

Student council life had its perks. As my girl and I sat in a room one day to organize a dance party, we realized there was boxes of bags leftover that appeared to be abandoned. We found pizza coupons in each bag. You know the one that Pizza Pizza would give out that allowed you to get a free slice? We struck gold. Now in high school, even the smallest things could be turned into a major thing. There was one coupon in each bag and there were soooo many bags, at least 60-70. Going through each bag, we took out the coupons. By the end I swear I had at least 30 coupons to myself. It was a great day. I knew I wouldn't be hungry for the next while.

It was Saturday April 22nd, 2006, me and my pregnant self decided that I wanted a free slice of pizza, only issue was it was a good walk from my house. I convinced my sister to come with me. I'll never forget that day. The pizza was especially delicious and my energy seemed to be different. Sunday April 23rd 2006 I woke up and headed to the bathroom except when I bent down to pee a gross amount of fluid gushed from my body. I freaked. Screamed for my mom. Despite our differences, I needed her at that very moment. Who was I kidding, I thought that I could have done this all by myself? Wrong. Apparently all that walking up and down to get pizza had my child anxious to come out. As we jumped in the car and rushed to the hospital I couldn't help but feel blessed; like this child was saving my life. The mixed emotions that I felt were overwhelming. The life that I was living was headed in the wrong direction, and even though I was making changes, it definitely wouldn't be enough on my own or even quick enough for the drastic changes that I needed.

I was driven to Oshawa hospital to give birth to my son. My mother was a nurse for a hospital in Scarborough, but we didn't go there even though she knew the doctors and nurses. She was too embarrassed to tell anyone that she had a pregnant teenage daughter. She didn't exactly say those words, but it was in her actions and she was against me having my child at a hospital where her co-workers could find out about the baby. It hurt. My mom was ashamed of me, just like so many people in the family; I was an outcast. I brought shame and disgrace to the family and they didn't shy away from letting me know every chance that they got.

Once I got to the hospital, that was a different scenario, the baby wasn't ready to come out but my water had broken so I was forced to just wait until he felt ready to come out. Since no one knew my initial due date and I needed to be retested for Chlamydia, they admitted me into the hospital to monitor my progression. Aaliyah came to keep me company. We played cards. It's the best memory I have of that day. I guess the nurses were jealous of how much fun I was having cause by 6 o'clock that night, they induced me. Induce means they began a procedure to stimulate my body to start natural labour. It was the first time I had really felt cramps. During my periods I don't ever really get cramps, so this was definitely a new experience for me; and it hurt. A lot. It was a surreal feeling. I had never been in a hospital before. The flow of people, the machines, the pain; it was all happening at once. *What did I get myself into?*

When I wasn't playing cards I was texting Romeo, he was on his way down to visit me and be present for the birth. I was excited to see him but then all of a sudden he stopped texting and didn't answer my calls. Worried about him and dealing with these cramps I could barely sleep. The cramps were getting worse by the hour. Finally, Romeo texted me late at night, a welcomed distraction. But he was in a car accident. He was okay but he was disappointed that he wouldn't be able to make it to the hospital. I was alone, disappointed and distracted from my own pain by worrying about him. My mother had decided that she didn't want me to get an epidural so that I would experience the pain and remember the consequences of my actions. I asked for one but the nurses kept delaying. I cried through the pain. With each contraction I clenched my eyes and fist and tried to roll to one side. It was my mom's friend who sat with me and held my hand through the night as each pain ripped through me.

By 9 am Monday morning it was time to begin pushing. *I had made it through the night. Thank God!* I was just ready to be done with this whole thing. 24hrs in a hospital was a long time. The nurse had come in wanting to do a final check. I thought it was just her, but then more nurses came in. It felt so awkward opening my legs to a bunch of strangers, like some kinda show I was putting on for them. I wanted to close my legs but they wouldn't let me. By the time the doctor finally came in the morning to do the epidural it was too late. Go figure. I had already dilated enough to start pushing. My mom comes in right before we begin to push. She was happy that I didn't get the epidural. From what I have seen on TV, I am supposed to scream as I push out this baby. Boy was that wrong. As soon as I started to scream my mom told me it was a waste of energy and that's not what I'm supposed to do. *Like I really know what I'm doing.* I laid there and awaited my next instructions. "Push" the nurses said in unison. I didn't know how to push. *What do they mean push? Push what?* I contracted my body and tried something, it felt like I was pooing but still very constipated. Ew. Gross. Apparently, I did something right? The nurse says, "Keep going, you're doing great " Ok, *I guess this is what I'm supposed to do.* I felt like I was multitasking. Trying to push, but not scream, or complain about the pain. I had to keep going, not allowed to stop. It was like having a personal trainer, every time I tried to take a break the nurses would say "Don't stop, keep going" *Can I breathe though?* I was supposed to be breathing continually throughout the whole time. I guess I missed that in prenatal care classes.

24 hours of labour with no epidural, no screaming, my son came flying out...literally. As I gave my last big push the foot of the bed dropped and the doctor caught him. I guess all those hours spent at the gym really paid off. My abs were in great shape. *I wonder how many babies he's had to catch in his career.* There I lay, no longer 16 and pregnant, but a 17-year-old single mother holding the most precious thing I'd ever seen. Kayshaun Antwoine Isaiah Bennett a.k.a Kaykay was born April 24, 2006 at 9 am. The name Kayshaun is actually two names that I combined to create one. Kay means happy and rejoicing, Shaun means gift from God. My friend Farrah actually gave him his middle names. Antwoine means highly praiseworthy and Isaiah means God's helper. When it came to the last name, that was easy, neither his father or his father's family wanted to get involved, so Kaykay took my last name Bennett, which meant little blessed one. This day in the hospital really changed my life.

Poetic Interlude

Twinkle twinkle little star how I wonder what you are
How I wonder who yu are
How true yu are
My little star
Started as an egg
Then yu grew
I was livin in denial
No thoughts in my head or my body
Through and through
Neva wanted to believe
That with that man I did conceive
Such a precious little seed which was you
9 months later yu took a breath of air
Born to one parent only and I kno it's not fair
How dare that sperm donor not even care
He brought life to this world yu ain't no teddy bear you're a boy soon to be a man

My lil man mommas yur biggest fan in life
So do what's right an succeed
Take heed
Don't let my heart bleed
From yu makin foolish mistakes
Everythin I do is to open up gates for you
to choose
Twinkle twinkle little star how I wonder what you are
How I wonder who yu are
How true yu are
My little star
Read read baby boy yu need to read
Feed feed baby feed yur mind
Weed weed boy stay away from the weed
No matta how bad things are your gonna be jus fine
Read read baby boy yu must read
Feed feed baby don't starve yur mind
Weed weed boy drop that weed
As long as yu have God you'll be jus fine
Twinkle twinkle little star how I wonder what you are
How I wonder who yu are
How true yu are
My little star
Twinkle twinkle little star baby boy you are my star
Sent from only God above
Born with mighty mighty love
Twinkle twinkle little star you're exactly what I wished for
and I'm blessed.

CHAPTER TWENTY-ONE

Peace To My Storm

Let her be as a loving hind and graceful doe, Let her breasts refresh and satisfy you at all times; Always be exhilarated and delight in her love.
-Proverbs 5 :19

My stomach knots and my cheeks flush every time I get a text from him. At 17 he's the peace to my storm. He writes me poems, sends me love songs, checks up on me every chance he gets, and he tells me "I love you". When he says it, I believe him. I've never felt so safe and secure, it's like nothing can get me down when I'm with him. I've shared my deepest pains and showed my darkest corners and he has stayed by my side. I've been able to share with him my experience with rape without feeling like he wanted to take advantage of me. I was nervous the first time I told him about my aunt's boyfriend. I didn't think he would believe me, but you know what? He believed me. I described to him every moment that man touched me or made comments towards me and he listened without judgment. When I was done telling him, he said "I will always protect you, I promise". I've never felt protected like that before, I knew that as long as he was in my life he would never let anything happen to me. I was falling fast and deep; not even two months yet but this feeling that consumed me was incredible. I've never talked to someone so constantly about everything, nothing and anything in between without boredom or fail. I was free to be myself; quirks and all and allowed him to be himself.

Even the transition from teen to single mom seemed a lot smoother once he was by my side encouraging me. He was a parent himself, so he understood my situation. He did small things to show he cared like stepping up to buy Kaykay's birth certificate for me. As much as Romeo had told me to leave my baby fadda alone, I couldn't give up so easily, yet I couldn't even get the guy to answer my phone calls to set up a DNA test, much less paying for a birth certificate.

Whenever I stayed home from school Romeo stayed home too and we would spend all day on the phone. He took time off school to be on the phone, just to make sure I was okay and keep me company. We spent all day talking and watching judge shows. Divorce court was our favorite show to watch because we would examine the different characters with their relationship problems. We used the examples in the show as scenarios of what we should avoid in our own relationship. Like cheating, that was something that I wasn't prepared to put up with because I was done feeling broken hearted. It's crazy how much you can learn and get attached to someone by just talking to them every day.

The closer we got, the more intimate we wanted to be, but with the distance we were forced to be creative. I loved his innocence. For him sex was straight-forward, for me intimacy happened on different levels. He had never participated in phone sex until he met me. Phone sex was a tool I used to flirt, and it became a very easy mind game for me. I enjoyed the power it gave me. I enjoyed the freedom of being very sexual without the touch. I wasn't even sure if it would be something he liked, and I was a bit nervous about it, so I started him off slow. I softened my voice and told him a story. Similar to how erotica books use descriptive words, I spoke slow, had minimal breathing and created an alluring image for him and listened to him squirm. Something like "You come home from a long day at work...tired. You open the door and find all the lights are off and a note that says meet me in the kitchen. You turn the corner towards the kitchen but before you can enter, you hear a whisper saying close your eyes. You find yourself blindfolded and smell a sweet aroma in the air while your lips are stained with chocolate. You taste the lips of familiarity and the unbuttoning of your shirt. Steam hits your skin as you enter what you guess to be the shower. As the water hits you, allow your mind to wander to freedom.

You feel a tickle, a smile and a warm sensation. Exhale stress. Deep breaths. Focus on love. Focus on me...."

It obviously gets more detailed than that, but this ain't an erotica book so I'll stop there. This was different with Romeo, I actually enjoyed the journey, the stories, the pursuit. The more we had phone sex, the more comfortable he got and the more we connected. He thought I was a freak, my response...define freak? *wink* It felt like a joining of our souls every time and my heart longed more than ever to be with him.

The most beautiful thing was knowing your partner feels just as deeply for you as you feel for them. We wanted more than anything to have a family of our own. We were both two broken souls latching onto whatever sign of love and life there was left. I felt so rejected by the family I had, and he was lacking the love that I wanted to provide. I already had a child, why not add wife to my life and be complete. I finally had a man who loved me unconditionally and wanted to spoil me rotten. He didn't judge me or make me feel insecure or less than. We finally exchanged pictures for the sake of knowing how each other looked but it didn't even matter. I mean it was like hitting the lotto once I saw that he was actually really good looking but to me his heart and words meant so much more. It was the same for him, he didn't see weight... he saw a beautiful woman with a heart and ass to match. He had gotten so used to women loving him superficially it became annoying. He wanted to find someone who was interested in his personality and not just his physical appearance. I loved his personality. He was funny, intelligent, sarcastic, understanding, logical and realistic. Iuno what he did for work, but he kept himself together well.

He was a great father and the type of man I wanted to help raise my son. Since neither of us had daughters we saw it as a blessing and a potential beginning to our family. I wanted to be able to give him his first daughter. I pictured us together after finally finding happiness in each other. We acted as if we were physically living with each other. We did everything together, we slept together - like never hung up the phone till morning, we sometimes ate together, shared recipes and watched movies together for our "date nights", all through phone conversations. All we had to do was meet up to complete the fantasy.

Since he missed Kaykay's birth we had missed our first opportunity to meet up. We set up a day for him to bring his son down to come see me and Kaykay. The easiest place to meet was at the mall close to my house. I arrived at the mall, which wasn't that big and waited for him to arrive. We had agreed upon a time when we spoke briefly earlier that day but not a location. I tried calling his phone to figure out the best spot to meet but his phone kept going straight to voicemail. I walked the mall looking for someone who resembled the picture I had but couldn't find him. I wasn't able to get in contact with Romeo until later that night when he called to explain what happened. He said he was at the mall looking around for me, but his phone had gotten damaged that same day and made it impossible for him to call. The thing that didn't make sense to me was that the mall wasn't that big to begin with and was majority white, therefore a tall black man would have stood out like a sore thumb - especially a man with a stroller. I was really upset and questioned his answer. Anything was possible, and it was only the second time we tried to meet. I took comfort in the fact that it wasn't the only time we were going to meet. Romeo would offer to drive down from Brampton to my house in Courtice to see me. I would be up talking to him then completely black out and only to wake an hour later to text messages saying that he was outside waiting for me. This happened on a few occasions. No matter how much I slept and tried to stay awake, whenever he was supposed to come check me I would black out. Eventually we had to stop trying to meet because it became taxing on our relationship. We had no explanation for the situation, he would get mad that I blacked out, and I would question whether or not he even drove out. I would normally wake up as he was driving back and got frustrated that he wouldn't turn around once I woke up even though it was a waste of gas and time. Nothing made sense. My friends warned me that he could be lying, but in my heart, I refused to believe that was true. I know his friends were telling him the same thing about me and he defended me each time.

It felt like the universe was keeping us apart. It was no longer something I could only blame on him. The circumstances presented were weird and unexplainable, but I only had the universe to blame...really truly.

CHAPTER TWENTY-TWO

Phone

Run away from youthful lusts--pursue righteousness, faith, love, and peace with those [believers] who call on the Lord out of a pure heart.

-2 Timothy 2:22

I couldn't control that situation, but what I could always control was myself, my body. This was my power. I reminisced on the first time I learned that I could fake orgasms. Ludacris had this song:

> "I wanna li li li lick you from your head to your toes. And I wanna move from the bed down to the down to the to the floor. Then I wanna ah ah you make it so good I don't wanna leave. But I gotta kno kno kno know wha what's your fan-ta-ta-sy"

I always had a lot of fun playing around with this song. It was pure pleasure for me to hear a man on the other line get off without me even touching him. Sexually it had no effect on me, I could turn the orgasms on and off while being completely detached. It kept men coming back for reasons they didn't even understand.

The longer it took for Romeo and I to meet in person, the more we connected sexually over the phone. It changed from every once in a while to several times per day. Sometimes we did it in my car other times whenever we could sneak away. I was drawn to his deep voice and the feeling of him needing me. The more I sensed he needed me the more I enjoyed it. For the first time, it wasn't just a game. It was love.

It was all new to him though so where two was fun, three had become a party. I'm not even sure how and when things changed but we progressed quickly. He always asked if I'd be interested in a threesome, and although I had thought of it, it wasn't something I ever went through with. When the opportunities came up I always found a reason why I couldn't. He had thought of it though and even had someone in mind. A woman he had previously messed with long before me who he knew was no stranger to threesomes. To be honest, since it was on the phone it made it easier to agree to. I wasn't actually doing anything, right? I wasn't attracted to women, not in the slightest, but Romeo wanted a threesome and I thought it would make him happy. Switch to game mode, block it out and it'll be fine.

The first time it was really awkward for the 3 of us. Neither of us spoke or knew how to begin. Usually I knew exactly what to do but I was nervous. She started the story, but her story described oral sex with Romeo and I got jealous. I didn't want him in her narrative. He was mine, I couldn't sit and listen to her talk about him, but I didn't wanna chicken out, so I turned the attention to me. I was feeling insecure. I didn't want his interest to grow for this other woman, so I changed the rules. What started out as a threesome became a twosome with just me and the girl while Romeo listened. Male fantasy, right? At least this way he had no other reason to cheat on me, right? I was doing everything I could to keep him happy.

It felt so unnatural, I didn't want to do anything, but the more Romeo liked it, the more I tried to get into it. Then I got too into it. The more I could manipulate the situation with her the more I enjoyed myself but then Romeo felt jealous and left out. Our "sessions" happened only a few times, but the more I did it the worse I felt. They were happy, but I felt so low. *This ain't you.* Parts of me enjoyed pleasing them, but there was that pull, that pulling at my heart that said it wasn't right. I started feeling more disconnected than anything and I knew Romeo could sense it, no matta how much I tried to hide it.

Around the same time I had begun a co-op as a teaching assistant for grade 1 French immersion class. It was a lot of fun and kept me busy, focused and grounded. I helped out different classes with various tasks and grew fond of a group of grade 7 girls I was assisting. During lunch, as they sat eating they would chitter chatter about boyfriends and relationships. *Grade 7 and they already talking about boyfriends.* This was different than what I remember talking about in my classes. While they were talking though, it hits me, this part of my life, the late nights of phone sex, had grown to be more than what I could handle without hating myself even more. What would I say if anyone found out? Could I stand proud or would I duck in shame and embarrassment? A part of me enjoyed being a mentor and role model to these girls but I was such a fraud. More than just the phone sex, I was reminded that I wasn't as in control of my life, my body, my mind, as I thought I was. Shame and disgust was not how I wanted to live my life. This lunchroom chatter reminded me of how dead I felt inside. At this point I was only doing things because I knew it made the other person happy, never anything for myself.

The first change I made to take my life back was telling Romeo how I felt about phone sex in general, but more specifically with the threesome. He ain't like it, but he understood. Although I knew he enjoyed himself, for me it was a matter of recognizing that cheating or no cheating, my happiness came first. It had become so easy to look in the mirror and literally hate myself. Most days I woke up with a smile, but I was like a zombie walking aimlessly through the world. Laughed on cue, cried at night. Would I be good enough to convince someone to stay with me even when I didn't do everything to make them happy? What was love if the same feeling that flooded butterflies in my stomach was the same poison that drained my soul? I was just another casualty. With each disappointment I died a little more.

Self-Reflection

This was a challenging chapter for me. It had forced me to be vulnerable and to face a part of my life that I kept trying to ignore. But I've learned that the best way to get over something is to face it directly because some things can only hide in darkness for so long. I debated whether or not to write this chapter. What would people think? How would people react? Would they judge me or act differently? Would they call me gay? These are the questions that matter when people are given too much power and control in my life. The longer I took to talk about this, the more it held a place in my mind and life. Romeo joked about it often and I carried a lot of guilt but came to a place of peace once I had prayed and repented. Then I had to forgive myself and stop beating myself up about it.

The best thing I had learned in my struggling relationship with God was that He loved me wherever I was. I was given the freedom to grow without judgment.

Forgive. Love. Move on.

CHAPTER TWENTY-THREE

Tested

So that Christ may dwell in your hearts through your faith. And may you, having been [deeply] rooted and [securely] grounded in love,

-Ephesians 3 :17

I had no clue there were so many Jamaican superstitions to be aware of as a mother. For example: my child wasn't allowed to leave the house for two months to keep him safe from harm. My son had to wear something red at all times i.e. string or shirt to keep the bod mind people away. Kaykay was born with a full head of hair and I wasn't allowed to cut it until he was either two years old or talking, whichever came first. The point of this was that my culture played a big part in raising my child. I love my culture though, I identify as Jamaican no matter where I go. In our culture, most people end up with nicknames. Even though my name is Nicola, all Jamaicans call me either Nikki or Nicole which comes out Knee-Cole. For Kayshaun, his nickname became Kaykay. Interestingly enough his father's nickname was Kay. He thought Kaykay was named after him, but it was clearly coincidental. Aside from culture there were other interesting mommy moments. I LOVE THE WAY MY SON SMELT. The way a baby smelt was so precious, and it just melted my heart. The innocence of a baby was so incredible, and God trusted me to raise him up correctly. I would have loved to have my son's father with me, but my situation wasn't set up like that. I chose to mess with someone who just wasn't ready for the commitment of a child.

Fortunately for me I had a good family, good friends and great teachers who supported me throughout the process. I only had to take a month off school, my teachers were really accommodating. I went back to school to write exams and finish up my grade 11 year.

My son's father still wanted nothing to do with me but having Romeo there when I needed to ask questions or advice was crucial. He helped lessen the burden of being a single mother as much as he could from just over the phone. Besides my son, Romeo was my everything.

Once I was home I was finally able to go through the stack of papers that the social worker from the hospital gave me. There was a lot of things I had to do. I got his short birth certificate, then I got the long birth certificate, then I had to register for baby bonus (gov money for women with babies, comes on the 20th of each month). I had to buy formula, diapers, I wasn't about to the take the bus with my child, so I had to figure out driving and getting a car. *AHHH!* It's a lot. My parents tried to start teaching me responsibility in their own way. My parents expected me to help pay the water bill, my food, anything for Kaykay. So how does a 16 year old with no money take care of a baby? Welfare. It was weird having to apply for assistance. It was all a new concept. The government hands out money to those who need it?? *Who knew!?* I was connected to a social worker and encouraged to attend teen mom groups. I hated those groups and never went. I felt so silly. Even though I had a baby, I wasn't ready to admit to myself that I was a teen mom. I felt like I was better than "those girls". My momma didn't raise me to take no handouts, this was tough.

I had so many expenses as a new mother plus the added expenses of being 17 and not having my family financially support me. Yes, I had a roof over my head but that felt like the only thing. I needed more support to even survive. I needed to get on welfare if I was going to finish school and raise my son. In order to get government assistance, I needed proof of my expenses, rent and food. I would need a letter from my parents saying I paid rent. My parents refused, I didn't formally pay rent although I did pay for a lot of my own things. They wouldn't write it. It left me in limbo. Through a lot of tears and arguments, they finally agreed to sign the letter. Teach me a lesson, ye, but this was such an unnecessary delay.

Once I had everything in place, money was coming in on the regular and I had two months left to bond with Kaykay over the summer before my final year in grade 12. I had to put him in daycare while I was at school. God has always had a way of working things out for me, he allowed me to find a home daycare that was a few houses down from where I lived. This was where my family came in handy, they were able to drop him off for me in the morning, and I would pick him up from daycare once I was home from school. Now that money was coming in, it was time to figure out my transportation. The bus system was horrible living in the suburbs because the buses only ran once every 30 mins. Not to mention taking a bus with a child seemed nearly impossible on most days. I would have to wait regardless of the weather, the bus could be crowded, people wouldn't offer up seats easily, people were annoyed with crying babies, there was no room at the front, or they would have to walk around the stroller to get off. Then there were the looks that people love to give teen moms, as if I was this horribly irresponsible person abusing their tax dollars. Now that I had a child, I was determined to get my driver's license and succeeded by getting my G1.

My parents each had their own vehicle, so once I got my license they let me use their car as practice. The car helped my situation but having a child in high school was hard. I won't even pretend like it was an easy thing, it was really hard. Since I was so involved in school I had help. After school, I had to balance homework and a baby. I loved to cook, and I loved making food for Kaykay to eat. I found joy in the smaller things which helped me keep a sense of self. One of the harder things to deal with was the atmosphere and family dynamic that was created by my pregnancy and past mistakes. My mother in particular still carried a lot of anger toward me and the situation. I would express how tired I was with school and everything I was balancing, and she would reply "Nobody told you to open your legs and get pregnant." *Hmm ok...I was jus saying, no need to be so rude.* I never expected any gold stars or hand claps, but I was making the best of the situation and I was met with harsh judgmental comments. I learned very early that I couldn't talk to my parents about anything. They weren't open. They didn't make any efforts to understand. I was the bad child and I kept making even worse decisions in their opinion. I had to constantly remind my mother of the fact that I could have been a lot worse. I could have gotten into drugs or ran away from home or been in trouble with the cops. It never seemed to make a difference though, nothing could be worse than a teen mom.

Kaykay was my new joy. To be honest a part of me was happy I got pregnant. I was happy to have someone to love who loved me back. He wasn't going to leave, as long as I treated him good, he would love me. For the first few months he felt more like a little brother than my son. Breastfeeding was an interesting experience for me. He always seemed fussy or gassy and I thought that maybe he wasn't handling the milk too well, so I tried different lactose free brands. My mom's friend suggested that I should have continued to try giving him breast milk even while I tried the lactose free types, cause when I tried to start him back on breastfeeding, he was already over it. I ended up breastfeeding for a total of 4 months. I felt a little like I failed and let him down cause I wasn't able to produce the milk he needed. I learned very quickly that motherhood wasn't as joyous as what I saw on TV. Once again, I was betrayed. Things didn't just happen so easily, I had to be patient and take the time to learn Kaykay's habits and understand it was ok to make mistakes along the way. As I got to know my child, I began to slowly understand that I could bring him everywhere with me. I took him to school, I took him to the movies- cause he was an amazing baby and slept right through without any noises. He adapted to me as I adapted to him. He allowed me to be myself and do things I use to do while I took care of him. He had a tranquil spirit about him.

Despite the drama going on, Lord knows how I was able to keep things together at school. I was caught up with all my courses and expected to apply to University; so, I applied to York University. As different as I was, I tried to maintain a normal life. I obviously couldn't go out much, nor did I want to, but I made sure to stay involved with my friends and my boyfriend. My average stayed above 80% and when it was time for my graduation photos, I was told I could bring along a prop...so I brought Kaykay. I dressed him up in the cutest suit and held him proudly as we took our pictures together. At least I wasn't left to feel like a stereotype and outcast who got pregnant and wasted life. I worked very hard and I got my acceptance letter from York University in May for the music program. The funny thing for me was that as students we were typically told to apply to more than one university, but I had made up my mind that York was the university I wanted to go to, so I only applied there. I prayed and left it in God's hands and never made a plan B. It worked out in my favor, but to be honest I was never worried about getting into university. Especially not for music. Piano was a gift and although I knew I didn't want piano to be my main career, I figured it was a good enough start. I was hoping to teach piano as a side hustle and use the university experience to figure out my main interest in hopes of developing a career. Before I could even get to that stage, I had to finish off exams and final courses for grade 12.

I was in the middle of writing my math exam when I got a phone call that Kaykay was in the hospital. He had a cold but it wasn't going away. My parents took him to the hospital for cautionary measures, but little did they know that one visit completely changed our lives. I couldn't even focus on my exam and my teacher was nice enough to not only let me leave in the middle of my exam but waved the final exam so that it didn't count towards my final grade average. In June 2007 I was told that the doctors had found elevated levels of protein in Kaykay's blood. Without any further explanation, we were sent to Sick Kids Hospital for more testing to determine what the cause of the elevation was. Needless to say, Kaykay got better and he got over the flu. While we awaited the medical results, we went on a family trip we had planned to Florida that summer which was a welcomed distraction. I absolutely loved road trips. From a young age, my parents often drove to New York and places all over the states. We got to experience traveling, and different environments which gave us a broader perspective in our young childhood. The trip itself was fun, meeting new cousins and realizing how big our family actually was.

In terms of relationships this trip to Florida really tested the stability of things between Romeo and me. I wasn't able to message him while we drove, but as soon as we got to Florida I sent him an email. "Hey, we reached here safely, trip was long but fun, how are you? I miss you." "Miss you too" I tried to message him as much as I could while on my vacay whenever I had Wi-Fi, but things started to feel a lil distant near the end of my trip. Romeo wasn't a good liar, so I confronted him about his strange and distant behavior during my last night in Florida. "I have something to tell you...I cheated." I was sitting on my aunty's couch watching American Idol when he first told me he had cheated. I wasn't sure I read it correctly. I didn't know how to respond. Instead of easing the pain like I thought he would, he added to it. "I met up with some girls and was unable to resist the offer of getting head." *Bullshit.* It ain't like he slipped right in her mouth, so there was no excuse in my opinion. "I didn't have sex with her, so I didn't really think it was cheating...it's only head" *Seriously?* Oh yea, Iuno if it was luck or not, but this was my last night in Florida, at least it didn't ruin my whole trip. I had the ride home to process all 24 hrs. It was the longest car ride. I'll admit I was a bit dramatic as I had Mariah Carey "Give my all" on replay as the tears fell. This outcome was everything I ran from. The very reasons I dreaded commitment was all broken with the words "I cheated".

Now I had two things to distract myself from Kaykay's medical test results and my failed relationship. I made myself busy with preparations for university. I was accepted to York University for their Fine Arts program and couldn't have been more ready to leave home and be an adult at York. I was excited to apply for the York University Gospel choir. Since I was pushed out of church I had been longing to sing and be a part of something special. The only thing was that I dreaded the commute from home to York. I lived an hour away not including traffic which meant I would have to wake up even earlier to get to class on time and I had a baby at home. According to my schedule my classes were for 8 am, which meant I'd have to leave by 6:45 to get to class on time, also which meant I'd have to wake up from at least 5 to get ready, feed the baby, pack a lunch and then leave. I could only imagine how I would feel once I got to school and let's not even begin to talk about the commute home during rush hour. So, I began looking for apartments that were suitable for Kaykay. I found a couple apartment buildings on York campus that I could have made work despite the fact that the space was tight and not too kid friendly; it was close to York and next to a daycare center. Perfect right? The only thing was that they needed a deposit of $800 and my osap didn't kick in yet. I had tried to make arrangements for them to hold the apartment for me, but money talks louder than compassion and the apartment was given to someone else. Although I was upset as it felt like a huge set back, I had just gotten my G2 license and my parents made me a lucrative deal. If I stayed home my first year of university than they would give me their car to help with my transportation. That was exciting! My first car, and it was a blue Chrysler neon.

My favorite thing about University was the fact that I didn't have to show up to school every day. Although classes were 3 hours long, there were breaks and if I was really tired I could take naps without being singled out. University was way easier to manage schedule-wise than high school. The one thing I didn't care for was that all my years spent learning from the Royal Conservatory of Music only gave me a slight advantage in some subjects. I struggled in those first few months. I was often late for class, which was frustrating within itself. I didn't always understand the material, but my other responsibilities took priority over waiting around for office hours. I was studying general music including sight singing which for the life of me I couldn't understand past my sound of music knowledge. The teacher was all over the place and was a challenge to follow but by the grace of God that class was only a fall semester course. I worked my ass off for that D grade and I'm proud of it. Good news is that I balanced it out with an A in Gospel choir. I made some pretty dope friends in that class. Being a single mother in university meant I missed out on a lot of group hangouts or opportunities. Not true for all mothers in university but especially because I lived far I was mindful of the distance and responsibilities. As the dynamics at home changed, I began to change as well. My parents had made it clear from early on that unless I was at school or church, they weren't willing to babysit for me. Even my sis I had to pay or bribe if I wanted to do something outside of school. For that reason, I either didn't go out or when I went to school I would find other things to do to take more time than needed. I tried as much as possible to avoid my parents to keep the peace within the house. Right as I was gettin adjusted to school and settlin into my new life I received a call from the doctors at Sick Kids Hospital. They wanted to discuss Kaykay's result, and it needed to be done in person. I had completely forgotten we were even waiting for results since he hadn't gotten sick again from that one time in June.

In November 2007 we arrived at the hospital and awaited the doctor with the diagnosis: Duchenne's Muscular Dystrophy. Three words that changed everything yet nothing at the same time. The doctor explained how Duchenne Muscular Dystrophy was only one type of muscular dystrophy yet one of the most fatal. DMD's a progressive deterioration of the muscles in the body caused by a lack of dystrophin created in our genes. Basically, the muscles wasted away over time because the body was unable to produce new muscles. As part of the due diligence of the doctor I was informed that boys with this disease typically required a wheelchair by age 10 and passed away in their late teens. I was also told that since Kaykay hadn't started walking as yet that he may not even walk, and if he did it would be with a waddle. I was warned he could potentially fall often, be delayed in learning and/or be delayed with speech. It was explained to me that women were carriers that passed on this disease to their sons; as DMD only affected boys. It was suggested that I get tested to see if I was a carrier of the disease who could still affect future children. I would need to test my individual eggs to see if any of them were affected; but at 17, testing my eggs was not a high priority.

The appointment felt like an information session more than anything else. As of now, I know the name of the diagnosis and how it came to be, but what were the treatment options? Slim-None. This disease had no cure. Even though there was no cure, the treatment option was a steroid that slowed down the progression rate in which the disease deteriorated the muscles. The doctor explained the full effects of the steroids, I was also educated on the long list of side effects to follow. May cause stunt of growth, excessive hair, weight gain, delayed puberty, mood swings, severe fatigue and potentially cataracts...among other things. My concern was with quality of life and wanting Kaykay to live free as a child instead of worrying about medication, especially medication that wasn't able to cure him. If it wasn't necessary at the moment for him to start taking them, I wasn't in a rush to start it.

With all the negative news I had heard, as my mom spoke I could sense the fear and frustration which was quite the opposite for me. I was overcome with a spirit of peace and calm amidst the storm. I was calm enough that I said, "It doesn't matter what the report says cause God would take him when he's ready." He could live to 18 or he could live past 18, it was all in God's design and I had no reason to question it. All I could do was love him wholeheartedly, make memories and cherish the time we were given together. This was where it became a useful tool to separate my child from the disease. The disease was in him but was not who he was. I made the decision to raise him as if he was a child with no disease. Meaning aside from certain precautions, I wouldn't trap him in a bubble. I let him be who he wanted to be and play as rough as he wanted. I let him laugh as loud as he wanted, and I spoiled him rotten, not because he was sick but because he was my child. I did all of this while maintaining respect and authority as his mother. He was being shaped to be the most well-mannered, respectable, intelligent, prove everyone wrong type of lil man. Did I mention he wanted to be a race car driver? Honestly the sky was the limit, this diagnosis was just one more thing for us to pray over and I still considered ourselves to be very blessed. It was just crazy that I was basically given a death sentence from a year old and I had to raise him in spite of that. *Guess God thinks I'm the right person to handle challenges.*

We were assigned to a rehabilitation clinic close to our house to begin treatment with physiotherapy, occupational therapy and speech therapy to get ahead of the game since we had received an early diagnosis. It was a blessing to have even caught the disease early, even though he was the youngest child there, for me it meant that we had a better chance at overcoming this disease. Despite what doctors said, my faith had me believing that he would one day be cured. Apparently, most kids weren't diagnosed until they are at least 4 or 5 once their parents notice a difference in their walk or speech. The decision to start steroids was one that wasn't made easily by my family. Initially my family wanted me to start the steroids in fear of the disease progressing, but my heart wouldn't allow me to get past the side effects. My take on life was this: I could start steroids to help prolong his life, but what kind of life would I be giving him if the same thing that extended life also created challenges. I know medical professionals would argue that the side effects weren't definite, but from the research I did, I saw a pattern of kids with visible side effects. Option two would be to monitor his progression, allowing him to live life medication free unless absolutely necessary with the possibility of revising the idea of steroids if it became visible that there was a decline. I was more comfortable with option two, cause I didn't want him to be on medication from such a young age. My main concern was that I did not get selfish. As a parent, I could seem that I was doing what I thought was best for my child but was in actual fact a selfish decision. If I could honestly answer that putting him on medication to prolong his life was a good choice for him and that he would suffer less; then I would have done it. But I couldn't convince myself that it was for him and not me. Instead I told myself that I would do everything possible to create an amazing life for him and trust everything else up to God.

Amazingly, a few months after the diagnosis, he began to walk. He had a small waddle, but it was cute, it added to his character. He did well when it came to rehab. Most people didn't even believe he had a disability because when they looked at him he was cheerful and rambunctious. From an early age as his personality developed, he was very charismatic. He loved cars. He would sit for hours playing with cars or playing with his hands, he was a quiet type but mesmerizing when he spoke. His favorite color was blue, he wanted to be a race car driver and loved anything that went fast. We developed an amazing bond, he fit me perfectly. He took a while to talk, though I don't believe it was related to the DMD, I truly believe he was just comfortable and lazy. He had gotten into a habit of pointing for everything he wanted and unless we challenged him to ask for it he found an easy way to get what he wanted.

Poetic Interlude

Dear dmd,
Deep in my womb yu attacked
Created some type of lacking of protein from my baby boys dna
Did yu even ask me, if it was ok?
Seems kinda rude don't cha think?
Poppin up without a cure
Talking bout yu some fatal disease
Who do yu think yu are?
Big topa top who can't be stopped?
21 questions I ask, Cause I don't understand
How yu come an try an ruin my plans
Showing signs only through weakness and immobility

Making me question my fertility had to get my eggs tested to see
If I was a carrier
And if this is how my son came to be currently stuck wit yu
But I pray for his health
And I pray I'm blessed with the wealth to take care of him to the fullest
I'm sendin a warning to yu now
Cause I won't back down
Imma fight,
Everythin I do will be to defeat yu
and every time yu attack I'll come back seven times stronger
Seven cause I heard that's the magic number they singing bout in heaven
No weapons formed against me formed against me shall prosper
It won't work
So yu see I've got God's crew wit me
And yu see it's only a matter of time that my son will be
Stronger than yu my dear dmd

CHAPTER TWENTY-FOUR

Confessions

He who loves [only selfish] pleasure will become a poor man; He who loves and is devoted to wine and [olive] oil will not become rich.
PROVERBS 21:17

I was devastated by the news of Romeo cheating. I wasn't sure what to think other than the fact that the bond we made was broken. I saw the images of the family I created in my head with him being ripped apart in slow motion. He didn't deserve my trust. It didn't matter how genuinely apologetic he was, I didn't want to build a relationship on lies. I was in too deep though. He was my escape, my foundation, my voice of reason, he understood me. For once in my life someone did. At least I thought he did. It felt like we were connected at the soul. I was so unsure...but I loved him. We figured we could work on strengthening our relationship and build back the trust. Then that phone call came. You know the Usher track confessions part two?

"These are my confessions
Just when I thought I said all I could say
My chick on the side said she got one on the way
These are my confessions
Man, I'm throwed and I don't know what to do
I guess I gotta give part two of my confessions
If I'm gonna tell it, then I gotta tell it all
Damn near cried when I got that phone call
I'm so throwed, I don't know what to do
But to give you part two of my confessions"

He now had the "pleasure" of explaining to me how his ex-ting ended up pregnant. He was never the relationships type. Apparently when Romeo and I had started talking he was talking to someone else already but broke it off to be with me. I had no clue. She didn't seem to take the break up well so according to him he went over one last time to "console" her. Guess they decided to end it with a bang. It's always that last time that'll get you caught up. One last drop, one last deal, one last hit. One last meet up, right before you get out of whatever situation. I mean damn, that's how I ended up pregnant. I was on a break from sex...that was one last time, except I didn't plan on getting pregnant. According to Romeo, this was their conversation:

- Hello? ...
- I'm pregnant...
- by who?
- You...
- how?
- ...we had sex
- I used a condom though, what happened
- I can still get pregnant even though you used a condom
- I don't believe you...I want a DNA test...you messed up everything cause you know I have a new girl
- ye I'll do the DNA test, but now I'm pregnant so you should be with me
- I don't want to be with you even if it's my kid
- Why not...I wanna be with you, you love me?
- No...I don't love you, I love Nicola and I wanna be with her
- What can I do to change your mind?
- Nothing....

Click.

Apparently, she later on admitted to him that she planned to get pregnant by him so once he left her house that night she used a turkey baster and extracted the sperm from the condom to insert inside her and voila! Crazy right? That's some Being Mary Jane or soap opera type of drama. I truly thought these things only happened on TV, but here I was as the girlfriend living through the experience. *What the fuck?* She honestly thought that a baby would keep him. He said it was never serious between them though, so a baby in the mix was just messy. He still left her with or without the baby. More than anything she was just a problem. She got caught up in her emotions and pissed him off, which was the opposite of what she wanted. I was cheesed, obviously, but what could I say or do? I was annoyed he didn't let me know his situation up front. Even if she was jus a side ting he never let me know, now I found myself in the unfortunate situation of being in love with a man who was expecting a baby that wasn't mine. He also kinda took away my right to be mad because our encounters overlapped, and I had no control over that. No matta how devoted he was to me, I felt like a side ting, next to his side ting, not including his first baby moms. She was trying to be in the picture just as much as I was trying to keep her out. Ugh! His baby moms in my opinion was special to say the least. Some baby mothers have a hard time watching their baby fathers move on. They seem to hold on to this fantasy of getting back together and raising their kids together, even going as far as wanting all their children to be from the same father. But how does that work when the father moves on? Exactly, it doesn't. Some people weren't meant to be together. Even though the situation looked bad and I felt very conflicted...I loved him, so I stayed. Couldn't even tell you why. All the red flags were there for me to leave. Couldn't even say it was the sex that kept me because we hadn't even met yet. My phone sex game was strong but not like that. Subconsciously he became my air. I became his drug.

Over the course of time, once things became more serious between us, I was introduced to his siblings. His twin sister and I would chat periodically, but his brother and I would chat all the time. I loved his younger brother as if he was my own and he seemed to form a bond with me, he always had my back. I felt more and more integrated into their family dynamic, and didn't feel like an outsider. I was well versed on the family drama and since Romeo was known for having a temper, they would call me whenever it got out of hand to calm him down. We both had tempers, but just as I was patient with him, he was patient with me.

We made a vow not to go to bed angry, so come hell or high water we were gonna solve our problems before we slept.

Things were good though, we were both raising our sons while trying to balance life. I loved his son as he loved mine. As much as our love grew, so did the problems. At least Romeo didn't have no baby fadda drama to worry about. I was stuck tryna deal with these two extra women who just couldn't recognize their proper lanes. Romeo told me that his first baby moms was expressing the desire to have more kids with him even though she knew he was in a relationship with me. Guess because she was first she felt entitled. Maybe thought it would bring them together. I don't even know, and I couldn't say exactly, all I knew was that she was trying to cause problems for us and wasn't a fan of me. My man's smart though, he told me it was stupid, and he wasn't going to do anything because he was with me and didn't want to mess up what we had. That was the last discussion we had on the situation and it had been put to rest.

The ultrasound came back for his second baby moms, and she was having a girl. I felt sick. Over the months, I tried to be ok with the situation, but it was hard. Now my dream of giving him his first daughter had been taken from me. It was an interesting dynamic to be with a man that was expecting a baby. Maybe it was the same way he felt when he met me, and I gave birth to someone else's baby and he stayed by my side. Even the chlamydia didn't scare him off. I think as time went on I became more upset with the fact that she had tried to trick him than the actual situation. It meant that a baby was being brought into the world in a less than desirable situation. A child should be given the opportunity to have the parents in their lives. Not the product of selfish drama. I felt bad for the baby more than anything. We could get through this though, one precious baby girl on the way.

Speaking of baby girls, within a few months I found out that Romeo's first baby mom was pregnant again but this time with a girl. Strangely, despite the fact that the baby was for her boyfriend, she wanted Romeo to be the godfather; my gut said something was off. "It makes no sense for you to be a godfather to her new child. So, you're daddy to one and uncle to the other? That's weird." It wasn't making no damn sense. Romeo stuck to his story for months, even as I stayed persistent. The feeling in my gut wasn't easing up, so in my softest voice, I said "You can tell me anything baby, I love you...I know you would never lie to me about anything because you respect me and trust me and would do nothing to ever hurt me. Right?" I laid the guilt on thick. Christmas had come around, many months had gone by and he was no longer able to keep his lies straight. He got really quiet when I asked what was going on.

- Who's the father of the baby? Silence.
- Romeo, who's the father?
- I am
- How? You said you weren't messing with her. When? How could you do this? You said you loved me...you lied. You lied to me this whole time?
- She's having a girl, baby. I'm so sorry. I do love you, I'm sorry, it jus happened.

Speechless.

He lied to me for months, but I knew. I knew something was wrong. I was trying to put the pieces together. When could this have happened? Cause we literally spent almost every second on the phone together. We went to bed every night together, we ate together, went to the bathroom together. There were barely any moments when we weren't together and yet he still managed to sleep with her. Along with some other females he confessed to sleeping with. I felt like the ground had moved from beneath my feet. I felt stupid, I felt lower than low, I felt tricked. I hated him for what he did to me. He completely disregarded how this would make me feel. The universe was cruel, on top of the girl getting pregnant, she too was having a girl.

- I HATE YOU! I FUCKING HATE YOU, I can't stay with you, you don't respect me, and you definitely don't deserve me.
- Baby, you said you weren't going to leave me if I told you the truth, you lied?
- You been lying, I don't want to be with a liar and I don't want to be with you.

Click.

I ignored his multiple calls and text messages for a day. I couldn't stop crying, I barely ate, I got so depressed. He turned out to be nothing more than a stupid asshole. All I could do was yell when he called. "You ruined our family, we were supposed to be a family, I was supposed to give you your first girl, but you ruined that. You took that from me. I can't trust you, I hate you. You can keep that bitch and your lil family cause I want nothing to do with you. Delete my number and leave me the hell alone". No amount of apologies were able to help.

Romeo: "Baby I love you, I'm sorry, I do love you, please talk to me, answer me, I need you, I can't live without you, I'm sorry, I can't live without you, you said you wouldn't leave, I'm gonna kill myself."

The more I ignored him the more frantic his messages became. He blew up my phone. He wouldn't stop texting or calling me until I answered. As mad as I was, his last message was troubling, so I called.

- Hello... why you text me that?
- I lost you, I'm such a horrible person, I know, I know I don't deserve you. I can't live without you, are you going to be with me?
- No.
- Then I'm going to kill myself. I have my gun and I'm going to shoot myself, where should I shoot myself...in the leg? No, I'm gonna shoot myself in the chest, where my heart is. Hold on.

I sat in deafening silence frantically trying to text his brother to get him help. His brother texted me and told me Romeo had locked himself in his room so that no one could get to him. I didn't hear a bang, I didn't hear anything at all until he came back and told me how much he loved me and how sorry he was and that he shot himself. I was shocked, I cried, I apologized. Within minutes the phone hung up. In my mind he was gone. About 20 mins later I got a phone call from his younger brother.

- Hey where's Romeo?
- Ambulance just came and took him. He shot himself in the chest. Said it was because you didn't want to be with him anymore. Said he was a bad person and wanted to die. Why would you do that to him? Why would you leave him, you know he loves you, you know he wants to be with you, why would you do this to him? You couldn't jus pretend and stay with him? He woulda done anything for you. This was all your fault.

Click.

Everything went blank for me. *How was this my fucking fault? I was expected to fix the relationship, ignore all that he had done and pretend to be ok with it all. How? Why should I? I'm 18. I'm fucking 18, what do I do now?* I can't even tell anyone this is my life right now. *How do I explain this?* I laid on my bed with tears flowing down. My brain felt scattered. Didn't know what to think at first. Then the phone rang. I hadn't heard anything else from his family until Romeo woke up. He was awake and wanted to talk to me. I was the first thing he asked for. Just as quickly as we broke up, we were together again. I couldn't deal with the guilt of being responsible for his suicide attempt, but he said as long as I stayed with him he was going to change. So, I stayed. I loved him, and he loved me.

CHAPTER TWENTY-FIVE

Custody

> But I say to you, love [that is, unselfishly seek the best or higher good for] your enemies and pray for those who persecute you,
> -Matthew 5:44

I spent months obsessing over Kendrick. I would send him messages on Facebook without response

> 2008 3:07 pm
> **Cola**
> Seeing how you check your Facebook I guess I'll write you a message....it ain't coo how you don't call back when I leave messages an what not.... I'm askin you one more time to get the dna test done and help me set it up...I'm sayin please...but this the last time imma ask.

I couldn't fight no more, so I figured I'd leave him alone for a while and focus on everything else I had going on. Kaykay's diagnosis was a lot to take on and I didn't want the headache, but my girl kept pushing me to not give up. She finally convinced me to at least seek financial support for my son. I began the court proceedings at the family courthouse in Oshawa and I was originally seeking to file papers for child support as well as DNA testing; however, I was advised by a court official that I should only apply for child support. He said that if I asked for DNA testing it would seem as if I didn't know who the father of my child was. As messed up as it seemed, he said to go after child support only if my son's father wanted a DNA test to prove he wasn't the father, then he would be responsible to pay for it out of his own pocket. I was initially uncomfortable with going after him for child support without the DNA test being done, but at the end of the day the system wasn't set up to help me win on my own. From the time I found out I was pregnant, I had always explained to Kendrick that even though things seemed confusing, the end result was that we were now both faced with parental responsibilities. I got pregnant from pre-cum and now he had to get over it and deal with the realities. A DNA test was the quickest way to clear his thoughts, but he was unwilling to work with me. I even offered to pay the full amount, all he had to do was show up, but even that wasn't good enough. He said, "The kid ain't mine, so I don't gotta waste my time taking no test". I was left with no other choice but to seek support payments.

I had to personally serve him with the child support papers to make sure he came to court. Easier said than done, I called up my baby fadda and asked him to meet with me for me to give him something and he agreed. However, the day we were meant to meet up in Toronto, he changed his mind. I drove to meet him, but he never arrived, so I called. Apparently, he had to do something on the other side of town and for me to meet him there. I drove to the other location and again he wasn't there. This time when I called him he says he's somewhere else and for me to meet him there. By now I caught the flex and as much as I didn't want to play his game, I needed to give him the papers to continue my application for court. He finally answered my call with the slickest grin plastered on his face.

- Oh, what do you need to see me about?
- I need to give you these papers to get the DNA testing done.
- Good luck trying to find me.

Click.

I was cheesed that I had spent an hour in travel time and about two hours driving around looking for this man, all for it to be one big joke. I was forced to go back to the courthouse in search of help. I doubt I was the first person who had trouble serving papers. I needed to know what were the next steps I could take.

This time the advice I received was that since Kendrick lived with his mother I could potentially file the papers to her on his behalf. Seems kinda dumb since his mother had nothing to with it, but I had run outta options. This was frustrating and very draining. I was feeling like I was backed up into a corner. I really didn't want to bring his mother into this situation, I only saw her a couple times when I visited the church. This situation turned me into a person I didn't like. I secretly hoped that if she knew about me, she would want to get involved in her grandson's life. Kinda like what you've seen on Maury, when the mother of the baby fadda was supporting the young girl.

Since I knew his family attended my god-mother's church I figured this would be the most convenient place for me to serve papers. Drama, right? If you thought things were bad for me being pregnant in church? It was nothing compared to what I was about to stir up. I really wish it could have been any church other than my god-mother's. I wouldn't have felt as bad. I felt horrible knowing what I was going to do but I also felt like a boss chic. The key was saying nothing until it was done, then I would play dumb and beg forgiveness. I nervously planned the day. There was a lot to figure out. *What time do I get to church? Will I be able to sit through the whole church service without gettin struck down by God for the evil? Should I go at the end? Will it look just as bad that I didn't even attend the church, but I showed up to do my dirty work? Are there really any right answers?* I was using church as if it was my personal family court proceeding. Damn, this seemed more and more like an episode of Jerry. Either way, I tell myself loudly: "I takes care of mines and since he wanna play stupid and play me like boo boo the clown, imma roll up on his church. Yep! Mess with me an I'll take ya down" I felt ready. I felt empowered.

That Sunday as I woke up and got dressed I felt scared. By time I rolled up to church late with my sister and cousin, I was ready to take care of my business. I entered the doors, waved at a few people and found us seats. I looked around for Kendrick but he was nowhere in sight, not surprised; but then I saw his mother and I smiled to myself. I sat in church sooooo distracted. I tried to be patient, but I just wanted service to be done so I could drop the papers and dip. When service was over, I greeted a few people, including my godparents. People were surprised and delighted to see me. They were like "Oh what are you doing here?" and I had to lie "Just in the area visiting." I lived over an hour away...it wasn't a usual visit. As people continued to greet each other I casually made my way over to his mother to greet her. Instead of greeting her I felt my hand extend the envelope towards her. I wish I coulda run, she looked at me so confused like "Oh what is that?" Then I said, "Please just take it". By this time Kendrick's younger sister walks over and takes the envelope from me. She asks, "What is it?" As I walk away I say "It's the papers for Kendrick concerning child support." By this time Kendrick's aunty had walked over. Out of the corner of my eye I see Kendrick's aunty open the envelope, glance at it then throw it on the ground. Man, I couldn't have walked faster out of there. In seconds, I saw Kendrick's cousins come over and I could hear them cussin me as I tried to keep my cool while walking out. "What kind of person comes to church and does this?" "Here, take it back, we're not keeping it" "Nasty girl" I couldn't let anything break my focus of gettin back to the car and peeling outta there. I probably woulda been more bothered but council advised that even if the papers hit the floor they are still considered served. In my opinion, my mission was complete. I'm sure I was gonna hear from my godparents soon enough once they realized why I actually showed up to church but in that exact moment it didn't matter. I vowed to always take care of my son and this was jus a casualty of my love for him. I just prayed that God and my god-parents would forgive me.

Once Kendrick heard what happened he was beyond pissed. If I had any hope of trying to save a relationship, that was a lost cause. Same thing with gettin his family involved in Kaykay's life. As far as they were concerned I needed to stay far far away from them with my fatherless child.

If my purpose was to piss off people, mission completed. My actions caused me to burn all bridges with Kendrick and his family. Rage built inside. My child was innocent, that never mattered though. I became obsessed trying to clear my name. Obsessed tryna prove that I wasn't crazy. He was my child's father and I was gonna make damn sure that he paid for this embarrassment. Thus far I hadn't acted like a crazy baby moms, but all that was bout to change real quick.

CHAPTER TWENTY-SIX

Mr. Producer

Israel's watchmen are blind, They are all without knowledge. They are all mute dogs, they cannot bark; Panting, lying down, they love to slumber.
-Isaiah 56:10

Ever have a crush on someone for so long and all you wanted was for them to notice you? This man was a dancer, he used to dance in a group with my cousin and for years I thought he was jus the sexiest thing. I would try so hard not to stare whenever I went to any of their performances. I always wondered if he ever liked me too. I was so over this whole love thing, but I would still get nervous around him. I guess it was a good thing that I never got a chance to be alone with him until I was in University, cause I never knew what to say.

University classes were different. This one class I had was next level boring so every time I stepped into this class, like clockwork I would fall asleep. Has that ever happened to you? You feel so energized until you walk into a room and jus drop asleep moments later like you hadn't slept in days? It wasn't like this class was hard, but it was just so abstract. Things were all over the place and the videos the teacher showed were weird as shit. I just didn't understand the point of the class, but it was a mandatory credit so yeah... no choice but to be there. Since attendance was a part of our marks, I made sure I was there physically, but mentally I was off in my own world. I would wear hoodies and set up my desk in a way that looked as if I was paying attention while I slept. The only time I paid attention was when we were assigned to a group project. This assignment seemed to have some merit and had potential to actually be fun...for once. It was worth a good portion of our work though, and I needed to get a great mark. Given the subject available, we wanted to make sure we did something equally entertaining. The topic of our project: life as a single mother, starring yours truly. The goal was to incorporate several different art forms like music, PowerPoint presentation and visual art. My brilliant idea for the music portion was to write and produce a track to accompany the presentation. I knew a producer, and I had been waiting for a good reason to get to know him betta; this might finally be my chance.

It jus so happened that my cousin's dance teammate was a music producer as well. I finally got the courage to contact him on Facebook and was thrilled when he offered his services. He had a home studio, so he invited me over to get started. Some crushes are better off uninterrupted. I wanted to get to know him better, but it ruined the whole flex, made me realize once you get close you see they aren't perfect like you thought. Everything was all cute until the flaws came out. He smokes weed, heavy. Although I preferred weed smell to cigarette, the frequency was such a turn off. It had been a while since I had seen him, and I remember him being a lot cuter; clearly, he aged. At least he had such a chill personality. He smoked, I chilled, we made music. This was working for us, we didn't have long to finish the project, so I drove up a few times a week to ensure we produced quality work. The more we worked together the more I was crushin. *I wonder what his sex game like.* I mean he talked a big game and we flirted, so why not? *Let's see what he's working with. Would he blow my back out? Foreplay or no? Does he kiss?* His touches were electric. Very intriguing, I had to find out for myself. The sexual energy between us was on another level. His laugh, my touch, the gaze in each other's eyes. The day we had sex was the day the magic died. It was lacking. It fell apart quickly. I had pictured it would be this sweat dripping moment where he would just bend me up and just turn me out. He was lazy though. He laid on his back...the whole time. I felt no power. He hyped it up so much. I shoulda felt him in my belly the way he was talking. Sigh. Now things were just weird.

Focusing on the project side of things we were on a great track to finishing early, but he was missing part of the equipment that we needed. The only thing stopping us was that he wasn't getting paid in time to buy the equipment before our project was due. So, he asked me to buy it until he could give me a cheque. At this point I jus needed to get this project done. It was too late to ask anyone else. We started off strong, but the little things started to annoy me, like the fact that he couldn't make music if he wasn't high, or the fact that he always needed money for something. The money was coming out of my account quicker than the cheques could be deposited.

The week my project was due Mr. Producer called me down to finish up. I showed him I didn't have gas but since he needed me down he offered to give me gas money for me to get back home. So, we were there working when he got a phone call from some chick. None of my business until he says he needs to go pick her up from down the street. Ok, no problem, right? Except that once she got to the house he conveniently forgets that we were in the middle of finishing up. To top it off this chocolate ass mutha was dissing me for a white girl. Really bro? And he didn't even gimme the damn gas money so I could get home. I had to wait for his momma to come home after 11 pm then watch him beg her for money just so I could get home, AND I STILL DIDN'T HAVE MY DAMN PROJECT.

Mr. Producer was a broke joke. Literally a broke joke, within days I had gotten a call from my bank to let me know that all the cheques deposited had bounced. Multiple bounced cheques flagged my account for fraud and everything was frozen. I was now under investigation. *Great! No project, no money.* The more I called him, the quicker he found the ignore button. He didn't even offer any apologies. I felt like I was kicked to the curb so easily.

After a week of trying I was going out of mind tryna come up with a backup plan for my project. I wasn't solo, it was a group assignment. My phone rang and it was Mr. Producer's mother. Her and her son had a conversation where he admitted to what he had done. She said her heart felt for me because I was a young single mother with a child to take care of and I had been taken advantage of in the worse way. She also schooled me and told me I shouldn't have given him anything. Point taken. Either way she felt bad. At her request I sent her copies of the cheques as proof only to find out that Mr. Producer was writing me cheques from his brother's account. It wasn't even his own money!!!! With that proof in hand, his mother made an agreement to pay me back until he was able to work and take over the payments himself.

He managed to give me the cd in time to perform my presentation and we received an A, but he wasn't worth all the hassle. Now came the hard work, forgiving someone who never truly seemed sorry, and forgiving myself for letting it happen. I learned from this that forgiveness doesn't mean that I have to keep a fake friendship going. It was ok to forgive and let go. That was a priceless lesson.

CHAPTER TWENTY-SEVEN

3 Times A Charm

Who shall ever separate us from the love of Christ? Will tribulation, or distress, or persecution, or famine, or nakedness, or danger, or sword?
-Romans 8:35

He kissed my tear stained cheek as I looked out the window after he raped me.

I could hear my friend Dela's voice in my head "What if you get raped?" The whole conversation replayed as my response "3rd time's a charm" was on repeat. "3rd time's a charm" "3rd time's a charm" "3rd time's a charm" My son sat in the other room with some other kids watching tv while I stood naked in my shame. I couldn't even process what the fuck just happened to me. At some point Kaykay entered the room and asked me why I was crying. I honestly can't say if it was during or after. Everything happened so quickly. But I remember his soft voice asking me if I was ok. My little hero, always. The one person who gave a fuck about me.

So, who was this guy? Some stranger I met at a mall one day with my girl Shay. We were always playing games, daring each other to get phone numbers and seeing how many guys would chop us. We had met him and his brother, I wasn't really feeling him, but his brother was feeling my girl so I took his number with no real intention of things going anywhere. Turns out he wasn't that bad. We kept in touch a few times. I ended up at his house purely out of boredom. I was down the street at Dela's sister's house and he asked if I wanted to hang out, even said Kaykay could play with his younger siblings.

Kaykay stayed with me while we talked until he felt comfortable to go hang out with the other kids. Once he left, my man started asking me all the personal questions. Where's your man? Why are you single? Can I take you out? He was flirty, fun, and genuinely seemed into me. He kissed me, and I let him. Getting lost in the moment. Laying back, kissing back. As he continues to kiss me his hands reach my pants and I stop. "No, don't touch there, leave it alone" "Why?" "Cause I'm not ready or looking for sex right now". "Ok".

I sit up contemplating if I should leave, but he apologizes so I stay. *Innocent mistake. He's kinda cute. He didn't know if I'd be down or not, but now that he knows, we can just chill.* "I just really like you, I'm sorry." "It's ok" At that moment, Kaykay walked in the room and says, "Mommy you ok?" "Yes baby, you ok?" "Ye" then he walks back out to the living room. This time ol dude asks if I want my pussy licked. *I mean I've had it done like once before, but it's been awhile. It would be nice, but I don't wanna give him the wrong impression. Shit...he already started.* I took too long to reply. As I look down I notice he begins. Definitely not Emmy worthy, but he asks if I like it, so I gave a couple of fake moans to make him feel like he hittin the spot. He tried to kiss me, but I turned my face. Yuck! Not interested in kissing a man that's kissing my pussy. Between the kissing and the fingering, I just laid there until I fell asleep.

I wake to his voice "Are you sleeping?" "Hmm? No, I'm not sleeping" I fully was. When I feel him tryna put his dick inside I sit up and push him away. "You're strong" "I said I'm not interested in having sex" "Yea, but I thought I was making you feel good...so I can lick your pussy, but I can't put it in?' "Hmm ye, plain and simple, I never asked you to lick my pussy" As I start to get dressed he apologizes and asks me not to go. "Ok I'm really sorry, please don't go, I just really like you and really like hanging out with you. You're so beautiful, I can't help myself." So, I lay back down on the bed with him. *I should go.*

This time when he touches me he's rougher. This time when he touches me he pulls my clothes back off. This time he pushes his dick inside. I'm the strong one, remember? But this time I can't push him off. "Stop, I said no already" This time my no means nothing. This time he's pushing me and asking me to relax as I push back. This time I lost the fight and waited for it to be over. I was finally able to get off the bed and I walked over to the window and just stared out at the sky. "I'm sorry" "I couldn't help myself" *Time to go.*

I hated myself. How do you tell your soul to stay strong when it's gone? I'm dead inside.

So, was this rape? Or did I ask for it? If my son wasn't in the car with me on my drive back home, I would have ended things right there.

I could hear my friend's voice in my head "What if you get raped?" But can I still call it rape if I let him lick my pussy? Where's the line drawn?

Poetic Interlude

Nocturne

They do not know sunlight
Lightness turned to darkness
But out of the tightest spot they
Breathe life
Eventually praying for the afterlife
She's holding the gun
As he holds the knife
Eyes are locked together as one
One night but two souls
Which one lives?
Living a lie where only the shadows know the truth
Truth is a piece of her soul was stolen
And since it happened she's been rolling in the sheets
Legs spread
Digging deep
searching for enough answers to keep her heart from growing cold
Molding to the darkness that creeps into her leftover soul
The emotional toll of the weight of his past
Last longer than his task
Hold her still is what they asked
Morally torn but loyal to his crew
Barely men themselves they hardly knew what to do
Yet they subscribed to the late night drive through

Then headed back to the corner
To make a few bucks from selling food
Dude forget her
She's a nobody
yet she stayed on his mind
Like Pause and rewind
Unwinding with a bottle in hand
Turned into a dependence that had him moving through the shadows of the land
She ran the distance only to fall slave to guilt and shame
Servicing pain
she slid her way to the top of the game
Every night they repeat to themselves the same
No eye shall see me,
They put disguises on their faces
Disguising any traces of the people and places
They used to be
3 year old masks
A delicate craft
Demanding the attention from soldiers of the moonlight
They do not know sunlight
So tonight they set off for work
The doctor and the rapper
She helps the block he feeds
2 blocks leading up to the destination
Her estimation is he has no clue that tonight is for justification and self-preservation
She thinks it's too late for the restoration of her heart
She started planning this evening ever since he showed up in the hospital a year ago
He's been searchin high and low for the
women who saved his soul
Putting the beat back in his heart
Allowing him to finally let go of the demons
His reasons to believe in love
Like two turtle doves
Is waiting around the corner
3 years
Two souls

One night
She says excuse me
He says I know you right
You're that guiding light who saved me
While you're that man who broke me
We have unfinished business
Triggering deep memories he offers his Forgiveness
You left me as a witness to my own pain
She's holding a gun
Now he's holding his knife
Both praying for a better afterlife
One night
Two souls
Same goal

CHAPTER TWENTY-EIGHT

Home...

But God, being [so very] rich in mercy, because of His great and wonderful love with which He loved us
EPHESIANS 2:4

Speaking about love and moving on, it had been two years since Kaykay had come home and even though home was supposed to be where the heart was, that concept seemed so distant from my reality. No matter what I did, it seemed like my image never changed in their eyes.

I felt like I was quarantined for a contagious disease that no one wanted to take the chance of catching. I knew my mother didn't want me. I told myself this often. It made it easier to numb myself to her direct method of parenting. It must be true, why else would she ask to send me to a group home? Despite my shame since Kaykay was born, I had to keep moving forward but even in my greatest moments it felt as though I was still not good enough. Not good enough as a daughter and most definitely not good enough as a young mother.

I had realized from early on that I was at a disadvantage as a mother for the mere fact that I was a teenager. As if my age meant I was disqualified to be a mother of good merit. I had some decisions to make. *Maybe some distance could ease the tension? Allow myself to figure things out. Be closer to school. Figure out motherhood for myself. I can do it right? It's gonna be hard with a toddler.* I finally decided I wanted to move. Things just felt really toxic at home and I needed air to breathe. Not only that, but I wanted my son to know me as his mother and in a home with 3 women the lines were getting a bit confusing. As a new mother, there was lots of wisdom coming from my elders and as much as

I appreciated it, it also felt at times like I was just sitting back watching my son being raised by other people.

I've learned that closed doors are real blessings. By the summer of 2008 I was determined to find an apartment. I started searching Google, Kijiji, an everywhere else for listings close to York University. To my luck, I found a program called Humewood House which was an organization dedicated to helping young mothers. They were in the beginning stages of interviewing teenage mothers for their new program at 1900 Sheppard. The program was designed to help teen mothers transition into society over 4 years by creating independent living with support from local programs and resources. The qualifications were that each participant had to be either in school or working and dedicate 5 hours of volunteer work per month. I was scared but excited to apply, I had to provide references. The building construction wasn't even complete yet, but I was confident that I was going to get in. It's amazing to me how God works; I started to shop and prepare for an apartment before I got it.

Throughout the year Canadian tire and Walmart were my best friends. Whenever they had sales I made sure I was the first in line. What sense did it make shopping for appliances when I didn't even have the apartment? Preparation for what was coming strengthened my faith because I trusted that God would provide, someway and somehow. I knew that when the time did come I would be ready. It took a whole year but by the time I had gotten my acceptance call I had only two weeks to move in, settle and find daycare before my fall classes began.

During the summer of 2007 I had put Kaykay on the child care subsidy waitlist in Toronto. With the time crunch I was facing I was praying that he would qualify. What felt like only God's favour, I received a phone call informing me that a space was now available for subsidy. I showed up to the office so unprepared for the meeting. The woman was asking so many questions. "What's the father's involvement? What was your income? Do you have your notice of assessment? What daycare were you hoping to get your son into?" Wow. Felt like overload. Since I just got the apartment I hadn't gotten the chance to look for quality daycares in the neighborhood. Sensing that I was overwhelmed the lady made a phone call then offered her suggestion. "There's a daycare that I used to work at that is down the street from your new apartment. The staff is really nice, and they have a spot available. Go check it out and let me know if that's the daycare you want." I left the office and drove straight to the new daycare. I was greeted by a sweet black lady named Dahlia. Everything she explained was clear and made me feel very comfortable leaving Kaykay at the daycare, especially with his disability. By the time I left I was already dialing the number for the subsidy office to accept the offer.

Within the week my parents helped me move in and got the place organized so that it was less of a burden while I focused on my studies. Everything was new and frightening. *Would I be good enough? Would I manage? At least I'm closer to school, but I was leaving my child with strangers. Would the daycare be good?* Truth is, I didn't really have an option if I was going to continue school. I needed him to be in an environment where he would be cared for and nurtured. Seems like I was nervous for nothing, within months he was potty trained. That was a relief. I always thought his dad would teach him, and I was kinda nervous for that responsibility to be left up to me. Thank God daycare eased this transition for me. With the good came the bad, I was in class and got a call saying Kaykay had fallen off a bike and hit his head off the concrete. He was fine, but it was a good reminder that we were both growing and learning how to adapt to new surroundings. With his disability I was supposed to be more cautious of outdoor activities, but I never wanted to limit him. I wanted him to enjoy life as much as he could. He was just a kid. He needed to explore some things on his own.

Things were finally feeling like they were working out how they were supposed to. I previously felt scared about leaving home at 19 with a baby, but this new-found freedom was growing on me. Love it.

CHAPTER TWENTY-NINE

Therapy

Just as a father loves his children, so the LORD loves those who fear and worship Him [with awe-filled respect and deepest reverence].
Psalm 103:13

Moving to the city had some real perks for us. Instead of driving back to Oshawa for therapy, we were transferred to Bloorview Kids Rehab in Toronto. It was a way bigger facility, bright and colorful, with a whole new team of nurses, doctors and services. It was an exciting process for the both of us. His new team took to him right away. From the receptionist to the nurses, and therapist, everyone seemed so happy to see us. They were all rooting for our success. It was such a blessing for us to catch this disease early enough that we were able to start therapy.

Our first appointment with the new doctor was spent explaining the characteristics of Muscular Dystrophy. Similar to that day, I felt very adamant that I was not comfortable with starting him on steroids at such a young age. I still believed quality was greater. Meaning, I would rather he lived a full life for shorter years than to live longer but to be suffering from the medication's side effects.

I already knew what it was like to be a chubby kid, I didn't want that for him. Irritability? Excessive hair? There was also the potential that once he reached puberty age it would be delayed. When I asked for the solution the answer was "There's a shot we can give" *Shot?? There's a puberty shot?* Didn't sound right. I'm no doctor, but I'm a mother, and my job was to protect my son. At this moment he wasn't showing any real obvious signs of the disease. I thought as long as we managed everything with therapy then we could prolong his life. If we did notice any decline, then I would be open to talking about steroids.

He started 3 types of therapy. Physical, occupational therapy and we went on a waitlist for speech therapy. Kaykay was such a quiet kid, he didn't speak much and when he did speak he had a bit of a stutter. I was trying to keep it all together. I felt like such a loser when I showed up to therapy by myself with Kaykay. I was always the youngest mom and I felt bad when I looked around and saw I was usually the only person who was alone with my child while the other families had two adults along with the child. From time to time, I would ask my sister or parents to come along. It was long though, a typical appointment was 3 hours by the time we saw all the nurses, therapists and completed all the assessments.

To measure if there was any deterioration from the disease they would have him complete a set of physical challenges and record his timing. If his timing slowed, then it was an indication that he was slowing down. His favorite test was when he was asked to walk up and down the hallway. He loved to run and show off how fast he could go. Then he was timed on his ability to get to his feet from laying on his back without any help. At first, he would use the wall as support, but once he understood how it worked he turned it into a game. He went through breathing tests, then finally his physical exam. His doctor would check his calves for the muscle mass and check his body for any sores.

At the time my only concern was that he would get severely constipated. My deduction was that he was probably having trouble pushing since the action involved muscles. At age two he was taking adult doses of stool softener. I was told it was harmless, but still. It seemed like a lot for one kid to deal with. Baby steps were key to managing his DMD.

CHAPTER THIRTY

Let It Rain

Faithful are the wounds of a friend [who corrects out of love and concern], but the kisses of an enemy are deceitful [because they serve his hidden agenda].
-Proverbs 27:6

Ever sit and feel like some people get away with everything? Yet when you try the exact same thing it somehow fails? Perfect example, my friends could drink, have sex and just live life, but I get pregnant from precum. It made me very aware that I couldn't get away with anything. It was the reason I never smoked or tried any drugs. With my luck, I'd get addicted right away. However, not smoking didn't exactly deter me from trying to sell it or doing any other hustles.

My main goal for going to York University was to get into the gospel choir, in which I did. Yay! So here I was sitting in class with Shay and we both notice this dark skin hunny sitting in the tenor section. After class we casually struck up a conversation. His name was Reign, he was 27, single, lived alone, lived down the block from me, and was an RnB singer. When he sang though, it was so blessed. His voice was so smooth. From that day the 3 of us became really close. He'd be at my new house at least once a week. He was easy to talk to and was helpful around the house, he helped with laundry, cleaning, using my car for errands and sometimes even cooking. It was great having a man around the house for the practical stuff but when it came to sexual needs...that was Shay's job. From early on I noticed Shay was feelin him deep, so who am I to interfere? Plus, I wasn't feelin him on that level. He was the bad boy type, he stole, he frauded, he smoked weed and did whatever he needed to survive. As long as he didn't do those things to me, we stayed on good terms.

We both loved music and harmonies, it was one of our main reasons for hanging out. I knew the theory and he understood the beauty of putting words to beats. He would smoke, and we would sit and feel the rhythm flow through our bodies. I think the best way to write music would be to feel it inside and out before adding layers. Whenever Shay would come over, he was invited too. My house very quickly became the "it" house. She used my house as a cover up to see him. At first it was fine, but once her step mom met me and realized I had a child, I was labelled a bad influence. Since Shay was no longer allowed at my house, she would go to Reigns, but when it was time for her to go home they would borrow my car cause she lived in the east. For at least 4 months we were the 3 musketeers. As their relationship blossomed, our relationship slowed a bit. Nothing bad, but Reign was getting into music more professionally with an up and coming Toronto RnB group. The only thing stopping him was money. He was in school and had revealed to me that he was receiving disability support, so money was tight. He wanted to pursue a music career but needed a lot of money, $3000 to be exact. He needed money so that he could rehearse with the group, help pay for studio space and such.

It wasn't out of the norm for him to ask to borrow money from me. It was usually only small amounts, $50 here, $100 there, nothing over $300; and he always paid me back within days. I trusted him. Since he was getting his monthly disability cheque, I was guaranteed to be paid back by the 1st. $3000 was steep, but it was supposed to help him advance his career so that's ok, right? Coincidentally a few days before he asked the government had given me exactly $3000 for backdated disability payments for Kaykay. I wanted to help but that money was to help me take care of Kaykay. To sweeten the pot, Reign made a deal that he would give me an extra $1000 for me helping him out. I still wasn't comfortable. This felt different, $3000 was many months of rent. *How did he know I got exactly 3 grand? Was this his plan the whole time? Is this* *why he asked for smaller amounts, to see how much I'd be willing to give? Damn. But he is good at singing, and sometimes opportunities only come around one time. At least he is trying to better himself. He has always paid me back though. Plus, that extra grand would really help me take care of Kaykay better. That seems like a pretty reasonable deal. Where was he gonna get the money from? Ain't no disability checks anywhere near $3000, so even if he did pay me, it was gonna take a very long time.*

Apparently Reign also had applied for a disability tax credit and was due a backdated amount. I guess he coulda just waited... if this music deal wasn't time sensitive. As proof of investment, Reign took me down to see his disability reporting officer to confirm that the money was coming. *Would he really go through all this trouble if it wasn't real?* It wasn't even a shady office either, it was a real ting, I shook the man's hand and left feeling comfortable enough to lend Reign the money. Everything seemed on point, I never felt pressured, but I had an internal sense of guilt. I felt like I had to help him out, the same way I would want someone to help me out. He showed me everything I needed to feel secure enough to make my own decision. Within a few days I had given him $3000 cash. It seemed like an early Christmas for him.

January came, and the money hadn't showed up yet, but Reign assured me that it was on its way. In the meantime, he would show me updates with the group. He was improving musically, it seemed like money well invested.

February had arrived, and no money had come yet, but it was government money... that always comes right? Osap had come but once I paid all my bills and courses, I was down to my last $1000 to get me through till April. I was panicking. I've heard of different investments to flip money and turn a quick profit, but in the hood that coulda meant anything. I just needed to make enough to get me through the next few months. Since Reign felt bad about the delay with his cheque, he offered me a quick money turn around; all we had to do was put up $1000 each and it would double within 24 hours. I wasn't so thrilled about giving up my last $1000 but the guy was a longtime friend of Reign's and he had done this before, so our chances of being ripped off were very slim. My morals have always stopped me from doing anything illegal but this money crunch had me bending the rules. The money we put up was to buy and sell weed. Not us personally. We invested in the weed man and he was going to give us our cut. I mean, it was just weed, everyone I know smoked it, it was honestly no big deal. 24 hours later the phone never rang. A week goes by before Reign tells me his friend wouldn't return any of his calls. I was devastated. Shoulda known better though, I shoulda neva expected to prosper from investing in weed.

I felt like I wasn't going to make it. *What did I do? Am I stupid? I realllly let him play me. I wanted to do something good. What about helping people out? I mean, I want people to believe in me and help me if I need it. Look at my life, my supports are nowhere to be found. From when I moved in, no one really visited or helped. Am I that desperate to please friends? Now I've put my son's well being in jeopardy. How will I pay for food? What if I need medication for him that's not covered? How will I pay for parking at school? How will I pay for babysitters? How do I put gas in my tank to get him to daycare or rehab? What the hell am I doing? You suck. You're a horrible mother. They were right, you can't take care of him. You shouldn't have left home. I'm still failing. How will I make it? God please, I know I don't talk to you often but please, please, just help me get through. Help me just make it to April. Thanks. This sucks.* I cried myself to sleep. Instead of having $1000 till April, I now had zero dollars to my name. I called the social assistance information line and quickly found out that I didn't qualify until April after my Osap period was done. I felt like the worst mother in the world. I wasn't able to provide the simple necessities that my son needed. The only choice I had was to try my best to manage my monthly baby bonus and pray to God it would be enough. My saving grace was that I would prepay my rent, so at least that was taken care of till May. At first my guilt and shame kept me from saying anything to Reign about the money, but as he kept receiving his cheques a bitterness grew inside me. I blamed him. I blamed him for putting me in this situation. I blamed him for gaining my trust. I blamed myself for ever letting my guard down and allowing myself to be so gullible. As he was able to continue living, he didn't even offer me a dime for repayment. To make matters worse, I found out that he didn't even apply for the disability money when he said he did. The government hadn't approved his case yet, the meeting I went to was jus an initial meeting.

I have always considered myself slow to anger, but I had just reached my limit with this man and his lies. He didn't see why he should have even offered any money from his monthly allowance. He would say to me "I didn't get the cheque yet, I said I would pay you from that money, I'm not paying you from anything else but that cheque. When it comes you will get your money". Talk about feeling betrayed. My heart felt like it was bleeding. "HOW CAN YOU NOT SEE YOUR FAULT IN THIS? I LENT YOU MONEY AND YOU PROMISED TO PAY IT BACK. IS IT MY FAULT YOUR CHEQUE DIDN'T COME? Months have passed, and you have refused to give me small payments from your monthly amount. YOU GET TO KEEP ALL YOUR MONEY, while I sit here and suffer. I can't even buy Kaykay food or pull ups cause I CAN'T AFFORD ANYTHING. You clearly have not lost anything. So, I guess I'm the sucker in the situation because I tried to do a good thing and help you." Reign looks at me, then walked out of my house. As mad as I was, I tried calling his phone and his answering machine picked up. He ignored me. Like I didn't exist. Created this mess and walked out on me. Leaving me with so many questions. *Was I wrong? It's my fault yes, but he did promise to pay me back and now he's walked out. Must be nice just to walk away like that. What a coward. Is he dumb? Stupid ass man. After all the times I tried to help. Yo how many times did I let him borrow my car? Him and Shay wouldn't even be dating if I didn't act as the go between. He clearly was just using me. He tested the waters and got me to a point of trusting him. He said he really cared about me and my son, so how does he just up and leave? We're best friends, that's how he treats me? What about Kaykay? Really? He's really not gonna answer the phone? So, what now?* Ain't it funny, how things were cool until I showed jus a lil anger. *Nice Cola would neva get mad.* Guess I was only useful to him when I stayed quiet, didn't talk back. What kinda friendship was this where I couldn't express my frustrations? How could I not be mad? Look at the situation I was in. He told me many times that the things I did for him as a friend were more than even his family was doing for him. But I guess it didn't matter.

CHAPTER THIRTY-ONE

Change

For if you *love* [only] those who *love* you, what reward do you have? Do not even the tax collectors do that?
MATTHEW 5:46

Spring had come and still no word from Reign. The man disappeared without a trace and left me to fend for myself. Thank God I could finally apply for social assistance until my summer Osap tuition kicked in. It had been 8 months in my new place and I had made some really close connections with the other moms in the building. Most of the moms would attend the programs held in the building which allowed us to get to know each other. My neighbour had a beautiful daughter close in age to Kaykay and they got along really great. It was nice to see him making friends. Most times he would play by himself, but this environment provided multiple kids for him to interact with. The move proved to be exactly what we needed. One of the key things for me to succeed was to stay connected and the requirement of volunteering helped that.

In terms of volunteer opportunities, I got myself quite acquainted with the building manager, nice lady, loved Kaykay and kept me up to date with any building changes. When a position opened up for tenant representative, she was the first to let me know. By default, I obtained the position since no one else in the building was interested. It was something positive for the community and I wanted to be a part of making a difference. The position was with Toronto Community Housing (TCHC). I enjoyed more practical work as opposed to sitting in a classroom. It was a bonus for me when I learned that it counted towards my volunteer hours each month. As Tenant Rep, my duties were to represent the desires of the tenants. I was also required to attend monthly community meetings to discuss and plan future events and community needs. Some girls embraced my new position, but others didn't like the fact that I wasn't born and raised in the hood. I felt like I had to try even harder to prove myself.

One of the first things I needed to tackle was getting additional security lights and cameras put up around our building. At night it was always too damn dark, and it became a safety issue for a lot of us mothers; especially with my apartment being on the first floor. Each apartment had huge windows which was great for light in the daytime but when it was night and you could see shadows of people walking it was scary. The lights and cameras would help us feel safer and if there was an incident it would be more visible. I was the youngest of all the tenant reps and I was living in a building for women, which meant a big part of my job was dispelling the rumours that my building was a shelter. A lot of community members had their own judgements of the type of people who lived here. My first goal was to prove them wrong and my second was to win us money. I needed to show them that despite being young, we were motivated and capable of taking care of our children; thriving despite stereotypes. When the day came where I had to pitch my idea to the group, I held my head up and strategically painted a convincing story to my peers. What I realized that day was that gettin funded was really a game about numbers, personality and popularity, the networking and politics mattered more than the presentation. After the presentations we were given time to network with other reps to convince them why they should vote for our projects. In the end I ranked in the top and was granted a green light for my fully funded project. I was on a high that day. I had pitched in my first allocation and I had done my building proud. I felt so strong, like I really could do anything I worked hard for. This gave me the courage to tackle my next project which was to have a crosswalk right next to the library that was under construction. I successfully raised the issue of the crosswalk with the city councilor for my ward and had a neighbourhood petition completed. The position was rewarding, I got opportunities to plan community events for back to school and Christmas, not just for TCHC but for Humewood House as well.

The work I did outside of school was shaping who I was and what courses I wanted to take in school. It gave me the direction I was looking for. I was taking music courses because I was gifted, not necessarily because it was my passion. Through community organizing I learned that my passion was helping others.

Poetic Interlude

She looked at him and said
Cash credit or soul
Cause it's the only currency that is currently available to you if you want to see your child grow
He replies
No I gave you cash last week
The quality of my credit runs deep
And my soul weakens at the notion that I only get a few moments on the weekends to spend raising my child to the best person that he or she can be
See a child needs a father just as much as a mother
Although there are lots of brothas who do not cherish this responsibility, I'm telling you straight up that that ain't me
I wanna be there
I wanna see the victories along with the defeats
Together we can raise a child who understands that love is more than skin deep
She's blinded by the pain of the division confused by the tugging of emotions
Hurt speaks the loudest
Anger does the most damage
Selfishness makes all the choices
She yells
Cash credit or soul
The cash you gave me is done
I'll take the credit as the only one financially capable of loving this one

Gave you my soul
Had it returned in pieces
So excuse me that my lease on life is trust no one
Life taught me that disappointments come
But I got tired of that familiar feeling
Feeling like I gotta always protect my child from the dangers of this life
Feeling like I gotta consistently take back the knife
Feeling like at this point we can just let the courts decide
Knowing full well that the courts usually fall to the mother's side
He's feeling rage and sadness inside
Formally oblivious to the detrimental
Emotional collide
Two people, Two paths
Growing a part
Creating a natural divide
Leaving only one left on the ride
Reminiscing on childhood memories
His wisdom provides understanding that a child thrives in organized co-parenting
But how do you parent open wounds?
How do you restore order where fear and distrust loom?
Leaving barely enough room to focus on priorities
Morals, Belief, Education, Celebration of life and freedom
Freedom to break free from a soulless society
Withholding Knowledge Sobriety
It's the reason why she seems to ask the same question
Cash credit or soul
Without any profitable goal
He caves in
Knowing in the end
He only wants his child to win
This might be his greatest sin
Deliberately choosing to do everything
He solemnly whispers
Soul
Hoping to lessen the toll
Of a stolen childhood

CHAPTER THIRTY-TWO

Truth

This [is what] I command you: that you love and unselfishly seek the best for one another.
JOHN 15:17

I've heard of stories where the father was trying to be involved and the woman was just hurting too much to be able to co-parent effectively. That wasn't my situation though. I was never the type of baby moms to bleed my baby father dry. In fact, to bleed him dry I woulda needed to get money from him first; and I couldn't even get a penny from him. A Toronto lawyer came to our building as part of the program at our housing complex. He had a lot of good information to offer. For example, I had no clue legal aid was available to me. Within a few days of his visit he was my new family lawyer. I had a lawyer y'all! Smartest decision I coulda made. Even though I had to start the whole filing process again since I moved, this time the heavy lifting was left in the hands of my legal team. All I had to do was provide them with the information I had on him. It wasn't much, but my detective skills paid off. I started googling phone numbers and names to figure out where his new crib was - I mean his momma's house. I searched using her name and phone number and found a couple listings. Then I called each one until I recognized his mom's voice. While I was diggin up dirt, I was tryna stay connected with him as much as possible. Despite everything, I still wanted him to have a relationship with his son. I love how holidays provide the perfect "Hey stranger" message.

Cola

Hey merry Christmas how are you? I hope everything is going well. Look I know we have our differences but I wanted to know if you wanted to see Kayshaun for the Christmas, anyway message me back please God bless and happy new year

He didn't reply even though it was marked as "seen". So, I posted Merry Christmas on his public wall. Finally got his attention, I guess it forced him to reply.

Kendrick
I'm not having a convo wit u on my wall
Cola
Ok then, you can talk to me on here what's good?
Kendrick
Nuttin is good .... how can I help u
Cola
You can start by being nicer to me after I never did you nothing... you can also try helping me out with your son an with all the court things I'm dealing with

I could barely get a response from him, but I could tell my lawyer was stirring up some trouble. Then to add to the fuel a few months later I got a strange message from his account.

Kendrick
Kendrick has a son?
What? Is this some kinda joke? Why is he asking me in 3rd person?
Cola
Hmm Kendrick? who is this?
Kendrick
No this is his girl
Cola
Oh ok, well that's something you should ask him then no?
Kendrick
Can you please just be honest with me, if he has a son then I should no
Cola

Ok well, even though he doesn't want to acknowledge it, he does have a son. You should ask him

The more I answered her questions, the more she asked. How did this happen? When? How old was I? How old was Kaykay? She wanted to know it all, at first I was like *"This is a bad idea, don't do it"* But then I was like *"Fuck it, he sucks anyways, why not tell the truth cause all he doin is lying".* After I got outta my feelings, I was more than happy to oblige. She seemed nice and I felt like if I was her, I'd wanna know if my man had a next kid. Speaks to his character and my life with him. She even told me he wanted to do the DNA test and get the courts over with. Apparently, he wanted joint custody; the fucking nerve of him, but hey at least the test was gonna get done finally. This all seemed too good to be true, so I figured I'd ask the man my damn self. No back and forth with some girl I didn't know, if he wanna talk about our son, he can talk to me.

March 19th 2009
Cola
So your sayin your gonna deal with the courts now and you wanna do dna test??
Kendrick
Fuck u u lying ass bitch
Cola
What did I even do to you?? please tell me
Kendrick
On here telling lies...I didn't fuck u and u kno that .....u kno u only sucked my dick....so u run around telling people bout I took a couple jooks...so u wouldnt look like the crazy bitch u are
Kendrick
Yeah nuttin to say now huh
Cola
Too bad i'm at school gettin an education i'm not gonna answer you right away.....no I don't have much to say cause i'm not gonna argue with you I told it like it is....you don't

like it sorry bout that....your girlfriend confronted me eh, I didn't start typin to her right away to make my story known so u can stay there an cuss me cause I ain't done nothin wrong and p.s.....i'm not a bitch ...don't disrespect me cause you're pissed off

Heated. I was fucking heated. This dumb ass mutherfucker has the damn nerve to come at me? Me? Plus, apparently he has been talking about my child so what the fuck was his problem now?

Cola
She told me you said if I pay you'll do dna.....where were you last year when I offered this to you? you're purposely trying not to solve this an that's fine you can keep not believing not carin or w.e it is you're doing.. as long as I try to resolve things that's what matters....so I take it you're not comin to court???...
Kendrick
U trying to fuck up my life right???.....well ur gonna fucking see what that fucking gets u........
Cola
Threats really??? I thought u were better than that....you don't kno where I live you know nothing about me....I would suggest that you don't try an intimidate me i'm not at all tryin to ruin your life I didnt kno u findin out whether or not you had a son would ruin your life. I just want to get more importantly the custody battle over with ....the rest has yet to come...
Kendrick
u shoulda told the true story......which is ....ima hoe...I can't remember who I was fucking at the the time...the next guys disappeared....I sucked his dick... somehow got pregnant...but I didn't know until I was due...so ima just try to take someone to court who I never had sexual intercoarse and lie that he took two jooks.. so u dont look like a big hoe in front of my pastor dad and the rest of my peoples..........that's the fucking truth
Kendrick

you can tell people u think its mine....but dont fucking lie about what happened....

No, he's really trying my damn patience. I've been nice. I haven't been like those crazy ass baby mommas on Maury. Nigga really think I know nun bout sex huh? Naw, what about the fact that he got me pregnant off precum? Didn't even get to enjoy the fuck before he buss.

Cola
I never lied...you're just in denial
Kendrick what are u not getting...I kno it ain't mine seeing as how we didn't fuck...3 years later and ur still thinking u can get pregnant from ur mouth
Kendrick
which part of this ain't true??????????. ....I can't remember who I was fucking at the the time...the next guys disappeared....I sucked his dick... somehow got pregnant...but I didn't know until I was due...so ima just try to take someone to court who I never had sexual intercoarse and lie that he took too jooks.. so u dont look like a big hoe in front of my pastor dad and the rest of my peoples..........that's the fucking truth......................... tell me????????

The more he talks, the dumber he sounds, like my man was a real heeediot!

Cola
I'm not a hoe.... don't get it twisted...I just made a BIG mistake..... too bad I was 16 when u were talkin to me....if i'm wrong i'm wrong ....regardless of what you wanna say bout what happened you still put it in an you can't get away from that small fact.....you can try but it still remains the same anywayz

Cola
.....I really REALLY need to get back to class an i'm not tryna argue with something you're in denial about...i'll just

talk to you another time when you're calm an not threatening me ....peace out homie P.s hmmm so I know that you're well aware that my lawyer is trying to serve you....
Kendrick
fuck off and may u and ur die a thousand death.........as soon as the hits come u ain't never got nuttin to say ....but a next time u wanna run ur mouth.....poor kid got u for a mom

I gladly saved these messages for my lawyer to help build a stronger case. However, the messages weren't enough evidence to grant me custody during the first court hearing. I had a male judge who wasn't moved by any of the messages that I felt were threatening. The only advice I ever got was call the police, but when I did they said unless he said "I will kill you" they can't do anything about it. I was scared cause my apartment on the first floor left me very exposed. If he had read any of the court documents then he had my address. I fought hard to keep it off record without success. How was I supposed to protect my son myself? I lost sleep thinking of the ways he could attack us. The reality was he probably didn't care enough to come find us, but the longer the case went the more unstable I felt.

It was a blessing when he didn't show up to court for our final hearing. I was a ball of nerves thinking I could potentially see him that day. I wasn't ready to see him. This was the day I was finally able to breathe a sigh of relief, cause at least I knew we just didn't matter enough. This judge finally granted me the gift of sole custody. Sole custody was especially important for doctor visits. If I needed to make any serious decisions, then the responsibility was solely mine, jus like it always was. It was always interesting when doctors would ask for the father's history and I would say "He's not in the picture". They always seem to give me some weird look like "Oh, you can't even figure that out for the sake of your child?" I always look back at them like "If it were that easy I'd have more answers for you" then I smiled at the end, so they knew to move to the next topic.

Before I could leave court we had to figure out the financials. Since we didn't know how much money he was making my child support payment was set to the lowest payment of $170 monthly. Still better than nothing though. I quickly learned that though I had successfully gotten a default judgement for finances, it didn't mean that money was gonna start rolling in. Since I knew practically nothing about him I didn't have any information like his work history or social insurance number in order to garnish his wages. Despite this temporary setback, my lawyer explained to me that the good thing about pushing to go to court was that the payments would now be backdated to 2009, so no matta when he pays, I'd still get current and past. The one agency that was trying to help me recover my payments was the Family Responsibility Office. They were a third-party agency that had the power to suspend drivers licenses or passports to force the payments to be upheld. All this fuss and fighting, but it didn't make one bit of difference. Just wasted energy since I never saw one cent.

CHAPTER THIRTY-THREE

Love

We have come to know [by personal observation and experience], and have believed [with deep, consistent faith] the love which God has for us. God is love, and the one who abides in love abides in God, and God abides continually in him.
1 JOHN 4:16

As much as I tried to change my situation and my relationships with people, I came to the understanding that I couldn't win with love. I love, and I don't get love back. I pour my heart out and in return it gets trampled on. I'm open but shot down by insecurity, regret and greed. I yell, I throw things, I fight, I cuss, I cry, I get the same result. Emptiness. I felt like my mind was being split and manipulated. I be giving my all when it came to my relationships. I would be late to class cause Romeo would say "If you love me, why do you leave me?" Sometimes it was a fight to get off the phone just to get to class. He missed me, I understood that. He wasn't used to me being in school while he was home. We usually spent most of the days together. Sometimes it was a hard pick between the two, I was torn, sometimes I skipped class just to talk to him. I loved him. Sometimes he would say he's gonna invite girls over while I was in class to keep him company. Then I'd get upset. I'd yell, I'd cry, then I stayed. He knew how to get me. Sometimes it felt like I should leave. Like we were toxic for each other, but I couldn't leave. I loved him. He was all I had. He loved me for me and he was the only person who stuck up for me. Whether I liked it or not, he had me for life cause regardless of the bullshit, when I was with him I felt safe. Unfortunately, this feeling of security was fleeting. This particular moment when I was talking to him I could sense something was off. I know when he's not faithful because I can feel it in my soul. Even when he tried to lie, I got a feeling in my stomach that wouldn't leave until the truth was revealed. He tried to manipulate me into thinking I was crazy. Who's crazy, huh? Who's crazy? The whole time he was tryna tell me I was hearing things and thinking wrong things. Yet I was probably right. Now I was stuck, if I left he'd attempt suicide again. It wasn't fair to be trapped in a relationship where I felt like I wasn't loved and respected. How does one say I love you and say I'm sorry for cheating so much?

I couldn't even keep count of the amount of girls I suspect he's been with. I mean, I knew when we got together that he was the type to get girls, but he said he locked them all off for me and I believed him. I friggin believed him. Why? Now look, I was stuck. I loved him, but he didn't seem to love me the same way. I wished it was easy, I wished I coulda just left and not cared. He said he's in love with me, he cheats, he lies, he apologizes, I believe him and then we start again. Love shouldn't even apologize to me no more because it's empty and void. Love is a thing I used to believe in. Not anymore. Fuck love. It can keep its unfulfilling results. I'm tired of being hurt and I'm tired of laying down dormant. From here on out, Imma do me. Romeo don't even gotta know. Game on love. Try hurting me now. I don't even exist.

CHAPTER THIRTY-FOUR

Hands

You who love the LORD, hate evil; He protects the souls of His godly ones (believers), He rescues them from the hand of the wicked.
-Psalm 97 :10

What age did you start drinking? Do you remember the first time? I was about 19/20 and enjoying the freedom of making my own decisions. Now that I had my own place I decided that I wanted to get drunk for the first time. It was always interesting for me trying to balance being young and being a mother. I wanted to still have fun and experience life, I just had to make it work for us. I had decided that any partying I did would be done either after Kaykay went to bed or when he was away at my parents' house. Since I moved out in less than desirable conditions, it had left a strain on my relationship with my parents. I had heard through the grapevine that my mom was telling people I had just basically taken Kaykay and abandoned them. I felt a little bad that Kaykay was missing out on time with his grandparents, but we just couldn't get along. It felt like a custody battle, even still I called my mom hoping to work it out. She expressed that she wanted Kaykay to visit on her weekends off which meant every other weekend. At first, I was kinda hesitant, I had left for a reason and I wanted to keep Kaykay to myself, but I knew my parents cared for him and I wanted them to form a relationship even if I couldn't. Plus, some time away would be helpful. Sometimes being a single mom and even more so a mom with a child with special needs was a lot to handle and this would at least give me a mental break.

I had my party on a Monday since I couldn't wait till the weekend. Tun up at the beginning of the week. The plan was to invite a few friends over and wait until Kaykay was asleep to party. He was always a great sleeper. Noise didn't bother him. He got that from me. We got some alcohol and we got some chocolate. The taste of alcohol was so bitter to me, but chocolate M&M peanuts were a good chaser. That bitter liquid slipped down my throat leaving a warm feeling in my belly. I felt like I had super strength. I went to get up onto the counter but misjudged the height. I landed on the ground face first, nearly missing the edge of my night table by an inch. I never felt a thing. My adrenaline had me running down the hallway convinced I could fly. I ran out the back door with just a t-shirt on in the dead of winter and dropped in the snow like a child.

My night was going well, laughing, drinking, talking, surrounded by people I knew for the most part; and then the sleepiness kicked in. I quickly learned that alcohol made me tired, so I retreated to my room to take a nap while the others continued to drink and smoke outside my apartment. I woke up when I felt a hand. I felt a hand in the dark, so I called my ex's name - Kendrick? No answer. I felt a hand and my head was spinning but I now saw the shadows of a body. I saw a body next to my bed, hands reached out, touching me. "What are you doing? Who are you? I'm not gonna have sex with you" I hear the words "Why not??" and I feel the weight of a body. So, I push and kick and scream. Knowing that people were nearby I yelled, and the shadow leapt back. I jumped up and ran into my bathroom, locking the door behind me while tears fell uncontrollably.

Moments of silence then a Tap. Tap. Tap. I was in too much shock to respond. I heard a female voice beggin for me to open up the door. Slowly pulling myself up from the ground I unlocked the door to see Dela's familiar face standing there. In between tears I managed to say "He tried to have sex with me. I don't know him, but he tried to have sex with me." Can't even remember her words to me. As she spoke I sat there trying to make sense of it all. Through the door I could hear the knocks and the whispers, why won't she come out, what happened to her? I laid still on my bathroom floor. I realized that the shadow was my ex's boy. He was the only one I didn't know previously. Again, the door knocks, except this time I hear my ex's voice. At first, I refused to open the door. I was humiliated and I couldn't stop crying. I wouldn't leave, so I finally allowed him to come in.

Kendrick, not my baby fadda, tha otha one, was never the emotional type, so I never expected much from him, but he sent his friend home and promised to sleep next to me for the rest of the night. He held me to make me feel secure. His gestures gave me back my control. We did end up having sex but this time it was my choice, and nothing was forced. Even if we weren't together and it was just for one night, at least that night I knew him, knew that he wouldn't hurt me. I felt the warmth as he held me while I slept. I wanted to get drunk for the first time in my own home, thinking that I had control of the situation, thinking I would be safe.... Thank God Dela was there to help me.

CHAPTER THIRTY-FIVE

Conflicted

Hatred stirs up conflict, but love covers all wrongs.
Proverbs 10:12

"You're probably too fat to fit into the pews" is one of the comments I heard when word got back that I wasn't goin to attend the funeral. Although I was taking a risk and making a firm decision, I was still extremely nervous. You see, the funeral was for the man who molested me and although I never wished him death; I didn't have any tears to shed either. It was shocking to find out he had been shot but I had conflicted feelings towards the news. No one should take pleasure in anyone's demise, so I didn't, but thinking about the abuse and the mystery of his death had me numb. Honestly I tried more and more to forget it even happened. It disappeared just as quickly as my innocence, leaving only me with the memories. Like a phantom I could still see his face or feel his breath even when I wasn't in that house. My aunt and her children had moved out of my grand ma's house at some point so I didn't have to see him in flesh when I went there, but the memories haunted me. His repetitive acts had me nervous to bend over or sometimes use the bathroom but despite the images that tormented me on the inside, I never revealed on the outside that it bothered me. The thing about being tormented is that the more I ignored it, the deeper I let it become buried. The nightmares, the visions, the flashbacks I buried it all and now I was faced with the decision to forgive and attend or forgive and stand in my truth.

It was quite clear to me that regardless of me speaking out about the abuse in previous instances, nobody seemed to care about the molestation or what I went through. Their silence told me everything I needed to know in those moments. I understood that with it being such a touchy subject no one may have known what to say or how, but the radio silence made me feel even more like an outsider. All the original emotions flooded my mind with this news of his murder. It brought great sadness in my family, he was only 47 at the time, and this tragic situation was even worse cause there were no leads or clues as to who would have committed such an act. Only whispers and speculation with no concrete evidence. All they knew was that it happened late at night.

Reality had set in and I was faced with a decision that shoulda seemed easy but was tearing me apart. I knew it was best for me not to take part in any celebration, but the attacks and insults that came as a result of my decision, made me feel so much worse about everything. I wish the attacks would stop because it made dealin with the situation that much tougher. It wasn't just the verbal comments, but it was the comments on my facebook pictures as a constant reminder of how trash I was, how fat I was and how much hatred they threw towards me.

One cousin commented below one of my pictures "U HAVE DIS ONE PIECE OF SWEATER ON ALL DA TIME IS DAT DA ONLI THING DAT FITS UR FATASS???" It felt strange enough having to live in this body but contending with their thoughts and opinions really made me feel worthless. It was my personal hell on earth that I couldn't escape. Worse because the same vile words they hurled at me was part of the reason this molestation started in the first place. *He was nice to me...* a thought that still played in my head. Who would have known that the simple gestures of protection would have become so much more and even shape a big part of my adolescents. He was old enough to be my father. All these thoughts played into my conflict and honestly death seemed sweeter than dealin with this bullshit. My sole reason to live at this moment was now the child that loved me back to life and taking care of him seemed like the one good thing I was doing with my life. No matta how many times I failed, my child's warmth, big cute eyes, love and dependence on me was enough to keep me tryna live for his sake.

After all my internal battles, my decision towards not attending the funeral felt like me taking back my power. In some odd way, part of me thought that maybe if my family saw how adamant I was about not going; they would finally believe that something had happened. In the end I had to realize that my peace was more important than the truth. As long as God knew that I wasn't lying, my honour would always stand and I needed God's help to get through this cause my emotions toggled between peace and anger. Not so much anger towards him, but anger over the situation, why did this happen to me? It caused division and caused me to alienate myself from my family. It made every visit and every holiday something I dreaded. Every time I got around them all I could think of was what names they had for me or what they thought of me, it was my own personal prison. But to my son that was family, and his connection to them was greater than my own wounds. My pain didn't need to spill over into his life as he was innocent and him being the first great grandchild, there was a special love for him that I didn't want to ruin. However, it was not lost on me the sacrifice I was making for him. The biggest wounds were from the people who were closest to me, designed to cut me deep enough to bleed, but bleed slowly, and internally.
I was so focused on surviving that I wasn't sure how to stop the bleedin. I wasn't sure what was going to help, or what would take this pain away but at the same time there was a slight ease knowing that I wouldn't have to see him or pretend anymore. Pretend that nothing happened. Pretend that I wasn't the family whore or pretend that I didn't feel disgusted in my skin every time I heard his name.

Clearly I didn't share the same pain as my family. I still had many wounds that I was nursing. Coming to terms with his death had many layers for me. I can't say for certain I had forgiven him in that moment, but I felt like I was embarking on a journey where the healing was finally beginning. I understood that healing could look different to many people and I wasn't sure how this process would look but I put my focus on being a mom, moving forward and letting God catch my tears every time I felt conflicted. The day of the funeral I sat at home. As my numbness was easing, I could feel winter turning into spring.

Self- Reflection

In a hotel room shower, in a state far away from home I spoke softly the words "I forgive you Winston". The warmth of the water mixed with my tears as I completed the final stages of my forgiveness process. For the purpose of this reflection, I'm going to jump ahead several years. It is the year 2021, and I had traveled from Canada to Tampa Florida for a christian Millionaire conference called Millions.

As I stood in the shower after service, I replayed what was said earlier. The atmosphere was electric and with one of the topics being forgiveness, I was ensuring that there was no unforgiveness left in my heart. I had thought to myself that I had forgiven everyone I could think of, but then ever so gently I was reminded of this teenage trauma. I had always spoken so freely about the rapes but the molestation always felt so much more personal. With it still feeling like a huge family secret, it always felt so weird talking about it. Whenever I have spoken publicly about it, I have been ridiculed back to silence with the same name calling I endured throughout my teens. This moment...this moment was a huge breakthrough for me. I cried real tears, I held myself tighter and I released what I had buried so deep down for years. When I felt completely empty I then said "I forgive you Nicola" for allowing this situation to rule such a huge part of my identity. No longer was I subscribing to the parts of me that felt undesirable and unsexy. No longer was I willing to hide myself and live under the shadows of guilt.

I understood my role and how I would now contribute to my own peace, happiness and full forgiveness.

I've learned that forgiveness is a decision and sometimes it can be instant and other times it can take years. Even if he had lived, I would still have to have figured out a way to forgive. Forgiveness is not because the person is no longer in play, but because I am choosing to release myself from the prisons and bitter roots that could manifest. In this situation forgiveness was an understanding, a compassion, and continuous. I may not understand why he did it, but I understood that someone who may have lacked self-control as a characteristic would have had trouble managing his own sexual desires and apetites. My compassion was for the little girl who knew no better at the time and who was navigating a challenging situation but was always taught to respect her elders. I have compassion for the same girl who never got to explore the beauty of setting boundaries, and valuing her temple as more than just the fat, ugly object many made her to feel like. From the time of the abuse she has had to continuously fight for her survival and ensure that typical emotions like hatred never took root in her heart.

In a hotel room shower, I spoke softly the words "I forgive you Winston for molesting me". This wasn't my first time speaking on forgiveness towards him, but this was my first time speaking his name and abuse out loud. My task now is to allow the same pain that tried to break me, to be the building blocks of my success as I step into my new identity; free, forgiven and loved. Now let's get back to the story.

CHAPTER THIRTY-SIX

New Friends

Above all, have fervent and unfailing *love* for one another, because *love* covers a multitude of sins [it overlooks unkindness and unselfishly seeks the best for others].
1 PETER 4:8

Back when Tdot wire was poppin I was all ova the online scene and I met this guy. Not my type but he was nice. Tall dark skin kinda mawga, his face was whatever, but like I said, he was nice. It started with an innocent message.

October 29
Duvall
Hi Nicola, How are you doing? Just want to say keep up the good looks and that thick sexy body, but most of all keep that sunshine smile on your pretty face...hope to hear from you soon cause I would like to get to know you better by having small conversation whenever you're not busy...msg me back and tell me what you think. (smiley face)

I hit him up and we kinda hit it off and spent time getting to know each other, basic questions; nothing special. We kept things on a messaging level but made plans to eventually meet in person.
I was driving past Davisville station when my phone rang.
Cola: Hello?
Anonymous: Hi... are you talking to someone named Kevin?
Cola: No, who's Kevin?
Anonymous: Your number is in his phone
Cola: What does he look like?
Anonymous: Tall, dark skin?
Cola: Oh Duvall
Anonymous: Yes, did he tell you he has a girlfriend?
Cola: What? No.... he has a girlfriend?

Anonymous: Yep
Cola: Wow, I'm so sorry, I had no clue and I'm not that kind of woman.

She said her name was Sheena. Apparently, her man had saved my name as a guy's name, either Nick or Cole, to avoid suspicion, but she felt like she needed to try the number and low an behold I picked up. As we continued the conversation we began to unravel the lies an we decided we were going to set him up. I was more than happy to help another female catch her cheatin man.

I was supposed to set up a date and give her the location and time so that she could show up and catch him. However, that same night when I called her on three-way, he had somehow caught on to what we were doin. By the time I tried to call him back he had changed his number. It didn't really matter though, she had already heard the conversation and he had already been caught.

> November 5th 2009
> Exchanging number on facebook...free..taking me out for dinner $20...hearing dial tone after your girl booked you on a 3 way....DAMN PRICELESS..HA HA HA HA So how does it feel to get caught???? Too bad you tried to change your number though....not cute....

At least I did something to help her out. Needless to say, she broke up with him, which she needed to do. Damn cheaters... Well at least she didn't cuss me out for it. Maybe we'll become friends after this. Women gotta stick together.

CHAPTER THIRTY-SEVEN

Choices

"Come, let us drink our fill of love until morning;
Let us console and delight ourselves with love.
-Proverbs 7:18

Speaking of friends, guess who finally called me?...Yep, Reign did. He gave some sorry ass excuse for why he ran off, talkin bout he was overwhelmed. Nigga please! Acting like he was the only one having trouble during that time. Yet as much as I still didn't trust him, I also didn't have time to be mad over stupid shit. What I did know was that it was time for another party to take my mind off things. Kaykay was gone to my parents' house that weekend. My life revolved around making sure Kaykay was good, but that meant that when he went away for the weekends I never knew what to do. It always felt like "So now what?" Being so young meant all my friends were out partying and they would invite me at first, but once I said no too often they stopped inviting me out. Now I was free but had nowhere to go so I would get lonely, even a lil depressed when I couldn't take care of him; but at least he was happy. He loved his grandparents, so I couldn't be selfish.

This time the party wasn't meant to be nothing big. Low key and I needed to know who was coming. The crowd was a bit different this time. Older group of people, 3 or 4 who knew how to handle themselves. We drank, we listened to music, we chilled, they smoked. Reign decided to show up with this dude I ain't neva met, as much as I was hesitant, I knew Reign knew me and respected my house enough to only bring someone he trusted. To my surprise it was this cool east African brotha. Nice hair, inviting eyes, definitely cute - mawga but cute. My favorite part of him was his eyes. Damn I would just get lost looking at them.

His eyelashes were beautiful. I couldn't help but feel weak. I could tell he liked me too cause while everyone was out smoking, he was inside chillin with me. By the time the party died down everyone had left - except him. We stayed up talking all night.

Nathaniel
Add me
Cola
lol heyyyyyyyy
February 17th 2009
Nathaniel
ok i have u now shorty

He was good company. We spent the day talking, then we spent the week talking, before we knew it, time had passed. He had his own place but he stayed at mine instead. We were young lovers tryna play grown up games. I thought I was hella mature, but my emotions were always getting the best of me. I was getting used to having Nathaniel with me. Day in and day out he stayed by my side. He was great help while he stayed with me. This fairy tale felt like it shoulda never end.

March 25th 2009
Cola
BABBBBYYYYYY oh my gosh i am soooo sorry that I threw the bottle at you i truly never mean to hurt you. or hit you. I was acting childish cause i wanted you to spend the time wit me an you just wanted to leave.... do you how it feels to want somethin or someone who doesn't feel the same at that present time. Like i feel like sometimes i gotta beg yu to chill wit me or show me more affection. I REALLY REALLY care about YOU. and im trying to make things work. I kno your gonna be mad at me...but dont be...cause im sorry i never meant it.... but i miss you and i want you to come home safe....so i guess i'll talk to you whenever but just know that i really care about an im sorry.....

Cola
Honestly baby i just wanna know that your good an you did what you had to do...so pleaase just come home. i know your not gonna see this message till maybe tom but i really have a feelin that your not gonna come back here tonight and im sad. Im really sorry babes...i kno you get mad for a long ass time but really just i unno ...just lemme know you ok please

He didn't answer my messages, but he eventually came home to me. I was happy he didn't leave, I wanted to work this thing out, whatever it was. We kissed. We made up. We continued. While I would cook he would sit and entertain Kaykay, sometimes soccer, sometimes video games. They really seemed to get along and my heart was delighted that Kaykay had someone to look up to. It was simple moments like this that I hated his father for not being around. Kaykay was such an amazing kid who had a lot of mobility function despite the disease. I loved that Nathaniel didn't see him as disabled but challenged him to move around. As the days moved forward Nathaniel took on even more of a role by picking Kaykay up from school and watching him while I went to meetings. I got home one day to see Nathaniel and Kaykay were already home. I was confused as to how they got there, cause I had the car. *How did they get home? Taxi?* I asked Nathaniel, "How did y'all get home" To my surprise he said, "We walked" *Walked? Kaykay's school was at least a 10-15 min walk for me, much less Kaykay. Could he even walk that far? We were always told by physiotherapists to conserve his energy* "What you mean walked? Wasn't it far?" "No, we took our time, we talked and played games along the way. He did really well, and when he was tired I carried him" *This shocked the hell outta me, he was only in daycare, still my young baby and he was like a grown man walking home.* It was so touching to see a man care so much for a child that wasn't his. He was so good with Kaykay and did things I woulda neva thought to do. My main focus was to protect him from everything and in this moment, I was challenged to look beyond his disability to see the abilities he did have. I respect a man for that. It was refreshing having the help, not just with Kaykay but also having another person on a day to day basis who truly understood me. He massaged me when I was tired, he cleaned while I was at school. We decided early on that he wouldn't cook after I came home to a burnt pot one day. However, he praised me when I cooked anything - I could make Kraft dinner and his praise made it seem like a high-class dish. I truly felt like a housewife, the more he enjoyed my cooking the more I did it to please him. *I never want this to end. Ye ok, don't get comfortable.*

The one thing I did know was that he wasn't chilling with me for my money. Despite being as broke as a joke, we made life work. He consistently reminded me that money wasn't everything. He showed me how to be happy with what was right in front of me and how to make the best outta a horrible situation. He worked casually and what he did make he brought back and shared it with me. This new mindset was working well for me until my birthday came. That was the first birthday that I had absolutely no money. Couldn't even buy a nice weave or special birthday dinner. *Like how is this really happening? Happy fucking birthday to me, this shit sucks. Fuck Reign, he got me here not even able to celebrate. I'm so broke I can't even walk outside.* It's like he could read my mind, guess who showed up offering to cook me dinner? Yep, Reign actually showed up and offered to do my hair and cook me dinner with whatever he could find in my house. *Nice effort for something ultimately caused by him.*

Truth was, it wasn't a horrible day after all. Nathaniel waited for Reign to leave before re-establishing his role as my man. He attempted to change my hairstyle; although it ain't work out, his jealousy was cute. He ain't have nun to worry bout though, Reign was always just a friend - nothing more. Between Reign and Nathaniel, a lil competition ain't hurt nobody cause I was the true winner in the end. I had my first orgasm that night when Nathaniel gave me head. It was such a memorable experience. I felt this man's tongue so deep that my toes curled, and my back arched. Sweetest gift I could have gotten, and it was free. *I guess money aint everything.*

By weekend money was expected to be in my account, I guess it wasn't the end of the world but I jus hated being broke and so dependent on money for happiness. The upside was that my girl had planned to take me away to Niagara Falls for the weekend. She paid for the hotel and all I had to do was pay for the gas. Blessed! As we stopped to fill up before hitting the road my card was declined for the gas. *That's weird, I had just checked my account that morning.* A call to my bank revealed that I had been a victim of fraud. The strange thing however was that my account was scammed for $300 and the exact amount that was deposited into my account that morning was $300. I was on the phone and the lady was grilling me, making me feel like I frauded my own damn account. "Miss Bennett this can happen when you share your account information. Is there anyone that has your PIN?" I replied No. *Yes, I lied, Reign and Nathaniel both had access to my account.* "If you gave anyone your PIN this is what can happen". Listen ma'am, I had nothing to do with this, and I am trying to go away so imma need you to help me please. I have nothing to do with this. *I know Reign is the type a nigga to do this, but he wouldn't do it to me would he? Plus, I only told Nathaniel about the money; wait, would he do this to me? I mean they are friends, I'm sure he knows what Reign does. What if this whole damn time he's been playing me. Oh man if that's the truth imma get him. Ok all you need to do is ask him and be cool.*

I called him right away.

-Yo, so tell me why my account was frauded today for exactly $300. You know anything bout that?

-Nathaniel: No, why?

-I just find it funny how the person frauded me for $300 and that's exactly how much I said was deposited into my account this morning. You talk to Reign today? You tell him?

Nathaniel: You think Reign did it? That's really messed up. I hope he didn't do that but try not to stress and just enjoy your trip.

-Yep, later

She ended up paying for gas and just about everything else on the trip. Thank God for her! The trip was a memorable one. I enjoyed the escape cause returning home only meant returning to what felt like a very chaotic life. My account didn't even get rectified until I returned home. At least I came home to money.

Month two with him and things were changing but still manageable. I wasn't sure if he could be trusted but he never gave me any other reason not to. Besides that, the bedroom magic was wearing off. Sex wasn't the same, sometimes he couldn't keep up or satisfy me and other times he just wasn't interested in sex or giving head. I felt too ugly, like maybe he wasn't attracted to me anymore or something. I felt bad sometimes cause when he did try, I knew he was trying his best, but it just wasn't good. Without the sex part we were just playing house.

My friends knew about him but it didn't seem like somethin I needed to tell my parents about. Not to mention that my relationship with my parents was designed in a way to keep them from ever meeting anyone in my life. My mom being the judgy type, I didn't wanna deal with it. God has an interesting humour though. I always felt like my parents kinda just moved me into my new place and that was it. They barely ever visited me unless I called them and said I needed something. Over time I had just gotten used to them being absent. I saw them to drop off and pick up Kaykay but that was it. I had learned to cope and since Nathaniel was living with me, I felt even less like I needed them to check in. This particular day, I woke up to a phone call from my dad saying they were on their way to see me. Shit! ETA? Kaykay was at daycare so this was really unexpected. Apparently, they were calling from the parking lot behind my house. I had no time to clean, and more importantly, what the hell was I gonna do with Nathaniel? I woke his ass up and told him he had to find somewhere to go by the time I walked outside. *There's a library next door, he can leave through the side door without them seeing him. What the hell though, they never come see me. I just hoped he was gone by the time I got back, and I hoped they didn't stay long. Oh man, imma be in so much shit.* Once I entered my apartment he was nowhere in sight. *Phew! I hope he's ok, I didn't give him much time to get out, oh well, I'll make it up to him later.*

My mother was like any other mother pointing out everything that needed additional cleaning. *Well if y'all told me you was coming I would have cleaned it to your liking, duh!* Her biggest pet peeve was that my bed was always unkempt. It bothered her to the point that most times she just made the bed for me. As she would say, "Why your bed look like mashed potato?" While she was in my room doing who knows what I was in the living room with my dad talking. "Ahhhh...NICOLAAA!!!" As I rushed to my room to see what the problem was, dread quickly fell on my face once I realized my mom was screaming because she had pulled back the sheets and was startled by seeing Nathaniel in my bed under the sheets. YEP! This heeeeediiiooottt decided to hide in my bed. *Didn't he fucking think? I said library, why the rass would he hide in my bed? I mean he's mawga as shit but still. Did this nigga really think that would work? Dumb ass.* Upon discovery he jumped up, introduced himself and listened and laughed quietly as I got cussed out by my mother. It was just a lot of angry words being hurled my way. Can't blame her, it's my fault I'm dating a dummy.

I really cared for him though, was it love? Lust? Or companionship? Wasn't sure, at times he was so immature I wanted to kill him. He didn't have a cell phone, so he was constantly borrowing my cell phone, my car, and a few times he didn't even come back with them till early in the morning. He was too damn comfortable. Then there were other times his jokes reminded me to laugh, something I had forgotten to do. Despite the ups and downs, for the moment, he was mine, I was his, this was us.

Going on to our third month together it began to feel like I had two kids I was taking care of. He was drinking and smoking more than usual and just acting completely out of character. He left his Facebook open while he went to smoke and as I passed by the computer a certain conversation caught my attention. He was talking to some chic telling her he was gonna pick her up from the airport. *Ye eh? Airport? How he getting to the airport? Whose car is he picking her up with? Lord knows he ain't got shit for himself. Let me find out this nigga tryna pick a bitch up in my car. I'm not the one and I'm not in the mood for this shit.*

- Cola: Sooooo, I saw a message on your Facebook
- Nathaniel: Oh ye? Where, what's it say?
- Cola: You tell me?
- Nathaniel: I don't know
- Cola: I see you telling some girl you gonna pick her up at the airport, but in whose car though? Cause we both know you ain't got a car, you barely got shit to your name so whose car, was it my car? My car you thought you was gonna use to pick this chick up?
- Nathaniel: Hmm ye
- Cola: You stupid, try again. This is what you do when I'm not around eh, you think I'm some kinna fool? You think this is some kinda game? Why? What's the point of talking to this girl?
- Nathaniel: She's just a friend
- Cola: So then why wouldn't you tell me about her or the fact that you were gonna use my car? Listen, I don't got time for you and your dumbass ways. I already have one child to take care of, I don't need two. Either you're gonna man up or you ain't. Truss me when I say I'm not forcing you to be here with us, you can leave at anytime. We ain't family, you don't gotta tie yourself down. Go and be free.
- Nathaniel: No baby I'm sorry, I'm so sorry. I'm not gonna do it again. I do wanna be here with you and with Kaykay. You're not forcing me. I just do stupid things sometimes and I don't think.
- Cola: Look I ain't doing this with you, I'll give you one more chance.
- Nathaniel: Thank you.

- While cleaning up around the house I started to notice my race car jacket and camera were missing only to see this man walking in the house with my jacket on and with my camera in his hand talking bout look at the pictures I took today baby. *Seriously? Take my shit off. Wait, did this nigga erase pictures of my kid?*
- Cola: Hmm where's the pictures of Kaykay? Did you erase them to take your own pictures?
- Nathaniel: Yes.
- Cola: Are you dumb? Why would you erase the pictures? THIS AINT EVEN YA CAMERA!! You cheese me so much, you just don't think before you do things.

This third month was draggin on long and living with this man made it feel even longer. I felt like I was always mad or crying or something. My peace was gone, and I was just about done with this man. He just needed to grow up. *What's the point of dating someone older when they still can't get their shit together?* It was a rollercoaster of feelings. He was messing up but these weren't individual deal breakers. It felt good when he introduced me to his cousins. We hung out a few times with them and Reign. He seemed pretty proud to show me off as his French speaking, piano playing girl. I had my shit together and it made him look good. His cousins ranged from younger than me, to the same age, to older - all guys. His cousins seemed all too familiar with his ability to fuck up a good situation but made sure I knew that he was good guy.

It was his older cousin who brought him back to my house the morning after he took my car and cell phone for the night. I spent the night using my house phone to call a cell phone that he just never answered. I had to take a taxi to get Kaykay to daycare that morning.

- Cola: I guess you brought your cousin thinking he was gonna save you
- Nathaniel: I know you're mad, I brought you flowers and I can explain, I was with my cousin all night doing some business stuff

- Cola: You think flowers can help you? You think I really want flowers right now? Get the fuck out, I'm done.

He left. I cried tears of anger. I felt like he just had no respect at all for me. He seemed so convinced that him being out "doing business" would excuse the fact that he left me here without a car or cell phone. Flowers were supposed to fix things? Really? I just needed to not be around him for a bit. He came back in a few days to move his stuff out. He had made his choice, and now I had to make mine. My motto had always been "On to the next one" and as much as I wasn't tryna rush into anything else, there was this one guy who was right there to catch me when things fell apart.

He was intrigued by my mystery and I was intrigued by his intellect. I wasn't physically attracted to him, but the conversation was good. He was much more attentive than Nathaniel. I knew he liked me from the first time Nathaniel introduced us. Nick was Nathaniel's cousin who happened to be the same age as me. He thought he had what it took to treat me better, so he started with the good morning texts. We had a few things in common, our belief in God, our ability to both speak French, our taste in music, our ambition and drive towards a better future. It was a nice change in pace, even better was that sex wasn't even a part of our conversations. We genuinely jus wanted to get to know each other.

Even though Nathaniel no longer lived with me, once the reality hit him that things were over, he tried harder to get me back. All of a sudden he wanted to give me head, back rubs, cook me dinner, anything to make things up to me. *"Muthafucka you had sooo many chances, naw I'm good, I'm on to betta now."* What I said in my mind didn't match with what I said out loud. All I said was "No thank you" He asked, "What about Kaykay, don't you still need help with him?" "Ye I know y'all had a kinda bond so you can still see him, you just gotta be consistent." I know that was gonna be a tall order for him, but I had to at least let him try. Most times when Nathaniel would come over Nick would accompany him. Then Nick got bold enough to come hang out alone. Then he would cum and hold me through the night, letting me know I was cared for in his arms.

Neither one of us had told Nathaniel about what we were doing, but this dangerous excitement could no longer be contained. One night it was the three of us hanging out and my ex had gone outside to smoke. There was a magnetic pull that overtook any sane rationale cause we locked the doors, ran into the darkness of the room laughing and touching and feeling and releasing. It felt good. Then I fixed my hair, clothes and unlocked the front door to see Nathaniel standing there frustrated. "You guys didn't hear me knocking?" "Nope sorry, you didn't knock hard enough I guess" *I hope he believes that* "Ook" I think that time he believed me, but it wasn't kept a secret for too much longer after that. The look he gave me when he found out I was sleeping with his cousin was heartbreaking. I felt bad cause it was the first time I fully understood his feelings for me. *Damn he actually cares about me? Why couldn't he just show me this when we were together? Why now?* All this drama and it wasn't even worth it. I got bored of Nick too, his sex was good at times and jus not enough other times. My pet peeve was a cocky nigga, the more he hyped up how great his dick was, the less I enjoyed it. He'd be like "Imma make sweet love to you that'll have your toes curling" Hmmm my back didn't even arch. Waste of energy and good pussy at this point. Once the magic wore off I realized how much I was not attracted to him, to the point I would tell myself, *Every Time you sleep with that man, there's a chance he could be your baby daddy. Is that what you want? Is that who you see as your baby daddy? Are you gonna introduce him to your friends, family? No? Stop fucking around and let him go. Dick is easy to get, there will always be a guy ready but make sure he's worth it. Make sure he's cute, stable and would be ready to take care of a baby if anything happens. Let him down easy or lie your way outta it. You can't tell the nigga he ugly, that's rude. Say something like, it's just not working out between us. Or tell him you feel bad about them being cousins.*

Welp based on my own advice I made up a lie and ended things with Nick. Oh well! Ugh, Romeo said this would happen, said I wouldn't find no one to treat me like how he do. Guess he was right.

CHAPTER THIRTY-EIGHT

Growth

He who covers and forgives an offense seeks love, but he who repeats or gossips about a matter separates intimate friends.
Proverbs 17:9

The house was quieter with Nathaniel gone. I was still mad at him yet what I missed the most was the help. There was just so much going on and it was challenging to make it all work. As much as Kaykay was a happy go lucky kid, we still had to navigate his severe constipation and his therapy appointments. It definitely was not easy having all these responsibilities while tryna complete a university degree. I doubt anyone in my class coulda understood my world. Young mother, it felt like people were nervously rooting for me. My mother would say she was proud of me but would also say "I don't know what to tell people when they ask what you are doing in school" I internalized this to mean that since I was studying for a music degree it wasn't as reputable as a lawyer, teaching, or even a nursing degree. I suspect her fear was in the security or stability in building a viable music career. Either way it hurt to feel how little she thought about me. I heard comments like "All she does is party, she ain't a good influence". No matta what I did, it wasn't good enough. The fact that I even made it to university with a kid would have made many parents thankful that I didn't give up, but not my mother. Well, she may not have been sure of me, but I knew other people who were.

There was a woman downstairs in the office named Audrey - the woman who interviewed me, who was in charge of programing. The way she would check up on me made me feel like she always had my back. Anything I needed I could ask her and she would do her best to help me. She gave me a heads up for different programs that were coming and was one of the people who encouraged me to take the tenant representative position. Our building actually had great programming for young mothers. Some girls had started a cooking class where we brought all our kids down to play with each other while we cooked a meal. More than ever I was happy I moved. I had a lot more peace around me and Kaykay was making new friends and playing with kids his age. Teen moms on the move was another amazing program run by an outside agency. That program would have different teen mothers from the area come in once a night, again we would have a meal prepared and we sat and talked about different relevant topics. These programs really helped me to change my internal message. I felt like such an outcast before, but here I was with other moms my age sharing our similar experiences. It felt like I was building a foundation as a mother. I was dusting off the word "young" and focusing on just being a mother. Every mother was going through their own battles, essentially, we all supported each other. As much as going to these programs meant giving up a night of studying, they were conveniently downstairs which was even more of a bonus since we didn't have to travel far.

Everything I was doing, every program I was a part of was shaping me and teaching me to handle greater responsibilities. Question, how come they don't teach us how to pay rent in school? Or how to manage money? I greatly appreciated receiving the maximum OSAP amount since I was a young mother, but without proper direction as a 20-year-old I had no knowledge or understanding on how to make $20,000 stretch for a whole year. My parents didn't teach me the fundamentals, which felt like the recurring theme I heard from my friends. Our parents dealt with their finances themselves and left us to figure it out... I guess. In life I was beginning to learn how to make the most of whatever cards I was dealt and to research everything I didn't know. While tryna figure out life and grow up, I had somehow survived school, not with the greatest marks but I passed with a solid C average. Classes like gospel choir and other arts/music related classes brought my average up, thank God!

It was almost time for my baby's birthday!!!!! April was almost done and time was moving so fast. He was the best kid in the world. God made him to fit me perfectly, like hand to glove. He was the quiet type of kid I coulda left to watch TV and he would just never move. I never had to baby proof the house cause he never did anything. He would sit and quietly play with his toys or simply his own hands for hours. He had a remarkably creative mind that allowed him to be patient with me as I was learning how to balance everything. Most of all he was loving!! He was so incredibly loving. It felt so nice to be unconditionally loved. No matta what I did he thought it was great, it was like I could never mess up in his eyes. He spoiled me with hugs and kisses and multiple times a day I told him I loved him. It was so important to me that he knew how much he mattered to me. Without him I was nothing. So, when it came to his birthday or anything he wanted I wanted to go above and beyond cause he deserved it. This year he actually had friends he could invite to his birthday thanks to the other women and their kids. Obviously, it was going to be a Cars themed birthday party, he LOVED cars. He had watched Disney's Cars movie a million times, no joke. I think he had played that movie almost everyday to the point that the bootleg CD got scratched so I was thinking of buying him the real DVD. Birthday parties as a single parent were challenging because it was a reminder that I was doing this all alone, and I felt a lil embarrassed cause I had always pictured doing all these things with a partner. Life didn't allow me to dwell on it too long though, I had to adjust my mind and keep it moving. My only hope was that I would find a man willingly to step up and be a role model for him.

Romeo called to speak to Kaykay for his birthday. No matta what we went through, Kaykay was always gonna be his son and so he made sure he checked up on him. Since Romeo and I had stopped talking his brother made more of a point to check in with me. My guess was to report back to his big bro that we were ok. Kaykay knew who Romeo was despite their interactions being solely by phone. I was surprised that he had the guts to call me, but I was happy he did. Even though he said, "I'm not calling for you, I'm calling for my son, is that ok?" "Yep, here Kaykay"

I handed Kaykay the phone on speaker phone and he put it up to his ear.

- Kaykay says "Hi Romeo, how are you?"
- Romeo: "Happy Birthday"
- Kaykay: "Thank you"
- Romeo: "What are you doing?"
- Kaykay: "Playing with cars"
- Romeo: "You excited for your birthday?"
- Kaykay: "Yea, what are, what are you doin?"
- Romeo: "Nothing" "Have you gotten lots of presents already?"
- Silence. Then I yell, "Kaykay pay attention or say bye."
- Kaykay: "Bye Romeo"

He was distracted by the movie on TV but handed me the phone and went right back to what he was doing. I was feeling conflicting emotions. I was hurt by him, but I had butterflies in my stomach. Romeo says "Ok, thank you, bye" Then I say, "Wait, that's it?" He replies "I didn't think you wanted to talk to me, but I thought I would at least try to call, to at least talk to my son" I missed him though so I responded "It's ok" It was as if a weight lifted, we began talking like nothing had ever happened. In my heart I was always gonna be Romeo's girl. He knew how I liked to be treated, and I missed not having to explain everything. I spent the rest of the time recounting to him how my relationship with Nathaniel was. It fueled many jokes between Romeo and I as I recounted the dumb shit Nathaniel had put me through. I could tell Romeo's cute lil jealous ass was tryna get mad, even though he tried to play it cool. I even missed how protective he would get over me. We break up to make up, and these in between niggas were just to pass my time. The truth was that even though we hurt each other...we understood each other...we loved each other. I guess it was better to stay with what I knew instead of being burnt by something new. Hopefully the time apart was enough to show him that I wasn't to be taken for granted. For the moment though, I was happy, it felt like we both had experienced some growth.

CHAPTER THIRTY-NINE

Caught Up

O sons of men, how long will my honor and glory be [turned into] shame? How long will you [my enemies] love worthless (vain, futile) things and seek deception and lies? Selah.
-Psalm 4:2

The phone call from Romeo was great, but not enough. I was tryna stay focused on life. I had heard too many promises to take him seriously, plus I was swimming in debt and my license just got suspended for non-payment of fines. UGH!! I needed my license back up quickly cause I was about to start my summer classes to speed up my degree. Mommy and daddy to the rescue, I had some RESP money saved up and they took it to pay off my debt and get my license reinstated. I had all intentions of fighting the tickets but I forgot, and it piled up till I wasn't able to pay for it. My parents came clutch at the right moment. I got a new start with my gud up gud up credit. My goal was to make it through summer school. I picked music classes that would be a no brainer to bring my GPA up. I was sitting at a C- average currently and at risk of being kicked outta my program if my GPA didn't improve. I couldn't be a single mother and university drop out. I'd be no betta than the girls in my building. Some of them were proud to be ghetto and going nowhere. Some of them spent time at home doing nun, and some of them wasted their time on the phone with niggas from jail.

My neighbour Sharie was one of those chicks who spent time on the phone with niggas from jail - one in particular. We had hit it off from when she moved in. She was nice and had a beautiful daughter. Maybe it was outta the convenience that we lived right next door, but we became close friends. She was my best friend in the building, anything she needed I was there, anything I needed she was equally there. It was a bonus that our kids got along very well. We were always at each otha's house; it was as dope as a friendship could get. So, when she was spending time on the phone with this guy from jail I was usually around somewhere. I honestly thought I was too good to get caught up in that. But the nigga she was talking to had a roommate that would always tell Sharie to tell me hi whenever he knew I was around. *Stop being such a snob, it wouldn't kill you to say hi back.* The next time Sharie was on the phone and his friend wanted to say hi, I took the phone and responded myself, "Hi" he responds, "How you doing?" *Damn his voice is sexy, I like his accent. I've always had a soft spot for American dudes.* He said he liked my voice. *Don't blame you.* Then he says, "Would you mind if I called you, can I get your number please?" Everything in me said *Don't do it, dis nigga in jail, don't do it.* But I respond "Ye, sure" he responds, "Don't worry I'll pay the bill" The price of the calls wasn't that much so it didn't bother me. His name was Jersey cause he was from New Jersey. I didn't know what he looked like, but he sounded mad sexy. We hit it off and the interest seemed mutual. Things with Sharie and her ting were going good and she wanted to go see him, but he was in jail in the far east and she ain't have no car. I was always down for a road trip, so I didn't mind driving her out there, plus I would get a chance to see my ting too. Only downfall was that by the time we drove down we wouldn't have made it back in time for me to pick up my son from daycare. She could always get her family to pick up her daughter from daycare, a luxury that I did not have, so I brought him with me.

The drive down was fine, but I felt hella horrible bringing my child to jail to meet a man who wasn't his daddy. *Damn are you this desperate? Jails aren't for kids.* I was hoping since he was so young he wouldn't even remember it. The looks I got was more than enough to shame me. I felt nervous about meeting Jersey. I know my voice was sexier than how I looked. Guys would say whoa you sound so sexy, sound like a phone sex operator...send me a pic. Feeling so gassed and confident I would send them a pic only to be met with silence, or the comment "You don't look like how you sound" I had gotten used to being invisible, so I kept my phone relationships and physical relationships separate. If they chopped me on da street than I knew they liked me, if they chopped me from online I tried to delay meeting for fear of disappointment.

I met Jersey, and he was sexy, but I could tell he was just putting on a good face. He seemed a bit taken back that I was a big girl. I'm sure it was not what he expected from a girl with such a sultry sexy voice. *Maybe you're overthinking this, it's not always about your weight.* The day I left the jail was the day the phone calls stopped, I heard he was released from jail a few weeks later but we never spoke again. *Told ya. He don't want no fat chick.* I hated it. Hated him. I was such a dope chick if only he coulda gotten past the weight he woulda seen how beautiful my soul was. But he didn't care bout me or the $800 bill he left me with. *Your mom was right, guys aren't gonna be ok with a girl who's heavy.*

One of Jersey's cell bredrin named AK who used to say hi from time to time found a way to get in contact with me after Jersey left. Said he heard I was in a situation an was gonna help out in exchange for some help. Said Jersey was a coward, but I didn't need to worry cause he preferred thick girls anyway. AK was this intelligent Arab dude. His maturity was next level, we actually held decent conversations. All he needed from me was to 3 way him to his mother in Windsor, so he could talk to her. It was easy enough. To avoid raising the bill, AK had me set up ghost lines to make the calls. Ghost lines were what niggas used to make phone calls without paying. It worked like this, I called the phone company and gave them a fake first name, fake last name, fake birthday and fake drivers license to set up the phone line. The company would send a technician out to set up the line and we used it until they discovered it was fake and cut it off. Then I'd call with a different ID to set up a different phone line. Sometimes we got a few weeks outta it, sometimes a few days, it depended on how good the fake ID was and how quick the company was to catch on. It was surprisingly easy to create a fake driver's license and a complete profile. This was a whole new world to me. I connected calls for AK, his bredrin Jigga and his bredrin Anthony. Jigga had family locally and Anthony would call his girl. It was honestly harmless. The main thing for me was switching up my voice, waiting for the technician and remembering what name I gave.

A knock at my door ended my exhausting wait for the technician. I was given a 12-5 window, which seemed to usually mean they'd show up closer to 5 than 12...go figure. I opened the door and could barely catch my breath, *damn he's sexy.* I didn't expect him to be so good looking. Most times I don't even notice the men who hook up my services. From my angle he's about 5'7, well-built, needs a line up but his eyes felt like they were piercing my soul. Although it may have only been a minute that I had this door open it felt like time had frozen and I was floating. I could imagine I probably threw him off guard. I was picturing the view from his angle. A door opened and revealed a woman standing in a long white T-shirt and a pair of batty ridas. All I could hear in my head was the T-shirt song from Destiny's child.

"I Feel The Fabric From Your T-Shirt
Flow With My Body
I Can Still Hear Your Baritone
In My Ear Telling Me You'll Take It Slow
And I Was In The Mirror Playing A Role
Like You Were Here, I Couldn't Turn Me On
So I Fell Asleep With The Music On
Woke Up Again Hearing The Same Old Song, Playing
(Oh) Give It To Me Deeper
(Oh) Giving Me The Fever
(Oh) Now You Got My Feet Up
This One Is A Keeper
Now The Second Verse Is Playing
(Oh) We Tried To Stand Up
(Oh) Hold Me While My Hands Up
(Oh) And The Music Picks Up
Now He Sees My Shirt Off
I'm Thinking To Myself Again"

A deep voice interrupted my thoughts, Andrea? You're Andrea, right? Hmmm yeah, yes, I am, I am Andrea. *Lies.* If I could read his mind, I could only surmise his response was...wow. With enough time passing between us as we stood there, he said "I'm here to activate some services for you, would you mind letting me in?" "Oh yea, sorry...I'll lead the way" I sashayed my way about 4 steps to where my tv was set up and where I left the phone. I knew the room he needed to get into to hook up my cable was locked and my super left from 4, it was now 5. I had AK in one ear on the phone asking a shit load of questions while I was tryna attend to the needs of this man in front of me. I put the phone to the side and in a low tone I said to him "Hmm I think the room you need is next door, but it's locked and there's no one here right now to open it. I had left a note on the file asking for the person to come before 4 but iuno if they got that message to you. Sorry to waste your time" To my surprise he says "Oh, I can come back tomorrow, but it's my day off." *All I want to scream is yes! yes! Yes! please come back on your day off.* Instead I say, "It's ok you don't have to come on your day off". Luckily, he says "Well I don't want to leave you without your services, so I don't mind coming back tomorrow. I get paid either way." He got my stomach in knots, butterflies all around, I couldn't stop looking at his eyes. As I walk him to the door I say, "Hmm, what's your name again?" "Roy" We exchange numbers and we both stood awkwardly before saying bye and I watched as he walked away. Damn I couldn't stop smiling.

I forgot this man was on the phone, "Hello, my bad...no he can't do it today, he's gonna do it tomorrow" I assured him by the following day everything would be connected, and I would be home, so he could get his calls done. At first the calls were far and few between, but then AK would feel a way when he called an I didn't answer so I had to forward my house phone to my cell phone, so I could connect the calls in between classes. It was gettin to be a lot, balancing the calls between all the guys but AK's mom had promised to send me some money to pay down the phone bill, so I kept making the calls. Besides the calls we spent time gettin to know each other. It was nice, but at the moment I had my sights set on someone else.

Roy would call me on his lunch breaks and we were constantly texting. Every time I got a message from him I couldn't help but smile. We talked about anything and everything and I felt so comfortable with him. From past experiences, I developed a habit of always asking a couple of key questions. #1 Do you have a girl? #2 What are your intentions by talking to me? I needed to know from the get go if this was a friendship ting, a sex ting, a once in a while ting. I needed to adjust my feelings accordingly and could only do that by asking questions up front. We brushed over the questions and conversations about our first date. There was jus so much to cover. With the way things were going, I just couldn't understand why he wasn't asking me out until I asked him directly "Are we still gonna go bowling? His response was "Unfortunately, I can't take you out because I have a girlfriend. I don't wanna hurt you, so I needed to be honest with you." *Didn't wanna hurt me? Too late. What the fuck man.* I'm scrolling through our text messages to see if I missed something or caught the wrong vibe. Nope, I uno how I coulda misread the signals. To make the situation better he says, "I like talking to you, if only I met you first it would be you and not her". This was crazy to me, if he felt that strongly, what was stopping him? *Here I am, you want me, I'm right here.* I could feel the anger and hurt in the pit of my stomach but there was nothing left but to leave him alone. I felt hella stupid.

Unbeknownst to AK, and while licking my own damn wounds, I was now emotionally available to entertain him. I was dissing someone who liked me while chasing a man who was unavailable to me. He was sweet, gentle, smart and he wanted me to be his girl. I said yes. Honestly, I gave it a chance, I didn't know how serious it really coulda been from jail but, at this point I didn't even care, he was happy. The phone calls had become a family affair once I started making calls for AK's brother too. His brother did the math for the fake profiles. It had been a long time since both brothers had been able to speak directly to each other, so I had one call my cell while the other called my house phone and put both on speaker phone to talk. It honestly felt nice being able to link both brothers since they hadn't spoken in so long. Only issue was the phone lines were gettin disconnected almost as fast as I was doing them, and when I called in they were inquiring about my apartment and who lived there. It was enough to scare me, I wasn't tryna get caught. Since I was now making calls for AK's brother he too offered to pay the bill, so I started using my house phone under my real name to connect the calls.

AK was as helpful as he could be from behind bars. I was looking for another car since my car had been giving me a little bit of trouble and he said he had a connect for a car, but I would have to travel to Windsor where his mom and other siblings lived. He also lemme know that his sister had a set of leather couches that she was selling that I could look at while I was down there. I had never met his mom and jus briefly spoke to her on the phone, but I figured, why not? I needed a car and if he had a link then why not? I planned it for a weekend when Kaykay was gone to my moms to ensure I could get things done without worrying about him. AK's mother happily met me as I got off the train and drove me over to the car dealership. Even though I didn't see any cars that I liked I quickly learned that welfare was not an acceptable means of "income" even if I had seen something I wanted. I also learned that having no credit was just as bad as having bad credit since I hadn't built up any type of trust with any creditors.

It wasn't a complete waste of a trip though, before driving me to the house, we stopped to see the leather chairs that were sitting in the lobby of the car dealership. Although they smelt like cigarette smoke, they were in great condition. She was selling two pieces of real leather reclining seats, a three-seater and single seater for $400 total. For an extra $100 AK's sister convinced one of her friends to drive the couch set from Windsor to my house in Toronto that same night. AK's mom prepared an amazing Middle Eastern meal before we left that night. The colors were so vibrant, the taste of mint was tickling my taste buds, it was so refreshingly different. The icing on the cake was when she gave me some money towards the phone bill. It wasn't a whole heap, but it gave me the security that they were gonna pay off the rest of the bill. I climbed into a truck, thanked his mom and started the 4-hour journey back to Toronto. On my way home, my mind was racing though. *Was this a good idea? I don't even know any of these people. What if something goes wrong? I didn't tell nobody where I was going.* I'd never been so happy to see my building. It was night by time we got back. The ride wasn't bad, they were extremely nice people, even helped carry my new furniture into my apartment. I didn't realize how bad the cigarette smell was until I brought it in my apartment. It was like stifling the air, but nun that some Febreze and a gooood wipe down couldn't fix.

AK was a good man, he checked for me, always made sure I was good. I respected that about him. What I didn't like was how jealous and possessive he was getting. From the beginning I made calls for his friend Jigga, but the more Jigga would call to connect to his girl, the more AK was jealous. Even if it didn't cut into his phone time cause I used different lines, it wasn't good enough. If he was gonna pay the bill he wasn't bout sharing. It got to the point that I had to hide when Jigga called to keep the cool on all sides. What was cool before was no longer cool. One thing about me, I don't do controlling relationships, so the more AK tried to control me the more I ran in the opposite direction. I never wanted to cut him out completely because I was grateful for the help and I knew he just didn't want me to get caught up. I could tell he cared but once he started to get rude he had to get cut off for a bit.

If AK was mad at me for making calls for Jigga, he definitely wouldn't have been ok with me delivering a package for him. Jigga had asked me to pick up a package from this one guy and pass it on to his brother. They were simple instructions to follow, pick up the package, don't look at it, pass it off. So, I did jus that, I picked up the package to give to his brother except his brother delayed our meeting by a week. My sister saw the package in my car and asked what it was, and I gave her the same answer, don't touch it, I gotta deliver it. My sister has always been rebellious though, somehow "Don't look", meant look to her. I always thought *that's how people get killed,* being too fass and asking questions that don't need answers. My sister thought it was stupid to not know what was in my possession. Ignorance was bliss though, cause once I knew what it was then I started to worry and got anxious. It turned out to be some bloody rag and now I was a sitting duck in an area that was a ticking time bomb of cops. It was at that moment that I realized the depth of this favor he asked. I could have easily gotten myself way more caught up.

This was a moment of growth for me. Between the favors and the phone bill, which by the end had been racked up to $8000 between AK's calls, his brothers, his sisters (at one time she was in jail too) and all the otha niggas I ran numbers for, the bill had accumulated and that $100 his mom had given me was nearly a drop in the bucket in comparison. I figure it was time I took a break altogether and re-focus on school. I had a taste of the life and decided it wasn't for me. So funny how I held my nose high and ended up getting caught up. It just kinda...happened.

CHAPTER FORTY

Take A Stand

He loves righteousness and justice; the earth is full of the lovingkindness of the LORD.
Psalm 33:5

Growth was such a common theme. I was growing, Kaykay was growing, school was starting back and even though it appeared chaotic and busy with the amount of commitments I had, things finally seemed peaceful. A routine was actually happening. Kaykay seemed to be doing well. I was constantly reminded of how far he came and how proud of him I was. He was talking, walking, even running and making new friends. It was the happiest I coulda been for him. Look at God, from being told he would never walk to having him walk home from school. We were in such a good space I wasn't even concerned about any changes when we were set for our fall check in, we went every 6 months to make sure we could stay on top of any potential changes. Although I thought I was prepared for news of any changes, given how well he seemed to be doing, our latest appointment left me blindsided.

September 15, 2009
My beautiful son ...Lord why?..I'm sorry for all I've done....but that's my baby...i jus dont get it....tried to be strong....i can't make a decision....

Comparing his new fitness test with the one from 6 months ago it showed that there was a slight delay in his function, which may have suggested a decrease in body function. This delay meant the whole appointment would then be focused on the steroids. I wasn't expecting to have this conversation for at least a few more years. This was when it was hard being a single mother. I wish I had help making these decisions. I was so confused, when I looked at

Kaykay he was happy, he was living his best life without the stress of side effects. That being said, how could I have missed the delay in function? Maybe I wasn't paying good enough attention. If I was gonna take on this disease I needed to stay on top of it. It was hard. In the end, I still wasn't ready to start him on steroids. As long as he kept running and smiling, there was no need to start treatment. We would just continue to monitor his progress.

I tried to find online support groups to help me to connect to other moms who were going through the same challenges. At first it was a bit frustrating for me because I couldn't find any other black kids going through the same thing. It felt like a very "white" disease. I figured it was because of the code of silence in the black community. Meaning we didn't talk out loud about a lot of things that affect us. Each person was left to figure things out for themselves. Here was a whole website dedicated to support and it was all older white women, so not only was there no black mothers, there weren't any young mothers or young single mothers. Majority of these women had their husbands to lean on. It was quite discouraging, but I tried to look deeper and took from it what I could. What seemed the most informative to me was that I found parents on both sides of the spectrum, some that had tried the steroids and some that hadn't. There really wasn't a clear decision on which was better. Some children had no side effects but then there were the other kids who were thriving but were having to deal with the side effects.

One of my greatest fears was that the steroids would cause Kaykay to gain a lot of weight. I didn't want him to grow up feeling less than. I didn't want him to be bullied or to feel like he had to go above and beyond to hide his flaws. I didn't want him to hide who he was. I didn't want him to be like me. Outside appearance was one thing, but inside I internalized more than I shared, and I couldn't do that to him. If he gained weight on his own that was one thing, but to gain weight because of a man made "suggestion" I felt would be neglect on my part as a mother. I went against the opinions of others, my family, friends, to protect him. They said I was selfish. I asked myself this question, was it more selfish to put a child through potential side effects in hopes he lived longer? Or was it more selfish to allow him to live life the way God designed until God was ready to either heal him or take him home? I was making these decisions all on my own and people didn't take my decisions seriously. As a single mother my decisions were often challenged. Even worse, because I was young, it was like I really didn't know how to make these kinds of decisions. Regardless, I stuck to my instincts. These moments now while I watched him walk, run and play were reminders that I made the right decision thus far. It felt good. At least there was something I was good at.

I think I was a very over protective mother. Having a son had me on alert like ten times when it came to him and other girl children playing. I realized very quickly that Kaykay was a follower. He would just happily and innocently follow along with what other kids did. I found myself having more and more conversations with him about the difference between right and wrong and how to stand his ground. He got along more with girls than he did boys. The boys were too rough, and he wasn't used to them. Plus, most of the women in the building had daughters. He was the type of child that if he punched you and it hurt he would start to cry then apologize for it. He had a big heart. His type of personality attracted girls; he was gentle. Being gentle was also a cause for concern though. I don't know what these other parents were teaching their children, but I found myself explaining to Kaykay why he was too young to be kissing girls. I was shocked when I saw little girls playing with naked barbies laying on top of each other. Or little girls running up and kissin him on his cheeks or calling Kaykay underneath tables out of the eye of parents. I knew children were impressionable but damn, it was far beyond what I thought 2 and 3 year olds were capable of. I did the only thing I knew, I told Kaykay "Kissing girls is gross". Then I decided it was a bit too immature of a response, so I told him "Kissing between boys and girls was something to be saved for when you are bigger. Until then, if a girl wants to kiss you, you say noooo and run away ok?"

"Okay" I was very nervous, this meant that I had to keep an even closer eye on him when it came to girls. He seemed like such an innocent kid and I didn't wanna corrupt his childhood. Kaykay wasn't the only boy that seemed clueless, I would watch as some of the other boys would run from the girls when they were called. How could I be surprised at these girl children though when some of these women joke about how their kids see them having sex or watching big people movies with kissing scenes?

I was so caught off guard with this kissin thing though, I always thought of it as something I would have his dad talk to him about first before I had to get involved. This was a self reminder that I played both roles, mother and father. It was my responsibility to ensure he understood right from wrong and he understood how to respect women without objectifying them. Even if a woman played temptress, he had to be mentally disciplined to respect himself as well as her. This was a very important lesson for me to teach him. I wished he had more positive male role models but at least he had Romeo who offered to help in some of these areas. I know he basically said the same things I said, but it was nice to have that reinforcement.

Things were also going good for Romeo. He had just started school downtown Toronto. I was so proud of him for finishing high school and deciding to move on. He never thought much of himself or that he could accomplish things, but he was now challenging that narrative of his old self to become someone he was also proud of. Undecided major, but at least he was doing it. He had dropped most of his "extra curricular" activities and was focusing on creating a career for himself. Just like he had helped me in school, I tried my best to help him get through some of the boring reading materials; like me though, he loved group assignments and projects that allowed our creative minds to shine.

It was around the end of October when he got his first group assignment. It happened to be in groups of two and his partner was a girl. *Great, here we go again.* He reassured me that I had nothing to worry about, yet my mind an spirit couldn't relax. Since he knew I would never be ok with him working with her at her house, he thought it would be better to bring her to his house. It was so hard to rebuild trust, we had been doing so good for a few months I was afraid to lose it. To ease my insecurities, he decided to keep me on the phone while they worked together to prove that he wasn't going to do anything. Everything was cool until she started complaining that he wasn't doing much work. I expected him to blow her off, *like who does this chic think she is?* To my surprise he said

- Romeo: I'm gonna go
- Cola: You're really gonna get off the phone with me for that chic?
- Romeo: I'm jus gonna finish up my work, then I'll call you back'
- Cola: Fine, love you
- Romeo: Ye, you too. I'll text you.

Click.

Did this nigga really not say I love you back? What, because she's there? Who is this chick? He really tryna diss me for a white chick? We were texting at first then it stopped. I was on edge and texted his brother to find out where he was, hoping to put my mind at ease. *He's just working on his project and you are being too clingy.* His brother texted back to say "His room is locked" I freaked. I mussa called his phone 30 times until he answered.

- Romeo: What Nicola? What's your problem? Why are you ringing down my phone?
- Cola: First of all, what do you mean what? Since when do you answer me like that? You tryna show off because you have guests? I'm not the one, remember that.
- Romeo: Ok yes, I'm sorry, what's wrong?
- Cola: What are you doing? Why'd you stop texting me?
- Romeo: You're crazy...we're just studying. What's your problem? Why are you being like this? I'm trying to get work done.
- Cola: Why is your door locked?

- Romeo: It's not
- Cola: You think I'm stupid? I know your door was locked. Listen, don't play games with me
- Romeo: (laughs) I'm not
- Cola: Why are you laughing? You think this is funny don't you
- Romeo: No sorry, I don't know why I'm laughing, but I gotta go. I'm not gonna do nothing, I'm working.
- Cola: Fine.

Click.

I hung up the phone thinking maybe I was crazy. I was letting my insecurities and our past get the best of me. It was such an unhealthy mindset to have, and such a horrible space to be in. *Did I hear noises in the background? Why was the door locked? He loves you, he's not gonna hurt you again. Stop thinking bout this, you're driving yourself crazy.* I wasn't able to function or think about anything else. I dunno how long I sat in place, but I was interrupted once he called me.

- Cola: Hello?
- Romeo: Ye baby wassup? You ok?
- Cola: Mmmhmmmmm mmm
- Romeo: Missed you, and I didn't do anything ok? You don't have to worry, I was a good boy.
- Cola: Ok
- Romeo: Baby, don't be like this, c'mon, let's enjoy the night. You eat? I'm sorry I got off the phone, but I wanted to get this assignment done. Unless you want me to fail? Maybe I should quit school.
- Cola: Why? Naw I'm ok. You need to stay in school.
- Romeo: I don't even care about school, I'm doing it cause it makes you happy.
- Cola: Don't do it for me
- Romeo: Why not? It makes you happy right?
- Cola: Yep, but I want you to want to do it. Not just cause of me.
- Romeo: It's ok, I'll just keep doing it.
- Cola: Ok

For the rest of the night, despite that my mind was on edge my heart was at ease.

Not even two days later I received an email from Romeo's group partner. I don't even know how this white girl got my email.

> 'Just want you to know that I was with your man the other night. It was fun. No wonder black guys prefer white girls, we're not as angry and we know how to please your men. He doesn't want to be with you. He says he has better fun with me. We had sex once you got off the phone and I enjoyed giving him head and he enjoyed eatin me out. You might as well jus leave him now so he can be with me.'

I don't know what was more disrespectful. The fact that she called me an angry black woman, or the fact that she says my man ate her out. That's never been his style...but then why would she say it? *How the fuck she get my email? This bitch is brave.* I didn't even know what to say back. Her email cut all the possible words from my mouth. Instead of wasting my time yelling at her, I figured I'd go straight to the source. *Wonder what lie he has for me this time.*

- Romeo: Hello?
- Cola: What did you do with the white girl the other day?
- Romeo: Nothing...why?
- Cola: Don't lie to me
- Romeo: Nothing baby
- Cola: Then why she emailing me...saying you guys messed around...and that you ate her out?
- Romeo: What? No baby, I would never do that, you have to believe me.
- Cola: I don't know what to believe, why would she say it then?
- Romeo: I don't know but all she did is give me head, I swear
- Cola: You're a liar, I don't believe you. You fucking promised me you ain't do nothing. "I was a good boy" memba dat? What the fuck Romeo, you really gon disrespect me like that? And with a white girl?

You have this bitch bold enough to email me talking bout black men prefer white girls and shit. You know how dumb you got me looking out here defending your dumb ass? Fuck you, I'm done with you, you can tell the white bitch she can have you. Y'all have fun.

- Romeo: No baby why? Please, I'm not lying, please don't leave me

Click.

My cell phone rang off the hook and I watched it go to voicemail with eyes full of tears. I felt so numb and confused. Wanted to talk to him but wanted to hate him even more. My heart felt so much rage but I couldn't move. It was like I was frozen, watching life happen to me. Sometimes I pressed ignore my damn self. There was at least 30 calls in a row and when he realized I wasn't going to answer he started calling my home phone. With 50 unanswered phone calls he decided to text me, he knew I'd read them.

- Romeo: Baby, I'm not lying. I didn't do that. I would never do that. I don't know why she emailed you or how she got your email. Baby you can't leave, I love you.
- -Baby, I'm sorry
- -Yo,
- -yo answer me, you can't leave me.
- -hello???
- -Yo answer your fucking phone
- He calls, and I answer
- Cola: Don't talk to me like that.
- Romeo: I'll talk to you however the fuck I want.
- Cola: Oh yea? Really? Bye

Click.

He calls back. I ignore it. He calls a few more times and I continue to ignore it. He texts me again. "Ok, I'm sorry, I won't talk to you like that. Please just answer your phone." He calls and I ignore the phone call again. "Ok since you don't wanna answer me then I'm gonna kill myself." I call him. He ignored me. I called again, then again, then again. He finally answers, but I'm so angry all I can do is yell through tears.

- Cola: THAT IS NOT FAIR. YOU DON'T GET TO SAY THAT TO ME. All you do is lie and cheat. You made me believe I was crazy, CRAZY!!! You told me there was nothing to worry about. You have no respect for me. You hung up with me and did whatever you wanted. I hate you...you don't get to play the fucking victim
- Romeo: I think this time I'm jus gonna drink. Can I die from too much alcohol? I didn't mean to hurt you, and now you don't believe me. Now you want to leave me, you said you weren't going to leave me. You lied to me too.
- Cola: You don't need to drink
- Romeo: Yes, I do, I upset you, I hurt you, I'm a bad person. I don't deserve you. I don't deserve to live. You don't wanna be with me. Are you gonna stay with me?
- Cola: No
- Romeo: Ok bye, nice knowing you, sorry I hurt you. Sorry I'm a horrible boyfriend. Bye Nicola. Tell Kaykay daddy loves him.
- Cola: Don't hang up the phone
- Romeo: Bye

Click.

I was numb but frantic at the same time. I tried calling back several times and each time he ignored my call. I rushed to text his brother to check on him but once again his door was locked. Within 20 mins I received a text message saying that he passed out and they were rushing him to the hospital. I sat in devastation. *What kinda person am I? I pushed him too far. I know he's sensitive. I shouldn't have gotten so mad or ignored him. I pushed him over the edge. What the fuck is wrong with me? This isn't fair though, how does he get to do what he feels like then hold my emotions hostage? How is it fair to blame me for this shit? He promised, he promised. I hope he's ok. I don't even know what imma do if he dies. What if he's dead? OMG his brother hasn't texted me with an update yet. Fuck,*

I can't live like this. Why me? What am I gonna tell Kaykay, someone else left us? I'm such a screw up.

I mussa laid there for hours until his brother texted me. "You need to leave him alone, this is too much for us" *What? How the fuck is this my fault again? Seriously?* As I sat in silence, my phone rang, and it was Romeo.

- Cola: Hello?
- Romeo: I'm sorry
- Cola: Are you ok?
- Romeo: Yes, I love you
- Cola: I love you too.
- Romeo: I'm sorry I hurt you
- Cola: It's ok, but I need some time to heal
- Romeo: Ok, how long?
- Cola: I don't know.
- Romeo: Ok, I love you
- Cola: Love you too, get better ok?
- Romeo: I'll always love you
- Cola: Me too
- Romeo: Bye Baby
- Cola: Bye

Part Two

Love is Bold

Rise up! Come be our help, and ransom us for
the sake of Your steadfast *love*.

PSALM 44:26

CHAPTER FORTY-ONE

New Years

Therefore, my fellow believers, whom I love and long for, my delight and crown [my wreath of victory], in this way stand firm in the Lord, my beloved.
-Phillipians 4 :1

I felt like I was constantly restarting life. I got moments of peace and once it was ruined then I'd have to start all over again. In the months leading up to New Years, since Romeo and I had stopped talking, I was really trying to find myself. It felt weird whenever we stopped talking. Interestingly enough, I had gotten an email again from the white chick saying that she made everything up. I didn't even have the energy to take her in. I needed desperately to stay away from that kinda drama. I had enough other shit on my plate, I was still bitter about Nathaniel stealin my shit and I wanted it back.

December 3rd 2009
Cola
you're an idiot, you obviously can't read I sent u a message from my sister fossbook cause I didn't wanna unblock you and I fully said its nicola....dumb ass.....do u have my bloody camera?

December 5th 2009
Cola
all now u still aint responded... I kno u get my messages ....you practically live on fossbook... I'm surprised u aint on right now

December 21st 2009
Cola
thats how u decline my friend invitation when u use to beg me to add you as a friend...rude much'???...wheres my camera nathaniel... I kno u been askin bout me...obviously u still wonder how I'm doin
December 27 2009
Cola
where's my camera natty?
Nathaniel
yo what the fuck are you sayin !!!!! I don't have your fuckin camera and I toll you dis from fuckin time so stop askin me!!!!!
Cola
who are u really cussin at though...like really????
Nathaniel
just stop f'in asking me, ask someone else
Cola
that's how you're angry and cussing? problems much?

He could cuss all he wanted but I didn't believe him. *Dis nigga ain't shit.* Moving past the bullshit I had to keep focused cause I was following a new diet from a doctor who I saw weekly to monitor my progress. It was actually making a difference and without effort I was losing weight. With my new-found confidence I decided this New Year was gonna be focused on myself, loving myself and creating healthy boundaries. But first, I needed to figure out what the heck I was gonna do to ring in the New Year for 2010. New Year parties were never a thing for me and this holiday fell on a weekend that Kaykay was with my mom which meant I did not wanna stay home. Growing up we always did church on New Year's Eve and I hadn't been to a church consistently in a few months. Someone had suggested this new church to me, so I figured I'd check it out. I needed something that felt a lil more like home to me. I got dressed that night in a form fitting red dress and headed off to church. I was looking good and walked with confidence! From the moment I entered the church my eyes caught the glimpse of a tall good-looking man. I brushed past him to go look for a seat inside the church but was unable to find one. I ended up standing in the front lobby across from him.

The rest of this chapter is written in poetic dialogue detailing that night and the following two months

Q: New Year's Eve has me post up inna di lobby
Listening to the preacha's message
(beat)
Back home as a lickle bwoy we always had to reach church (beat) especially on special occasion but since coming here in dis country I have not been on the church tip
Cola: It's New Year's Eve
(beat)
I pull up to the church
Damn I'm looking so fly and my confidence is peaking
Q: I been hearing dat di gyal dem dat reach church is usually sweet like suga
And here comes the sweetest one
Cola: As I reach the entrance I already feel many eyes on me, but I keep my head straight and walk
Q: As I lean up against da wall and turn mi head to di lef
A vibrant red dress walks tru di door
Tru di door and holds unto my thoughts
Cola: Parting ways with just a glance I'm stuck standing around trying to get comfortable
The problem with reaching church late is that there's never any seats left
Q: *Dere's times when I swear my thoughts are not my own*
Own...what do I own
Betta yet what do I own that I can use
Use to get into dat pretty red dress
My eyes do not lie
Cola: *Tonight especially I see everybody and their mommas packed into the sanctuary*
Q: *My tongue will not rest*
Cola: *Damn*
Q: *Until I get into dat pretty red dress*
Cola: *I guess even thugs need prayer too*

Q: *My eyes cannot lie*
Cola: *Too many bod mon with their sunglasses on stand on either sides of the walls like soldiers*
Q: *My dick will not rest*
Cola: *Soldiers for Christ waiting patiently for church to finish*
Q: *Until I am inside dat pretty red dress*
Cola: *Finising off one year and welcoming a next*
sending off texts checking up on the party they can't wait to get to
too many people with wrong intentions and false hopes
Q: *My eyes are watching her body move*
Place to place making memories of her groove
My tongue dances
my spit flows
Cola: *Hoping that God will bless 'em for their efforts*
bless 'em for showing up one day while ignoring 364
For several others like me
we
be
constantly searching and learning to keep the Gospel in our hearts
Q: *I catch her glimpse and give har a wicked smile*
Cola: *Hearts filled with love*
love on the mind
Q: *Dis is hardly a challenge*
she gon tek mi home tonight
Cola: *Mindlessly trying to stay focused*
some focused on the grind
Q: *Di gyal too easy*
Cola: *Some focused on the preacher's words*
words that are swirling around
like the symbolisms of smoke hanging from this man's neck
puff puff and pass to the next
I'm sitting in the next room watching the pastor on the giant screen
when the glimmer of a weed necklace catches my eye
Q: *I catch her off guard by my sight*
Winking my eye
I watch har eyes roll back
As she kiss har teet' (beat)
but watch dis

If I wave her ova and she gon come near
Cola: I kiss my teeth and laugh
Warm brown eyes and a friendly wave in a constant rhythm
Coming from a fly guy who has the audacity to wear his sins around his neck
no judgments
But I've never met a man so bold
boldly watching me (beat) his hands move but it's his eyes that are calling me
so inevitably I make my way closer to him
now standing close enough that I can feel his breath tickle my ear
Q: "Hey, I saw you was watching me from so far away"
I am overwhelmed by her cuteness
I am lacking the ability to resist her
her seductive smile
smiling and revealing the space between her teeth
hmm how I love to fill that space beneath causing great fulfilling relief
Lawd!
Cola: "Actually I swear it was you watching me"
I can't help but smile crazy
Tryna listen in church but I'm so distracted
his words tickle my mind as he tries to speak loud enough for me to hear
but not too loud to disturb the others in churchhhhh
Q: "You seem to be deep in thought and I thought that maybe it was me you had on your mind"
body's intertwined
messing up all the sheets

Cola: "Don't bright yourself
I'm here tryna listen to the message just like you"
He is smiling
Smile back
Straight teeth
Damn this man is so gorgeous
Q: "Well I was thinking that when church finish you and me coulda go somewhere an talk"
da beat of our body's
louder with each touch

much appreciated
Appreciating the curves of her hips
her batty when it tips side to side
Cola: "What if I'm busy?"
looking like a tall glass of light chocolate milk
milking the hell outta his charming good looks
Q: "My apologies, what kinda plans a girl like you has tonight?"
The feeling of her leg as it glides through my fingers
my stinger causing the high notes of this new-found singer
and the sweet smell that lingers
Cola: "So typical. You don't even ask my name but you wanna know my plans. Boy please"
Q: "Ok so Miss Sexy Red Dress, can I know your name, please?"
Tryna keep my game face
There is an energy that has overcome me
cause when she looks at me
I get lost in her eyes
Cola: "I'm Cola, you?"
Damn it's like he can see right through me
reading my mind
watching me sweat
Q: "My name is Q"
she wanna keep di feelings inside
feelings I refuse to hide and ignore
Why should I ignore and store di sexual emotions?
patiently waiting to be released
Cola: "Nice to meet you"
Oh yeah (beat) I'm alone tonight
Q: "Now that I know your name, lemme ask you again
Do you have any plans tonight?"
my ex-gyal release me of my duties to her
by refusing an abusing my basic needs as a man
so for the body of the hotty hotty in the red dress, it is her luck
that I am stuck and determined to have her
Cola: "Yep sorry.... I'm unavailable tonight"
There's a strong energy that is pulling me closer to him
The pastors words are now a mere distance away

as my mind is overcrowded by
hot thoughts
warms hugs
sweet kisses
Q: "Oh you're gonna stay at church and praise God all night?"
Determined to wrap her up inna di bed
I am aroused by dis challenge
dere's no challenge I cyaan overcome and my buddy jumps
thinking where to cum to alleviate
the pressure when I am done
a few more sweet words and she's mine
Gotta put in overtime
to really mek dis pussy mine
Cola: "You make it sound like a bad thing,
essentially that is why I'm here
I take it you have other plans?"
Focus
I didn't come here for this
Q: "That depends... on what you're doing tonight"
A week a day whatever it will take
I am known to make the pussy break free from the bondage of the panty
No gyal's eva resisted me
Cola: "I already told you (beat) I'm busy"
heart melting
body lusting
Q: "With what? How do I know you're not just telling me lies...remember you're standing in church. You're not supposed to lie .... especially in church"
Maybe if I friend her up
And gain her trus'
Cola: "Fine you got me, I don't have plans at the moment but it's New Years, I'm sure there's a million things I could do"
He has plenty of slick words, yet there's humour
Thoughts interrupted
This man tries an old school play
Q: "I just wanna get to know you
gimme a chance nah?"

She is so beautiful
Cola: "Why? Why should I?"
props to the man who has yet to give up
Q: "Cause I know you like me, I can tell"
It's a must
Di gyal stole my heart
an' now all I need is to bus'
Cola: "You're full of yourself and it's the other way around, I can tell"
I feel his eyes burning holes in my red dress as I walk away
Q: "Come here gyal. What's the worst that could happen? Do you like hanging out alone?"
Cola: "Who said I'd be alone? Don't eva assume..."
Q: "So you have company? Or just imaginary friends?"
Frustration rising. I wanna take her away to a place where she can be mine
Cola: "Well either way I wouldn't wanna keep my imaginary friends waiting"
Girl you haven't had fun in a while and Kaykay ain't home so live it up. What's the worst that could happen? You wanna be alone for NewYears?
Q: "Ok well I might as well bring mine too, so we can party"
I cyaan rest till I am in dat pretty red dress
red dress red dress
"Baby, please don't walk away"
My mind's racing tryna find a way to make har stay
"Baby girl, joking aside how bout you take my number in case you change ya mind. Are you afraid you'd have a likkle fun?"
Cola: "I'm not afraid of fun"
Q: "Tell me what has you so hesitant? Just take the chance to get to know me before you judge me"
Cola: "I don't judge people"
Q: "Seems like you're judging me. You don't even know me but won't gimme that chance"
Cola: "Ok gimme your number...maybe you'll prove me wrong"
Damn I just met him, what will people say?

Q: "Beautiful gyal, I will be waiting for your call, hope you do not mek me wait too long"
Sexy body
Sexy dress
Straight sexiness
Cola: *It took me till I walked outside to decide that I was gonna invite him ova so I call him up and he answers on the second ring.*
Q: "Yeah, wha gwan?"
My lips divide into an instant smile
As my mind pictures har bent ova
Another long night wukking hard

Despite what he might have thought he was gonna get that night, I did not give up the cookie. Instead we spent the night talking and making out. The tension between us woulda made the sex alone good on anotha level, but I really wanted to start off on a different level. I wanted to date, not just have sex and he seemed down for that too. He lived down the block from me which meant we saw each other almost every day. Our first date was to Dave and Busters. He wasn't much for conversation, but he was hot, so I didn't mind. Two whole months without sex. What an accomplishment. I felt like I had made him wait long enough. I had already said no a bunch of times and he was still coming by, so he was obviously here for more than sex. *He isn't afraid to take me on dates, he hasn't pressured me for sex, this was a good look for him.* Sex with him for the first time happened so beautifully and so naturally.
Cola: "Be gentle"
I am awaiting his enter to my center *s*
low to start initiating the drip of my lakes
Q: *With each touch her body shakes*
drawing me to cup my lips over her lakes
Syrup filled juices will feed my cravings
Savouring the taste lingering in my mouth
Cola: *chills run up my spine*
I
am
dizzy
Just breathe

Kissing and
Slivering his tongue
The length of my back
feeling and filling the crack between our bodies
My eyes roll back
Photographic memory
Memorizing the lines
The dip in his back
Q: *It takes great restraint*
Not to bite down too hard
On her bosoms blessed by eve
Leaving Eden open for my drive thru
Paradise paralyzes penetration
Mentally causing me to Stevie Wonder her body
I love this feeling
Cola: *Just breathe*
Q: *Just breathe*

I run my soft hands through his rough braids
Watching his fists pound the bed next to me

Cola: *Slapping and clapping spaces* **Q:** *Slapping and clapping spaces*
kings and aces *kings and aces*
Q: *I'm tearing up sheets, her pussy has me weak, overcome by sweetness*
Cola: *Plunging deep into my river striking me like candy rain releasing all fears*
Q: *Slip and slide side to side out and in I'm drowning*
Cola: *The depth he is establishing*
sends walls collapsing
Q: *Asthmatic breathing*
Sweats dripping
knocking the boots off her body
Cola: *Loving his sweat*
loving the drip drip all ova me
my nails grab his back
Q: *Painful loving*
casualties of worship

Cola: *Singing praises* ***Q:*** *Singing praises*
Just... breathe *Just....breathe*
Q: *Exhaling her ecstasy*
Ingesting her crack love
Cola: *Exhaling his crack love*
Ingesting his ecstasy
Q: *She's got me feenin*

Cola: *Just...Breathe* ***Q:*** *Just...breathe*
Cola: *me* ***Q:*** *me*
you *you*
we *we*
be *be*
Cola: *Climbing higher heights*
Q: *Exploring this territory*
Cola: *Exploring our territory*
Q: *Trapped by her beautiful body*
Sweet lady, what am I gonna do
Cola: *My minds enslaved tryna break free*
Q: *I jiggle my key unlocking unblocking and opening the door to her freedom*
Cola: *Can't hold back the rain my hearts crying out to him*
Q: *One bite*
Cola: *Our flesh connects*
Q: *One taste*
Cola: *Our spirits emerge*
Q: *One sniff*
Cola: *Our minds entangle*
Q: *Minds blank*
Cola: *All mighty three connect*
Q: *Flying high above*
Cola: *My soul is dying*
Q: *My soul is dying*
Cola: *Our souls are dying to become one* ***Q:*** *Our souls are dying to become one*
Cola: *Poetically connecting* ***Q:*** *Poetically connecting*
Q: *I reach her peak*
She screams loudly
but whispers my name
Cola: *Back , back, forth and forth*

Q: *How deep is her love that is causing my April showers*
forcing my moments release
and pulling my insides inside her

Cola: *Pulling his insides inside me*
I need him
My body screams
he groans in satisfaction
Q: *Justifying*
Cola: *My*
Q: *Need*
Cola: *This fast pace*
Slow pace
Hard pace
Love
Q: *This fast pace*
Slow pace
Hard pace
Love
Q: *Is*
Cola: *Justifying*
Q: *My*
Cola: *Need to be*
Q: *Right here in her arms*
Cola: "Stay next to me"
Q: "Couldn't move if I wanted to"
I will await my next fix

Self-Reflection

Ever have sex that felt magical? I felt like I was filling a void, but the feeling was only temporary. Once the high was over, the feeling of nostalgia was replaced by self-disgust and shame. I thought this was what I wanted yet now that I had it, the game was over. I started remembering that my initial reason for going to church on New Year's was to start life over, but here I was laid up doing the same shit I was running from. Sex was beginning to feel so mundane for me. It was like a drug but started losing power and was no longer strong enough to satisfy me. I think this was why I never experimented with drugs; my personality was too addictive.

In that moment, I hated myself. There wasn't even a reason to have sex anymore, if felt more like I was doing it to keep men happy more than myself. These feelings weren't new, but they were getting stronger. I thought that by taking more time to get to know the guy the sex would be more meaningful, but I was clearly just wasting my time now. There was something else missing that I couldn't fix with dick. Not even good dick. Good dick or not, my pet peeve was a man that got too comfortable. *Ain't nobody tells you to stop trying, just cause you got pussy don't mean you impressed me enough to stop trying.* Even though he lived close enough to my house to walk, I always picked him up or dropped him off in the morning. I expected that if he wanted to see me, he would walk or bus it even when I couldn't pick him up but all he did was make complaints. Yet again I felt like I had picked up the title mother instead of girlfriend. The more he complained, the more unattractive he was looking.

Dating was such a challenge as a single mother. To find a man who wasn't worried about you having a kid was one thing, but then cause I usually had my son with me it was a bit of a challenge sorting out when, how and the time. Time was valuable, between appointments, programs, school and being a mother, I was surprised I had time to breathe let alone date. For this reason, most of my datin interactions were during the nighttime hours and after the last rape I decided that I would never travel to a man's house. If he wanted to date me or even interact with me, then he needed to put in the effort, pursue me and travel to my house. Most men I "Dated" "Chilled" "Kicked it with" or had over to my house could only come after my son was asleep and they had to leave before he woke up in the morning. I wanted to protect my son, but still have some kind of fun. The more fun I had, the more bored I got. Something was missing.

Finding a church that felt like home was a challenge. I had been to a few here and there previously but even if it felt like somewhere I could potentially build, eventually that feeling wore off. Not to mention that at that same time I was still sexually active. I didn't wanna be a hypocrite to be in church and having sex, so I was forced to pick. I wasn't ready to give up sex yet, it felt too good, but now with how I was feeling I knew I needed to find myself back to church. It normally helped ground me when things felt really off.

The vibe from the church on New Years felt like home. The Caribbean medley and preaching resonated with me, so I decided to go back a few times. As per usual, I received a warm welcome whenever I showed up, no matta how long it took me to return. Speaking of friendly, I even stumbled upon Sheena there. Memba my no new friend's motto? I was shocked when I saw her. First thing I said to her "What you doing here? Long time no see how you doing? How's the guy you were seeing, y'all still together after all the drama?" "I go here, this is my church, and no we aren't together right now" "Wow, small world, and sorry things didn't work out. *Sorry not sorry, he's a dog.* "Well, we go here now so maybe I'll see you around. Take my number, let's keep in touch". Ok God I hear you, *this must be a sign.*

This time I was gonna choose church over sex. I was gonna stay on the right path. The more I attended the church the more God's message spoke to me. "NO SEX before marriage. SEX IS SACRED." What was I doing to myself? I was searching for that missing piece of me from Q but all he provided me was empty conversations and headaches. Now that sex was off the table there really was nothing between us. I never noticed before how we had almost nothing to talk about. I was too caught up in how cute he was, but I could no longer deny the shift that was happening in my mind and in my heart. He had to go. For once I was putting my needs before everyone else's.

CHAPTER FORTY-TWO

The Shift

Steadfast love and truth and faithfulness meet together;
Righteousness and peace kiss each other.
Psalm 85:10

I called up Q on the phone and let him know that I couldn't do this relationship no more. It didn't go well by phone, so I let him come over so we could talk it out.

Q: "What can I do to change your mind?"
Cola: "Q this just isn't what I wanted. Beyond being physically attracted to you I'm struggling to feel anything else. To be honest, I should have never given up church simply to avoid the guilt. I haven't been to church in weeks. Church is my foundation and after all my torment and struggle, I gave it up for you, to prove I was capable of finding love but even with you here, something is still missing"
Q: "What am I to do? How can you jus' end it like this?"
Cola: "I'm sorry. I just can't. Beside the fact that you get frustrated easily, I literally have to do everything in this relationship and you command so much of my attention sometimes even more than my son. To top it off you don't even take me out anymore, it's been a few months that we've been dating and since the first time you haven't taken me out again"
Q: "You know money's been tight for me. I've heard you mention things but I neva understood how serious you were till now"
Cola: "Yeah well, I'm serious, I can't do this anymore"
Q: "Baby please. I'll do better. I love you. I want to work this out. Maybe in the beginning I took this for granted but I'm ready now. I even took the bus here. It was long and cold. I did it to prove to you I want this to work"

I had a habit of passing out and not remembering anything upon awakening. Sometimes I would wake up and realize I had not put Kaykay to bed and he was just up watching TV. It would be like 3 in the morning and this kid was jus sitting quietly watching TV. Sometimes he would ask me if I enjoyed my nap. It was beyond my comprehension that he seemed more in control than I was. Sometimes it used to happen to me as I drove the long distance from school to my parents' house. Only God knows how I made it home sometimes, which was another good reason for me to move, to cut down on the commute. It happened a lot when Romeo was trying to come visit me. I couldn't exactly pinpoint when it would happen, I just knew it had to do with exhaustion. I felt like such a mess and a failure just tryna hold it together for one more day. Tonight, I guess my body was over exhausted and I passed out right in his lap. Once I woke up I realized I was in my bed and Kaykay was in my bed right next to me. I could barely remember what I was doing right before, but I vaguely remember Q had been over.

Cola: I picked Kaykay up and put him back to his bed.
Back to bed
back to bed
baby sleep and be still

Wasn't Q laying beside me? Where is he? Did he leave? Why would he leave when he coulda slept next to me? Lemme check the living room. Oh, there he is, aww, he looks so cute and cold curled up sleeping in his boxers.
"Q wake up! Q wake up! Come lay down"

Q: *Awaken from the cold*
She offers a warm place of refuge
by allowing me to share her bed
Familiar spaces
Untouched places
The warmth of her body draws me near
Cola: As I hand him a blanket I ask, "Is this better?"
Q: "Yeah. It's nice and warm thanks"

Overcome by her morning beauty
my dick hardens instantly
I am thirsting for that candy
Cola: "Welcome"
Q: *I climb on top with ease gently pushing down her waist*
I need to please her
And please me
Cola: *I told him he could lay next to me*
so, he mussa thought he was blessed to be next to me
but it wasn't good enough
Q: *The initial touch already has my head rolled back*
Familiar spaces
Untouched places for any other man but me
Cola: *On top of me*
All ova me
I tried to make him move
"What are you doing?"
Q: *Finally reaching the spot*
I hold tightly for leverage
Cola: *Wanting to scream*
wanting to fight
fight the enter in my center
"Q What are you doing?"
Q: "Hmmm"
The first thrust sending chills all through my body
Cola: *the initial dig to my soul*
has me laying helpless
Q: *I feel hands reaching*
Pounding grabbing my chest
Cola: *Pounding*
punching his chest
Q: *Testing me*
letting me know that she is ready
Cola: *My hands fight my battle*
Q: *Love battles in the bedroom*
my soldier overcome with the sweetness that runs
Cola: *My baby's laying right in the same room*
Not wanting him to awake to a boom boom boom
And a stop stop stop
I'm silently pleading

Pleading for my pussy's life
"Stop please"
A life that has seen better days
Better days is now just a haze
Maze I'm stuck in a sexual maze
Running (beat) looking for a way out
But trapped
"Please! Please!"
Q: *Swirling images in my head*
I feel high
As I lay
Plunging deep into her thighs
Getting lost
Sweat dripping on her face
Cola: "Q Why?"
Q: *Her body keeps sucking me back in*
I am a slave
My dick falls out
My body shivers
Craving her touch
Cola: "Get off of me. What you tryna do"
This man won't even look down
At my sad face
All he can think of is giving his dick a taste
Q: *I put it back*
taking more time
putting more power in each thrust
Cola: *I feel unfamiliar hands*
rough
Unfamiliar hands
Grabbin at me
gnawing at me
My face twist with disgust
Disgusted at how he merely pushed my panty aside
Q: *My mind is too far gone*
but in a distance I hear a cry
Cola: "Why Q?"
Q: *Why?*
I cannot lie

I try
Cola: *My body fills with his lust*
I must stop this
trus'
I don't want to be
The reason this man finally bus'
"Stop"
Q: *I am so close to the end*
Cola: *The bastard's smiling*
Release me from this pain
"Stop Q"
Q: *Loving this ride*
Cola: *Showing every moment he is loving*
He loves it I hate it
It's my body he's playing with
"Stop Q"

Q: "Stop why? It's only sex. What is the big deal?"
Cola: "I don't want to have sex with you. Get off. I don't want you"
Q: *Her words hit me like a ton of knives*
Heart hurts
Mind a spin
I tek a pause
Cola: *Momentarily he pauses*
then keeps on going
Q: *Dis pussy too good*
Cola: *Going and growing rougher*
Q: *Messages*
misunderstandings
she tek me for a fool
Love me den leave me
No different from the rest
A test to have me lay in her bed
without even a touch
not nice
blood a boil
dis ride is heavy
My breath shortens

My eyes shut tight
Cola: *With every juke juke juke*
I shake
and he takes away
A piece of me
Now leaving me
In a mental bondage
That I am stuck with
"Stop. No. Don't"
Q: *Yess*
I hear her call out
"No Don't Stop"
Q: "Baby I won't"
Cola: *Tired of fighting*
But not wanting to give up
there's a pain in my body
my pussy feels like it's cut
Liquid flows
my body's turning numb
Q: "I buss"
Sweet sweet relief
followed by silence underneath
No condom use, she's condemned
To feel my youth swim
Attached on top
Blood drained down below
A look of sadness in her eye
Blue flowing
Flowing like her soul
Floating away
Whispers of
Cola: "Why. Why. Why"
sweet loving turn stale
Q: *I try*
She try
We lie
Foolishly trying to make sense
Of this
Of us

Of me on top
Squeezing teasing needing her love
No exhale of her ecstasy
for me to ingest her crack love
I realize I am alone
Red and white blend on my dick as I pull out
My quick satisfaction
my thirst to burst
leaves me feeling empty
no sugar high
no sweet cravings
"What did I do that was so wrong?"
Cola: *I ran outta the room*
all I feel is all alone
Where can I run to be safe if I am not safe in my own home?
I lay here stuck
what should I do?
should I call the cops?
Q: "Why you so vex? What did I do you?"
Cola: "Why would you do this to me?"
Q: "Do what? Didn't you want me to?"
Cola: "You didn't even use a condom. Did you say you bussed?"
***Q:** "Yes"*
Cola: "Are you friggin kiddin me? So you have money for plan b?"
***Q:** "No"*
Cola: "Seriously get the hell out of my house. My son is about to wake up"
Q: "Can we talk?"
Cola: "GET OUT"
Q: "You seriously gonna get vex cause we had sex?"
Cola: "Get the fuck out! Leave!"
Q: "Will I ever see you again?"
Cola: *Unable to think*
eyes choosing not to blink
attempting to comprehend the morning events
school today
should I go?
this feels familiar yet different

why didn't he just stop?
Why did I have to call him back into my bed?
No really, should I call the cops?
"SHIT!"
Kaykay's calling me
can't I have one second to myself to cry
Life is crazy
time is a heartless monster. won't even stop to let me catch my breath for a second
I'm a mother yes, but I'm also human
I cry tears of blood too
breaking into my thoughts of consciousness
Shit! a million things to do today
daycare
school
now..... doctor's
what the hell am I gonna say to get this plan B?
I ain't got no money to pay for this, But I need it
these doctors at these clinics are always so damn nosy
Kaykay's crying even louder for me
"Baby I'm coming!"
I can do this, I just gotta get through this day, just like all those other times
keep smiling

CHAPTER FORTY-THREE

Soul

In return for my love, they attack me, but I am in prayer.
Psalm 109:4

He raped me. He raped me and there was nothing I could do about it. My son laid in his bed two feet from me. Thank God he wasn't in my bed. Would this man have still raped me if Kaykay was in my bed? I really hoped he didn't sense any of that. I felt like such a shit mother. All I could think of was getting Kaykay off to school and out of that environment. I couldn't even comprehend what was happening to me. He was my man though, how the hell would I explain that? Why did he think it was ok? I said no, I pleaded, I even tried to push him off of me. Fuck me! Like not again. How does one say they've been raped multiple times? People are gonna start thinking I asked for this, but I specifically made sure I didn't dress in a suggestive way when I knew he was coming over. I did everything right. I shouldn't have passed out. I shouldn't have passed out. Why would I pass out and leave someone in my house? This was not safe. I was not safe with myself. Poor Kaykay, this could have been worse for him, I'm so dumb, I put him in danger. What kinda mother am I?

The routine was automatic. I got Kaykay ready for school and dropped him off then drove to the clinic over on Bathurst and just sat in my car rehearsing what I was gonna say before going in. Once I had enough courage, then I went in. The elevator ride seemed to take forever, and I was a ball of nerves.

I waited patiently in the room before the doctor called me in. She asked me a bunch of questions to which I answered as honestly as I could. I was numb, I was frozen, I didn't even speak once to the doctor. All I could do was nod my head. When the doctor asked me if it was rape, all I could do was look down. Tears flowed but I couldn't answer. I didn't want to believe the answer. I wanted this all to go away. I wanted to hide in shame, but I couldn't have this man's baby, so I was forced to wear my shame in public. I HAD NO MONEY. I just kept reasoning and tryna figure out how to get this pill with no money. I kept my head down the entire time I was questioned and when the doctor asked me if I had any money for the pill, I looked up and started to cry and shook my head no. To my surprise she gave it to me free of charge. I definitely felt like God had his hand on me in that exact moment cause I ain't neva heard of nun free. She offered me a space to talk to someone, but I declined. She asked me about talking to the cops, but what's the point? I declined. All I needed was to take the pill and to figure out my next steps. It was a Tuesday when this all happened. I'll neva forget it cause then I drove myself to school cause I knew I couldn't miss my Gospel choir class. I'd just have to smile a lil while longer.

I have no clue why I decided to go to school. I guess I was tryna stay as normal as possible. I was hoping the images and feelings would go away. I was hoping I would wake up. I was hoping. Whenever the tears welled up in my eyes, I quickly ran to the bathroom in hopes of catching them before anyone else did. I was angry, I was angry with everything. This was the first time I had experienced this kind of deep emotion. I guess with the other rapes I had told myself that it was partially my fault, but with this one, I did everything I had taught myself to do in order to protect myself. So why did it still happen? In this moment I understood that I had compartmentalized the other rapes and had hidden them so deep within me that I had no feeling towards them anymore. But this? This was another level of pain. How do I contain this? How do I manage my feelings and keep it together?

The truth was, I wasn't containing things as well as I thought and people in class were starting to take notice. I had one guy friend from my class who caught me running back and forth and asked me point blank what was wrong. Even though I didn't know how to explain it, I knew he was a safe person, so I did my best to put into words what I felt. It felt like the end of my life. I was so scared for what he was gonna say. Probably thought I was a bad mother, which I felt like I was. If I involve the police, then CAS was gonna get involved. I couldn't give them a reason to take away my son. I needed him. This would only prove to people what they already believe of me. As I was explaining what happened my mind was racing, and I kept feeling like I need to defend. I was in my home. I wasn't out where I wasn't supposed to be, and I had been with this man sexually before and he was as gentle as he could be. He wasn't a stranger to me, we knew each other for at least a few months. Nothing made sense. My clothes weren't suggestive. Once I was done explaining, my friend hugged me. He hugged me as I stood there crying.

That day felt incredibly long and as I laid myself in that bed it felt like a betrayal. Not unlike the betrayal that awaited me in the next few days once this man started calling my phone. Just seeing his number made my body jerk. Every time I ignored the calls he called right back. *What is wrong with this guy?* I finally answered to tell him to leave me alone and block my number.

Q:"I'm sorry, it felt too good to stop. I don't know why I couldn't stop. That's not rape though. I'm not a rapist. I'm not some bad guy in the streets raping people. I didn't drug you or beat you up. Don't call me a rapist."
Cola: "You pinned me down with your hand. Didn't you hear me saying stop. Beggin you to get off me. Didn't you feel me pushing you off."
Q:"Yes but, it felt too good, it's just sex"
Cola: "Rememba the very first time I met you, and we made out and you wanted to have sex?"
Q: "Yes"
Cola: "Didn't I say no and you stopped?"
Q:"Yes"
Cola: "Memba the first time we had sex?"
Q:"Yes"
Cola: "Wasn't it me who said it was ok, wasn't it me who gave you permission"

Q: "Yes"
Cola: "So what's the difference then? If I gave you permission to have sex and when I said no you stopped, why was this time different?"
Silence.
Cola: "Hello?"
Q: "I don't know, but don't do me like this, come on, I didn't rape you."
Cola: "Goodbye Q, you obviously don't get it, stop calling me!"
Click.

When I thought it was over, he showed up at my house. Came right to my front door. It was a living nightmare. I didn't wanna let him in, but I didn't want my neighbours to hear. I compromised and cracked the door slightly.

Q: "Yo lemme in"
Cola: "Go away, I don't want to see you."
Q: "I just want to talk to you"
Cola: "Go away, I have nothing to say to you"
Q: "Please, I'm sorry"
Cola: "No, just leave me alone"

He puts his foot in the door to stop me from closing it and I'm yelling at him to move his foot. He finally gives in and I close the door and I hear a bang on my door followed by silence. I was too nervous to peep through the door, but I did it anyway to see if he was gone.

I spent that week on automation. Kaykay was at daycare early and I left here a lil bit later to give me time during the day to just think. For that whole week after the rape my phone rang multiple times per day. I spent days tryna console him.

Cola: "It's ok, I hope you learned a lesson so you don't do it to anyone else. When a woman says no, no matta what you feel you need to stop"
Q: "Ok, are you going to call the cops?"
Cola: "No, I won't, you just need to stop calling me though"
Q: "So we can't fix things, we can't get back together? I miss you"

Cola: "Nope, we can't, sorry"
Q: "Please, I haven't been able to eat. I need you.
Cola: "No, sorry"
Q: "Damn that sucks"
Cola: "Yep well, that's what happens"

I started to feel bad for him. He was crying on the phone, he was quiet and sad. He seemed remorseful. He seemed like he truly just made a genuine mistake. I felt like what happened between us was something that was culturally accepted. I felt like as a society we teach our children that rapists and bad guys are the scary looking people on the road. That's who we all look out for. We also talk about the blurred lines between consent. A woman can say no, but she didn't really mean it. That's the message most of the guys I know grew up with. He genuinely believed he couldn't have raped me. The worst part was that I realized that I too had been conditioned with that narrative because I still found him attractive. It was like my mind couldn't comprehend that someone good looking was capable of doing such a thing. He didn't have a face of a monster which would have been easier to digest if he did. I found myself trying to justify what happened, even though my body felt violated. Not to mention the time I was taking to talk to this man to console him. I was concerned he wouldn't be ok for some odd reason. He made me believe that he needed my help. Made me believe that maybe this was just a mistake and I didn't need to involve the cops. Plus, what would they do for me anyway? Anytime I had called the cops they found some way to blame me for the situation I was in. When my ex threatened me, they said I shouldn't have antagonized him. What would make this situation any different? Especially since it happened in my own house.

Kaykay would be better off without me as his mother. I was the common denominator in all of the rapes, it must be something I was doing, and I was putting Kaykay's life in danger. His house was supposed to be one of protection and I was doing a shitty job with one child much less two. I spent weeks agonizing, waiting for my period to come before I was able to breathe normal. What if I had gotten pregnant? How would I cope? Unlike before, my rapist lived down the street from me. In the same hood. I had nightmares of this guy showing up at my house or seeing me on the road. I couldn't sleep at night. We lived in the same area. I wanted to slip away. Sometimes I was afraid of driving in the area or walking anywhere for fear I would see him. Then it happened. Few months later...I saw him.

Poetic Interlude

You walked outside in the night air to light your cigarette
Light skin good looking man standing tall
Bastard
Without a care or thought in the world you stood there smokin your life away
I sat in my car and wondered
Was this really you?
Ppl been sayin you cut your hair
Ppl been tellin me they see you all the time
I've never cared
I've wondered what it would be like to be in yur presence again
Would I be ok?
Would I cry?
Would I be nervous?
What is there to say to the man who betrayed me?
That morning still fresh in my mind
Jus like it was yesterday
But I now question myself
Did it even happen?
Y didn't I tell anyone?
The shame of it all was too much to bare
There's somethin to say about someone who's been raped 4 times
The world doesn't view situations like mine in a kind way
Who would really believe me?
I regret doing nothin about it

Here yu stand free, smokin, chillin
Walking amongst the very likes of me
All because I did nothin about it
N now everytime I see yu I feel trapped inside a world of disgrace, shame, guilt and 21 questions
I honked my horn to see if it was really yu or if I was drivin myself crazy for no reason
Yep
Tabernack
Je suis fâché contre vous
Mais j'ai fait la décision de rester silencieux
I'll n'y a rien je peux faire maintenant
There's nothing left to do, I made the decision to stay quiet
So I left
Went home
And cried myself to sleep
Damn thought I was over this

CHAPTER FORTY-FOUR

Snitch

And this I pray, that your love may abound more and more [displaying itself in greater depth] in real knowledge and in practical insight,
PHILIPPIANS 1:9

How does one function after being raped? I never thought it was possible to feel lower than I had felt. What was I good for? Romeo was outta my life, I tried this new relationship and it just didn't go as planned. Was there anything I could do right? I had visions of taking the knife and stabbing myself in my belly. Stabbing myself in my fat. I saw myself bleeding on the floor. Alone. *Who would raise your child? Your mom?* My mind always snapped back. I could never actually pick up a knife to do it and pills seemed like it wouldn't create the type of pain I deserved. I was scared for Kaykay to leave me alone. I was scared when he went to my mom's house. Not cause I thought they wouldn't take care of him, but I was afraid of what I would do to myself when he wasn't home. He was the only thing that was keeping me alive. If he wasn't in sight, if I didn't have him to live for, what was the point? What was the fucking point? To keep myself in this hell hole? I hated this house. I no longer felt safe. I hated my bed. I hated my room. I hated myself. I couldn't sleep. Nightmares kept me awake. I wanted peace so bad but it wasn't coming. To be asleep forever, what a goal. *I hated alcohol so that wasn't gonna work. I don't smoke weed. I ain't neva done no drugs. Why not? I should, maybe it would ease this pain. Where would I even get drugs? See you can't even do that shit properly. Fuck I'm such a disappointment, just like my family said I was.* I needed to keep myself busy and keep my mind preoccupied to avoid the negative thinking. My own mind was scaring me.

Thankfully there was always some kinda program happening in the building. I jus had to push myself more to get there instead of secluding myself. It was so hard. It was easier to just stay in my apartment. Sometimes some of the other girls would help me out by taking Kaykay to program with them to allow me time to get work done. Sometimes I needed them to take him to get him away from me. I didn't want to push my negative feelings on him. His happiness and growth was my main priorities.

Things started turning around for me when the Literature for Life program started up in our building. It created a space for us to read books and have group discussions as well as have group writing sessions. Despite my high school teacher saying I wasn't no good at writing, there was something about it that connected with my soul. Our program instructor was a super dope emcee by the name Motion. She had such a calm personality and was very patient with us. When she performed for us, when she spit a line, it was like magic. My mind was like, *what is this rhythm with words? I love it!* I learned that what she was doing was called spoken word. I had never heard of it before meeting her. The more I looked up this spoken word artistry I noticed that those people spoke a lot like me. They didn't all use proper grammar, but they were still able to evoke feelings and tell a story in such a creative way. I fell in love with metaphors, flow, rhythm, word manipulation and storytelling. It was like God knew exactly what I needed. There were only a few of us who showed up for the program because it took place during the day when most girls had school. We met weekly and were given different writing challenges to respond to. At first, we were all nervous to share, but we were all supportive of each other and the atmosphere of support allowed us to open up and share. It was kinda therapeutic in a way. The small group made it more intimate and safe. I got to know the women better here than in any other program.

I met a really dope chick named Whitney with the most amazing spirit. She was love and she was life. Although she wasn't from the building and didn't have any children herself, she offered such color to the group with her contagious smiles. There was another woman who was from the building who had locs and made amazing vegan dishes. Her way with words really inspired me. She was a poet effortlessly and seemed so wise. She was like a mother to many. There was another girl from the building named Leah, she was from the states but was in Toronto on her own, kinda like me. She had a colorful personality, always cracking jokes and loud but she had a genuinely big heart. There were a few other women who would drop in from time to time but for the most part we were the main participants. Our group dynamic was good, and I looked forward to this program every week. The more I wrote, the more I worked on myself and the more free I felt.

I was at a point where I wanted to celebrate the freedom I felt. One of the staff members had pulled me aside, asked me to look out for Leah, and take her under my wing. She seemed like a cool person and hella funny, so we started to hang out outside of the program as well. I would invite her over to my house for dinner which also allowed us to get to know each other as our kids played together. Her daughter was two years old and such a beautiful toddler, but she just lacked some broughtupsi. She drove me mod, when she would jump on my couch or walk and open up my fridge. I hadn't raised Kaykay like that, so it was very different for me to experience. Like what do I do? She ain't my kid so I couldn't give no time outs or nun. Kaykay tried to follow her one day and jump on the couch, I shut that shit down quick. "We don't do that round here, please sit down, Kaykay you know better" He mussa lost his damn mind too bout he gon jump on a couch. Hmm, nah.

I was used to my house being a hot spot simply because I was well equipped. From kitchen supplies, to a computer, to TV, internet and a home phone. I was set up better than most of these women, so they would often come by to hang out once I was home. Leah was one of those women who made herself right at home. I enjoyed her company to be honest and even though she lived upstairs sometimes she would sleep over if it got too late. She would cook at my house, admittedly I wasn't the cleanest, yet she helped to keep the house clean. She said she loved the company and didn't like being alone. That resonated with me. It's not always easy feeling alone. Plus, her apartment didn't have cable or internet, so there wasn't much to do when she was up there. I was cool with everything except that her daughter would be running and yelling around the small apartment and misbehaving. The way the house was set up, there were many potential points of injury and it made me nervous as hell having her run around. Leah made a suggestion "You should kid proof your house to avoid any injuries". What I wanted to say was: *That's a greeeeaaatt suggestion, except for the fact that my kid sits still. Da fuck I need to kid proof when my kid doesn't run around? My house was designed for my kid, not other kids. If you would just take care of your child betta this wouldn't be an issue now would it?* Instead I said, "Uh huh, good suggestion." I really needed to say what was on my mind more, but I didn't wanna hurt no feelings. Things became increasingly uncomfortable watching the two, mother and daughter get into yelling matches with each other. I swear I couldn't hold my facial expressions together the first time I heard this lil two-year-old yelling at her mom. *Yo who this kid think she yelling at? Kaykay betta not pick up none of this damn bad behaviour.*

Things seemed to always resolve so I would try to ignore it, also cause I knew Leah was doing the best she could. I mean her daughter was only two, I remember Kaykay when he was that age. He'd grown a lot, but it had been an adjustment. It wasn't always the easiest thing to do. Consistency was one of the biggest lessons I had to learn with him. But that wasn't always second nature for some people. As a mother I learnt to try, fail, then try again. She seemed overwhelmed when she tried to discipline her daughter. Sometimes I wondered if she could even manage, but her daughter was always fed and never looked out of place. She always had on the cutest dresses. For discipline, she started with timeouts or slapping her daughter, but it was inconsistent thus ineffective. Some days she would yell "Don't jump on the couch" *Ye dat's right tell her.* Other days she'd be like "Aww are you having fun?" *Fun?? Get yo damn legs off my couch.* I couldn't keep up with her mixed messages, iuno how her daughter was going to.

Since none of those tactics worked, she got advice from my neighbour about using a belt to slap instead of just her hand. Not only did we endure yelling and crying on a daily basis but when her daughter would misbehave Leah would walk into my room, grab one of my belts and woop her daughter in front of me and Kaykay. Even though I was slapped with the belt growin up, it was nothing I encouraged or even did to Kaykay. We were all living in a modhouse. I didn't think it was cool, but I didn't know what to do about it. I was tryna mind my own damn business in my own damn house. I felt bad for her and her daughter. Leah looked so embarrassed every time her daughter acted out but in reality, my apartment really didn't have the space she needed to run around. Crazy enough, whenever I asked her daughter to stop and spoke with a stern voice she listened. So, I realized it wasn't a matter of her not being able to listen, she was just used to getting her way with her mom.

I was feeling a bit overwhelmed but figured it was nothing more than I could handle. Until this one night. We were cooking while the kids were watching tv. Out of excitement her daughter started jumping and yelling and shouting. Kaykay was gettin frustrated cause he couldn't watch his tv show and Leah was tryna talk to her with no prevail. She tried to get her daughter to sit but all she would do was kick and scream louder. Leah lost it really quickly and she grabbed one of my kitchen knives and put it in her daughter's face and asked, "Do you want me to go to jail tonight?" her daughter answers "NO" to which she says, "So why won't you listen and behave?" She marched her daughter back to the couch where she sat quietly the rest of the night. I had no clue what to even say or do. I was shocked. Everything in me was like, *yep this has gone on way too damn long now. You need to separate yourself cause you do not want to be associated with any of this. Just figure out a way to cut yourself off.* I tried coming up with excuses as to why they could no longer come over. I would tell Leah I had meetings, or I stayed at school later just to avoid bumping into her. I would park my car in the back of the building and moments after I got in I would hear a knock at my door. I had to start parking in the second parking lot, out of sight and go through the front door to avoid running into her. My living situation felt so fucked. Just as I was tryna put things back together, shit goes left again. The only thing going right was the fact that I was still losing weight, by now I had lost a total of 80 pounds. At least my confidence was peaking, I noticed that for once I was catching the eye of some pretty cute niggas who weren't old as shit.

As I was leaving the Jane and Finch mall with my groceries this dark skinned brotha caught my eye. Anthony Smith. That's how he introduced himself to me. He had a cute smile, so we exchanged numbers. *This might be the distraction that I need.* He made me laugh at a time when I felt so out of control. He lived down the street from me which made it convenient to see each other. We clicked naturally, nothing was forced. He even had a friend that I hooked my girl up with. Him and his friend were like botty and bench - they went everywhere together. Most time all four of us hung out together but it was also nice when it was just the two of us together. It gave us time to get to know each other, understanding that we were both parents on a grind to make a better life for our kids. He said he was a construction worker that often went out of town but when he was in town we spent time together.

Whenever we had sex I had to stroke his ego a bit to make him feel good about himself. "Yes, the sex is good, no your dick isn't too small" He asked me once if I was into anal which made me feel hella uncomfortable. *Is this nigga on the DL? - Down low? He does seem to like backas a lot. I guess just because a man wants to do it in the ass it don't make him gay. Iuno though, still kinda weird. Ain't no way I'm finna let him do it though cause it's also givin me flashbacks to the time I was raped.* Lil comments here and there really made him feel like he was a man. He used to say it felt wrong being driven around by a girl. Since I was so used to driving, I didn't complain when he started driving my car. At least I was getting a break. Besides all that, he was doing the lil things that Romeo had warned me to look for in a man. No matta who I was with, Romeo always stayed on my mind. I was always comparing the new guys to him. How he treated me and what he taught me. He would always say "Don't eva let a man sit in the car while you pump gas" A man should never let you pump your own gas. I didn't have to worry bout that, neither did I have to worry about always being the one to cook, cause Anthony often cooked for me, I felt spoilt.

It also created an excuse for me to avoid seeing Leah whenever she tried to come over. She had knocked my door one night while he was over, I let her in cause she said she needed to grab something. Once she came and noticed he was over she made herself comfortable. That girl can talk! Damn. I tried to give her subtle hints that we was tryna chill, but she was dodging all hints. I finally had to say it plainly that we were tryna chill before she even moved. At least I had a witness that I wasn't crazy, chick just never wanted to leave my house. She literally had no boundaries and didn't respect my boundaries.

So, I found out that construction worker was code for drug dealer. *Seriously? Not again*, I'm not even bout that...*but I like him* though. It should have been an issue when he brought me with him to re-up on his supply, but I kept ignoring any part of me that was tryna reason with sanity. Very rarely did I ever let him take the car on his own, but he had asked to run an errand and take his son home. He was taking kinda long, so I called him up.

- Anthony: Yo
- Cola: Where you at? You been gone for a minute
- Anthony: I'm in Hamilton, just had to run an errand.
- Cola: Why the fuck you in Hamilton? You only asked me to run a local errand and drop your son home. How does that translate into driving to Hamilton?
- Anthony: Relax, I'm coming back soon
- Cola: You need to find your way back now, I'm not even fucking playing bring my car back now!!

- Anthony: Why are you swearing so much?
- Cola: Cause I fucking can, did you hear me? Don't play with me, bring back my fucking car cause I have shit to do.
- Anthony: Listen, don't get loud with me or talk to me like that
- click.
- It's night time and I still have yet to hear from him, so I get to calling his phone again.
- Anthony: What?
- Cola: What you mean what? where's my damn car? It's been hours now.
- Anthony: Did you even look outside? No? Look outside and don't call back my fucking number.

When I drew back the blinds my car was parked at the back. Great! Except for him to park it and leave, it meant he still had my spare key. *You need to get your keys back, what if he comes to get your car without you knowing like before. Just call him up and ask him to meet up to get your keys.* I called him a few times with no response. I text him. I call again. Finally, I get an answer.

- Anthony: What do you want?
- Cola: I just wanna get my spare key back
- Anthony: Sure, no problem.
- Cola: Thank you, when can I get them?
- Anthony: When I have time

Click.

Things very quickly turned into a cat and mouse games. I would call him, I went to his apartment, I texted him and he ignored me every single time. I was still worried that he would come after my car, so I broke my own rule and well known hood rule - I called the cops. *You ain't this kinda chick, you ain't no damn snitch. Put the phone down. What will people think if they see you talking to the cops? Why can't he just gimme back my damn keys so we can go our ways He's so fucking immature.* Within about an hour two cops showed up at my door to take my statement. "What seems to be the problem?" "Well I was dating this guy and I let him borrow my car and he refuses to give me back my spare key." "How long have you guys been together?" "Hmm, a few months maybe" "Really? And you already lent him your car? What do you do for work?" "I'm a student and a single mother." "Well you seem like a pretty smart girl, you should know better than to let some guy you barely know drive your car" "Hmmmm, lesson learned" "What's his first name?" "Anthony" "Last name?" "Smith" "Where does he live?" "Down the street, in those tall buildings at the corner" "Ok we'll look into this and get back to you." "Thanks" *Maybe now he'll know I'm serious about my keys.*

Within a few days I got a call from one of the cops saying he had information that I needed to know. He was in the parking lot by the time I got outside. He rolled down the window and said we needed to make it quick before anyone saw me talking to him. He then proceeds to pull up a picture on his screen and asks me "Is this the guy you know?" "Yes" "And you know him as Anthony Smith?" "Yes" "He's known to us, but that's not his name. His name is Marvin Black and he's not someone you want to be around. He's not a great guy, and definitely not someone you want around your son" "Ok, what about his friend, he lie about his name too?" "Yes, and he's the one you need to be more careful of" "But he's so quiet" "It's normally the quiet ones that are more dangerous, and your car was pulled over recently with two males and two female passengers. He told the officer he was driving his sister's car" "Wooooowww really? His sister? Really? His sister? That's just great. Ok, how can I get my car keys back?" "We'll try to contact him and see if he can just return them to you, you should go back inside though, you don't want anyone around here to see you talking to me." "Ok, thank you." I tried to stay calm but inside I had some many questions and emotions. *Sister? Marvin? Whoa this was jus more than I wanted to deal with. All I need is my keys back and I'm good. I need to cut ties as soon as possible. But what about my girl? I introduced her to his friend. What a mess, I've essentially put her in danger as well. Known to police, what does that even mean?* I couldn't even dwell on this too long cause I was about to start summer school.

Not long after I returned inside, I heard the door knocking...it was Leah. "Sorry, don't mean to bother you but would it be possible if I used your phone? I also just bought some pork chops and thought maybe you'd like me to make you some dinner." "Sure, come in, ye we can make food, I haven't gotten a chance to make anything yet." Today was baby bonus day which meant Leah was up from the crack a dawn with her daughter at Walmart making sure her house was stacked. This time I noticed she was alone, so I asked her, "Where's your daughter?" she replied, "Oh she's upstairs taking a nap, I'll check up on her" "Oh ok" *You feel safe leaving her all alone? Man, I could never leave Kaykay alone.* By the time I looked at the clock, the day had flown by and there was just enough time to pick up Kaykay. We had a routine, once he got home he ate, he played a bit while I tried to do some homework and then he went to bed. Even with Leah over Kaykay was still in bed by the same time every night. Tonight ended pretty good and Leah left at a decent time which gave me enough time to relax and rest up for my class.

Summer school was a lot harder than what I expected. This one class in particular I thought was more of a social anthropology class, but it turned out to be a lot of math. Ugh! Not my strong suit, and since it was summer school everything was condensed and challenging to retain all in one sitting. Turns out I wasn't alone in my expectation since after the first week a group of classmates had dropped the class. Regardless I convinced myself I could still get through it. *Don't quit.*

I was driving home from school when I got a call from a private number. I answered "Hello?" *Breathing heavy* "Hello?" Click. Within a few minutes I get another call. "Hello?" *Breathing Heavy* "Who is this?" Click. As I approached my apartment a third call came in, I answered but didn't say anything at first. Then I heard the caller say "Snitches get stitches" click. *What? What the fuck? Is this a joke? Snitches get Stitches? Who I snitch on? Oh man I bet you it's*

Anthony, I mean Marvin calling me. Within a few minutes of that call, Anthony calls me.

- Anthony: "Why the fuck did you call the cops, I told you I'd give you the keys when I had time."
- Cola: "Did you just call me?"
- Anthony: "Nope"
- Cola: "This is your first time calling me?"
- Anthony: "Stop asking me stupid questions, and answer me, didn't I tell you I'd give your fucking keys back? DIDN'T I TELL YOU? You betta be careful. You betta be careful cause snitches get stitches"
- Cola: "YEAH EH, YEAH EH, THAT'S WHAT YOU HAVE TO SAY TO ME? YOU CAN'T DO SHIT TO ME" *Yo calm down, why you shaking, why you yelling back, is that smart?*
- Anthony: memba I warned you, just memba I warned you. I know where you are.

Click.

I couldn't slow down my breathing. My first thoughts were of Kaykay. *You done fucked up now. You put your son's life in danger. What if the apartment is shot up while he's home? How will you live with yourself? You live on the first floor with huge windows, it would be nothing to have your windows blown out. Look at the mess you got yourself into this time. What kinda mother are you to put your son in danger? Even if you don't care about your life, it's not fair that you put him in danger as well. You ain't no good for that lil boy. What you gonna do now?* I was unsure of what to do, but I found the number of the officers who were a part of my case. I was hoping they could assist me now that he was threatening me but to my surprise I was told "Since it wasn't a direct threat there's nothing we can do to help you, but you should come in to make a formal report since he hasn't returned your car keys yet." I hung up the phone and balled. While crying I heard a small voice that said, "Why are you crying mommy?" all I could say was, "I'm ok baby". In that moment his hug was exactly what I needed. I put him to bed in his room, away from the window and I fell asleep sitting up in the couch as I tried to keep a lookout.

I was a paranoid mess, I barely slept anymore, couldn't concentrate in school, but I was passed the deadline to drop the class; I needed to get away. Since it was my mom's weekend to have Kaykay I decided to go with him. We lived far enough out of the city that it felt like a mini getaway. At least I knew Anthony couldn't find us there. Since Leah knew I was leaving she asked if she could stay at my place while I was gone. As much as I wasn't sure it was a great idea, after a lil nagging I gave in. I just wanted to be out and away from everything.

As happy as I was that I moved out of my parent's home, there was something peaceful about waking up to sounds of birds chirping. It sure put my mind at ease if only for a little while. Just as I thought I was free from drama, on my second night I got a phone call from Leah. She was panicking so much I could barely understand her.

- Leah: "She wouldn't behave, she wouldn't behave so I beat her. I left marks on her but she's ok, she's taking a bath. I have a magic potion that'll make the bruises go away."
- Cola: Wait hol up, you what? Magic potion? I don't understand what you saying.
- Leah: Ye it's some witch hazel concoction my mother used to use on me. It takes the marks away. I already got CAS in my life, I can't have them taking her away, and you know she's already light skin so I can't have any bruises showing up on her.
- Cola: Hmm ok, but what do you mean you beat her? Like you slapped her?
- Leah: I used the belt.
- Cola: Is she ok? So, she's sitting in my bathtub right now? I gotta go but I'll be home tomorrow night.
- Leah: Ok bye

This chicks insane, this is the last damn time I leave her in my house. She just be doing the most. No boundaries eh? I really didn't know how to handle this. Now I had two reasons I dreaded going home. *I can't handle all this pressure. This ain't right. Something ain't right. And I still gotta go catch up on these classes.* I returned home but didn't attend any school that week. I was tired. My relaxing weekend was anything but. Everyday I kept the blinds closed, I was too afraid to open them. I jumped every time I thought I saw a shadow of a person walking past my window. Or anytime my door knocked. I was a prisoner in my own home. I still had to make it down to the police station to give a formal report for my missing keys. I drove to the police station uneasy, I had to pass his building to even get to the police station. All I heard the entire time was *Snitches get sitches, snitches get stitches.* Once I reached the station they sat me in a big room and I waited what felt like hours until the officers came in. I know I was supposed to be there to get help, but it seemed more like I was being grilled and judged rather than assisted. Things didn't get better once I admitted that I had been on a few runs with Anthony. They wanted to know where the house was and what else I knew that could be used against him. I didn't know shit all. I just wanted my keys back. They pressured me to help them out. "You help us, and we help you" "Look I can't remember what house, I only know the general area". I didn't give them any type of information that was helpful, but what the fuck I look like? A detective? They kept telling me about the hood code of silence but still expected me to break it. *Y'all can't even protect me, what do y'all do again?* They said in terms of threats, since he didn't say directly "I will kill you", then there was nothing they could do for me. I just had to sign some papers then I was free to leave. To add insult to injury they said, "If you think of anything, then just let us know", yeah like that's gonna happen. Fuck me! It felt like I was waking up every morning thinking today I might get shot. I know I felt so often like I wanted to die, but my fear for my son was at an ultimate high. How do I prepare for the unexpected? I felt like a sitting duck, but I kept moving forward everyday praying to God he would protect me despite my downfall. *Spare my child from my missteps.* My whole visit to the police station was a big blur but I found out a lil later on that the form I had signed was actually for domestic assault. *Domestic dispute? Was that what it was? I just wanted my car keys, I wasn't a weak person, he was just a super jerk.* It felt weird being identified as a victim of domestic dispute, I always thought it would look and feel a lot more violent. I felt a lot of shame that I had put myself in that situation.

Speaking of situations, I was back to dodging Leah. Anytime she asked me to come over and I couldn't accommodate she would say "Ok I guess I'll just hang out in my apartment, all alone, with nothing to do. No phone, no internet. Just me and my daughter." It was sooooo manipulative and I used to give in, but after that last incident, I really couldn't take on anything else. I tried to just get through each day but it was increasingly difficult. At times when things got to be overwhelming I would go down to the office to vent with Audrey. I was mad when she was let go. It was complete bullshit. They had the middle-aged black women, Audrey, do all the interviews to fill the building and had the new young white girl, Sarah, running all the programs. Once the building was full they said they needed to restructure the jobs and had them both "apply for the job". We all knew who was gonna get the job, but it didn't make much sense to us because the building was filled with predominantly black young single mothers. How was this out of town white girl gonna relate to us? I mean the new girl was a cool person, but she didn't speak the lingo. What we lost was a role model, a mothering figure, someone who didn't take no bullshit. Either way when the switch happened we all adjusted accordingly and soon learned to embrace Sarah. She had creative ideas and was hella nice. She still kept her office open for communication so if we needed something we could always reach out. It did help having someone I could talk to cause right now I needed to figure out what to do about this Leah situation. Everything was closing in on me and I needed some guidance.

I got to the office and at first, I was just venting about how I gotta park far to dodge Leah and how I was under a lot of stress from school and from my ex not giving me back my keys. Then once I started, it was hard to stop, and I spilled the tea on everything. How Leah slept at my house, how her daughter ran around, how she would guilt trip me into letting her stay, and how shocked I was to get the phone call from her once I was away. Bit by bit as I was asked questions and I continued to talk, the look on Sarah's face told me that things were not ok. She said she understood my stress and was glad she could be a support to me. Once I let it all out I felt better and the way in which she was so supportive it felt like I had done therapy or something. But once I calmed down the vibe changed, and she said to me "I gotta report the abuse to her CAS worker" So I'm like "What? No, no, no, I jus wanted to talk it out, I wasn't tryna get nobody in trouble" I wished it was that simple. Even though Sarah wasn't much older than me, she was still an employee, not a tenant, which meant she had obligations that went beyond my "feelings". She said "I have to call CAS it's part of my obligation and you need to call as well" I get why she needed to call, but why me? So, I said "I'm not gonna call. Worst thing you could do as a mother is to call CAS on another mother" but then she says "Well since the abuse you described happened in your house, with your personal items i.e. belt, knife, bathtub; you are also legally responsible. If anything more serious happened you would also be held accountable. Which meant CAS would get involved in your life as well." *Shit, so now because of some crazy bitch I gotta be a snitch and CAS could open a file on me? Fuck that. I can't have no CAS in my life. I still don't wanna do this shit though. Why me? Why'd I come down here, I thought we would just talk like we normally do. I feel like this was a set up. I miss the black lady, at least she understood the code of not snitching; or at least not forcing me to snitch.* "I don't wanna call and I need to go pick up Kaykay". She said, "I understand" and with that I left. She planted a seed that had me worried, but I had bigger shit to worry about. I didn't have to pick up Kaykay right away but I sure as hell wasn't gonna stay downstairs.

It had been about three weeks of agony before my phone rang. It was Anthony telling me to come get my keys. It was light out, so I was hoping he wasn't too brazen, but I really had no clue what I was walking into. The drive up the block seemed like it was taking forever but I kept telling myself to keep a stern face. I drove up to the back of the buildin and breathed a sigh of relief once I didn't see him. It was like *Phew ok, so far no traps.* I got knots in my stomach when I had to dial his number.

- Anthony: "Hello?"
- Cola: "Yeah i'm here"
- Anthony: "Coming"

Click

I saw him in the distance. He walked with a confidence like I was intruding on his territory. He looked at me with cold eyes. I tried to ask him why he lied or treated me this way but all he did was smirk and throw my keys into the dirt as he looks up towards a balcony. I follow his gaze to see two women lookin down. I hear them laughing as I bent down to pick up my keys. By the time I stood up I saw him walking away. I got into my car and cried as I drove home. I felt low and so disrespected.

The very next day I was sitting home chillin when I got a call from my social worker. *Odd, she don't normally check up on me.* Said she wanted to come see me if I was home. My only guess was it had to do with my rant yesterday. My social worker was a super dope Asian woman. She checked in every now an then but she never micromanaged me, just let me know she was available if I was ever stuck. It didn't take her long to get to the building. Apparently, she had gotten a call from the program leader who so intently explained everything that happened including my reluctance to call CAS. *What a snitch. Thanks for nothing, guess I won't be coming down here no more.* For the second day in a row I felt the heat and guilt of choosing to stay silent. But then there was Kaykay. Iuno what I'd do if I had to deal with CAS in my life. Lord knows I do my best, but who knows what the standards are. They said I could be anonymous as they dialed the number for me. Retelling the story was one of the hardest things I had to do in life. I couldn't even get through it without bawling. *How they gonna play me like this? How they gonna guilt me? I can't lose my son. I'm jus tryna keep this shit together. How'd I even get in this situation?* By time I finished the call I was mad. *Fuck all y'all. Y'all can leave me the fuck alone now. Don't call my damn name for any help.* This felt like such a huge betrayal. I'd hate for anyone to call CAS on me. As it turned out a few of the other girls had been making their own complaints and a case had been building against Leah. Either way I played my part and now I was done, right? Wrong, Iuno if these people did not understand anonymous, but somehow my name was whispered to the CAS worker and she wanted to meet me. So now I had to retell the story in front of the CAS worker. Just my luck. *Can't they jus leave me alone now? This is exactly why more people don't get involved. Who the hell wants to repeat this story? Who wants to risk their identity and sanity since these people clearly don't know what the fuck anonymous means.* I answered a few questions and got the hell up outta there. The CAS worker assured me I would be anonymous, but I already knew not to get my hopes up for that.

It had only been a few hours and Leah was knocking at my door telling me how someone had called CAS on her and she had a pretty good idea who it was. I felt like my heart was beating out my damn chest. At any moment I was about to start sweating and pass out. She asked me if I knew who had snitched and I flat out lied... "Nope, I don't know". Then she told me how she was downstairs speaking with the program leader and was told that I was the one who called. *SHIT! Shit, shit, shit, shit, shit. You gotta get yourself outta this.* I looked her dead in her face and said. "It wasn't me". She smiled, cracked a joke then said she was gonna go back up to her apartment. I smiled back as I closed the door ready to explode. I didn't even wait for the elevator, I ran downstairs furious. I had tears streaming down my face. The second I saw our program manager I quietly yelled "You said it was supposed to be anonymous. Why, why, why would Leah knock my door saying that you were the one who told her it was me?" I was flailing my arms, she was tryna calm me down as she said "I would never do that to you. I didn't do that to you. She's just tryna get a reaction outta you. You know she's trying to make you feel guilty. It's manipulation, but I promise you it wasn't me. I could lose my job if I did. You should also know that she told me that you gave her the belt to discipline her daughter and that it was all your idea" This was just too damn much to handle. My brain couldn't cope with everything. How was she gonna blame me? I didn't tell her to grab my belt, that had nothing to do with me. She'd really accuse me of that?

After a few weeks of trying to avoid Leah again, I finally decided that I needed to tell her the truth. I couldn't see her and not say something, I wasn't that type of person, I wasn't fake. I couldn't smile with her knowing what I had done. I took her out for breakfast somewhere public. *She's gonna hate you. Abort, abort. Don't do it, don't do it.* I was soo nervous I couldn't speak. How does one even breach the subject? *Hey, I called CAS on you, I hope we can still be friends? Lord please gimme the words to say and I pray she will receive it in love and not hate me or fight me once she knows the truth. They left me no choice.* I tried to strike up a conversation

- Cola: How's things going for you?
- Leah: Good
- Cola: That's good...so, what's new in the building?

Leah had intel on everything going on in the building. She knew who was getting beat down, who's baby daddy left, who was cheating, she damn well knew everybody's business, hence why I didn't tell her all my business. When she was done it was time to spill the beans.

- Cola: I have another reason for bringing you out for breakfast. I have something I need to tell you. I know you'll probably hate me, but I want to be honest with you...It was me who called CAS on you. I didn't mean to, I was really stressed about a lot of things and I went downstairs to vent and by the time I was done talking they said I had to report you. I hate conflict, which means I have a hard time communicating my feelings with people. You were over all the time and I've tried to talk to you, but then sometimes you would say you had nowhere to go or you were gonna be all alone and I felt bad. I didn't mind having you over but sometimes it was a lot for me. This was worse though, I'm so sorry. I'm so sorry. This was so hard for me. They said that if I didn't do it then CAS could also come after me cause I was legally responsible. They even called in my social worker to convince me to make the call. I said no at first, I really did.

- Leah: Who, who told you to call?
- Cola: Program leader
- Leah: That bitch, she makes it seem like she's being helpful. I knew I couldn't trust her. What did you tell them?
- Cola: Everything...I just went downstairs to vent, I was only trying to let go of some steam. I didn't know she would call CAS.
- Leah: How could you not know?
- Cola: I've never been in this situation before. I just went to talk, I told them so many times I didn't want to call.
- Leah: It's ok, it's ok. I know how to deal with them.
- Cola: Another thing though, I was told that you've been saying that I gave you the belt to discipline your daughter. But you know that's not true, I never gave you the idea. You told me you heard that from my neighbour. You just ended up using my belts because you were at my house. Why would you say that it was me?
- Leah: I never said that. I mentioned I talked to you about it, but I never said that you told me to do it.
- Cola: Why would they tell me that?
- Leah: They're lying. They're gonna say whatever they need to. They're out to get me.
- Cola: Ok, iuno what's going on or who to believe. Thanks for having this conversation with me. Is there anywhere you need to be right now? I'll drive you anywhere you want to go. Just name it.

I had hit my breaking point. I emailed my teachers the next day informing them of my decision to drop out of their class. I passed the deadline so I couldn't get any money back or get my grades dropped off my record. My record was now tarnished with two beautiful F's but in the moment none of it mattered. Although, I had heard through the grapevine that I could potentially have my grades reversed if I had probable cause. To claim mental illness I would need a counsellor to sign off on it, so I signed up for school counseling. I needed an appointment as soon as possible if I was gonna stay afloat. It felt like I was crashing faster than I could keep up. Depression couldn't even begin to express the emotion I was feeling. I didn't wanna leave the house, didn't trust anyone to talk to, didn't know where to go to get support anymore. More than ever I missed Audrey. She had looked out for me since I moved in, taught me how to change a tire, how to get insurance, told me to keep my head up. I wondered if she woulda done the same thing and left me stranded. Leah stopped coming by so in a way I got what I wanted, but I never wanted it like this.

I had my first counselling appointment the following week. I was a lil uneasy cause I had never had counseling before, so I never knew what to expect. I was hoping for a black lady but they only had an older white woman available. It only made me more nervous. She started out by asking me a ton of questions. It felt like an interrogation more than like the therapy I had seen on TV. When she had finished asking her questions, like word vomit I began spilling everything. From my ex and how I lived in fear over my property to calling CAS and living through the shock of being implicated in the CAS case. By the time I had expressed my own experience with corporal punishment or discipline as a child the look of discontentment that spread across this lady's face had me questioning my own damn upbringing. *But I was raised black though, discipline was just a part of our culture.* The story also had the counsellor running for the phone to make a report to CAS. *What is it with these white people and snitching?* I had to sit in silence and wait as she reported what I just told her. I felt so uncomfortable. I understood the legal obligation, but it added more stress than peace. That was my last day at counseling and it reaffirmed my position, trust no one. I wasn't gonna leave without getting somethin out of it though. I convinced the counsellor to at least sign my paper that would give me the support needed to reverse my failed grades. *At least it wasn't a full waste, but I ain't doing this shit no more. She don't seem to understand me.* In the end I felt we lacked relatability. I didn't have time to explain everything, there were some things I needed her to just understand and she couldn't.

When I had thought things had gotten as bad as they could I was now hearing from other people that Leah was saying that I was dirty, kept my house dirty and how she always had to cook and clean up after me. Then she added that she would have never slapped her daughter if she wasn't around me because I was the one pressuring her to teach her daughter to act a certain way. Every story of abuse, including the bathtub incident she told people that I was also involved. It had gotten to the point where even Leah's CAS worker called me to the office to tell me that Leah had implicated me in her stories. I was getting such dirty looks when I walked through the halls. Girls would see me and whisper or stop whispering as I walked by. *What are you looking at?* It was so obvious. I was crushed. When it wasn't the women from the building telling me stuff, it was strangers on the street, literally. There was nowhere I could go to escape.

Even the old man on the block was looking at me weird. Every neighbourhood has one, that one old man who side glances women way younger than him. Ours had these incredible blue eyes, even though he was old enough to be my dad he looked young. He was nice and would often spark up a conversation that usually ended in him asking for my number. Though I was never interested, I was never rude to him. Jus simple conversation and kept it moving. Even he came to tell me how Leah had told him about a thick girl on the first floor with a son who was a disgusting whore that always had revolving men coming in and out of her house. Doesn't take a rocket scientist to know she was talking about me, especially since I was one of the very few thick chicks in the whole damn building let alone the first floor. The nail in the coffin came when my neighbour had come and told me Leah told her how I was a shitty mother and treated my son horribly. I knew better than to let her win, but she was already in my head. No matta what I did, I was still wrong. I couldn't believe she took it this far, was there nowhere I could go without hearing my name being dragged through the mud?

'Call now I'm off the phone.' These words wake me from my sleep. I stare at those words over and over only to realize that the message wasn't for me. Cause see the message came from the phone of the man that I just hung up the phone with. And see, he told me he'd talk to me another day because I laid there sleeping and unable to speak. So, you see my dilemma, the message wasn't for me. At 12:35 in the morning that message came and I immediately thought it was a girl cause that man don't really eva be talking to dudes so late. Almost instantly I felt like I was having déjà vu. First year university I sat in my car parked at school while me and dude was fighting. I suspected he was talking to another g and sho nuff when I clicked that phone in his ear he sent me a text. The moment I read those words they stung my heart like a thousand daggers. The message wasn't meant for me.

Now back to the present I sit here listening to the smooth voice of Anthony Hamilton trying not to cry cause I don't wanna be a pussy. This feeling! This feeling I feel won't allow me to put my pen down. Water flowing like a river, the ink flows outta my pen. An like a mod woman I write as this man rings off my phone. This man, this man was supposed to love me, yet he sits here tryna make me feel guilty and tries to ignore the fact that there was a text sent to his phone. No explanation given, at least not a proper one, just excuses and lies, but I am tired and four years later I refuse to go through troubles again. I refuse to be lied to. I refuse to be pushed aside. I refuse to allow a man to have control over my emotions because I am a strong woman and I refuse to put up with this cause I deserve better than this. "Call now, I'm off the phone," that's what he said.

Poetic Interlude

Does my sweet aroma please you
Tease you
Make you fall to your knees with wonder?
Wondering if the experience will be everything you fantasize?
You fan the size of your lies
That seem to have made you blind and fall deaf to my stare
Cause I still said no
You heard me though right?
There's no miscommunication
Excommunicate yourself from the thought of my thighs
Glide your eyes to a different part of my body
I do not bend for you
Merely thought maybe I could lend my heart to you
But I already know I wont get it back in one piece
I can picture you breaking it off piece by piece until there is nothing left and I cannot be apart of your detrimental regime
I am not the woman for you to practice all your self hate
Self wait
Cause that's what you want me to do
Wait until you're a betta manz still
Still like riva wata
Quiva and sorta laugh
Let me move out of your gaze
To weigh the cost of this mistake
You only see sex
I only want love
Woven through the tapestries of complexities
You are not who I thought you were
Your lust for pussy has your mind divided
You tried it
Now i'm forced to walk away

Poetic Interlude

ODE TO CLYDE
He is strong, reliable, my ride or die forever
He's my best friend, my main man who leaves me never.
We have several commonalities
We like the same color blue
You like to ride n I like to ride in yu to
Do yu memba when we first met
Ya I kno yu do
I knew right away that I loved yu and I'd always be true
True you and I had our ups and downs
You've made me cry and you've made me frown but
regardless me n yu always be crusin town
Made me look good when mans dem be around
Yu was born is 02 an me in 89
But together we both shined
I gotchu
Boo hoo I heard the horrible news
The man at the shop hit me wit these big ass blues
I loved yu more than a brand new pair of shoes
Heard yu was dying got me sighin..jus all crazy upset
Jus here reminiscing again bout when we first met
Hmmm how could I forget
Got all my belongings set
And I was free
And I see my baby was stuntin like me
gotta be grateful for yu sharin yur life with me
Yu been alive for 8 and mine for 4
I'd never close the door
But once more
I love yu
Yu were always by my side
I was yur bonnie and yu my clyde
My ride or die
goodbye to my supa fly

Car

CHAPTER FORTY-FIVE

Ode to Clyde

You love all words that devour, O deceitful tongue.
-Psalm 52:4

I was re-learning how dope metaphors could be. This wasn't a lesson I learned in high school cause it was hella boring; yet somehow the things we learned about in this writing group came to life in different ways. I wrote Ode to Clyde to challenge myself. I realized how beyond blessed I was to have a car once I saw how most of the women in my building were struggling to take the bus with their kids. Instead of cherishing my blessing I took it for granted. I sped, got tickets, I waited too long for oil changes. When it was new, I took the utmost care for it, but once I was comfortable I forgot how valuable it was to me. I would drive it everywhere as if mileage or wear and tear wasn't anything to worry about. I spent so much time in my car I practically lived in there but with gas prices rising I was forced to slow down and keep my ass at home more.

This summer I was desperate, I hadn't saved and had no money for food. Dropping out of summer classes and not getting the money back screwed me over. I overheard some of the girls talking bout how Money Mart would buy jewelry, so I gathered up what gold I could find in the house and headed down to Money Mart. I never thought life could get lower, yet somehow it always did. Always. Couldn't catch a damn break. My heart broke when I had to pawn our 10k gold necklace and didn't even get much in return. $25 was all my precious jewelry was worth to this store. But to me I had sold so much more that day. *What kind of mother are you? You weren't raised this way, you can't even provide for your son, are you sure you should be raising him? He's probably betta off with someone else. At least he wouldn't starve.* Despite my feelings, I took the $25 to Price Chopper trying to stretch it as much as possible. This was life I guess. The cheap food I bought was only enough to feed us for a few days.

All the stress of everything was also taking a toll on me physically. I couldn't afford the veggies like I had before, and I had developed something called gout that was extremely painful. It started out as a small bump on my foot but once I scratched it my whole foot became extremely swollen to the point that I couldn't walk without being in pain. I had taken a taxi to drop Kaykay to daycare or keep him home. Once the gout cleared up on one foot it jumped to the next. The inactivity plus cheap food had my weight on the up and up and it felt like there was nothing I could do about it. I got very depressed. I had worked so hard to get the weight off - 80 pounds, but I realized how unrealistic the methods were for the first time. Very quickly I was feeling less humane.

I was so sick and tired of being sick and tired. Having no money for good food made everything worse. Being poor meant being unhealthy. What was worse was that anytime I went to the doctors all they would say was that it was weight related. Everything was classified as weight, I sprained my ankle and they would say it was because of my weight. Doctors were not my favorite people. When I finally made it to the doctor this time they diagnosed me with having gallstones. The gout plus gallstone pain was too much. I was in pain all the time, sleeping was hard, moving was hard, taking care of Kaykay and the house was hard, and all the doctors could say was wait for surgery and manage things myself. Otherwise there was no support.

Taking care of myself was almost impossible with no food, no ambition or ability cause I was in pain 80% of the time for a period of three weeks. Just like that, my hard work slid through my hands as the weight was back, not fully but enough to keep me miserable. I tried to start back the diet but every time I would start I became immensely sick. What I learned from personal research was that the gout and gallstones could have been caused by the rapidness in which I lost the weight - 10 months. The shame of being heavy and the push from the outside to look a certain way and be "healthy" led me to try and lose as much weight as possible in the shortest amount of time. My body couldn't handle all the changes plus all the stress I was currently enduring. When I needed it most, even my body gave up on me. No other worse betrayal than from your own body especially when I was trying to actively take care of it.

Being confined to a couch for weeks didn't help my depression, I was home every day watching it happen and it was driving me crazy. To make it worse, when the weight started to come back I was so ashamed that I wanted to hide. I didn't want to face people. In my experience society does this thing where they make it such a big deal that I lost weight that it felt like I wasn't a person until the weight came off. They'd say, "Omg good for you." "Good work" "Hard work pays off" or my favorite "Omg you're so beautiful" Like what the fuck was I before I lost the weight? These messages I understood to mean that I was finally desirable. Reign was the only friend who told me not to lose too much weight because I had a cute figure and nice ass. So, with the weight being put back on, I felt unworthy, ugly, disappointed, like I had let people down. As the weight went back on they didn't say anything, but the "good" compliments stopped. I really wish people didn't put so much emphasis on me losing weight, maybe I wouldn't have felt so disgusted with myself if I thought people liked me either way. At this point, I only left my house to drop off and pick up Kaykay, run to the bank or do groceries.

One day I was in the process of leaving the bank and this guy approached me and asked me if I wanted to buy some perfume. "No thank you, I'm not interested." So, then he says, "Why don't you buy something for you boyfriend" *Hmm, he thinks he's slick.* After weeks of isolation and feeling horrible it was nice to talk to someone, so I replied "I don't have a man but I'll take a look at some of your perfumes since you're persistent." "Hey, I'm Pierce" "Cola, nice to meet you." I shook his hand then turned my attention to his bootleg bottles. He wasn't much taller than me, but he had these amazingly cute dimples when he smiled. His beard was nice, and I was feeling his dreads and stocky build. He was completely different than the type of man I typically went for, but his charm was on point. He kept me laughin till I finally bought a small bottle. We exchanged numbers and I sashayed my hips all the way back to my car just in case he was watching me walk away. *Don't get caught up, this man sells bootleg perfume on a street carna. What can he provide for you? He's cute though, can we have just a lil fun? Jus a lil? Maybe he can help distract you from this drama. Don't be such a boogie chick. Don't act like you betta than him. He ain't your typical type but give him a chance. You neva know.* I decided to send a quick text now that I was home.

- Cola: Hey, thanks again for the perfume, you out there often?
- Pierce: Ye, but it's jus a side hustle while I try to get my music career started. I'm a rapper.
- Cola: Oh, that's nice, I'm in school for music right now. *Ok so he's a local rapper, I swear everyone in this damn hood is a rapper.*
- Pierce: Oh, you sing?
- Cola: I can but I'm in school for classical piano
- Pierce: Oh wow, how long have you been playing?
- Cola: Hmm since I was 3, so about 18 years. How old are you?
- Pierce: So, you can teach me then, I'm 21
- Cola: Sure, no problem, oh we're the same age...89?
- Pierce: Ye, you got kids?
- Cola: I do, I have one son, you?
- Pierce: Naw, where's his dad if you don't mind me asking?
- Cola: Naw it's cool, his dad is nowhere around
- Pierce: Oh, he doesn't live here?
- Cola: No, he lives here in Toronto, he just wants nothing to do with us.

- Pierce: Oh, damn, I know what that's like though, I'm not really close with my dad either.
- Cola: It's not fun no, so where your girl at? Or are you single?
- Pierce: Ye, so that's your car?
- Cola: Ye it's mine, you drive?
- Pierce: I have my G1
- Cola: That's cute, when you going for your G2?
- Pierce: I just need to practice a few times before I can go for it. I have a car, I just need to get the license and I'm good.
- Cola: How do you get around now selling your stuff?
- Pierce: Sometimes I take the bus, other times I sell with my boys.
- Cola: All y'all from the same car? That's a lot
- Pierce: Ye it can be, that's why I'm tryna get my own whip going. I wanna ask you something
- Cola: Ok?
- Pierce: How would you feel about renting out your car to me?
- Cola: That's a bold question, how you so brave? What you mean rent out my car? What I gotta do?
- Pierce: I'll pay you \$25-\$30 a day, not including gas to drive me around while I sell.
- Cola: What time though, cause I have to drop my son to daycare and pick him up.
- Pierce: No problem, I'll work with the times you have, this would help me out a lot. I could probably sell a lot more.
- Cola: Hmm, I dunno

This is crazy, I've done some crazy things, but this is crazy. Should I do it? I can't do it. I'm really gonna drive around all day? Ok but if he gives me \$25 a day for 5 days then that's \$125 a week. That's more than I have right now. I don't have no otha *funds coming in till September. That's still 3 months away. What you gonna do? I really needed money and maybe it would help me get out of the house.*

- Pierce: Not even for $25 a day? How bout $30?
- Cola: When would you need to start?
- Pierce: As soon as possible
- Cola: Ok, I'm down.

Right now, feeding my son was more important than my ego. At least it was money coming in. This felt like a saving grace and I realized no beginning was too small. It was a welcomed change since most niggas I met tried to use me or robbed my shit. With Pierce it was different cause he made sure I got paid daily, no excuses. I never even had to ask him. He automatically gave it to me when I dropped him off. He had his G1 but didn't know how to drive so initially I did all the driving. But eventually I let him practice. I think it does something to a man's ego having a woman drive him around, so I figured it would be better if I taught him how to drive, especially since we mostly drove circles in the parking lot. We spent hours driving around which gave us plenty of time to get to know each other. We flirted here an there, gave a lil extra laugh. We both made sexual comments, he brushed up against my titties, but everything seemed to go nowhere. I felt the sexual tension but knew the boundaries and we tried not to cross them. The focus was always business first. Make money without all the emotional bullshit cause none of us had time for that. We both weren't interested in a relationship, I was over it and he said he always ends up hurting the people he cared about. I respected the honesty. What we did agree to was to have each other's backs. Through our stories we realized we had so much in common. Was it possible to be this close and just be friends?

He was one of the first men I introduced to Kaykay since my ex Nathaniel. The men in my life that I fucked came only at night and left before morning, no strings attached, no feelings. Since Pierce was with me when I picked up Kaykay the introduction was outta my hands. It was cool though, Pierce was great with him. They formed an interesting bond which had Kaykay referring to him as uncle Psy. I was so nervous in the beginning. This was my child, I wanted him to have positive role models, but it had to be someone consistent, not someone who was here temporarily. Knowin how that fear felt Pierce promised he wasn't gonna go nowhere. He said "Cola, I gotchu, I got your back, imma be here for you and for Kaykay. I promise."

I tried to snuff out the feelings that were growing for him. It was hard though, his smile had me weak, the money I was making was enough to keep me going, when I needed help he was there. His vulnerability and insecurities made his genuineness feel so real. He shared stories about his childhood and disappointments from friends. It made me feel relatable. Made me feel like he had been through some real shit like me. The times when we drove around it was as if we lived in our own bubble away from the problems an stress of life.

We were driving on our way back home, laughin, making jokes like usual. He joked about how my titties were big, which I denied, but he kept insisting so I told him to feel them and tell me. I just wanted him to touch me to be honest. It was like it was written on his face how much he wanted me, but I guess he didn't wanna blur the boundaries. He was always saying how girls caught feelings too fast but what he didn't know was that I wasn't the type to catch feelings. My motto was fuck feelings. I had trained myself to be completely detached. So, he ain't have to worry bout me catching feelings. He didn't believe me at first, but I think he was starting to trust me when he asks, "Do you give becky?" I was clueless

- Cola: "What's becky?"
- Pierce: "If a man asks for becky he's asking to get his dick sucked."
- Cola: I've never heard that term before and no I don't give head.
- Pierce: Oh, why not?
- Cola: For me there's shame attached to it, it feels degrading having my head lower than a man's head.

- Pierce: Why would there be shame attached to it?
- Cola: There just is, it feels weird
- Pierce: Why though?
- Cola: It just is, next topic.
- Pierce: No tell me, tell me why, there's gotta be a reason. We've been talking, sharin, I told you stuff I didn't wanna say either, so what is it?
- Cola: Hmmm
- Pierce: Just trust me

Why he gotta know, I hate talking bout this, he's right though, he has opened up and we have talked about a lot of other deep shit. Fine. But people always get so weird, iuno how he's gonna react.

- Cola: Ok well, when I was young I was in a situation...I was gang raped and that was one of the things I was forced to do. Ever since then I haven't liked it.
- Pierce: So, you haven't done it since then?
- Cola: No, I'm not saying I haven't, I'm saying I don't like to. He'd have to be extremely special if I were gonna do that again and he'd have to promise to keep it on the dl. I don't need my business out there.
- Pierce: I wouldn't say anything.

I was doing my best to shut down any feelings but it was gettin harder.

- Cola: You know I've never had an orgasm from sex yet?
- Pierce: No? You must be fucking the wrong guys
- Cola: Who's the right one? You?
- Pierce: I mean, I'm ok, but I only like to give backas
- Cola: That's my favorite position.
- Pierce: Oh ye?
- Cola: Ye, I love how it feels, I love the sound, I love moaning. I can turn it on and off.
- *Moans*
- Pierce: Shit
- Cola: What?
- Pierce: You like to tease, don't you?
- Cola: Not at all. You like hearing your name?
- *moaning voice* Pierce, Pierce

- Pierce: Ok stop, I'm driving, I gotta focus
- Cola: Oh, my bad

He takes my hand and puts in on the bulge in his pants. It excites me. *Damn. I can only imagine what this feels like. I wanna hear him buss.* We reached my house with more than enough time before we had to pick up Kaykay. It was one of those rare times when the selling had slowed early. I watched as he dropped his pants to the floor as I sat him down in the couch and put his dick in my mouth. His initial reaction excited me. I let my mind go blank and got to work on him. I loved watching his eyes roll back, I loved hearing him moan. It meant I was doing my job to satisfy him and he was pleased. I loved pleasing him, it made me feel good inside when he would say my name in excitement. "Cola, Cola, shit, you're good at this. You're the best I've ever had." Before I could finish he'd bend me over and slap my ass hard. I touched my toes and took it like a boss. It felt good. Like a release of happiness in my body and the more he hit the more I wanted. Even after he buss I wanted more. Didn't want him to stop, but at the end of the day, this was straight fucking, no emotions, no strings attached, just business with a lil side of play. I always warned him

- Cola: "This is all fun an all, but don't catch feelings for me."
- Pierce: "You don't catch feeling for me either"
- Cola: "Don't worry, I won't"

We enjoyed each other frequently but were always free to see whomever else we wanted to.

I was walking outta the building one day and this tall skinny dude called me over to him. He was handsome and I wasn't in a rush. Turns out he wasn't typically from the area but he was gonna be staying with an aunty for the summer. All Dre wanted to do was to kick it, and I had no objections against it. So, I let him come over to chill but I ain't had enough food in the house to share so he bought pizza. There were a few benefits to having him buy food. #1 He let me keep the change and #2 I kept the leftovers to feed Kaykay the next day. Sure, it meant I had to endure a couple of sloppy fucks but faking it was my specialty and whenever he asked for head I said I was allergic. I did what I needed to do to get by.

The time we spent driving around was good, but Pierce felt he could hit another crowd late night if he was able to take the car after we picked up Kaykay. So, we re-negotiated the terms to make it a bit more flexible. If Pierce made more money, then he could drop me a bit extra, if he made less money, then he would give me a bit less. We worked well together. It felt good having more physical help on the days that Pierce would pick up Kaykay for me. I cared for him more than I wanted to, but whenever I felt anything for him, I reminded myself that he said he didn't want a relationship. He thought he was slick though, said he didn't care who I messed with but once he found out I was messing with Dre he was texting me off my phone.

- Pierce: Is that guy gonna be at your house tonight?
- Cola: Ye, imma hang wit him tonight
- Pierce: Is he any good?
- Cola: Wouldn't you like to know?
- Pierce: It's cool cause you let him hit it but it's my money that pays your bills
- Cola: Excuse me? Don't get fucking bright, it's my car you driving, this is the business. You can't say you don't want a relationship then catch feelings when a nigga shows he's interested in me...it doesn't work both ways."

He's jealous, I told him not to catch feelings. I get it, there's jus something about me, I've heard it before. It's confusing as hell cause we act like a couple, but neither of us can commit to the title. It's good that he cares but this is jus business though, don't forget that. Don't catch feelings for him.

As much as it was fun keeping Pierce on his toes, Dre and I kept it casual for only a couple more weeks before his nostalgia started to wear off. I tried to find something else for us to do other than sex but there was nothing. He was useless when it came to building furniture, he didn't have a car to take me out but more importantly he didn't stimulate my mind. He was sooo handsome but we couldn't keep a conversation going. What purpose was a man who couldn't leave me feening mentally or physically? There was only so much pizza I could eat, and my body felt tense the more I faked my way through our nights.

I'll admit it was nice when Pierce would drop off the car early and hang out with Kaykay, either by watching a movie or by playing with his toys but I was still holding my breath. I told Pierce

- Cola: "Eventually you'll leave, cause no one ever stays" He looked me in my eyes and said:
- Pierce: "I promise to never leave, I know what it feels like and I don't want to be like everyone else"
- Cola: "Don't make promises you can't keep"

Girl don't fall fo it. Everything is cool now, but he playing games. Stay focused.

- Pierce: You wearing dat niggas watch now?
- Cola: Oh, ye he left it here the otha night, it's nice ain't it
- Pierce: Ye, lemme see it *puts watch on* Nice...it's mine now
- Cola: Naw I gotta give it back to him, why you want his watch anyway?
- Pierce: It's a nice watch, you don't need it. Just tell him you lost it.
- Cola: Ugh fine, you lucky

When Dre came looking for his watch I played it off. "Naw I ain't seen it. I don't think you lost it here" *Girl you sooo wrong fo dis. You betta hope this Karma don't come back to you for it. Anyway, you lucky you cuttin things off with him, no betta time than now.* Things tapered off slowly between Dre and me. I was never free when he wanted to come over anymore and he eventually got tired of asking.

I was used to men chopping me, neva had a problem with that, but it was very rare that I would push myself up on a guy. There was a local Caribbean restaurant in the area that was my go to whenever I needed a quick and cheap meal. I could get chicken, rice and coleslaw for a decent price, a single mother's dream. There was an Asian guy who worked the register that just made my panties wet

whenever I saw him. I knew I probably wasn't his type but man I wanted him. I made sure my sexy voice came through whenever I would order from him. Made sure the lipstick was good, I caught him looking at me a few times, so I know it wasn't just in my head. Since the only time I saw him was at work, he never got the chance to make a move so it woulda been up to me. I went back a few times before I even worked up the courage to hand his brother my phone number to give to him. I was so nervous. *What if he doesn't text me? Well then, I guess he wasn't interested. You think he likes black chicks? He probably wants some slim Asian woman. Don't get your hopes up. He's probably gonna text. I can't believe you actually handed him your number. You're bold girl.*
He texted the next day!

- Josh: Hey, it's the guy from the restaurant

Omg he texted me, play casual

- Cola: Oh hey, wassup

From the conversation that followed I learned he was Cambodian, loved poetry and was Christian. Cha ching, the same kinda things I was into. I checked out his poetry on his Facebook and it was beautifully dope. He talked about the struggle between being a Christian and wanting to be in the streets. Being Christian came with a lot of weight. Most of the Christians I knew were all holier than thou, like they ain't neva experienced life or been through some shit. Not Josh though, he seemed to understand the delicate balance of wanting to be better yet constantly falling short. I loved that we had things in common and things we could talk about. He said he wasn't tryna be in no relationship. I said I just wanted to fuck with no strings attached. "What we do ain't nobody have to know, and when I see you on the streets I'll act like I don't know you". Truth was, I didn't think I was his type for a relationship, not jus cause of my weight but I wasn't sure he was into dating black chicks. For me it was easier to have sex than face the truth he wasn't into me. I don't regret my decision cause he was everything and even more than what I expected.

The first time we had sex it was a bit awkward, but once we got into a rhythm he turned out to be a good fit.

He kissed me with intention, his touch was gentle, and for an Asian man his dick size had me singing praises. His depth was incredible, the more he gave the more I wanted to give back. We mutually cared for each other's satisfaction and he didn't leave quick once he bussed. It was a nice change; chillin, fucking and talking. I looked forward to him cummin and I was enjoying my time with him the few times a week he came over after he was done at the restaurant. He was someone Pierce didn't need to know about right away. If it came up I'd tell him, but I wasn't gonna go out of my way. For the time being we were just gonna enjoy each other's company. It was times when I was with him I was able to ignore all the other bullshit going on in my life. One of those things being this stupid disease. Muscular Dystrophy was infiltrating our lives like dandelions through the concrete or ivy on a brick wall. Everything we did this disease surrounded us. The food we ate, the appointments, the doctors' visits, the rehab, the constipation. It felt like we couldn't breathe.

At the previous rehab therapy appointment everything I was fighting so hard against was now dropped onto my lap. We had done the running tests as always except this time his results showed that his time was slower than the previous time. When they did the physical check of his legs they noticed that his muscles had become tighter which could impact his walking. It was causing him to walk with a bit of a waddle. The only solution was to get a foot brace that would be used to keep his muscles stretched for a few hours a day. It was a scary thought for me. I tried to deal with his DMD very minimally. As much as I could I tried to ignore it but still deal with it at the same time. He had the unavoidable constipation, but as far as things were concerned he was doing pretty good. Most people didn't even know he had a disability, he played, ran, talked just like all the other kids and I treated him no different. Even I forgot sometimes, I really didn't want him to feel bad about himself.

The reality of this conversation about braces was just more than I could wrap my head around. The price of the brace was more than $1000, which I didn't have. But then I found out that we were eligible for partial coverage through his government disability plan. Besides price, this conversation about foot braces was the last thing I wanted to discuss. If his mobility was slowing down it meant the disease had accelerated. I wasn't ready for that. I wasn't ready for the talk about steroids and wheelchairs. It was a lot to handle. I felt very alone, my family was there, but I ran the day to day activities with Kaykay, and I alone had to apply for the braces. I tried to stay positive, I never wanted him to see me crying or upset. I just didn't know how to process everything. I tried to think of all I could to make enough money to pay for the additional costs of the braces. At the same time, I realized that not enough people truly knew of our situation. Most people didn't know what DMD even was.

I had an idea to throw a fundraiser in our program room downstairs that would serve as a way to not only raise funds but would educate people as well. School was about to start so I would have to juggle both my classes and planning this event, I just needed to find performers for it. Growing up in church, whenever we needed to raise money we would put on fundraisers. *I know a bunch of artists, maybe that same idea could work here.*

August 23, 2010
Many of u dat know me, know dat my son has a disability...recently I found out dat he is in need of a foot brace 2 help his walking.. I am holdin a raffle 2 help raise money....da gov pays 75% which still leaves me 400$ 2 pay...da raffle prize is a euro gourmet slicer, shredder, scissors and metal peeler...da winner will also receive an extra peeler...tickets are 1 for 5 and 2 for 10..plZ link me if ur interested.

The business with Pierce was doing great, but not enough to pay the difference for the cost of his braces. Not to mention the dynamics of the business was about to switch up now that school was starting back up. Part of the change was that I no longer had the time to drive around with Pierce everyday which meant he now had more responsibility. He had to get up earlier to take Kaykay to daycare, then take me to school, then he had to pick me up from school before picking up Kaykay. To make things easier on him I would prepare to stay at school longer, closer to the time we would pick up Kaykay. Even though it was longer days it helped me save time looking for parking. The business wasn't so much of a need for me once OSAP had kicked in, but he still needed the car so any money I made was extra. As much as he could he was tryna build himself and his career, he worked later into the night and on weekends. His ambition was sexy. I always admired a man who didn't give up. I watched all throughout the summer how he worked hard to finish up his high school credits, make money, make music, build himself up and take care of his mom and lil brother. I had judged him in the beginning for being a street hustler but he was bringing in decent money and maintained a living, something I could barely do. I was all kinds of proud of him and I told him all the time. "You're doing good, you're makin something of yourself. I'm proud of you, I think you're smart, you're handsome, you got this" He didn't seem to believe in himself the way I did.

Since I was no longer able to drive around with him he asked if his girl cousin could drive around with him to fill the gaps, as long as I met her, and he didn't let her drive I'd be ok with it. I wasn't even supposed to let him drive but I trusted him. We understood that if anything happened he would absorb costs and blame. I met her on our last ride together. She got in the back and Pierce introduced us. "Hey Cola, this is my cousin Melissa, Melissa this is Cola." We both replied "Hey" but from that point on it was one of the quietest rides we had. I couldn't tell if we'd hit it off and admittedly that first week was challenging at times to see her sitting upfront where I used to sit, but I kept telling myself it was jus business. The switch didn't seem to affect us, if anything it brought us closer. Since we didn't spend hours together in the car it seemed like he made more of an effort to chill with me and Kaykay at the house. The time at the house gave us a chance to talk on a deeper level, more focused when we weren't tryna sell in between. It was nice though cause *I missed him. Missed his touch. Missed the way he looked at me.* I appreciated our time cause I felt the difference every time his cousin was around vs. when it was just us two. I couldn't understand why there was a change, but I felt it. I would tell myself *you're crazy, don't get jealous. You really gonna get jealous over a cousin? Naw ignore that.* But it was a continuous thing, so I had to ask him wassup one day when they picked me up from school early.

- Cola: Why you always quiet nowadays? It seems different ever since your cousin has been riding with you
- Pierce: It's nun, just got a lot on my mind.
- Cola: Ye, but every ride? You barely say anything in the car, we don't laugh, don't joke, like wassup?
- Pierce: Nun
- Cola: Iight cool, I'll try to leave it alone

Sharing the car was becoming more of a challenge. We were going on month two and between the time Pierce had to do drop offs and pickups, there was barely enough time for him to get into a rhythm to make enough money. He still had the same amount of bills but the money coming in was less. We needed a quick solution which happened to be his car. The problem was we had to get the car moving on the road but for the time we weren't able to make those adjustments, so we just had to balance things out better. Which meant he would take the car overnight. From when he dropped us home, I was without a car till the next day. It also meant our time chilling was short.

- Pierce: I missed you
- Cola: Oh ye? What you miss?
- Pierce: *slaps cola's ass* This
- Cola: Oh yea, so come get it then
- Pierce: Come here
- Cola: Ain't ya cousin waiting in the car outside?
- Pierce: She's ok, so you don't want none of this then? C'mere, bend over, just like that.

There was something about the way we connected. Seconds seemed like minutes. Maybe it was his force, maybe the way I held on tight. Maybe the way he seemed to give it his all. We'd never made love or even had sex looking into each other's eyes but there was still something there. I think we were both afraid of what would happen if we looked at each other and saw each other on a deeper level. With each slap I said his name and kept saying it until he bussed. Then he cleaned himself up and went back out to his cousin in the car. *You really let him fuck you with his cousin sittin in the car? What kinda disrespectful thing is that? This don't mean shit, know your place. Notice how he seems to dip right after?* I wanted to like him, I wanted him to like me, but I knew my place so whenever emotions came up I reminded myself that no matta how things appeared, I wasn't his girl. He was honest with me and even though his actions showed he cared, showed he wanted me, showed he wanted to be in our lives, he said he didn't want that. His words, his words were important. As long as I knew he didn't want this, until he came and said to me "I want you to be my girl", we were gonna stay in the same situation, one I couldn't lend my heart to. So, I occupied my heart with other things - men, food, workouts and being a mom to KayKay.

I had met a really dope woman trainer named Nikki and I hit her up whenever I had money to keep me on track with my workouts. What I loved about her was that she was mobile, so even when I didn't have the car I could still schedule in a workout session. She got to my house one day and says, "Who's that girl I saw outside driving your car?" I'm like what you mean? There ain't no girl driving my car. I walk outside only to see Melissa in my driver's seat. I was livid. I didn't have many rules but that was a big one for me. I shouldn't even have Pierce driving my car, especially not after he bumped into another car. That day when he called to tell me I thought I was gonna lose it. I nearly threw up, I had nerves and butterflies running all through my body, it felt like I couldn't breathe. Luckily for me, the damage was done to my car and the other person agreed to let it go. I saw my license flash before my eyes. To go through that and to still have him letting this chick drive my car? Naw, this was too much. Cousin or not, they weren't worth the risk.

- Pierce: I'm really sorry, ok? I messed up, I promise I won't do it again. I won't let her drive. I'm sorry

It was like next level betrayal to me. How do I trust him and go forward? I know he still needed the car though and I didn't wanna come off as some crazy jealous chick. At least he apologized, hopefully from this point on we could build back some kinda trust cause his nostalgia was wearing off. I guess only time would tell. All I knew was I was putting too much energy into just one guy, it was clouding up my mind, I had to switch things up a bit.

At times it was a challenge balancing the guys I was seeing. I had to keep them organized and keep my feelings compartmentalized for all of them. If they caught feelings that was their own fault, I wasn't gonna be played like that. I usually spaced out the days and weeks to make sure there was no overlapping. This week though somehow I was seeing them each on a different night. Monday was Pierce, Tuesday was with this Spanish guy I met at the bank, Wednesday was Josh the Asian guy and Thursday was another random. Shit I didn't even know I had that many dudes running at the same time. It was gettin a bit confusing but as they disappointed me I cut them off. In the end it was back to Pierce and Josh. I loved Josh's poetry and ability to communicate and with Pierce I loved his security. For the moment we lived in a fairytale. It was cute when he would come home and show me his marks from school. I cooked for him and he brought home the money.

Having steady money meant I was mobile again but the issue of the car kept rising. When I really needed the car, Pierce brought it back but at the sacrifice of losing a day of money. It couldn't be avoided though, we were left with no choice but to get his car fixed. We were hoping he woulda gotten his G2 by now but there jus wasn't enough money to make it all work. He bought his Chevy from a friend who had said it only needed "minor fixes". $800 later and we still had to register the car and get insurance on it. It seemed more like his friend was just trying to dump a car on him than help him out.

I offered to put the car in my name until he got his g2 and could legally drive the car. Since the car was going in my name initially I brought it to my mechanics at Keele and Eglinton. As I stood at the counter this tall light skin brotha walked in with his friend. He walked with a swag and a step, he was cute. He looked old, but he also looked pretty fly. I was trying not to pay him much attention while hopin he wouldn't notice me, but he did. We made small talk while I waited for my car to be brought around. His name was Leo, he was about 11 years older than me and he was some kinda businessman. His voice was alluring, he tried puttin on a whisper as he spoke to make himself seem sexier. Before the conversation could go any further my mechanic came back with my bill. I ended up paying for all the repairs, the transfers and everything the car needed to get it ready for the road. As I go to leave Leo hands me his phone and says "Here, put your number in my phone" I was kinda shocked. *This man was damn bold. Who does he think he is? Can't say please? What makes him think I'm gonna put my number in his phone? He's so damn bright.* It was kinda intriguing though, so I put my number in his phone and in return he gave me his number then I sashayed to my car forgetting all about him. He had contacted me the day after, but I had no real intentions of actually talking to him, so I blew him off.

Pierce and I wrote out an agreement that he signed stating that he would pay me the sum of $800 once he got his g2 and I would transfer the car into his name. It was easier now that we had two cars cause he didn't have to pick me up and drop me home. It also made it easier to pick up my supplies for my fundraiser.

Finally, the day came for the event and I was nervous, would people show up? It was forecasted to be horrible weather and not many people had accepted my invite on Facebook. I at least had my performers confirmed. I was doing a spoken word piece along with some of the other girls from my writing group; even Pierce was going to take time out to support us and perform. I had designed educational brochures filled with games to create a fun teachable experience for people who knew nothing about DMD. It was a lot of hard work, but I was proud that I was pulling it off. I had ordered a cake with Kaykay's face on it and had everything lined up. That night was one of the most fun nights we had since we learned about DMD. Even though it was a blizzard outside, I had friends who traveled the distance just to show their support. It was quite a humbling experience. It let me know that I wasn't as alone as I felt. I invited his father, but he wasn't interested in coming. He was still singing the "I'm not the father" tune. Which was fine, I couldn't force him to do something he didn't want to.

Based on my experience that night I wanted to start a charity to provide scholarships to mothers with children with disabilities, but I needed to get a few more people on board with my idea to really execute a working plan. For now, I was tryna keep a handle on school and this side hustle.

Things were easier with 2 cars but unfortunately that didn't last long. My Neon had run its last course within the month cause it needed a new transmission, money which I didn't have. I had spent nearly $1000 on the Chevy and this Neon was going to be at least $1000-$1500 to fix. It just didn't seem worth it yet. I temporarily said goodbye to my neon and started using the Chevy as the new driving source, but I was hopin to fix my first love once I got all the money together or transferred the Chevy back to Pierce.

The colder it got the less sales Pierce was able to make which was stressful for him. People weren't on the road as much which made it challenging to sell. Since his business was changing he was hoping to slightly change our agreement to lessen the daily rate but if I lowered the rate then it wouldn't even be worth it for me. It wasn't personal, it was just business. There was still the wear and tear to think about. Although we were technically driving his car, I had still put a lot of work into it just to get it running. I was still expecting that he was going to pay me for the repairs, but this damn car became our ultimate demise. How conveniently he tried to ignore all the work that went into the car once his business was slowing down. I was just leaving my mechanics when I decided to call Pierce cause he was texting me on some bullshit bout the car.

- Cola: Pierce we had an agreement, I put the car on the road and you would pay me for everything once you got your G2. It's not my fault your friend sold you a lemon, but with repairs, emission test and winter tires, the cost is $800. That's what we agreed upon, that's what we wrote down.
- Pierce: Why am I paying for tires? Naw I think I should only pay $500 for the car, it can't be worth more than that.
- Cola: I don't give a shit what it's worth, I'm telling you what I paid. And what you mean why are you paying for tires? Your tires were busted so I had to buy new tires for the car. $500 ain't gonna work, that still puts me out money and this ain't even my damn car. Listen just pay what we agreed and you can take your car.
- Pierce: Why am I paying you so much for my own car?
- Cola: That's not my problem, you signed the agreement
- Pierce: Jokes on you, I didn't even sign my real name, so I'm not bound to that.
- Cola: Are you dumb? That's the name I know you by, so even if you tried to pull one over on me that's the name you go by, that's the same name the judge is gonna use. You think you're slick? Listen gimme back my fucking money or I'm keepin the damn car. Don't come to me with less than $800.
- Pierce: You're really gonna steal my car from me?
- Cola: How the fuck am I stealing your car? You think I want your lil shit box bucket? Once you pay me imma fix up my other car, stop playing games and send me my money.
- Pierce: How I know you gonna gimme the car back?
- Cola: Are you not listening to anything? You're a fucking idiot, I DON'T WANT YOUR SHIT BOX CAR. You really think I need to steal from you?

Don't insult me. Listen, imma say it again, gimme my damn money or I'm keeping your damn car.

Click.

Dis nigga stupid, he had me up in my damn feelings. How could he think I wanted to steal his 1998 Chevy when I drove a 2002 Neon? His shit box car was nothing to write home about. Plus, the car was in my name... He wasn't about to play me though, if he didn't wanna pay the money then I would just keep the damn car. It seemed like people were just out to cheese me that day. Still vexed I called my girl Sharie from the building to tell her how this nigga tried to play me. I was expecting her to laugh with me but instead she said, "Oh so you gonna sue him like you sue everyone else?" Bish wha? Wha you mean like I sue everyone else? Do I not have a right to defend myself? She was referring to a story I had told her about an ex friend who had screwed me over.

She was talking about Dela. The same Dela who was at my house party, the same Dela I grew up with and our families went to church together. The same Dela that was like a sister to me and Kaykay's unofficial godmother. My sis an her brother were tight. It was a bonus that their family were French speaking Africans and we spoke French, so I understood and fit in for the most part. Whenever I needed my hair braided she was the one to do it. Normally I would just pay her for her work, but this time I wanted to do something a bit different. Dela could never keep a phone, either it broke or she lost it or something. But recently she was telling me how she had tried to help her brother out by putting a phone in his name and he ran up the bill and refused to pay. Even though she needed a phone she couldn't even get one because her credit was damaged. Instead of paying her for my hair I offered to not only buy her a phone but to put the phone in my name as well. It sucked what her brother had done to her. She ain't deserve that cause she was always tryna help other people out. She was family, as long as she paid the bill I had no problems. No sooner after I got her the phone did she run up the bill. I only found out after getting a call from the phone collection company. I was shocked, they said that she ain't paid since the phone was activated. When I called her on it she said it was some issue with the phone company, but she would start making payments; so, I got it sorted out and paid the $300 owed. Months after that I got another call, this time the bill was more than $600, so I had them shut her phone off. She clearly didn't care to tell me wassup and was making crazy long distance calls. I didn't even tell her shit, I was wondering how long it would take until she contacted me. Didn't take long before she called me saying

- Dela: Yo Nicky they cut the phone off, is your phone working?
- Cola: I had your phone turned off. You ran the bill up again to $600? Who the hell is supposed to pay that? I paid off the first bill to help you out, but this is getting out of hand. You clearly don't deserve the phone. You're doing to me exactly what your brother just did to you; why? I've always tried to help you out so why would you do this?
- Dela: So, it's like that? You're really gonna treat me like this and cut the phone off on me? You didn't even let me know. You coulda asked me about the payment but now I'm gonna pay nothing on it. Goodluck
- Cola: What the fuck you mean you ain't gonna pay nun on the bill. Are you dumb? Who you expect to pay that? You really gonna stick me with the bill? You're on a brand new contract that has years left to pay off.
- Dela: I'm not paying anything
- Cola: Some family you are, if you ain't gonna pay then imma have to take you to court.
- Dela: Do what you gotta do.

Click.

It had taken me a whole year to fight her in court. I had never sued anybody and since she lived back where my parents did I had to drive to and from Toronto to make it to the court appearances. I didn't really wanna sue her but it was the principal of the matter. I had gone outta my way to get her a phone and she took advantage of me, not once but twice. When I called the phone company my only options were to transfer to her name, or to pay out the contract which still had over $1000 left to pay off. We clearly weren't on any good terms to put it in her name, plus that would mean she rightfully inherited her debt which she wasn't tryna do. In the end I had more than enough evidence to win my case, plus she didn't even care enough to show up for court. It was a short-lived victory when I won cause I learned winning was only half the battle. I still had to get her to pay which was hard cause she never held a steady job.

Luckily when I moved into my building my neighbour Sharie and I had become such good friends that she offered to take over the payments for me, so I no longer had to pay two phone bills. But I was feeling the shade heavy from Sharie about her court comment. She added "I gotta make sure I pay my bill so you don't try to take me to court" We laughed but I was like damn that's what you really think of me? I guess I shouldn't have shared that story huh, whatever, I didn't have the energy to over analyze it this time. As for Dela, our friendship was done, besides not paying the bill she had all kinda talks for me. How I'm a horrible mother, I don't take care of my kid, I'm with all these different men. None of this was ever a thing when we were on good terms. Callin me a slut was one thing but talking bout my kid was not okay. This bitch was crazy and I no longer had time for her ass. She was family but apparently family don't mean shit until tragedy strikes. All that drama happened in 2008/2009 but in the summer of 2010, Dela's younger brother was murdered as he tried to break up a fight. All that drama with the phone didn't even matter anymore. I was there for the moments that mattered. It was like old times. After the funeral Dela and I tried to maintain the friendship, but I couldn't get past the names she called me, and she couldn't get past the fact that I had taken her to court. Hopefully one day we can meet on even grounds. When it counts, she's still family. I always hated that money could ruin a friendship. It seemed like I hadn't even learned from that situation, here I was again fighting a nigga for money.

Pierce and I were at a standstill. He was still laughing saying he wasn't gonna pay, I was laughing telling him to get used to taking the bus again. The friendship was over once he started calling me out my name. Said I was a crazy fat bitch and a hoe he used to get his dick sucked. Funny, I thought I was the best he eva had. I wasn't a hoe, bitch, crazy or fat when he was deep inside me or when I was helping him out, but I guess that didn't matter once he couldn't get his way. He coulda been mad all he wanted but I didn't stand for no disrespect. As quickly as he entered my life he exited. Like I told him before "Don't make promises you can't keep" Foreva was neva gonna last. I always knew that.

That wasn't the only thing that didn't last that month, my Asian fling was done the minute I found out he had a girlfriend. I believe fossbook gave it away. He neva had one when we started sooooooooooo, I guess somewhere in between fucking me he was whispering sweet words to anotha ting. It was neva anything more than what it was but my number one rule for myself was not to mess with men who were already booed up. I had seen a cute pic of them together and inquired who she was. It wasn't my style to be with no next chick's man, I wasn't a homewrecker, I respected women and relationships enough to leave things as they were. *Damnit Cola, you always end up in this situation. Always a side bitch neva the main dish. What's up with you?* I didn't even know if we had messed around when he had a girl or if I was finding out just as they started. But as I questioned him bout his Asian boo it seemed more an more like there was an overlap. He has the nerve to say, "My girl said it's cool if we still mess around though" Hmm pause, so I said, "What you mean mess around?" He must of lost his mind when he said, "You can still suck my dick cause she doesn't do that". *So, what the fuck I look like? Some desperate chick feening for leftovers? The nerve of this fucking man. Bruh if I coulda reached through my phone I woulda slapped him so hard.* Yes, I was damn up in my feelings, so apparently, t's cool to be the black bitch on the DL, but to the world he shows off his slim Asian ting. Everything I thought was coming true and this man had the nerve to act like all I did was suck his dick. Da fuck? Apparently I missed the memo. All I had to say was "Go focus on your relationship and Imma keep doing me". The level of disrespect I felt had me feeling like it was time to make some major changes again which usually meant it was time to hit up church. It always made me feel some kinda special, no matta how long I stayed away, church was always a place of familiarity which was exactly what I needed cause I couldn't recognize myself or the people around me no more.

CHAPTER FORTY-SIX

Miss Independent

Turn to me and be gracious to me and show me favor, as is Your way to those who love Your name.
-Psalm 119:132

I moved out of the bedroom when I could no longer sleep in there. Recurring memories of the trauma wouldn't allow me to have any peace until a few friends suggested that I "pray out my space". I didn't know what that meant. I knew you prayed for a space before you moved in, but I was already here. What could God do about the space? It happened, things happened, it had already passed, yet when I let them pray through my phone speaker phone there was a shift in my atmosphere. The air felt lighter. I wasn't as afraid of the dark as I used to be. It wasn't an immediate; Hooray, I'm free! It was an unexplainable shift. Before the call ended my friend said "I see your book becoming your ministry". Such a simple sentence, but it became a defining moment for me. As desperate as I felt, I decided that no matta what happened to me, I would write it down and let the pain be the bricks to my foundation.

My sister had come to live with me since I lived closer to her college. It was nice having my lil sis with me. I mean she visited practically every weekend, but it was good to have her at the house more regularly and I know Kaykay loved it. They had this incredible bond, it was always fun to watch cause she was the "fun" one and spoiled him rotten with anything he needed. With her at the house we lived in the living room and Kaykay got the bedroom. I had switched around the bedroom to give Kaykay his own space, he upgraded to the big kid bed, had his own tv, and had his toys all set up; now that he was four, he was grown.

I survived to December. This was a huge deal. It didn't feel like I would at times, but I'm here.

> December 7, 2010
> Dear girls....yall make me sick....the end...

It had been months and Leah was still running her mouth bout me. Last I heard she was telling some guy down at Yonge and Sheppard about me. She was just out of control but if that wasn't bad enough, I had just lost my best friend in the building and I couldn't even begin to understand what happened. For the short time I had been living in the buildin Sharie and I had become close, like even her family was like family, you kno? Anyway, I had invited her to church one night and she wasn't able to come, no problem, but then the next day all hell seemed to break loose. I mussa answered a text message wrong or not answered it, iuno. Alls I knew was that she started bringing up shit she seemed to have kept in her books against me. She started saying how this one time I had made a comment she didn't like. But from what I remembered there was more than one person who made a comment and we was allll laughing. All of a sudden it was a problem. Then she said how I always throw the things that I do for her in her face. So, I'm like "Gimme an example so I know what you're talking about". I'm still waiting. The most she could say was this one time I got mad that she brought my car back late and made me late for class. Besides that, I couldn't think of anything else I said, *or at least I didn't think I did.* Then she said how I never offered to babysit anymore. *Didn't know I was supposed to but ok.* Then my favorite part was when she said "You're mad that I didn't go to church with you last night, that's why you didn't talk to me this morning".

Church was a personal thing so there was no reason for me to get mad if someone doesn't wanna go. She agreed to go an then cancelled last minute but that had nothing to do with anything. I was working out my own shit. This was the time BBM was gettin ppl in trouble. That same day she had asked me for a huge favor but I didn't see it until hours later when I got home from church. I guess it looked like I saw the message and ignored it. By time I got home there were text messages saying she didn't wanna be friends no more. I felt like she jus woke up one day and decided she no longer wanted to be friends and was looking for a way out. I was crushed. I had seen her cuss other people out, but I never thought it woulda happened to me. Within a few days her and her whole family unfriended me on Facebook. *It's that serious guys? Really? Facebook? Really? Me... Mad? I don't even get mad like that. How do I throw shit in her face? Do I do that? What shit? The times I've helped her? I don't even say nun. She used my car whenever she needed, no problem, where is this shit coming from? Damn, the one person I truly thought I had here in Toronto. Like the family away from home. This is why I don't trust people, nothing sticks, nothing's real anymore.*

It got worse when I heard she was talking behind my back just like Leah was. *Fuck females.* Imma keep that love like Jesus but keep my distance like Ye - Kanye. As much as I had been hurt by men, at this point I'd take a man over a female any day. At least with men I expected the betrayal so when it came, I already knew it was coming. With females we supposed to look out for each other, not cut one another down, but it seemed like no one had gotten that memo. Then just when I thought life wasn't gonna get worse, it does.

December 14, 2010 ·
wow....all my mistakes catching up with me all at once...lord help me...

I hate cops. Not just cause I lived in the hood and they harassed me every second they could. Not cause when I needed protection from a verbally abusive ex boyfriend and baby fadda they told me they were unable to actually do anything unless they both physically attacked me. Naw, I hate cops because they're trying to take away my independence.

One morning I was rushing to get Kaykay to daycare, so I ran out of the house, threw him in the car and drove the 5 min, a few blocks drive up the road to his daycare. As I drove back from his daycare, a block away from home I noticed a cop car in the lane next to me. Damn, I realized I didn't have my seat belt on so I tried to slickly put it on as I waited for the light to turn green and prayed he didn't see me. Whoop whoop! Within seconds this cop pulls me over on a side street. As he walks up to my car I look for my ID because I already know he's going to ask; except my purse wasn't in the car. Damn. So, I was tryna play it cool now that I realize I have no ID on me. I answered his questions as politely as I could, and I found an expired insurance leaf in my glove compartment that I handed him while promising him the up to date papers were in my purse at home. He took what seemed like forever to look up my information then calmly walked back to the car and handed me three tickets. Three bumbaclot tickets, with such a smug look on his face.

ASDHJHDSFHA!!! That's how I felt on the inside, but on the outside I said "Ok, thank you, have a good day!" *THE FUCK? THREE* TICKETS? THREE tickets? three.... tickets, UGHGHGH! One for not wearing my seatbelt, the other for my missing driver's license and the last for my missing insurance card. As mad as I was I thought ok, no problem. I have valid insurance papers so I'll just fight these, no problem!

Within two days I got a call from my broker asking if I was recently pulled over by the cops. "Yea, why? I was gonna fight the tickets he gave me" Not so fast, apparently after he gave me the tickets he made a phone call to the insurance company and reported my insurance as fraudulent. "That's crazy, I'm not a fraud" That wasn't the issue, the issue was that the address on my insurance and the address of my driver's license were listed as two different cities. My insurance address was that of my parents in Courtice, from when I lived there, and the address of my driver's license was that of my apartment in Toronto. The main reason for the difference was that the car used to be in my mom's name and with me being in the JnF area I was constantly being stopped by the cops. One cop had informed me that if I was temporarily living in the area then I should change my drivers license for the sake of not being harassed as much.

When I had sent in my information to my new broker he didn't mention that there was anything wrong, so I assumed all was correct.... until now. With the cop calling me in as a fraud the insurance company had looked up my name and realized that I had an apartment registered in my name in Toronto. They deemed this as misrepresentation and gave me only two options. Either I pay the difference in what the rate was between the two areas at a price of $3500 within two weeks or they would cancel me and unofficially black ball me for material misrepresentation. Either way I was stuck and super annoyed. I was advised to contact the ombudsman of the company as it seemed like they were dealing with me a bit harsh and the minute I got off the phone I drove right down to the police station looking for the jerk who set off the grenade. Technically, I was away for school and would be returning home once I graduated, so what the hell was the problem?

Lucky for the asshole, I didn't know his name so complaining was useless. The cop with whom I spoke to said there was no need for the cop to report. I guess he did it for shits and giggles, but it was fucking up my life. I wish he coulda seen the damage he cost me. I feel like some cops like to provoke people and mess with some people who are just tryna live life while crimes were ACTUALLY happening all around me. I couldn't get no help when threats were coming my way but lemme try to be a good mom and shit just went real left on me. The ombudsman declined to help me even when I said I was a single mom with a child with a disability that I needed to take care of...it didn't matter. *What the fuck is an ombudsman good for?* My only option now was to take the money from my student loan. That was just a lot of money to lose all at once. With all of this bullshit going on I looked forward to the fact that the writing program was still going strong in my building. That support was so needed. We were about to launch a website that had all our writing on it. How dope! Finally published!

·December 28, 2010 ·
Women with words got some real hot writing going on...to all my friends plz support me an check out wasssup wit the site.. womenzwordz.wordpress.com

The high of the new website was enough to get me to New Years Eve. Not to mention I just found out a new writing program I applied to called A.M.Y. had jus accepted me into their program. I had applied to two, A.M.Y. was run by white people and Obsidian was a black theater company - I wasn't accepted into their program. I always had this weird thing where I wasn't black enough for the black kids, yet I was too black for the white kids; this oddly reminded me of that but who cares? At least I was accepted by someone. Leah had applied to the same program but didn't get in soooooo I needed to just count my blessings. It didn't start till the new year so I still had time to focus on that, but for now I needed things to make sense again. I needed things to be ok again. I needed God. I had barely been to church throughout the course of the year, I mean I tried, but I was never comfortable. The only church I knew was the same place I met my rapist and I was scared that I might see him, so I avoided church all together. I would go every now an then when the guilt hit, but nothing consistent. My heart was aching though. Sometimes it felt like I was a kid looking in the window of a candy store seeing how joyful everyone was, but I was left in the cold, broken and miserable.

Christmas came and I had my usual sense of dread going to my grammas house. That place was filled with so many traumatic memories, not to mention the bullying from my family. They weren't actively calling me names or talking about how bad I was, but I still felt unwelcome. Kaykay was my saving grace, everyone loved him and he was a good buffer. To avoid everything I just usually stayed on my phone, chatting with people. I got a "Merry Christmas" text on Christmas from a number I didn't know.

"New phone who dis?" "Leo" *Who is that again? Oh, right, the car mechanic, sweet talking light skin nigga with ol swag.* I love those texts, people who haven't spoken all year seem to reconnect for the sake of Saint Nick. Anyway, he had invited me over for New Years but I made the choice to choose God instead. This was gonna be good.

What I didn't know was that they were doing baptism that same night and I had arrived early enough to catch it. Now baptism has been a soft spot for me ever since my church essentially pushed me out. Well it was more than a push out, they flat out denied me only minutes before I was to be baptized. My heart still hurts just thinking bout it. I still haven't been baptised yet. The memory had been too painful to go back and revisit that. *What if they just rejected me again? Two-time rejection was more than enough for me.* Since I was already here, I decided I'd sit and watch. As I sat in the church that night the candidates for baptism were giving an account of why they wanted to get baptized. Most of them said "I really have to thank my mentor for praying with me, checking in on me, and helping me to stay on this good path even when times seemed hard. With all the changes I've made internally I really wanted to show the world externally what God was doing for me"

That's good, right? Right? *Soooo where was my mentor? Where was the person who was supposed to check up on me? I heard "I'll call you hun", and I never got a call, and yet here they are, a plethora of mentors. God you didn't think I needed a mentor? You didn't think that could help? So wha? I'm jus expected to get through life when everything keeps happening to me? I have yet to catch a damn break. Everywhere I turn there's something else happening, another sickness, another bill, IT NEVER ENDS. Am I not good enough for you? I tried to get baptized, I tried. I tried to show the world I was ready and what did they do? They chased me out, they told me no, they stopped me from singing, they wouldn't allow me to participate. They kept their kids from hanging out with me. I was the SCUM of the church because I was pregnant and I wasn't good enough then, but this whole time I coulda had help and you sent NO ONE to help me? Why? What have I done to deserve this? Because I got pregnant? I'm sorry, I'm sorry. I love my son, I'm sorry I'm not good enough. I don't think I ever will be.*

As quickly as I wiped the tears away from my face they would fall right back. I was immensely hurt. I had never questioned God before, it was never my place to, but I was hurt. I felt like my heart broke into so many pieces. I felt like if even God didn't want me, then what the fuck was the point? Where were my mentors? Where was the person who was to help me get back on track? Where was the person who cared enough to text me and check on my spiritual well being? Why didn't God love me enough to send someone my way to help me out? Why did I have to figure out everything on my own? Why was I not allowed to get baptized? Was I really not good enough because I had my son? Did God really turn his back on me for what I did? No love for the unwed mother? No love for the sinner? No room in the church for mistakes? I walked out of the church as quickly as I could. This anger in me was boiling. Since it was a celebratory night, most of my friends were already out having fun. I dialed Leo's number desperate not to be forced to return to my empty apartment. *I remember this guy. Just like at the mechanic's that day, this man still has his swag on point. He had a grey fedora hat, long black jacket, pimped out shoes, man was styling. The dark colors looked good against his light skin.* I chilled with him and his cousin for a bit at a local restaurant before Leo and I made our way back to his office.

Wasn't long before he had me spread out on top of his desk and penetrated me with his tongue. I've often heard this saying from Jamaican men, bodman nah nyam fish; translation, gangstas don't eat pussy. Lies, on top of his desk he penetrated me in several different ways, and when he was done, I sat up and cried. *This is a new low, even for you. Did you really do that? No wonder God don't want ya ass. You really have no respect. You don't know how to just say no?* My anger and rejection had caused me to have sex with a complete stranger, in an office, on a desk, and I didn't even know his real name. He held me as I cried, confused as hell he said "Why are you crying?" I sobbed silently without response. He tries again "Is it cause you think imma judge you cause we jus had sex?" I nod my head yes "Baby girl, I'm a grown man, that shit don't phase me, I'm not judging you and I'm not gonna leave you just like that, I'll always take care of you" I guess that was all I needed to hear cause I brought him home with me and we spent the rest of the morning enjoying each others company.

My morning was full of regret. I'm looking at this man and all I can think of is his age. *This nigga 11 years older, really Cola? Really? You couldn't find no one your age eh? What's the number one rule? No niggas over 3 years, 5 max. You jus go let some old dick up in you eh?* I didn't know what to do with myself. I'm looking into his eyes and they're beautiful, warm, and caring, he spoke so gently as he said, "Don't tell anyone I ate you out, not even your girls" "Don't worry I won't" Once we got up he took me out to eat and he said he'd text me later. As I was driving myself back home I realized *old nigga meant he wasn't a broke ass. Maybe there were some perks after all.* This was just the beginning for us. An the minute I got home. "Girrrlllllll guess what happened last night...." I had checked all the Happy New Years messages and realized Nathaniel had left a message on my wall asking for my number.

January 1st 2011
lol here nerd....my house phone....*******an my cell is ******...lol don't lose it now

womenzwordz.wordpress.com ...check it out...under miss cola....

Nathaniel and I reconnected enough to be cordial. He had moved out of town after we split and was coming back to Toronto for an appointment. Only thing was he needed somewhere to crash for a couple days and thought he'd ask me. Actually, it was more than a couple days...it was three months to be exact and he was kinda scared to ask based on how things ended. Truth be told I didn't hold grudges like that, if he needed a place to stay than I'd help him out. I rather he stay with me than at a shelter, plus it wasn't going to be a long stay, only three months. I had to try to explain this to my sister, it's reasonable right?

Poetic Interlude

I've heard stories that the straighter my weave
The more I should believe that success would be inevitable
Incredible
Because the style of my hair could not even compare to the fact that my skin is still
Black
Backing me into the deep corners and shadows of my history
If I even tried to solve the mystery of kinky hair the only results I would find is that God truly made us a special kind of people
Not special as in better
Or superior
That's not the message we want to be teaching the next generation
But this newest population needs to understand the powerful det-onation resonating in solidarity instead of separation
Especially if the nation adopts a notion of criticism and discrimi-nation
Lets increase our community support
Supporting one another
Like sista and brotha
Raising our voices to the sky
Hi
My name is Cola and
I
Am
Just like my hair
Funky and free
Sometimes wild like a tree
I may braid it to tame it
Shave it

Color it
Wave it or shape it
Its beauty knows no bounds
My beauty had to re learn the sounds of love
An emotion that now makes me proud of this creation from the creator up above
Love
My soul urges and searches the highs and lows
To give love
To get love
To show love
To know love
Cause to know love is to know peace
But when there's no love there's no peace
Piecing together my comprehension I've heard mention that we've been crafted with a purpose and released to a destiny filled with choices and opportunities greater than any style that our hairs could be
See no matta what the world throws at me
I'm ready
Whether we become
Bus drivers
Inventors
Teachers
Doctors
Or preachers
Our ability to succeed
Should never exceed
Our appreciation
That we are free
Like John 8:36
Free to forgive and be forgiven
I feel the rhythms of change
Salute to our hair
I've developed a beautifully Multifaceted
Love affair
I declare that we are royalty

CHAPTER FORTY-SEVEN

Jus Right

You love evil more than good, and falsehood more than speaking what is right. Selah.
Psalm 52:3

Being the business man he was, Leo assured me he could get me different insurance without falling victim to their high-priced scam. That being said, I lost my independence January 5th, 2011. That's the day my insurance company terminated my insurance. Don't matta how many months or years I was a faithful client or paid my damn insurance on time.

According to Leo, for just $1300 I could get new insurance and my bad record wiped clean of all infractions. Sounded like a hood deal, but to me it sounded like a way to provide for my son within a budget that I could manage. That wasn't all the tricks this business savvy man had for me, and I always loved a man who was good with money. Pillow talk was good for more ways than one. Usually in January I spent money on my books, my rent, my courses and before I knew it March had come and money was dried up. Leo was offering me the secret for how white ppl stayed rich - they invested. I had heard of investments but to me they were usually long-term investments that couldn't help me in like the next month.

Since I had just spent an unexpected $1300 I needed to figure out how to keep my flow of money coming, I hated seeing Kaykay suffer and go without food while I tried to finish my degree. I was offered an interesting opportunity to invest my money for a period of 6 weeks with a weekly return of profit while protecting my initial investment. At the end of each 6 weeks I had the option of either re-investing my money or pulling it all out. I was so skeptical because people were always so damn sketchy and after the countless adventures I've had with money, there was no guarantee that this would actually work. Everything in me said *Nooo, don't do it,* but then I thought *well, what do you have to lose?* My initial investment was $3000 and I made sure I got a guarantee and a drawn-up agreement from Leo to ease my conscience. As long as I had proof and a signed agreement I could claim my money back...right?

A week went by and guess what...Cha ching ching, I met up with Leo and he handed me my profits. Bruh! *This shit actually worked!!!* And the week after, an the week after, money stayed in my account. I mean Leo said "I see potential in you, you can go far" I didn't know what he meant but I've always had a love and a sense for business and money. I wasn't always the best with it, but I knew I was a quick learner once given opportunities.

So far, my new year was off to a good start, then I got this message from this blast from the past baby fadda that sent my mind into a frenzy.

January 15th 2011

Kendrick

hey

Cola

hi

Kendrick

Lemme know when ur free in the next 2 weeks...cause I'm booking the test

Cola

I'm free monday an tuesdays..

Kendrick

Alright then, Ur still convinced right?

Cola

yes I am... what's makin you change your mind?

Kendrick: Just wanna prove my point... And so u can stop tryna get money outta me

Cola: fair enough....well I'm free before 4

Kendrick: So wat would u do if he aint mine? Where would u go from there

Cola: I'd apologize an try to fix the situation...do the best I can do....but what if he is yours...where do we go from there?

Kendrick: Then ima do my half

Cola: k

Kendrick: Wat happened to the next guy? Thought there was 2 of us?

Cola: What I was telling you was that your the only person I remember around that time... I understood where u were coming from...but it still came down to you....the otha guy I mentioned to you... I've spoken to him he's seen my son....he said we didnt have sex that day...eitha way like I said if he's not yours... I apologize..an imma do what I gotta do to fix things....but if he is yours....dat means u lost out on 5 years of his life....

Kendrick: we didn't have sex either... buts it's watever... this has been a huge waste of time...but we need to deal wit it once and for all......have a daughter they look nothing alike, hey wats ur #?

Cola: My number is********, my son looks exactly like my sister and my family....ye I agree we do need to deal with this

I hadn't heard from this man in two years, yet here he was. I had long since given up on the fact that he would ever come around but I guess it took time to change. Even though he was singing the same tune, at least now he was ready to deal with the situation. He called me and we spoke about setting up the DNA appointment. He was finally ready to get this over and done with just to prove me wrong. He was even willing to pay for the whole thing. Either way I didn't care, I just wanted him to follow through. The date was set, the time was set, time was ticking down to the reveal.

Speaking of follow-through, Nathaniel and I had previously spoken bout him stayin by me short term and even though my sister wasn't happy with it I was still going ahead with the plan if only Nathaniel could get his shit together long enough for me to actually help him.

January 17th 2011

Cola

you know what Nathaniel....we've talked and I offered my house to you jus tryna help you out....but u come to toronto from thursday....an u say u didnt have my number till I spoke to u on facebook that night...said you would call...but never did...its sunday...and u haven't bothered to get in touch with me....or lemme kno anything thats going on....so since u clearly don't need my help an are fine on your own...then I wish u the best of luck.... I hope your friends are able to help u out the 3 months that you are staying here....

Nati

hey so sorry about everything I had to say what I had to say wit some people and don't sit there putting shit on me like I dont have shit on me already. I thank you for all that you are doing 4 me but if you feel what you feel the fuck you!!!! I am in a trouble moment and the last thing I need on me is people that give up on me easily you FUCKIN FEEL ME

January 18th 2011

Cola

Fuck me?....k coool.....it's not bout givin up on you u.....its bout yu havin the courtesy to call me or message me an lemme kno what's going... I don't mind if you do you.... I don't mind if u check your friends....but let me kno whats poppin....don't ask for help then ignore me.... I still have a life I was tryna make u apart of...u was all mad an shit sayin u have nowhere to go.... I said I gotchu....wouldn't it have made sense to come to me so u have a place to leave your stuff?.... I'm hard on u because I care...an because unlike some ppl u kno... I'm a true friend...if u can't handle me tellin u the truth...then you're right...fuck me...an you should move on with life.... I'm not tryna hold shit on you...not tryna rub it in your face that I was helping u....jus tryna make u see u gotta hold yourself accountable when u mess up...you apologize an you move on.... I hope shit works out for u still.... I don't wish nun bad on you...like I said before...goodluck.....

January 22 2011

Nati
hope all is well with you.
Cola
I am fine Nathaniel thank you

I knew he still needed my help, he still didn't have a place to stay, so yet again I offered him a place to stay on two conditions: he wouldn't drink and he respected my space, no late nights, no disappearing, just get to his appointments and get life together. He agreed and showed up later the next day with his clothes, his PlayStation, and my camera...my missing camera. I woulda been even more annoyed if I wasn't preoccupied with Kendrick and this DNA test. I was nervous as hell. *What if you're wrong? You woulda messed up his life for nothing. I didn't really mess up his life but still, but what if I'm right? What a jerk.* We were supposed to meet later on that week and even though I wasn't sure if I wanted to do it on the inside, on the outside I kept a game face on.

January 24th 2011
Kendrick
Hey lost ur number...msg it back please
Cola
Hey...k it's ********...can yu send me yurs too please...an jus to double check the time is 4 30 right?

I dunno if I was relieved for me or for Kaykay when his dad said we had to postpone. He wanted to use a different center with more flexible hours, so we postponed the test. He couldn't get the time off during their hours of operation. I honestly felt happy. *Phew thank God, I was not ready for that yet.* I wanted to know the truth but it had honestly been so long I was afraid of the same truth I was hoping would vindicate me. More than jus vindication, I had gotten used to life being jus the two of us, and as selfish as it sounds I did not want to share him. Not yet anyway. I knew eventually we'd have to get this done but for now we decided to try again next month which woulda given me time as I was still adjusting to my new guests.

So, it was me, Kaykay, my sister and Nathaniel in my one-bedroom apartment and it was about to get even more crowded. Leo needed a favor from me, he had a cousin in town that needed a place to stay. Mind you there was no room at all, but he asked for me to do him this one favor for only a couple days till he could find him somewhere else to stay. How could I say no to helping someone out? ...Then there were five people in my home. It was an adjustment for sure, and if my sister wasn't ok with Nathaniel this next one was gonna be even more drama. We had different views on helping people, my sister always thought I helped too much and I thought she didn't help enough, either way it didn't change the current situation. Leo's cousin smelt like he hadn't bathed in months and made it even more uncomfortable. I didn't wanna be rude but damn, his scent permeated my couch. It was definitely a nose adjustment, even Kaykay was like "Ahh what smells? Mommy something doesn't smell right" Even though he was right I was still hella embarrassed, why kids gotta point out the obvious? All I could say was "Go to your room" At least he still had his space to himself until his aunty invaded it, tryna get away from the rest of us. What do you get when you put one ex and one yardi in a house full of women?...Jealousy. My ex didn't like that another man was staying in the house and Leo didn't like that my ex was staying at the house. Both men were tryna flex but it didn't phase me. Good thing it was my house and my rules.

Leo's cousin was a budding artist with an upcoming performance so I decided to go and support him. It was a Friday night, Kaykay was already at my moms for the weekends, I had work the next day so I didn't wanna be out late but I went regardless and met Leo there. It was a great performance, great night and when I went looking for Leo so we could leave I found him at the bar flirting with the bartender. It wouldn't have bothered me so much if the first time I asked him to follow me out he actually paid attention. I wasn't familiar with that area of town enough to find my way back home. "Leo, can we please go? I got work in the morning". "Ye, ye, I'm coming" Yet he was still running jokes wit di gyal, so I left. *The fuck I look like standing here waiting for him to finish up his jokes? Imma find my way home and his cousin can come later.*

The subway station was across the street and I was sure there was someone who could tell me which train to take to get back to my area. As I walked into the station the attendant comes out of his booth. The way he was looking at me had me thinking *is he gonna try an chop me? Why he looking at me like that? Just ask him which way and leave.* By now it was two in the morning and I didn't even know if the train was still running but I asked "Which train will take me to the Jane & Sheppard area?" He says "You'd wanna take the westbound train to get home, so where ya man at? Do you have a man?" *I'm smiling cause I knew this was coming. Nigga!! I'm jus tryna get home.* "No, I don't have a man, is the train still running?" "Why are you still single?" "I just am" "Can I have you number?" "No" "C'mon maybe we chill sometime" Before I could even answer, out the corner of my eye I could see Leo and his cousin walking into the station. *Oh shit!* Leo thought he was really slick though. He walked passed me and passed the attendant on the other side of the turn point and positioned himself behind the attendant and faced towards me. He stood and stared me down. *Yo what's he doing? Why he looking at me like that. I ain't even do anything. Damn.* The attendant looks at Leo, then looks back at me and says, "Is that your man?" all I say is "Look I'm jus tryna get home" then I walked passed him towards the stairs while Leo walked behind me. By the time we hit the steps to go down to the subway Leo yells "WHAT THE FUCK ARE YOU DOIN? ARE YOU TRYNA FUCKING EMBARRASS ME?" *Who the fuck this nigga yellin at? If he had left when I said let's go this shit wouldn't of happened. I DIDN'T EVEN DO ANYTHING? WHAT THE FUCK?*

Even though I was screaming on the inside, on the outside I was silent. I just stood there looking at him like he had lost his damn mind. *This man, who's not my man, is yelling at me like I'm some likkle kid.* I think if he coulda boxed me down he would have cause I seen his whole body twitch. But we were literally on the third step. Too many witnesses. "Leo, I was jus asking the guy for directions" "You think I'm stupid? You think I didn't see what was going on on?" so I reply "I don't know what you saw, and I don't care what it looked like, I was jus asking for which train to take to get home, I can't help it if that guy liked me, I said no anywayz", I was afraid to even raise my voice at him. Iuno why, but I was scared to do anything, even to move off the steps. We heard the train going by and tried to run down the steps to catch it. By the time we reached the last step the attendant had already made it down. *How'd he get down here so fast?* We had just missed the last train for the night and now had to find a new way. *Could this night get any longer? I just wanna go home.*

We climbed those steps in silence as we made our way out of the station to catch the night bus. *Where was his cousin this whole time?* It was like his cousin jus appeared outta nowhere cause I didn't see him anywhere on those damn steps with me. We all stood at the bus stop waiting. Leo unable to let this shit go says again "I know what I saw, I know what you were doing, you think I'm stupid" "Imma say it again, I was just tryna get home" then Leo goes "So he wasn't asking for your number?" "Yes, but I said no and that has nothing to do with me" Too Toos Leo walked back to the subway station leaving his cousin and me

He only came back in time to catch the bus as it pulled up. Apparently, since Leo was convinced I was a liar he went back to ask the guy for himself and the guy admitted he was hitting on me. *Well no shit! That's what I said. This man don't listen to me.* Then he says to me "I asked him if he was willing to pay to have sex with you and he said yes." *What the hell? I'm not a prostitute, why would he even ask that? He's fucked. So, he was willing to pay to have sex with me, based on what conversation? I felt so dirty, why would he do that?* I couldn't even look at him anymore, I was so ashamed I kept my face towards the window. "He said he'd pay a good amount for you too. That's what you want, you wanna be a hoe? You tryna embarrass me and lied to me. You wanna be a hoe, you can be a hoe" I couldn't move.

A man sitting in front of us turned around as said "Hey, that's not nice, you shouldn't talk to her like that. You should treat her better than that" I was apparently nothing more than a sellable hoe. *Fuck this dude.* Leo explodes at the man "CAN YOU MIND YOUR OWN FUCKING BUSINESS, IF I WANNA TALK TO HER THAT WAY THEN I'LL TALK TO HER THAT WAY. YOU DON'T WANNA GET INVOLVED CAUSE I'LL GIVE YOU SOMETHING TO BE NOSY ABOUT." "You should treat her better than that". *Wow that was brave, that poor man. Lord please don't let him get hurt. Jus lemme get home please.* Once we got off the bus, Leo put his cousin and I in a cab and went his own way. *This is why I don't go out unless I know how I'm gettin back. Never again.*

If I didn't have so much money tied to Leo I woulda left that same night, but I had about two investments worth $5000 with him and if I didn't call him at the end of each week he seemed to forget to put the money in my account. *This is so wrong but think about the money you'd lose, what about your car insurance?*

Within a few days of that incident Nathaniel shows up to the house drunk tryna pick a fight. "Nathaniel, just chill man, I don't know why you were drinking and I'm not in the mood, I will break your skinny ass in half if you don't calm the hell down" That didn't seem to phase him, he got in my face "Do it, do it, you think I'm weak but I'm strong" "I'm not laughing with you and shut up before you wake Kaykay" I pushed him outta my face and he came back. "Yo chill, or you can't stay here tonight, you promised you stopped drinking" "You don't want me here? Ok, I'm gonna go, I'm sorry" With that he stumbled out. I had no clue where he went. He was back the next day, hella apologetic. I was hoping things would have changed but a few days later he was back to his antics, except this time I couldn't find him. I was not down for tryna keep tabs on a grown ass man.

January 31 2011
Cola
So I'm cheesed...but I'm sending you this message cause I don't want yell at you... I've tried to help you out...but clearly u dont want my help...you wanna keep livin the life you have...hangin out with friends...drinkin....not reachin my house...not callin....k so today I lent u my keys because u were complainin about being on the road for long until I came back.... I said the only way I'd give you the keys is if u cleaned while I was gone...soft...u said ud call...u didnt call me till 10....then I said ud better be back by the time I get here cause I shouldn't have to buzz to get into my own house...you said ya you'll be here....it's almost one... I gotta take my son to school.... I have work...an your not here....so you need to leave my house....there's no point in you stayin here an me tryna help u...if u have no respect for my words...or my house....so I'm sorry it has to be this way...but ye... I don't trust yu an u haven't proven that you've changed...

He showed up the next day and I had his clothes waiting by the door. He wasn't allowed in the house to take nun, I learned my lesson the first time. Without a place to stay he was in need of money. He had posted on Facebook that he was looking for someone to buy his brand-new PlayStation 3 - the PlayStation that was sitting in my house. Since it was already with me my sis and I decided to split the cost and buy it off him. I hit him up asking the price and he got back to me sayin:

February 2nd 2011

Nati
so its 220 and the camera

Camera? I know this man ain't tryna sell me back my own damn camera. Sure enough he was tryna sell me his PlayStation AND my camera. Ain't that a trip. We paid the $200 for the PlayStation and I told him to keep the camera, he had it the whole time anyway. With the purchase complete I was done with Nathaniel. One gone and the other was on his way out. I was over being nice. I may have been stuck with Leo, but I could no longer be stuck with his cousin. I could only tolerate his cousin at my house for one more week. I always had to wake up at inconvenient times to let him in and that smell seemed to have gotten worse. I tried, but it wasn't going to work any longer.

It must have been the week to test my damn patience cause Pierce text me bout "Can I get the car?" and I hit back with "You got my money?" then it was silence. *I'm so done with alla dese fakes.* Things were like a whirlwind for me, I could barely catch my breath. I had classes, program, volunteering, and business meetings with Leo. Leo still had me going to all these fancy ass restaurants, no sex, just teaching me business and some real street education shit. The stuff you learned from an OG on the streets, the importance of time, the freedom of business, the possibility of better. I still wasn't comfortable with the age thing but I was learning a lot so I soaked up as much as I could. As I waited for my insurance to come through this man kept me protected and making my own money, like some miss independent shit fo real. As much as I was mad at God on New Year's Eve, it seemed like he was back to blessing me and it was only getting better. *I guess he heard me.*

A.M.Y was a blessing and a turning point for me. It was the best decision I could have made, it started in the dead of winter but Leo hadn't gotten my insurance yet so I had to take the bus.

One day, Leo and I had been riding the bus talking about goals, dreams, and the future and I said "What I really wanna do is get into plus size fashion. I'm tired of the cheap quality ugly looking clothes they have here. If I want anything cute I always gotta travel to the states" to my surprise Leo said "Ye we can make that happen. If you wanna know fashion you gotta check out a show in Las Vegas called Magic. If you're really serious I can get you in." I thought about it, it was winter, and I could really use some warmer weather and I found a cheap ticket. *Why not? This could be amazing, and it'd give me a break too.* I had only been to about two sessions of A.M.Y. before I had to fly off to Vegas.

Thank God for friends, my girl was watching Kaykay for me which allowed me to plan my trip and execute it on the lows - I called my parents from the plane to say I was leaving. I paid for the trip but Leo provided media pass access under his media company.

Guess who texts me right before I left though?...Pierce. Hear him bout "Hey, just wanted to let you know that I graduated." So I hit him with "Good job! I'm headed off to Vegas right now, so I'll hit you up once I'm back." *Smiling on the inside, that's right, you fucked up!* My plane arrived late to my connecting flight so I spent an extra night in Chicago. I eventually made it to my destination but my clothes did not, and I was expected at expo, so I had to take a bus to a mall, buy clothes and get back before the day was done. My job as media was to make contact with viable businesses and gather as many look books and business cards as I could during my time there. Besides catching a cold, and losing my luggage, my first time traveling alone wasn't bad. It was quite memorable, something I could definitely get used to. It was too short of a trip but I had things waiting for me at home: #1 my dope ass program A.M.Y and #2 DNA testing with my baby fadda.

I hadn't heard any new info from Kendrick so I sent him a message.

February 17th 2011
Cola
Hey wassup Kendrick.... I've been tryna reach you... I'm back in the country...can u message me an lemme kno wassup... I kno we were to do the test this saturday...so if it won't work so jus lemme kno please...hope everything is ok

No response. DNA test didn't happen. So, I carried on with life. On to bigga and betta tings.

A.M.Y. Artist Mentoring Youth is an amazing project aimed at helping young woman develop their talents as young writers, actors, theatre majors, singers, dancers, you name it. One of the best decisions I made this year was applying to this program. I wasn't even sure if my writing was gonna be good enough and I was right at the cut off age but man, this was a dream come true for me. *It was a good thing I never listened to my writing teacher in high school.* I didn't know how far writing could really take me until I joined this program. For a period of months our group of women were expected to meet every Monday night for dinner and program.

My only hesitation was babysitting. I didn't have consistent babysitting for Kaykay and thought I might have to drop out, but then the co-founder calls me and tells me that they were gonna try to help me with babysitting by getting some of the alumni to help out. *They really wanna help out a single mom like me?* I cried. It wasn't often that help like this came. I had learned that since he was my child I needed to figure things out myself. Whatever happened to that "it takes a village" saying? Modern day was like "your kid...your problem." An yet here I was with an amazing offer and an amazing solution. SOOO, I GOT IN YAY! The best part for me was that I knew that Kaykay was the type of child that was well behaved in public. If he had a couple cars and a book he'd sit quiet for hours and he adapted quickly to strangers. It meant I didn't have to stress out while trying to advance myself.

I don't think I understood how much I loved writing until I started this program. I also didn't realize how shy I was or how much I cared about appearances. Lemme just say this: theater people were weird as hell...an I love em. They challenged themselves to be different without letting the fear dictate their emotions. It was brilliant.

Normally, seasons wouldn't bother me cause I had a car. Without it, winter had become a huge adjustment. Not to mention I had a kid traveling from the west to halfway across the world to the east of Toronto. Kaykay's legs were getting weaker. He couldn't walk as long as he used to. The distance was too long for him and most times when he fell asleep I had to carry him but I was too tired. It was such a struggle that I wasn't used to. Sometimes I brought a stroller with me and would have to deal with the looks from strangers cause KayKay clearly looked too damn big to be in a small stroller. Once I got past the looks then I had to deal with the fact that most TTC stations on the route I was taking weren't wheelchair accessible. Straight fuckery. And bus passes or tokens? I was new to this life of TTC and I wasn't adjusting well. *Toronto has been around for how many years? They still don't think people with disabilities need to get around?* Sometimes I would have some generous men stop and help me, but most time people walked past like we were invisible. I saw a different Toronto anytime I had to travel. If I didn't believe in the program, the journey alone woulda convinced my ass to stay home. I was ringing down Leo about the insurance, it was supposed to have been set up by now.

At first when I looked at the group of girls and how they acted, didn't think I fit in. They were talking about high school... I was in University. Having a child matured me in such a way that I didn't even realize how much I had changed. I never really left my house to do any social things. *Is sex social?* Regardless I stayed inside, I was so out of the loop and most of these girls were also in some type of theater, so all the weird theater exercises we played they already knew. Why was it cool to make weird noises from my mouth? Being the biggest girl there physically I definitely didn't wanna play any games that required me to move my body. What if I couldn't control which way it went? Naw what if the fat fell out of my shirt? Embarrassed my ass? No thank you, yet they won me over slowly, some of the games weren't so bad and they weren't watching my fat as much as I was. Kaykay won them over too. His personality was infectious. We would be focused on writing and in the dead silence there would be this loud giggle or yell and everyone couldn't help but laugh as I died of embarrassment. "Sorry guys" Or the times we would have break and he would take his car and run around the room. It was so hard not to love him. He was so damn cute.

The writing process was different for me. The goal of these workshops were for each woman to write a story, personal to them, based on a theme. Once the individual stories were written a team of alumni would weave the stories together to create one play and we would each be responsible for acting out our writing. Each week we had a different exercise that would help us in writing as well as time to write, edit and practice our stories. To kick things off we started brainstorming ideas for the initial theme. One of the ideas were about different statistics. I knew my idea was very personal, but I wanted to know the statistics of rape, how often, men vs. women and I was challenging myself to think about what went through the mindset of a rapist. My rapist. I wanted to understand his intentions and bring closure. Rape was not something anyone wanted to talk about, but by me writing on it, it forced more people to be aware and uncomfortable. *Did I just make you feel uncomfortable? Talking bout how I was raped? At least you weren't on the receiving end.* I didn't want to jus write on rape. I didn't want to just relive it. I needed to understand it. Like he did. This group of women so fearlessly challenged me to write and speak my truths. I had finally found people who understood art, expression and passion to be free in writing. They challenged me to be a better writer. I love em for that. Each and every one of them.

It was the end of February and I was tryna figure out where the hell my insurance was at. Wey it deh? Soh mi wann kno. How come Leo can't deliver all now? Why was me an mines still taking the damn bus. What the fuck I put $1300 up for? Listen at this point I was thinking I shoulda just paid the damn blackmail money of $3500 and be done. The fact that he was supplying me with fake bus passes was nice, but it wasn't my car. I was tryna play it cool cause I knew he was tryna help me out but damn. Anyway, you know my bday was coming up and last year was a shit storm, so I was really tryna make up for it this year by doing something fun. Being a man with many connects Leo offered to set me and my friends up with a booth with food, drinks and entry into a nightclub for the night. It was like night an day compared to last year. Since it was music week in Toronto different artists were performing at various local clubs and this Canadian Idol singer Caleb Simmonds was performing at the same spot I was at. *That's cool. Canadian Idol? Who is he again?* Ye I had to look him up, but his music was gwaning, so it added an element of intrigue, plus Leo had a surprise for me that night, I could hardly wait. But nothing was set in stone yet. Honestly, it couldn't get any better except I couldn't understand why someone would put this much effort in making sure I was ok. Remember...I'm the invisible girl who didn't mean anything to anyone except for some dollars.

It had been going on three months since we'd been kicking it and maybe I was jumping the gun here but I needed to know in what direction we were headed. Do I put feeling into this or naw? He was putting in all this effort doing all this "I'm your man shit" but I hadn't asked and he ain't say nun, so I asked. Realistically things were on more of a business level. I invested money, he gave me a return and we flirted. But still what were his intentions with me? Did he like me? Wanna date me? Keep it casual? Or keep it business only? The first time I tried to ask in a text message he casually tried to pretend he aint seen it. Days before my birthday event that I wasn't even sure was gonna happen I figured since I was sittin there lemme ask him directly to his face, "So.... what is this between us?" He looked me dead in my face and said, "If you're pushing me to give you an answer then the answer is that I'm not your man." Bruh you coulda hit me with a ton a bricks and I wouldn't have moved. I was numb as shit.

My brain was tryna register like... *Ok, cool, I get that, I guess...so you doing all this shit for what? Just because? This ain't actually going anywhere? So, I'm wasting my time then? Iight message received. Fuck you too then. Anythin I had for you is going right over there in this box called "feelings" with a lock around it called "lock that shit up" and Imma bury it, deep. Memba you asked for this shit. I'm not gonna get played like this again.* This was exactly why I ask niggas from the first day what do you want from me, so that I knew how to direct my emotions and any future emotions that tried to creep up. This was my fault though, I let my guard down and was swooped up by the fancy dinners. I got slapped back down with the truth and sting of rejection. Even a man who didn't want sex from me and treated me great wasn't able to see any good enough qualities in me to want to be with me. It was ok though, cause two could play this game.

I was tired of all these games that I seemed to be playing with people. I felt like I was constantly jus on pause as they did what they needed to do. I still hadn't heard anythin from Kendrick, so I sent him another message:

March 1st 2011
Cola
k so I dunno if u saw my last message or if u care... I jus wanted to kno straight up if u dont wanna do the test...then jus lemme kno...if u changed ur mind...cool...my son an I have been doing good...but atleast jus lemme kno..send me a message or somethin...
Kendrick
I do wanna do it.....I had a family emergency ...had to go to Jamaica
Cola
I'm very sorry to hear that...is everything ok?.... I messaged u when I got back from vegas wonderin if u was iight ...but I dunno if u even saw that message....well I hope things are going better for u now....cool yu wanna do it..then lemme kno when... I doubt u kno but my b day this thursday...an I'm not even sure what I'm doin for it...or if I'll be in toronto lol...but lemme kno the day u wanna do it..an I'll make sure I'm around cause I think this jus draggin on too long

No response. But I didn't have time dwell on that cause IT WAS MUH BIRTHHDAAYYYYYY!!!!! Despite that hiccup between Leo and I, he actually came through and made things pop off for my birthday. I was surprised he pulled it off. It seemed so sketchy but I was ready to rock and roll that night. It would certainly be a night to remember. The club was hella fun and Leo's surprise was that he got Caleb Simmonds to sing me happy birthday. AWWWWWW! Ok, well done. The only messed up part was that Reign showed up to celebrate and hijacked the damn night. We were supposed to go straight to the club for a specific time but Reign needed to pick up something and made us late, but the time we showed up, instead of being free we had to pay to get in. SUPER annoyed. Can this man do anything right? Catch this, Reign made us late and threw a temper tantrum and didn't even come to the club. Imagine. Grown ass man. On my birthday. This nigga. Still gotta give Leo the credit for pulling through. Wasn't sure with this insurance being such a flop. Tick, tock, April was approaching and so was Kaykay's birthday.

April 3rd 2011
Cola
I unno what you're up to...hope everything's cool...you haven't really said anything to me since the last message...anyway...my son's birthday party is comin up so if your interested in coming then let me kno.

No response. I was trying my best to keep the communication line open and to help him be involved in our lives if he wanted to but I wasn't getting anywhere. With the show coming up on the 9th I didn't have time to wait on him.

After months of hard work we were about to debut *Check Out, cash credit or soul* from the A.M.Y project. I had never really acted before, didn't know how. Everyone had to find their own style to perform, we had some girls singing, some girls doing monologues and I was doing spoken word. It was where I felt the most comfortable. I understood rhythm and the rhythms of words was what made it easier for me to get on stage and spill my truth. It was an interestingly rough yet rewarding night, I had four pieces of my story woven between the stories of everyone else and in my final scene I got to play a piece on the piano that I had written. What an accomplishment.

Although Kaykay wasn't there that night he had been such a crucial part in my story and as I stood on the stage I felt like I had done him proud. I had also done myself proud, it was the first time that I had publicly spoken about being raped and I felt like I had finally gotten back some of the power in the situation. I was scared to invite my parents, they had no clue I had been raped and based on how they handled it the first time, this wasn't a conversation I was ready to have. How does one even bring it up? I invited a few friends and Leo who showed up late and left as it finished. I guess I should be happy he showed up, I asked him why he left right after and he said "I know some of the people in there" so I guess he wasn't tryna be seen with me in public. Whatever. Everyone else was proud of me. I felt amazing. I was heard. Funny how God works cause I really wanted to get into Obsidian theater and I was kinda sad when I didn't get in, but it turns out that this was a better program for me. I couldn't have asked for better support. Lesson learned, God wins again. Here is the final piece I performed that night, titled: Overcome. I can't wait for it to be developed into a full play.

Poetic Interlude

What would they say if I say that he raped me on a Tuesday
Nothing but a whore
Why was he at your house?
my house is not my home
My home is not safe
Safe is a place full of love and embrace
Embrace what I long for because I just been raped
But for fear of ridicule
My mouth remained taped up and silent
Silently my tears fell
Thinking back to every time I'd been raped
The four times that is
Tormented teenage years
Searching for love, but only finding sex the love I had had me wishing for death
Injecting and subjecting my body to sex
sex is never just about sex
every man I've laid with left something behind
something that I've been left to deal with
luckily for me a couple times it's been temporary
temporary devotions causing long lasting emotions
suffering in silence

silently suffering
Wondering why I never said a thing
Do you hear the sad melody my heart sings
Ring a ling a ling
I'm dealing wit a mash-up ting
A mash-up ting
called life
Do you think I'll ever be good enough to be called
someone's wife
I've been interrogated and slapped
Slapped with the hurtful words that humans use
Use me and abuse me
They say I'm a slut and a whore
Fat bitch a disgrace
Disgraced this family
When all those men had a taste
Taste good don't it
Look at the way I was dressed
How could I not expect men not to look at my big old chest
I was blessed with this body
Wait, Maybe it's a curse
Every part of my body evenly dispersed
Awakens men's thoughts, the young and the old
The first time I was raped I was only
14 years young
Young child with a pretty face
Heart so cold it could freeze this place
Don't judge me
Don't judge me
Just love me
That's it
Sometimes I wish I could just spit
on all a dem who hurt me
lacking the ability to continuously pick up the broken
pieces
Depression swirled engulfing me closing the door to any
chance of self-forgiveness
Words beat me harder than bricks
Still it was easier to forgive them

Him
Than myself
How could I allow it all to happen?
Play or be play(ed)
Words I used to live by
Today I have chosen to rise above and set an example and make my son proud
I'm letting go of past messes life's stresses
I'm obviously still here for a reason
So why fight it?
I'm a survivor not a damn victim
Victim defines a person who suffers from an event
raped by a group, an acquaintance, a friend and a past lover

betrayed by their touch
Don't touch me
God freed me from their foreign touches, that left me
clutching my favorite drug was isolation I was
suffering from an overdose on sin
Please I needed an intervention to my soul To win
I am no longer bound
Can no longer drown
In this unfair game called life
So What would you say i f I say that they raped me on a Friday?
Would you stay silent? Or learn ways to fight against the violence.

CHAPTER FORTY-EIGHT

The Journey

And may the Lord cause you to increase and excel and overflow in love for one another, and for all people, just as we also do for you;

1 THESSALONIANS 3:12

I was still on a clear high from the A.M.Y. performance. As the Lit for Life program was ending we decided it would be a super dope idea to put together a book entitled "HOLLA". It was an anthology of stories written by various women who had come through the program. We weren't launching till summer, but we needed to start organizing our stories and themes. The end of the program was bittersweet for me. I loved the writing, but the girls I once knew and kicked it with were less than kind to me so many seasons later. Leah had done her best to damage my image and I was experiencing backlash from some of the other females as well. It was the most loneliest place to be, in a place where no one cared or wanted me around. I had increased my investments with Leo by a few thousand and was finally in a steady position but the money couldn't even help with my situation. Not to mention I felt like I was being dragged through the mud with Kendrick. We still had not set a new date for the DNA testing and I was losing hope we ever would.

April 15th 2011
Cola
ok so I'm pretty convinced that you ain't really tryna do no dna so imma leave you be an continue taking care of my son like I been doin. There's no point in us tryna work nun out cause you jus have me here waitin an you ain't contacting me or messagin me no more...so I wish you the best with you an your family..but you ain't gon

hear from me no more...peace n blessins.

Kendrick
don't jump to conclusions. I've been hella busy.... I've been to yard and back cause of my family... it's a money thing... I'm working tryna save money so I can do the test....take it easy
Cola
I understand that...but I've sent you how many messages....you couldn't send me a text or w.e an lemme kno your family is good an everything is cool?...
Kendrick
don't have the same phone... don't have the same number... don't have ur number
Cola
yu have my fossbook though... I'm not tryna get at u im jus sayin...it's been a couple months...haven't heard from you. I'm tryna get my car sold right now so I'll message u lata on tonight...here's my number if anything. You know Kayshaun's birthday is in like a week right?

No response. It was starting to become a pattern. He never finished the conversation if he didn't want to. I was always left hangin, wondering, *where do we go from here?* He always got my hopes up only to crush them again.

Since I no longer drove my car I realized that some girls no longer came around me. It had been months and I was losing hope of ever driving again. My car was gettin tickets for being on the road and at the point the most my $1300 had managed to do was partially clear my record. Once a company asked for my insurance history from another company the quote jumped to $10,000 for only 6 months. Not one damn company would touch me. I cried when I had to sell both my cars for a mere $600 in total. That was painful, but not as painful as finding out the car plates I had let Leo put in my name had racked up unpaid fines. Somehow months after my cars were parked I was still getting parking tickets. If that wasn't enough bad news my grades had slipped too low and I was kicked outta the honours program which essentially meant I was wasting my damn time. Who goes to school for 4 years only to end up with a 3-year degree? The only way I could get back into my program would be to increase my GPA before the end of my program. SHIT! I hate school. It was all bullshit anyway, I only liked the fun music classes, I learned way more from my volunteer work that I did. That's where my heart was. I just wanted to help people and get paid. Was that a thing?

May 5, 2011 ·
mothers day weekend... I wanna go to the movies...to bad I have no friends loooool

Tunnel vision had me thinking I had no friends, truth was I just didn't have any friends who lived close to me. I left most of them back in the east end. How lonely.

May 7, 2011 ·
Its mothers day...and I really wanted to thank my sperm donor for givin me the best gift of life, i.e my baby boy kayshaun antwoine isaiah bennett...love this little boy..so THANK YOU...for allowing me to have him all to myself....

My understanding of his father not wanting to be in our lives came years prior. Sometimes it stung on special holidays but then I watched the drama that some of the women in my buildin went through and thought thank you Jesus for his blessin. It's true God knows what I can handle, and a bruk down baby fadda wasn't one of them.

Even though most of the girls and I had fallen out, I was still required to attend programs and volunteer. I was going through a pretty bad spiral but I couldn't stay upstairs anymore. It was like living through an episode of Mean Girls. Everyone turned so quickly. Oh, how quickly they forgot any good I had done. At the program today we had a speaker named Nova, she was from L.A. and she was coming to speak to us bout self-confidence. As she told her story I felt like she was telling my story. I felt like she was reading me. I felt like she knew me. I felt like she understood. When she was done she reaffirmed our self-worth as women. She challenged us to speak life, speak confidence, speak love to ourselves. *I don't deserve this. I just wanna die. I just wanna disappear.* I tried to smile even though my eyes were filled with tears. I tried to wipe away the tears hoping no one would see me. The embarrassment if people realized I was crying. *They'll ask you why you're crying. I hate when people ask. I don't wanna talk, I don't want people to know my story cause they might look at me different.*

If I could just talk to her, maybe she would see me, maybe she would hear me out. Maybe I'll feel human again if even for a second. *Just try. Go talk to her when she's done.* I felt so connected to her. *Ok, here I go.* "Hi, I'm Cola" I don't even remember what she said, but I remember how she made me feel. Warm. Like it was ok to breathe. Like she saw me. She saw right through to my soul. I cried on spot. *So embarrassing.* We exchanged emails with a promise to keep in touch and that was it. I retreated to my apartment as fast as I could. I finished making dinner for Kaykay, let him play for a bit before bed and spent the rest of night drowning out my mind with music.

Sun, May 15, 2011

To: Nova

hi Nova,

how are you? my names Nicola, I met you at 1900 when you came to speak, I was the one in the front row seat. I'm very inspired by your story and what you've overcome. I picked up more on the small things like the fact that you're married. To know that you've been assaulted and in abusive relationships an still found love is a blessing. I've been raped 4 times and in countless failed relationships and I've really gotten to the point where I have convinced myself that I am unlovable. The only man that eva "loved" me was a man that I never physically met but put me through a lot...its a crazy story really. Aside from men hurting me, women also have hurt me, so it's really hard for me to put it all aside. Every time I try to give someone new a chance...in ends the same way...and otha than keepin myself away from ppl I don't understand what I was doing wrong...cause id fix it. Some of the girls who were sittin right in the same room with me have been girls who have hurt me. One in particular has made it her duty to spread constant rumours about me, and I kno it sounds petty, but I have a higher position like a leader type volunteer position that I took and it's a challenge tryna get these girls to trust me when they hear the worst of me.

Anywayz all of these situations are jus more things that I plan to add to my book. It's hard to love yourself when you're not even happy in the skin you're in. I've been teased for my weight for years...and I know the best thing to do is have patience and work on it, but in the meantime it's a struggle...but jus like you said, ppl can either take chill wit the card they are dealt or take it an use it as a challenge to move forward...i'm tryin to graduate from my music program in university and move on to starting a business, plus size and curvaceous fashion is what i'm interested in. It's a shame that canadian curvy or "phat" girls can't find clothes like american girls. All in all I really loved meeting you and hearing your words...you started out jus like where i'm at and you've been very successful...so there's hope...you say 20-25 was the worst years for you...well mine started at 15..the first time I was gang raped...and im still learning and growing from it all...once again it was a blessing and a privilege to meet you....thank you....

Born into a family of two
A little girl struggles an wonders what to do
Cause see her folks be workin hard
Tryna get that money right
While she ends up all alone night after night
They don't see the pain an anguish they cause.
Too busy preachin' the gospel an followin' bible laws
Picked on and tease this little girl can't understand
Y god would allow her to be placed on this cruel land
full of hatred and trouble.
This girl was double in size
And no one realize the sadness in her eyes
Her parents were too busy for love so she found it somewhere else
A group of guys all different size came and ripped open her

thighs and took somethin' she'll never get back
Thought it was love but it wasn't
Love couldn't be so cold
But how would she know
She was only 15 years old
Never had the courage to stand up an be bold
And tell the truth
It was rape
Like blinds hidden behind a drape
The secret of this encounter would remain taped up and silence
For her knowledge only
But when the truth came out it only left her lonely
Her mother never understood and wanted to send her away
But her father seemed to lover her enough to let her stay
love what a funny word to be said
Cause this so called love makes me wish I were dead.

17 May 2011
To: Nicola
Thanks so much for reaching out and for trusting me with your story. I'm so sorry for what has happened to you - I actually had a nightmare about the incident after reading your email (before bed, not a good idea) so I guess you and I are connected deeper then we thought. I'm sure it was no accident that I sat knee to knee with you either. :)
making the choice to move past the trauma of my rape (age 22) and be open to love was a huge thing for me. I was still messed up, having flashbacks and the whole 9, but I had to be honest with myself and with him as to what happened, how I was choosing to deal and being clear as to how he could help me. you can't get a yes if you don't ask.
there is no question that you are loveable - STOP convincing yourself that you are not. again, the SELF, yourSELF, is that bright innocent little girl that lives in you. stop telling her she'll never be loved...its hard, and weird to wrap your head around, but when you slander her, diss her and tell her she's nothing or not worthy, I promise you, a little piece dies that can never come back. knock it off!

icegrill angry face
we have to talk ourselves INTO it rather then OUT of it. and that goes for everything. you have done it before. into keeping your adorable son, into applying for 1900, into moving in and making it work and to stay when haters start to hate (which happens...it says more about them then you.). you've talked yourself into things that have benefited you before...keep doing it! love is one more thing and when you are strong, ready, walking tall, feeling confident, you'll be putting those vibes out rather than unsure, doubtful, mistrusting vibes. like I said, if that's what we put out, that we'll meet the person who will confirm that everyday all day. follow me?
your poetry and writing seem like a useful outlet. keep writing. what other creative methods to you use to relieve stress?
keep in touch with me. i'm on you now girl! :)
nova
May 21, 2011
To: Nova
hey so its real early but I figured id write you back...I get what u sayin, and I understand it but it's hard to put into practice. It's more than feelin unlovable I began realizing that because i'm so unhappy in the skin i'm in its hard for me to truly do anything. Everything I do everywhere I go I seem to have somethin tellin me that i'm too fat to do it or deserve it, and I guess when things go wrong for me I take it heart and attribute it with my weight. I feel like at this moment my weight really holds me down. Last year I lost 80 pounds over 8 months because I was on this crazy diet thing and once I came off I gained it back, so I went to finally havin more confidence, back to living in a box. everyone says if your unhappy...do something about it but its not as easy. I think also from years of emotional abuse an allowing myself to be used an abused it has only reinforced my insecurities. Because I am thicker i've always attracted an older crowd so from the time I was first gang raped when I was 15 havin at least one man being 24, it's been a constant thing that older men are attracted to me.

They say they love my size and I guess it leaves me feelin like i'm too fat for men my own age. it's definitely a tough battle, but I don't believe that we sat across from each other so coincidentally. I don't have a variety of very positive women in my life that I feel I can really talk to just because my experience with women has been a horrible one so I do appreciate the time you take to read and answer my emails. Most time I put on a face for other ppl because I know deep down that showin insecurities aren't positive. For awhile I was positive and caring an all that good stuff n it really jus attracted ppl who wanted to use me and took my kindness for granted..so to find a happy medium is weird...I dont wanna trust anyone especially in my age range because I feel like ppl my age jus don't understand. pretty much otha than writing I used to do piano quite often i'm in school for piano...but I lost my confidence within myself so i've taken a break for about 5 years now...around the time my son was born. otha than that...jus tryna get into fashion...i'm hopin that it will help me overcome some of the frustrations an insecurities I feel. My insecurities come from not findin clothes that fit my figure an look good...that's when I get the most upset...so to fix it...I figured...y not do something about it. Only thing is...i'm not girly at all or into a lot of fashion so its all new for me...but anything creative artistic even event planning are things that I get very passionate about in terms of destressing.

After so many years I was so confused, and I convinced myself I was gang raped at 15 instead of 14, not wanting to face the truth. When I sat down and recalled my own trauma there was one comment that will always stay etched in my brain. The moment the female cop said, "The age of consent is 14" and I said "Ok, well, I did it then" She single handedly gave me my "out". As many years have passed I'll never forget her words. Now the words of Nova were the words I clung onto to get me over this hump. I was given the opportunity to see Miss Maya Angelou with the same girls from our writing group, but who really passes up a chance to see Maya Angelou?...It was Maya Angelou.

May 25, 2011 ·
Hmmm seeing Maya angelou's tonight...yay

It was a memorable night. Inspiring to say the least. She made a living out of writing poems and it gave validation to a career in the arts. Listening to her speak reminded me of how blessed I was to live in a building that worked with organizations such as Literature for Life to create such amazing opportunities to challenge our minds to push beyond normal. It left me feeling like I had finally found a place that accepted me for who I was. Ms. Maya reminded me that at the end of the day my purpose was to be a blessing in someone else's life. Though I felt at times like I wish I neva met Leah, I realized that the times that I did help were not a curse or mistake but were a blessing and this was the beginning of my forgiveness for her and others who have hurt me along the way. Instead of just living, I wanted to make an influential difference in the lives of other people. This realization meant that I had unlocked the beginning potential to my purpose and it felt like I was now... home. I just had one last thing to take care of.

May 31st 2011
Cola
So this is pretty much gonna be the last time I message you...after dis...imma jus close this chapter of my son and you ever meeting and havin a relationship. The last time we messaged each other was in april and I haven't heard anything from you since. The dna test is something that you wanted and it would have been nice, but my sons doing jus fine with jus me raising him. once again..God bless and I wish u an your family the best..

I had come to an understanding that he wasn't ready. I couldn't hate him for it, I just had to accept it and move on. God had been providing for us without him. An ye, sometimes I wish he was around and we coulda shared in this journey, then sometimes I was happy I was on the journey without him. It was a process, but I think when I started to understand that he couldn't give us what we needed I stopped hating him. I stopped being angry with him. I wanted to see him do well in life even without us. I just couldn't allow myself to be drained anymore. Waiting for calls, messages, acknowledgements. He didn't value my time and suddenly I did. I valued my own time. That's when forgiveness started for me. It was when I was able to let go and be free.

7 Jun 2011

To: nicola,from Nova

Thanks so much for reaching out and being so so honest.

I apologize for the delay. You sent this to me at the end of my trip, my nephew was born, I went back to L.A and a few days of not checking my email can get things buried.

all good.

I can't tell you what to do girl, 'you a big 'oman!' :)

but I can remind you how important your self-esteem and confidence is. not only to your well being, to those who turn to you for support and advice (and I have a feeling you are a girl they go to) but for an example for your too cute son. these little people feel our energy and when its low, low, low they sense it too.

you've lost the 80 pds. and that took determination and serious will power. no one gave that to you.

you got over unspeakable trauma and opened your heart again. you have to be really brave to do that.

you chose to keep and raise your son. that took courage and no one gave that to you.

stay creating, stay close to people who build you up. make goals, have someone hold you accountable and be clear on what you expect and what you'll accept for YOUR life.

you are so bright Nicola, I saw it in you right away. but that light is no good if you can't recognize that it's there all the time. keep it burning. and when its hard and you hear the negative tape repeating in your head...stop...gather...take a minute and tell yourself 'from THIS moment on' and keep it moving.

I hope this helps and please keep in touch with me.

nova

Jun 7, 2011
To: Nova
honesty Is the best policy.
yay babies congrats to your sis...babies are so cute.
things seem to be working itself out....i'm back to doing what I do best...tryna help ppl out...as much as I possibly can...it's a great feeling....I jus do me...an the girls I use to talk to who been givin me grief I ignore...and focus on my life and if need be the girls around me who seem to appreciate the things I do far more. Things got kinda bad in terms of my self esteem but it's gettin better...I got my personal trainer back and I started working out again...plus I jus started on the jenny craig plan lol...im so busy it's the only way I can manage to eat without skippin meals.
anywayz..i'll definitely keep in touch there's a book launch for my writing group at the end of the month...it's exciting times....we'll see what the future holds....
how are things with you?

My Jenny Craig plan lasted about a week. I never really ate three meals a day but the moment I realized one meal consisted of only five fries, I figured starving myself wasn't the way to go either. I may have only ate one or two meals a day but at least I was full when I was done. There was a saying that when life goes good old flames try to creep back in. With life the way it was, I guess it should have been no surprise when I got a message from Nathaniel.

June 14th 2011
Nathaniel
hi, how r u?
Cola
hi, fine thanks relaxed
Nathaniel
nice, hows kk doing
Cola
he's great thanks
Nathaniel
is he sleeping
Cola

ye he jus went to bed, we jus got home
Nathaniel
oh yea from?
Cola
the gym
Nathaniel
nice
Cola
yep
Nathaniel
I just seen Reign, lol, hows the work out going
Cola
oh ye ? tru, its cool I jus started a real work out today...but it was great
Nathaniel
your working out at a gym or your house
Cola
both
Nathaniel
lol nice, is that guy still with you
Cola
livin wit me?
Nathaniel
yea
Cola
naw he hasn't been wit me for awhile
Nathaniel
are you still in school? don't you get horny after you work out
Cola
ye i'm still in school, hmmm...nope...I really dont get horny ever
Nathaniel
bull shit
Cola
not really..I think of men...an how they piss me off an they not worth the headache...an I forget all about any hormones
Nathaniel

lmfao, really that's how it is, fuck !!! it got to you that much ay
Cola
its been years of niggas pissin me off...it was bound to happen
Nathaniel
so you must hate me. I think I contributed to that still.
Cola
I don't hate ppl, not even the ppl who did me the most wrong, I jus feel that in life right now...its money over love...I dont need love...I can't survive on love if it's not the love of jesus...but money makes the world go round..
Nathaniel
true, I am with you on that
Cola
an to have sex mean i'm willin to deal with the consequence if things mess up an I happen to get pregnant...an I dont got time to get pregnant with nobody's baby n I don't love the man
Nathaniel
I understand
Cola
good
Nathaniel
lol good, are you also trying to say something else
Cola
nope
Nathaniel
hows the book thing going
Cola
it comin
Nathaniel
nice I would love to read it some time
Cola
i'm part of a poetry book that should come out the end of this month
Nathaniel
sweet

Cola
thanks
how u doin?
Nathaniel
I am doing good again it's been about 2 months now that I haven't had a drink.and I put on 10 pounds. I also work out 2. I have my new place
Cola
oh that's good...I thought u were goin back to you family...where u live
Cola
anyway i'm off to bed...night

I appreciated him asking about Kaykay, there was no love lost when it came to him, we just weren't good together. We always rooted for each other though, somehow I think he woulda been disappointed in me if he knew I was selling fake bus passes. It wasn't so much for the money that I sold the passes to the other girls in my building but more so to help out other single mothers who struggled. Only a couple of rules they had to follow, don't get caught, never give the name of the person who sold them the pass and never give up the pass. Since I started using the passes myself I had only been caught once. I got out of it by dropping the correct amount, apologizing for the misunderstanding and continued on my way. Soft tings. But jus as quickly as I started sellin, I stopped. People can be hella annoying and I didn't wanna deal with the headache. They started complaining that the fake bus passes looked tooo fake. Sometimes the customer ain't always right....

Poetic Interlude

Inspired by Maya Angelou
Let me be a rainbow in your life
Let me shine my many colors and brighten up yur day
A brightened day that soon turned to night as I'm quickly dying with anticipation an stuffed with delight
Delighted for the reveal of what awaits on the other side of these doors
Let me be a rainbow in your life
Let me shine my many colors and brighten up yur day
Maybe ill smile so big my lips are permanently stuck
Running stumbling yet full of joy
Even when I buck my toe an nearly fell
I played it off an kept going
Doors fly wide open
Givin way to an enormous room
Filled with a rainbow sea of races
Traces back generations to generations
Interrupted message
Ladies and gentlemen the show is about to start so please no cameras and enjoy the show
A woman's voice can be heard echoing through the halls
The keys touched an so delicately rang out sweet classical music
I enjoyed it and was tickled with admiration
Knowing that I was sittin on the balcony
With a group of the most talented females waiting and waiting the arrival of the nights special guest
Curtains open and I'm entranced and
Dazzled as a beautiful bright brilliant red dress flows onto the stage
Damn ms Maya Angelou looks so gracious
So confident
So beautiful
She tells a story
A story that sticks

Like honey and peanut butter
This is what I learnt from her
Let me be a rainbow in your life
Let me ease the fret
And start a legacy
Let me sing that song
Rub that back
Play taxi for a day
Even throw money your way
Let me play that jam
Boogie down with one hand in the air
Today is yur day to smile
Even if for a little awhile
I could be a stranger in the street
But a rainbow in yur life
Maybe it will encourage yu
To do something nice an become a rainbow in someone else's life
Passed down from generation to generation
Jus like crippled willie
From the words of maya angelou
"He taught me my times table"
An although he was not fully able
And stable with a portion of his body
His mind his words his teachings
Reached a white man
An I was blessed with the opportunity to hear this story
An inspiration that could potentially heal a nation
I took the time to listen an I let the words settle in that
I could be a rainbow in someone's life and someone could be a rainbow in my life

CHAPTER FORTY-NINE

Summa Summa Tyme

Oh, how I *love* Your law! It is my meditation all the day.
PSALM 119:97

July 2, 2011 ·   Hmm I'm realizing I'm allergic to insects an bullshit...my body reacts in a negative way
July 3, 2011 ·   Soo last night preacha said how u a christian but aint been changed, still cussin n carryin on, well although I'd really like to cuss right now I think imma refrain

Some people will make you lose your salvation if you ain't careful. I refuse to let this hefa drag me to hell, but my patience was being tested. FO SURE!

July 4, 2011 ·   frustrated...but i keep on writing..

We made it to launch day and despite all the bullshit it was a very deserving night for all of us. We had worked hard. We had poured out our souls. This was our night to roc and shine. We did it! Holla 2011·

July 6, 2011 ·   rejection makes you stronger.....wise words from my bet friend...guess im buildin up my brick wall
·July 6, 2011 ·   its funny how some ppl could meet u one day, then act like u never existed...meh that's ok..one more brick to add to my wall..

I had landed my first summer job in a long time. Only it wasn't a job, more like a slave opportunity. I was hired by a company to stand on the corner to raise funds and my pay was only a portion of whatever money I was able to raise that day. If I had a shitty day, well that was supposed to be incentive to work harder. My paycheck one day was 11 cents. They literally sent me a check for 11 cents. After they stuck us at a shitty location for hours. This "job" wasn't for me at all but while working outside of a Walmart in Rexdale my charming baby fadda walks right past me. I was shocked. I hadn't seen him in years. YEEEEAARRRSSSS. Last I was told the muthafucka had his driver's license suspended for non-payment so my ass was hella curious if he actually drove himself cause I seen him and his bredrin walk in an I was jus waiting. *I wonder if he saw me?* I didn't have to wonder long, as he walked out of the store he waved, didn't say a word and walked to the driver's side of the car, got in and drove off. He was sooo bold!!! The man treated me like I was a stranger. Wow! I mean I didn't expect no hugs but shit, not even a hey, how's life, how's my son? I guess that was too much to ask from a man who still refused to claim him. Wasteman to the fullest.

> *July 10, 2011 ·*
> *Yo yo yo I'm a hood celebrity dawg, so keep hatin*

The first part of the summa was rough, but the ending was about to get sooo much sweeter. I just keep my head straight.

> · July 24, 2011 ·
> some men have disgusting mentalities, yall comment on weight cause yall think its the best way to cut someone down, please just like u tryna dis a "fat girl" what makes u think that a "fat girl" would even want a man like you....tired of nonsense remarks, jus continuin the circle of hate, kiss teet

Apparently it was like the ultimate dis if a big girl turned down the advances of a next man, as if I should be grateful just cause he looked my way. "Why thank you kind sir for loving a poor fat girl like me" Pfft, fuck that, I was in no mood to deal with unnecessary comments. It was ok to say no, yet this nigga tried to make me feel bad. He wasn't even my type. I LIKE CUTE NIGGAS. NEXT...

August 1, 2011 ·
jus woke up n now I can't fall bck asleep...uggg

·August 3, 2011 ·
Jamaica then rock the bells, woot woot best summer ever

I was anxiously counting down the days till I could leave all this shit behind. I was mostly excited about bringing Kaykay home to Jamaica to meet his granddad. On anotha note it was Leo's birthday but I ain't had shit planned cause I wasn't his girl. You know this nigga had the nerve to tell me he loved me? We were on the train headed downtown and as he sat across from me he asked me "Do you miss me, miss my kisses?" I laugh it off then he says "I love you" an I reply "What? I can't hear you" so he says it again and I said "What? Sorry the trains too loud. What did you say?" So he tried to say it again and I just happened to look down and missed it again. Whoops. Two big middle fingas up. Where was love when I was tryna care for you? Love don't live here. Next

August 4, 2011 ·
Soo I jus passed my g test ahhh god is great, now its really the best summer eveeeerrrrrr

I had failed my G test two times and passed the allowable date for any more tries. Had I failed this 3rd time I woulda had to start from the beginning. The first two times weren't my fault. Have you seen Toronto traffic at 4pm? Who the hell was gonna drive that fast on the highway? "Sir I can't speed up there's a car in front of me" = failed. The second time definitely wasn't my fault. Yellow light means slow or go through the light if possible...it was possible. And I'm pretty sure right turns on red lights are allowed so iuno why this man was picking on me. Anyway, on the very last possible chance God pulled out a miracle and my instructor wasn't a complete dick, so I passed. YAY!

·August 9, 2011 ·
many of you know that my son has been diagnosed with dmd, there is a walk on september 10th that i jus registered for. It's important to raise money to try and find a cure for this disease, i am asking all of you for help, either by participating or by donating. Raising awareness is key..get at me for more information...

August 9, 2011 ·
My goal is to raise at least 500 towards findin a cure for muscular dystrophy...to sponsor my team click on the link on my page, imma be out of country for a week so please ppl help an donate towards the cause, my greatest i accomplishment would be to help my son an see him grow old...i refuse to out live him

Kaykay was such an important part of my everyday life. I loved being a mother more than anything. I was still tryna grown and figure myself out and I was at a place where I wanted to figure out this thing called Muscular Dystrophy. If I could aid in anyway then jus maybe they could find a cure for the strain he had. My vision was to see my baby grow strong and healthy and let God prove them all wrong. It was gonna happen. My mind was focused on the future when I got an unexpected message in my inbox.... the messages were from Melissa.

August 11, 2011
Melissa
hi do u still talk to Pierce? just curious
Cola
Hmm hi, every now an then y?Yu his cousin right?
Melissa

do u talk to him on the phone or just the computer? and when was the last time u seen him i haven't talked to him in a while

Cola

I swear u an him were so close being family an all, hmm I haven't seen him, my sis has, I spoke to him recently jus to say wassup that was on the computer though, he hasn't called since a couple months ago...yu an him fall out?

Melissa

oh, he's close to ur sis? naw we just dont talk as much ye me and him are close but i just haven't been around, but u said u do still talk to him and now it just wats up? lol i thought u guys were close

Cola

Naw he's not close with her but her saw her at a bana party. N asked for her pin, otha than that we both stubborn so since our fall out its neva been the same

Melissa

Oh kk cause I never knew what was goin on between you. You guys never told me anything was there like something going on tho. Its kinda looked like u liked him in a way but i could b wrong lol

Cola

Goin on like what? We was real close or so I thought did he have a girl? He said he didn't?

Melissa

Well did u guys kiss or do anything

Cola

Kiss? Hmm a couple times, not really we fucked on a couple occasions

Melissa

What! R u serious how many times

Cola

So I'm being honest with u yu wanna lemme kno wassup? Were yu his girl or did he have a girl?

Melissa

i don't know but how many times did u fuck?and what he used to stay at ur house or something

Cola
Yu don't know? Yu aint even bein honest, if he didn't have a girl or yu weren't his girl u wouldn't be so interested in what happened between us, now i'll continue to answer u n be honest if u can do the same with me
Melissa
ye i am his gurl for 5 years so how many time u guys fucked
Cola
So that whole time yall was lyin to me n usin me for my car, cool I had a feelin but he said he didn't want no relationship, well I'm not that kinda girl. If I knew he had a girl I wouldn't have messed with him, to be honest I don't remember how many times we fucked maybe 3 or 4 or more, do yu memba one time u was waitin in the car? Well we fucked while u sat outside, hmm he said he only wanted to fuck me from behind, dunno if that makes a difference, he pretty much acted like my man we jus didn't have that label, everyone else thought we was together, not tryna put myself out there but if imma be fully honest I might as well tell u I gave him brains too, I did that often. Hmm dunno what else to tell u except I neva knew, did he tell u y we stopped talkin?
Melissa
Ye me too so how many times u fucked and how many time did he stay over
Cola
He neva stayed over, yu didn't read that long paragraph I sent?
Melissa
What? Ok but u didn't answer me how many time did u guys fuck
Cola
Ye... I said I don't memba but probably like 3, 4 times or more, we had sex on different occasions I can't remember all, but it was more than 2
Melissa
Wow ..... What else should I know
Cola

I'm honest with u but I don't want no drama. Everythin u should kno I wrote in that paragraph for yu
Melissa
Can I call you?

It was quite the damn call. I felt played, like you let this damn man introduce you to me as his cousin? Naw y'all was tryna run game. "Why didn't you say something? ". She ain't have no answer for that. I had a feeling it wasn't his cousin, she moved different when I was around. Obviously she picked up some vibes that I liked him a bit, I had gotten in too deep emotionally and broke my own rules. As much as I felt guilty for sleeping with a man who had a girl I felt like she was just as responsible. This chick had issues for real though, asking me "How can you just suck his dick?" Hmm iuno, how do you suck a dick? There ain't no rules if he single. It was obvious the call was to try and shame me, figure out how often and when, where, she took no responsibility for her part. I said what I needed to and got the hell off the phone. I don't do drama. This was the reason I wouldn't mess with people man. Ain't got no time for dumb ass questions. I'm sorry your man preferred me for the times he was with me. Shit check ya man, not me. This was why I cherished my friendship with Sheena so much more, at least she had the nerve to step to me correctly, like a grown ass woman. Mind you, I neva fucked her man but still, she was classy. What do you expect when ya man stands and introduces you as a cousin to a next chick, eitha y'all tryna play me or you're getting played ya'self. Now that drama had found me, it was time to give Pierce a piece of my mind.

Cola
so this is the only thing imma say to u before I delete u off my facebook....I memba yu told me one time u were a bad person an all u do is hurt ppl....now I understand y...what u did was fucked up...yu coulda been honest me wit, I asked u many times if u had a girl, you lied bout everything. Tried to make me seem crazy like id catch

feelings, and the whole time u acted like u were my best friend and had my back. I had yu around my son, had him callin u uncle, I feel stupid an fucked up for that, what bothers me is u played such a victim, made me feel sorry for u, and the whole time u used me, used me to learn how to drive, used me to sell your perfumes, said we'd always be friends and like a fool I fell for it...told u everything bout me an my past...opened up to u..you listened knowing the whole time I was jus a temporary throw away. I memba when I found out your "cousin" was drivin my car we fought an so many ppl warned me about u and I thought with everything we went through wit ur dad an all dat that u were honestly different. from the beginning yu jus didn't give a fuck about a friendship...but its cool though, if anything ive learnt is to never trust anyone, never let them get too close, definitely keep men at a distance when it comes to relationships. an most of all most men are fucked up. Its guys like u who fuck up girls like me who intern do it to other ppl, anyway u tried to call me on some bullshit, if anything, be a man n tell ur gurl wassup..regardless I wish yu two the best of luck with yur relationship, I wish u the best with music and writing, an I thank u for the life lessons, most of all, I gotta forgive u to close this chapter of my life...maybe you'll read my book when it comes out...goodluck pierce

He never responded. Oh well. Fuck him. I got betta shit to think bout.

·August 23, 2011·
listen I'm on vacay nobody text me call me or facebook me bbm only

Jamaica always has my heart. From day one, it holds so many childhood memories for me and I wanted to create the same kinda memories for Kaykay. He wasn't as fond of the heat as I was, but it was a blessing to see him, my dad and granddad all together. Three strong men. My favorite part of the trip besides watching Kaykay drink from a coconut was bringing him into the ocean. Sun shining. picture perfect moment. Forever remembered. And after an amazing family trip, once we returned to Canada my sis, my friend and I bussed it to NYC for the Rock the Bells concert on Governors island. The lineup was fire and we had V.I.P status which jus meant we didn't stand in the hot sun and burn cause we got a bit closer to the stage than the others. It was my first non-Christian outdoor event and I loved it. Seeing my favorite artists, singing their songs, nothing could have made this summer better. It was a great way to end before going into my last year of school.

•September 6, 2011 ·
happening this saturday we've only raised 20 dollar so far thanks for the donation, much more is needed please ppl click this link support either with a donation or come out with us this saturday...

I think we might of had maybe $100 by the time Saturday came but we came out ready to enjoy the day and mingle with other families... Except, we was the only black family there. I guess fundraising walks wasn't a black thing or maybe not enough black families had been affected by the disease. Then I thought there was gonna be this whole interactive thing so that families could come together, but it really seemed like every family for themselves. They had a few lil stations here and there but not at all what I thought it was gonna be. Needless to say, that was our first an last fundraising walk. I figured if anything...I'll just send the money.

Poetic Interlude

I'm stuck on a relationship rollercoaster
Forever chasin those that don't want me
Yet rejecting those that do
With each beginning
The ending remains the same
Yur a cool person
A great friend
But somethings lackin
To make the greater connection
Greater transformation
From friends
To lovers
And beyond
With each fail
I tack a nail in the box holdin all my love
Love for another
Who's not my father sister motha true friend or seed is stale
I finally realised
N devised a plan to keep my love secure
When there's a cure for heartbreak jus lemme kno
Jus lemme kno when its safe for real love to flow
Or when yur man enough to see a real relationship grow
I showed yu the type of woman I am
Showed yu I'm the type of woman to stand by her man
Showed yu everythin I could provide
I mussa seemed too good to be true
Yu ran up
Grabbed my heart
Broke it in two
Then dipped
tripped n trampled on my
Emotions n self esteem
Leavin me to ask questions
Is it me?
How could it be that I allowed myself to get caught up?
I seem to be runnin a drive thru

Open late
Attractin the same kinda customers
Through my gates
I'm a mcdonalds tryna be a montana's
Tryna up my game an clientele
But my addictive goodies and low standards keep em comin back for more
N keep the same crowd knockin at my door
Its a damn shame
Got no more love running through these veins
Got no more love fo all dese games
Terrified of rejection
And unwilling to seek a new truth
I stay bounded
An strapped on to this rollercoaster
Taking me through the journeys of relationships
No stops
No release
Travellin high speeds
Screamin my lungs out
Butterflies in my stomach
As I drop
Built up tension to the top
What appears to be forever
Was over within seconds
Take deep breaths
My heart races
Then I open my eyes to see I'm right back where I started
As much as I'm afraid of heights
I keep comin on the same damn ride
As much as I'm afraid of relationships
I keep occupyin my time with the same type of guys
Will I never learn?

CHAPTER FIFTY

Evol.ve

Love is to be sincere and active [the real thing--without guile and hypocrisy]. Hate what is evil [detest all ungodliness, do not tolerate wickedness]; hold on tightly to what is good.
ROMANS 12:9

My summa was hella fun, but something was missing. He was missing. What is love if not to be loved from the depths of your soul? I couldn't let go. The undercurrents of his love haunted my very being and every time I was rejected, I was pulled closer to him. By now I was jaded but I needed his love more than anything. He had been working hard to show me how much he was changing for me. He wanted to be a better man, one I could be proud of. His love hurt, but it also sustained me. How could I say no? He never missed a birthday or anniversary; kept his distance but always let me know he was there. He would call me whenever I was in the midst of turmoil. It was like he knew in his spirit I needed help and he reached out. It didn't matter how many times I told him to leave me alone or changed my number. He pursued me relentlessly, always letting me know I was his one and only from the first day we spoke. He knew how to calm me, by now we had grown a few years together. Still hadn't met up and yet he knew me better than anyone else around me. Was this real? Besides being on the phone constantly we would have movie dates where one of us would pick a movie and we would both watch it at the same time. I loved our movie dates. One of those dates we watched this movie that completely blew our minds.

Have you seen the movie the *Adjustment Bureau?* Well I lived a life very similar to what was depicted in that movie. Every time we planned to meet we would constantly be missing each other by mere minutes at times. For those who haven't seen the Adjustment Bureau lemme give you a quick synopsis. Basically, there are these "angels" who are responsible for keeping people on their designated schedules. Each angel or man in the hat is assigned a caseload of people who he was responsible to keep tabs on. At times they would either allow people to spill coffee or misplace keys in order to either delay them for something good or divert them from a crisis. In this story a man and woman meet by chance when the man in the hat made a mistake and didn't create the proper diversion at the exact moment needed. This in turn allowed two people to cross paths who never would have met any other way. Make sense? Romeo and I have no clue how we ended up on each other's msn list. We met by chance. As you keep following this whole movie you begin to see how these two people go through the motions of the adjustments. The man in the story falls in love at first sight and spends his time trying to figure out why the man in the hat won't allow them to be together. The girl is completely oblivious of the angels but also finds herself deeply connected to this man after their initial visit. The man tries everything in his power to make the relationship work, but the "angels" block his many attempts making him look uninterested and a complete jerk to his mystery woman who doesn't even know this is going on behind the scenes. For example, when the man would try to call her they would block the signal. Even if he did find her at an appointment, all of a sudden, the appointment would be rescheduled. After multiple attempts he is finally offered two choices. Either he stay with her and risk both their careers for mediocre jobs or he stay away in order for them both to reach their full potential. It came down to love or destiny. Which was more important? In the end, Love won.

It was like someone had been following our relationship and wrote a story about it. It made no sense but felt eerily familiar. Hoping that at some point in our journey love would win as well.

People around me thought that because I hadn't met him in person that it was not a real relationship, yet it was the realest relationship I've ever had. I didn't need to question if he liked me, wanted me, needed me. I needed him. He was the only man Kaykay had any type of relationship with and I didn't want that to end. Kaykay obviously never had a physical relationship but they talked. His dedication to Kaykay and to me was admirable. I couldn't ignore my attraction for the man he was trying to be. Even if he had broken me. I was no angel either. When I reevaluated the situation between us I realized my own wrongs. Since I knew Romeo wasn't physically present I took advantage of the situation. I would lie about where I went when I knew I was going to see other guys behind his back. One guy in particular I used as my rebound nigga. He was a cute lil nerd but whenever Romeo pissed me off I called the next dude up just to get back at him. I got sloppy one day and got caught and when he asked me, I couldn't lie to him. But the sound of his voice, the pain in his voice when he found out made me feel like shit. Even though he deserved everything based on how he disrespected me...two wrongs didn't make a right. Tank's *Maybe I Deserve* was a heavy track during these times. My man used to play this song on repeat and sing to himself.

"Maybe I deserve
For you to go out and find some other guy
Maybe I deserve
For you to stay out with him all night
Maybe I deserve
For you to do all the things I did to you
Maybe I deserve (oh yeah)
Maybe I deserve
For you to put on a sexy dress
For me to ask you Who the hell you trying to impress
For you to laugh it off like it ain't nothing
I know it's something Maybe just maybe
To sit at home and wonder where you are
Is he kissing you touching you holding you what
Take a drink and help ease my mind
I want to be mad after all those times

For me to ask you where you been
For you to say I better stop tripping

To grab your neck until you let me know
For you to run crying, crying out the door
To grab my coat and chase you down the street
To say it ain't you it's my own insecurity
For you to say yes I cheated on you
I won't care cause after all I put you through I deserve
I deserve yeah yeah yeah
To be mistreated sometimes
To even be lied to sometimes
Maybe you should go cheat on me"

It wasn't entertaining in the least to be the cause of the pain. I gained nothing from hurting him. It would have been better had I just left him alone completely knowing that I couldn't trust him. What I did instead was string him along for the ride while I ran games on other men. Allowing them to plunge deep into my body while disregarding my heart, hoping I'd find someone betta. But did they eva love me? During the time that we had taken a break from each other there were a lot of changes. Once we both figured out what was important, neither wanted to let go.

His love was my syringe, his pain was my drug. It ran through my body like an endless supply causing me to fall time an time again. He would say "Didn't I tell you that you wouldn't find nobody like me? No otha man is gonna treat you like I do". He was right, I hadn't found anyone to treat me betta. So we had come to a place of understanding. I could see the changes he was making and wanted more than anything to make it work. Every time I wanted to say yes I remembered the cheating. We tried being friends but even that had problems. His past wouldn't leave him alone. I started getting text messages from different girls saying that he was still up to no good. One girl named Weezy text me to say that she had just hooked up with my man. Funny, how did she get my number? Not one to waste time I asked him "What the fuck? This is how you win me back?" He denied it but by the next day she texted me back saying Romeo had beat her up for lying. *Guess she shouldn't have lied. But why the hell he puttin his hands on her? That ain't cool.* "Yo don't be puttin your hands on no next female, I don't care if she lying. I don't like it and I don't accept it and if you gonna be with me you gonna have to cut that shit out. Seriously." He said "Ok, I promise".

His first baby moms was another chic I had issues with. I hated this woman. She didn't respect no boundaries between us. He went over to her house to check the kids and I guess he fell asleep an the hefa felt like stirring up trouble, so she took his phone an started texting me some bullshit. "Your man is here laid up in bed with me. He wants me, not you. I'm the one who has his kids" She was trying me on some next level. I rang down his phone till he answered.

- Cola: Where the fuck you been Romeo?
- Romeo: Hello?
- Cola: Don't play games with me, don't act like you was sleeping, why you give tha bitch your phone and have her texting me bullshit?
- Romeo: What are you talking about? Baby calm down
- Cola: Don't fucking tell me calm down, ask that dutty hoe why she texting my phone.
- Romeo: There's no text messages in my phone
- Cola: Oh no now I'm a liar? Fuck you then
- Romeo: Whoa why are you swearing at me, I didn't say you were lying.
- Cola: iight lemme take a picture of the messages right here and show you. The dumb bitch been texting off my phone. ...You get em?
- Romeo: Ye hold on.

She shoulda just left things alone, once he figured out what she was doing he beat her up. I don't condone what he did even though she was sneaky. I knew he had a temper but damn, violence was never the answer, at least not with me. As much as it wasn't me getting beat it very well could have been. Deep down I felt like he would never hit me though. I was the only person who was able to calm him once he got mad. When it wasn't crazy girls tryna hit me up then it was his phone ringing all times of the night. It became a game, I accused, he denied, then I cried, and he promised it was done. How do I forgive enough to move forward?

CHAPTER FIFTY-ONE

Educate

He executes justice for the orphan and the widow, and shows His love for the stranger (resident alien, foreigner) by giving him food and clothing.
-Deuteronomy 10:18

During the best summa eva I met Brooklyn. I loved Romeo, I always would, but I just couldn't adjust, couldn't evolve to being the person that was ready to forgive him for all the pain. I wasn't looking for no man when Brooklyn saw me. His head did a double take as I walked past him on Yonge street during the beautiful Caribana night. Tall, dark skin, bald and full of charm. His smile literally lit up the night sky. Y'all know I have a thing for American dudes, his accent was making me all kinds of wet. He ain't even try to hit that night, *respectable*, not like I woulda done it anyway and even though he licked his lips while looking at me like a snack, I respected that he came at me proper, asked for my number then we said goodnight. He flew back to New York the next day so I didn't get to see him again, but he called. Said he produced music and traveled often but he'd keep in touch whenever he travelled to Toronto. It was cute, I admired the effort but I wasn't looking for no man.

Money over Love. I was gettin cold feet over my investments with Leo, the money kept comin but I was tired of depending on him, I wanted to break free. He kept the money coming through, there was never an actual problem with that. I had a lot of whispers in my ear warning me to be careful, but that didn't bother me; it was the fact that I felt like I always had to beg for the money. I was at the end of my investment cycle so I had asked him if I could get my $11,000 back. At first he was working on withdrawing the money but then he came back to me with a different proposal. Instead of taking my initial out I could use the same money and put it towards another lucrative deal. If I dropped another 5k I stood to make 30k by the end of the deal which was set to be ready right around the time I was supposed to move out. Instead of taking the money now and potentially wasting it I could have it ready right when I needed it. *Take the money now! Don't re-invest.* Instead of listening to myself I locked myself in to this new deal. 30k? I could pay off my osap and still afford a decent apartment in a better area. We were running outta space, the sleeping arrangements at the apartment were tighter than ever and I figured if I could afford somewhere nice then I wouldn't have to deal with roaches or bed bugs. *Ew!*

I lived in a brand-new building, there was no reason why roaches should have been in our building. Yet after only three years we had roaches, not an infestation but still. My apartment wasn't bad like the others cause the minute I saw a roach I had the whole place fumigated. *These girls are so nasty man.* Some women in the building just kept their house in disarray and I wasn't the cleanest but I damn sure didn't have roaches chillin up in my place like that.

The worst thing was when the bed bugs came. I had just finished a training on bedbugs as part of my tenant rep responsibilities and I was to bring the information back. I didn't even know what a bed bug was until then. After learning about how quickly it could spread and how to clean once infected I was so afraid I was gonna catch them, so when I heard some apartments were getting treated I figured I would ask them to treat mine too. Treatment was a long ass process. It involved washing all our clothes and even spraying the couch. Spraying the apartment was more work than I imagined it would be even with the knowledge I had attained. I started the process but felt like *Is this all necessary? I don't actually have bed bugs, I'm tryna protect against it.* I decided to wait until the man came to my house to ask him what exactly needed to be done. He came once he had finished the other apartments, so I asked him "Hey do I really gotta do all this work? Cause I don't have bedbugs, I'm just tryna prevent against it." At first he says yes, then my superintendent said "If you don't have bed bugs then you don't need to spray, the treatment is only if you have bed bugs" *I thought this treatment was like how you spray for roaches. I spray before so you don't get them later.* Turns out I was wrong and causing more work for myself then needed. *Now I gotta put it all back? Ughhh!*

So, it turns out I was being too overprotective, but then Saturday morning I woke up scratching a lil bump on my arm. *That's weird, where'd this bump come from? Don't overthink it.* I carried on with my day. Sunday I woke up with more bites and more scratching. *Something is definitely wrong here. What could this be? Bed bugs? Noo, I don't have bed bugs. How could they have come int-NOOOO that man was in my house. The inspection guy. Naw, this can't be.* I look up the symptoms of bed bugs and sure enough, they were the exact same symptoms I was experiencing, and not jus me, my sister too. Now I was freaking out and tryna put two and two together. I didn't have bed bugs, then bed bug man came in my apartment, didn't do the spray and now I have bites??? Nothing was making sense. *Maybe they were on his shoe or something cause he came to me AFTER he treated them otha apartments.* I had to wait till Monday to alert my super but I was beyond mad. *How do I try to protect against it and end up gettin it? That make sense? What, the world just wanted to give me a first glance at what it feels like so I can educate others effectively?*

Early Monday morning I was in the superintendent's office tryna calmly explain to her that the man brought bed bugs into my house. To my damn surprise she was like "No, I don't think that's what happened. Maybe you had them before and just didn't know, or it's probably not even bed bugs" *How? How dat make sense, so it may not even be bed bugs but if it is then I had them previously, but they only decided to bite me after the man was in my house? I'm not an idiot.* "No, I didn't have bites until AFTER he was in my house, how do you explain that? Well now this was a huge inconvenience cause I gotta pack my house up again to get the treatment". Without proof they weren't willing to spray again. For that week my sister and I took turns tryna stay awake during the night to catch them. We were afraid to sleep because we didn't wanna get bitten. Suddenly that saying "Night Night don't let the bed bugs bite" made sense. *Why do parents say that to kids? That's horrible, do they know what bed bug bites feel like?* I had some supplies that I had taken from my training class on bed bugs that I was going to use to catch one if I ever saw one.

One night I woke up randomly at 3 am, looked over at my sister sleeping and saw something crawling down her stomach. I screamed, jumped up and grabbed the tape thingy to get it off her. She jumped up and freaked out too once she realized the bug was crawling on her. Amidst the chaos we caught the stupid thing and put it in a bag to later use as proof. Instead of showing my super - I no longer trusted her - I called public health to inspect. It didn't even take long for the woman to show up and make inspections. She inspected my house and couldn't find any trace of bed bugs, but when I showed her the thing I caught she said "Yep that's definitely a bed bug and given how you explained the situation and my investigation, it most likely came in by the guy who did the inspection. Reason being, bed bugs can latch onto even the smallest of clothing and that man was going from apartment to apartment. Plus, I see no evidence of it being anywhere." *That's cause I didn't let him in anywhere but right here in the living room. Dis man tried to blame me. Sigh!!! Finally, justice.* I didn't always like to be right but I didn't like being made to feel like I was stupid. What I said made logical sense. I never did get an apology but at least they were now forced to treat my apartment properly AND I asked that it was done by a different company.

After that ordeal my leather set needed to go. Even though bed bugs don't really live on leather I wanted to be extra careful. Plus, it was not comfortable to share with my sister and she was here to stay. After a long discussion and negotiating my dad helped me purchase something better. A large sectional. I planned to use the money I was making from Leo to pay for the new furniture but my investments were tied up and it was easier to buy everything on store credit. The goal was to find one piece of furniture that provided sleeping arrangements for both my sister and I, two beds, one couch. We settled on an L shaped sectional with a built-in bed. She got the bed and I got the chaise.

Such a fancy word...chaise. I was attached to the leather couch merely because of how I acquired such beautiful pieces for cheap. Now I had to spend real money, it was like an investment and our return was that we no longer had to scrunch up scrunch up on the couch. If you woulda seen my apartment then you would understand there was no way that this L shaped sectional should have fit, but it needed to fit, so it did.

As tiring as all this was, it couldn't take away the excitement of the milestones we were embarking on. Everyday this beautiful boy was growing. It was scary, challenging, yet rewarding. Eva look at ya child an be like whoa dats all me? I was looking at my baby as I helped him get ready for kindergarten. HE MADE IT!!! I was so proud that God had trusted me to be his momma. He graduated from daycare to kindergarten and thank God too cause I was gettin tired of asking "Hey, what did yu do today?" Only to hear "Playing" Apparently that's all they did before kindergarten, jus enjoyed the days playing but it was time he started to learn stuff, you know? Abc's, count money, tell time...sumthin. With any new establishment I always set an appointment with the person to give them a full rundown of Kaykay's disability, his limits, what to watch for, what to listen for, how he behaved, the whole nine yards, and I also tried to educate the teacher about what muscular dystrophy was. As many years as Muscular Dystrophy had been around it was definitely not common knowledge. Either way I never had any problems, most people thanked me for the info as a heads up but chose to get to know him for themselves which was totally fine.

At first everything seemed cool, then I got a call saying I needed to meet with his new principal. Confused as to why the teacher ain't call me if she had an issue, I showed up to school a lil hesitant. It was a black vice principal so I was thinking, *"light let's see,* she introduced herself then says "The reason I wanted to talk to you was because his teacher had some questions". *Funny I don't see her in this room to ask me the questions but ok...go on.* "She wanted to know why Kayshaun was not in a special needs class." If I coulda choked the teacher out I woulda. Neva has a question sent my blood boiling from zero to one hundred so quick. *Special needs? What the fuck? No disrespect to the people who need that but where's this coming from? If she's talking bout the same special needs classes that I saw while I was growing up...I'll pass.* I responded "If she had all these questions, why didn't she ask me herself? I gave her all the papers and said if she had questions to ask me...why isn't she here?" "She wasn't able to be here but if your son has all these needs why isn't he going to a special needs school? There are many good schools in the area"

I'm trying my hardest to calm my nerves as tears are running down my face. "He's in this school cause he doesn't need to be in a special needs school, what is it that he needs that she feels she can't provide for him? She hasn't even met him yet, how does she even know?" I'm back and forth with this VP and she's really tryna defend this lady who ain't even here "I'm not exactly sure what it is" I was trying not to yell "So how can you tell me y'all can't accommodate him? If you want him to go to a special needs class you're gonna have to show me what the problem is so I can get the help he needs. We have outside therapy programs that have been involved with him and if there is a problem I will let them know. Until then your teacher is gonna have to find a way to teach him or move him to a different class." After she apologized for upsetting me I finished off by saying "You can tell the teacher to contact me, betta yet, I'll be back to talk to her myself" Then I stormed out of the office.

Admittedly Kaykay was a bit behind, I wasn't sure if it was a condition of the disease or just life itself, but I wasn't about to let some lady who ain't know him label him. Listen, she was just gonna have to find a more creative way to teach. If after she tried there was an actual issue I had no problem getting him help. Kaykay was the type of child that it might look like he wasn't catching on but the moment it clicked, he got it. Even with reading he was a bit slower than the other kids but one day after sitting with him and getting him to sound out words, he said c...a...r...s an looks at me and says "I'm an intelligent boy....which is another word for smart"

He knew himself that he was smart, therefore it was my duty as his mother to prove it to the unbelievers and those hesitating. By the next day his teacher apologized and tried to say it was a misunderstanding, but I was over her. Mind you I had given her a lot of information to process and so not all of it applied to him, but instead of meeting with me and asking questions she went above me and damn near insulted my parenting. Now I wanted more than anything to prove her wrong. She thought he was behind? Then I was getting the tests to prove he wasn't.

I had a good relationship with his rehab team. As I was learning more about the disability and his needs I was learning that I had access to more agencies. It was a beautiful blessing. This lady stirred something up in me and I ran with it. I started researching agencies for help, I tried to see what I could tap into through the school board. We already had physiotherapy, occupational therapy and speech therapy going, but I needed a school advocate, someone to do my fighting for me in a more politically correct way. I didn't even know people like advocates existed for mothers like me but I found one and she was a God sent. She helped me understand EAP - Education Assistance Plan and other school lingo they use against the uninformed. All I had to do was provide her with the info I collected from the doctor and we were well protected. I requested that Kaykay had a psychological assessment done from his rehab team in order to understand his learning better so that I could bring it to put in his school file.

This didn't feel like this was the right environment for him. Only thing was that I was told this was one of the better schools in the hood, so where did that leave us? I just needed to spend more time teaching him in between class, programing, volunteering and life. Welcome to motherhood!

I was still learning the ins and outs of motherhood and as much as I was still hoping for some fairytale relationship with my mother I had come to my own understanding of our relationship. Either way, I was still hoping to find some type of mentor along the way. I prayed, and she came. She came in the form of an arts educator. Tish and her friend ran a creative arts program for women of color that combined digital media, recording and other forms of art into a unique outlet opportunity. It was a program unlike any other which was probably why it didn't last long in our building. Apparently there seemed to have been a misunderstanding where the people at my building weren't aware that the program was for women of colour only. Sara left and we had a new girl, still young, still white. She had the same task of coordinating programs and local agencies into our building. She was running around tryna play middle man between her bosses and Tish. Shit was crazy. It didn't make sense to me, I kept hearing the phrase "We do not feel comfortable...we do not feel comfortable having a program here". We had enough girls interested in the program but there was some issue about how it wasn't inclusive of the ONE white girl we had in the building who didn't even have an interest in the program. *Sigh! This building is 90% black, who is it hurting? White people always gotta find a problem where there ain't none.*

I loved the program, it was refreshing to have another type of program that gave me the opportunity to connect with other women-and other women of colour. As tenant rep I tried to see if there was anything I could do to keep the program in our building but it was a losing fight. We ended up moving the program next door to the library. Annoying but at least we had somewhere to go. *That ain't right though, I don't like that.* At least we got a chance to kick it with a variety of different women. Some were mothers, some were younger, all were women of color. Things were so chill I wanted to be involved as much as I could. One of the program leaders had a mothering type of personality that I gravitated to. She thought what I did was magical. I was a black girl who did classical piano, who also did poetry, who also was a kick ass mom, who also did this, who also did that. I was just tryna get a balance on everything, surprisingly she was willing to help me. The way the program was handled left a bad taste in my mouth and a strain on my relationship with the building staff. I no longer felt like I could trust them. It was my last year of tenancy, I was set to move out in the summer and I had no clue where I was gonna go.

We were in the midst of trying to figure out a deal with our landlord. By the end of the year the first group of women were all set to roll out as we had completed our four year agreement, but from speaking to the other women, none of us knew where to go. There was a lot of pressure. A lot of pressure. Whenever things felt overwhelming it was always nice to connect with Nova - she gave me life in so many ways.

24 Oct 2011 To: Cola

Hey pretty lady!

Just thinking about you and I saw that we lost touch a little while back. I was going through some videos, saw your face, your crazy cute son and wanted to check in ... see you are doing and all that good stuff.

:)

keep in touch, i'd love to know how you are doing!

Nova

Oct 24, 2011 To:Nova

Omg hey how are you?

Ye I thought of you the other day and some of the things you said when you were here in terms of relationships and how you were able to move on.

Anyway I am doing good thanks. I'm back in school full time for my last year. I will be graduating in 2012.

I am busy with my volunteer work for toronto housing.

My son is doing great, he jus started sk and he seems to really enjoy it.

I am so glad you emailed me

How are yu doing? How's the book? How's life?

Can't wait to hear from you, Nicola

25 Oct 2011 To: Cola

Good to know we were both on each other's mind! :)

what about relationships were you thinking about? i'm actually doing a tele-seminar tonight and for the next 3

weeks about getting IN, OUT and OVER relationships. you basically call the number, i talk, you listen, i answer any questions and then do follow-up questions on twitter.
haaaaaay to graduation! that's incredible and so fantastic! AND volunteering on top of it!? go YOU!
your son is too adorable, i'm sure he'll really excel in a school setting.
how are YOU doing? how are the girls at Humewood?
Nova

I was experiencing a new kinna stress. Helping my baby boy was a priority but I was also in my last year of my program and I desperately needed to raise my GPA. This meant more studying, more long nights, more assignments and more courses as I tried to squeeze in enough classes to pull out a miracle. I was surprised when Brooklyn called and said he was in town and wanted to take me out. We talked on the phone a few times but never anything serious. *I was happy. I can't believe he wanted to take me out.* He was calling me at the right time now though cause I was itching to chill with someone low key. So, we're chilling in his car after our date, touching, kissing, rubbing and kinda like second nature I began to remove my clothes. He stopped, looked at me and said "What are you doing" *What's happening, did he jus ask me what I'm doing? Iuno, following the flow. Well this is embarrassing.* I reply "Iuno, thought you wanted to have sex" Brooklyn says "No, I'm jus tryna kick it with you, you need to have some more self-respect girl, hold yourself to a high standard. You're beautiful" *I feel so dumb. I'm not sure if I should cry of embarrassment or jus sit here.* "Baby girl I love your body, I love your size, I don't want to rush into having sex, let's just go slow, I'm not going nowhere" This was the best date I had been on thus far. Anytime I talked bout going to the gym he got mad. "Baby you perfect as you are, quit with the gym talk" I didn't know how to respond. I was happy he liked me for me, but I had never had my weight celebrated. He really educated me and raised my standards that I didn't even know were so damn low.

He had other gems for me during our time together.

I said to him "My next baby daddy gon be different" He got so mad "Why would you strive to have another baby daddy? Do you even know what that word means? How you ain't got no problem with saying that? Instead of saying you want to have a child with your husband you're saying you want another baby daddy? You should want more for yourself and for your child" He was right though, I didn't get it, but I knew I was meant to feel stupid. I didn't want any other baby fadda, but ain't no husband was kicking down my door till now. We had kicked it long distance for five months, talked when he could, and he always saw me when he was in town. I tried not to complain about his absences. I understood he was focused in the studio but once a week barely seemed like much. It still seemed like it was something real special we had growing so I tried not to let my insecurities get the best of me... except they were gettin the best of me. I couldn't help but feel like it was too good to be true. Like with my complaining or naggin he was gonna tell me it was over. He was gonna leave me. I didn't even deserve to be with someone like him, but before he left me I was gonna leave him. I called him up and left a voice message saying it was over. He never answered often anyway. "I'm sorry, I can't do this, the distance is too much, you never have time, I just, I miss you but can't see you. I'm sorry I just can't." I waited for a response but it never came.

Oct 25, 2011 To: Nova

Hmmm well in terms of relationships, I met someone back in july an I guess we've been talking ever since, but its not an easy transition for me. I am not used to relationships or talking in a serious matter with someone who actually truly likes me. Its hard. There's times I tell him I jus wanna stay friends because I don't believe I deserve to be in a relationship, or I'm just scared that my past will repeat itself. Relationships are just weird to me.

How much do yur phone conversations cost?

An I am, hmm tired but good, working hard to figure out what I wanna do in life, an how to achieve it all. Feeling sluggish, so I know I gotta make time for the gym, but with my life up an down it seems almost impossible.

So how is everything else with you?

Nov 7, 2011 To: Cola

Hey girl, sorry for the slow reply...

if you sluggish, up those vitamins, ditch any caffeine and powerwalk!! before that snow hits! i'm a big advocate of WINNING in the morning. if possible, before your son is up, or once he's out to school - MAKE time for you. 30 minutes to start. this could be a great time to walk, listen to inspirational music or a book on tape on your iPod, stretch, pray, journal ... but something just for you.

you might even feel guilty at first, but don't. the time you take to fill up will effect what you do for the rest of the day. TRUST!

if you don't take care of YOU, you will resent the people who need you because the time you give to THEM is time you could be giving to yourself. and who wants to live like that?! is that something you could do?

one thing i've learned about relationships is that you have to BE what it is that you want. if you want LOVE, be loving, if you want RESPECT, be respectful, if you want TRUST, HONEST, COMMUNICATION ... its got to come from you and that's not just romantic relationships, that's dealing with people period. you don't get to control what happens on the outside, but you always can control what happens inside.

if you aren't ready for something serious, then take your time! its all about YOU boo!

the calls are free and tomorrow night is the last one where i talk about getting iN a relationship. could be the ONE to listen to.

Nova was right. I needed to be everything I was expecting from this man. I just hope it wasn't too late to reach him.

Nathaniel
whats up
Cola
nun u

Nathaniel
chilling at home
Cola
oh ok
Nathaniel
how you been
Cola
good thank u, what's new
Nathaniel
working, lol, I c you have a man. I been 3 month no alcohol, you should see my guns
Cola
how would u know if i have a man... that's good that u gone that long, where you at, t dot?
Nathaniel
what
Cola
how would u know if i have a man
Nathaniel
cause that what you said
Cola
and i said that it's good that you've gone so long without alcohol im proud of you... are u still in toronto
Nathaniel
yea, i wish to see you
Cola
you wanna see me..y's that
Nathaniel
cause your very special to me in my life
Cola
fo real...i neva thought that
Nathaniel
you have done so much, and yur so really
Cola
do u mean real
Nathaniel
yea what the fuck
hows your kk
Cola

to be honest after last time, i didn't really think i meant that much the way things went down

Nathaniel

i love him

Cola

he's good, he's sooo big now

Nathaniel

going to be a strong boy

Cola

yep he talks a lot an he's doin well in school, i'm proud of him he's so cute

Nathaniel

goood

Cola

thanks

Nathaniel

im happy to hear

Cola

ye thanks

Nathaniel

if your down to chill im down

Cola

depends on where an when

Nathaniel

your place or my place

Cola

public place..aint tryna chill in homes...plus my sis lives wit me now..an she dont like u

Nathaniel

why?can i call you, how bout that

Cola

hmmm because of how shit went down last time an u tried to hype, do u still know my number

Nathaniel

fuck i now i fucked up SORRY

Cola

y u cussin...u asked why she didn't like u an i told u the truth

Nathaniel
can i call you?

I gave him my number, we talked and caught up. He always had good intentions but it wasn't a relationship I wanted to revisit. Occasional support sure, I mean, I was still tryna put my own stuff together. Right now my focus was on my school, my child, my programs and Brooklyn. Who I was having trouble tryna locate at the moment. I tried calling with no answer. Then I heard a knock at the door. Standin outside my door the week after Christmas was Brooklyn and his sexy chocolate goodness with a goofy grin on his face. *Love. Him.* "Baby girl, I got your message, but I figured I should come see you instead. I'm sorry I eva made you feel that way. I promise things are gonna be different, Imma call more, Imma make the time despite being in the studio, but you gotta promise to work on your temper, please." "Ok, I'm sorry"

That was a great surprise, had I known he was gonna show up I woulda gotten him a present like he had done for me. I invited him in for the night and presented him my body. Naked. He had empowered me. He made me feel comfortable. Beautiful. As he laid me back he plunged his love inside me for the first time. After a climactic five months we had both let down our guards as the magic of Christmas left singing sounds all around us. When he was done he asked me to sit on him. *What's he mean sit on him?* "Come sit on my face, I want you to suffocate me" *What kinda weird shit is this? Suffocate? What the fuck I look like? Welp here I go.* "How do I know when to stop" "I'll tap you" This was the most uncomfortable shit I had ever done. I didn't do sexual exploration like this. I did the regular shit. Missionary, Doggy, not Suffocation. Women around me talk about masturbation. But for me it was like masturbation? What's that? Not for me, I didn't think it was my job to do. What's the point of fucking a dude who can't do the exploration himself? This whole suffocation thing was just beyond me. How does it work? Do I sit? Put some weight? Little weight? Wait...is this why he likes my weight?

Oh, hellllllll no, I'm some...fat fetish? Sigh. *Just try it. Am I hurting him? Will he die? What if he stops breathing? This shit is weird.* He tapped out when he had enough but it jus left me feeling so strange in my own body. *Way to ruin it for me.* I'm thinking damn he thinks I'm beautiful while he's probably thinking damn she could really sit on my face. Despite the weird ending I was happy that I had gotten to spend time with him.

He kept to his word once he was back in New York. He called more, checked in more, we started off the new year great and was moving strong. Seeing as me an my new beau were good, and my bestie Aaliyah was having a bday coming up, when she asked for bday suggestions I had told her about a couple's night comedy show. She was more than happy with the suggestions so we set plans in motion and started purchasing tickets. Before buying Brooklyn's ticket I had to be sure he was actually gonna be in the country, so I call him up. "Hey boo, my bestie's having a bday in a few weeks would you like to come with me? I'd have to buy your ticket early though" "Hmmm, I'm not sure if I'll be in the studio or not, it's kinda too early for me to plan" "Iight well, how bout this, I'll buy us the tickets and if you can't go jus lemme know and I'll sell the ticket cool?" "Ok baby girl, I'll let you know, gotta go, talk to you soon". Like clockwork later on that night, Nathaniel was hittin me up.

January 28th 2012 10:06pm
Nathaniel
hi you
Cola
hi
Nathaniel
what you doing
Cola
tryna buy tickets to a show
Nathaniel
so what u saying for tonight
Cola

chillin doin wrk
Nathaniel
kk do your thin
Cola
ye wat u up to
Nathaniel
at home, an you?
Cola
ye im home
Nathaniel
u want to chill, i want to eat something
Cola
i have a man..hanging out is not a good idea sorry
Nathaniel
wtf, what ever
Cola
there should be no issue...u can't possibly expect me to drop my man for you...regardless of you apologizing an the fact that we gettin along... you're still my ex...an i gotta keep you at a distance..especially since I know you miss me an wanna fuck
Nathaniel
well said kk

My new boo got me swerving my old boo but as the date approached and I was calling his phone I was gettin no response. I called, I called, I called. *Yo why this nigga ain't picking up? It's so simple. You want the ticket or naw? I can't believe he's doing this to me, really? I hope he's ok, what if something happened to him?*

The big night comes and still no word from Brooklyn. I was excited to celebrate with Aaliyah but I was literally surrounded by couple's jus as my couple had left me hanging, even my lil sister had a man at the show. With the understanding now that he wasn't coming I gave the ticket away and headed inside to make the most of the night. I tried so hard to keep from crying. *Am I really that big of a loser that I had not one guy I coulda called tonight? Not one that could be my date? Wow. Yo focus, it ain't about you tonight. Smile and keep laughing.* I'll admit, the jokes were hot, and I was really starting to laugh and enjoy myself. *That's it, enjoy yourself.*

This night was a two in one comedy and dance show. Once the laughter was done the floor opened up and the music started to pump to let way for the rhythms of the night. *Hey that's our song, girl you never let loose, shake off this dude and have some fun.* I hadn't had much to eat but for the night I was gonna make my money worth it. I went to the table and asked for a drink and had a rum and coke mixed. WHOOO HAPPY BIRTHDAY!!!! And Aaliyah shouted IT'S MY BIRTHDAY We were happy. Once I finished my first drink they poured me another. "Girl you never drink, have another" My sister chimed in "She's not a big drinker, Nikki slow down on your drinks" *You got this, don't let em tell you wassup. You know your limit. Go ahead, have another.* 15 mins with 7 rum and cokes running through my system I took a bow. Everything was a blur as I swayed my body and arms.

Yo what happened last night? How did I get into my bed? Where's Aaliyah? WHAT HAPPENED!!! I woke up the next day with no recollection of how I got home much less how I got into my bed. As my sister explained things to me, I was carried out by the men in the group once I threw up on Aaliyah's shoes. *Are you good fam? You need to call her, try to explain...something.* I have never behaved in that way. "Hey.... happy birthday, girl omg I'm so sorry. I don't even know what got into me or what happened last night. That's not like me at all. So many things were happening, please, please, please say you can forgive me." She was clearly mad. *Shit, did I just lose a best friend? Cola you need help man, like seriously.* I literally had to beg for forgiveness. I didn't know what else to do. *What the fuck are you good for? Maybe you should jus disappear. How easy it would be to take a knife and end all this pain. You just keep hurting those around you. You suck. You really think she's gonna wanna be your friend? Look at you, you're pathetic. Brooklyn ain't call cause you naggin and he over your bullshit. Who's gonna wanna be with you? You couldn't even find a man to go with you last night. You unlovable piece of shit. Nobody's eva gonna love you. Nobody. This is it for you.* Was this rock bottom? Could it get any lower? Would the pain stop now? Why couldn't the voices jus leave me alone? Could I just lay here in the dark? Why wouldn't life just leave me alone? I didn't eva wanna move. Fuck life.

Poetic Interlude

Regrettably
I've had one of those nights
Those nights when everything becomes a haze
No matta how hard we try our minds are stuck in mental mazes
And we party way too hard
Worse
We black out
And leave the safety of our body
In the hands of whomever we've surrounded ourselves with
I
Have had one of those nights
One of those nights
One of those weeks
One of those months
When the annoyance of my past weighs heavily on my mind
Ingested with every sip of alcohol
The feel good drink
Makes me feel good no more
As I project all my hurting pain
Onto the dance floor
Wondering
What the hell happened?
When did things get so wrong?
I guess I've been lying to myself for quite awhile now
I've been stacking issues in my life like a brick house
Building from the inside out
On the outside I appear to be
So beautiful an strong
On the inside I've created an establishment
Where I can be separated from the world
Surrounded by thoughts of me myself and I
I feel as though I'm no longer strong enough to survive

I'm tired
Weakened by the years of deprivation
My heart and head are feeling the separation and frustration of life
My hearts cold as ice
Fueled by cruelty
I've been spit on
Disrespected
Robbed
Relationships have broken me
Taken everything and left me
Abandoned in my house
These are the thoughts that haunted me
As I drank more and more
Tumbled to the floor
and woke up in my bed
Regrettably
I've had one of those nights
One of those nights
Where for the first time I couldn't see past
The negativity cloudin my head
Tryna be happy an smile for my best friend
Cause see it was her birthday
I've never behaved that way in public
I've never allowed my emotions to spill over an take control in a public setting
I would normally jus wear a happy mask
Masking the true identity of my soul
With the pressures of graduation
The foundation in which I built my life
Is fastly unraveling
Revealing the true pain
Stuffed into a jar
Like a grain of salt
My wounds are still burning me
Imma half to dig real deep down to pull myself outta this
I pray God will forgive me, Forgive my sins
Maybe i'll finally be able to forgive myself
And do away with those regrettable crazy nights

CHAPTER FIFTY-TWO

Need

Even so husbands should and are morally obligated to love their own wives as [being in a sense] their own bodies. He who loves his own wife loves himself. EPHESIANS 5:28

When I needed him most Romeo was here. Everything else was going shitty and all I needed to do was hear his voice. Out of fear or missed opportunity it had been awhile since we tried to see each other. Even now when we attempted to see each other things failed. It was hard on him cause he got his hopes up only to have his heart broken each time it was unsuccessful. He spoke with a gentle voice and did everything in his power to show me how much he changed and how he was ready to be with me seriously. I had not made an attempt to visit him since I moved to Toronto, yet he was only a 20 min drive away. He had moved recently to a new house but I got his address and googled the directions to his house to ensure I didn't get lost. He was hesitant to let me drive down to him, afraid it wasn't going to work, but I was determined. It had been way too long and I needed him. His touch, his love, I didn't care about the past, in this moment... I just needed him. *I have the directions to his house so there's nothing that could stop us from seeing each other. My phone's charged. I'm ready!* The plan was to stay on the phone with each other until I got to his door.

Anticipation grew the closer I got to Brampton. I tried to laugh it off by sayin "Yo what if the phone cuts" He's not laughing with me "Why would you say that?". It was all fun and games until the call dropped as I approached his exit. He called me back and we both tried to laugh it off, *that was close.* I didn't have GPS so I was kicking it old school using the printed paper from mapquest trying to follow it as I drove. *I thought it was just a 5 min drive from the exit. Hello? Hello? Did the call just drop?* My phone rings again *Hello? Hello? Romeo? I can hear you, can you hear me? K hang up and I'll call you back.* We hang up and I try calling him again. *Romeo? Can you hear me? I can hear him, why can't he hear me?* My phone rang again it was his brother "Are you ok? Romeo wanted me to tell you not to waste your time, it's not gonna work" "I'm not going home, can you tell me the correct street address please?" "It's the new house, I don't know the address sorry." We hang up and within another few minutes I receive another call, this time it was from his twin "Hey, what's going on, is your brother ok?" "Iuno he jus asked me to call you to see if you're ok" "I'm fine, I'm jus trying to find your house. Can you tell me what street to go on?" "I don't even live there sorry, I wouldn't know where it is." *So they can both hear me and respond but he can't? That's weird, it doesn't make sense. Here we go again with this stuff.*

An hour had gone by, then two, but I was determined to find this house. I finally pull over and asked someone where this street was. *Iuno why I didn't think of it sooner.* The man said he wasn't 100% sure but he believed it was just two streets over in the new suburb. It gave me the first glimmer of hope in hours. As I started to drive there my phone rang again. "Hello?" "Baby, if you can hear me, then go home. I knew it wasn't going to work out, just give up and go home, don't waste anymore of your time on me." I knew he couldn't hear me but I yelled "No baby, I'm coming". Then he hung the phone up. It was the most heartbreaking call I've ever gotten from him. I stepped on the gas and I was driving these two streets over in a fury.

Once I turned down the street I started looking for the number. *Look, it's there on your left. Yess!! You found it!* I jumped out of my car, ran up to the door and rang the doorbell. *Omg omg, finally.* My smile could not have been any bigger as I waited for this door to open. I almost wanted to kick it down and run inside into his arms. I heard the footsteps to the door then heard the unlock as I got ready to embrace him. *Romeo!!! Hug first? Kiss first? What?* The door opened...and as I was about to lean in I saw a white man standing in the doorway. *What? That's not Romeo, what number house is this?* "Sorry, I have the wrong house" I couldn't get my legs to move fast enough as I ran back down the steps to my car. *What just happened?* My heart sank. That was it. My one chance gone. *How could it have gone so wrong? I had the directions. What did I miss?* As I made it onto the highway home my phone rang and it was Romeo's brother again "Hey Cola, you home yet? Are you ok? What happened?" "Ye, I'm ok, I'm on my way home, thanks for checking in" I hang up with him and Romeo finally called me again. "Baby? You ok?" "Ye Romeo, I'm ok" I'm trying to hide my tears, I didn't want him to know I was crying. He sounded different, like a shell. He kept me company until I had made it safely home.

I tried to let it go but this thing was gnawing at me, *how did I go to the wrong house?* As I got inside I headed directly over to my computer to google the address again. From what I could tell from the maps I was on the correct street, however there were two adjoining streets with different names. I was at the top of the street and he lived on the bottom of the street. Had I kept driving down I would have found his house. I had driven right past his house on my way to the highway. Now that I knew better, I wanted to try again but Romeo was done trying. "My heart can't take anymore disappointments. Every time we try and it doesn't work it hurts a lot, and I keep reliving this pain. There's no point in us trying anymore. We should just stop trying, stop talking" *Stop talking? It's like that? No, I don't wanna stop trying.* "You don't wanna eva talk anymore?" "It's jus not meant to be, goodbye" I had no words, I jus cried in silence.

CHAPTER FIFTY-THREE

Dim light

"Catch the foxes for us, The little foxes that spoil and ruin the vineyards [of love], while our vineyards are in blossom."
-Song of Solomon 2 :15

Mar 14, 2012 To:Nova

Hey nova how are things going? I know its been a while since we spoke but I just wanted to say hi and see how your doing.
Nicola

Mar 14, 2012 To:Cola

So nice to hear from you! You're on my mind allll the time!!:)
What's the latest from Finch?

Mar 14, 2012 To:Nova

That's good to know....hmm I'm moving out of finch by June and I'm graduating university by June....I've been involved in programs, and performing. I recently started writing for an online magazine as a lifestyle editor. What's new with you?
Nicola

I had all these good things going on around me except I couldn't find a place for us to live. Things were only getting even more tense at the building for me. Nobody saw me unless I wanted them to see me. My relationship with the staff was nonexistent cause they looked like the enemy to me. I had stopped overextending myself. I was no longer at every event, every beck and call. I was no longer the shining success that I once was, so now it was even more important for me to find my own place and prove to them I could do shit on my own. Yet I looked everywhere and couldn't find anything. It was early, but still, what area was I gonna move to? What schools would KayKay go to? There were a lot of factors to figure out. Two-bedroom or Three? My sister was gonna move with me wherever I went so I had to find something for all of us. Inside I was drowning. I was tryna find reasons to smile for longer than a minute. Connecting to Nova always gave my heart something to hold onto. In my darkest moments either she reached me, or I reached her. It was like a light that never went dim.

> March 24, 2012
>
> Even though my child has Duchenne muscular dystrophy, I thank God that it is not visible in the way he moves...my son was blessed with RIDDIM

KayKay was literally my reason to breathe, my reason to get up, my reason to keep my heart beating. Whenever I saw him dancing it reminded me that he was OK. If he was ok then I was ok. We had a few bumpy rides along the way, he'd fall but he always got up. There was something about watching him grow that always amazed me. I found it hard to believe that God would trust me to be his mother the way I felt so messed up. I was a failure in life yet my child loved me without fault. As much as I felt like dying, truth be told, there wasn't even time for that. Like I was so busy that suicide wasn't even an option. *Who will take care of your child if you go?*

Thank God I had people who looked out for me and made me feel not so alone. Tish took me under her wing and was my unofficial mentor. I was meeting her at the library so we could create a plan to help me organize my mess of a life. Regardless of anything I needed to graduate this year. I had been in school too damn long and she had a plan to keep me accountable. It felt so incredible to finally have some direction. I thought she was gonna jus help me organize my subjects and assignments or something but from the stories I had told her about Leo and Aaliyah's birthday (which still haunted me) she said, "You're a hot mess and you need to get help" She wasn't wrong. I just didn't know where to start. When she said I need help she meant a therapist, someone who I could just lay all my shit out with and help me establish healthy boundaries. The second thing she said I needed to do was to cut free from Leo and leave the money behind. *She crazy, that's too much money.* She ain't know him but her impression was that he was too old to be preying on girls like me. That was gonna take time though, I wasn't ready to give it up. I thought the list was done but then she was coming for my fake passes. She said "If you get caught you could end up in jail and lose your son, is that what you want? Is it all worth it?" Well the answer to that question was obvious but with more money locked into the investment I didn't have the extra cash to pay for the bus pass and why should I if Leo was supplying a cheaper option? I was here tryna save money and she was tryna get me to give it all up. Nope! She often came off really bossy but it was only cause she cared. She really got invested when she was tryna help someone out.

I loved that Tish was Christian, but not Christian Christian, not like all holier than thou cause she still understood life. She had that hood Christian vibe, loved God but understood the streets. The way she talked about Jesus made Him seem so much cooler than I remembered as a child. She said she talks to Him just like she would any of her friends like "I see what you tried to do there Lord, I see you" *I didn't even know we could talk to him like that.* Truth was there wasn't any major rules on how we spoke to Him as long as we weren't being disrespectful, just like with anyone else. I mean sure, He's God but He's not so far away that He couldn't relate to us on our level; I mean damn, He made us. She would tell me stories and I'd be like wait, that was in the Bible? Like how she said Jesus rolled with the prostitutes and the bod mon and the rejected. I mean I had heard that, but not like that, she made the Bible come alive and she was always animated when she reenacted the stories. *Maybe He can relate to me. Who is this man she speaks about?* I needed to find God in my own way, not jus cause I was the daughter of a pastor. *Maybe they should teach bout Him more like this. I think people wouldn't feel so rejected. I wouldn't.* I decided that from then on I wanted to get to know gangsta Jesus, the man who loved sinners and fought for the oppressed yet remained very respectful. For the 100th time I wanted to make another attempt at attending church more consistently.

CHAPTER FIFTY-FOUR

Subway Love

And may the Lord cause you to increase and excel and overflow in love for one another, and for all people, just as we also do for you;
-1 Thesselonian 3:12

My quest for Jesus brought me to a new church in a movie theatre at Yonge and Sheppard. This church was different but good, refreshing. It was multicultural, they sang unfamiliar songs, but it started on time and was done on time. I was used to hearing Jamaican medleys. Whenever someone started singing "Goodbye worl, I stay no langa wid yu.... reel reel reel Christ so reel to mi, hI luv (h)im, cause he give us di victori" my heart felt so full. These songs were my childhood. It was the one thing that made a church feel like home to me. Even without those songs I could still see myself going back if it wasn't so far by bus. A year had gone by without having my car and I was slowly adjusting. Public transit was not as comfortable as taking a car, it took forever to get to a destination, but I always saw interesting people. As I stood in front of the subway doors waiting for them to open our eyes made contact. I was on the inside about to step off and he was on the outside about to step in. Time paused as I watched this gorgeous tall light skin sexy eyed brotha walk onto the train. I smiled as he watched my hips sway. *Phew! Omg, hot damn, how can man be that damn fine? Lord have mercy! He's giving me butterflies. Who's touching me?* The butterflies intensified as I felt a hand take my hand. *Wow*, I look up, and it was him. *AHHHHHH, yo play cool, stop smiling so big.* In that moment there were no words. Just actions. Here it goes: This is Subway Love...

Poetic Love Story
On the subway subway subway
One day
I was on the subway

Sunday
I was on the subway
Comin from church
Got lost on the subway
But found your love
On that same subway
The sheppard way
My final stop
one bus
To my destination
One must wonder how it came to be
You an me
Beautiful sight to see
My insecurities an my past have haunted me until you came and set me free
Showed me a love that I never thought existed
Told me to love myself and be me
And thats real
In that moment as I stepped off the train
I looked up yu looked at me
an for a spit second life and time jus paused
Doo doo doo
Doors be closin
I be walkin
Felt a hand
Take me hand an lead me away
Lol what the hell
I got lost in his brown eyes
Hmmm his brown eyes
Wasn't tellin no lies
Said he loved my thighs
He smile I smile
What's ya name
Cola yurs
Chef
Cute so wassup
Nun yu
Oh boo I had to holla at yu
Cause yu be mighty fine in that tight ass skirt
Ass so big an poppin

Almost lost my shirt
I chuckle a bit n my bat my eyes
Pinch me I'm in a dream
This mans way to fly
Down to business
How much kids yu got
3 yu
One
Man
Naw
Girl
Naw
Numba
Pause
We walking an talkin tryna find my bus
Saw the sunlight shine bright and glisten off his beautiful face
Truss
6'3 to 5'3
Tall to short
Light skin with braids
Made me weak in the knees
Please Lord please
Don't let this man tease me
He leans close
I can feel his sweet warm breath on my neck
As I hold my face away
He leans closer to my ear an all I hear him say
Is your so beautiful damn
Gimme ya numba girl please
I wanna chance to make yu smile
N imma do it with ease
My bus is here
I gotta go
I give him my numba an walk away
Ooo damn damn damn
Is what I hear him say
Sittin on the bus
Ring ring

Hello
All I wanted to do was hear your voice one more time
Maybe we'll meet up soon
But for now it's just goodbye
Click...

I can't believe that jus happened. No, he didn't. Girl stop smiling so big you look goofy. Is he still standing there? Are you gonna call him? Naw don't call him. You just came from church. Focus. He was fine though, jus call him. Who cares if you met him today, nobody has to know if you don't tell them. Pheww deep breath. He had me all bent outta shape. *Live a little!* I called him. We agreed to meet later on that night at my place since I was gonna be home alone...Poetic Love story continued...

Hey I jus met yu today
On the subway
Love
My eyes couldn't look away
My feelings I tried to
Shove
In my back pocket
Yu see
Where they will remain
With the dust an the lint
All my disgrace an shame
I've been emotionally beaten and bruised
My heart shattered in two
Too many pieces
I figured would never get glued
Back together again
I'm no humpty dumpty
I can't even compete
I'm too ugly
I'm too fat
I am a hoe
Used by others to clean their messes
Angry that I provoke thoughts by wearin red dresses
Forced to face reality an make self confesses
What is going on
What is going wrong

My life's a sad song
Blah blah blah
4 rapes
4 rapes that left me longing an wantin for a single delicate human touch
I say human cause them be monsters
Monsters that haunted me an left me feelin unworthy unloved worthless
No man's prize but everyone's
Bitch
Take a picture an frame it
Welcome to my perfect life
Where black is white
An I'm never right
6 years I been feelin this way
My subway love came
Made me a part of his play
I called him that night
To my beckon call he ran
Grabbed me tight in his muscular arms
My fear and excitement was so alarming an present
Felt like a king holdin a peasant
Not deserving of such kind words
I'm like a bird
But I can't fly away, his soft large hands
Rests peaceful on my face
Ahh the first kiss
And it was gently placed
From lips to lips
Then hands to hands
My bodies intertwined with his body
An his body's all ova my body
Still jus kissing
No grindin yet
Lips are wet
Then I'm floatin through the air
Me
Wow
I neva had anyone pick me up then lay me down

My insecurities always had me down
But wait
Breathe
Relax
And think
Think think think
Deep breath out
My insecurities are gone
I'm prayin for that new song
What's my name again
Live life to the fullest
Cease moments
I kno we jus met
But get ready get set
Go
Sweet lovin till the break of dawn
Touchin
Teasin
Squeezin
Screamin
Pleasing
Then
Cuddling
Cuddlin my new found love
An even if it was only one night
I was grinin ear to ear
We fit hand to glove
Made me feel brand new
It was a pleasure to meet yu
If yu allow me i'll treat yu
Right he says
Be my lil secret
An ill be yur lil secret
That's how we should keep it
He treats me to another sweet yet zesty
Kiss
Then he walks out my door
Damn my legs be sore
N my mouth hurts
Don't get it twisted

Hurts from grinin so much
Thank yu for yur blessed touch
My
Subway
Love

That was magical. I've never, wow, that was, he really did that? I haven't even, I didn't know I was that flexible. Damn, that was good. He lifted me up so easily, I always thought I was too big to be lifted. He didn't even struggle. He was jus, breathe. I'll always remember this night. Good thing I called. This man was a gentleman. He didn't come to my house with his expectations known. He didn't sit on my couch arrogantly waiting me for to service him. He was sensual in every way. Our foreplay? He told me to sit and put my feet up while he finished washing my dishes. "A woman as beautiful as you doesn't need to be labouring while a man is around, I'm here, let me take care of you." He did just that. That night, and the next. It was an exhilarating feeling, my breath shortened with each thought of him but I didn't want to be jus merely a secret. I couldn't have the sting of secrecy cloud the moment we jus shared. Although I wanted more, the fairytale was over. I needed to protect my memories. Protect my inner self. Protect... my value.

Poetic Interlude

I am searching for the definition of l.o.v.e and all I can find is f.u.c.k
Thinking that can't be right, I try again.
L.o.v.e
This time I find
L.u.s.t
Lusting for attention
I realize we are a bunch of lonely souls searching for an emotion that at times does not seem to exist
Existing mostly in the shadows of happiness or coincidence
At least..that's whats it seems like to me
See I set out on a journey determined to find love
On my first stop I remember I got high off kissing
Missing the touch of anotha
Anotha lova who played my body like the keys under the hands of Stevie wonda
Gracefully
Allowing me to injest the crack love
And fragrances of connectivity
While exhaling the sweet sounds
Of emotional flexibility
Willingly exploring the sharp sounds of singing from above
Thinking damn this must be love
And if this path of l.o.v.e is intertwined with f.u.c.k or l.u.s.t then I am perfectly fine abandoning my search and trading in one for two with a sprinkle of a few
But after a few late nights of continuously addictive electric shock
My heart stopped
And this love running through my veins
Keeps numbing my brain
Draining the highs
Containing the lows
Lowering the heat circling my body
Lowering the happiness in my toes

Until the familiar feeling I know
Dissipated
Dissolving
Delirious
Desires
Driving me forward
To path number two
Too many nightcrawlers
With tall secrets
I found messages of I Love you and I hate you simultaneously
Synchronizing my heart and mind to understand that l.o.v.e can be the same as h.u.r.t
Even when it's not done intentionally this hurt becomes a blinding poison
Injected by words
Digested by taste
This quest for love got me slowly dying
Trying to make sense of how I abused f.u.c.k confusing it with l.o.v.e
Following everything I see on t.v thinking damn this must be the reality
This must be love
This must be the l.o.v.e that I've been searching for
Gimme more
Gimme more
More of this love that takes little effort More of this t.v idea that produces a happy blissful life full of money, sarcasm, coincidences and imagination
Imagining im in a world where Nikki and professor oglevee are an everyday reality without the chase
Facing reality forces me to
Break free from the stigmas and run in the opposite direction
Forging connections between my soul and restoration
My desperation for truth brings me to
Another level of understanding that the definition of l.o.v.e
Is synonymous for m.e

CHAPTER FIFTY-FIVE

Circumstance

Hatred stirs up strife, but love covers and overwhelms all transgressions [forgiving and overlooking another's faults].
PROVERBS 10:12

I was in summer school for hopefully the last time ever. I had brought up my GPA but it wasn't quite enough yet to get back into my honours program. Plus, I found out that some of the classes I took didn't even count towards my degree requirements so this was my last attempt to complete all the requirements and raise my GPA. The stakes were high. At this point I had been in school for five years and had borrowed $100 000 from the government for a classical piano degree so it was time to get the hell up outta school. I was tired of school, tired of people, tired of my neighbourhood. I needed a change.

> *May 21, 2012 ·*
> *My fortune cookie says I need new friends....I agree 100%...*

Too many parts of me were clashing and I didn't know what to do about it. We had a new agency that had come to our building called Women's Health in Women's Hands. It's a health agency that catered to women of color. The woman who came to speak to us was one of their therapists. She spoke about the different types of programs and resources that were available to us if need be. *Therapy? But I already tried that.* Something about her presence drew me to her. She spoke in a calm voice that soothed me, it was like I could feel her vibes of peace. *I didn't even know they had black therapists that were accessible. You're a hot mess, you need help. You're a hot mess, you need help.* Tish's voice was ringing in my head about how messed up I was. The stress of school, KayKay, a place to live and feeling like I wasn't good enough was constantly weighing on me to the point that I figured I needed to do something about it. I made an appointment and went in. I was scared. When she looked at me and said, "So tell me why you wanted to come" I couldn't think of no otha answer but "My mentor says I'm a hot mess and I need help" She kinda looked at me perplexed and said, "Well do you think you need help?" "Well ye" I then proceed to explain to her the things I had been through. That appointment was the day that life started to change for me. No regrets. It felt great to speak with someone that made me feel instantly comfortable.

June 3, 2012

I wanna forgive those who have hurt me....but its hard...years later they try to talk to me as if they never hurt me in the first place...how am i to feel?

Mr. Producer hit me up asking if I could join him on a track he was working on. *Damn stranger, ain't heard from you in a while.* Instantly I was reminded of the encounter, he still hadn't paid me a dime since when his mom gave me the money. I thought I had forgiven him but the minute I saw his name in my inbox I just got mad all over again. How was it fair? How was it fair to me that he never rectified his wrong but he was gonna message me like we were on good terms for me to do another project with him? *How is this ok? I'm kinda happy that he thought of me in terms of my artistry but how he gon jus act like we don't have unresolved history? Naw. I can't. All this anger inside and clearly, he don't even know. Tell him.*

Cola

I know you been trying to visit me when your in the area but truth is I honestly haven't been ready to see you. Like i'm still out 1000 bucks because of you, and that's hard to just put behind me and move forward and act like nun even happened. I saw your music video..well done..i wish you the best of luck with your future endeavors. But as for me, there's just too much unresolved anger to act like nun happened.

Mr Producer

I hear you cool

That wasn't so bad. Breathe. It felt better to say how I truly felt. I had been tryna avoid him. I would make up reasons why I couldn't meet up when truthfully, I was still angry. I think that's when the healing started, years of anger finally at peace.

June 14 2012

Nathaniel

hallo cola, how you been

Cola

wassup

Nathaniel

just wanted to stop by and say hi, how you been, hows kk?

Cola

i'm good doing well thanks, he's doing just fine

Nathaniel

nice, you still at the same place, what's new, how's school

Cola

not for long, i'm moving, and i just finished school today

Nathaniel

what!!!!!!!!,all done university

Cola

ye my last class was today

Nathaniel

congrats

Cola

thanks

Nathaniel

your parents must be very proud of you

Cola

i believe they are. yep so everythin else good?

Nathaniel

yea girl just been working. saving and just fixing up my new place
Cola
dats proper
Nathaniel
you should stop by my new place sometime
Cola
when i get a chance mos def
Nathaniel
nice thats whats up

I never made it out to his place. I never wanted to be mean to him, but I was just tryna move on. That's why my number changed so often. I always felt like I needed a fresh start from something. Once a relationship was over, to me it didn't make any sense to keep the communication open. I just never knew how to tell him that. I wanted the best for him, yes, and I didn't mind the updates, but it was a chapter that was already closed.

In the midst of all my chaos I always found time to travel. Money or not, I made it work. Traveling and journeying to a new place always carried so much peace and temporary relief from the strains of life. For the time that I was away I didn't have to be this girl with all these expectations, I could just be a tourist tryna find my way through the city. My parents always traveled somewhere with us, it felt like life was unbalanced if I didn't travel. I honestly had no clue if my parents were really proud of me. It had taken me five years to get to this point and with my GPA being so low and my degree being in music, I wasn't sure if they were proud that I finished or just happy they didn't have to tell people I was a dropout. Even with this degree, I still wasn't convinced that piano was my only path.

I had bigger dreams, music was jus an easy choice to silence the voices. One of those dreams was that one day Kaykay would get to have a relationship with his dad. I had forgiven him for all the otha drama but hoped one day things would change. It was always such a trip when he hit me up outta the blue.

June 14th 2012
Kendrick
hi...msg me back need to speak to u
Cola
Wassup?
Kendrick
We need to do that test
Cola
ok, when
Kendrick
Next month
Cola
ok, jus lemme know when
Kendrick
Ok, Im supposed to serve u with some paper for a motion to change so that I can get a paternity test...but I'm not into the whole waste of time court drama ...do i'd rather we come together and do this like grown folk

Cola
ye im cool with that
Kendrick
What's ur #?
MissCola
*******...wats yours?
Kendrick
Phones down right now...ima hit u up with the number as soon as I buy a replacement... In the meantime, Link me on here whenever
Cola
same to you, id like to get it done before i move
Kendrick
Where u moving to and when u moving?
Cola
im moving in august

I hadn't heard from this man in over a year. Here he was again. I wanted to get the test done just as much as he did. I was hoping we could really just move on with life. So as long as he was trying, I would try too. Some people I couldn't give up on. I wasn't doing this for me, I was doing it for my son. Every now and then I would pull up Kendrick's facebook account and show Kaykay pictures of his dad. He never had any questions, but I always wanted him to know who his dad was and what he looked like. It was the least I could do so he never had to wonder. Even when my sister would say "Kaykay that's not your dad" or "He's a waste man" I'd always said, "Don't talk like that in front of him." *Waste man or not, he was still Kaykay's dad.* I had grown a respect for him as the father of my child cause when I looked at Kaykay I saw a part of me and a part of him. We may not get along but it was the best gift he could have ever given me.

There were many changes in my life. My peace over things with my son's father was giving me peace in other areas too. I was understanding that just because I had forgiven a person it didn't mean I needed to keep in constant communication with them. Polite or not, it was fake.

June 15 2012
Nathaniel
hallo cola, how are you
Cola
good thanks
Nathaniel
what you doing
Cola
goin to the library, lata
Nathaniel
oh okay

Just tell him you're tryna move on. No point in keeping this back and forth thing. I still couldn't bring myself to say anything. I just didn't wanna hurt him. *Ok next time I will.* Instead of saying anything to him I just kept my focus on the future. I still hadn't found a place to move, I had to be out by mid-august and my baby was about to hit a milestone.

> · June 27, 2012
>
> my baby graduated yesterday, it's a milestone in his life. I thank God for allowing me to watch my child walk across the stage. I pray i'll get the chance in the future to see him walk across other stages as he strives to defy his disability and work towards great accomplishments. Thank you to my two sisters Aaliyah and Roti who came...among the others...it meant a lot to me to have the support.

He did it!!!!! My baby did it. He showed them. He stayed in the regular class and graduated! It was one of the best moments in my life. I cried. We fought so hard to be here for a lil boy they said would never walk, he walked across the stage. It felt like we could do anything. I was hoping that I would get to follow in his footsteps very shortly.

> July 9, 2012 ·
>
> what scripture can i read for encouragement? or anything to strengthen my strength?

Trying times tryna try me during these times. Lord help me get through this.

> · July 12, 2012
>
> **Cola**
>
> Hey Nathaniel, I know you've tried to call me a couple times, but I haven't been honest with you. Im happy that your life is going good now and i'm glad you got the help that you needed, but i'm not interested in talking even on a friendship tip. I've moved on from the shit that we went through and i'm doing great. Too much happened for us to be friends. I appreciate you apologizing and keeping me in your thoughts, but thats really as far as it'll go. I wish u luck, i hope you will treat

the next girl you are in a relationship with..with respect and you find happiness...

I had too much going on in every other aspect of my life to continue this relationship leading nowhere. I needed to stay focused on everything happening around me.

· July 12, 2012

How can there be a limit placed on my child's life. What choices have I been given? 20 years old or steroids? Really...why can't he live forever without medication...there's nothing more to say

It seemed life never let me smile for long. We had another rehab appointment. Things changed, again. Things were moving beyond my control. As hard as I tried, nothing I did helped. We were using the braces, I had limited how much walking he had to do, tried to switch his diet, *why is he getting worse? I don't know what else to do. I feel so helpless.* We were at a crossroads. It was time to start the steroids. That word *steroids...was there really no other way? He jus graduated, I just saw him walk.* I just can't. I can't take in anything the doctor was saying. It was one big blur. I would explain his fatigue and they would explain it was a part of the disease, but one thing I could do was get him a wheelchair. *I don't wanna see him in a wheelchair. This is too much.* It felt like a battle of the minds, between how my mind said he should be and the reality in front of me. It was as if I had never fully accepted this diagnosis. Maybe that was our downfall, maybe it was our saving grace. In the moment, nothing felt real.

Understanding my discomfort with the look and function of the wheelchair they offered a solution which was a device that looked like a stroller but had some of the functionalities of a wheelchair. My fear with a wheelchair was that if he had to push himself around it would tire him out too much. With the stroller I would push him, but the wheels were bigger which meant they pushed smoother.

The main point of the stroller was to conserve his energy. It was enough to ease my mind at the moment. Since I had completely shut down when the doctors talked about the steroids, we left the subject alone for the moment. The focus now was gettin the stroller ordered and luckily his occupational therapist was there to help me cause I had no clue where to even start.

July 12 2012

Cola

hey just wanted to know if u still wanted to get this test done?

Kendrick

yea

Cola

Ok

Kendrick

hopefully end of the month, how u been

Cola

Oh ok, i'll be working the last week of July and kayshaun won't even be with me. At this moment things could be better, I just came from rehab with kaykay and I didn't get the news I was hoping for. Other then that, we are perfectly fine. You?

Kendrick

Trying to get by...what was the news?

Cola

Oh i just have huge decisions to make in regards to kayshaun and his future, his doctors are suggesting that I start him on the steroids to prolong his life expectancy and quality of life

July 15th 2012

Kendrick

What are the side effects?

Cola

Stunt of growth, hyperactivity, osteoporosis, mood swings,weight gain, acne, delayed puberty,cataracts, hmm that's what I know so far..and they wanna put him on other medication to counteract the effects of the steroids...

Kaykay and Kendrick were complete strangers. Kendrick had no knowledge of what was going on with Kaykay. I had told him bits and pieces over the years to gain an understanding of his medical history but he never seemed interested, so I never shared any more. If that news wasn't enough to handle, time was running out for me to find an apartment and money was slowing down. I was tryna contact Leo about my money and I was gettin the runaround. The money was still tied up and he wasn't sure if it would be accessible to me by the time I moved. I had put all my hope, trust, and faith in that money and now he was telling me there was no guarantee that it was gonna be ready.

I was searching through internet sites for apartments but it was impossible to find anything. Nothing was all-inclusive, if it was, it wasn't wheelchair accessible, the prices were too high, or I needed proof of income. I didn't have a job because I took care of Kaykay full time. Welfare was my proof of income, yet it wasn't good enough for these landlords. *This is crazy to me, you would think that people would want welfare as a proof of income, at least it's a guarantee that imma get money every month.* Most places were turning me down, but this one place, this one place rocked me to my core.

I finally found a potential apartment. It was a two bedroom with two bathrooms with ample space for me, Kaykay and my sister to move in. *Perfect and it's within budget.* I called them up to see if there was any availability and lucky for me there was. It was a long bus ride from Jane and Sheppard to south Etobicoke and I didn't know the area well at all. But what I did notice was all the schools, grocery stores and bus routes along the way. I got a lil lost on the way but once I arrived at the building I walked towards the office and waited patiently for the lady to finish up her conversation.

Once done, she looked over and said, "Can I help you?" I responded, "I'm here to see the two bedroom" to which she replies, "I'm sorry it's no longer available." *I came all the way down here an it's not available? I called just this morning. This don't make no sense.* "Oh, but I called a few hours ago and they said they still had it available" "No, I'm not sure who told you that, but it is unavailable". *Weird. That sucks.* I was so discouraged. I thought I had found a great apartment and just my luck, it was gone. I left the building and started the long journey back home. On my way I called my mom and explained the situation and she said "What do they mean it's not available? So how come when you called earlier they had something. This doesn't sound right." I uno why but my gut was saying something was off and my mother confirmed my same sentiments. On a hunch I called the office "Hi there, I was calling to see if you had a 2-bedroom available? Oh ye? Would it be possible for me to view it? I can come later on tonight around 7pm. Great, thank you so much. Have a great day". *Huh, so it is available?* I wanted to be sure I had heard correctly, so I asked both my mom and sister to make similar calls. Each was told the same thing, they had a two bedroom and even a three bedroom available. *That don't make no damn sense.* I waited for my sister to get home from school to drive us down cause I didn't have enough time to bus and make it back to pick up KayKay.

We pull up to the building but instead of me going in, I let my sister go in and ask while I stayed in the car with Kaykay. Not even five minutes later my sister walks outside saying "They said the apartment is no longer available" *What the hell is wrong with these people. Is it cause we're black? Seriously? They can do that? No, it can't be. That can't be what's happening to us. They made us waste our gas to drive back down and nothing is available? I've spent my whole day on this bullshit.* I can't figure this out. To test my theory. I call again from the car right outside to see what they would say. Once again, the lady confirms there was a two bedroom available. Yet again, I say I'll be there right away to see it. The second I hung up the phone, I hopped out of the car with Kaykay and ran up in the spot pumped with adrenaline. From the top of the stairs I looked at the women and said, "Do you remember me"? *Gotcha.* The look on her face was priceless. She was silent at the moment, then proceeded to say, "Oh did you just call?" "Yes, I did, and you said there's a two bedroom available and I would like to see it". Instead of letting us see the apartment she had us sit to fill out an application. I've never experienced anything like that in my life before. I've been in situations where I've had to ask myself *wait did that seem a bit racist to you?* but this, this was just blatant to me. Both my sister and I filled out an application. It had been a long and exhausting day and I just wanted to get this over so we could go home. Time was ticking and we needed a place to stay. By 9am the next morning our application had been denied. *Ouch, I guess I shoulda seen that coming.* So not only did I not have a place to live, but I didn't have a place to live...because I was black. How does one make sense of that?

Often when I felt lost I would write. Seemed like perfect timing when I got a call from the A.M.Y. program leader asking if I was able to be a part of their summer program. It was gonna be a condensed workshop but I didn't wanna pass on this opportunity cause it would have given me an amazing chance to perform with such talented women as part of the Summerworks festival. I already had a story ready, last time it was about rape, this time it was gonna be about KayKay, his illness and my challenges with being a young black female mother.

June 17th 2012

Cola

Hey the week of the 29th to August 4, kayshaun won't be at home with me...just a heads up and I'm doing a show downtown after that so my schedule is hectic...

Kendrick

When u free?

Cola

Well next week and August 5-8 after 3.... After that not until after I move

Kendrick
Wow... Ok
Cola
Ye my summer job kicks in July 30 and its crazy along with the move...when are yu free? When did yu wanna get it done?
Kendrick
First week in august
Cola
I gotta work and daycare is closed, can we do it the second week?
Kendrick
Ok, What u up to?
Cola
Right now I'm packing and cleaning....yu? Just let me know where we meeting...and if it can be after 3 plz
Kendrick
Ok np
Cola
Thanks
Kendrick
I'm just here chilling
Cola
Oh word, you still hang in rex?
Kendrick
Ye.... Where you at now?
Cola
Same place, Jane and shep, How's your daughter?
Kendrick
No daughter
Cola
I swear you told me yu had a child one time?
Kendrick
Nah
Cola
Oh ok Tru, so what yu been doing with yourself?
Kendrick
School and work....story of my life
Cola

Still studying paramedic or ems something like that?

Kendrick

Yes and tuner school

Cola

Wats turner school?

Kendrick

Cars

Cola

Oh interesting

Kendrick

U still in school?

Cola

Naw I just finished...graduation is in the fall

Kendrick

Congrats

Cola

Thanks, 5 years

Kendrick

Wow, Ur moving with the hubby?

Cola

Naw no hubby right now, just Kk...and I'm letting my sister stay until she finishes school, Yu live on your own?

Kendrick

Ye

Cola

Oh ok, how much longer do yu have for school?

Kendrick

1 year

Cola

That's a good accomplishment

Kendrick

Then I'll be torontos # 1 bachelor, Thanks

Cola

Oh really, where did all the girls go

Kendrick

I can't get no girls lol

Cola

Lol why's that?i swear your Facebook page has pics of wifeys

Kendrick

Years back lol, Ur pics should of been up

Cola

Quit playing, I was never wifey lol, So your all grown up now

Kendrick

U could of been, Yes I am

Cola

Hey your bday is tomorrow ain't it?

Kendrick

Yep, Remember the last bday present u gave me?

Cola

Do yu remember? It was soo long ago, How old r u 26?

Kendrick

I'll never forget

Cola

You'll never forget?

Kendrick

Yes...it was a wonderful night

Cola

Yu do know that was the same night I got pg right?...but I'm curious of what yu remember

Cola

Well it's almost 12 so lemme be the first to say happy birthday, Wish yu many more

Kendrick

thank u mama cita

Cola

How's your birthday so far?

Kendrick

alright...what u up to?

Cola

I'm downtown right now enjoying a sick ass dinner..some summerlicious ting...what are yu doing for you bday

This was the first decent conversation we had in years. I felt like he was tryna flirt with me, which caught me off guard a bit. *Thought you hated me? Thought I was just some dumbass hoe.* It was interesting, but I went along with it cause it felt good to finally be able to just talk. We used to talk before all the drama started. We used to have great conversations. In this moment I missed that. I missed the dude I could just kick it with on the phone. I felt like a part of me would always care bout him a bit, we connected deeper than just the surface, our child was growing strong and beautiful. The more love I had for my son the more I respected his father. I was hoping this would be the beginning of a cordial friendship. Kaykay loved cars just as much as his dad did, maybe it was something they could have done together. Maybe just Maybe... I won't get my hopes up though.

July 21th 2012
Cola
hey how are you...what did u end up doing for your b day?
Kendrick
I'm going out tonite
Cola
oh cool have fun
July 27th 2012
Cola
So I'm doing research for a play Im in this summer and I want to know what you look for physically in the opposite sex?
Kendrick
Someone that's real... Loves to laugh...respects space and adventurous in the bedroom and out
Cola
I respect your answer..thank you...but her physical attributes is what I'm curious about
Cola

like bodywise...breast, ass, smile, anything that turns u on sexually by the way a woman looks...what kind of women would u typically date?
Kendrick
Phat ass... Nice breasts and a killer smile
Cola
LOL thank you....
Kendrick
Lol...sounds shallow I kno
Cola
it's an honest answer...i respect that, i'll take that over bull shit anyday
Kendrick
What u like physically in a dude
Cola
oh wow lol no ones asked me back before ...hmmm...i'm intrigued by nice eyes an cute smile...bodywise...someone taller than me..lol which isn't hard...i'm 5'3..but i like a thick dude who can grip me..i'm not attracted to mawga men...and at the moment...in really attracted to american dudes...i'm kinda over toronto men...i haven't met any that have something solid to offer me
Kendrick
Ok ok
Cola
what u doin? ye my bad i realize i got carried away with that response lol
Kendrick
Just came out the shower... I'm a lil nude
Cola
oh my bad..do yu...

I had asked a few guys what they were attracted to and I always got some interesting answers. One of the characters I was working on needed some more depth and since I wasn't a man, I thought I'd go to the source. I dunno why I thought my baby fadda would be a good person to ask, but since we were on talking terms, why not? *Girl stay focused, get this test done with, stop being so damn friendly.*

July 29th 2012
Cola
Hey how are you? Have yu gotten the chance to book the test yet?
Kendrick
Not yet but ima book it this week
Cola
For next week after 3 right? Don't mean to be on yu so much, but with my shows,moving and me going to Vegas for business...I jus wanna get it done. An I'm sure yu wanna get on with life too. Your good though?
Kendrick
Yea im good, What u up to?
Cola
I'm just getting back from Windsor...bout to go drop kaykay off in the east end
Kendrick
Ok ok
Cola
What yu doing?
Kendrick
Nuttin....bored as fuck
Cola
LOL boo,That sucks. What do yu normally do for fun
Kendrick
Go out ...stay in..don't matter, U?
Cola
I don't go out unless I'm traveling a distance...I usually stay home and chill

July 30 2012
Cola
Thanks for Yur input the other day...so far it made it into the show I'm doing
Kendrick
No problem

August 3 2012

Cola
Wats gwaning
Kendrick
Just drinking
Cola
Sounds like fun...Wat yu drinking?...I can only drink specific drinks cause i hate the taste of alcohol...I like a porn star cause it taste like candy
Kendrick
What do U taste like?
Cola
porn star is the drink i like..it just happens to have a crazy name ....and i don't know what i taste like...you dont remember?
Kendrick
I didn't get to taste
Cola
fair enough
Kendrick
Now I'm curious
Cola
y now?
Kendrick
All ways been
Cola
i never got that memo...we kinda just lost touch, i think your sister might have told me once that u liked me...but we wasted so much time fighting
Kendrick
I kno
Cola
so it's true then..there was once a point that u liked me, good to know i wasn't the only one then, so no bana for you today?
Kendrick
I used to love u off
Cola

i never knew...but i used to love u off too, funny cause i dont look like your type...according to all the girls i see u hanging out with
Kendrick Suuuure
Cola sure what?
Kendrick U used to love me off
Cola
i did...we never hung out cause i lived far...but i loved when we talked on the phone..and physically..yu were exactly what i wanted,but you started calling me a hoe...and i guess that's all i was to u at the time. I'm sorry for everything that you went through when we stopped talking...i really am..but the fact remains we still have a crazy past to deal with...things could have been so simple...but it never happened that way....so have you booked the test yet?

It's a dangerous thing when people start to reminisce. I couldn't tell if he was playing games with me or not. He never liked me after that first time. *Was I crazy? One minute he wanted to be my man, the next he was calling me a hoe. Which do I believe? Was I starting to have feelings for him again? Nawwww that's crazy.* Right now my goal was to keep the conversation going to make sure this DNA test happened. The fact that we were on good terms was a miracle and I didn't wanna mess this up, but I needed to organize myself and it was time to learn the truth.

August 5, 2012
SUMMERWORKS FESTIVAL....COME CHECK OUT THE SHOW DERAILED....FILLED WITH DRAMA AND HEART FILLED STORIES.....TICKETS ON SALE..CHECK YOUR EVENTS FOR MORE INFO...

August 7th 2012
Kendrick no, ima book it for next week

Cola

I'm moving next week....Monday to Thursday I'm moving...Thursday to Sunday I have a show everyday...then Monday to Thursday i'll be in Vegas......

No. Response.

He don't respond when I need him too

I was set to move outta my place even though I didn't have another place set up yet. I felt like everything was moving faster than I could catch up to. Everything was happening at the same time and when things got heavy, I got traveling. Aaliyah and I settled on a three day trip to Vegas cause it allowed me to go back to the Magic fashion show during the day yet still make the most of our night. This trip to Vegas couldn't have come at a better time. I knew after this Summerworks festival I was gonna need something.

It was a beautiful performance. One to remember. I had never tapped into so many raw emotions about Kaykay and muscular dystrophy before. It was like an overflow of love and release of the pressures that I felt being his mother, making all the decisions and having not one clue if I was doing anything right. There was a strength that came from standing on stage and telling my story freely. There was an outpour of love that was exchanged for your sorrow. How do I explain the unexplainable? Theater is full of live emotions, feelings, movement, and unspoken words even if I'm shouting at the top of my lungs. It's beautiful. And suddenly I didn't feel like the black woman that was rejected or the mother of a child with an incurable disease. I was Cola. Daughter to two loving parents, though they had different ways of expressing it, they loved me jus as much as they loved their grandchild. This moment created a new understanding of life and gratitude. I was never as alone as I felt, God made sure of that. But at this moment of high, there was always a low. Life and love never let me smile longer than I had to.

The beauty of therapy was it was always there to catch me before I spiraled. In therapy I was learning about safe boundaries and core morals. Things that no matta what would never change. My faith in God was something that was always constant and my love for my son, friends/family (interchangeable at times). My ability to survive all my trauma had been rooted not only in the foundation of those I have chosen to surround myself with but also by my morals. In my heart I believed that suicide was wrong, therefore no matta how much pain I was in, no matta how many thoughts would come, it was never an option for me personally. But there were moments that no matta how much sunshine was around me the darkness seemed never ending. My therapist reminded me "Have faith that things will work out" I knew that saying inside and out, it was written in my bones, yet I often forgot how to be grounded in the midst of a storm. Only when the sun shone again I would say *Lord you were faithful.* I had caused myself to be physically ill with all my stressing and worrying about finding a new apartment. I felt like shit that I couldn't provide a place for son, but I was determined to keep searching.

In the very last moments, jus mere weeks before I was supposed to move out, we had found a place. It was another Toronto Community Housing building but the price was gonna be market rent as opposed to subsidized. It was a huge change but one that made me feel like "Welcome to the adult world" even though I still needed my mom to co-sign for us. It was originally supposed to be ready for the middle of August. I was ready to move but they needed more time to work on it which was a blessing in disguise cause the investments still hadn't come in, so I needed to find another way to get my first and last paid and now I had more time to find it. Lucky enough, my current building extended my stay for the few weeks it would take for the new place to be ready.

To my benefit I was already in the TCHC system so it was an easy transition from uptown west to downtown west. From when I stepped in the office I had a feeling I was leaving with an apartment, I just didn't know which building she had available. Instead of looking for an apartment to suit us I looked for a school that would suit Kaykay. My mentor Tish had told me of this school that was full of bright colors and was almost magical once you walked in. She knew of it because she lived in the area. We decided to visit the school and from the moment I walked in it felt like home. The first thing I noticed was the decorated piano in the lobby. There were colors everywhere and the open space in the front made the school feel larger than life. I got to sit with the vp to ask her questions. *Oh damn, a black lady. I neva had that growing up.* I had a bunch of questions. What's your EAP program like? What if he needs breaks? Is this school accessible? What are your class sizes? How many students? How many grades? Will you guys work with his outside agencies?

I left that meeting feeling confident that I had found his school. Coincidentally the apartment that was available for us was right down the street from the school. Before accepting the offer the woman had told us to view the apartment. At first glance, it was a bit of a wreck. It wasn't the cleanest, floors were scratched, garbage everywhere, meat left on the counter, but I fell in love with the potential of the apartment. It seemed like a match made in heaven. Ready, set, paid. Move in date September 1st 2012.

My highlights from my Vegas trip were the connections I made while networking and apparently I saw French Montana. I love that I am kinda oblivious to celebs so I don't act like a groupie. Only thing that sucked was unless I had a reason to meet the person I missed out on certain opportunities. One night we decided to do bar hopping and that was incredibly fun. It was kinda suspect the way we were sold the tickets but I met so many interesting people that night. I'm not sure what it is with me, whenever I travel I get hit on by white guys who find me really beautiful and fun but back in Toronto I guess I blend in. I can't even get a white guy to look my way. Overall it was an amazing trip and a polar opposite for the hell that was patiently awaiting my arrival at home.

August 25, 2012
Cola
Wha gwan?
Kendrick

hey
Cola
What's going on, how are you? We still doing that test?
Kendrick
i'm alright and yes we are
Cola
Ok cool...I just got back from Vegas so i have a lil more, time now. So what are yu up to?

No response.
Will this test ever get DONE?

CHAPTER FIFTY-SIX

Battles

No one has greater love [nor stronger commitment] than to lay down his own life for his friends.
JOHN 15:13

August 26, 2012
Crying on the inside and ain't nobody that can help...damn

The trip was dope but I was in my own turmoil. I had my own emotions going on, my own shit to deal with. By most standards my bestie was beautiful. So, I let her do most of the talking whenever I seen dudes we were tryna get info from. It's a weird thing, I willingly stepped back and let her shine while feeling horrible that I seemed so invisible next to her. Its just how things were, I guess. All our lives it was never hard for good looking men to hit her up. I usually got whatever was left over. I don't mean that in a rude way, *maybe I do?* I just wanted to know what that feelin was like. I felt like too many people were playing with my head. Romeo was sexy as hell, sometimes I still didn't know why he liked me. I just had a bunch of different things that I felt like were at war inside me. I just didn't feel myself, didn't feel good, just sad for no damn reason. I was trapped within and I was tryna get things organized. Life felt scattered.

August 29, 2012
Cola
So schools about to start...do yu know when your planning to book the test?

No. response. *Here we go again.* Iight well, nun else I can do but focus on the move and wait till he's ready. We're all excited to move in. Apartment packed. Furniture bought. We opened the door to reveal a floor literally covered in dead roaches. There was nowhere to step without stepping on them. *EWWWWW, I'm gonna be sick.* It was apparently a shock for everyone including the superintendent. They had seen a few roaches but had not realized that it was actually an infestation. The fumes from the newly varnished floor and the treatment they had done must have triggered the roaches to come out of hiding. *This is not ok. We're supposed to move in, everything is already set for delivery.* My mom said, "Is it too late to get your money back?" I wish things were that easy. Kaykay was already enrolled in school, there wasn't any other apartments, everything was bought and I had already handed in my keys to my other place. Noticing the state of panic that we were in the super makes a few phone calls and says "We're gonna do some more treatments and if it is still a problem then you can temporarily move your stuff into an empty apartment upstairs until yours is ready. That way you don't have to cancel any deliveries. Try not to get stressed out." *Too late.* I was really hoping things would have sorted themselves out cause Kaykay was about to experience his first day in a new school and in a new grade.

September 4, 2012
ahhh my babys first day of grade 1...can't wait to pick him up....ahhhh...moving life is too crazzy, still not settled in this house..so much work to do

While I was gone my family had started to move our stuff in. My sis took one bedroom and Kaykay and I shared the other room. I had bought him a custom made top bunk with stairs while I fit my queen size underneath. My sister and I had a love-hate relationship. It was great for her to be around Kaykay but while she was tryna live her life as a young teen I was tryna live my life as a young mother. Those were two different types of ideals, opinions and interests. Despite my wilder life up west, once I moved downtown I no longer had the desire to replay or relive the haunted shadows of my vagina. I wanted to just focus on being a mother and figure out what the hell to do with my life. Even though we had gone through a lot of arguments I felt like she had too much attitude, she felt like I was tryna parent her but she was my lil sister and also needed a place to live closer to school. She had put in a lot of effort into helping us find a place. Since we were both living together my parents offered to cover a part of the rent and helped us furnish the place.

This place still had a lot of work left to do. The roach problem wasn't rectified but it was a hell of a lot better than it was before. My skin crawled every time I seen a roach and I was worried about how the fumes from each treatment would affect Kaykay seeing as his immune system was already compromised; I was hoping the treatments would have minimal effect on him.

The thing about being in a new apartment was that I had to install all new services. It was such a process. New phone, cable, internet. Luckily, I knew a guy. Roy and I had stayed in touch over the years and although he was now married and with child, as he stood in my front hallway years after our first interaction, it felt like no time had passed. *Damn he's still fine. Still takes my breath away.* From my place on the couch I could feel his energy. I was surprised at how strong it was. In that moment my mind was saying *do something.* But I could do nothing. He installed my services as once before and we just stayed in the moment. What if? What if we? How come we never? It felt so crazy to be this attracted to someone I had only met once. The vibrations were soo strong. "Can I see you again?" "Ye, tomorrow". It felt as if we were finally going to explore this feeling, explore this dimension of us. What is and what was. He leaves. *Ah man this is actually gonna happen?* Chills run down my spine. I can feel his breath on my neck, the touch of his hands. *What about his wife? Shit, oh ye. I'm not that kinda chick. I just... I can't, he has kids. I like him. Shit. I want him. No, I can't.* He said "If I had met you first...I would have chosen you". I can't stop thinking about, "what if we? " As amazing as those words sounded, as much as his voice rang in my ear, the truth was even though he didn't meet me first he met me before he was married. *I want him, but he's not mine. I don't do seconds.* The guilt weighed heavy on me so I sent him a text. "We can't do this... you have a family" "I know, I can't either, I'm not a cheater". Maybe this was something we weren't meant to explore. For the second time, we had to go our separate ways. I mean, we both had families and kids to think of and that priority was greater than any other.

September 12, 2012
Ug at the hospital with my child who just had a couple seizures and threw up...pray is definitely in need right now....

I don't know how it happened. It had been years since it happened last but we were all watching TV when Kaykay started to shake and became unresponsive. My sister and I both jumped to his aid, called his name "Kaykay, Kaykay," no response. We grabbed the keys, ran outta the house and tried to flag down a cab to take us to Sick Kids hospital. Luckily the hospital wasn't too far from the new apartment cause we were able to get him there in about 10 mins. He became semi-alert then threw up in the cab before we left. Once we got him inside he went back to his normal self-talking and playing with his hands. I hated needles so watching him get an IV put in was painful. I was crying on the inside. *I hate seeing him sad.* To make the situation better my sis and I had told him that the IV was his super power, like spider man. But I guess he was too smart to believe in our trick.

September 12, 2012
So we told Kk his arm is like spiderman and he asked me how come no web is coming out....

He didn't have any other episodes while we were at the hospital so they sent us home with no real explanation of what happened. In fact, they didn't think it was a seizure at all, they just didn't know what else it was.

September 14, 2012
I feel like my son an I are in for the biggest battles of life so far....

It seemed like things had changed so quickly. One minute he was healthy, the next minute we are running back and forth between hospital visits and doctors appointments.

September 16, 2012
think i'm gonna go to church today....got a lot to be thankful for...and im not ungrateful...where I end up, who knows...but im going from downtown to the west so if I hit up your church and im late...I apologize....

I didn't have the answers I needed but I was thankful that it could have been worse. I was hoping and praying that God would turn things around cause in this moment I felt completely hopeless.

September 17, 2012 ·
I am strong..stronger than this hurt I feel...

·September 17, 2012
I love kayshaun antwoine Isaiah Bennett...he is my world

September 17, 2012
Cola
hey wassup, haven't heard from you in a minute..you good?

I had no clue where this man had gone and yet again I set myself up for failure. I thought this was gonna be different. *I thought he loved me, jks.* Naw, I knew he didn't love me, but I did think he was serious about this test. It was going on too long now. I felt like a puppet and I was really hurt for Kaykay. He deserved to know. Then I felt like a horrible person. I brought him into the world with a man I knew wasn't ready. I woulda never done an abortion but I just held a lot of guilt in my heart for him not having a father. Felt like I failed him.

September 22, 2012
I love when my child blames me...says I got him sick cause I fed him too much junk food.. he only ask for one chip...but ate the whole bag ...apparently I should know better next time

He kept me laughing. That's what I loved about him. No matta how much pain he was in, his inquisitiveness kept me laughing. He was adjusting to school quite well despite missing days due to illness. He loved his school. He had no problem walking the 10 minute walk, but we would take our time, . walking and talking and learning about our surroundings. Watching him walk was always a miracle, that's why it was one of my favorite things to do with him. I just wished I could have shared this with someone. The journey of a single mom was rewarding yet lonely at times.

September 23, 2012
sometimes I feel like maybe I should settle down in a serious relationship...then I meet some of the men this world has to offer...and I thank God I have my freedom

Serial dater. I was more accustomed to short term dating. If I wasn't with Romeo, relationships just didn't make sense. I spent 6 years on and off investing in Romeo and I hadn't found any other man that was able to love me with the intent, magnitude, protection and desire that he had. I wanted someone for me, I wanted someone for Kaykay, but the someone I wanted I couldn't have. It was frustrating. I was honestly giving up on love. Love didn't love me. So, I'd live free. Unattached to anyone, anything, jus me and Kaykay in our own world writing our own story.

September 26, 2012
Some people live with unbelievable truths

I was writing down the tales of my life and this was the title that I came up with. S.L.U.T: S.ome people L.ive with U.nbelievable T.ruths. I wanted to reclaim the power people had stolen from me over the years. The names they called me, the things they said to break me. To my family I was a dropout, a disgrace, a nobody, but I was living a life filled with so many unbelievable truths. My friends would ask, "Can it get any worse?" Somehow it always did. It's hard to believe I survived to this point, or that the only person who loved me was a man I had never met. I was fighting but life was jus exhausting.

Even with 4 treatments for roaches it was like they multiplied by the dozens. They were literally everywhere. I couldn't open cupboards without seeing roaches. I couldn't keep food in the pantry. I couldn't shower without roaches. I couldn't sleep without seeing roaches on the ceiling. I was downstairs once a week complaining and begging for more treatments. I looked online for treatments. I had bought about 6 bottles of caulk that I was going to use to seal every crack I could find in my apartment including the walls between me and the adjacent apartment. I didn't want to take a chance with bed bugs or any other roaches coming in. Apparently, every time my apartment was sprayed for roaches they ran and flooded other apartments. I needed to protect my space from them coming back. The treatments weren't good for Kaykay. Even though I always sent him away when we sprayed I still had borax powder and other chemicals spread around the place to kill anything that moved. I couldn't sleep. I stayed awake to kill anything I saw. I didn't feel safe or comfortable. *I can't take this. Why'd I bring Kaykay here? How could I bring him into this?* My mind felt very scattered. I was always on edge. *I can't breathe.* I loved cooking but hated cooking in the house. I couldn't cook freely or enjoy the beauty of the apartment. *I feel like I am losing it in more ways than one.*

September 28, 2012
I am exhausted....n I look like a scary hot mess walking through sick kids ug

It happened again. And again, we rushed him to the hospital. I had no words. It's a scary feeling. It's a scary thing to watch. What's even scarier, being forced to film it instead of helping cause we needed "proof". Kaykay had another seizure. We were in the hospital tryna figure out what happened. I may not be a nurse but I knew what a seizure looked like. I explained myself multiple times "He had a seizure" to which they responded, "What did it look like?" I tried my best to explain what I had witnessed. I got the sense that they didn't believe me. It was confirmed when the resident doctor said to me "It doesn't seem like a seizure, it seems like a behavioural thing" *Yes cause my son starts shaking and eyes fluttering and being unresponsive, just to get attention. Yep that makes the most sense.* I was perplexed cause I couldn't understand how this could be behavioural and not exactly what I said it was. After she left the room it happened again. But this time instead of helping him I had to get my sister to record it so we had proof of what we meant. When he had stopped I called the resident back in and showed her the video to which she replied "Ye that looks like a seizure, lemme go show this to the doctors" *No shit sherlock. I wonder what gave it away?* Why did it have to be this difficult to get genuine help?

The video prompted them to admit us to the hospital. We spent hours at the hospital running tests. In terms of the seizures, the end result was that it wasn't a seizure, but they referred us to a seizure specialist regardless. As for any other results we met with the cardiologist who had explained to me that they had noticed a small decrease in function in his heart. The heart being a muscle, and the biggest muscle in the body, it was cause for concern. The solution? He was put on meds that would help maintain things. The medicine was supposed to help his body get more blood flow so he could preserve more energy. They scheduled a follow up appointment for the following year and sent us home. On the one hand I had some answers but on the other I still had so many questions. I understood they did the best they could. I was just frustrated. I had a rollercoaster of emotions. *Decrease of heart function?* I was just scared for him, you know? His life lately, had been full of doctors, hospital visits and medicine. I wished I could provide a better life.

October 3, 2012
I have an interview tomorrow for a playwright program I'm trying to get into.....yea buddy.....*dancing to myself*

Between the hospital visits, tryna get the house under control and my baby fadda, it was amazing when opportunities opened up for me to pursue my writing. I wanted to use my poetry from the A.M.Y show to develop it into a full-blown play. I applied to Tarragon theatre's young playwright's unit and was called in for round one interviews. This was a fancy ass white people theater and I wasn't sure if my language would have fit but I mean I grew up around white people, so I knew how to flip the switch if need be. I was hoping I'd get in cause it would give me something to do while balancing out the negative. I was unable to get full time employment cause I needed to be home for Kaykay. Even though he was at school I needed to be accessible in case something happened. This meant a lot of hours spent at home since I wasn't in school. Even though I had time at home, I still hated feelin like my time was being wasted. I had planned to message Kendrick one last time.

October 3, 2012
Cola
at this point I think it'll be best if you just go through the courts if you want a dna test. If you don't want one, then that's fine by me cause I'll continue to raise my child like I been doing.
Kendrick
I do want one....I'm in school paying my rent and all that...be patient
Cola
Listen I get that, I'm doing the same thing...but all I ask is that yu keep me updated with what's gwanin. I messaged yu and asked if yu were good, and you never said

anything. To me it seems like your not interested. I'll be patient, if yu serious bout it. His heart is gettin weaker and he been in and out of the hospital, so I got a lot dealing with too. Feel me?

Cola

Since you low on money, we can do this...i'll find a place and we split it half...

Kendrick

Ok...I'm sorry...we can do that

Cola

Thank you, i'll message yu when I find a place...but my graduation is next week, so I get money at the end of the month. How's school anyway?

Kendrick

Ok, School is a Fuck.....feel like quitting some days, How u been?

Cola

ye school sucks, but as much as you might wanna quit, it'll be worth it once your done and start making good money for all those cars I see you love. I been exhausted

Kendrick

Lol...I do love cars

Cola

I don't understand, my son insanely loves cars..wants to be a racecar driver. I use to love the car I drove....but you take it to a next level. lol

Kendrick

Why not lol, Every boys first love should be cars

Cola

its past love...every birthday since he was born is cars....and every toy he owns is cars. Anyway what u studyin thats so hard?

Cola

do you mind sending me your number? k well I gotta check a couple places tomorrow for the test. K I think the Keele street lab that yu mentioned way back is gonna be the cheapest...385+ tax so I'd say we get about 225 each....how long will it take yu to get that?

Kendrick
I'm good on the first
Cola
Does that number work that yu sent me?....and what day are yu free they open 10-3... Imma book it soon an call you
Kendrick
Any day
Cola
K November 1st ...yu driving?...cause I moved so I'm not close anymore...I'm takin the bus
Kendrick
Yeah I'm driving
Cola
I probably should have checked but yu wanted the legal test right?
Kendrick
Yeah that's the only way
Cola
The only way ...to prove your not the dad?
Kendrick
If it is either way we need one that admissible in court
Cola
fair enough, I get you...iight well kk knows about it, and he knows who you are so I guess we will see you there...an ill message you closer to the date. But please keep in touch with me if things are going hectic...I really hope we can get this done without further delay..but I get life is crazy
Kendrick
We should be good this time
Cola
cool, thanks

He may have loved cars like his dad but he definitely got his swimming from me. I researched to see what kind of activities could help him and swimming was the most effective and gentle. There was a swimming pool not too far from the house. It was a moment of happiness whenever I got to see him swim. I was really hoping this time we could get the tests done. It was an interesting conversation that I had to have with Kaykay. I had to explain to him that we needed to do a test to see if Kendrick was his dad. He didn't ask much questions, he jus said "Ok". This woulda been the first time he met his dad. The only other time Kendrick has seen Kaykay was maybe when he was only a few months old. Kaykay would only know him because of the pictures I showed. I was nervous for them to meet. *What would it be like? Would they get along? Would Kaykay talk to him or just ignore him? Would Kendrick have anything to say? What if Kaykay asks questions? Well he was never the questioning type. Oh man. Does this mean joint custody?* I tried not to get my hopes up cause I knew Kendrick's plan was solely to prove he wasn't the father. Still couldn't help but enjoy the fact that we were still on friendly terms.

October 5th 2012
Cola
Hey wasup?
Kendrick
Hey
Cola
why u up so early lol
Kendrick
Lol...why u up so early?
Cola
cause kayshaun has school, and the bus comes for him ....an he takes forever and a day to get ready....I thought u men got ready quick lol
Kendrick
Lol...only when we want to
Cola
lol ...not cute at all, so what u doin today?
Kendrick
School...maybe work, U?
Cola
nun much got some ppl coming to do work in my house and meeting up with a friend
Kendrick

Oooooo someone's got a daaaate
Cola
lol it's not really like that...I don't think lol
Kendrick
Suuuure
Cola
nothin is concrete
Kendrick
Lol, U like him?
Cola
I duno yet
Kendrick
Don't know yet?
Cola
jus met him, an he's not really my type, but he's nice. lol but enough about me an my non existent love life lol, yu datin ?
Kendrick
No I'm not dating
Cola
ys that?
Kendrick
Whats ur type?
Cola
I like men who a real, ...my physically I like thick guys, real, but with a personality..have fun and laugh
Kendrick
Ok ok. I don't date cause chicks are crazy
Cola
I believe the opposite lol, men don't know how to treat women
Kendrick
Yeah right. Y'all don't know what u want and on top of that y'all are never satisfied. ....don't even have sex anymore
Cola
...I dont have sex cause no man can do it right...so selfish....some women know what they want....some men just can't live up to it.

Kendrick
What u mean no man can do it right?
Cola
they rush, don't take the time...it's all about them bussin an thats it. It's more like a transaction than romance. Overrated
Kendrick
I can tell u never had sex with me
Cola
Ye every man claims that , I just think there needs to be some kinda connection to have good sex...
Kendrick
Definitely. ..and I can't speak for other men
Cola
Ye I realize you can't. I uno I got tired of same ol thing....why'd yu stop? Have yu ever missed me...or wondered what it woulda been like
Kendrick
All the time
Cola
Which question are yu answering
Kendrick
The second
Cola
...thanks for answering ...I've wondered too
Kendrick
Have u ever missed me?
Cola
There's been times, but then you just got real mean and hurtful, it's hard to like someone an not have them feel the same way

Slippery slope tryna reminisce. This can only end in disappointment. Something about me still wanted him to want me even if I didn't want him. I had felt so rejected by him, this felt like a small win.

· October 6, 2012

My mom keeps waiting for me to act/be normal....ha...not gonna happen

She didn't understand me. I mean she tried. We tried. Years of animosity were finally at peace for the moment. I had realized that she was always gonna be the same. Instead of constantly getting mad or hurt, I needed to find something else to focus on. It was not an easy task, I often had to just ignore her comments, pretending like I didn't even hear it or just let it bounce right off a barrier I built. She was trying in her own way and even though it wasn't the way that made the most sense to me, I accepted that this was what it was. I don't know if I could ever make her happy with who I was, but I just had to be happy with myself and all my flaws knowing that my flaws made me unique. Ain't nun wrong with being unique. Bein unique got me this far in life and will continue to give me the confidence to make my own decisions.

October 8, 2012
Cola
hey I gotta ask you something...so say for example the test proves that you my childs father...are you gonna respect my decisions in terms of his medical care...or would you try an challenge me?
Kendrick
What do u mean medical care?....give me a example
Cola
Well there is no cure for his disability but there are steroids that he can take to slow down the progression of the deterioration of the muscles. But I'm choosing not to start the steroids because I don't like the side effects....so would yu support my decision or challenge it?
Kendrick
What are some side effects?
Cola
weight gain, mood swings, cataracts, osteoporosis, an hyperactivity, but they would give him more medication to counteract the effects. hmm stunt of growth, he may start puberty later...but they would give him meds for

that too....the difference is with the steroids he may live to 30 and without he may only live to 20 according to doctors..but at least he wouldn't have to live with the side effects of meds....plus he is already starting heart medication this week cause his heart is getting weaker...I know this is a conversation that should wait till we know whether or not you're the father but i'd just like to know as well as u know what you may have to deal with
Kendrick
Wow...ok
Cola
ye I know it's a lot to take in...thats why I wanted to talk bout it with u from now
Kendrick
U have a lot to deal with
Cola
ye I do....so would you try an challenge my decision? Or is it too much for you to grasp?
Kendrick
I wouldn't challenge u
Cola
Cool I appreciate that...have yu seen any pics of Kk lately?
Kendrick
No I haven't
Cola
Oh ok
Kendrick
Do u have them up?
Cola
Ye I have a lot of him. Yu wanna see em?
Kendrick
Ye
Cola
K I'll send a couple. Whats your email? Hey do yu wanna meet up before we do the test?
Kendrick
When and where?

October 9th 2012
Cola
That's what I wanna know from you. I'm free during the days...n where ever a bus runs. The week of the 22nd. There's places downtown if yu wanna drive down there

I hated the idea of starting the heart medication but at least it wasn't the steroids. I could at least try it. I was so protective of him taking too many meds. I wasn't sure how involved Kendrick wanted to be but I also realized that this was gonna be a whole new world for him and I wasn't sure if he was ready for it. I've at least had 6 years to get used to this. I was also nervous that he would try to make decisions above me. Even though I had full custody, as his dad he still had a right to an opinion. To be honest I was torn, on one hand I wanted to make all the decisions but on the other hand the idea of sharing some of the burden was nice. It wouldn't jus be left up to me. *What if I made the wrong decision?* More than anything now, I was just happy it seemed like we were finally gettin this thing done. Seemed like the impossible was happening all around me.

·October 10, 2012
Definitely a proud moment to walk across stage today at graduation...best part is...my child got to see me in a positive light. Thank you lord for my fam who showed today...you have brought me this far...phase 1 complete

I did it. First to graduate University. They counted me out and I rocked it. I rocked it, 5 years and I graduated with an Honours Degree. Nicola Jovita Audriana Bennett, Bachelor of Fine Art, Honours program. I had worked extremely hard, shed a lot of tears, dealt with plenty of fear but no greater feeling than knowing that I did it. I increased my GPA in the nick of time. If you ask Tish she would say "It's a good thing I was there to help you" As grateful as I was for her help, I wasn't a fan of her taking so much credit for helping me. Iuno, something just didn't feel great about it. The more she tried to "help me" the more I pulled away.

It was great when it started but now it was more aggressive and I was being passive aggressive in my responses. Either way I wasn't bout to let her steal my shine. I was graduating at the same time as some of my classmates that I started with, except I had the additional challenges of being a single mother. It was like a double bonus for me. To see Kaykay so happy I could only think I was making him proud.

> October 11, 2012
> thanks to all who have supported me..and to those I have met walking through the halls of york...it's been real, I appreciate the opportunity to study with yall without judgment and with an understanding that doing school while raising a child with a disability is hard..but not impossible..now on to phase 2

Phase 2 was looking pretty good. I had jus learned that I had gotten into the playwright program. It seemed like such a transition for me, from full time student to full time stay at home mom. It also seemed like the minute I finished school all these health problems arose. *You think it's all the treatments? How would you even prove it?* I didn't know how to prove it, but I know I needed to do something. I would open cupboard doors and still see roaches crawling even when they weren't there. It was a horrible feeling to consistently be haunted by invisible images. No matta what I tried I just couldn't regain the balance. I felt like I was slowly suffocating. Normally I would try to seek help from my therapist but *what can she do to help me? Can she find me another place? Can she get rid of the roaches?* My mind was playing tricks on me. I was tryna get life to slow down to a better rhythm but while the house was in complete mess the rest of life just kept on dancing away to the style of the quick step. I kept dreaming of the moment I'd be able to take a breath. *Naw you're good, you can handle the pressure.* Now this thing with his dad? The closer we got to the date of the DNA test the more nervous I got. *I feel like a mess. Please let this result be in my favour.*

·October 11, 2012
Cola
Yu good? I haven't really heard from you since I sent yu those pics...yu reconsidering us meeting up or something?

Kendrick
No not at all, I'm here. He looks just like his beautiful mother
Cola
Oh ok good, thought maybe I scared yu away or something Lol. Oh wow thanks, it's a great compliment. Hey guess what ...I graduated yesterday:)
Kendrick
Congrats, So what's next for u?
Cola
Thanks, hmm well I just got into an arts program to create and write my own plays,....hmm I'm in the process of writing my autobiography...and I'm starting up a fashion line/ business....n once my house is set up imma start teaching piano on the side LOL....I know its a lot
Kendrick
Wow
Cola
What? Lol
Kendrick
Ambition is sexy tho
Cola
Ye eh..dats why I'm Tryna be a boss. More importantly I gotta be available for my child and any type of family I try an create
Kendrick
I feel ya
Cola
So what are some of your goals...aside from school?..I'm mean your still pretty young
Kendrick
My own business...I want to build a car from scratch...travel all corners of the world...maybe find someone
Cola

See...being a boss is sexy...we have similar mindsets ....I'm not surprised with the car idea...I think it's a good idea...can yu fix any cars? And if yu could leave right now....where would yu go?
Kendrick
Japan
Cola
That's smart...most ppl say somewhere tropical
Kendrick
Not me
Cola
Y Japan? Business? Or pleasure?
Kendrick
Both
Cola
Oh la la,I seen what yu said bout maybe finding someone...that shits hard to do truss...relationships are difficult
Kendrick
I know
Cola
I hate the awkwardness when two ppl first meet an they tryna get to know each other
Kendrick
Well we are opposite. ..I don't like when everyone's too comfortable and don't appreciate and are boring. At the beginning it's exciting
Cola
Ye I get that...in long term relationships ppl forget how to have fun...
Kendrick
Exactly
Cola
Ye at the beginning there's nerves Tryna figure out what the real feelings are
Kendrick
Ye
Cola

See I have not been in any long term relationships so I don't get to that point Lol plus I'm weird ...the fun doesn't stop
Kendrick
Never?
Cola
Naw. My longest relationship is a mystery ...I've been talkin to a guy I've never met...but he's been there since Kk was born
Kendrick
Online?
Cola
I met him online, but we talk on the phone everyday...
Kendrick
Ok
Cola
What's your longest relationship been?
Kendrick
5 years
Cola
Damn
Kendrick
lol ye
Cola
So what happened?..if yu don't mind me asking. See I actually want something long term and stable ...I eventually want more kids
Kendrick
Don't wanna get into it
Cola
No problem
Kendrick
Don't know if I want kids
Cola
Ys that..?
Kendrick
U scared the shit outta me
Cola

Oh boo, wasn't my intentions...what exactly is it that's messed with yu?
Kendrick
Wats u mean?
Cola
Yu said I scared the shit outta yu...yu mean recently or with how everything has happened between us?
Kendrick
From before
Cola
Oh, ye I get it shits messed up...I understood y u were mad, to an extent, but I didn't understand y yu treated me so bad..you really thought I was a big hoe?
Kendrick
Its how u went about things
Cola
I didn't even know I was pregnant.Naw but for real...yu really thought I was a hoe though?...honest talks...I can't get mad
Kendrick
Nope...thought u were the dumbest person on the planet
Cola
Dry ...it's all good...cause I didn't know I was pregnant? I was working out everyday, losing weight...I was in denial...I was 16, didn't wanna think about the fact that I might be pregnant. I didn't even have symptoms
Kendrick
Plus I thought it was unfair that we didn't have sex and u were on me. ...but u admitted to having sex with someone else and disregarded that
Cola
I'm srry it took me so long to tell yu, or that my dad called to talk to yu...those were not my intentions.I don't remember sayin I had sex with someone else, not sayin your lying..I just don't remember..and I talked to dude bout me going to see him, neither one of us remember having sex. The thing between me n yu had me spooked...I didn't understand it either...the only

explanation I have is that because I was giving yu brains it might have caused precum N those two seconds yu put it in might have done something...I mean I know it's hard to believe but it's not impossible
Kendrick
U told me u did some guys hair then y'all ended up having sex
Cola
And that's y I really just wanted us to the test from the beginning cause I understood what yu were thinkin
Kendrick
I had a condom on
Cola
Ye it's the same guy whose hair I was doing...but I don't remember I uno, I could have blocked it out
Kendrick
I've had sex multiple times after getting head...even raw...and nuttin has happened. That was my problem...why block it out and focus on me
Cola
I was young, scared and I fucked up, I can admit to that...I uno I guess it made the most sense to me at the time...But y wouldn't yu just do the test and prove me wrong?
Kendrick
Cause I didn't even take it serious...come on
Cola
I get that, but I offered to pay for it..it woulda been so easy for yu to humor me an get it done...yu never once thought what it be like to have a son?
Kendrick
A girl who u never set wit calls u and lets u know she just realized she's 8 months pregnant by u...Don't sound weird
Cola
To yu an other ppl ye...to me? My whole life is weird and nothin made sense, it was just another thing for me
Kendrick
Humour u? Ur father shouting at my mom? The other guy doesn't make sense?
Cola

When I say humour me I mean by taking the test even though yu believed otherwise just to show me I'm wrong. I can't speak for my dad...the situation was messed up

Kendrick

U shoulda talked to me alone. Not Ur dad. Not my mom

Cola

I spoke to the other dude...I stopped talkin to him same time like yu...it was hard for him to understand and we tried to sort it out...but he said nun happened and I was convinced it was you. I know I'm srry about that...my dad yelled, and scared the shit outta me....didn't leave me much choice living under his roof. I didn't know what else to do..

Kendrick

Wat u mean he told u nothing happened?

Cola

No I was sitting across the room from him in the kitchen, I stalled, I begged, I pleaded..he didn't care..he wanted to talk to yu and he wouldn't let me leave the room until I told him. I was put in a tough spot...an I was too immature to handle it any different. To be honest I never planned to tell yu. I already planned to take care of my child by myself cause I knew yu would never believe me...I mean shit after 8 months, even I was having trouble Tryna figure out what was going on

Kendrick

What u mean he told u nothing happened?

Cola

I was there, I member he asked yu about my pregnancy and what yu were going to do

Kendrick

U said"I spoke to the other dude...I stopped talkin to him same time like yu...it was hard for him to understand and we tried to sort it out...but he said nun happened and I was convinced it was you "....wat do u mean by that

Cola

Oh ...Damn I thought yu meant somethin else. He remembers the same shit I do...I showed up I did his hair..then he left me stranded ...he doesn't remember us having sex. You're the only guy I remember doing anything sexual with

Kendrick

That's not wat u said before

Cola

I have no clue what I said to yu before...but I guess it would make sense y yu had such anger towards me

Kendrick

Why don't u ever remember anything...I don't get it. U even said u don't remember wat happened with us that night either

Cola

Yu remember me tellin yu that I was gang raped when I was younger?..well I used to cope with shit by blocking it out...or selective memory to deal with the situation as best as I can. I memba yu came...we talked...had some conversation bout wanting to be together...maybe yu was just saying what I wanted to hear...I gave yu head...hmm yu tried to put it in, I told yu I didn't wanna have sex...yu took a shower...chilled on my computer...then yu left...did I forget anything? Writing helps me remember...hence y I been writing my book...I do remember what happened..I just forgot details like whether or not you used a condom. An..it hurts to remember...so unless I'm writing, id rather not. I thought we stop talkin cause I didn't want to have sex with you that night...which is why yu never heard from me until my dad called

Kendrick

We will see next month, U don't know how much that fucked me up. But hey it is wat it is

Cola

I have an idea...the shit fucked me up too...I wish we coulda had this calm conversation 6 years ago

Kendrick

This is where we are now

Cola

Can yu ever accept my apology, for how things went?

Kendrick

What if it comes back that I'm not the father?
Cola
Well I can't fix what has already happened to yu, and an apology won't be enough..but i'll fix it with the family responsibility office as much as I can
Kendrick
Not me....Wats next for u
Cola
What If yu are the father? Nothing is next for me...I keep raising my son how I been doing
Kendrick:
Wat if I'm not
Cola
Yu already asked me that....life goes on for us if yu aren't. An if yu are....life changes....what would yu do
Kendrick
Haven't thought about it
Cola
k
Kendrick
But if I'm not Ur just gonna accept the fact that u had a miracle baby
Cola
That's my plan...I have goals I have to meet...I don't have any more time to chase the shadow of a man who doesn't wanna be in our lives. This thing with you started so long ago, but I no longer have the time an energy to invest in it...I'm happy the test is finally gettin done. We can move on with our lives. I'm glad we finally got to talk without the hostility. Yu seem more mature...I like u better this way
Kendrick
So do u
Cola
Thanks. Well since we spent all this time talking about all that happened...we really don't need to meet until the 1st when we do the test. It'll be stressful and a big day for us both

Kendrick
A stressful week u mean
Cola
Oh shit ye it takes 5 days...don't think imma sleep that week
Kendrick
Lol, If he is my son...I still don't want to deal with the courts
Cola
Ok, well I already have custody, so I don't have any involvement with the courts really. If he is your son, i'd like us to get along...like we seem to be now...an I'm cool with no courts
Kendrick
Alright...if he is...I promise u I'm gonna help u out
Cola
Ok cool, glad we could get this far. It's not money I care bout eh?...
Kendrick
I'll be there
Cola
Good, It'll take some getting used to but I'm willing to try
Kendrick
Ok. Well until then
Cola
Ye feel free to message me if yu want
Kendrick
U too
Cola
Thanks

In just one conversation the war was over. Years of animosity, hurt feelings and misunderstandings were forgiven, at least on my side. I knew he just wanted to prove me wrong but regardless I was jus happy we could finally get to this point. I always understood why he felt I was untrustworthy, I just wished we coulda just done the test. We spent six years fighting. As bad as I felt for going to the courts and the way things went, if a third party hadn't suspended his driver's license and passport he wouldn't even be here talking to me. His whole goal was to get his stuff reinstated. So, in a way, this was bound to happen the exact way it happened. No regrets. We were spending more time offline via text or on the phone than we were online. It was just like it used to be. Talking about a potential future together or wherever life would bring us as parents. Talking about future dreams and aspirations. We just needed to get through these results first. *Why? After everything, why? Keep your emotions together, don't get caught up. If these results say he's not the dad, he ain't gon claim you. He jus wants to prove you wrong and move forward. He ain't change that much.*

October 15, 2012
pet peeve: ppl who make me wait without communicating what's going on....I have a life too

We had plans. We had made plans to connect and he stood me up. Without text. Without conversation. *Just when I thought....*I mean, who was I kidding? I knew I shouldn't have gotten my hopes up, but I thought just maybe. We're both grown, maybe time jus needed to pass but here I was mad, afraid, hurt, scared. WHHYYYYYY????

·October 11, 2012
Cola
K Im assuming your busy, but I really had a feeling to talk to yu, so I guess i'll message yu on here and you can get back to me when yu have time. I'm scared. everything I did, I did for my son but for once in 6 years I'm so scared of the results, I'm nervous to see you, and I'm scared to even do the test. After our initial conversation I messaged the other guy to try an help clarify some things for me and he basically told me to fuck off. I guess I have a special quality that makes people hate me. I don't even know y I'm rambling to you, guess I'm hoping you understand or can relate. I'm starting to care bout yu more each time we talk...thinking we kinda on the same page but hell even that makes me nervous. I know you've been open about your feelings and what you want from

me one thing I don't get is why now?...what changed to make yu feel the way yu do about me?... Ug so many Damn questions I can't wait till the test so I can have some of these answered. I guess with us...only time will tell how close we become, and how much we can do like what you said and just move forward together. Soooooo...ye...feel free to answer my modness

No response

My fears didn't ease up the closer we got to Nov 1st. I didn't get much sleep, it was this constant back and forth agony of what the truth was. I tried my best to prepare Kaykay but how do you explain this to a six year old? I didn't wanna lie or try to make it sound better than it was, so I said "Kaykay, we are going to do a test to see if Kendrick is your dad or not" "Ok mommy" I was hoping the more I said it the more he would understand.

The day had finally come and we took the hour long ride up to the west end to the test facility. It was my first time seeing him in a long time. He was way different than what I remembered. He was bald, grown a belly, just different. Kaykay looked like a mini version of him. It was such a crazy thing to see cause I had never seen them together. Kaykay was super nice and Kendrick had candy that he shared with him. If I coulda taken a picture in that moment I woulda done it. Kaykay was so receptive to him. Before long everything was done. It happened so quickly I was still daydreaming. Kaykay's infectious laugh pierced through my thoughts. Kendrick held Kaykay's hand as we walked out on our way to the bus stop. We said our goodbyes and now the real worrying began cause we had to await the results.

· November 9, 2012
6 years and the truth finally came out...feels like a big weight has been lifted

We were at swimming when we got the news. I got the email and then my phone rang. Kayshaun was 99.99% Kendrick's son. No other chance it was someone else's. So, my miracle condom wearing non-sex having baby was Kendrick's and he was left speechless. I think he had convinced himself so much that there was no possible way he could be the dad that the news hit him like bricks. There was a lot of silence on the phone as I continued to watch Kaykay swim through the glass. He needed time to adjust. I finally got vindication. No matta how things went down, in the end I was right. I always knew in the pit of my stomach but there was so much outside chatter, outside voices that I couldn't silence until right in that moment. It felt amazing. But to be honest, I wasn't sure how well he was gonna process the information. My only guess was that he was feeling exactly how I felt when I found out at 8 months that I was pregnant. *How did this happen?* With this news now out, and with the outcome coming out in my favor I was feelin like nothin could stop us. Despite the fact that it had been months since Romeo and I spoke this news was way too good not to tell him.

November 19, 2012
its me and my son against the world..dun kno we run tings

People didn't know what to say. Those who judged me were silenced for once. But I had a feeling that even my closest friends low key thought I was wrong and were just happy I didn't embarrass myself. Romeo was happy to hear from me and not surprised by the news in the slightest. Things kinda just picked up where they left off except now he was in Vancouver. He and the kids had moved there during the time we had stopped talking. He was miles away yet very close to my heart. I didn't have time or energy to be mad at him anymore. This news was way too big to stay angry with him. Plus, it wasn't like we had to start datin again, we could focus on just maintaining a friendship. That's all I could manage, just friendship and comfort. The comfort he provided was all I needed in this exact moment cause I hadn't yet had a decent sleep since we moved in. I had constant headaches, I was spending money like crazy and I'd sit up and just cry. I no longer slept in my bedroom but I didn't trust the living room. *Is this what it feels like to lose your mind?* I couldn't keep the thoughts straight. *You think this is best for Kaykay?*

I couldn't see much encouragement around me. It hadn't even been that long before my sister and I were gettin on each otha's nerves. I hated feelin like I was picking up after her and she hated feelin like I was tellin her what to do. We argued more often than not, and unless it had somethin to do with Kaykay things jus moved at separate speeds. Anyway, I made comments but tried to keep things to myself. I already had other things on my mind. I was still at a loss when it came to this roach situation. Most of us were at a loss on what to say in this situation yet I would still hear "God doesn't give you more than you can handle." *Wow that's amazing news!!! Wish I thought of that. Why did he make cockroaches anyway? What's their purpose but to annoy and disgust me?* Ok, I agree that the statement is true, and I'd often repeat it to myself for self-motivation, but while going through this kinda personal hell that sentence produced bitterness more than encouragement. I'm just being honest. That's not what I wanted to hear. Truth was I knew God was with me, however in the moments when I was hurting bad what I preferred was a hug or some personal understanding. Like "Hey Cola, I understand life is really difficult right now, everything is happening all at once, if you need me I'm here for you. We can pray, we can talk, just know that I know things kinda suck but I gotcha back." Straight up. I woulda appreciated that on a whole different level. It would let me know that cool, even though you probably may not understand what I was going through, you were willing to listen and try to feel my pain on some level. My perspective on friends, life, and family were changing. The deeper I sunk into my hole the harder it was to see things any differently.

> November 19, 2012
> My friend pool is very small, joke is ppl assume that we are friends when they are simply acquaintances...

There were a lot of changes happening internally. They didn't see it, but it was happening. People were being shifted based on how I felt in the moment. Those who supported me, those who didn't. Those who wanted the best for us, those that didn't. It all needed to shift so we could focus on bigger dreams.

November 23, 2012 ·
My child wants to be a race car driver.....so who am I to stop him

He wanted to race cars. He loved how fast they were. His love was like his dad's. For the simple fact that most people saw him as disabled was the exact reason that I didn't wanna crush his dreams of being a race car driver. The last thing I needed to do was tell him how to live his life. I felt like my goal as his mother was to teach him the fundamentals and guide him as best as I could, but ultimately the choices of his destination were left to him. At this moment I chose to start fresh.

November 23, 2012
Sometimes it's hard to see how much ppl care bout me...my heart is made of stone

Love. I keep hearin this word but it has no meaning to me. What the fuck is love? And why does it keep tryna claim me? Love just slapped me with a six year truth. Love just slapped me with another look at myself. Love jus had no damn place in my life, cause love, love has drained my last ounce of energy, my last hooray, my last fuck I gave, and I was through with love and all its selfish ways.

Nov 26
Cola
k so communication is a BIG thing for me. We all got our own problems and things we deal with but I still feel like that aint no reason for a person to just not communicate. I been raising my child with his disability for 6 years on my own, got my unI degree and it wasn't easy but im here, the LEAST you could do is call me or message me back when I text you. Or communicate to me a lil bit of

what you're going through so I don't feel like you just don't want any part of your son's life. I get that you're still in shock tryna figure out how you have a son but real talks, you need to get over this, cause he needs you to be there for him physically and if you can't do that then its cool...you aint been there so nothing changes. But I just thought it would be great that he gets to bond with you SINCE you are his dad and you both could easily learn to love each other. I understand that money is a problem right now and that back child support is hard to deal with, but it's owed to the son you chose to ignore. I would never have taken you to court if you didnt act like a complete asswhole to me. We could have worked this out together, but now it's too late...so now we just gotta move forward. I am not gonna chase you no more, from now on it's up to you whether or not you have a relationship with your child. Do you realize that you haven't even tried to see him since the test? anyway you have my house number, you have my new cell number...no more excuses...find a way to communicate with me..the same way I make time for you

I fell for the trap. I actually believed he wanted things to be different. I actually thought for a second that a nightmare could have a happy ending. From the day he saw us we never heard from him again. It was a different kind of sting, different kind of hurt. Like rejection on a next level. I understood before things were muddy, but now, now he knew the truth. It wasn't ok. Nothing about this was ok. So, I did what I had to do as a mother. I mailed the DNA test to his mom's house. I was hoping she'd know the truth and would wanna meet KayKay. I don't know how much time God was giving him left on this earth, but I want him to know his other family, I want them to know him. I wanted them to know his smile, his laugh, his energy. I want to know their family history; how does it connect to Kaykay?

Within a week he called me, threatening me, warning me to leave his family alone. We both called the cops on each other. He told the cops I was harassing him, I told the cops he was threatening me, yet I was the only person warned in this situation. The cop that came to take my statement said I kinda deserved it since I sent the DNA test. Said what did I expect? *I expected his family would care. I expected an apology. I expected the cops wouldn't come into my house to blame me.* They walked into my apartment, looked it over and asked me how I make my money and how I was able to afford something like it. It was such a crummy feeling to be interrogated like that. It wasn't until after they left I got a separate call from another cop from another division saying Kendrick had called to report me. After weeks of texting and phone calls back and forth this was where we now stood. Strangers all over again. I suspected it was because of how I looked. I suspected it was my weight. I suspected the embarrassment was too much to handle. I suspected that with years of denial there was no explanation. So, we left it there. He went back to his life and I went back to being a mom.

December 1, 2012
Kk picked this Tree said its perfect

We called it his Charlie Brown Christmas tree. There wasn't much room in the apartment but there was at least more room here than at the last place, so I didn't want to complain. He never had a tree before. He saw the display in the store and his eyes lit up as he stood next to the tree and pronounced happily "It's cute just like I am". *How can I deny that?* Him and the tree were the exact same height and it came pre-lit. We bought stockings and other Christmas decorations. With everything going on around us it felt good to see the joy on his face. *Maybe I am doing something right.* I think being a mom, as challenging as it was, was the only thing that kept me moving forward. As much as we struggled we were blessed. I loved Christmas shopping for Kaykay cause he never asked for anything. He was spoiled but didn't have a spoiled attitude. He literally appreciated everything I did for him and it made me want to spoil him more. I bought him gifts, Leo bought gifts, his aunty bought him gifts. It was a beautiful sight to see under his tiny Christmas tree. The smile on his face every time we put a gift down or we baked cookies made being a mom such an amazing thing for me. I didn't know how to be anything else, even the small things like taking him to the dentist made me smile. I remember how much fun it was for me as a child cause I always got a treat after.

> December 3, 2012
> Why is my Child's dentist such a sweetie though...

There's certain professions that I just don't expect to see someone sexy and young, a dentist was one of them. All the dentists I ever met were old and white but damn what a change. I tried to find joy where I could and honey he was fillin me with joy all ova. It was a welcomed smile. I think a super power of mothers was somehow making everything look and seem alright in the midst of storms. The great thing was, despite the mayhem, Kaykay loved his new school and he said he liked living downtown more than in the west. I don't blame him. I once witnessed a kid stare him down in the hallways at his old school and from then, I told myself that I would find a better school for him to go to.

> December 6, 2012
> So I met the kid bullying my child today...for no reason at all he said he hates my child and doesn't care if he cries...his mother just sat there and couldn't control him..not gonna let this go

One of my biggest fears came true today. I witnessed it and could do nothing about it. I've always been protective of my child, maybe even over protective. He has such a beautiful heart and I always feared he'd be picked on because of his disability. As I witnessed it I was angry and then I cried. *How could a child be so mean? How could his mother sit there and say nothing? And yet if I drape up the kid I'll be in the wrong.* People think black women are angry? Touch our children and we'll show you angry! I don't care if it's a kid, imma protect mine. I walked up to the kid to have a talk with him. I towered above him and I gave him a lil shove. *He wants to pick on Kaykay? Nahhh. But what if I wasn't here? Would he know to stand up for himself and tell a teacher?* It broke my heart to hear him explain it to me with sadness in his voice. How do I teach him to love when all this child does is hate? These battles of life continue to challenge me every day as I search for inner peace. *Will it ever come?*

December brought new changes. I was done tryna fight with the roaches, done tryna fight with Kendrick, done tryna fight bullies and by this time my sister an I were done tryna live together. I felt like I was tryna talk to her but it was falling on deaf ears and I snapped. We had an incident where the kitchen almost flooded, my sister was yelling at me, calling me dumb for something I didn't do an I lost it. I called my parents and told them we could no longer live together. After only 3 months she was moving out. I felt bad but I could not manage everything at the same time. It jus felt like there needed to be changes.

The potential of the apartment was really starting to shine through. The roach problem was finally under control after months of hell and we were finally able to decorate and settle in. Even as we settled, it felt like there was always moving parts. Tish always had one way she was pulling me, Kaykay the next, life the next, Leo was somewhere in the background, my sis was gone which meant the money my parents paid for rent was done and I took over the full amount. There were just many shadows to live up to. It was a welcoming break when I met another single mother named Té at the local welfare office. She was nice, had a son just like me, she was younger than me but she was tryna get life together jus like I was and she had a dope afro. I normally don't talk to anyone when I go to the office but our conversation opened up when she asked me to watch her sleeping child while she met with her worker. We exchanged numbers cause I wanted to know how to make my hair grow naturally. As much as I said I don't trust people, every now and then I gave in a little cause sometimes I met people and things jus clicked. I think life so far has taught me not to judge anyone, some of my best friendships came from the craziest of places. I've accepted from early, that I lived in an unconventional world which was full of many strange things without explanation so I stopped tryna explain them and just lived through them. It created beautiful memories and lessons. What's life without adventure?

Poetic interlude

Man's property
Common sense would tell you that right now
I'm pissed off
Common sense would tell you no matta how soft you try and make your voice
It cannot erase the words that you said to me
The embarrassment you caused when you called me a bitch and untrustworthy
Yelled at me in front of others
Thinkin you was justified
By the lies you continue to let flow through your mind
The embarrassment you cause was not to me but yurself
Cause common sense would tell you that by me walking away
Your words have no affect
Like play
Stop
Delete

Growing pains
You neva took the chance to get to know me
Neva took the time to understand the beauty
Your physical attraction
And your dicks reaction to me
Blind sided you
An almost had me in a trance
Trance feeling so high
Wantin to do a victory dance
Thinkin after all the hurt an pain
I'd finally found the one

But mr one yu were da wrong one for me
Lettin sex guide my way
Only led me astray
Thinkin sex is equivalent to love
Dumbin down my feelings
Cause yu said you aint ready for love
An yu aint sure what yu want
But like a fool I waited
Hanging on yur every word
Even as yu ignore me
An store me away
For what yu consider to be a rainy day
Yu neva took the chance to get to know me
Neva did yu see potential in me
Neva did yu see the wifey in me
Neva did yu see a mother to be
Somebody to love n care n hold yu down
No matta how much yu made me cry
I stayed layin around
But like they say what goes around comes around
So yu neva took the chance to get to know me
But he did
I used to love you, I used to love them
But they neva took the the chance to get to know me
Goodbye to past relationships
I'm embracin my new future to be
Cause he's takin time to get to know me
N its a beautiful thing

CHAPTER FIFTY-SEVEN

Focus

"Many waters cannot quench love, nor can rivers drown it. If a man would offer all the riches of his house for love, it would be utterly scorned and despised."
SONG OF SOLOMON 8:7

Whenever Romeo and I connected it always felt right but wrong. I don't know what this pull was. I don't know why we break up to make up. I don't know why I felt like I needed him yet couldn't have him. I had given up on meeting him in person cause truth was, it wasn't the most important thing. Over the last few months we had movie dates, we listened to music, we did everything together. The distance didn't take away from what we had. He knew me better than anyone around me. He took more interest than anyone else around me. I jus blocked out the otha shit and focused on our friendship.

So, I'm talking to Romeo one day and I hear noises in the background. *Is that the tv? Yo that sounds like a baby. Maybe you're just hearing stuff. Lol why would there be a baby there? Let it go. Don't say nun.* "Hey, what's that noise in the background...it sounds like a baby" Silence. "Hello? You there? Why you quiet?" "What if it was a baby?" *No this nigga didn't. What did he jus say to me? What if it was a baby? What the hell that mean?* "What do you mean what if it is a baby, like is it? Just tell me the truth. Over anything you know the biggest thing for me was lying. I don't like lies or liars or anything in that nature. What do you mean what if it is a baby...is it a baby?" I hear a deep exhale followed by "Yes, it's a baby." *NO, he betta be playing some trick on me. This ain't even funny, naw he's joking. Where the hell would a baby come from?* "SOOOOOOOO how old is the baby, with who, why didn't you tell me, why lie? Why would you hide this and how did you hide this?" "I didn't wanna hurt you or disappoint you or get you mad. I hate when you get mad. My son is a few months old and it was with my baby moms." "You know what Romeo, fuck you. You wanna lie? You wanna be with your baby moms? Go ahead. I'm so tired of you living your life and expecting me to jus be here on pause for you. You're clearly living your life, what is this, the 4th kid? You know I still only have one, right? I coulda had another kid but stupid me thinking naw I don't wanna mess up jus in case we get together".

"I'm a fool. I'm a damn fool that I been sittin here keeping my heart on pause for a man who has CLEARLY moved on. Well you know what? I wish you the best of luck but I need to move on now. I need to live my life, I need to be unattached and give other people a chance. There are some really great people out there that won't lie to me and who value the woman I am. I just can't do this shit with you no more. DON'T CALL ME NO MORE, you're selfish and I don't deserve this shit." Click. He rang down my phone, left me messages, he seemed so sad but I couldn't even care. He always says he doesn't want to be with anyone else but me and that I have his heart and yet here I am findin out about another child. How many kids does he need to have before I truly give up on him? And with her too? Her? Really? He said they were done. Said he didn't want nothing to do with her, said she meant nothing. So how does he keep fallin on to her? To be so dumb and blind to the truth. I have jus been slapped by reality. *Dis nigga really tryna have his cake and eat it too, well I ain't got the time for this no more, he gon have to play someone else.* He didn't have to do me like this. He could have showed me the flex and his movements and I wouldn't have held on. I would have tried harder to move on.

I just couldn't deal. The nerve of this man. He had me wasting my damn time. I didn't know what to do but I knew I needed a distraction. I finally gave in, got an Instagram account and created an online dating profile. It turned out that Romeo was wrong. There were otha men interested in me. He said "No otha man will love you like I do. You're a difficult person to love." Yet an still a man named Bruce was in my inbox. 28, good looking, Fed-ex worker and American (yum) from New York which was close enough by bus. Conversations were good...when he had time. He worked a lot but more importantly he was a shy guy which meant I did most of the talking. It was exactly the distraction I needed. It felt good to be wanted by someone otha than Romeo cause I really didn't think anyone else would want me. I was damaged goods.

I was worried about all the damages that was happening in Kaykay's body. This new medication was causing him to be overly active. It was great to see him so excited but he just couldn't sit still for nun. Even his teachers noticed a difference in his behavior at school. It was the first time I had been gettin calls from school. He just wasn't himself. I tried to have a conversation with him about the effects he was feeling since he started taking the medication. During our conversation he said, "Mommy I don't want to keep taking the medication." "You're tired of all the pills?" He nods his head yes. *Damn, what do I do now?* I hated having to give him the meds, I could barely remember to take vitamins. Doctors said it was to make him better but if he didn't wanna take them, I didn't wanna force him. He had a right to give his opinion on the things that he was puttin in his body. I respected that. After all, he knew his body betta than I did.

Kaykay said "I'm not gonna say my disability makes me slow like a turtle cause I can hop really fast like a kangaroo...watch me!" "Where is all this coming from?" "I told you...I'm smart!"

Between the changes I noticed and him not wanting to take the medication, I figured I'd talk to his doctors to see what other options we had. I had set up an appointment to see his cardiologist. She seemed detached. Not emotionally invested. I mean I get it, sometimes it's dangerous to get too emotionally invested in patients, but she was too removed. It never gave me a great feeling when we had to meet up with her. All that to say, I wasn't surprised when she said she didn't think there was a correlation between the medication and his hyper activity. Actually, it sounded more like she thought I was making things up. The response I got was "There's no evidence to prove that the medication causes hyperactivity." Translation, not enough kids have displayed an adverse effect for us to care enough to do something about it. *Great. Gotcha!* That wasn't a good enough reason for me to keep giving him the medication and she wasn't offering any other options, so I stopped the meds. We'd just have to figure things out a lil at a time. There was a possibility that he was hyper because the medication helped his heart function better which in turn made him feel better and allowed him to have more energy. But it was such a drastic change. No matta what was going on there was always something to make me laugh.

I had been asking Kaykay to clean his room for a couple days and he just flat out didn't do it so I stopped asking him, and then the greatest thing happened. He walked into his room and all I heard was "Who am I kidding? I need to clean my room" Then to my shock he cleaned his whole room. As much as things were unbalanced, small moments like that helped to keep my smiles up. The best part of our apartment was the balcony. I was on the 6th floor but since no one was above me it would snow on my balcony which worked to my benefit. I got Kaykay dressed in his winter attire: hats, boots, mitts, jacket, and snowsuit and I let him go on the balcony to play while I stayed inside. I could easily watch him from the comfort of a toasty apartment while he made snow angels on the balcony. Win win. The best part of parenting was the compromises, cause although I wasn't a winter person, Kaykay was. I uno how cause he has Jamaican blood but the Canadian part of him loved winter and playing outside.

I often felt guilty he had to live life kinda trapped. Even though he was happy I found joy in him doing "normal" activities. At school all the girls said he was cute so they helped him do everything from putting his shoes on for him to buttoning up his coat. He lived life like a rockstar making me proud at the Christmas concert when he landed the starring role as the little drummer boy. I held my breath the whole time just praying he would remember everything. When we practiced earlier on he seemed to remember nothing but pulled it off beautifully during the concert. Music runs in the blood, so I guess I'm not even too surprised that he was like a mini me.

January 10, 2013 ·
I am happy

The roaches were gone and I could finally breathe...slightly. I didn't see much of a way out but the months had gone by and I had survived. Without the extra money from Leo and my sis gone my rent was more than half the money I made so I stayed broke, but we were making things work. I had a few other things causing me to smile. Even though my conversations with Bruce had slowed down a whole lot I found myself on another dating site and had caught the interest of this cute Ghanian guy named George. To be honest I wasn't looking for anything in particular but he approached me in a decent way so why not give him a chance? He had a job, his own place, his own money, no car yet but I was wit it. Based on my past it was like hitting the jackpot. He was a construction worker...like a real one, not a drug dealer like I had in the past. This man actually got up and went to work in the downtown core. When he asked me out I was hesitant. *Have you ever dated? No strings attached?* This was new territory for me. I mean I had been on a few dates here and there but this felt so different. I was gonna have to get dressed and go meet a complete stranger. As nervous as I was to say yes we had a lot in common so I was curious how this was gonna play out. *What do we talk about? What do I even wear?*

We met up downtown at a southern style restaurant which was a really dope spot for food but horrible for dates. The live music made it virtually impossible to keep any sort of conversation flowing. We made the best of it nonetheless. George looked just like his picture, maybe even a lil cuter. He was thick but not much taller than me, but at 5"3 who am I to be picky over height? The first date we hit off really nicely, he didn't try to kiss me or feel me up at all, it was a really simple first date which I appreciated. It put my mind at ease. The more we spoke the more it felt like we just knew each other from time. It was great that I was able to have a deep connection with someone otha than Romeo. Every time I met someone new I heard Romeo in the back of my head saying that he was the only one for me. It made me try harder to prove him wrong. As much as I felt like I was unlovable, George was really opening my eyes to the potential.

That first date was the start to a few more within only a few days. It had me feeling like I was enjoying normal people stuff. I was very comfortable with him, comfortable enough to have him over to meet Kaykay. For the first introduction I made dinner and we all watched a kid's movie together. He was actually really good with Kaykay, they got along instantly which was extremely important for any guy I was gonna see. By the 2nd week I was spending nights at his house. I actually took the bus from downtown up to the west end in a snow storm to chill with this man. *Girl you crazy, this is going way too quickly. But it's nice though, it's something normal. He's cute, he's good, don't overthink this.* It was like someone hit me on the head or I caught amnesia or something, cause I don't travel for men...ever. That was one of my rules from time, never travel for dick. Once I left my house I was no longer in control and anything could happen. He could leave me stranded, he could kick me outta his house, there were too many variables to entrust my safety to a man. Yet somehow he had me desiring to bend the rules, maybe cause it felt like a real relationship for once where I wasn't the only one contributing or putting in work. This man had me making him lunches and dropping them off at work for him, not cause he asked but cause it felt like what I was supposed to do. This was like real crazy stuff that I never really did.

He knew a lot of history that I didn't care too much for but I loved his ambition when he would talk about his dreams. As quickly as things were going, they were being deflated. The first issues was with the sex. Sigh! *Guess you can't always have it all. Great guy, boring sex vs. Wack man with amazing sex. Not hard to pick between the two. Just have to get a lil creative.* He wasn't too blessed in the dick department but it was more about angles, so that wasn't the problem. A small dick I could work with but what I couldn't work with was a selfish lover. Always wanting me to give head but didn't wanna give head himself. *Ye eh.* See how quick I got lock jaw. To top it off he never waited for me to buss. Sex was like being at a fast food drive through. Took my money and was quick to deliver on the food but the products were less than satisfactory. Missy Elliot knew what she was talkin bout when she made the song <u>One Minute Man</u>. In my head I would sing,

Break me off, show me what you got
'Cause I don't want, no one minute man
Break me off, show me what you got
'Cause I don't want, no one minute man

I would have been willing to work on improving the sex if he actually tried. He didn't really see nothing wrong with it. Sex was not the deal breaker though. George had very deep personal wounds from his mom and with me being a mom and having a "mothering" personality it was breeding grounds for constant arguments. Literally over the dumbest shit. Whenever George left my house I would ask him to let me know when he got home safe. Dude told me I was too fauss and controlling. *How?* Even just me reminding him of things HE ASKED me to remind him about was a problem. Said I was needy and overbearing. *How? You're the one who asked me to remind you. How is this somehow my fault?* I guess the little things I did his mom never did so it triggered something in him. *This is the way I show love though. I don't know how to change it.* It was far more complicated than it needed to be and I was losing my patience. It was like whatever I did I was still somehow wrong.

We're nearing the end of January and his birthday was coming up. Although we had known each other for less than a month I wanted to do something special for him because this was his first birthday since his dad had passed away. I remembered from one of our many conversations he said he had never been to a Raptors game, so I bought us a couple of tickets in a decent row. The plan was that he would come over for dinner and we would head out from my place since I was already downtown. My one last surprise for him was a handmade birthday card. He talked about wanting to put together pictures of his dad since he passed and not having time to do it. *Hey, I should put together pictures of him and his dad in a birthday card for his birthday. I mean, it's a little weird, maybe even stalkerish but hopefully he'll like it. I know he's been having such a rough time.* I wanted it to be a surprise so I went through his facebook pictures and gathered the pictures of his dad he had posted online to use as a collage in the form of a birthday card. I take a look at my handy work and think, *this is actually pretty dope.* Even my sis and otha friends were kinda jealous of how nice the card was.

I had recently read the book Think Like Man by Steve Harvey and I was definitely picking up some of the cues and applying it to this situation. One of those helpful tools was about listening to how a man introduces you to his friends. His birthday came before we were set to go to the basketball game and he already had plans that day to celebrate with his friends and I wasn't invited. He said, "I'm a private person, I'm not ready to introduce you yet." *Really? That don't make sense. Here I am going outta my way for this man, telling my friends and what not and he out here playing games. Ok, I see you.* I had already bought the tickets and had everything ready so I wasn't gonna be petty and cancel, but it definitely lemme know he wasn't as into me as he claimed he was. No matta how much he said he cared about me or loved me (he said he was falling in love with me, we even talked about being exclusive) his actions showed me something different.

The day of the Raptors game rolled around and while he was working I was prepping the food. It was a man's dinner, steak and potatoes with some sort of veggie. Real gourmet type ting. He was supposed to be done early that day so I wanted to make sure everything was ready for when he came. I had Kaykay with me this weekend so I had Té to watch him for me. Té and I had gotten close and often used each other as babysitters which was great to have options for weekends when he wasn't with my parents. The game started at 7:30 but 6:30 pm came around and I hadn't received no phone call or even a text to say he's late. I tried callin him but no answer. Dinner wasn't a surprise though, we had planned ahead of time that he was gonna come early, instead he rolls up after 7 wondering why I looked so cheesed. I couldn't even hide my face. *So, his phone clearly works, he didn't have the decency to call and say he's running late, yet he wanna show up here an ask me why I'm mad? Seriously?? Is he dumb? I must have the word "take me for granted or boo boo the fool written on my head".* I didn't even get an apology...I got nothing. We jumped in the cab to the venue and I handed him the card, he looked at it kinda weird and says "Wow, I'm gonna need to change the privacy settings on my facebook." *Ouch! It was like I had no feelings. I was jus taking punches tonight. Guess he hates the card, I mean I know it was kinda weird and caught off guard, but he didn't even try to hide his feelings. So now I'm a weird stalker girl...great. Great start to the night.* As we were getting out of the cab he left the card on the seat so I grab it for him, then he tells me to hold onto it for him. *I should just throw the shit out but I'm not gonna let him ruin my night. There's no way I got a babysitter to waste my night. With or without him this will be a good night.*

The game was good, he was having fun and so was I. We put aside the rough start and jus enjoyed the night for was it was. Everything was going great until we bumped into one of his friends and he introduced me as...his friend. *Friend? Did he jus forget the girl part of that word? I mean I'm not crazy, he did ask me to be his girl, he does say he loves me yet I'm standing here as...his friend? Oh really? This is why I don't spend money on niggas. Rule number 2, avoid all holidays and birthdays so you neva have to spend any money. Damn he caught me off guard with this one.* By the time the game ended we were both visibly miserable. The conversation on the ride home wasn't any better once he accused me of being "loud and ghetto" in the streets when I tried to confront him about what the hell happened. I was taking all kinds of character hits from this man who clearly couldn't appreciate not one thing I had tried to do for him. He told me to keep the card so it didn't get "ruined" on the bus on his way home. *I deserved better than this shit. I had ignored the fact that he was on facebook flirting with other girls cause he said I was acting "crazy" and "jealous". I didn't wanna come off as insecure but this shit.... naw this shit was over the top for me. So, I'm expected to continue to let a non-communicating, quick bussing, disrespectful ass man continues to waste my time? No thank you.* To top things off after we broke up (or not since we were never together) one of my girls asked me if SHE could have his number. *Say wha? This chic really tryna talk to him?* As shocked as I was I gave it to her anyway and went right back to minding my business. That was a month full of drama and I was done. Even my therapist was applauding my growth and realization of my own true worth. Oh well, I learned I couldn't force nobody to treat me right. It was a lesson worth living. Plus, I was certain more than ever that Canadian boys just weren't for me. They lacked a lot of experience... something American men didn't. Anywayz, now that I was free to be me again, those conversations I had with Bruce were resumed, as well as a new man from New Jersey named Chris popped up via Insta. So really there was no love loss, just time and it was time for me to focus again.

February 15, 2013 ·
Today was the first day my son wasn't able to walk up the stairs to his bed and he's in a lot of pain...for once I dunno what to do...can ppl please pray

His bed had a set of stairs that he was used to climbin. It hadn't been an issue, he loved it, but tonight he couldn't do it. I looked at him and just didn't know what to do. My heart broke as I tried to imagine how he was feeling. He was visibly upset that he wouldn't be able to sleep in his bed. The only thing I could do was to lift him up onto his bed. It's not an easy thing lifting a six year old up onto a bed but impossible was a word we just didn't know. My love for him grew every moment I saw him overcome a difficulty with a smile. Was it possible that I loved him too much? Kaykay's life was my life. I was consumed with making sure he was ok. I never wanted to let him go. *Will he be ok without me?* When Kaykay went to my parents every other weekend I didn't even know what to do with my life. I had no desire to go out and it was like this feeling of sadness hit ten times harder.

I hated being alone without him. I was left alone with just my own thoughts. I used to picture myself with a knife in hand stabbing away at my stomach, instead I ended up crying myself to sleep. Any time the thoughts got really bad I noticed my phone would always ring and it would be one of my friends calling me to check up and I had to play pretend that I was good. "Hey Cola, just wanted to call and see how you were doing" What I wanted my response to be was *No, I'm not ok, I'm never ok, I make it seem like I'm ok, but I never am. I just know how to smile big. If it wasn't for my son I'd probably just kill myself but I don't want him to even find my body, and I don't trust anyone enough to leave him with.* My response was always "Yep...I'm good" then I suck up my tears and pretended like everything was ok until things started to feel normal. I don't know why it happened like that. Just anytime my son left I felt abandoned all over again. Whenever I felt abandoned it normally meant I had travelled too far away from God and just couldn't feel His presence. This meant I needed to drag my ass to church to let light back into my life. No matta how hard things were I needed to overcome, keep pushing and focus. I kept using these men to keep me numb to the fact that life was happening around me. It kept me dreamin. Dreaming that one day I'd finally be in a loving relationship with a man who loved me, loved Kaykay and embraced all that we came with. More importantly I dreamt that Kaykay was healed.

February 19, 2013 ·
For those of you who know what I went through...this next statement will make sense....I settled my human rights case today...!!! I am more than my skin color and I will continue to fight

Healing was needed all around. The scars that were left from my housing nightmare ran deep. Luckily for me I had met a team of social justice people who had a mission to help others fight against discrimination. Denying me an apartment just because I was black was not right. Even though they denied it, they had no other explanation for why things went the way it did. Today I was victorious though and they agreed to pay a small settlement. The sun was shinin a bit brighter today. It was God's restitution for a messed up situation.

I had a couple of healthy growing situations gwaning on Insta. It was so easy to get sucked into different pages. There were a couple of pages that would do features. For example, they would say send in pics of you wearing red and they would post it up. So, I sent it in and once they posted the pictures I received a lot of comments. The amount of men that hit me up reminded me of that DMX song What These Bitches Want...

There was Brenda, LaTisha, Linda, Felicia (okay)
Dawn, LeShaun, Ines, and Alicia (ooh)
Teresa, Monica, Sharron, Nicki (uh-huh)
Lisa, Veronica, Karen, Vicky (damn)
Cookies, well I met her in a ice cream parlor (aight?)
Tish, Diane, Lori and Carla (okay)
Marina (uhh) Selena (uhh) Katrina (uhh) Sabrina (uhh)
About three Kim's (WHAT?) LaToya, and Tina (WHOO!)
Shelley, Bridget, Cavi, Rasheeda (uh-huh)
Kelly, Nicole, Angel, Juanita (damn!)
Stacy, Tracie, Rohna, and Ronda (WHAT?)
Donna, Ulanda (WHAT?) Tawana, and Wanda (WHAT?)
were all treated fairly but yet and still
bitches is on some other shit now that I'm fuckin wit Dru Hill
But I'ma keep it real (WHAT?)
What the fuck you want from a nigga? (c'mon)
What the fuck you want from a nigga? (c'mon)
What these bitches want from a nigga?
What you want.. (what you want)
What these bitches want from a nigga?

Really want..

It was all about gettin to know each other. Out of the men I spoke to, only a few made a lasting impression. I had this cool funny guy in ATL, a serious but mother friggin gorgeous guy in Chicago, this cute ass freaky nerd from Cali, a dude in North Carolina and one in New Jersey. The guy in Jersey really caught my attention when he hit me up. Under one of my pics he writes "It's too bad that you live in Canada cause I would love to see you". *Challenge accepted. Dude don't know me, I'm a worl class travela.* When I checked out his page I saw abs galore. I was always a visual learner, I processed everything I saw and internally my body was excited!! He literally had a page of jus different angles of his abs. We moved our conversation from Instagram to Facebook, within two weeks of us talking he had asked me to be his girl and I was on the next flight to New Jersey for May. Lucky for me, my girl Sheena was crazy enough to follow me down to see him. I was so happy we reconnected cause she loved to travel just as much as I did.

> April 4, 2013 ·
> It's official...American boys are my fav...can't wait to travel!!! love<3 them!

Besides being attractive, Chris was everything I had hoped to find: he was honest, funny, he listened, he was gentle, non-judgmental, and he was sweet. I loved that he was taking care of his mom and siblings. He had a job with UPS but had bigger dreams. He checked up on me regularly without it being a chore, he encouraged me and he supported me as I did for him. He valued me and I couldn't wait to meet him. I was falling for him fast. It was scary but good to know I wasn't alone. He said "I love you" I said "I love you too" *Love? How does he know he loves me? How can he love me? I'm damaged...I'm crazy, I'm worthless. I want him to love me but I don't.* What did this mean...love? How can I trust him to love me fully? *I already know I can't be loved.*

Just as things were picking up for Chris and I, I started receiving phone calls and text messages from George asking if he could come over and pick up the card I made for him back in January. *Well look who's tryna come back. Now you want the card? I thought you hated it...it's been sittin here for weeks and you never asked about it.* There were so many times that I wanted to throw it in the garbage but it just sat around in my house. It was a memory of his dad and it was hard to just throw that in the garbage. His call surprised me a little bit and as much as I wanted to say no, I let him come over to talk in the hallway. "Cola, I'm really sorry for how I acted towards you. I'm happy you kept the card for me, it means a lot to me that you would do that and I didn't handle the situation correctly. I wasn't used to the way you tried to love me. I need to work on my relationships, especially with my mother and my anger. You are the best girl I've had and this has been a great relationship for me but I messed it up. I miss you, I want us to try again. I'll be better this time, I'm more stable cause I've worked on some things." "I'm sorry, I can't, I have a man in Jersey" "Oh, really, already?" "Yep" I could see the tears in his eyes. We hugged, said goodbye and that was it.

I know he didn't expect me to move on so quickly but a good girl like me never stayed single for long unless by choice. I was coming to understand my worth and I wasn't gonna waste it waiting around, my bounce back was real. I realized in life the main priorities would always be Kaykay and myself, anyone else was extra.

CHAPTER FIFTY-EIGHT

Family

Love bears all things [regardless of what comes], believes all things [looking for the best in each one], hopes all things [remaining steadfast during difficult times], endures all things [without weakening].
-1 CORINTHIANS 13:7

I found him. The one to love me past my pain. The one to love me despite my faults, but I was scared. He was everything I thought I wanted yet I was still unhappy. I was on hyper alert about him and other potential women. *Am I good enough?* I was comparing this to my relationship with Romeo and it just wasn't the same. We didn't talk for hours, he didn't always text me goodnight or good morning. There were so many things he did right yet every time he liked a girl's pic on Instagram or Facebook I felt so demeaned. I felt like I wasn't worthy, I felt like it was exactly what I was running from. Romeo was great except when he was cheating and controlling and even though I had gotten away from him it felt like I hadn't fully gotten away. I wanted him to love me more than he showed. I wanted to feel his love on deeper levels. *Maybe my expectations are too high. At least he says he loves you.* Things felt like they were on a next level fast. Then as I was tryna put the details of my upcoming trip together Chris had completely ghosted me. I couldn't hear from him on any platform. Felt like I had given my heart foolishly. Felt like I had been shot down. Felt like I had been abandoned all over again. He couldn't know how much this hurt me. I had no clue if I was gonna hear from him again but I knew I had already paid for my full trip to Jersey.

I guess it was a good thing Bruce and I were still talking cause at least then I knew my trip wouldn't be a complete waste of time if Chris didn't get back to me. This was the plan, Chris lived in Jersey and Bruce lived in New York. Practically neighbours right? Chris didn't drive but Bruce did, so we picked a hotel in Jersey so that Chris could come see me easy enough by bus and Bruce could drive over and see me. Sheena and I also rented a car so we could get around without stress. The most important thing was that Chris and Bruce knew nothing about each other. It was awkward enough that they worked for rival companies. I had to always remember which was UPS and which was FedEx. We were only staying down 3 days which meant we needed to make the trip as efficient as possible. I was long overdue for a trip. I started daydreaming and counting down the days.

My definition of family wasn't always blood. I had friends who treated me better than blood. So, the word "family" hasn't had much meaning to me for years yet I didn't want my views to be Kaykay's views. My views were skewed by experiences he'll never have to go through. I was happy that he was closer to my family than I was. He had drawn two pictures one day. On one side it was just me and him and on the other side it was me, him, my mom, dad and sister. Even at 6 he understood that he had two families that loved him and love him we did. It was great when my sister visited even after all that otha drama cause it allowed her and Kaykay to grow their relationship which was pretty fun to watch.

April 18, 2013 ·
My sis says: kk why you home from school
Kk: I'm sick
Sis: so what you gonna do all day
Kk:watch the cars movie
Sis: again
Kk: don't judge me
Me: ah ha ha ha ha classic!

April 18, 2013 ·
My sis says: come here booger
Kk says: mommy she's judging my face
Me:lol

April 18, 2013 ·
i swear its like i don't know my own child anymore...a week before his birthday he chooses to unload mind blowing comments that I can't seem to understand. Like he just came to me and said: i'm gonna get some privacy in my room, do you mind? ....damn how do i answer this lol...ahh the blessings of children
Privacy? What did this child know about privacy? Who taught him this? AHHH I loved him. He gave me so many gems to cherish when things felt so unstable all around me.

April 19, 2013 ·
Ppl don't understand the life I live....I am tired

As hard as I was trying to move forward I constantly felt like I was being held in place by a lack of finances. As best as I was tryna juggle my finances I was feelin like a failure and my annoyance with Leo was growing. My relationship with Leo was becoming more and more strained as I was becoming more agitated that there were no updates as to when the money was going to be released. 30 grand was a lot of money to wait on in my situation. Paying market rent was the real deal. Welfare didn't gimme enough to cover my full rent and baby bonus wasn't enough to pay all the otha bills plus groceries. It felt like a struggle every month just to get by. When it wasn't the financial stress I was just tired of being tired. I wasn't in school, wasn't doing volunteering yet I felt drained. It was like no matta how much I slept I was always tired. I focused on taking care of Kaykay but this disease felt like it was taking over. Even though the seizures had stopped the amount of times he was sick with a cold, constipation, or had a stomach ache, it felt like sickness was a never ending curse and it had me worried all the time. He was falling behind in school and I was doing the best I could to keep his readin up and to help with his homework but it was tough. My only escape was my playwright program. It was new and exciting territory I was embarking on. The ability to develop 4 monologues into a full play was something I didn't even know was possible. I needed someone to look over my work so I reconnected with Tish hoping that she could help me. As overbearing as she felt she had a beautifully creative mind filled with really great ideas and a great perspective that I truly admired. She happily agreed to help me so we worked on developing a title and worked on the story line. We came up with the title Play(ed), it seemed fitting for my story about a woman who was on a journey to find love but tries to play her way through it, gets played but comes out victorious. I was working hard towards having a staged reading done but for the moment my focus was on another beautiful milestone.

April 24, 2013 ·
AHHHHHH HAPPY BIRTHDAY TO THE COOLEST KID ALIVE...BIG MAN TURN 7..LOOK HOW FAR HE'S COME..THANK YOU LORD FOR KEEPING HIM EVEN THROUGH HIS DISABILITY...I WISH US MANY MORE YEARS TOGETHER...LOVE HIS LIFE!!!!

April 24, 2013 ·
So this is how the morning conversation with kk went:
ME: KK come get ready for school
KK: Aww, but i thought i was going to my birthday
Me: No that's on saturday
KK: So why did you tell me happy birthday
Me: Cause it is your birthday today but your party is on saturday..you still have to go to school
KK: Awwwwwwww
Me: ye im done with you

April 24, 2013 ·
Me: Kk lets get get you dressed for school, gotta look sexy for your birthday

KK: or handsome, cause i'm a handsome guyyyyyy (singing)

The best gift of life was the day he was born. Every year he lived was a testament to the blessing God has given me. It felt like my very own gift every year I got to plan another party, buy more gifts and grow with him. It was such a special moment I can't see how anyone would opt to not be a part of his life.

He kept me on my toes and made me question my university degree several times. Somehow he managed to make me feel slightly less smart in the most innocent of ways. He was growing to be the lil man of the house. I was hoping my relationship with Chris woulda taken us to the next level to provide more stability for Kaykay, so he wouldn't have to take on the label "man of the house" so young. But after like a month gone I wasn't sure Chris was gonna come back. Then he did, and it created so many mixed feelings for me. *Where did you go? Why did you leave me like that?* Apparently he had no way to communicate with me since his phone had been disconnected and he had only just reconnected it. I still felt unsettled that I was tryna build something with someone who could leave at any moment. So, he's back now and he noticed that a guy was liking my pics and he asks me bout it. I didn't wanna lie to him so I told him the truth "It's a guy I was talking to" *I shoulda lied.* The way he got so mad, "So just cause I didn't message you yu found another guy?" "I didn't know if you were coming back" "That's no excuse Cola, so how many guys you talking to huh?" "Just that one, so you expected me to just sit here and wait for you? I didn't even know if it was gonna really go anywhere" "I asked you to be my girl" "You were serious serious? You ain't say all that, we hadn't even met yet." So somehow I was in the wrong even though he ghosted me so hard. *My bad, broke my own damn rule, don't get caught.* I had hurt him yes but then I looked on his facebook and all I saw was him commenting on otha chics pics, liking pics, sharing pics and I snnnaappppeeeddd. *HYPOCRITE.* All the pics he liked were of girls in provocative positions or barely clothed, jus no. He said he was jus looking, but why he gotta look, like and comment though? He said "You know you're crazy right? I'm doing all I can and I'm not good enough for you Cola" *Why do I always end up with these guys? What is wrong with me?* To know he jus lectured me over the same shit was jus maddening. Plus, he called me crazy the minute I started confronting him? *This is why you don't give only one man your time. They always playing games.* Not to mention he was giving me the silent treatment. It was driving me crazy and I felt like I was gonna get hurt even more and needed to do something to stop the bleeding. "Chris, I can't do this"

May 5 2013

Hey Chris,

So I wanted to write u something quick I guess to explain why I felt the need to have space from you...even though I really didn't take it.

So i'm feeling better...I needed to be in church...too many things weren't at peace and the pastor today touched on a lot of the things that I been dealing with.

The stuff wit my family has been affecting me cause like I said I feel kinda abandoned and part of me was hoping you'd magically rescue me...but that's not reality...you have your own family problems that you are dealing with.

part of me not feelin loved is mainly jus cause I wish you would pay more attention to me...simple..

the same love I show u and the same attention I show yu...i'm always tryna call u...you're always too tired or sick or working...so its hard...long distant relationships require more I think cause we so far apart.

hmmm, in a way I wish we could start over...like I forgive u for anything u've done that's hurt me...and I wish u would do the same...

I appreciate you going through the roller coaster emotions with me while I try an sort my feelings out...

I still wanna be wit you...but I need you to answer me a question...how do I know that when u mad you aint gonna try an get back at me?

cause I don't really wanna be on your ig no more cause it bothers me and u don't even really check for on

there like u use to ...I wanna know how we avoid hurting each other outta anger?
relationships take work...and we both aint perfect...so I wanna work on this....

my minds always running and I've forgotten how to just relax and have fun...so I'm really hoping Jersey will do that for me...

May 3, 2013 ·
i wish my balcony was ready for summer...tonight's the night i would lay out there and talk to God

I felt like God could hear me. There was nothing more peaceful to me than laying down and looking up at the stars from my apartment. Looking at God's work, *oh how beautiful!* I needed these breaks and moments to take a breath and respect life for what was. It was always a great peace before the storm.

May 7, 2013 ·
Yooooo why did the school bus drop off my child without me there
and left him in the lobby cring.
..chhhhhheeeeeesssssseeeedddddddd

I wasn't late, I had gotten no phone call to say they were coming early. I went down at the normal time only to find Kaykay was already there, in the lobby, alone. *How the hell he get in? Where the fuck is the driver?* Fuming I called the bus company and gave them a piece of my damn mind. How they jus gon leave a 7 year old outside with no one there? I know some 7 year olds were advanced, but my poor baby was so scared. I never let him out of my sight when he was with me. Never. Anything could have happened to him. What's an apology if someone had taken my damn child? I don't know if some of the drivers have kids cause they jus on a next level of not thinking. By the next day he had a different driver. Iuno what happened to the otha man, but I was glad he was gone. It was a good thing he left cause I was contemplating how I was gonna get my kid to and from school. I had been working with his occupational therapist to have equipment available for Kaykay. We got him a padded toilet seat, a chair for the bathtub so he could sit under the shower to conserve his energy-he really got a good use outta that one and a stroller. We were blessed to have the president's choice charity pay for his stroller for us. It was a huge benefit not to have that financial burden. With the way things were warming up I was able to pick him up on the sunny days and walk him back home. I loved our neighbourhood. The colors, the trees, the people. It was home. It finally felt like home. Deep breath.

May 9, 2013 ·
I know no man is worth the heartbreak...but is that really my heart breaking, or the dream I'm waking up from...

Well my ticket was non-refundable and the trip wasn't just for me, so despite all the fights and arguments I figured I might as well just go. Sheena was already excited for our first trip together. Three weeks later, the night before we are supposed to leave, Chris let me know via email that his phone was about to get disconnected and that we could only communicate through wifi. *How am I supposed to see this man if I can't even call his phone when I get there?* He gave me his address and we planned that I would show up to his house at 10 am after we landed. All I had to do was ring the doorbell when I got there. Sketchy as hell but what choice did I have? I googled the directions to get to his place and took a screenshot since I wouldn't have data down there.

Am I dreaming? In a movie? We landed safely at JFK and proceeded to pick up our car rental. Apparently a major credit card was needed to rent a car, something that had been accidentally left at home. We literally tried everything to try and get this car rented and in the end all they could suggest was that we purchased a prepaid debit card and used that to rent the car. Sheena was sooooo upset that she had forgotten the credit card but we didn't have time to dwell, we had to figure out Plan B. My main goal was to stay calm, somebody had to. The issue was that we took a bus to New York assuming we would drive to New Jersey where our hotel was, so we were currently stuck with no way to get to Jersey. I had to call my phone provider to put U.S. calling on my phone then phoned Bruce to see if he could help out but he was stuck at work and nowhere close to where we were. He did suggest for us to take a shuttle bus to New Jersey airport which was near to the hotel. By the time we went to catch the bus it was already 1pm and we had landed from 10am. It was already a long ass day but we rolled with the punches.

I felt bad for how bad Sheena felt, I kept tryna reassure her like "Naw we good don't worry about it. We landed safely, we didn't get robbed, and we still had options to rent this car." The only thing that sucked was that I was several hours behind meeting Chris and had no way of letting him know.

I handed the address to our bootleg taxi driver at the airport as we headed off towards East Orange New Jersey. It was 4pm and I had no clue if Chris was still home but I figured I'd try anyway. I had no clue where we were going but when we entered their ghetto shit was a real eye opener for me. *Shit this is some real ghetto. Even our Canadian hoods don't look like this. Sheena probably wondering where the hell I'm takin her. Maybe we just driving through a rough area. Hmmm, are those abandoned buildings? Where the hell this nigga live? Really? It's really gonna start raining right this moment?* The taxi pulls up to a building and I'm looking outside and looking at him askin "Are you sure this is the place sir?" *Breathe.* "Hey Sheena, stay in the car, I'll be right back" I'm walking slowly towards the building. *Please God, don't lemme die. I know this was a pretty crazy idea and I know this is the wrong time to pray but please God. Please let this man be home and please let this not be no catfish. Maybe I should have skyped him at least once before I flew over here. Shit. Ok. Breathe, don't be scared. He said he was on the 2nd floor, ok just up these stairs I guess. What apartment number? Oh ye, ok, calm.* I got to the door and held my breath as I knocked the door. *This waiting is killing me, maybe he's not home, should I knock again?* I knocked again and the door flew open as a woman yells

HELLO? *Shit, speak. Don't just stand here, SAY SOMETHING!!!* "Hi is Chris here?" she yells his name CHRIS! *Phew ok, at least someone named Chris lives here.* He appeared at the door and we both jus stood there in silence staring at each other. *He's real. Omg this actually worked.* "I'm so sorry I'm late, it's been a crazy morning but my girl is downstairs waiting for me." "Ye no problem lemme get dressed and follow you."

It was a hell of a day. I had my debit card that could be used to at least withdraw cash. The plan was to find a bank, withdraw the cash then find a store to purchase the debit card. We used the wifi from Wendy's to transfer money then walked to the bank to withdraw the cash, then walked to the Walgreens to get the debit cards, all while pulling our suitcases around. Lucky for me Chris did all that heavy lifting. After all that work we anxiously walked to the car rental place to finally get our car. "Sorry we can't take prepaid debit cards for payment, it has to be a major credit card or a debit card" *Seriously? We did all that work and y'all can't take our debit card? But the otha rental place told us to buy the stupid card in the first place. Not fair but ok, debit card? I've had my debit card this whole time.* Ok so Sheena sends me more money to keep on my debit card and we return to the counter. "Oh, where is the visa logo on your card?" "What logo?" This was the first time I learned what Canadians call debit vs. what Americans call debit. Apparently, they meant debit visa, but that was new technology in Canada so I hadn't even gotten my card yet. "Sorry without that we can't rent to you". Once again we had no way of renting this car and now we got stuck with two debit cards full of money we didn't need. To make things even better, as I read the fine print on the card I notice that only U.S residents could use the card because they need their social security number to activate the card. *Great! Just what we needed.* Money we cannot access. We left the car rental frustrated, tired, hungry, with no way to get to the hotel except to find a taxi. Eventually Chris was able to chase down a taxi that took us to our hotel. It was about 6pm by the time we finally reached it.

The tension was sooo thick. Our room was

surprisingly beautiful for a two-star hotel but the way the day unfolded jus had everyone on edge. I felt horrible that Sheena had put money on two debit cards that were now essentially useless to us, so even though it was my first day meeting Chris I asked if he'd be comfortable giving us his social security number just to activate the card. *This is so awkward asking. I hope he don't think I'm some crazy chic.* Surprisingly he said yes. *I did not expect that. Aww he's so sweet.* His gesture was enough to break the tension in the room. Now that we were all calm it was time to relax. *Deep breath* after such a long trip.

Sheena decided to take a shower which also gave us some privacy. As soon as the bathroom door closed he kissed me deeply. *Whoa!* He pushed me up against the wall then proceeded to lift me up. *Omg this is not happening, did he just lift me? Omg he jus lifted me, damn he strong.* Normally I would object to him lifting me but my mind was going a mile a minute. *AAHAHAHHDSHJFSHK damn he sexy, shit. His kisses are ...damn...breathe...ahahdasjkdahjdskah, this is happening.* He kisses my neck as he lays me down on the bed. I've only had one other man lift me up. My mind was going numb. I felt his presence overtake me. I felt chills up and down my body as he laid on top of me. His kisses were making their way up and down my body and I was just lost in him. *..........shhh shit don't make noise, you don't want her to hear you. Hmmmm, he feels good.* I grabbed his back tighter and pulled him closer, and closer, he entered me *Hmmmm. Exhale.* "I love you" "I love you too". *He jus said he loved me; looked me in my eyes and said he loved me. Wow.* Our bodies were in rhythm with each other and we moved to the beat of adrenaline. I could feel his heartbeat as my hand rested on his chest. I didn't want him to stop. *Wait, did you hear that? Is she done?* His kisses left my head feeling dizzy. "Did you hear that?" "No" *Focus. Hmmmm* He continued to kiss me, he continued to flow with me, he continued... then he held me, looked at me and said, "You are so beautiful" *Really?* It never gets easy every time I hear those words. Although it was a beautiful ending to what felt like a magical moment we shared, nothing felt forced. When he stood me up and helped me fix my clothes and my hair I knew he was for me. It didn't feel like it was our first day meeting. We spent the time talking, sexing, eating, chillin, sleeping, then he left me early the next morning to get to work.

Day 2 had far less drama. The plan was to stay lowkey, check out a mall, chill at the hotel, and see Bruce. Shopping in the states was always a great thing for us. Canadian plus size clothes were always overpriced, cheap quality and ugly. It was great when we had an choice that allowed us to feel sexy and beautiful without breaking the bank. It was like all Toronto plus women had similar styles and clothes cause we ain't have many options. Not having the car wasn't such a big deal cause we were close enough to the airport that we had a shuttle bus that took us nearly everywhere we needed to go. We were very low maintenance girls so we never needed to be on road long. It was refreshing going back to the hotel early enough to just relax.

When we got back to the room we ordered pizza from some local shop. Have you realized how sexy delivery guys can be? *Shit, they don't make em like this back home.* I welcomed him in while we got the money together and even though he waited patiently the silent attraction was deafening. His eyes were piercing, his lips were inviting. I wanted to reach out and touch him but he was in Muslim attire from head to toe. He interrupted the silence by rubbing his hands together while saying "Damn you girls are so beautiful. I converted to Muslim a little while ago but if I wasn't, things would be different right now. As part of my custom I can't even shake your hands but there's so much more I wish I could do". His smile was huge, as I imagined he was envisioning all those things he was forbidden to do. We invited him to chill with us for a bit but he had already gotten a call telling him that he was taking long. We finally got the money together to pay him for the pizza and he left unwillingly. Sheena and I might be thicker girls but we knew how to rock the charm and our personalities were banging. I loved being in the states cause American men just appreciated us on a different level. In Toronto it was almost a sin if manz got caught liking a thick girl.

Girl focus, you have a man remember? Wasn't like I was gonna do anything anyway. The delivery man was just fun to look at. I didn't expect how quickly or how strongly I would feel for Chris. Yes, technically he had asked me to be his girl even before we came down but then there was that whole weird thing with his disappearing and I just didn't know. I already had made plans with Bruce, not to mention that since we no longer had a car we no longer had a way to get to the airport in New York to catch our 6 am flight. Our best bet was Bruce since he drove which meant no matta how I felt about Chris I needed to ensure we had a ride home. Chris wasn't coming over that night so I had time to sort through my feelings cause Bruce wasn't coming to check me until after work. I don't know what I was expecting to feel when he showed up but as handsome as he was, I didn't get butterflies or chills. We sat up and talked, "So why did you get a hotel in Jersey instead of New York?" "Oh, cause the hotels are cheaper out here" That was only a partial lie. "Since we couldn't get the car we now gotta figure out how we gonna get to the airport. Our flight is way too early in the morning and we have no way to get there. I mean I guess we can take taxi, but iuno how much that's even gonna cost us. Ugh what a mess" so he said "Don't worry, I'll take you to the airport" "No fo real? You'd actually do that for us? That's incredibly sweet. Thank you so much cause I had no clue what we were gonna do. I really appreciate that." "I can't just leave you stranded" *Mission accomplished.* We spent the rest of the time gettin to know each other. I tried so hard to stay engaged with him. He was shy so the conversation didn't flow as easily. "Why won't you look at me when you're talking to me?" "Cause you're so beautiful, I'm really shy and I can't look at you." *Aww, shit I feel so bad...I feel so bad. I really wanna like him more than I do. I feel guilty having him lay here in bed with me.* He never tried to make a move on me, we never had sex he jus held me as we slept, yet it still felt so wrong. He woke up early to get to work and within a few hours of him leaving for work Chris was on his way from work to our hotel. *That was close.*

It was our final day in Jersey and we needed to make the most out of it. The plan was to chill with Chris during the day and get Bruce to pick us up and take us out during the night. Timing was essential and lucky for me Chris wasn't the clubbing type. He had come to spend the final day with us and showed us around Newark. He knew exactly where to take us. Places like Jersey Gardens mall and a few shops in downtown Newark. It felt like I was floating anytime he was around. He was so open to love me, holdin my hand in public, kissin me, he just made me feel like I was everything he ever wanted. I never had to worry about my weight or feel insecure cause he never gave me any moment to question or doubt. I never wanted to leave him behind. We got back with enough time to change and say our goodbyes to Chris. *That was really hard. It felt like I was leaving a piece of my heart behind.* Bruce returned to our hotel like 30 mins after Chris left to pick us up. Bruce wasn't much for dancing or parties so he wasn't too familiar with the dance scene but had agreed to take us somewhere with reggae. Difference between Toronto and New York parties was that Toronto was a melting pot of culture and sounds whereas most American parties were full of rap music, so it was great when *Murda She wrote* came on cause we got so hype compared to the rest of the crowd when 50 cent came on. As much as Bruce wasn't much for the dance scene he did make efforts to dance with me but I honestly couldn't get into it. *This doesn't feel right.* Sheena pulled me aside right quick and said, "You need to dance with him, he's our ride to the airport so suck it up and take one for the team" it sucked but she was right. There were also a lot of otha brothas in there that were tempting but I couldn't even look in their direction. I had to stay locked down. *Is he my man though? He ain't even my man. Suck it up. He's a really good guy.* We left the club shortly before it closed and stopped at Mcdonalds where he bought us both food right before he drove us to the airport. *Awww he's such a sweet guy. Damn I wish I liked him more.* He brought us to the airport and sat with us in the car until it was time for us to go inside. *You're such a jerk, he's been a gentleman every step of the way and all you care about is getting home.* We said goodbye and Sheena nudged me to give him a proper goodbye. "Don't do him so bad" He had finally worked up the courage to kiss me goodbye and promised to keep in touch. *I didn't feel anything with that kiss though.*

Chris was all my mind could think of, my heart smiled when I pictured his face. I couldn't wait to go back and see him and thanks to plus size fashion week I didn't have to wait long. Fashion still had a hold onto my heart and I just wanted to be around other beautiful plus size women as we celebrated self-love and this journey. I had no clue where I was gonna stay or any other details but with the money I had left I bought my tickets for the show and my bus fare. I had no extra money for a hotel but I was hoping things would work itself out. I still had a few weeks to figure that out. More than anything I missed my baby. Three days felt long cause I was that much further away.

June 8, 2013 ·
So kk wakes me up this morning to make him breakfast telling me he was nice enough to let me sleep in....it was 8:30 in the morning lol...on a Saturday...

He really kept laughing. This kid had the nerve to say he let me sleep in. He was never the cereal type of kid either. Breakfast meant eggs and bacon with toast or something hella fancy. I bruk him bad to expect full breakfast meals. Anything for my baby though, even when I was tired I never got tired of making him food.

June 11, 2013 ·
My sons in a lot of pain today..can we please pray for his legs...pray that the disease attacking his muscles with slow down and be non existent....don't really know what else to do

My ticket was already bought, plans were already in motion and Kaykay was doubled over in pain. It was always the most heartbreaking thing to endure cause I had no way to help him. I was sooooo over this disease. I hated it. I was at such a loss on where to go from here. I hated leaving him. Even Tish had convinced me to follow my dreams and here this disease was tryna ruin things. I felt incredibly guilty about the thought of leaving him during a time when he needed me. The pain came and went, one minute he was in pain, the next minute he was playing. He really understood the concept of pushing forward. I didn't wanna leave but in the end, I also wanted to try to make some contacts to see how I could use fashion to build a platform that would allow me to take better care of Kaykay's needs. I had adjusted the amount of time I spent talking to Bruce to minimal but I did inform him that I was coming back to New York. In conversation I also casually mentioned that I had nowhere to stay to which Bruce so graciously offered up a place to stay. He was even willing to try to make it work around his work schedule. It made sense for me to stay there cause he lived in New York if it wasn't for the fact that I had a man. Chris wasn't having it. He was not bout to let me stay at a next man's house. He rather I stayed with him...in his home...with his mom...sister...and two nephews....in a one-bedroom apartment. It made no sense for me to travel from Jersey and his momma ain't even want me there, but Chris was adamant that it was gonna work. I could respect that and I had to turn Bruce down. There was no way to explain to Bruce that I was gonna stay in New Jersey without showing my hand. I didn't even have the guts to tell him until the day of my travels. There was no way I could have gotten out of the situation as clean as I wanted. It was painfully obvious when he said, "Where you gonna stay?" "In Jersey" "Why would you stay in Jersey when the show is in New York?" I could barely get the words out. *Damn, damn, damn. I did not want him to find out like this. I was hoping that we'd just fall outta conversation and we could fade things out slowly, not this.* "I'm gonna stay in Jersey at a friend's house" "I see." There wasn't anything left to say, I could tell over the phone that he understood exactly what was happening. I think he was just starting to like me. *He didn't even wanna go to church though, that woulda never worked long term. He doesn't express his feelings in the same way. He's usually too busy for you. You're right.* I had to be true to myself about whether or not there was a future with him. Once I got off the train in Jersey and saw Chris standing with a rose in hand, I knew I had made the right decision.

My decision to pick Chris meant that we would share a single mattress in the living room with his mom's bed on the other side of the living room with just the floor that separated us. No curtain, no door, no nothing. Somehow, we managed to both fit on a single mattress for almost a week that I was there. I didn't care though, I was so humbled that I had a place to sleep, I didn't even focus on the details of how. Their apartment was so cute and cozy. My biggest worry was how I was gonna sleep cute. I had worn a wig down. *Do I take it off or jus sleep in it? Shit imma jus sleep with it on. I ain't bout to expose myself like that. Next thing I know he gon wake up and find my wig on the floor, no thank you.* As far as his family knew that was my real hair and I woke up gorgeous every morning. *Keep it tight girl.* It was jus great to be back with him, I normally didn't mind distance but I missed him greatly. From the moment I got off the train he paid attention to my every need. He rubbed my feet, massaged my back, cooked me food, fixed my shoes when they broke, made peanut butter and jelly sandwiches, sat and talked to me for hours about life and soothed my wounded heart. He let me cry. *It's ok to cry? He said it's ok to cry.* I was so not used to this, all he wanted to do was take care of me. It was almost like I didn't know how to receive it all. Then when I saw him playing with his nephews I knew him and Kaykay would get along without any problem. He sealed the deal to my heart. This relationship was not what I expected. *Is this what it's like to be in a real relationship? A loving relationship?* Something about him seemed committed to making sure I felt love in every sense of the word. *What is love?* He was everything I wanted. A breath of fresh air, a change from the abusive past I had, a potential father, a step-father. I loved him. He gave me baby fever.

In a cozy space like his the only place of privacy was the bathroom cause it was the only place we could go, shut the door and not worry about anyone else coming in. After a long bus trip I needed to shower and to relax. I must have felt hella comfortable cause I wasn't even nervous to strip down in front of him. I had turned the water on and just as I turned around to do something Chris was knelt down on one knee with a ring held up towards me. "Cola I know in my heart that you are the love of my life. I know that God is bringing me the one thing missing in my heart and you mean everything to me. You gave me a chance to love you and I'm grateful. Baby, will you marry me?" *Shit, wha? This is real, omg this is real.* ..... "YES" I bent down to kiss him and pulled him up towards me. Creative spaces make creative results for creatively harmonized energies. My pleasured moments were muted by the sounds of the water falling. My flexible nature had me folded in half with toes in hand. He kissed my back, the steam increased, his pleasure released then we started again as the water bounced off our skin. He held me tighter that night. He held me as the future Mrs. McCall and welcomed me into his family.

Poetic Interlude

When I think about writing on the topic of l.o.v.e
Nothing seems to come to mind easily
Mindlessly so many of us spend time and money trying to buy a love that is binding our souls
Tieing us to unattainable visions
Frustrating our hearts along the way
Weighing on my heart was the sound of a distant voice
Distant love
Distant choice
Choosing to ignore the tugging
I kept lugging around my stresses
Doing the same thing over again searching for better results
Raging
Rapidly
On the road to
Ruination

But the restrictions of the bottom had me ripping my way to
Restoration
My destination led me to my knees
Where I begged and pleaded for a love that was always available to me
See I said yes to a true love who I know will always stay
May I introduce you to my l.o.v.e spelt J.e.s.u.s
Less fortunate are those otha brothas who tried talking to me before I started walking with Christ
Righteous love is my new aim since Jesus showed my heart a fresh love game
Schooling me on the importance of positive attitudes
Instead of submitting myself to latitudes
Then cussing
Nagging
And feuds
But now I am submitting to the covering
Governing and producing
A love like 1 Corinthians 13
Written into so many wedding vows
I am reminded to be patient and kind
Eyes opened to a love that is no longer blind
Blinders gone
My mind has learned to compromise
My heart has learned to trust
My mouth has learned to hope
The scope of my understanding of l.o.v.e when covered by J.C provides an impeccable bond that never fails
Exhaling all defeat
I hear the sweet sounds of new experiences beating at the doors of my heart
Today I start enjoying this beautiful art journey
With a better comprehension of a redemption song
Life supplied me with my first key to l.o.v.e
Which is to have faith and always love me
It just took me awhile to see

CHAPTER FIFTY-NINE

Fears

I love the LORD, because He hears [and continues to hear] my voice and my supplications (my pleas, my cries, my specific needs).
-Psalm 116:1

I was back home and in awe of this man that I was about to transform my life for. On one hand I was scared about what everyone would say and on the other hand I didn't give a shit. Some of my friends were happy, some were shocked, some didn't know what to say. One person who had a lot to say was Tish. She always had the opinion that a fluffy girl shouldn't expect to be with a fit man. Unbeknownst to her, my man was fit and had no problem with the fact that I was bigger. When I told her I was engaged she was dumbfounded, her expression was priceless. She looked like how did cola get a man before her...*what like it's hard? - (legally blonde voice).* Regardless of what people thought, I was happy. The only thing I was nervous about was how I was gonna tell my parents. As much as we weren't close they still needed to know. I had made a promise when I was younger that I wouldn't introduce them to anyone until I was engaged. I jus wanted to avoid my mom's negative comments altogether, but now that I was in the situation I felt like they deserved to know.

I wanted to be the first one to tell them but unfortunately my cousins didn't allow that to happen. These people talk too damn much and get into people's business. I had my cousins blocked on my facebook simply because I didn't trust not one of them. It had been years and I still felt like they were out to get me. I posted a picture of my engagement ring but tried to edit my settings so that only a few people could see it. My attempts at keeping my engagement news quiet failed. I mean obviously I told my friends who were shocked to say the least. Somehow one of my cousins saw my engagement ring and told my other cousins who told my grandma who told my mother. It was like déjà vu. Now I had to explain to an angry mother how I went to New York for fashion and came home engaged. *Well damn. Am I ready for this?* I was on a high from the trip to Jersey every time I thought of him. My heart was happy, it seemed to be happening very quickly. Truthfully, I never thought I would get engaged. I never thought someone would love me to this extent. Neva thought someone would wanna build a family with me. I been telling myself the damaged goods narrative for so long it was all I believed about myself. Then there was the fact that I had only been with him for a short amount of time, yet it felt so natural. I was still tryna navigate through the relationship world as well as my own feelings. I always try to check in with myself like *Cola why do you feel this way, why you letting something like social media get you upset? Why are you jealous?*

I absolutely hated the phrase "I'm a private person" cause it felt like a gentle way of rejection. *How you on social media with thousands of pictures but say you're a private person? What's private?* There was this chick on ig that seemed to be riding his dick, the minute he put up a pic of himself she would like it in 0.00 seconds. So I wanted him to put up a pic of us or me on his ig so these thirsty girls knew wassup...but he wasn't tryna do that which hurt. *Am I ugly? Why can't this man claim me? All the girls I see him liking are ugly, what does that say about me?* This may be the insecure part of me talking but I wasn't into this hidden love type a ting which was what it was starting to feel like. It seemed like his love for the attention was greater than my own feelings. I asked him who this chick was and his response was "She's just a friend, someone I used to talk to, but I don't put up pics of girls cause I'm private like that." *Really? Ok soooooo.... maybe I'm being too sensitive. But if that were true why did I scroll through his insta and see a pic of a girl up who ain't his momma or sister?* When I scrolled down a few weeks, actually through his entire insta history, I saw he posted a picture of the SAME girl who be riding his dick. Underneath the picture he was claiming how special she was to him. *So how private could he be when he had already done the exact thing I was asking him to do?* He said, "We're jus friends, I'm jus tryna be nice" *Women don't need nice, they need a man to check em an tell em back off.* "You act a lil nice and they misinterpret that for something completely different. Can you please take the picture down?" He kept coming with his convenient excuses like "I'll do it later" or "I'm busy" or "I'm focused on you right now, that don't matter to me" I wasn't buying none of that. Then he says to me "Since we so far apart and I know you got needs, it's ok if you wanna hook up with otha guys" ????? *What does that even mean? Really? It's ok for me to hook up with otha guys? Did we not jus get engaged? What am I missin here? All this over one chick? Who is this girl really? They don't even live in the same city and he tripping over her and she ain't even cute.* He was saying everything to get away from just taking down the picture. *Am I just some cheap whore? This is like Leo all ova again. What is it with these men thinking I'm their property to rent out? As a man wouldn't you want to claim me and not want me talking to other guys?* "Why? Why would you want me to sleep with other guys? And you're giving me permission? Am I your property? All this shit cause you don't wanna take down a pic? Who is this girl to you?" "For the last time, she's nobody. No, you're not my property, I just know I can't satisfy you sexually right now and I wanted you to be able to have your needs met" "Did you see me complaining? This makes no sense, you would wanna see me with another guy? That wouldn't bother you?" "It would but what can I do about it? I'm not there for you when you need me" "You know what, I'm just gonna take some time to myself right now, keep the damn picture if you want to. I don't care anymore" *Is there no one that will eva jus love me without the bullshit? This always happens to me. I'm sooooooo tired of it. All because of some girl's picture. This is insane. At least when I was with Romeo this neva woulda happened. He neva put ANY girl before me in this way. He cheated ye, but at least I knew his heart. At least I knew that if it came down between me and another girl he would always pick me. He woulda never suggested that a next man "satisfy" my needs and we've been in a relationship way longer than this. He jus wouldn't allow it. He don't even like when next man looks at me much less. Wow, this is some real fucked up thing I got myself into. I miss Romeo but I just can't go back to that anymore. Maybe I'm jus betta off alone. All I seem to be is property to these niggas.* I needed time to sort myself out. As I opened up I opened myself to a world of hurt. These relationships were just not worth the emotional strain but I had already fallen for him so what was I to do? Chris's phone jus got cut off which created the perfect moment to take some time apart and really jus think about what we wanted.

July 14th 2013 To Cola

Hey baby I hope u get this I love u and I will start listening to u for now on

.... I didn't respond

Baby I missing u like crazy hope we can talk I might get my phone on today so we can talk on the phone I want to listen to ur voice

To Chris

Hey, I miss yu too

You wanna know why everything bothers me so much. You been claiming that you and this girl were jus friends...yet you had her picture up on facebook and ig claiming she's your queen only ONE MONTH before you met me. I had to BEG YOU to claim me on facebook in a stupid relationship status cause u say your a private person but you had no issue with having her picture up there and that stupid card she made. How am I supposed to feel? when that's how u felt about someone only a month before we met. And you're not even takin down the pictures voluntary...I still have to force u like you aint ready or something. If all this REALLY MEANT NOTHING to you...you'd show me that instead of arguing and expecting me to believe that you care nothing bout her but wanna keep her pictures and keep her as a friend when I showed you it bothers me that she likes every single picture and status. If that's what u like...two girls giving you attention..then lemme know...cause...i'm not gonna fight for attention.. but if you can call a girl your queen and post up pics...there must me something there...cause you're a private person...right??

I never thought social media would play such a role in my relationship. Most of the guys I dated weren't even on social media and although I met Chris on social media I didn't think it would become a topic of arguments. This time apart really did help though, when I looked at the whole situation and I looked at my engagement ring, it meant that from when I said yes, no matta what I was gonna try my best to make things work.

To Cola

I love u so I deleted my Facebook for u cuz u think im in love with this girl and u have a idea of me being with her or something but ur wrong I haven't talk to her in months. I am only with u I didn't want us to fight. I understand if ur leaving me over this. I get it I don't deserve u, ur beautiful smart and intelligent u deserve the world u deserve to be happy I love u and I get why u upset cuz a friend that I never had interest in was nice to me and took interest in me but she knew I didn't want a relationship at the time so we stopped talking after but u deserve better then me I get that to u can have whatever u like cuz u deserve the best

To Chris

I told yu I'm with yu forever...I'm not leaving I just wanted yu to understand...being nice is cool...but that's in the past and UN like the other girls on your Facebook they are not liking every picture and status. Obviously she likes yu. I never said yu were in love, I Jus wanted to know why yu made such a big deal about it. I thought yu woulda just deleted it and moved on since it meant nothing. You deserve to be happy too...if we together it's cause we both deserve each other...but we Jus gotta work at communicating and understanding one another. As yu saw, I took down my Facebook as well. I want yu to believe that yu deserve me. It's not ok for me to be talking to ppl as long as I don't hook up and it's ok for yu to say that...yu deserve respect that's why I don't add guys and I deleted any guy that still likes me...cause I believe yu deserve all of me and my attention...and I feel I deserve the same from you...as your future wife...I love yu though we promised forever...and I intend on keeping that promise

We could only talk by email since we had deactivated our Facebook accounts so we sent messages back and forth.

- Cola: So what should we do now?
- Chris: What do u want to do
- Cola: What do yu wanna do. How do yu feel about my email are you ok?
- Chris: Yes I'm ok r u ok how do u feel about emailing me
- Cola: I mean it's ok, kinda weird cause I can't see if you've read my message ...did yu get my response email
- Chris: Yes I got ur response
- Cola: How yu feel
- Chris: I feel bad cuz I didn't listen to u
- Cola: My phone might die...but I love yu...so yu wanna go back on Facebook
- Chris: I deleted my Facebook
- Cola: Deactivated or deleted?
- Chris: I believe I deleted it
- Cola: Oh ok...I miss your voice
- Chris: I miss your voice too
- Cola: when do you wanna get married...date?
- Chris: I'm hoping next year
- Cola: September 2014?
- Chris: yes
- Cola: Ok it's a date :-), I love you hubby
- Chris: Love u too

I didn't wanna give up yet. I couldn't. I wanted to try, I didn't want to fail. Plus, he needed me. I couldn't wait to go back and see him. My parents and grandma were planning a trip to New York which gave me the idea that they should meet him. *Crazy, I neva thought this day would come.* On one hand I wanted to introduce him but on the otha it was such a weird concept I just wanted to skip through it entirely. I thought most kids did this in their teenage years so this made me feel like I was a kid again as opposed to a grown woman introducing her fiancé. But this was a new decade so hopefully they would react in a more positive light. I was more excited for him to meet Kaykay. They had spoken on the phone every now and then and when I talked to Kaykay about it he seemed happy. "So, I'm gonna have a new daddy?" "Hmm, something like that." "Thank you, mommy, you're the best". When he hugged me I felt the excitement and it made me feel like I had finally done something right. I wasn't about to ruin any of that for him. We were gettin ready to go on road to get some food and I had quickly thrown on a mesh shirt over my bra, before I could even leave my room Kaykay sat on my bed talking bout "Why are you going outside dressed like that?" "Dressed like what?" "Like that" (points to my stomach through the mesh) "You don't like my outfit?" "No, you should change it." "You know what just go put your shoes on" "They're not shoes they're boots" "Ye thanks kid."

I loved our dynamics, I loved that I could talk openly with him and clearly, he felt he could speak openly with me too which was exactly what I wanted from him. He was innocently honest. I wanted to build the relationship with him that I wished I had with my parents. When he asked for something and I didn't have the money I let him know "Mommy doesn't have money" and I would often tell him why I don't have the money. Of course that didn't stop him from gettin what he wanted. He was quick on his toes. My sister had come over so he says to her "Aunty can you buy me frozen yogrit cause mommy says she doesn't have any money." My sister replied "I don't have money either but how can I say no to you, ok I'll get you frozen yogrit" *"Yay!! Thank you aunty"*

We were building something that was so special, I had only hoped that when Chris came he would add much more to what was already here. We had discussed Chris coming to Canada and trying to get a job here since I had Kaykay and all of his medical doctors and therapists set up. Plus, I already had my own apartment. I didn't have my car but honestly, with me being downtown I didn't notice it as much.

This summer felt like it was going by so fast. Té was

coming over more often as she was going through her own situations in her relationship and my place had a lot more room to breathe. Our kids got along really great despite being 5 years apart cause Kaykay had such a playful spirit, he could watch Treehouse for hours and just laugh and laugh. It kept him very innocent. While the kids played Té was working on gettin her business launched. She was building a natural skincare business that created holistic benefits for the body. It was real interesting stuff. I jus wanted to learn how to get my hair to grow and she was opening my mind to all the harmful chemicals we put on our body everyday. It made me think about Kaykay and how the environment could be creating even greater problems for his already compromised immune system. I was doing my own research as well as tryna take in whatever Té was tryna show me. I was learning bout body butters, the benefits of scrubs, all kinda tings. It just made a lot of sense to me. Since it was summer time she had all these trade shows she was headed to so I would try to help out in whatever way I could, either by babysitting or by tryna mock up some marketing material on my computer. It was one more thing I was adding to my plate but I really enjoyed it. I forgot how much I enjoyed doing computer design and arts and crafts. Ownin a business was an aspiration of mine, watching her work hard at it made me realize how possible it was. For the moment we were jus caught up with wedding talks and the who what and where that comes with the excitement.

Once I got over the shock of actually being engaged and the embarrassment of my parents finding out, I was allowing myself to get excited about it. But as excited as I was it was being overshadowed by the fact that he was always sick. He was always tired and sleeping, never had energy, always in the bathroom, pains up and down his arms, sometimes he'd pass out. I was scared for him. It made phone conversations challenging when I either couldn't get him on the phone or when I did, he sounded horrible. I tried to encourage him to see a doctor but the fear of the truth kept him home. From looking up his symptoms it seemed like it could be diabetes but only a doctor could confirm and he did not want to hear those words. He wasn't getting any better and I felt so helpless since I couldn't help him. I had Kaykay that was here sick and now my fiancé was miles away sick, for both men I loved, for both men I could do nothing. It was frustrating. Even more so cause at least Kaykay was a child so I understood if he wanted to complain but Chris was a grown ass man and was refusing to get help. He literally only agreed to go to the doctors if I dragged him there myself. We were only a few weeks away from me traveling back to the states so that was exactly what I had planned to do. It felt like everyday I was adding one more thing to my plate.

I had experienced so much success with the readin of my first staged play that Tish wanted to work with me to develop it into a full production. Our plan was to leverage help from the community to make it a community project. To kick start the planning I had invited her over to my house. It had been awhile since she had been here but it was always great catching up. We talked about plans for the production, talked about my upcoming trips to New York and Atl, talked about her new job prospects. It was jus a genuine conversation about life while I was in the midst of making dinner. Things were going well until she said "Why don't you make him a green smoothie instead of noodles for dinner? The noodles can be extremely harmful on his immune system" *Is she serious right now? She's already starting on this again? She hasn't even been here long.* "Well it's already made and it's his favorite thing to eat" "Ye but you're his mother, you're supposed to take care of him and guide him the right way. How hard would it be for you to make him a green smoothie right now?" *I'm sorry do you have kids?* "He'll be ok, thank you" "Maybe if you stopped spending so much money on all these trips you would have the money to buy him the things he needs. " "I get it, I always make sure my son is taken care of before I go on any trips. Kaykay has everything he needs to ensure he is taken care of" "A single mother shouldn't have any extra money to be able to go on vacation. Especially when you live on welfare and you're wasting MY money. It's MY TAXES that allow you to have housing and it's being wasted on unnecessary things. It frustrates me watching you constantly on vacation when I have to work so hard just to pay my rent. You went on a trip in May, and then June. YOU DON'T NEED to go on another trip. You should take the money and spend it ON YOUR CHILD."

"Back when I was young my mother never had any extra money for vacation. She spent her money making sure we were ok and she worked extremely hard for the money she made. That's a GOOD mother, she spent time with us and took care of us. Your son always needs the money. You could take the money and buy him the green smoothies I keep telling you to buy. You have no priorities, you would rather go away on vacation than give your son the nourishment HIS BODY NEEDS. If you're not going to buy him good food then put the money away for other things he may need. Or with the extra money you have you should take it and give it to your TRAINER because you are MORBIDLY OBESE and it would be a better use of your money. I can no longer be a part of your life and we can't go forward with this project because you can't even get your personal life in order and I can't have that effect the work we do." *Did she really jus say that?* I stood there frozen as she gathered her things and left. I couldn't even wrap my head around what was said.

Those words cut deeper than any other wound. I tried to bury the pain by focusing on the love I did have around me. My family was about to head to New York but I decided to take the bus down a few days early to spend a few days with Chris. Every time I was around him he took my breath away. Nothing mattered once we were together. It didn't even feel like sex, it felt way deeper than that. I woke up the morning after to breakfast in bed before he even got ready for work. *He's such a sweetheart. I don't remember the last time I had breakfast in bed.* As I'm looking at him in awe I notice he's holding his arm. "What's wrong baby?" "My arm feels numb, I feel hot, I don't feel well" "I think we should go to the hospital" "But I have to work" "And if you don't make it? What if you pass out? You said the only way you'll go is if I bring you and I'm here, so let's go" "FINE, I don't wanna go but whatever you say". I knew something was wrong based on how quickly they admitted us into the hospital. That night was the roughest sleep I'd had sleeping halfway on this hard metal chair. I had no phone, barely enough blankets to cover me and everything around me was so unfamiliar. Chris begged me to go back to his house but I didn't wanna leave his side. By morning the results confirmed that he had diabetes. It was sad but not entirely shocking. All he ate was processed food. Vegetables weren't even a thing in his house. I asked him once for a salad and he looked at me as if I was speaking some kinda vegetable foreign language. The good news was that the doctor said with proper diet and exercise his diabetes could be reversed. *Maybe it's something I can help him with.* Chris wasn't taking the news very well. He kept talking about how his life was over. It was a little hard for me to hear being in the position that I was in with Kaykay. I would give anything to hear the words reversible. That there was something I could do to change Kaykay's life, but there wasn't. So ye excuse me if I didn't join in his pity party.

The first day everything was a shock but by the second day I just couldn't manage. His negativity had turned bitter and he was sayin a bunch of things. Like I should find another man, that I didn't need to waste my time with him, that life was over, that he was no good. It was draining and I had to leave the hospital to get some air. As I turned to leave his room he grabs me by my arm and tells me not to leave. *Did he jus put his hands on me?* "Let me go" "Don't leave, where you gonna go" "Let me go right now" *Ow that hurt.* I pulled my hand away and left as fast as I could. I could hear him calling me but I kept moving. I didn't know where I was going, I just kept walking until I recognized something familiar. There was a Jamaican restaurant a few blocks down from the hospital. *There's nun like finding a piece of home.* It was like a safe haven, a place that's familiar. It was so warm and welcoming I stayed for a few hours, eating and watching whatever movie that was playing. Once I was calm I returned to the hospital. "Omg baby, you came back? Where have you been? I'm so sorry for how I treated you, I didn't mean to hurt you or grab your arm, please forgive me, I love you. I just...why would you wanna stay with someone like me?" "Cause I loved you before you were sick, I wouldn't just leave you now. I'm sorry I worried you, I found a Jamaican restaurant down the street, it was nice" To be honest I had been through so much stuff in my life that I mostly only knew and tasted bad so I cherished the good and got through the bad with a level head.

The medication brought his body back under control and once he improved he was ok to go home. I was gonna cancel the meetin with my parents but he insisted he was ok to come. I had kept in touch with my parents to let them know what was happening with him as well to warn my mother to be on her best behaviour. We met at Ruby Tuesdays in New York, me, Kaykay, my mom, dad, grandma, my sister and Chris. Everything seemed to be going well. I loved watching Kaykay and Chris interact as they laughed together. The dinner wasn't as scary as I thought it would have been. My family actually asked pretty normal questions without screw face. Questions like what are your plans for work? What are your plans for your health? Are you ready for marriage? When are you coming to visit Canada? I had been encouraging Chris to get his passport so he could take the bus up to see me. I wanted him to get familiar with Toronto especially since he had never been. Now that it seemed as if I had gotten their approval we could now focus on planning the wedding. Destination Jamaica!!!

CHAPTER SIXTY

Work

"How beautiful and how delightful you are, My love, with all your delights!
SONG OF SOLOMON 7:6

After a successful trip to New York it was time to get loose in ATL. Sheena had always wanted to go and since she followed me to Jersey to meet Chris I wanted to follow her to ATL. Plus with how hectic everything was I really needed a vacation just to cope with the last vacation. When we originally planned the trip for labour day weekend we had no clue what kinda parties were gwanin but upon a quick google search of labour day weekend parties this thing called Luda day weekend popped up. *Luda was always my baby daddy.* Whooooooo LUDA DAY WEEKEND ye ye! This time when we travelled we made sure we had brought the credit card to rent the car. Somehow we managed to get lost along the way an ended up at a best western to ask for directions. They pointed us in the right direction but when we rolled up to the hotel things just seemed...wrong, very wrong. The "hotel" looked like a run-down apartment building and there were kids running everywhere. Against our betta judgement we checked into our hotel and proceeded up the shifty elevator to our room. The place smelled horrible. Anyway, keeping a positive mind we opened the door, turned on the lights and I literally watched roaches scatter. This the type of hotel room that I would catch something just by stepping in the room. I had already experienced bed bugs at home and would be damned if I brought any of those blood suckers home. Sheena was saying "We just gotta make the best of it". "Bump that, have you ever had bed bugs? I ain't staying here, I ain't even putting my bag down inside." In the elevator on the way down I witness a man slap his girl then proceed to barate her through the hallway. *No way in hell I was tryna stay there.* We called the booking company and got the hell up outta there. To our surprise we ended up right

back at the best western. *Thank God, at least that place looked clean.*
This trip was one big fun blur. We packed in as much things as possible. We found a piano bar one night, we visited a campus party, found a couple of dope clubs - we ended up at a spot that played all the hottest reggae. The highlight for me was the celebrity basketball game. We ended up waiting in a long line jus to get good seats but it was more than worth it to sit close up and only a couple rows away from Monica!!! *The boy is mine...ohhh dat was my jam.* As exciting as that was, I was there to see my main man Luda. I saw him from a distance at the game but got to see him much closer later on that night. *Woo! Damn he fine.* Picha dis, we dancing with the riddims of the reggae that finally played causing our hips to sway, I looked up to see Luda smiling and laughing. As he looked down in our direction I kept his glaze till WE MADE EYE CONTACT! I swear we did, even Sheena noticed. It happened twice actually, I'm sure he was laughing at us dancing so hard but I didn't even care. We were dancing near the back of the club next to the video vixen groupies. They danced with eyes constantly looking up at the VIP section tryna look sexy. It was fun to watch when 1 of the 3 groupies finally made it upstairs. *Good for you girl, you put a lot of work into that.* My dancing slowed once the rap music came back on. *How do Americans dance to this music?* Anyway, the rest of the night went beautifully and I got to touch the tips of Terrance J's hand.

We opted to save money on a hotel room that night and slept in the rental at the airport. But once we got to the airport we found out that our flight had been delayed. *Worst timing ever.* I needed to get back cause I was gonna miss KayKay's first day of school plus my sister who was taking care of him couldn't miss her first day of school either. In a twist of fate, instead of flying straight to Toronto our flight was making a detour to New Jersey. *Ohhh lemme see if Chris will come see me at the airport.* When I messaged him to give him the good news he was excited but he wanted me to spend the night at his house instead of him coming to the airport. I didn't wanna leave Sheena cause dats my girl, she comes first you kno? But she was tellin me it was fine, to leave her and go see him. Actually, she was putting in more effort to convince me of the reasons I should go instead of staying with her. She said, "I'm a grown woman capable of being alone for the night, go see him". *Aww, dat's my girl for real though, I love traveling with this girl.* Gotta love friends with good understanding that also love to see you happy and encourage you. Each visit for us was like an eternity of time and we made every moment count. With the amount of trips I had made down to the states it didn't even feel like a long distance relationship. I'd been hoping he woulda had his passport by now but we were still waitin for that to come through. Each time he would say "On my next paycheck." Unfulfilled promises seemed to have us both on defense.

Until I got into this relationship fo real fo real I didn't really know or understand what I wanted or expected, except for church. I have always made it clear that church was important to me. I thought Chris was on board with me, I thought we wanted the same things but the more I brought up the conversation the more he disconnected from me. More and more I was understanding he was jus telling me what he thought I wanted to hear, he was more of a see you on the holidays type of church goer.

September 16th 2013 To Chris

I understand that you need to do things on your own time, I do...with regards to opening up about your anger issues I have a question for you...should we really be getting married right now if you're not even ready to open up about your own feelings? I'm still confused about my feeling about religion, it's a major part of my life and I need the man I marry to be able to support and grow with me. I don't know if you can or will grow with me because of the boundaries you have already set for yourself. You say you're open to church but not every week...I don't wanna fight with you about coming to church with me.... that's just something I am not up for in this relationship...so I dunno...lots of unanswered questions as to if this relationship is gonna be right for us both...can we grow together and spiritually if we are not even on the same page? And should we be planning the rest of our lives together?...

Chris: Do u want to break up if so tell me cuz it sounds like u r and that u don't care about me and my feelings?

Cola: I do care about yu...how could yu think I don't?...do yu understand my feelings? You know everything about me and I wouldn't say yes to marry yu without telling yu everything...all I said was...yu say you're ready to marry me but still can't tell me stuff about your feelings and past....how does that make sense?...I'm willing to sacrifice a lot for you...but not my religion and if yu knew me you would know that

Chris: The religion is not my problem I never said I don't want to marry u but u r confusing me on if u going to be with me or not I love u but u going to break up with me over religious beliefs

Cola: church is my life...I'm not all into church yet...but that's the way i'm gonna go...at least I'm making an actual effort to make it a part of my life and try to grow spiritually...you can't grow with me or even make the effort...why are we wasting our time? even with your anger issues I wanna be there to support you and I wanna know what it is, to be honest I don't understand why you aren't able to talk to me about it...but are able to marry me and say I do. I'm trying to look out for us as a family...not jus me...if we can't grow together...what are we doing? if you're not truly open minded to the things that I believe...I'm not gonna force you...but understand that this is who I am

Chris: Fine u win I will do everything u say ok damn I will be religious I will be more open I will do whatever u ask whatever

Cola: Chris that's not what I'm asking you to do...please understand I am not forcing you. You don't have to be religious...all I'm saying is I thought you were open to coming to church and growing with me...I didn't realize you had a problem with coming with me to church...even if that meant every week...

No response
Cola: I don't really understand why you haven't responded...I've never once said I don't love you....and I haven't said I don't want to be with you...I was nearly stating how I feel and I was trying to be honest with you about what I'm thinking ...I am trying to think for the both of us...its not jus about me...we should be able to grow as a family and be even more connected...but iuno you ignoring me and getting mad so...when you are ready to talk...i'll be here for you...I do love you Chris...always will
No response for about a week

I could only hope and pray that things would work themselves out. In the meantime I was excited to start planning our wedding. I was allowing myself to dream again. I was giving myself permission to be excited. I was giving myself permission to feel all the emotions attached to this engagement. My dream wedding has always been a destination to Jamaica. Something different, beautiful and free. I also loved how it limited the amount of people to invite. My list was short but his was even shorter...just him. Even in the groom's party he didn't have anyone willing to travel to Jamaica for his wedding. It never bothered me that he didn't have many friends until I began planning the wedding. I felt guilty that he didn't have the same kind of support that I did. It made me realize how blessed I was to even have the friends I did.

September 17th 2013 To Cola
Chris: Beautiful as a scented rose ur love blooms for my attention to look directly at ur heart. Ur eyes glow like the morning sun and ur smile brightens my day full of life and energy the attraction of one so beautifully correct makes a man want to explore the mind of xstacy and get high off of the aura that is the beauty of u. Ur kiss gives me passion to want more it tells me words that doesn't have no means but one and that's love and ur heart brings power excitement joy but im here to shield ur love from ever being in pain and show u the other side of what true love is and why u mean so much in my world

He was the reason I smiled. There was always a lot of shit going on. Now with this wedding? I was happy but it seemed like the people around me had a million and one demands that had nothing to do with my own needs. "Jamaica is too expensive, I don't want to take too much vacation time, I don't wanna stay down there that long" I was hearing it all from those around me. The resort I wanted was out of the budget for the majority so I switched it to a boat cruise wedding. It was short term and more budget friendly but even with that people were still complaining "I don't like boats, I get points with a different company, ew don't use that company, I still can't afford it, I don't wanna go away for so long" *Sigh.* To top it all off my parents said they couldn't afford it and really didn't seem interested. *What a let down.* Chris wasn't even helping me plan. When I brought up wedding talks he seemed distant, like maybe he was changing his mind. *Was this too much for him? New country, new family, a kid that's not his?*

I had so many feelings but I couldn't even process them cause KayKay was starting grade 2. Another year, another milestone, a new teacher, new class, new friends and new education plan to fill out. He needed some extra help and would be pulled outta class for a few hours a week for remedial work. Since he seemed to move a bit slower his school wanted to modify and limit the amount of time he was gonna spend on his feet. The irony of the situation was that if you asked KayKay what his favorite subject in school was, it was gym. Outside of school he loved to swim. He stayed very active, swimming was gentle and didn't cause any additional stress on his body. It was suggested that he be encouraged to stay inside during recess and that he not participate in gym class. He was already using the school elevator to avoid problems with the stairs which I agreed was necessary, but no gym? That was harsh. He was still a kid, I understood they were trying to do what they felt was in the best interest of my child and avoid lawsuits if he ever became injured. I raised him to be fearless and do whatever made him happy. My response was "KayKay's able to make his own decision in regards to gym class and recess. If he's tired he'll let you know and he can stay inside to play but I'm not gonna put those limitations on him. He knows his body and capability more than me" Especially since he had this disability I needed to teach him independence from me.

Independence was something I had to develop on my own over time. The bitter lessons have taught me how to be guarded and protect myself but sometimes I jus cracked under pressure, sometimes I couldn't hold it all together, sometimes jus sometimes I needed reassurance cause my insecurities got the best of me.

September 26th 2013

Cola: Do yu actually wanna be with me? Between yu saying it's too early to get married and Jus having no reaction to me saying that we need yu...I'm second guessing myself...maybe it's too much...if so lemme know cause I've been tryna organize this cruise day in and day out ...haven't heard yu ask me about it...I Jus...iuno

Chris: Really cola u really trying to leave me fine go just go ok cuz I am here loving u and u saying I don't care if u feel this way about me the leave cuz I am trying my best but u being impatient with me

Cola: ....I was Jus asking...you don't need to yell at me and get upset. Nvm I won't ask yu nothing any more. I didn't know yu wanted me to leave

Chris: No I don't want u to leave it's ur choice if u leave or not I do care about everything that is going on but I also have stuff going on too

Cola: I know yu have stuff going...it's ok there's no point in talking bout this carry on with what yu been doing

Chris: Really u going to act like this to me fine I got u

Cola: I'm not gonna interrupt your life and what yu already doing

Chris: U not interrupt anything

Cola: don't worry, it's cool

Chris: So this it huh u leaving me u upset u going to talk to other guys cuz I am doing nothing to make u happy fine say no more hope it's worth it day a fun life

Cola: I dunno where this is coming from but I'm gonna ignore it. I been telling yu that yu don't seem to take much interest in the wedding...I asked yu the other day if yu wanna get married in November at justice of the peace and the first thing yu said to me was why so soon...so clearly you're not ready to marry me...I said it's cool...don't worry bout nun...I'm good...I'm always good, I take care of myself
Chris: I asked that cuz u had a lot on ur mind with u and ur family that u wanted to push to November and it had surprised me. I been ready but now u leaving me fine ok have a good day just hope u find happiness in the next guy u left me for
Cola: I thought we already talked about gettin married this year so I can start the application for you to come here? and we do a symbolic ceremony next year ...but I guess we weren't on the same page so I felt like u were jus having second thoughts
Chris: Now I know that I will never be happy cuz of shit like this I should of killed myself
Cola: honestly fuck you chris, you don't have the right to assume I'm leaving every time and leaving you for another guy, I haven't even spoken to another guy in months and I've been stressed out tryna plan this wedding ALL BY MYSELF...like wtf I wouldn't be tryna help yu if I was leaving...u think I have time to waste...say it one more time...jus one...an i'll grant you your damn wish..
Chris: I didn't have second thought about anything
Cola: you wanna kill yourself then do it...I've been by your side an whenever I try an express my feelings or ask for a lil help you get mad sayin I dont give u time and I'm leaving...like..it's honestly annoyin cause I don't know what else I could do to help you anymore. I asked a simple question an you're going off like I don't get it, its not always about yu hun...I'm doing the best I can as well...all I hear is either I'm leaving...I'm talkin to a next guy...or yu wanna kill yourself...those are some serious issues that you need to work through...ill support you through them...but...damn homie..
Chris: Really so fuck me fuck me fuck me ok I have a good day hmu when u tired of saying fuck Chris cuz honestly u

just say fuck chris. Ok so now u want me to kill myself fine ok I will do whatever cola says
Cola: I love yu...I don't want yu to kill yourself...I want yu to stop saying it. Are yu ok? I thought we we're good...
Chris: Baby hit me back in a few minutes

This relationship triggered so many thoughts of Romeo, what was it about me that made men wanna kill themselves over me? *I'm really not that special.* I know it's not really about me but this tactic was jus not cool and I was tired of them using this against me. *Am I supposed to beg you? This was just way too much. I wanna help him but how? I already had a kid to take care of and now this?* I was tryna help him with his eating plan, remind him of his medication, soothe his every needs, plan the wedding, and remind him to get his passport. I was just doing everything and it felt like the role of a mother as opposed to his fiancé. *Is he even trying?*

<u>October 18th 2013</u>
Cola: I'm telling yu right now that if you can't get your passport and come see me by Christmas then I know yu truly don't love us enough to make the sacrifices and I'm gonna cancel the wedding. I have family and friends who wanna meet yu and get to know you. I have made the effort to come down there and meet your family and I'm not gonna continue to do this all on my own. I've been tryna tell yu but you get defensive and you're not listening to me... I wanna come for Thanksgiving Please tell your dad that I would love to come out there but if you aren't able to at least APPLY for your passport to show me that yu want us as a part of your family. I don't wanna be the only one supporting this relationship. You had the money from September all you have to do is get the picture and send in the application form. I don't get it...do we really not mean that much to you?
Chris: I'm out with friends celebrating right now, ill talk to you later
Cola: It's cool, I'm over it
Chris: Wtf is wrong with u huh all I am doing is paying bills
Cola: Don't cuss at me, pay your damn bills and leave me alone

Chris: Ok I will if u want wont bother u have fun good night
Cola: whatever It's nothing new, I'm used to this
Chris: What u want me to do just sit and talk whenever the boss message me or call and do nothing else ok I will do that to make u happy I will start doing what u want for now on u in control u the queen u rule I will do whatever u want
Cola: Are yu kidding me? Don't do me any damn favors. Always tryna make me seem needy and fucking greedy well yu know what I'm good I'm fucking good so don't do me any favors. It's cool leave it as is, we don't gotta talk I don't ever fucking beg a man to talk to me to marry me. I always gotta do everything but it's cool enjoy
Chris: Fine if u don't want this anymore then leave cuz u don't care u don't want me u want someone u can tell what to do cuz u don't give me a chance to get things done fine u won't have to worry anymore. I was the one to ask u to marry me u the one that doesn't want to wait until we can afford one so u don't have to do it urself but I never beg ur ass to marry me I picked u cuz I love u u were different but different turned into difficult
Cola: Ok yu win....
Chris: I don't win shit u win I bow to u I do what u want
Cola: At least I know the truth...ok..
Chris: What truth instead of talking it out u planned all of it for next year I didn't want next year I wanted the year after
Cola: I'm so broken I don't care anymore...I won't be difficult,
Chris: No my heart been broken u haven't noticed it
Cola: Ok....the wedding next year is canceled, I'll let everyone know. Of course...poor you, it's all about yu...I forced the wedding...you only asked me to marry yu to keep me...you were never ready for it...I'm stupid..I fell for it and forced something that wasn't there...have a good day Chris..thanks for the truth
Chris: No I ask to marry cuz I love u
Cola: Don't worry bout me, I'm good, I heard the truth it's ok even though I asked yu a million times if yu were ok with the wedding plans...I did it on my own, yu never wanted any of this...so your wish is granted..

Chris: Wtf I do want this I still do I want to just give u ur dream wedding
Cola: It's not my dream anymore...yu never wanted this...yu said yu wanted to wait another year but I rushed it. Yu said yu didn't have the money but I bullied yu ... It's ok ...I wanted to work together but obviously that's not the case. Jus gimme time for me to tell everyone that it's canceled.
Chris: U don't have to cancel anything. Let's get married ok. U don't get why i love u so much
Cola: How could I understand when yu say I'm difficult and bossy...and yu leave me to do everything. You don't make time to talk and then tell me I'm needy. You don't send me the information I need for the wedding then tell me I chose to do this on my own. If yu really wanted this wedding yu would show interest so thank yu but no thanks you've showed your colors
I was hurt but the silence was excruciating. To me, the worst thing a person could do was ignore me. It's as if they're saying that I am just not worth their time, not worth their energy, not worth the hassle. It made me feel so inhuman. As mad as I was at a person it would take a lot for me to ignore them for a long period of time. They woulda had to do something really bad to me. But in this case who was right? Who was wrong? Anytime I stood up for myself or expressed my feelings in any relationship it was like I was expected to just take it. *Shut up, don't say nun, jus be grateful.* That wasn't ok. I'm a person....with feelings.

October 20th 2013 To Chris
Cola: I miss,..my best friend...I wish it didn't have to be this way. I'd give anything for yu, I duno why yu couldn't do the same..it hurts..my heart is crying cause it's so sad
....
No response

October 25th 2013 To Chris
Cola: I lost my bus pass today, actually the bus driver took it from me because its fake. I can't afford a real one. I can't afford food, I can't afford to take care of KayKay. I don't

know how I do. I was late picking up kk from school and I had no money except my friends money in my wallet and I had to use a lil just to pick him up from school. I'm exhausted, mentally, physically, and I've never had my heart hurt like this, I have ppl calling me to make deposits on a wedding I wish will still happen, but am unsure. I have no money, I feel like a horrible mother, I have no future right now, I'm lost and for the first time in a long time I was wondering how life would be without me in it. If I just slipped away...would it matter? it feels so dark the place I am in. And I don't want to hurt anyone anymore I don't wanna keep failing KayKay. He did really good with swimming today...I am so proud of him...so proud. I just want to be happy...have a family..be someone important. I'm so far gone...i'm sorry chris. I really am. I just want you to be happy, I love you...like a lot. more than myself. please always remember that. Hope you had a good day at work. I have some good memories of us.

....

No response

<u>October 27th 2013 To Chris</u>

Cola: Rhetorical question: how does a person claim they can't live without someone yet they let days pass without even one message

Chris: Hey my phone is off I had no way of message u

....

No response

<u>October 28th 2013 To Cola</u>

Chris: Good morning love I miss u hope u ok

<u>November 2nd 2013 To Chris</u>

Cola: Sadly I knew yu weren't gonna call...this is what the relationship has become...goodnight

<u>November 7th 2013 To Cola</u>

Chris: Together forever glad to call u my wife the drive u give with soft words sings to my heart it felt like heaven open the gates for me with ur words of love I love u always for every minute hour day ur love will never go away it keeps me focus on ur heart and me loving it when u smile knowing its real its just the way u make me feel u save my heart from loneliness and heartbreak crying myself to sleep but u lift my head up and gave me a reason to try again to be a better human I love u my queen nothing will ever break our love apart

Cola: I feel like it's my birthday lol sweet words awe I love it Mr mccall. I do feel like you are my husband. We should talk...but not on your birthday I want yu to have an amazing day

Chris: I will can we still have sex when u come

Cola: I dunno gotta figure some things out before I can give myself to you again. I know you're a man and you need sex or you're just gonna cheat on me but I'm being honest I would need to know what we have planned for the future...what ideas you have for us

Chris: Nevermind sorry I asked and I have to think of the plans

Cola: No it's good you asked...I never said no Chris ...I Jus want us to be sure. I miss you but I'm haunted by the fact that you don't wanna marry me next year...it hurts and sex is gonna confuse things when we don't even know if and when we are getting married

Chris: Fine no sex then

Cola: I miss kissing you...riding you....feeling you go deep...we fit perfectly together

Chris: So let's make love when u cum

November 8th 2013 To Cola

Chris: Ur my wonder woman so strong so beautiful so amazing so gifted ur power of love gives me strength to be ur superman u give my heart the power of love its like looking into a mirror a reflection of ur heart next to mine

......

Chris: Every time I think of u I am lost for words everyday is a passion of love with u. Ur love satisfy my heart when u step thru the door I love when u smile more ur mind is so unique my heart never will face defeat. Ur kiss so tasteful so right even when we kiss goodnight I can still taste ur love. Ur skin soft as a bed of cotton and smooth as ur words just know what to say just having u on my mind brings love towards a brighter day

Chris: Hope u got the poems I sent u

Cola: yep, they were really nice thank you
Chris: Its how much I love u
Cola: I'm gonna take this time to get myself together as well
Chris R u going to date
Cola: I don't trust anyone...I just need to be alone and get myself together. If you wanna date, do you..I can't stop you
Chris: R we still together
Cola: honestly I don't even have anymore tears, my hearts just cold...I mean..I uno I'm torn up..I get it...you don't feel any responsibility. I uno why you asked me if I'm gonna date,
Chris: I ask u cuz u r going to talk to other guys and stuff and say fuck Chris he dont want me and I do want u
Cola: naw I'm so done I'm so done, I've been tryna figure out love since I was 14 and I've been through countless relationships that don't work and I'm jus ...I'm so tired...I can't go any further...I can't keep allowing myself to get hurt like there's something seriously retarded about me cause I keep opening myself up...I just don't have the strength to go through it again...so no I can't even begin to feel safe enough to date...I'm better off keeping to myself
Chris: U not coming for thanksgiving
Cola: I don't have a choice I can't give my ticket back so i'll be there
Chris: in reality u don't want me anymore
Cola: I didn't say that...I'm jus...I'm tired chris...I'm happy for you I am..I hope God will bless you...I just don't want a wedding anymore...it hurts that I believed it was gonna happen, and now...I just don't want it...so you kinda got your wish

....

Chris: The first day I met such a beautiful angel sent from heaven my heart was in an eternal bliss. The way u walk the way u talk the way u feel the love must be real. Ur love open my eyes and made a smile to my heart, god gave me u so how should I start..... with love honesty trust loyalty and respect we can deep in love that my heart don't know what's next. The passion u give me to love again I am very thankful that ur my lover and my friend. Our love will last forever its never meant to end. Holding ur love in my arms

I feel warm and grace as I look into ur eyes ur love puts a smile on my face. With every beat of my heart draws me close to u no matter what I will always be with u forever more I will always be urs

November 9th 2013 To Chris

Cola: I never took the time to fully read your poems cause. I was really hurt by you and to be honest didn't want anything to do with you. But I love poems, and I love that you write and send me poems...i've always wanted a man who would write me love notes...especially cause I'm a writer I appreciate it that much more. Thank you for your kind words, I do love them and I won't take them for granted. Have a good day, God bless!

November 10th 2013 To Cola

Chris: ok love you

Cola: I really hope you do

November 14th 2013 To Chris

Cola: I put my ring back on

Chris: Really why

Cola: well, we aren't officially married...but I did promise to try an work things out with you and give you another chance to fix things between us, and until we officially break up, which I hope we don't cause I like you, I want to wear it to remember my commitment to you, even if you can't commit to me

Chris: I can commit

What I learned growing up was that you don't give up on someone jus cause there were a few problems. I made a promise and I was doing my best to keep it. Plus, since I was headed down for Thanksgiving we had to at least start to work through things.

It was hard to even talk to any of my friends about this. *How do I even begin to talk about this? They would just tell me to leave. I couldn't let go yet though.* I could tell Sheena cause she met him so I kinda felt like she would get it and otha than her I was able to talk about it a lil bit with Té. She was actually a really good support for me during this time. Té was coming over more and more to do work on her business but saw firsthand how I was dealing with things. *I was not handling things well.* Her own relationship situation gave her perspectives that she was able to share, that was comforting. I think both of us were jus tired of the bullshit and were tryna focus on more positive things... like growin a business.

Things started off as me jus helping. It soon turned into a full-blown business. I was doing research, helping with back office and with marketing material. I knew the information inside and out and was still learning more. I neva thought about the products I put on my skin before but now it was all I could think of. How naive I had been all these years. Now it was like I couldn't get enough of this information. I had no problem helping Té out with her business cause it came so naturally to me and it was a great distraction for me. I guess all the work I was doing was paying off cause Té had asked me if I would join the business as her partner. She loved how much I was into it and how much I was learning and bringing to the table so effortlessly. I was excited but unsure cause I had no problem helping her out just to help her, but to join?? That was a whole new commitment that I never put much thought into. She was right though, I did enjoy it and I mean since I was doing it anyway.... why not? First thing I wanted to do was build a website. She already had her products set and had been to a bunch of trade shows. Now she just needed to build her online presence. I had no clue how to build a website but how hard could a drag and drop be when I knew the basics?

So now I co-owned a business, I was undecided about a wedding, I was tryna sort out my own damn feelings and I was trying my best to make sure I provided all the supports that KayKay needed. The more I tried the more I failed. I had no one who understood the day to day tasks of trying everything but falling short. These are the times I hated being a single mother. *Can I get some support? Please....*

November 18th 2013 To Chris

Cola: I know you've asked about kk and I forgot to tell you, we were in the hospital last well for a follow up

appointment. They said he has a minor obstruction which is part of the reason he has trouble sleeping. They prescribed me an inhaler big I haven't gotten it yet.
His report card came home last week, he's struggling in school with math and reading. Other than that he's average.
And we are at rehab today cause they are doing a psycho evaluation on him to see how he thinks and how's he is developing. We are gonna be here all day.
So Ye, Jus wanted to update you...feel free to ask me anything or give your opinion.

We were finally able to speak by phone. At least he reassured me that I wasn't a failure of a mother. KayKay had already had a preliminary psycho evaluation and we were doing a follow up. As he aged I needed to stay on top of all and any changes, so I knew how to get him the help he needed. There was too much going on to actually leave, it had taken me two weeks but we were about to launch the website. I had become really good at escaping at the right moment and since I had already bought my ticket it made sense to go. Plus, I had never been to an American Thanksgiving and I needed to figure out this thing with Chris. It felt like I was dating two different people. Once I was home, we fought, we argued, we didn't talk much, he was too busy or too tired or tryna deal with his diabetes. But in person? He was amazing, treated me like a queen, doted on me, took an interest in everything I said and we never fought.

He hugged me like he never wanted to let me go. *Dammit it's like I have temporary amnesia with him.* His dad didn't live in jersey so it was a further ride out which gave us plenty of time to talk. I was excited to meet his dad and step mom cause from what I heard he liked me which was a welcomed change from his mom who didn't seem to like me much. *We have to talk but where do we begin?* It's like we were tryna avoid the real conversation needed. Neither one of us knew what to say except "I missed you" "I missed you too" "So what kinda food y'all eat for American Thanksgivin?" We didn't talk much for the rest of the trip, I just spent the time laying in his arms.

I had such a bomb ass chicken salad sandwich with potato salad on the side. The veggie was flavored and the pies oh man the pies. It was the best first American Thanksgiving I coulda had. His dad was soooo welcoming, he even hugged me as I got there. I was all smiles when the dinner conversation was about our relationship and how Chris needed to step up as a man and make sure he treated me good. *That's right, you tell him.* His dad was saying how it was time to step out and get his own place. Since he was the "man" at his mom's house he was heavily involved with making sure bills were paid, groceries were done and his nephews were taken care of. He was always putting them before himself, it was the reason he hadn't gotten his passport yet. It was great what he was doing but it was to his own detriment. When he wasn't working or sleeping he was playing with the boys or putting them to bed. It was kinda hard not to get mad when he would say he'll call me back then 3 days would go by. *How do I compete with kids?* Even his relationship with KayKay was being affected. I mean he would always ask about him but the minute I said "You wanna talk to him?" it was like "I can't, I'm doing something with the boys." I thought maybe I was over jealous or crazy, but here his dad was sticking up for me. His step mom and dad actually cared about our relationship and knew Chris had a tendency to sit back and let his family walk all over him.

I guess the talk really opened his eyes. After they had gone to bed and he spread out our bed on the floor he took my hands and said to me "I know I haven't been a great fiancé to you but I promise I will do better if you let me. I love you, I need you, I want to marry you. I'm sorry I took you for granted. I jus got scared. It's a lot all at once. I wanted to wait to marry you and I felt like cause you wanted it to happen right now I was tryna make you happy. But I don't have the money to pay for the wedding. You wanna do it in Jamaica and none of my family can come." "Why couldn't you just say this to me instead of making me feel like you didn't want any of this or like I was bullying you?" "I didn't wanna disappoint you" "Ye but instead you hurt me. Like you really hurt me." "I'm sorry, I never meant to make you feel like I didn't care." "If you're not ready we can wait, it's fine" "No baby I'm ready, please, don't leave me...I can be the man for you. Will you marry me please...again? I won't let you down" The makeup sex had me forgettin all about anything otha than being Ms. McCall.

So, the wedding was back on but the when, I wasn't sure of. For now I wanted to take it day by day. Hopefully with my being back at home we could still keep the momentum going.

While Té made all the products at her house I slowly created an office and storage area at my house to hold our products and trade show supplies. I had given Té a key so that she could come in with ease to get work done or when she would babysit for me. She was such a gentle spirit, funny, a good mother and I trusted her with KayKay. We were working on tryna get a partnership agreement together and a business plan together but tryna figure out our pricing had taken priority. *How much should we charge?* I thought high, Té thought low. So, we enlisted the help of Té's mentor and husband to help us figure it out. They were a dope Christian couple that knew how to keep it real. I felt an instant connection with them. Their experiences in the music and beauty industries allowed them to give us realistic advice and plans to follow. "Get a partnership agreement and let your pricing be reflective of your time, production costs and materials" This meant the higher pricing that I was suggesting was the better price but Té still wasn't sold on it. We were both stuck at odd ends. Irregardless of that we needed to move forward. Té was about to graduate from a program called The Remix Project which I had never heard of, nevertheless KayKay and I showed up to cheer her on.

December 16th 2013 To Cola

Chris: I love u honestly I never meant to hurt u at all I love how beautiful u r how u talk to me the way u look at me ur smile the way u love me the way u care for me I been a fool I am stupid I never wanted to hurt u all I want is to give u love cuz without u coming into my I would of killed myself a long time ago but it's not about me its about u and what u deserve to have u deserve love a good man someone to give u everything u want no matter what I am just stupid I lost u I am a failure

The happy bliss didn't last long once I was home. Everything we discussed only lasted like a week. There were gaps when we spoke and he still was no closer to gettin his passport. *You know how embarrassing it is to feel like I have to beg a man to check for me? As messed up as Romeo was, he never let a day go by without asking me if I was ok. The "good morning beautiful" and the goodnight texts were desperately missed. I wasn't used to not being chased. I missed that.* I had told Romeo's brother that I was engaged and not too long after received a "congrats" text from Romeo. He was in shock that I was actually getting married. I don't think he expected me to move on. By now he had a girlfriend and was doing well for himself. It was good just to catch up. I talked bout how my fiancé wasn't checking for me and making me feel like I was nagging, and he talked bout how his girl was impossible to please. *Pfft that ain't gonna last.* He checked for me, he asked how KayKay was doing. *Why can't Chris do this? What's so hard?* Even though he bussed it to work he didn't have time to talk to me then and when he finished work he was just too tired. I tried not to let Romeo back in but the more absent Chris was the more Romeo was free. It didn't help when Romeo told me "I told my girl we could kick it but if Nicola comes back into my life you gotta go" *Damn...that sucks for her.* I was torn. *I love Chris, I just wish he knew how much he was pushing me away. I missed Romeo but we just had too much history. I can't give up on Chris, all he needs to do is get his passport and we'll be good.*

Sheena and I wanted to do something fun for new years so we planned a trip to New York. We always did New Years in Canada and needed to experience something different. It was only a two day trip but we were gonna make it work. We were staying in Queens and Chris was supposed to come down so we could exchange our gifts. I was excited for him to get his gift cause I had bought him almost everything he wanted. I love how thoughtful and sweet he was. He had originally bought me a bracelet but returned it because he thought I deserved something better. Amazing right? Except by buying me something better he spent all his money, including bus fare. *I would have taken the smaller gift if it meant he kept money in his pocket to take care of himself.* I was hoping he would stay the night but the hotel we were staying in was too small to sneak him in so we would have been responsible for an extra person fee which I was fine to pay except he didn't want me spending money on him. He said he'd come back the day after but with him not having bus fare I was worried he wouldn't make it. Anyway, he was grown and we ain't come to New York to jus siddung.

We were two good looking women dressed for a night out on the town. I was wearing a handmade tutu on the streets of New York. The amount of looks I got was funny as hell. *Yes, I'm grown, yes I'm plus and yes I'm wearing a damn tutu, stop staring.* Sheena and I ended up at a white people party and lemme say...white people know how to party. Just saying. It had food and crazy dancin white people. It was actually an excellent night, we didn't starve, we didn't freeze and we got to dance with some fun personalities. *Best New Years ever!!*

I spent hours trying to get in contact with Chris the following day. We procrastinated in the hotel a bit hoping he would show up but when he finally answered his phone it was apparent that I had jus woken him up outta his sleep. "Hey, are you coming down to meet me" "Uh, I can't baby, I don't have any bus fare" "I fucking knew it, didn't I say this shit last night? Ain't this why I told you to stay? I knew you weren't coming, jus go back to sleep. I'm not gon waste no more time waiting here for you" "Don't worry baby, I'll find the bus fare and come see you" *I knew it. Is it me? What is it I'm doing wrong? I've made myself available and still nothin.* I didn't even have nun else to say to him, I jus hung up. Like I was so cheesed. I was in no mood to shop but I followed Sheena around while she made her purchases before we headed for the bus back to Toronto. The whole day had gone by and just as we were standing in line waiting to board the bus Chris showed up with this goofy grin on his face talking bout "Hey I told you I would make it". *Da fuck? You missed the whole day my nigga.... look what time it is, and you expect points fi wha? You showed up before I left New York? Get outta here with that nonsense.* Showing up 10 mins before I leave doesn't do nun for me. I left him standing there and got on my bus. I ain't have not one damn thing to say to him and unless he got his passport he wasn't gonna see me no more, I didn't have the time or energy to keep wastin.

After Té's graduation I knew I needed to be in The Remix Project to help me figure out my next steps in life. Essentially what the Remix Project did was help refine the raw talents of young people in order to help them find success on their own terms. Once they started accepting new participants I put in my application then waited for a reply. I wanted to further develop my talent with classical piano, hip-hop as well as work on the natural skincare business jus like Té did.

Part Three

Love Cannot Be Sold

He who loves purity of heart and whose speech is gracious will have the king as his friend.
PROVERBS 22:11

CHAPTER SIXTY-ONE

January 2014

He who loves money will not be satisfied with money, nor he who loves abundance with its gain. This too is vanity (emptiness).
ECCLESIASTES 5:10

Things with the business had slowed down a bit so to drum up some interest we threw a home party. We invited a bunch of girls to come over for food and a home spa party. The whole point was to allow our potential clientele to try our products in a controlled, relaxed environment. I loved planning events, all the years I volunteered as a tenant rep definitely came in handy. I made a variety of hors-d'oeuvres like tuna stuffed in cucumber, spaghetti served in cups and pigs in a blanket. We lit candles and had the air smelling sweet and fresh. Unfortunately on the day of the event there was a huge snow storm so it impacted the amount of people that came out to our party, nonetheless it was a great success. We used my storage closet as an aromatherapy room for facials, everyone else took time testing the products. My apartment may not have been big but it set the tone for the type of potential we could have as a business. I brought a lot of fresh ideas to our presentation and marketing and Té was really creative with the types of products we produced.

As well as things were going sometimes things were hard to balance with our different schedules. I was an early riser because Kaykay had school and she was a late riser. Being a young mother and entrepreneur were very new and a bit challenging for her to balance. We seemed to be on different pages with work ethic but the real shift came right after we attended a networking party. We met business consultants, a couple of photographers and graphic designers that we had hoped would take us to the next level of branding. There was one photographer that seemed real interested in working with us. Té seemed to like him but I never really liked his vibe. He wanted to elevate our brand and completely re-do our product shots and website however his ideas were too expensive and not the direction that I thought we needed to go in. Again, we were at standstill. Té and I couldn't agree.

Speaking of standstill, I was holding firm against Chris. I really wanted to work things out with him but all we did was argue over his damn passport.

January 13th 2014 To Chris

Cola: It's hard to help you more than I have. I feel like I've encouraged you and tried to support you and although you've let me down I'm still here waiting. All you gotta do is get your passport and come to Canada and I will help you reach your potential after that. I just need to see that you are serious and I'll be there for you helping you l, building with you forever

Every time I travelled I had to make sure my son was healthy and had people to take care of him. I couldn't leave him with just anyone because of the special care he required. I was putting a lot into this relationship and it was starting to feel one sided. I didn't wanna play the fool or worse, get my heart broken. It wasn't just about me but Kaykay also. Even when it came to Kaykay he made me feel like I was trying to force it. *Ye, but if you can't even build a relationship with Kaykay now, how can I trust it'll jus work out later?* I told him he needed to make a decision of what really mattered.

January 19th 2014 To Chris

Cola: I would never tell you not to take care of your nephews but if you want kaykay in your life, you're going to have to make time for him as well. Or just be honest and tell me you can't handle both

I understood that he still has responsibilities at home but I also felt like his mom was being way too greedy. It was one thing to give some of his cheques, but he was giving the whole damn check. Where did it end? When would he be able to take care of himself if every dime was spent on them?

CHAPTER SIXTY-TWO

February 2014

"For God so [greatly] loved and dearly prized the world, that He [even] gave His [One and] only begotten Son, so that whoever believes and trusts in Him [as Savior] shall not perish, but have eternal life.

JOHN 3:16

Not usually my style but I had a story to tell and Facebook was my platform to vent.

Sunday February 16th 2014
my mother woke me up at 7 am to say my son was having trouble breathing and I needed to get to Oshawa with his health card as soon as possible. So I jumped up and although I had my business partner Té and her son at my house I trusted her enough to leave her at my house and allowed her to have a key to lock up and leave when she was ready, plus my mind was only on getting to my son and since I no longer drive..the Go bus was my only option. I arrive in oshawa and my son was throwing up a lot and we took him to a walk-in clinic and the doctor determined that he was in so much pain that he gave us (my parents and i) a note to take to sick kids emerge..We get there but we sit in the waiting room for 3 hours and since they said they were extremely busy there was no guarantee that my son would be seen promptly..so we left thinking that it was just a problem with constipation and we would try to do something at home instead of him sitting in pain in the hospital..

Monday February 17th
I woke up after having a dream about walking with a rod that would change into a snake and change back into a rod...and then change into a snake and then back

into a rod. I woke up remembering how odd that was because I know dreaming with a snake means I am walking with enemies but I was unsure of who my enemy was and who that status was meant for. However that day I spent time trying to give my son everything I could think of to get him to poo as he was still in pain...Nothing worked. Until monday night I gave him a little bit of a natural laxative in milk hoping that it would help him go poo.

Tuesday morning at 6 am
my son finally goes poo and I am thankful because it eased some of the pain in his stomach. After being at my moms house for 3 days I decided to return home, plus My business partner and her son were still staying at my house...not unusual, but it was time to go home since my son had missed so much school already. I return home tuesday night and my business partner decided it was time to leave because she had other work to do. That night via text message I confirmed that we would be talking on a radio show the wednesday night. Everything was a go.

Wednesday February 19th
as I am getting my son ready for school I receive a text from Te saying that we needed to put the business on hold and she would explain to me at a later date why. For those that don't know, I joined this business October 31st and I was asked to be a 50/50 partner in the business because I have a drive and I was already helping behind the scenes without being a part owner. First order of business was a website because there was 400$ being spent on a website that was barely getting built. Now I don't know how to build websites but from the day I joined the company, in just two weeks I had the website completed enough to be launched. I jumped head first into a world I new nothing about but

created positive outcomes. Nuff said

Thursday February 20th
I got a text early morning from my business partner Té asking what time my son had his appointment because she wanted to come by and grab some of the oils for the products that she was making. Kaykay had to go to rehab that day for doctors to monitor his progress with the disease. I explained that I was available only up until 11 because wheel trans would be giving me a ride to my sons appointment by 11:45 that morning and I had to pick my son up from school. I waited and by 11:20 I called to find out where she was, she explained to me that she thought she was suppose to meet me at my house for 11:45 so I said I can't wait I have to go, but she could go grab the oils she needed. Until now she hasn't explained to me why the business would be on hold, so when she mentioned that money came in for the business I messaged her and she said to call when I had time to speak.

I called Té and she said that the business took off faster than she was expecting and that she wanted to slow it down and go back to school and that we have had difference of opinions about pricing our products and that it would be best if she did her business and school and I went back to doing music and writing. So I ask is it that you want to put the business on hold, or is it that you no longer want to be friends.. She replied..both. I felt like I was jus hit with a ton of bricks. Then she goes on to explain that she would like to pay me for the website I built and I also mentioned that there was 500$ on my credit card that I had paid into the business along with other money that I would need to sort out so we hung up the phone.

Is she fo real? Is this really happening right now? What does she mean I should do my music thing? So natural products can't be my thing also? Joke cause I was fine jus helping her out for free. Té slowly put the pressure on me to get me to join but I never intended or needed to join. My work ethic and commitment to the business got simple things done. Instead of paying someone for graphics and a basic website I did all the foundation work to at least get us a platform. I organized the receipts, did company research and the little things to free up time for Té to focus on just making products. I had wasted so much time and stayed up so many nights. I coulda used that time to build my own company. Her timing couldn't have been anymore inconsiderate. She knew what she needed to say; she could have at least given me the decency to wait until I was home and had nowhere to go. Instead of focusing on the appointment I had other things on my mind, that was unfair to Kayshaun. I was disgusted about how she treated me in private, I tried to jus manage but it needed to be said in public.

> I am now on my way to rehab with my son as our ride has arrived and receive this message from Té that says: I'm going to send you $165.00. Please remember I love you and I appreciate everything you've done for me, my son and the business. Hard news is never easy but I believe it'll be for the best and I'm praying nonstop it doesn't hinder or put a dent in our friendship. I love working with you and I've gone further with you then I could've made it by myself and for that I thank you and I'm not sure what the heck I'm going to do without you, but, I have to keep it real or I've learned nothing throughout my journey...I'm letting God take the wheel on this one. Talk to you when you're ready. Balance due: $335.

As part of my rant I included our conversation by text message.

> Cola: trust less..

Té: I understand, it was a swift decision, but you can't 'trust less' with the people who aren't hiding anything. It's just a choice and some choices hurt. I understand how you may feeling, I took that it into account before I came to this conclusion. Hopefully you can sleep on it and shrug it off in the morning. If anything I'm the one who's losing out and I thought of that too.
I got a notification from my phone that said "email login fail". So I text Té and asked if she had changed the email passwords...no response

I continued to try to log in to our business email but I keep getting the same message "password fail". Our wheel trans pulled up to rehab so I put my phone away till I had a moment to deal with it.

Kaykay's timing assessment during this appointment was a little bit slower than usual which indicated his body was slowing down. The stroller helped to preserve his energy which meant it had been a good decision to get but even with the stroller there was still a decline. To conserve even more energy we were in the process of getting him a computer for handwriting exercises. Overall it was a great appointment and we left feeling good.

The reality of what just happened came back and I needed to keep ranting.

Upon returning home at 7:30 pm I sat at my desk and while talking to a friend of mine..and broke down in tears once I realized that not only did Té change the passwords on the email but she locked me out of the website that I built and she took all the original receipts (left photocopies) took all the products, the debit machine everything to do with the business and while on MY computer she also deleted the business plan that we were working on and updated the changes so that I could not even recover any of the information and then she left my house...all while I was at rehab. I call her several times with no response..and finally I sent a message saying that I would be at her house in the morning to retrieve my house keys and I would have an invoice with all the money due for her to sign.

I'm checking out what else was missing so I head to the storage room to find it empty. *She took it all...she cleaned me out.* I had split the cost of everything with her from when I joined. Technically, I was part owner of everything she took. It was hard enough as a single mother to sacrifice money but to have it all taken away...just like that? *In my own house. She robbed me clean.* I gave her that key. That same key she used to clean me out. *I feel so violated.* I broke down crying. This pain in my heart was so intense. *I never saw this coming.* To kick me out of the business was one thing, but to completely rob me while I was at rehab with my child jus seemed cold and unnecessary. I don't hate easily but I hated the chic. *Used and discarded.* She needed me to get her to a certain level and I guess she thought she was good to take care of the rest by herself.

Friday February 21st
I arrive at the house of Té with a letter for her to sign jus documenting everything that I am owed. Since my credit card pays for the website that I built it. She refused to sign and refused to write down what she acknowledges she owes me. She actually looked at me and asked me Why am I mad? she felt like as a business owner she had a right to protect herself and her assets from me..and she had a right to lock me out of everything. LUCKILY i recorded the conversation whether she knows it or not so I at least have some legal footing to stand on. I ended up leaving her house with my keys but no paper signed.

It was like talking to satan, this chic was cold hearted. No soul. No remorse for what was done. Straight wicked man. I thank God for my morals cause I was ready to tump her in her damn face the way she was smirking at me. When you approach someone and they laugh in your face it does something to you but there's no sense arguing with the devil.

Saturday february 22
from Thursday February 20th when I realized I was locked out I emailed the website begging for help because my personal information still on the site. The site says that because they were able to verify my identity as the owner of the website by using the last four digits of my credit card they were able to override and give me access, and I just have to thank God because I really felt powerless like I had lost everything and God saw me and helped me long enough for me to remove my name and house information from the website, the only problem was when I looked at the billing information Té didn't have the decency to take off my credit card information, leaving it on file so that I would be on the hook for future payments of the website. So I shut the website down, changed passwords and sought legal help with the situation.

My stress level was through the roof. I didn't know what she had taken from my house. I had to report all of my cards stolen and wait for new ones. I attempted to get my credit card info off the billing cycle but to no avail. I would contact customer service and convince someone to let me in. By time I got in and changed the password Té would call to have me locked out again. Damn puta!

Business was failing, Kaykay was sick and now Chris was sick as well. He wasn't taking his meds or eating properly. It was hard to hear about his hardship knowing there was nothing I could do. I tried to encourage him but words only travel so far.

February 2014 To Chris

Cola: I don't want to have to bury you, and I don't want a life long sickness that you could have prevented. I get that you're sick, but that's why you gotta do everything you can to beat it...i've tried encouraging you but you gotta tell me what's missing, what's wrong why can't you get this. Is it that you're 27 and you feel kinda lost? like you don't know where you belong?
Chris: I just need to come home to u
Cola: ok but what's going on like i need you to be open with me right now wassup? be honest
Chris: I feel lost like everyone depends on me like my job my mom u everyone and i don't know how i can satisfy
Cola: the only way to stop feeling lost is to take control of your life and determine that it has to be different and start living it like that. Your job will always depend on you, but maybe you need to find a job where there's more reward and satisfaction. You may think I'm constantly pushing graphic design on you, but I think you'd be really great..I saw your work..the least you could do is try and get back into the habit and rhythm. Did you think it would be this hard to have a long distance relationship? do you wish you could take it back to before you fell in love?
Chris: No it's not hard i just made it hard
Cola: what do you think you could have done differently?
Chris: Be more aggressive and depending
Cola: but things gotta be different like you gotta take care and turn things around...i don't wanna keep talking about things that you already know...i hate having kaykay ask when you coming and then sayin..oh he don't know...kaykay likes you..you have a son who looks up to you. If you have the money, why haven't you gotten the passport? you really don't wanna be up here with us..is that it?
Chris: I want to come up
Cola: ok but when? What day will you go get the passport?
Chris: I don't know ok
Cola: I'm trying to help you, if you don't want my help then do it on your own and don't complain

It's crazy how drastic things could change in just a short time. For the business, for Chris but especially for Kaykay. Both were failing at the exact same time. It took us 3 visits over 2-3 days to get the doctors to take a serious look at Kaykay. On our very first visit I had to persuade the doctor to run x-rays to check for stool back up. They finally agreed the x-ray showed he had stool backing up into his stomach which was causing a lot of his other symptoms. They gave him an Advil and an enema in hospital to bring down the fever and to get some stool out, then sent us home hoping the rest would come out. Once the Advil wore off the fever started back along with the vomiting and the fatigue. Day 2 was very similar to day 1, diagnosis was constipation, Advil for fever then they discharged us home. By day 3 I had refused to leave the hospital until they provided a better solution. *I can't jus sit here and watch him in pain. This is horrible. Why can't they do somethin, why is it I gotta make suggestions? Why am I fighting? Something is wrong, this isn't jus constipation, it's different. SOMETHING IS WRONG.* There's been times he would get constipated to the point that it affected his breathing cause his stomach was so distended. But it never lasted this long. Normally, after an enema he would be ok. It has been 3 days of labored breathing which meant he wasn't eating, he couldn't keep food down, he barely spoke, he stopped playing, all he did was sleep and he was in so much pain he couldn't even sit. *These doctors are too nonchalant, they can't see he's in pain? He's not even playing, Kaykay is always playing.* Kaykay could smile through the toughest pain, he wasn't whiny which sometimes made it seem like he was ok. I've had doctors say to me "Well he looks good, he's playing, laughing, he'll be fine." But this time he wasn't playing, or laughin, he wasn't himself even in the slightest. So, it was day 3 and they went through the regular checkup, blood work, heart tests, blood pressure, oxygen levels, but this time...they admit us immediately to the cardiac floor without any explanations otha than "it's for further observation"

February 27, 2014 ·
Don't know if I've ever wanted prayer more than now...still at the hospital...he still hasn't eaten, his heart rate is high and there's been a drastic decrease in heart function..so please pray, even if you're my enemy please pray for my son..thanks..

February 27, 2014 ·
Still smiling

February 27th 2014 To Cola
Chris: hey r u ok i hurried home to check up on kk
Cola: Hey kk heart rate is high and they said there's been a lot of Decrease of function in the heart since September and he might have a virus attacking his heart
Chris: oh no did they say anything about the choices they want to with him like surgery
Cola: No tomorrow they will do more tests
Chris: ok he needs all the help wyd r u ok and i will get my stuff asap so i can make my way to u did u rest

February 28, 2014 ·
So kaykay thinks he's in the hospital cause he drank too much water and it caused him to start coughing. Kaykay says: mom how come you didn't tell the truth about my coughing to the doctors. You should tell them I love drinking tasty water and I had too much and it caused me to cough...Good morning Fb thanks to those who prayed, there's been a big improvement since last night. The support will never be forgotten..

I was brought into a separate room for the doctors to speak with me in regards to Kaykay's condition. *Why are we on this floor? How bad could it be? What do all these numbers mean? Why are the nurses being so mean? Why did it take so many visits for them to take us seriously?* A blonde-haired woman enters the room with a team of other people behind her. She introduces herself as a cardiac doctor that works as part of the Sick Kid's team. *Oh, she speaks French, we have something in common. Her accent weirdly made me feel more comfortable.* She says "The tests reveal that your son's heart has deteriorated to 5% heart function in only 4 months. We've never seen anything like this, it's very rare." She then touches my knee and says "I'm sorry but he might not make it through the weekend, there's nothing we can do for him, so you should make any necessary arrangements. Call your family and let them know. If there's anything I can do to explain further, please just lemme know". With that she left me in the room. Left me to sit...take it in. First thought. *How could this happen?* Second thought. *He can't die. I'll die with him. If he goes...then I go.* Third thought. *God is able.* Fourth thought. *Smile for KayKay, don't scare him.* I feel like an empty shell.

February 28, 2014 ·

Update: even though he looks better, his heart is very sick and deteriorated very quickly. The possibility is that he will only live a couple more months if it continues to deteriorate and there's no cure.. so we need to pray harder, for those who have met him he's very bright and I serve an awesome God who has the power to change things, but I can't do it alone...

How do I do this? How do I keep going? I wasn't really sure how to cope so I turned to facebook to ask for prayers. The influx of people who sent me messages or who flocked to the hospital only hours after I made the post was incredible. People literally dropped everything to offer support. I spent my days trying to smile and my nights bawling. I didn't know who to contact, everything was a fog. *Chris was supposed to be here. I wish he was here. I wish I could feel his strength.* I tried to call him but his phone was disconnected again. I emailed him but I had no clue when he was gonna get it.

February 28th 2013 To Chris

Cola: Honestly Chris I can't keep doing a relationship by email, something had to change

Chris: I know but my phone broke again. I'm pissed off and I'm sorry for not keeping u happy, how's kk?

Cola: I'm getting sick from taking care of him an I'm tired. I just woke up. I feel like shit ugh Update: even though he looks better today he's still very sick and. The doctor thinks it's caused by his disability and it's very rare for his heart to deteriorate this quickly there's no cure and she doesn't know how much longer he has to live essentially

Chris: omg baby there has to be something. I'm hurt by it. I would give up my life for him to live. I'm going to cry. It hurts to know how badly this is for him. I am scared to know this condition. I don't know what to do anymore to come home to find this out i would tell them to cut out my heart to give to him i cant stop crying

Cola: Jus get your passport so that when he's better you can be there waiting for him

Chris: ok i will get it baby i love him

Cola: He loves you too and he needs you right now even if jus for a couple days

I was annoyed that I was having to email him instead of him being here. We had planned for him to come down that same weekend but he wasn't able to get things together. Although I didn't feel like I could count on him I had a friend from university who had brought some otha friends over to pray.

When they laid their hands on me and started to pray I can't even begin to explain the peace that overcame me that day. I went from wanting to die to believing that God would turn things around for us. Not that I didn't believe that before but it was always challenging to stand firm in the face of adversity. The presence of God and faith was all I needed during that time. Funny how people find God in times of need. I was surprised He even recognized me.

MARCH 2014

Love does no wrong to a neighbor [it never hurts anyone].
Therefore [unselfish] love is the fulfillment of the Law.
ROMANS 13:10

The doctors were asking me a bunch of questions about Kaykay's medical health and I didn't have all the answers so I messaged Kendrick hoping he would have some of the answers they were looking for.

March 2nd 2014
Cola
I need to know if anyone in your family had issues with clotting or bleeding or heart or liver problems. Doctors say kayshaun is dying and I need to know this information.
Kendrick
No.. Never... What's wrong with him?
Cola
Heart failure
Kendrick
So young? Did they put a time on it?
Cola
No, but they said it can be sudden they don't know
Kendrick
Fuck, Why is this happening?
Cola
I don't know Kendrick. I jus wanted to know the history so they can take caution with the blood thinners
Kendrick
Ok
Cola
But he has muscular dystrophy...so that's what they say is causing the decline in the last 4 months

I was hoping he'd wanna come see him but I wasn't holding my breath. There were so many people I was dealing with, my phone was buzzing non-stop and as great as it was,I was happiest once Chris finally messaged me. What I didn't expect though was his hysteria. That was more stressful than comforting. *This was not helpful.* It was good to see him so moved but I couldn't handle how emotional he was and I ended up trying to calm him down more than the other way around. I had jus gained some peace. I wanted him to be my rock but I felt like I needed to find my own strength, especially cause I neva knew when I was gonna hear from him.

March 2nd 2014 To Chris
Cola:It's Saturday and Chris you haven't even said nun to me ...
Chris: I don't have internet right now so I have to use my sister's phone. You get upset at me too much. Our main focus is kk. We don't need to argue every time. I am limited to everything. I dont have money for a phone. The internet is off. I don't know what to do to communicate. I am trying but u dont like a try man sorry if i m no baller with the best job. I just try to give u what u want ok i don't feel good im very dizzy i might need a hospital idk but i dont want u to stress anymore i will give u what u want i am not making excuses i am just trying to tell u im trying to give u as much as i can with little that i have. I feel bad for hurting u
Cola: I'm not angry, but I thought I would have heard from you at least once to ask how things are going. No one ever asked you to be a baller and you're wrong,, I love a man that tries. I jus didn't hear from you how do I know what's going on over there. I'm here stressin bout kk and jus needed support. Hope you feel better, hope you can get help for the dizziness. Hope you're eating and taking meds. I'll talk to you whenever you see this
Chris: hey baby im ok been doing good missing u i am here for support dont stress let me do it for u i love u beautiful ur my foundation it keeps us together. Is kk ok? i miss him

Cola: Awe love you baby, he's doing better today. Hey question, would you ask your dad if he would want to travel to see you get married. I still wanna get married but with all this stuff happening with kaykay I was wondering if we could do it in Canada cause I want kk apart of my wedding
Chris:I can ask but it will be expensive but if it makes us more together I will. How is my wife and son
Cola: I'm ok ...it's my birthday kk is ok

We made it through the weekend. 7 am. March 3rd. The doctors came to our room wanting to talk to me about our options. Since Kaykay had the underlying illness of muscular dystrophy he didn't qualify for any type of heart transplant. With his heart being so weak the potential was that he could pass at any moment and so they needed to know what the procedure would be in the event he stopped breathing. They wanted me to sign a DNR (Do Not Resuscitate) meaning that if he stopped breathing we would let him go instead of trying to revive him. *I can't even process this. Can I just enjoy this time with him without all these extras? I jus wanna enjoy my birthday.* I was 25 today. I still hadn't processed everything but what I did know was that I didn't wanna deal with this shit. I wished I could just disappear. I wished it was me laying in bed and not Kaykay. I wished...just for my birthday for things to be normal. Whatever normal was, if it meant not being here I wanted that. As the tears rolled down my cheek all I could muster up to say was "It's my birthday and I don't wanna make any decisions or deal with paperwork on my birthday. You can ask me tomorrow, but just not today" "Oh, happy birthday" "Thank you" Before the doctor left she introduced me to a group called a PACT team who were like my advocates in the hospital. They helped relay my concerns back to the doctors.

I called up Romeo hysterically to tell him and even though he was in disbelief he was tryna get me to calm my breathing. *I can't breathe. I can't breathe. Omg I can't breathe. Why him? Why not me? Iunno what imma do. Trust God...trust God. Why am I crying to this man, it should be Chris not Romeo.*

<u>March 4th Message to Chris</u>
Cola: You missed my birthday :(
Chris: happy bday no i didnt i remember it everything i had missed i will make up i notice it's almost our anniversary one year together so exciting huh so what u do for your bday i miss u happy birthday to u ur beauty gets younger every year stay loving happy and sexy cuz u deserve greatness passion sex and together forever u r mine til the end of my journey but i never want u to stop giving me that beautiful smile i love so much

March 5, 2014 ·
Update: prayer is working...lets keep going lets keep remembering kayshaun...his favorite color is blue and he loves cars

<u>March 5th 2014 To Cola</u>
Chris: hey i want u to know i be thinkin of u and i miss u im not doing well. My sugar level was high close to 500 i'm sorry i let u down
Cola:Why is it so high? Did you get your passport?
Chris:baby i paid for it but i wont get it right away the same day ok sorry baby but i dont to hear about it no more and idk why its high
Cola:It's ok, the fact that you finally paid for it puts me at ease.. now we wait for it to come and don't let your mom and family steal it or hide it from you. Are you eating? Or taking your meds? You gotta do it to keep you good cause I'm gonna need your support during this time...it's already hard you not being here to help

March 6, 2014 ·
Dang...he jus threw up everything...ok..back to the drawing board

March 6, 2014 ·

I need someone who can pray out my hospital room tomorrow please..important!

March 6, 2014 ·
Kaykay did good today, but he says his heart is tired...

March 7, 2014 ·
Kaykay says: I know how to spell please...P..L..E..E..Z :-) enjoy the day

March 7, 2014 ·
Is anyone free to pray over my house tomorrow?

After a week of ups and downs we were exhausted. We still had so far to go and he wasn't out of the woods but it was time to go home. As the staff had put it, "We've been generous enough to let you stay till the 7th and we need the bed" *He ain't betta yet. Y'all said he could die at any time but you wanna send us home?* It was a pretty hard thing to hear. I understood that there were other kids who needed saving but we were here already. I got the impression that since there was nothing they could do for him then there wasn't much sense keeping him. One of his doctors kept saying "Well at least he'll be home where he is comfortable." I wasn't ready though. I broke down. I went mute. I didn't know how to verbalize what I was feeling. The PACT team tried to help but in the end I thought *fuck it, they don't want us here then we'll leave.* It was probably the most hostile departure eva. After much insisting from the doctors I ended up signing the DNR papers before we left the hospital. But otha than that I wasn't talkin to nobody and I dipped before they could finish their charting. *They can finish that shit without us. Gotta get the fuck up outta here. Fuck this hospital.* All I needed was someone to help pray out my house. I needed that house to be filled with God and with positive love so that Kaykay could continue to heal once we were home.

March 8, 2014 ·
Home now

<u>March 8th 2014 To Cola</u>
Chris: hi ms bennett how r u me im not well my chest been hurtin my arm is numb by the way how is kk hope he is ok miss y'all alot
Cola: Have you not been eating or taking your meds?

I had a sick child and a sick fiancé. *This was a lot. A lot of pressure. A lot of worrying. A lot of stress.* What made it worse was the hours that would go by before I could hear from Chris. In his absence Romeo stayed by my side for a play by play of everything happening. I didn't have to wait till the end of the day to recount things, I was able to get more real time support from Romeo. He always acted like a stand in father for Kaykay anyway so he had a right to know. While Romeo took care of the emotional needs my sis helped me out with the physical day to day needs of Kaykay. Since she was a nursing student she helped decode the messages from the doctors. It felt really shitty that I had jus gotten into the Remix Project and I had only been at a handful of meetings. I was trying my hardest to learn it all but everything was constantly non-stop and I jus needed to catch a breath.

I got my first uninterrupted sleep in over a week the first night back in our apartment. I can't fully explain the feeling but I woke up the next morning with a very heavy heart and feeling very overwhelmed. My first thought was *I don't think I'm ready for this marriage.* Especially not with everything going on. I would barely hear from my fiancé and my focus was on Kaykay getting better. *You gotta make a choice.* Both needed me but only one could get 100% of me. Without question that would be Kaykay cause he came before everyone else, even me.

That night the same young woman who I had previously met when she prayed for us with the group had come over alone to pray and talk to me. I called her T. It was important to surround myself with the right people and right vibes during this time. *At least I'm not alone.* I felt like the only way Kaykay could be healed was if I did everything in my power to live correctly so once we had finished sharing life stories with one another I decided to give my life over to God. We prayed while sitting right in Kaykay's room and as I prayed the sinner's prayer I felt a different kind of peace overcome me, I felt free.

From this place of freedom we spoke about relationships. She shared her stories and I shared mine. I talked about my relationship with God thus far and how important he was in my relationship. When I first started dating God was important, but I was flexible not wanting to offend Chris. As I grew and matured I understood God played a much bigger part in my life. I could no longer compromise my own spiritual beliefs and we were growing at different paces. As much as Chris proclaimed his love for God it felt like we were on different pages and moving at different paces. The more I grew the more it seemed like he was trying to catch up. I didn't want him to love God solely cause I did, I wanted him to love God cause that was in his heart. He was trying to hold on to me by saying the things he thought I wanted to hear, like "hey baby I prayed today" or "I listened to a pastor today". It was cool that I inspired him but the minute we spoke about church and how it was a weekly commitment his conversation was, "why can't he go only sometimes...not all the time." I was living in denial until I no longer could. We weren't on the same page spiritually and as long as I stayed with him it would hold me back. My relationship with God had become too important to me to allow him to come between us. So again, it came down to choice. God was my peace and my relationship with Him I could no longer compromise on. It was ok that he wasn't into church, it didn't make him a bad person, just not the right person for me. Religion and spirituality were always so tricky. I never wanted to make him feel bad for not being a Christian, hell I was still learning, but as I learned more about myself I needed to show up for myself.

After we spoke about God and where I was at spiritually we started talking about the actual relationship. I didn't mention to her that I was second guessing the engagement but the more we spoke the more I felt that tugging coming back. *I'm not ready for marriage.* Through the conversation one piece of advice she gave to me was "Jus cause he's a great guy doesn't mean that he is THE guy for you at this time. God always wants to give us His best." It felt like she was reading my mind. I was so heartbroken over how I was feeling inside because the reality was that he had been the best man I had been with and he was trying his best to provide and be everything he could for me. I felt guilty that even at his best I still wasn't fully at peace. I felt like I was being overly picky. *You have a man that loves you, just be happy for that.* Either way, her conversation with me had struck a chord in my heart and regardless of what my mind was telling me I knew that Chris and I needed to slow things down, work things out better and understand ourselves completely before we jumped into marriage. *How will I tell him this?* He still didn't have a phone up and running so I had to put it in an email. My fingers struggled for a bit figuring out what to write but I knew it couldn't be put off any longer. Hopefully he won't be too upset.

March 9th 2014 To Chris

Cola: I wish we could of had this conversation face to face or even on the phone, but i'm left with no choice but to message you by email. This has been the best relationship that I have been in, and you have taught me so many things about love and about being good enough and about having more self esteem but unfortunately, I can't marry you and I can't continue in this relationship. I love you dearly, but I am going through a lot with Kayshaun right now and I need to focus my attention on him.

I don't know what direction my life is going to take, what kind of job I will have, or what kind of mother I will be, much less wife and girlfriend and I need time to figure all these things out.

There has been an overwhelming outpour of support from friends and family and prayers to help Kayshaun be brought back from a place of nearly death. And I need to obey God and I need to turn my life completely over to him in order for my life to take a change for the better. Kaykay is on his way to healing, but he's not there yet and I need God to heal Kayshaun cause he's my world.

You are the best man I've ever been with, treated me like a princess and more..it's not about money, it's about me not being ready, and not being certain of the future.

I need to spend time praying and understanding where God needs me to be and only if it is his will for us to be together will that happen.

I think you are an amazing man but there's too much distance between us and not enough communication, and not enough support and I need to separate myself from this world until I am able to stand on my own before I can join in a relationship and get married.

Thank you for everything you have taught me, thank you for not judging me, thank you for listening to me, thank you for being there and looking at me and telling me how beautiful I was, thank you for loving me for what I look like and who I am. I will always pray for your healing with your diabetes, and I only wish and hope you will come to know God not because of me but because he can give you the strength you need to get out of the situation you are in right now. You are a wonderful man of God and even though it may not feel like it right now, you will get through this, just pray and lean on God for guidance. As hardworking as you are, I hope a fire will be lit in your life, I hope your ambition takes flight and you become that graphic designer that you studied for. You are not dumb, so please stop calling yourself that, I speak life over your life so that you come to understand and love yourself.

I understand if you hate me, but I want to wish you the best and know that I will always love you, you have changed my life...and I'll never forget you. Please forgive me in time...

Cola..

That was hard to do. I knew he'd be heart broken. If this were a typical situation, knowing how upset he was gonna be I would have just let the guilt convince me to stay without ever bringing it up to him. I never wanted to hurt him but with the way I was feeling and with the conversation I had the previous night, I had to put aside emotions. T didn't even know she was saying the things I needed to hear. I felt like if I stayed I'd be signing my life away, cuttin down my own potential just to make sure he was ok. It felt like life and death to me. To stay with him meant to continue pouring into a future I knew we didn't have and it meant pouring out my empty emotions to him. I was already drained and he wasn't getting the love he deserved from me either. He was gettin only a piece of me which wasn't fair.

If things couldn't have gotten any more stressful Té was tryna push me right off the damn cliff. *What now satan?* I had seen Té only 24 hours prior. She had asked me if she could come visit Kaykay at the hospital. *Why would I say no to that?* Now I was regretting my decision cause beyond her fake smile and helpful nature, bitch was plotting against me. The bitch had gone too far,and I was losing my damn mind, I felt so hurt and violated...and so it continued, my facebook rant.

March 9, 2014 ·
I am honestly tired, tired of fighting... the amount of evil one person can do is unfathomable to me. Please just pray for me as I deal with this mess. To visit me in the hospital but at the same time work behind my back...i just..i can't.. This one is directly to you.. Té

March 9, 2014 ·
We are out the hospital and as I wake up to check on some work I realize that I can't login to the website, I check the reset button and I realized that she used her

email to regain access to the website and lock me out again. Now please understand that I was told by the website, the only way she could have re gained access to the website is if she uses my credit card information... Which was on the receipts that she took from my house. So while I was in the hospital with my son and while she was visiting me in the hospital and telling me she's praying for me she was also using my information to regain access and re lock me out meaning I again have no control over the website and once again I do not kno whether or not my credit card information is still on file on the website.

March 9, 2014 ·
Please understand I just finish praying for many situations in my life last night and forgiving and releasing people from the hurt that they have caused me..and I wake up to this.. I am not ranting because I am angry. I honestly feel like I have had this in the dark for too long and have been dealing with it along with dealing with my son and it's draining me of all my energy and I just need help praying cause I am tired...I can't fight this right now and she knows this... Té knows that I am dealing with my son which is why this was the perfect time to get back at me...So please don't take this as a rant or a negative thing...I am shedding light on a dark situation and I am asking for prayer and positive thoughts while I deal with this..updates are coming soon..THANK YOU

I desperately needed to refocus my attention on Kaykay. I had my sis with me to help cause we had left the hospital with a list of new medications that we had to adjust to. Along with a new home nurse and new home doctor, there were a lota new changes happening. Things were moving faster than I was able to adjust to.

March 9, 2014 ·
Update on kayshaun, although he is complaining of

tummy pain he has been holding food down so I give God all the praise. I could be here without him but he's improving by the grace of God

March 9, 2014 ·
The gas is overtaking and stopping him from eating...:(poor baby

My faith was all that was keeping me balanced. Just as I celebrated one victory, a defeating situation would attempt to make me feel as though the breakthrough would never come. My emotions got the best of me and I was still learning and growing with God, trying to get rid of my "trust no one" mentality. T was now someone I could call a friend and a support. She had an organization called The Love Movement – they're a community outreach organization and they had bible studies and praise & worship. It was perfect for a baby Christian like me still trying to sort out all my emotions. I was surrounded by a group of young people on fire for Jesus with a heart full of radical love. It just so happened that I met them right as they were accepting new members into the group for their summer outreach. Without question it made sense to be surrounded by love to balance out the dark in my life. I too wanted to have a radical love like Jesus, I wanted to learn my bible and see it as more than just a boring book, I wanted the stories to come alive and I wanted someone to walk with me through this new journey. Every time I tried before people would pray with me then leave me alone to figure things out and I went right back to old behavior. I couldn't go back this time, it didn't feel right and I needed to make sure I did everything so that Kaykay would get better.

March 10, 2014 ·
life on the other side is so positive..so much faith..so much prayer..so much potential

March 10, 2014 ·
I know that many of you are relieved that the doctors have released us from the hospital, but let me explain further..they released us from the hospital because they said there is nothing else MEDICALLY that they can do for us. They have sent us home to let kayshaun die and to let him live out the rest of his life (in the comfort of his home) which they don't expect to be very long. Medically they are at a loss but spiritually we are not, I am not...please continue to pray...If you want to visit and pray we are very open cause we can only beat this with everyone's help. Y'all have been amazing and taught me soo much..still keeping the faith..we got this..update: He's throwing up again..its a blessed day, but has not been a positive day for kayshaun. Thank you

March 10, 2014 ·
I know my posts have been a bit sad so here's something to add humour to the day. I gave kaykay all his meds (he takes 6 meds) and when I got to the tums he was refusing to take it and he said to me : mommy do you know what tums taste like....tastes like bad candy :-) he he he

It was hard to get comfortable enough to fall asleep. Knowing that Kaykay was so ill and was constantly waking up I just wanted to be awake anytime he needed me. I feared I'd sleep too heavy and he would cry out and I wouldn't be there. Just as I was about to close my eyes an email came in. It was from Chris. My whole body went numb even before I opened it up. *I don't wanna hurt him. What if he doesn't get it.*

March 10th 2014 To Cola

Chris: So I paid my passport for nothing and u going to leave me. I knew it, I just came out the hospital from a heart attack now I have nobody. What I'm going to tell my dad now u hurt me I been heartbroken too many times and u want to put more pain by leaving, wow how I knew this happens to me all the time. I feel like killing myself. We suppose to get married to go thru life together what I suppose to do now? huh I'm trying but u didn't wanna be patient I know ur son needs u but I need u too. I thought I found what I was looking for but now I know nobody wants me. Fine go all I could do is try to make it work I'm lost and about to cry all I had was u don't leave I want to be there with u I don't know what to do. What did I do wrong? I try to be a man for u. I don't deserve love anymore my heart really hurts.

Cola: What did the doctors say?

Chris: I will never be happy ever again. I'm not moving on cuz I just lost everything. I'm done with relationships tired of not having love after u I don't want anyone u stomp on my heart now I have no heart idk what to look forward to I don't want nobody but u but it wont happen since I am waiting for my passport minus well rip it cuz I cant come to canada to be with a girl I fell for now I feel like my life is a lie why I'm still alive why I'm still in pain idk I will never be happy ever again........... ever. if u felt this way u should've chosen someone else it hurts that everyone I been with did the exact same thing its on replay but with a different girl my life is over

....

Cola: What did the doctors say

Chris: doctor said its due too much stress

Cola: Chris breathe take a break from heartbreak. You've always wanted to travel and see the world...why can't you come and still visit Canada and experience something different? Will you pray with me right now? How are you messaging me?

Chris: oh so now u care but u still want to leave huh

Cola: I've always cared, please don't act like that or there's no reason for us to continue talking. You know I care what happens to you.

Chris: I wanted to see the world with my wife and son and my internet is on the only experience I want is to spend my life with u

Cola: Can we pray? You still need to do better...with or

without me you need to experience life abundantly and see what it has to offer, you've been down and depressed for too long now

Chris:i been eating and takin meds but it's not about that is about u leaving my heart and love i am trying get there but u decide to leave

Cola: Can we pray? You're right to some extent I did up and do this out of thoughts from my mind but I didn't confirm if this is what God wanted me to do, I'd like to share this with you and ask that you give me some time to pray and seek God. Understand I nearly lost a child last week and you weren't there for me like I wanted you to be there. So I'm gonna ask one more time. Will you pray with me through this?

Chris :but i don't want u to go, ok we can pray, if this what u want to do is to break up to seek god for ur son then ok but i really hope the next man can give u more then me and tell kk i'm sorry but u have to explain why u did this and what u want for him ok now lets pray

Cola: Lord I thank you for kayshaun and the ability to have him laying next to me because he is a very important person in my life. Another important person to me is Chris McCall lord you see my heart, you know my thoughts some thoughts have been judgmental and presumptive without being patient enough to hear the other side, Lord I feel like I've been in this relationship solo and left to only have email disconnected relationships but I come to you and ask what is your will to be done. We need guidance on our relationship, we need to know if it is your will be done. I am ready and willing for you to use me and I want to change my life over to you and I ask that you help me on my journey to understand clearly what needs to be done. I love Christopher your son but I am also experiencing that the timing may not be right for us to get married. I pray that you will touch Chris heart, physically and spirituality that he may come to know you I understand your will and your promises for our life. Please comfort us on this journey and help us to make the right decisions regarding our future together, in the name of Jesus..amen

Ok your turn
Chris:dear father i come to u in prayer for life and love for nicola and her son. My journey on that path is over but please give her the strength to continue on the path with her son i come to u to give thanks for kk to live another day watch over him as he sleep and protect him from harm also shower nicola bennett with ur love and guidance so she can live a healthy loving life in her new life going forward findin u God a new male companion and happiness for her son i also need u to make sure that they're safe and well for me i'm lost for words but in spirit i know u can give what she seeks amen
Cola:You're supposed to pray for yourself as well.Look I never said it won't ever happen between us, I said in my email if it's Gods will...I have a lot of learning to do, you could do it to if your heart was ready...I jus said with the stress of kaykay I'm not ready for a marriage at this time
Chris:i also come to u lord to give us guidance on where should we go from here there r questions we seek to make our love a fighting chance and to bring me closer to cola and kk i love them i will give my life to give them many if i had the power i need u we need u please show us they way ur name jesus amen
Cola:Before you up lift yourself you're praying for a next man for me...I did not ask you to do that. You need more confidence Chris...what If we were meant to be but jus not now...instead of praying with me and seeking for answers you're praying a new guy will come in...I didn't ask for a new guy that's not even on my mind. My kind has been you kk and God but I need God's favor so I need to focus more on God right now..and you're not even trying to understand and walk with me
Chris:i am understanding but u was pushing me away without thinking and making a decision before giving me a chance it hurts to feel alone i know the feeling but honestly listen to what u said u have god kk and me ur only support u have u never in it alone i dont care i will fight for my family
Cola:How do you plan on fighting for us?
Chris:whatever i need to do i will make the changes to

make us work
Cola:You said you've been praying for us...what have you heard from God? I don't know where you're heart is...I know you don't want to be at church every week but I also want you to want to change because of you and your life and not jus because of me
Chris:i haven't got my answer from god yet be i will be patient also if u want me in church everyday i will for us i will change my life for us to have better

I fell asleep for what felt like seconds before I was up with Kaykay tryna rub his stomach.

March 11, 2014 ·
Belly troubles...I'm so tired...long night

His home doctor has been coming for regular visits and we've grown to really like her and her us but I can see in her eyes she doesn't believe he has long. She's trying to prep me for the end. She wasn't used to dealing with children. Her regular patients were all older adults but Kaykay was the best kid she could have gotten cause he was very outspoken with what hurts and where. It helped cause she didn't have to guess plus half the time he tried to help her or played with the medical equipment.

March 11, 2014 ·
I understand that the nurses and doctors are trying to help but the term "end of life care" really bothers me...especially since I know God specializes in long term life care...still praying

I can barely grasp everything happening, I'm scared all the time, but if I'm scared...how does Kaykay feel? I couldn't even begin to imagine the effects it was having on Kaykay. He stayed smiling throughout, even when it seemed hard. He smiled. Since he wasn't able to attend school I had arranged for a music therapist to come to the house to keep his spirits up. Just like his momma, he loved music but I was too drained to actually teach him. I always wanted to but with everything goin on, I figured if someone else could come with instruments and put a smile on his face it was worth it. So, every Wednesday became music day.

March 11, 2014 ·
Kaykay says he's scared and all he sees is black in his mind :-(praying against all darkness and fear...speaking life into him

March 11, 2014 ·
For those of your who have been following my post, this one is important. I need a break through, I've been praying..but it's time for the next level, trust me when I say I've never done a fast let alone liquid fast but this is my sons life I am fighting for. So I am asking please please join me in fasting from thursday to Sunday and we will pray specifically for the restoration of kayshaun antwoine Isaiah Bennett. I will be doing a liquid fast, but for those who can't I am asking for a meal a day fast. This is definitely my life taking a new direction. Thank you for the support.

March 11, 2014 ·
For those who are non religious and don't want to fast, but still want to pray please I ask to set aside some time every day from Thursday to Sunday specifically to send positive vibes say a prayer with kayshaun specifically in mind and we can all bare witness to the miracle that will happen.

A woman from facebook contacted me to ask if she and her sister could come over and pray. I wasn't in a position to turn down prayer so bright and early they made the drive from Brampton to downtown to see us. They then prayed throughout every single room and you could just feel the weight lifting all over. Just as she was done praying over the house she said "By the way, God said the man you are with is not for you. God has someone completely different who is better for you, who will help you pray over your business and is God's best for you." *What she jus say to me? YOOOOO how did she know though? God...dat's you? Wooooow, ok. I hear you. I prayed and you sent a VERY clear response.* I thought that maybe Chris just wasn't for me at that time. Now there was no clearer message that God coulda sent me. As I stood in shock I removed my ring and put it on the table. I'm not one to go against God and I needed him to save Kaykay. Whatever it takes, whatever I gotta do to see my baby back to health imma do. I'd rather be obedient than pay for it later. *Now how am I gonna tell him. This will kill him and I will be responsible.*

March 12th 2014 To Chris

Cola: I've prayed and we prayed together, and I've received my answer this morning, sent from God as a message. I love you dearly, but this relationship is not going to work for us. I pray everything works out for you, and you will start to figure out your life and what you want out of it. I hope one day I can see you in Canada and you get to enjoy it.

Love always

Cola

Chris: fine whatever bye cola. I knew u was going to do this take my happiness away fine do what u want I'm tired of having ppl not wanting to be in my life I was ready to go but no u left me for no reason what I do to deserve this its very selfish of u to do this to me I try to be the man for u but its still no good find go have fun. my health is better my heart is not in pain i been fine up to this point in my life no its ruin i have nothing to look forward to and to help me start over u took away everything why did u be with me in the first place to end up hurting me at the end it's not fair u dont want a chance with me do u do this to everyone what i do to hurt u huh now what i'm going to do i loved u and u crush my heart

Cola: Other than the communication issues we have and the fact that you're promises to me always get delayed, you've been the best fiance I could ask for at this time in my life. And I love you dearly. You are an incredible man and I know God will take care of you. Kayshaun is doing better, thanks for asking. See my life is not my own and my son needs me, I jus can't be a great mother to him and in a relationship. I need to be focused on him getting better. So yes, you are right I am being selfish...and it's to save my child's life. I'm sorry things worked out this way, I would hope you can forgive me and we can be friends but if not I understand.

Love always cola

Chris: well i hope ur happy leaving me

Cola:I'm glad your health is better...keep it up...I honestly want to see you in Canada one day jus traveling. You have lots to look forward to...talk to God he's waiting and he will give you peace and understanding.

Chris: we can be friends but we can't never get back together ever but friendship we can have ok

Cola:You can lay guilt all you want...I told you I'm doing this for my childs life and you can't understand so if you'd rather we don't talk at all then fine

Chris: i did talk to god i got my answer and it was to be with u to start my life a new with the one i love and to finally have peace in my heart. we can talk i told u but we just can't be in a relationship anymore we can only have friendship ok im not mad i took a deep breath just not and just thought of this and ur right ur son needs u so u right about leaving me

Cola: Thank you, understand it's nothing against you I still love you. This is just something I have to do right now. :-) love you Chris...you're gonna be ok honestly. By the way God said that kaykay is healed and will live....:-) give thanks

One of my girl's asked me "Did you even love him...cause how could you walk away like that?" *Did I love him? Yes, of course.* Love was the reason I was walking away. Love for myself, love for Kaykay and love to preserve the relationship we had so that we didn't end up resenting one another. I loved Chris, he was the first man to show me I deserved better, took me on dates, proposed, did whatever I needed. I didn't want to lose that but I had to be obedient not just to what God was saying but also to what I felt deep in my heart. As I recalled the morning out of the hospital I woke up with that overwhelming feeling. "I'm not ready for this" my inner gut knew something before my heart and mind could process it. The confirmations I had gotten allowed me to be true to what I had already felt deep inside. The hardest thing was reading the answers I had already expected. Even though I knew, it was still hard to read them on paper. He really tried to be supportive, he did, but I needed more than he was capable of giving me. I was happy that he finally got his passport but it had been a year of me asking him before he got it. These things didn't make it a failure, we just were growing on different paths of life. It wasn't fair to me to keep holding myself back until he was ready.

Instead of depending on him for support I looked to the sky and let God be my guide. *(Prov 25:19 NLT) Putting confidence in an unreliable person in times of trouble is like chewing with a broken tooth or walking on a lame foot.* From the day Kayshaun took his first breath I promised to always protect and put him first. I went from contemplating suicide if he died to praying and believing that God could heal him completely. Not many things made sense but being single did... alone to grow.

March 12, 2014 ·
Good news..Kaykay kept his food down last night and he woke up saying he had a good dream and a good sleep...Praise God!

March 12, 2014 ·
You know what's so special about kaykay, no matter how much pain he is in, if you ask him..he will always say "i'm good". God is keeping his spirit strong...stronger than any child i've ever seen before..

I needed to fast to silence all the noise around me. I had never taken fasting seriously cause the minute I denied my body food I had horrible headaches and fatigue, but maybe my head just wasn't committed before cause this time when I fasted it wasn't so bad. I was fasting to know what the next steps were for me and for Kaykay so whenever I got hungry I reminded myself why I was doing this. *This ain't for you...it's for Kaykay, suck it up.* I welcomed this change to our lives. I needed answers.

March 13, 2014 ·
I know fasting isn't about the food, but I find it funny how I seem to be taking in more nutrients through liquids only than I would on a regular day. Gotta reevaluate my daily food intake

March 13, 2014 ·
Update: kaykay says his mind believes in God and he can picture himself running and he feels free
From when I told Kendrick, Kaykay was dying, I hadn't heard from him and it was really disheartening. I thought for sure, he woulda wanted to be around him. I wasn't stopping him. It's heavy news to take on, but still. I mean I had to suck it up and every moment I wished I could do more.

March 15, 2014 ·
I know as single mothers we tend to get upset when our child's father is not around, but I feel strongly that at times we just have to thank God because only he knows the type of man or coward we would let into our children's lives. Just because they are the biological father doesn't always mean they are suited for the role as parent.

Bounce back and celebrate small victories.

March 15, 2014 ·
Kaykay says: mommy my heart is hurting like crazy
Me: it's cause God is reformatting your heart and making it smaller so it can function

Kaykay says: so God is fixing my heart so I can eat chicken and burgers and salad?
Lol he's been asking for chicken for about a week

March 15, 2014 ·
Update: he ate a little bit of food and he said mommy I feel free...today is a blessed today trust me...day 3 still fasting...to God be the glory

March 15, 2014 ·
Kaykay was bored of just eggs so I added a salad....he says:hmm impressive :-D he's eating right now

Keep on going.

March 16, 2014 ·
Update: kaykay is doing so much better today playing and talking....I'm mentally drained today..so imma say goodnight I'll post more tomorrow

March 16, 2014 ·
I agreed to give God thanks every day at 12, thank you lord for complete healing. Kayshaun is asleep and yesterday was the very first day he held down multiple meals. No throwing up and increased appetite. Thank you Lord:-) ok goodnight again

March 17, 2014 ·
Been a good day..after a morning throwing up we saw the home doctor who said the fluid is no longer in his lungs and his heart rate came down to 120 :-) progress, we gotta conquer the vomiting and the large liver but great news kaykay went to his school for a visit today

His class was very supportive. His school was jus as amazing as I thought they were going to be. He was blessed to have several teachers and both principals visit him. They made us food, they brought gifts, they came with guitars to sing songs. It was truly a blessing to have such a positive experience with such a loving school and class. It was interesting to watch the interactions from children so young. They didn't take it for granted that Kaykay was well enough to be in class. He was a superstar whenever he was in class. All the girls help him with his boots and jacket, pinch his cheeks and gave a lot of hugs. All the boys wanted to do was play games. Even the child that used to bully him was super understanding. These kids taught me the biggest lessons about appreciation.

March 20, 2014 ·
Update: it's a down day today :-(:-)but I know Gods got this..

March 22, 2014 ·
Update: so far today is going well praise God. Kaykay is eating again and able to keep it down, thankful for small victories. Sooo...we should be in church tomorrow :-) excited to see everyone

Despite the home doctor visits we still had weekly visits to the hospital so they could get a more accurate read on his blood levels and heart function. Sometimes the visits were encouraging and at other times it felt like I was fighting a losing battle. I had kinda gotten over my bitterness towards the hospital. He needed as much help as he could get.

March 23, 2014 ·
Update: if you see how his stomach has grown...nurse says his heart is growing and is running out of space...gotta keep the faith..gotta keep smiling cause he is still smiling

March 25, 2014 ·
Update: kaykay looks exhausted today but he's still smiling, he's on and increased dose of medication and added a new medication to conquer the nausea..

It was a matter of finding the right balance with the new meds cause he was now sleeping for hours at a time and I found myself always anxious. *Don't die in your sleep please. Is he breathing? Is he ok? Why he sleeping so much?* I checked him often to make sure he was still breathing. I wouldn't even let him sleep in his room because I was scared something could happen. We all slept on the couch in the living room: me, my sis and Kaykay and I kept lights on at all times in case they were needed.

March 25, 2014 ·
Despite the added medication to stop the vomiting, he still threw up and says he can't move his arms cause they are too tired.

March 25, 2014 ·
I need a break through....this is not the way of life..
How do I stand firm when things look so bleak.

March 26, 2014 ·
Update: doing better today praise God he's smiling :-) during our regular conversations ..kaykay says the girls in my class like me because I'm cute...lol

March 27, 2014 ·
Update: kaykay jus woke up...says his legs hurt like it's tired and his body has been exhausted. The doctor wants to explain to him what's going on cause they think his body is tired as a result of his heart getting weaker...we know that God is still in control ...

Despite all efforts to help him feel better he was

constantly on the edge of things going south. The doctor thought it would be best to explain to Kaykay that he was dying. *How am I supposed to be ok with this? He's gonna be fine. He has to be fine. I don't wanna scare him. Can he just enjoy life without worry?* I'd rather he knew nothing about it and continued to enjoy life without fear. It's not fair to rob him of the little happiness and tarnish it with thoughts of death. *I'm not ready...it's too soon.* I don't believe it, he's worked so hard to keep pushing and I gotta respect that.

March 30, 2014 ·
Headed back to the hospital....

March 30, 2014 ·
Update: there is a clot in the left side of his heart that can cause a stroke..so we are most likely getting admitted again.

We were trying everything we could. Looking at different options to help overcome some symptoms. We were still getting many visits from friends, family, church family and my parents' friends. One of my parent's friends suggested this homeopathic doctor they had heard of that was supposed to be really good. I was open to the idea. I mean doctors ain't have any otha plan, they were jus waiting for him to die.

The natural path doctor showed up with her sidekick asking what was wrong with him and reassured me that she could help. Said she had some herbs and a tea she could hook me up with that could help get rid of the fluid. She said once he started to take the stuff he would start to get better. *Herbs? Tea? That's it? That's all he needs? This don't seem right.* My parents wanted to do all they could to help. My dad kept saying "It's too soon" "Not yet" and as much as I believed my mom was tryna be positive, fear turned everything she spoke into the opposite. So, when this natural path doctor came and said she could help they strongly held onto the idea that she could make a difference. It put our family at a divide. I didn't wanna spend money on her herbs. I had drained my accounts paying for food and taxi rides and parking for my sister's car. My supply was limited yet I was made to feel like if I didn't purchase the herbs then I wasn't truly doing everything I could to save his life. I didn't see no one else putting up the money though. *I do care, I do wanna do everything for him. Fine, I'll try this.* In the end to make them happy it was me who had to pull out the money to pay for these services. *This betta work. I feel like shit. I'm a good mother. I am.* I didn't wanna see Kaykay in pain. I paid the money to the doctor and waited for the delivery.

The herbs were delivered, unlabeled in a brown paper bag and were only half of the herbs that I thought we were getting. *How do I even know what herbs these are? How can I trust this? Really? Unlabeled herbs? Brown paper bag? This has to be a joke. Great there goes my money...I really could have used those couple hundred dollars.* Even though she called me to explain what the herbs were and how to make it for him I felt uneasy. So, I went back to the person who had suggested her and asked her, "Is she credible? How do you know her? What can you tell me about her?" As I found out they barely knew each other. *Fo real?* As for the special tea she was giving me...it was Organa gold organic hot chocolate. It was available through a wide range of vendors. It cost me $260 at a time when I could barely feed myself. I completely understood my parents' position as grandparents cause it was hard to watch Kaykay struggle to walk and breathe but because we were divided that's exactly how she was able to take advantage of our emotions.

March 30, 2014 ·
Sitting in emerge at sick kids he's still smiling...rock star kid bringing joy this Sunday

Behind all the madness there had been some relief. Kaykay had a spirit that was so deeply loved by all that met him. No surprise. Between Sick Kids and Make A Wish there were some truly amazing people who were working hard at creating the best memories possible. Someone at Sick Kids heard of Kaykay's obsession with cars and arranged for him to visit a Ferrari dealership in Vaughn. I couldn't wait to tell him, he was gonna flip out.

My friend had been determined to get him to Disney World since he had never been. She's been doing a lot of the background work to ensure he gets to go. It's been a complete blessing to have someone work so hard for us. I couldn't actually take on any more than simply taking care of him. We contacted G98.7 and other organizations to help us get to Disney World but Make A Wish heard the story and stepped up. I didn't even know organizations like this existed. It was amazing. They came out to our house to see Kayshaun to talk to him. Before Make-A-Wish had come I explained to Kaykay what was gonna happen. "Hey Kaykay, when they come, they're gonna ask you what you want your wish to be....say Disney World. Nothing else but Disney world...ok?" "Ok mommy" "Good, cause if we get to go to Disney World then you'll get to meet Mater and Lightning McQueen, ok?" "Yaaaaaaaaaay!!!"

When they came he said exactly that. I mean he looked at me first for approval and I tried not to make it so obvious that I had told him to say it, but regardless we were on our way to Disney World and it was the best news we could've ever heard. One of the requirements for Make-A-Wish was that the child have a life-threatening illness. It sucked that he qualified but I knew it would be an opportunity to make great memories. Even better news was that his doctors said that he was strong enough to travel. This is how I know God worked in our lives. Make-A-Wish said they could only send two adults to Disney with Kaykay. Presumably that would be a mother and father situation. My sister was automatically the fill-in for the second adult ticket. However, my dad refused to stay back. "This could be a chance of a lifetime, whatever I gotta pay or do I need to be on this trip with him". A day later I received a phone call saying that the resort we were supposed to stay at was full and they would have to put us in a resort that was a short drive away. I explained that I wasn't comfortable driving in the states and the only person who I trusted to drive was my father. After a bit of back and forth I was told that they would pay for my dad to go on the trip so that he could drive us between the resort and Disney World. With three of us going, all that was left was to get my mom on the trip. Although they couldn't pay for her flight they offered to pay for her tickets and accommodation. All we needed to do was pay for her flight. They went above and beyond anything that I could have hoped or wished for. When I thought things couldn't have gotten any better we got a call a few days after that explaining that the original resort now had the space to accommodate us so we wouldn't need to drive if we didn't have to. *Great...are they still gonna pay for my dad?* Since they had already made the accommodations to include him and pay for my mom's tickets they went ahead with things as planned. God moved in such a way that we were able to get 3 paying adults and only have one additional plane fair to pay for. *He jus amazes me. He keeps on blessing me.*

March 30, 2014 ·
This needs to be a week of healing. I know a lot of you have been praying and thank you very much. What a lot of you don't know is that make a wish foundation has set up for kaykay to go to Disney world April 10-16 and with the ups and downs I know this trip is blessed by God. So this is the week for healing so that once kaykay is in Florida he can be free from pain. I claim this! Keep praying. Keep believing. He is already healed. His fate is in Gods hands.

March 30, 2014 ·
Oh Disney world is also a surprise for kaykay so shhhhhhh! Lol

Despite the ups and downs he was finally given one final all clear to travel. We just had to bring his portable oxygen and other equipment with us. Either way we were just hoping the trip would bring a change to his spirits. I was hoping that being in Disney would bring the miracle of healing into our lives.

March 31, 2014 ·
Update: he's on new medication to clear the clot from the left ventricle of his heart. And we are trying to control the nausea. God is good and is keeping us, what more could I ask for...

Now that things seemed a lil bit more stable I wasn't holding my breath as much. I brought Kaykay with me for a meeting at the Remix Program. With everything I was going through I still felt immense guilt that I wasn't living up to the expectations which I soon found were more of my own expectations. They understood that life happened and still wanted to support me in anyway. So instead of kicking me out of the program they told me to keep in touch and come in when I could. *Amazing.* Facebook had been a powerful vehicle of communication and connections. I was meeting people left right and center who were touched by our story and wanted to help. One of the women I heard that I should connect with was Tara. I had heard that she was a powerful woman with a heart for the city. If anything, she woulda been another great support to have durin this time. I had reached out with hopes of connecting. We agreed that the next time I was in the hospital she would come visit cause she lived close. God was at work again cause while I was sitting in my meeting a woman with her dog in hand walked up to the desk across from me. I overheard her say her name was Tara. *What are the odds? Go introduce yourself, don't be scared. This is so weird.* I delayed but wanted to catch her before she left. I introduced myself and Kaykay. At first Kaykay was nervous of the dog but soon got used to him. She says she was willing to get involved in any way possible and to let her know how she could help. *Wow ok God, I see you!*

CHAPTER SIXTY-FOUR

April 2014

Love bears all things [regardless of what comes], believes all things [looking for the best in each one], hopes all things [remaining steadfast during difficult times], endures all things [without weakening].
1 CORINTHIANS 13:7

For a moment, Disney World was in jeopardy. We were back in the hospital to get some of the fluid out of his body. It felt like we were there for so long, the days felt like weeks, and the weeks felt like months, but he was finally stable enough for us to go home again. Nothing was for certain.

April 2, 2014 ·
Morning, we are supposed to go home today ...he did really good last night and this morning he woke up throwing up and complaining of exhaustion and headaches...still praying for a breakthrough

April 4, 2014 ·
1st day home yesterday and everything went well the next week is going to be quite busy, but I will make sure to post pictures. Tonight is a raptors game, Sunday is a baseball game and we reveal to him that he is going to Disney World yay!, Monday he is getting a test drive in a Ferrari at the Ferrari dealership in Vaughan, getting a tour and meeting race car drivers and Thursday we leave for Disney World. EVERYTHING HAS BEEN DONATED..LOOK AT GOD. HE IS BLESSING US MORE THAN I COULD EVER HAVE ASKED FOR! thank for you the continued prayers we are all winning this battle together. still praying that the blood clot is gone and we will continue to see a breakthrough with the side effects

and "symptoms of congestive heart failure" God is sooo GOOD..AMEN?..Amen!

Bennett meant little blessed one and it really felt like God was raining down blessings on us. We had activity after activity planned and I was jus hoping his body was gonna allow him to do it all. The countdown of activities began and we kicked things off with a raptors game. He's finally old enough to enjoy them!

April 4, 2014 ·
On the road with his kinder surprise going to pick up his raptors tickets...he said he's excited to eat food and watch the game at the same time lol

Well, I learnt that Kaykay wasn't really into basketball. His favorite part of the game was the dancing at half time and the fact that I got him food to eat. The simplest things made him happy. Welp, basketball was out, but what about baseball?

April 6, 2014 ·
Twins. Jays game...why do they look alike? Lol

Him and his aunty were like best friends. Like me, she never left his side. She was on this journey with us in every way. Today she got to enjoy a baseball game with him. He seemed to enjoy watching baseball more than basketball. Most importantly he loved the free popcorn. This day was a reveal party that Make A Wish was sending him to Disney world. They bought him two cakes and all he cared about was eating popcorn. It was as if the news of Disney World went right over his head.

Day 3 of the activities continued. It was Ferrari day. The craziest thing for me was that Kendrick shoulda been there with us. Some days I felt guilty that I got to do all these cool things with him. *He made his choices.* I was happy to be there with Kaykay. I knew he was going to love it. My only worry was that on every other day Kaykay wasn't able to go long without vomiting or getting exhausted but today the most amazing thing happened. He got out of his wheelchair and began to walk unassisted all throughout the dealership. He was walking and looking in amazement and asking questions I didn't even know he knew. All I kept hearin was "This is amazing! Cool!" He walked out the whole place without even a limp or stumble. He got to a red Ferrari on the showcase floor but was too scared to get in. Even though the car had no engine he was afraid he would press a button that would cause the car to move. He said, "I'm too young to drive." We finally convinced him to get in and the look on his face was priceless. Once we had finished upstairs the real fun began. He was offered a test drive in a black Ferrari. I let his aunt go with him as I sat back, watched and filmed his happiness. I never wanted to take this moment for granted and I was making sure I captured moments that we could look back at and smile upon as he grew older. Once the tour was done we headed off to do Kaykay's favorite thing...eat.

April 7, 2014 ·
My child says when he gets older he's gonna buy me a Ferrari yay! Too excited! This is why we must support our children's dreams

I always thought that eating was a right. My experiences have taught me that eating was a privilege. Do you know how gut wrenching it was to make the decisions to deny Kaykay water because I knew it did more harm than good to his body? Having congestive heart failure meant that his body was full of fluid, he was on diuretics to keep the water off so I had to limit his water intake. Not to mention that sometimes when he would have water it would cause him to vomit. Withholding water was the only way to help him avoid throwing up. Not fun at all. We had jus finished an amazing time at the dealership yet I had to sit and watch Kaykay cry over the fact that he couldn't drink water. *This feels so inhumane. How is this ok? I feel so horrible.*

April 7, 2014 ·
This is one of the first times I've seen him so upset...he wants to drink water but can't because he keeps throwing up please pray for him today he's really tired

Every moment counted, every minute made a difference and every day could change quickly

April 9, 2014 ·
We went for a check up yesterday. Heart rate is down to 112, blood pressure is good, chest is clear of fluid and his stomach is soft...God is amazing he is honestly so good we are still praying that he will stop throwing up but for now his appetite is back and he's holding down food so we are blessed :-) one more sleep till Disney..lol still have to pack

April 9, 2014 ·
Hair cut done...getting ready for Disney

April 9, 2014 ·
Whoever is up..emergency prayer please kaykay jus woke up complaining of being dizzy bawling up stomach pain and throwing up...please pray for strength cause he was doing so well today

It was the day before we left for Disney and things seemed to be going horribly wrong. I refused to watch the trip be ruined for him. I was holding on through the storm, looking for the morning breakthrough as we assembled our final belongings for the trip.

It was an early morning wake up with a limo ride to the airport. Nothing could be more amazing. Kaykay stopped throwing up long enough for us to board the plane. A few spit ups on the descend but manageable. I think we've developed a system to handle everything and my dad had stepped up 100% to take the load off me. I never realized how draining things were until the little things were handled without me.

He's not supposed to get sick on this trip. It's Disney, he needs to enjoy this. Lord please allow him to enjoy this without gettin sick. I thought that because God had worked things out for us to be here it meant he was gonna heal him. I thought his body would give him a break from the havoc. I guess I was living in a fairy tale. Everything at Give Kids the World Village was adorable and like a story book. We had our own villa and we had gifts awaiting us as he entered. It was handpicked for us and designed to make us feel welcomed. *Things don't ever go wrong in the fairy tales they tell us.* The first time he threw up there was the first time I became very angry and disheartened. I cried. Hard. *How is he still throwin up in such a magical place.* It was almost too much to bare for me. Thank God for my dad's personality. He kept us smiling and laughing throughout the whole trip. His excitement was just as big as Kaykay's.

I've never been to Disney World so I definitely took advantage. I felt like a big kid. Since Kaykay was in a stroller/wheelchair we got automatic line bypass which made the day bearable. Since the stroller was mostly for the times when kaykay couldn't walk, when it came to a ride that didn't accept the wheelchair he simply hopped out and hopped onto the ride. For me it was a simple reminder that even though things looked bad it was still better than most. Some children weren't able to get out of a wheelchair...not once. Not every day went great though, we went for 5 days but weren't always able to get off the resort. On a day like that the resort had train rides and merry go rounds. They had themed movie nights and they had Disney characters show up to the resort. Dreams do come true.

A few weeks prior Kaykay woke up and told me he had a dream that cars 3 was coming out. I knew that meeting them would be one of his biggest highlights. When I googled cars 3 he was in fact correct. Cars 3 was set to come out in 2016 and he couldn't wait to watch it. He was always asking "Is it 2016 yet?" Although it wasn't 2016, here in 2014 he got to see Mater, Lightning McQueen, a car stunt show and even got to drive a go kart with my sister. I lived for the smile on his face. The decision to travel as a family was the best decision we could have made. When the trip was over and we returned to Toronto not one person could have been less grateful for the experience that could have only been God led. In the words of Kaykay "It was awesome!"

April 16, 2014 ·
Wanna give a shout out to God for blessing every step of the way...he's the greatest

I went to school for classical Piano for a reason. My field of choice was creative and fun, not science and nurse things. I wasn't a fan of doctors or needles. I cried every time I got blood work done yet told Kaykay to be brave. The medication we had been giving him wasn't working and we needed to try a different method. Only this method included me giving a needle once a day. *I hate needles.* Did I say that before? Not my specialty or interest. Now I was given the painful task of giving my son a needle everyday. *I don't want to.* I wasn't given much of a choice cause either I did it or the chances of death increased. *I can't. I can't. I can't stab him. I'm not a nurse for a reason. I have two nurses in the family, can't they do it?* Watching him go through pain was hard enough. Now I was expected to be a different source of the pain. I cried for the whole day. I couldn't bring myself to it. I just ...I couldn't. But there was no one else. As much as my sis was with me she had school and wasn't always available. At this point I couldn't even attempt to learn what was required cause my brain was stuck in shut off mode. I closed my eyes wishing that when I opened them it would be a dream. *I CAN'T DO THIS, I CAN'T, I CAN'T HURT MY BABY.* I couldn't breathe, no matta how many doctors, nurses or family members talked to me I couldn't calm down, I couldn't think, I couldn't move. I sat in the corner clutching a teddy bear and crying to myself. *It wasn't fair.* My responsibility as his mother was to love him and take care of him, not to cause pain. Kaykay had come over to give me hugs and wipe my tears. *This is to save him.*

You gotta do it. I still don't know how I found the strength to do it. It took me a couple of tries. The first time I gave him the needle, with a face full of tears he looked me straight in my eyes and said mommy it hurts, as his cries got louder there was nothing I could do but tell him "I'm sorry baby" "I'm sorry baby" I felt like a monster. It was one of the most heartbreaking things I had to do. I locked myself in my room and broke down crying. *This can't be life.*

April 19, 2014 ·
I cant even believe its been two months since I received the news from the doctors that my son wasn't going to live much longer, and look at him today...hes progressing slowly but surely by the grace of God he will live..its indescribable the feeling of having my best friend back, he saved my life when i was 16 and carrying him and he has changed my life again more than he will ever know he's one of my role models..the new medication has him getting a needle once a day and even though sometimes it hurts his pain is only temporary and he smiles again at the end of it. God has given him a patience and calm and obedience that is unimaginable and I'm a proud mother:) Monday we have an appointment to see if the blood clot is gone. I AM BELIEVING THAT THERE WILL BE DRASTIC CHANGE!

April 21, 2014 ·
They say the vomiting is a side effect of his heart being sick so as long as he still throws up then we know his body is still sick. ...so they are prescribing morphine to numb the pain.

As much as I knew that the morphine could potentially help ease the pain I was unwilling to try. Sometimes the things prescribed as a remedy caused more problems than solutions. The risk was too great. So, I held off and continued to pray.

April 23, 2014 ·
I love my son, it bout to be his birthday man I feel old...he's bout ta be 8 praise God!

April 24, 2014 ·
AAHHHH HAPPY BIRTHDAY KAYKAY!!!!GOD HAS KEPT YOU! This is an important day for me. I always say life has changed because of my son 8 years and I feel blessed every single day to have my best friend by my side. No matter what they throw at him he overcomes every single thing. the love I feel is incredible. yay!

April 24, 2014 ·
For those that don't believe in God and for those who's faith needs rejuvenating , let my son be a testament of God's love. When he was laying in the hospital and the doctors looked at me and said "i'm sorry there's nothing else we can do, enjoy your time with him because it could be any day now that he passes", the only person I cried out to is Jesus. There's no other person who could raise my child off of death's bed to be the dancing smiling happy child I see standing in front of me today. When they said "there's nothing else (medically) that we can do. That's where God comforted me, gave me inner peace and strength because God is the supernatural healer able to overrule everything humans fall short of. Keep the Faith. I was born and raised in church, daughter of a pastor and to be honest it wasn't until this moment that I fully began to understand God's love, his ability to heal, and his ability to keep my calm amidst the storm. Another honesty I was preparing myself to go with my child because I can't see or understand life without him. So when I say God and my son have saved my life, that's what I mean. No more depression, no more complaining, new chapters..new beginnings..we are blessed and we plan to pay it forward. :) have a blessed day! Remember to Thank God you are awake and to Thank God you are still

breathing. I hope this message touches at least one person today.

I had a party planned with all his school friends. It was a time to celebrate. *What do you get a child who needs life more than anything?* I paid for the party, all his friends and god parents and my friends had come to bowl and celebrate. He got sick once but we were just happy to celebrate. Once he returned home he had a present waiting for him from Romeo. He got him his very first tablet. He never did forget about us.

With months of ups and downs I was happy for any type of positive distraction. Sheena was gettin married. An although I wasn't 100% convinced that this man was for her, I couldn't be happier for her. Relationships take work so it was a privilege to be invited to the wedding, especially cause of the history with her man. I understood that he wasn't a fan of me but that didn't matta cause I was always loyal to the people who were loyal to me. I celebrated with love and smiles.

April 25, 2014 ·
One of my closest friends is getting married today and I couldn't be more excited and happy for her. Love you Sheena Taffe you are an amazing person and I pray for longevity, happiness and most importantly wisdom to your marriage. May God truly bless you and your groom Duvall and enrich your lives abundantly. Can't wait to party with you both tonight!!!!!!!

What a party it was! The ceremony was beautiful. Sheena looked incredible and the music at the end was bumping. Leading up to the wedding I was helping wherever I could to assist with the jack and jill and anything else I could do. The jack and jill was held at her house and I played the role of hostess for the night. Fun! It helped me take my mind off things for a bit.

April 28, 2014 ·

Important announcement....kayshaun has not vomited yesterday or today... Praise God!! This is huge news not even a spit up...God is alive and working. Full recovery is in the midst. We go to sick kids tomorrow to find out about the bloodclot

April 29, 2014 ·
So we are back from sick kids and the tests show that there has been NO MEDICAL CHANGES...but for those who saw my son two months ago and saw him today would understand there doesn't always have to be medical changes for a person's life to change. He is NOT the same person. I am NOT the same person. Kayshaun is doing so much better, he's had increase appetite, no vomiting, no headaches, he's laughing it doesn't matter what the tests say..yes I want the bloodclot to be gone but God is still working, he's jus not done with us yet. It's a journey and a process that he is bringing us through and strengthening us as individuals and as a family unit. We continue to feel Gods love everyday we wake up and take a breath to start our day. Thank you to those who have been praying. Keep praying for us. The enemy is trying to attack in dreams but we are stronger...update: God is good...and we are more than okay right now!

Besides Sick Kids appointments, home doctor visits, and nurse visits we still had visits with the specialist monitoring him for the seizures. We had gone in to see him and after months without answers all the tests we had done finally came back confirming that back in fall he was indeed having seizures. *I knew it.* It felt kinda nice knowing I wasn't crazy and I had fought for something. At the same time this wasn't a pleasant appointment. Behind the eyes of the doctor held much more than I wanted to acknowledge. This was gonna be our last appointment in his office.

Do you know what it feels like to have a doctor look at you and all you see in their eyes is despair? The look in their eyes tells you that they believe this will be their last time seein you. Do you know what that feeling is? They look right past you like they seen a ghost and you're looking in their eyes and see the heartbreak they try to hide. They feel helpless and there's nothing you can do to unsee the look in their eyes or the feeling it leaves you with. You just know. You know it's over, the fight is done. You take on their sadness, try to shake it off, but that feeling seeps in and you gotta fight harder to release it from your soul.

April 30, 2014 ·
I've been battling with whether or not I should cancel my tv. I feel like it has become a sense of comfort and addiction for kaykay and I and in favor of more reading and freeing our minds we would be forced to be more creative with entertaining ourselves. Well I've officially made up my mind today, kaykay came to me and said my mind is thinking of bad things, it's thinking of robots and monsters. Instead of letting kaykay watch tv alone I know all the shows he watched and even watch some with him and they are riddled with monsters and robots and other poisonous material. Certain shows we choose not to watch but admittedly some of the other shows dance around and even make joke of robots turning evil and taking over the world. Anyways I guess this long post is to say be mindful of what your children watch, no matter how harmless ...the good thing about this...I've introduced him to veggie tales

Has this ever happened to you? Maybe you don't swear too much but then you watch something riddled with swear words then you begin to swear a lot more. You wondering when did I start swearin? Or you watch a show with all these sex scenes and you start feelin a way? Or you watch love shows with all these happy couples, then you start to feel lonely, unsatisfied and reexamine your whole life??? The power of influence was so real to me. As an adult it was easier for me to block things out. I also knew right from wrong but with Kaykay he would be fine until he went to sleep, his mind was too active and it scared him. I had to monitor what he watched. I thought *hey it's a kid show, it's fine,* but I've watched some "kid shows" and felt myself questioning their intentions. Once I changed the programming his mind and actions improved, the nightmares went away and he went back to being happy.

CHAPTER SIXTY-FIVE

MAY 2014

"I love You [fervently and devotedly], O LORD, my strength."
PSALM 18:1

May 8, 2014 ·
I haven't done an update in a while, Kayshaun is doing well, He throws up from time to time and has pain in his body and gets tired easily BUT he is doing well considering where God has brought him from. As of right now he has an increased dosage of the blood thinner to help remove the clot which hasn't moved. May 21st we go back for testing, so we just keep believing that the clot will leave.

He was back to playing and acting like his inquisitive self. Just gotta be grateful for the small things. The little victories were enough to keep us going. Breathe. Appreciate the ability to walk. Appreciate life.

May 11, 2014 ·
I cried..my baby is alive. God is good..

Today I cried. Every year when we celebrated Mother's Day at church the children were responsible for giving roses to their mothers. Today Kaykay walked across the stage to get the rose and poem for me. He walked. That's all that mattered. As I reflected over the past few months I thanked God for the progress. Peace was something we had to fight for in this house. At a time when we should be grateful my mom was up in her feelings again. She was upset that my dad hadn't said happy Mother's Day right away and didn't make dinner plans because taking her to Niagara on Friday and Saturday wasn't good enough. As she complained I said, "It's Mother's Day jus remember to be grateful for the little things" She responded, "I have nothing to be grateful for."

What she mean she ain't got nun to be grateful for? Haven't we been watching Kaykay fight for his life? HE WALKED TODAY that's something. We aren't in the hospital...that's something. He's eating, that's something. I cried. It was a hard thing to hear when we were going through so much. It didn't even make sense. With many things to be grateful for I *kept my focus on only one.*

May 12, 2014 ·
Status update: (tear) kayshaun will start school tomorrow...one period a day, but he's going back and he doesn't lose the year, he will continue to grade 3 next year

Watching Kaykay's classmates react to his return was priceless. Couldn't have asked for a better welcome. They had cards made and all the kids could barely wait to take turns showing him their games. He was instantly famous. It was a beautiful moment.

May 13, 2014 ·
In 6 months, there will be a change ....

May 17, 2014 ·
Kaykay seems to be fighting restlessly all night and he jus called out saying he threw up over himself and his whole bed...he and his bed are completely soaked. I'm jus asking for prayer because we've been working hard to keep his fluid levels low, and his weight is down to 20 kg yet his cheeks look chubby and he threw up a good amount. Iuno, I haven't lost hope I'm jus asking for prayer as I try an make sense of this and re adjust how we live.

May 21, 2014 ·
The clot is gone the clot is gone! God is soo good to us. The doctor refuses to admit that it is gone completely because it's supposed to take longer to leave so she said "i don't see it" but will not completely say it is gone, but I know the God I serve he dazzles and amazes, he is

awesome, I'm crying with happiness. Thanks for prayers and support...we continue battling against all sickness.

I got accepted into the Love Movement program and felt like I was on the right path. God's approval for me always came in the form of peace over my decisions. My parents made themselves available to help take care of Kaykay so as I took the time to focus on my life Kaykay stayed with them which was a big help not to have to stress over his care. The program kicked off with a 3-day retreat that included a liquid fast, bible study, solitude, connecting to God and deliverance. This was the first time I was doing a liquid fast, no food for 3 days, I wasn't even sure if I would make it. It was exactly what I needed though. I really connected to myself, confronted my insecurities-vanity, my weight, my fear of abandonment, rejection, confronted elements of my past that had plagued me-sexual assaults and family rejection, confronted judgements of myself and the judgement I placed on others. I prayed for a release of the negative and to be filled with the positive allowing me to forgive and heal.

I really prayed for God to reestablish the relationship I had with my mother. As I prayed I had a vision of my mom and me when I was 10, when we used to sing on stage at church events. It was the last good memory I had of my mother and God allowed me to remember it. I also saw God erasing my past. Like when someone wiped clean a drawing board, I was left shiny and new to reset and restart. God closed the chapter to all the men I had slept with, giving me a brand-new identity through Him, an identity of a woman who was gentle, kind, creative, healed and living out my purpose to inspire others. Next thing I had to tackle was deliverance. Deliverance is to pray and be set free from addictions or oppression. At first it sounded so weird but I had some addictions I needed to get rid oflike sex, and I was definitely oppressed by depression, anger, unforgiveness and abandonment. I had anger against Romeo and I hated my cousins for how they treated me. I was revictimized every time I was around them. I held so much guilt. I couldn't see myself as beautiful no matter how much I tried. I felt like a dirty broken shell, undesirable to anyone for anything more than sexual gratification. These were all things that needed to be prayed over and removed. I needed my freedom.

Deliverance was an indescribable and incredible experience, one that really got me looking at life in a different light. Although it was hard leaving Kaykay for the 3 days, by the end of the retreat I felt refreshed, renewed and rejuvenated. Not to mention the fact that I survived a 3-day liquid fast and I had hit a new personal record. *You got this.* My faith had been restored. From the weekend retreat we moved into our summer program. This required a greater commitment in order to be a part of the bible studies and other activities that were planned. It started off great for me, I was even using wheel trans to get around because I brought Kaykay with me to the sessions which helped with the commute. I loved it but it was a challenge to balance everything going on. Most of the people in the program were single with no kids and I felt disconnected. They were able to stay late but I hated getting Kaykay home late. By time we got home Kaykay and I were just exhausted. Sometimes jus leaving the house seemed like such a daunting task. I felt like I was failing as a Christian cause I wasn't able to keep up. *God loves me despite my faults, my imperfections and he sees my heart and desire to do well. Above all He honors this.* I decided to create a schedule that allowed me to still participate without showing up to every outing. Some of the days that they had bible study I would call in instead of traveling. I didn't go to every single outing and no longer felt pressured and guilty because as much as it was helping, Kaykay had needs. I developed such a love for the team. They continued to support me and pray for me and for the first time in a long time I felt like I was right where I belonged.

CHAPTER SIXTY-SIX

June 2014

For I shall delight in Your commandments, which I love.
PSALM 18:1

June 2, 2014 ·
So something amazing just happened. God answers prayers and concerns and encourages even when we least expect it. When we first learnt about the diagnosis when kaykay was only a year and a half, the doctors told me that he may not even live to see post secondary school and we would jus have to take things slow. Despite their warning, I set up an education savings plan (resp) so he would have money for post secondary, and later found out there was a disability savings plan (rdsp) that the government put money in regardless of my contribution which is key cause money has been tight and the government puts in a lot more than they do for an resp. The benefit is he can use the plan for either school or medical bills. I did this because I didn't accept what the doctors said, and all I want is for God to prove them wrong through my son. Well a friend of mine jus called and said God gave him a dream where he saw me in a stadium but didn't see kaykay, then he realized we were at a graduation. Confirming that the doctors are wrong, he will live and he will graduate. I've battled schools who suggested he be placed in special needs school, he was diagnosed in January with adhd and I've been battling ever since to get the help he needs, as much as I have support from family and friends, I am only one person and no one lives close enough to help, so every time these teachers attack with words it cuts deep cause I'm doing the best I can to get him to school on time after a night where he didn't sleep or a morning he was throwing up. I jus gotta give God all the praise, cause he jus

answered prayers and has encouraged me to keep going, I'm right where he wants me to be and I will keep fighting for kaykay cause God has a plan, and in the end it will all be worth it. I read a scripture the other day Hebrews 12:11 no discipline is enjoyable while it is happening, it's painful! But afterwards there will be a peaceful harvest of right living for those who are trained this way. I will jus keep training and preparing kayshaun for the battle ahead with Gods direction. ...I'm in awe of his mercy and I'm crying with happiness...

June 3, 2014 ·
My strength comes from God

Looking back on my nights in the hospital I remember trying to sleep on a makeshift bed or chair. I remember how I barely went home for showers. I remember how I would quick clean in the bathroom cause I was too afraid to leave him at the hospital. I didn't want him to think that I was abandoning him. I needed to make sure he knew I was always there. We'd had many people visit and bring food which I was truly grateful for, now we were home and didn't have the same support. I didn't have a nurse to watch him while I ran downstairs to grab him food. It was just us two which was great but with it being just the two of us, my body was gettin run down. I wasn't eating properly, I wasn't sleeping well, I was stressed out and I had gotten really sick. I neglected myself making sure Kaykay had everything he needed. The hardest thing for me was not being able to cook the food he needed cause I always made sure he was ok first and I had literally pushed myself to the point that I couldn't do anything at all for him. Mentally and physically it was a struggle.

One night, I needed to get Kaykay food and I wanted to get soup to help with my cold but it was too late at night and too cold to bring him outside. I lived on a corner that had at least two 24-hour restaurants. One being Subway and the other McDonalds. I was on the phone with

Romeo and he convinced me to run across the street to get food while he stayed with Kaykay on the phone. Having both a landline and cell phone meant that while Kaykay stayed and talked to Romeo, if anything were to happen Romeo could at least message me on my cell so I could run back home. Subway was literally a 30 second walk from my building. I had never left Kaykay alone at home but I knew he was the type of kid that would sit in one spot until I returned. I trusted that Romeo would keep him talking until I got back. I left quickly and returned to find Kaykay and Romeo deep in conversation. *Cute.* Romeo was more surprised than anything that Kaykay remembered who he was and that they were able to maintain a conversation. That night was such a blessing to me. Those were the comforting moments that kept me going. With the ongoing stress I was sick, I was gaining weight, but I always smiled around him. I wanted to do something special for Kaykay so I looked into purchasing him a bed in the shape of a car. It was rough, but God was greater. I was finally able to gain access to his resp that allowed me to alleviate some of the money stress so I was able to adequately support myself while I took care of him.

CHAPTER SIXTY-SEVEN

July 2014

And now there remain: faith [abiding trust in God and His promises], hope [confident expectation of eternal salvation], love [unselfish love for others growing out of God's love for me], these three [the choicest graces]; but the greatest of these is love.
1 CORINTHIANS 13:13

Kaykay's home doctor had come for a visit but it was short lived as she advised us to go back to the hospital. I watched as she bravely tried to keep a smile on for him as she said goodbye knowing this might have been her last time seeing him.

July 17, 2014 ·
Hey so kayshaun and I are in the hospital he jus did blood work and the results are that his kidneys and liver aren't functioning. They haven't said much else to me other than the fact that the results are really bad...please jus keep us in prayer. The battle is not over, we are still in God's hands. Thanks

July 17, 2014 ·
They think he only has the weekend to live based on his blood work...God will show up this weekend!

July 17, 2014 ·
Even though I post the update, I am not in agreement with death, I pray against all reports of death, kayshaun will live well past expectations, this is jus another bump in the road. God is good all the time, no fear!!!

July 17, 2014 ·

Since there's nothing medically the team can do we are basically going to be at sick kids until he passes (they give him 1-2 days) or until he gets better (God is more than able!) so if you need us, we will be here on the cardiology floor, thanks for all the prayers

Once again, we were faced with predictions of death. I brought him to the hospital and they looked at me like I was expecting them to work miracles. The doctor asked me "What do you want us to do?" I stared back at her while my mind was racing. I'm not sure how to even answer this question. *Hmm iuno? Take care of my child?* Not knowing what else to say I said to her "We have tickets from Make-A-Wish to attend the Honda Indy tomorrow". She then presents me with two options, we could either go back home or we could be admitted to the hospital. At home it was only me and I didn't know what else to do, at the hospital at least they would monitor him and I would have support. She says, "Well if we admit you then you forfeit going to the Honda Indy" *So wha? Is she making sense right now? So, admit him then. Is she really trying to convince me to not admit him? He needs help. I need help.* "Ok admit him" I began to understand that because they expected him to die they weren't willing to put in the extra effort. Once they admitted us the doctor came back in and said "We're gonna see what we can do about gettin you a day pass so that you can go to the Honda Indy, we'll get you a ride there and back." *Oh, what happened to the forfeit? Did I just call your bluff? You think I would pick Honda ova my child's life? But since you found a way to make it work, good.* That night his doctor signed off on allowing us to go to the Honda Indy. I longed for the French doctor we had met back in Feb. She was way nicer, it was obvious how far removed this doctor was from the situation. Anyway, even though I hadn't heard from Kendrick, I figured I'd just keep sending him updates.

July 17th 2014
Cola
Kaykay is back in the hospital, they give him one to two

days
Kendrick
What? When did it get so bad?
Cola
I jus brought him in today. It's only been a week since he's had trouble and he has had home nurses and doctors monitoring him
Kendrick
Can't they be wrong?
Cola
Well God always proves them wrong but they did the blood work today which is where they came up with the diagnosis. Your welcome to come see him
Kendrick
Sick kids?
Cola
Ye.

He stopped replying. *What is goin on, I just told him his child is dying. Does he not care at all?*

Cola
What yu thinking? You're so quiet?

He finally responded later on that day

Kendrick
How are things?
Cola
He's spitting up but in good spirits make a wish and Sick Kids let him come to Honda Indy for a couple hours . His stomach is hurting but otherwise ok, and I think they wanna transfer him to a hospice
Kendrick
Hospice?
Cola
A home for children who are dying
Kendrick
When?

Cola
I haven't made the decision yet. It's either hospital hospice or home
Kendrick
What time is visiting hours?
Cola
It's flexible cause they think he's dying

No response and he didn't show up. I know his birthday was the next day but still.

July 18, 2014 ·
And we are off to Honda Indy!

We had just met James Hinchcliffe! We were really excited that he got to meet a racecar driver. After we said goodbye I asked Kaykay "You wanna go ride the dirt bike or you wanna go back and rest?" to my complete shock he said "I wanna ride the bike." *Damn I thought fo sure he was gonna say he was tired.* He had never ridden a dirt bike but he was hella excited. We get over to where the bikes were and luckily it wasn't too crowded. Even with the IV in his arm he put all the equipment on and went out there like a champ. He even caught the attention of CBC news for the amazing job he did. If you ask Kaykay how his day went he woulda said...it was awesome!

July 18, 2014
Update: despite a lil throwing up and his stomach hurting he is in good spirits today! Amen! and the doctors are talking about moving him to a hospice...

The topic of hospice came up today. I wasn't sure how to feel about it. *What's a hospice?* This whole experience has been draining. It has been mostly me fighting against what doctors said or fighting against them sending us home or fighting to get admitted or fighting to stay. You would think it should be easier but once a child was on the verge of dying with an underlying condition it was as if people had thrown in the towel. Since I refused to take him home they came back with another option of hospice. *Why?* In their opinion he's been dying. *But he hasn't died, so why move him? Why move him to a facility with minimal care? Is that all his life is worth at this time?* I refused the hospice and forced them to come up with another option. As for now, he had a great day and we stayed in the hospital. At least his team of nurses were amazing. My child, my choice. Make the next move.

July 19, 2014 ·
Ahhhhh God's grace hmmmm so good, when you trust him amen! Doctors say he is a MYSTERY this morning, they dont know what's going on but he's doing BETTER today, we may go home tomorrow. 2 days without ANY medication and his appetite increased he's peeing on his own AMMMMEEEENNNNNN! TRUST IN GOD! DO NOT FEAR

Tara had officially become an adopted member of our family. She was over every day for hours at a time. She was over so much Kaykay began calling her aunty Tara and he genuinely appreciated whenever she was around. Plus, he loved her dog. Tara asked the questions I didn't want to and was always looking to create new ways to make him smile. She had posted information about Kaykay and his story and his love for cars while asking people to donate cars to cheer him up. Many people were touched by his story and answered her plea by sending several toy cars, car collectables, drawings of cars, you name it. It was like Christmas in July.

Christmas was actually his favorite holiday. Randomly one day he yells "Aahhhh" we jump up and ask what happened, he said, "I miss Christmas" and sheds one single tear. He still had months to go before Christmas came back around. With all the toys that came in I told him "With all these cars I'm not buying you any for Christmas." He groans and says, "That's why I didn't want to open my cars, can I save them all for Christmas so I can be surprised." He's sooo dramatic yet he still opened a few of them regardless. Besides the toy cars that came in Tara had arranged for a group of Ruff Rider bikers and car riders to come and show off their cars to him. Right outside the doors of Sick Kids Kaykay had his own personal car show. It was dope! Every time was more impressive. At the end of the day the smile on his face made everything we had dealt with worthwhile.

July 20, 2014 ·
Update: to be honest the doctors don't have much of a plan at this moment, they've stopped all meds even cancelled future appointments, so we are going to go home and continue to pray for full recovery! He's gonna be fine! Thank you for all prayers and encouragements! God is teaching me a lot and my heart and love for people continually grows.

July 20, 2014 ·
Good news the blood work came back and his kidney function is back to normal. No more kidney failure! God is good!, his liver and heart still need work, but baby steps God is restoring his body

July 20, 2014 ·
Y'all are witnessing this miracle no denying its God the same God who moved mountains took a child with creatinine levels of 400 and in kidney failure on Thursday to normal levels and normal kidney function by Sunday. This isn't about me pushing my religion...I dont belong to a religion I have a relationship with God and an understanding that he loves me and never let's me down. Undeniable truths!

July 20, 2014 ·
Let me explain, kayshaun had a sleep study this Wednesday at Sick Kids, and they were so sure he was going to DIE that they CANCELLED the appointment.....! When God speaks, no one else can change the destiny!

July 20, 2014 ·
We are home!!

July 20, 2014 ·
Just called the ambulance headed back to the hospital with chest pain and fast heart beat pray for us...round 2 !

We weren't even home for long before he was sick again. Maybe it was something at the house because we spent most of our time in the hospital. I started thinking maybe our house wasn't the best place for him. *Maybe all those sprays and powders for the roaches?* It may just be coincidental but these new health problems started once we moved downtown and had to do all that work to get the house to living standards. Obviously, it's nothing I could even prove cause he had an underlying issue but with his immune system so weak, who's to say it didn't affect him?

One of the community organizations that Tara ran was an organization called the F-you project. The F stands for Forgiveness, *how fitting.* As part of this project she creates safe spaces to talk about forgiveness, what it looks like and how to establish forgiveness in our daily lives. This year the F-you project was a part of Youth day and Tara asked Kaykay if he wanted to be a part of the special day to which he responded yes. When the day came she brought him on stage and asked him one question: "What does forgiveness mean to you?" He paused too long, and I thought he got too scared to answer. *Please...Lord please just let him answer the question.* In the smallest voice he says, "It means saying sorry to someone else" *That's my baby.* He got up on the stage in front of all those people an gave his own definition of forgiveness.

July 21, 2014 ·
Been a hectic morning but kayshaun is doing ok, we are unsure of what the chest pains and headaches and increased heart rate is but still trusting God for guidance we will do some heart tests today or tomorrow and ill keep updating. Thanks

July 22, 2014 ·
I'm sorry I'm bout to get mad in this hospital. Ain't nobody hearing me yet..tomorrow is gonna be a different day. Update: can't hold food down, he's back on IV fluid, his blood pressure dropped to 67 his sats are low, he's having constant headaches and he's constipated...still giving God praise for peace and sanity we will come out of this by his strength and love...

Sometimes we gotta get a lil crazy while we fight the good fight. God was still in control in the spiritual world. In this physical world the doctors and some nurses were getting on my last damn nerve. His sats (saturation levels) dropped really low and they were holding their breath waiting for him to go. They brought me in a room and tried to convince me to go along with their plan. The way they worded it sounded like they were tryna say they've let me play around long enough and live in denial and it was time to wake up. In the most diplomatic way I said "Y'all keep tellin me he's gonna die and he hasn't. Every time you think he's gonna die he lives past your expectations. Stop waiting for him to die and figure out a way to help him. Don't give up on him just cause he has muscular dystrophy. Figure out a way to help him beyond that diagnosis. He ain't dead yet and he's not gonna die. We ain't leaving to go home or to go to a hospice, so figure something out." I wasn't playing games anymore. I had had enough of their 'laid back wait till he dies' attitude and I was ready to give em hell until something was done. Within a few hours they had scheduled him for a blood transfusion. *Yep...try me again.*

July 22, 2014 ·
Update: kayshaun is going to get better today God is in control

July 24, 2014 ·

Update: doing a blood transfusion and iv food and breathing test tonight, kayshaun has been getting lots of rest and is improving

July 24, 2014 ·
Pray for me, I'm feeling weak and tired ..

July 25, 2014 ·
Ugh mi need sum lime an honey an sum red pea soup

The stress was wearing down my immune system. It was all worth it if it meant things were gonna get done, but I was struggling.

July 25, 2014 ·
My goal for today that we will accomplish is for kaykay to start eating by mouth. He has been progressing well over that last few days, We will be here over the weekend. My long term goal is for him to leave the hospital completely healed, without feeding tube, or iv, or oxygen. God is able!

July 25, 2014 ·
Mid day report: ate half a slice of bread and kept it down yay! Praise God for even the small victories. Still has extra fluid in his body but so far he has peed out more than he did yesterday. Slow improvement towards total body restoration. Amen! What a magnificent God, oh and my symptoms are drying up and strength is returning, thanks for the prayers.

July 25, 2014 ·
We are going to be here at least until Monday, we are running the breathing test tonight to see if it improves oxygen and heart function. This is my belief and my prayer for the weekend, that by the time we leave this

hospital kayshaun will have complete body restoration and healing. From Duchenne muscular dystrophy, from heart failure, from adhd, from seizures, that his liver will return to normal function and size, that his stomach and lungs will not be filled with fluid that his kidney levels will be normal and that he will no longer struggle with constipation. In the name of Jesus every illness will leave his body this weekend and we will leave this hospital healed. We have been here since last Thursday fighting for break through. I can picture kayshaun running and free and healed. So please pray and stand in agreement with me this weekend. Please share this post and let it reach as many people as possible, God is going to work some miracles in my son's life.

July 26, 2014 ·
Kaykay says: I am happy and I'm thinking happy things, how are you doing mommy ? love him soo much, always looking out for me.

July 26, 2014 ·
So I said kaykay I'm gonna take a nap ..and he says Ye I'm gonna let you take a nap....Hmm ok lol

July 26, 2014 ·
Kaykay went from 0 to 100 today, Amen! Eating, drinking, peeing, he even walked to the play room. For the first time since Sunday he's strong enough to walk a short distance out of the room, let's keep praying cause God is moving

Never give up! No matter how bleak. No matter how depressed. No matter how frustrated. Never give up! It's never too late for miracles. Even just having this outlet and community on facebook helped me balance out my emotions.

July 26, 2014 ·
Funny moments today
Kaykay calls the nurse for assistance to get to the bathroom, then tells the nurse, "i need some privacy please"...Lol wha does he knows bout privacy?
After we put on his breathing mask for the night...kaykay says: this smells weird....it smells like someone's bum... Hmmm I had to laugh out loud for that one..at least im getting my baby boy back to his normal personality. Love him.!! Thank you Lord

July 27, 2014 ·
Early morning update: kaykay is doing good today, still peeing, and talking a lot which are good signs. The iv has caused his arm to be swollen and he has a bit of a fever but he's handling it like a big man and he's wrapped his arm in a prayer cloth he calls Jesus Complete healing!

I was extremely mad that the nurse failed to check his IV properly and it had caused his whole hand to swell. Thank God my sister was with me cause she was able to check and bring attention to the situation. Damn I felt like I couldn't even trust the staff sometimes. For the most part though, there were amazing nurses. They kept me calm and they encouraged me to fight back and some even tried to fight on my behalf. I developed a special connection with the nurses on 4D at Sick Kids. I won't ever forget them.

July 27, 2014 ·
Mid-day update: jus woke up from a nap, doing well, says he feel a free not being attached to the iv machine. Goal for the rest of the day is to get him to eat way more and drink more or it will be an extended visit and he will be back on the iv.

July 27, 2014 ·

Kaykay jus threw up his food and says: this is the worst day ever, now i'm never gonna go home. Can you pray for my me please? So I've prayed and I'm extending this to everyone to help pray cause He is scared he will have to have the iv put back in.

By now he was tired of the hospital. I was just as sad that he was trapped inside the walls of a hospital and a bed. I kept telling myself it was for his own good cause I refused to go home and wait for him to die, this was what we had signed up for. The staff could tell a difference in his behavior and would suggest activities we could do in the hospital to keep his spirits up. We got him car puzzles to do, we had him paint, he did handprints in a mold and he did a 3D sculpture. The 3D sculpture was my personal favorite. We had never done anything like that before and there was a nurse on one of the lower levels who happened to know how to create them. He did one on his own giving a thumbs up and another holding my hand. *Unbreakable bond.* That was one of the most meaningful activities we had done.

July 28, 2014 ·
Good news we should be going home on Friday...after two long weeks in the hospital with ups and downs he is looking good and talking a lot and walking to the playroom God's grace and love is amazing. I know he was upset last night and even he was starting to doubt but he believed in the power of prayer and today has shown the importance of never letting go of God.

July 28, 2014 ·
This is gonna be a week of praise and thanksgiving the end is near

July 31, 2014 ·
Still doing good, we should be leaving the hospital

tomorrow

CHAPTER SIXTY-EIGHT

AUGUST 2014

There is no fear in love [dread does not exist]. But perfect (complete, full-grown) love drives out fear, because fear involves [the expectation of divine] punishment, so the one who is afraid [of God's judgment] is not perfected in love [has not grown into a sufficient understanding of God's love].
1 JOHN 4:18

August 1, 2014 ·
Been admitted since July 17th and we finally get to go home. Praise God!

August 1, 2014 ·
We are home!!! God has beeen really good to us.

August 2, 2014 ·
You know that moment when you just get angry at sickness and medicine...i'm so over it...building life back from scratch

I had been praying constantly for months. We had been back only a day but the change in his body was enough to temporarily break me. I decided to go to my parents' house after such a long time in the hospital so I could get some more help from them. Only thing was my parents lived in a house instead of an apartment which meant there were stairs. Kaykay was so weak he couldn't even climb or slide down the stairs I had watched him climb so confidently months and years prior. My dad had offered to carry him up and down the stairs whenever he needed but watching how much his body ballooned changed me. We had family from Jamaica over and I felt like I had to try even harder to keep a smile on my face.

Today I couldn't. I went to the basement where no one could hear me and I bawled. For the first time in my life I understood why some mothers resorted to killing their children in hopes of relieving them from suffering. I don't agree with it, would never do it, I could never do it...but I understood it.

It was devastating to watch Kaykay lose complete function in his legs. His body was filled with so much fluid it looked painful. I hated how helpless I was. I hated every moment of it. As I cried I told God "Just take me instead. Please, don't let him suffer, please just take me instead. I can't watch this no more" In a heartbeat I would easily take the pain so that Kaykay didn't have to feel any of it. I would give anything to have him back to his regular personality - playful, happy and inquisitive. This kind of pain hit the depths of my soul and I couldn't control anything in that moment. Just as I was losing grip there was a peace that took over and I was calm. It was so eerie. Once I finished crying I tried to come up with some kind of plan. I started looking up different natural remedies that could help with some of the symptoms he was having. I was desperate to find anything that could help or give me direction to ease some of the pain. I looked for a natural blood thinner, a natural diuretic, vitamins that could boost his immune system and liquid sources of nutrients for times when he couldn't hold down any food. I was desperate.

August 5, 2014 ·
Update: kaykay has been resting his body and doing well overall, we got nothing to lose. Jus going on the up and up God is good. Putting natural life into action.

While reading my bible I felt like God was saying to me whatever happens was not what it appeared to be and to remain calm.

August 5, 2014
A lil swollen but still smiling, love him!

August 9, 2014 ·
GoFundMe
Growing up I've learned not to ask people for help. But i've reached a point in life where the "village help" could make a life or death difference in a world run by pharmaceutical companies.

We were back in Toronto awaiting a visit from his rehab doctor. From what she saw it didn't look good. She cried. She had gotten so used to him she couldn't help but get upset over how bad the situation looked, she said bye knowing it was for the last time too

August 14, 2014 ·
Go back to hospital

August 14, 2014 ·
We are going back to the hospital. He is Coughing up blood, they said there's not much they can do and they feel like he's dying so today will be a day to praise God for all Hes done. Not even prayers asking for healing cause Hes healed, today we will celebrate and thank God for what is already done.

August 14, 2014 ·
After you've done all you can...you just stand

August 15, 2014 ·
Still standing, no changes except he hasn't coughed up blood this morning, he is still having trouble breathing but I am still rejoicing and giving thanks that he only needs a lil bit of oxygen to help breath. He doesnt need a breathing tube, nor feeding tube, he is still very capable on his own. God is great...today will be another praise day.

August 15, 2014 ·
The peace of God is so important, I jus watched the fear of death in the eyes of the nurse as she reports he's getting worse and there's nothing else they can do. They feel stuck. I thank God that he has given me the strength to be at peace. I'm excited for the constant miracles! Praise God

With all the pain from coughing he looked exhausted but was still playful. The doctor had suggested giving him a small dose of morphine at one point and although my family was for it I refused. I was still firm in not wanting to give him any type of heavy drug. My family was questioning my decisions, they wanted to know how I could just watch the pain and not do anything. To them it seemed like I was being selfish. *Maybe I am being selfish*? Sometimes I wish I had a husband or his dad to support me and to help me make the decisions. Feeling guilty I caved and decided it would be ok to give him the smallest dose of morphine.

After months of back and forth Kendrick's mom, Kaykay's other grandma came to visit him today. This was her second time being introduced to him and I was happy she had made it out. I stayed in close contact with his lil sister but to see his mom come meant that she finally accepted the truth. She brought him the coolest headset and he spent the afternoon pretending he was a race car driver.

Kaykay had this saying that I was super mommy. I took care of him and did anything he needed me to do. He was my everything. My mom, dad and sister came to spend that night with me. We all jus sat and listened to music; Kaykay was tired. He was in and out of sleep mumbling along the way so we let him relax. He looked peaceful like his body was finally getting the rest it needed. Early the next morning my dad had to leave to perform a wedding ceremony. Before they left my mom kissed Kaykay and said, "Hey my prince I'll be back to see you a little later." Within an hour we woke up to the sun shining in the room.

Kaykay woke up and said he had to pee so I jumped up and called the nurse to help remove him from all the machines so I could walk him to the bathroom. The nurse arrives and unhooks him from everything as my sister is talking to him. She asks him if he needs to pee and he sounds a bit incoherent but still formulates the word yes. As we lift him off the bed my sister notices the bed is wet. She asks Kaykay if he wet the bed and he says yes. As the nurse an I get him to stand up his legs give out and he falls back in my arms. As I put him back on the bed with my arm still around him he takes his last breath. We try calling his name but he doesn't respond. We shake him but he doesn't respond. My sister screams and I jump up and start praying as the nurse runs to call everyone. I had rescinded my DNR request months before so they began to revive him.

> August 16, 2014 ·
> Everyone who can see this pray....His heart jus stopped and Hes coding

> August 16, 2014 ·
> They are about to pronounce him dead...but he's jus sleeping...keep praying.
> JOHN 11:11 (AMP)
> He said this, and after that said, "Our friend Lazarus has fallen asleep; but I am going there to wake him."

The moment he took his last breath all I could recall was to remain calm and pray. I never actually thought he was going to die with the amount of close calls we had gotten. Even the doctors had been made aware of how "lucky" he had been over the past few months. They worked on him for as long as they could before asking me for my final decision. I kept praying.

> August 16, 2014 ·
> Time of death 9:38....now lets wait for the miracle

Over and over they said he was gonna die and he

always bounced back. *Bounce back baby!*

> August 16, 2014 ·
> God is greater than death...please dont lose hope, please keep praying and stand with me while we await the miracle...

Since February they've called death on him and he hasn't died. Prayer has kept him alive thus far, prayer can bring him back. *Bounce back baby please!*

> August 16, 2014 ·
> For those at home praying Ezekiel 37:1-10

Keep praying, miracles are all around, we've had so many miracles over the past six months. *Bounce back baby!*

> August 16, 2014 ·
> Psalm 91....keep praying

As the doctors were forced to stop and looked at me with despair and sadness I had so much peace in my heart. I kept praying. *He's not gone.* I called my parents and texted my friends who weren't on social media and sat and waited for people to show up. They were visibly upset by text or by phone, but I couldn't take on their emotions, all I did was sit in prayer. I couldn't explain the reasoning but I was calm. I heard God say it was going to be alright but I never thought he was going to die. I remember reading scriptures about when God had healed Lazarus. The possibility of a miracle of that magnitude filled my mind. I mean we sing all the time that God is great, and we read about miracles in the Bible, so why couldn't He do that for us? *If we have faith even as a mustard seed we can move mountains.* Since Kaykay wasn't healed in the natural world then I could only depend on healing in the spiritual world first.

I began praying and reading different texts surrounding resurrection miracles and instances when it occurred. The God I had come to personally know since February was not capable of being placed in a box. His love was mighty, His peace was indescribable, and His miracles were awesome wonders. Fear and doubt basically tied God's hands together whenever he wanted to bless us. How could I truly manifest anything if I didn't truly believe it was coming? I prepared for an apartment that I didn't have and God provided. Whenever I didn't have food or a bill was due the money would come or the food would be provided. I applied to only one school, got in and succeeded, there was no plan B, God was everything and anything I needed at all times. This situation was no different to me, I began to pray and believe and prepare for Kaykay to come back.

I had the room set up with gospel music and I sat calmly and waited for people to arrive. I changed my clothes, put a summer dress on full of color and sat by the window across from where Kaykay lay on the bed. *He looks so peaceful. He looks like he is just sleeping. I can't wait for him to wake up.* I couldn't allow myself to cry cause I didn't want him to see me upset when he got up. As each guest came to the room to visit I hugged each one and calmly told them if they were going to cry they needed to do so in the hallway. I wasn't trying to be rude but I was holding things together an being surrounded by crying faces wasn't helping. My family and friends came and the Love Movement group showed up and began to pray with me. The main goal was to keep good vibes and positive spiritual energy flowing through the room. Since I was believing for resurrection I didn't want anyone to say goodbye or R.I.P. for fear it would cast doubt.

As much as I would not force my opinions on anyone I also expected people to respect my beliefs. My mom and some of my friends who didn't understand it felt very uncomfortable. They would have preferred I kicked out the people praying in order to let them see Kaykay. *I don't know why they won't just go in. We are all family and friends.* I never stopped anyone from seeing Kaykay but I let everyone who visited know that they were more than welcomed to enter the room as is. My mother tried to act like I was ignoring my family since I was unwilling to kick out T and The Love Movement group, but the truth was that the praying and the music kept me at peace. I didn't want to be run by my family.

August 16, 2014 ·
Please please stand with me, I am not crazy stand with me please
JOB 19:19 (AMP)
"All the men of my council hate me; Those I love have turned against me.

I could never give up on Kaykay, I will keep praying until the results manifest and he's back in my arms. Keep praying, he's always beat the odds. *Bounce back baby!*

August 16, 2014 ·
Start thanking God, it's not over jus thank God for the miracle coming

I was used to miracles, my faith had increased so much in the past 6 months that anything and everything was possible. Who else but God could do this thing for us? I awaited my next miracle.

With the ups come the downs and even though I was in a state of peace I almost hit my mother. She pushes buttons too much. She likes to get loud and speak her mind without filter. Since I was ignoring her request to kick people out she got up in my face waving her finger, giving me attitude. She felt as though she couldn't say goodbye with everyone around. She started yelling about how I was disrespectful and putting my friends before my family. I wasn't in the mood. I had been smiling the whole day until she started up. We had to be physically separated. Outta respect T had and the few others had chosen to leave temporarily to allow those who wanted to say goodbye some time. Either way, the music stayed on. Not agreeing with me was one thing but trying to tear me and my opinions down was aggravating. They didn't have to agree with my decisions or agree to my prayer for resurrection but what I did expect was for people to respect my wishes. We stayed in the room for hours praying and believing he was going to wake up. I was in a state of shock but the prayer and singing was keeping my spirit calm. The continued peace even allowed me to endure watching the blood pour from his eyes as he laid still on the bed. Somehow, I still didn't crack in that moment.

When it came time for him to be moved downstairs I was heartbroken but not defeated. He still had not gotten up and I didn't want to leave the hospital without him. I didn't want him to think that I was leaving him behind. I would never do that. It was a very numbing experience leaving him at the hospital. I kept looking back for him expecting him to be there. I stared out the car window vowing to return to get him and bring him home. He couldn't be gone. This wasn't the end for him. It wasn't the end for me. It couldn't be the end of us.

August 17, 2014 ·
Please keep praying. God is in control! Christ can do all things. Keep the faith dont waiver! it looks tough but dont give up

I had made the decision to do a water fast until Kaykay woke up. From the moment I left him at the hospital I was fasting.

August 18, 2014 ·
It is well...

It's been two days and my soul was still at peace, I knew this wasn't the end. I left him at the hospital but he's coming back. *He'll understand why I had to leave once we're reunited. Bounce back baby!*

August 18 2014 4:12pm
Kendrick
Hi
Cola
Hi, How are you
Kendrick

I'm so sorry about kaykay. Not too well
Cola
He's your son
Kendrick
I know
Cola
Don't beat yourself up
Kendrick
Why not? I deserve way worse
Cola
Well I won't be the one to do it to you. God is taking care of him and it's not the time to get at you for anything. Plus God told me he's gonna bring him back and he's not gonna get buried. The funeral is this week but God said Hes gonna do a miracle. As his father you need to pray please . It's not over . You can have a second chance , you jus gotta be there for him. I love you I don't hate you
Kendrick
Thank you so much.. And I have been and will continue to pray

My mother was having a hard time coping with the loss of Kaykay and understanding my newfound faith. She was angry and had lots to say. When I woke up I overheard my mother telling my friend who was at my house that I was in a cult. I walked out of my room and said, "Please stop saying I'm in a cult cause that's not what was happening." I was doin nothing different than what my mom had been doing for years - prayer and bible study. The minute I turned my back she had begun saying the exact same things I had asked her not to. She acted like I wasn't even standing right there. "Didn't I jus ask you to stop saying that? Did I not just explain to you that I'm not in a cult? Why do you keep talking about it? Stop saying that"

She then followed me into my room and said, "What about arrangements for the grave?" "No need cause Kaykay's coming back." *It's true, he is though. Why would I need to make arrangements?* So, then she says, "I REBUKE YOU, YOU'RE CRAZY." I yelled back "HOW AM I CRAZY?

We read in the bible so many times about resurrection, who is to say it can't be happening now again? There's so many Bible scriptures that I read as proof" "Those are just stories" *What?!* "WHAT DO YOU MEAN JUST STORIES? That's been my whole childhood, we GREW up on these 'stories'. You don't have to believe but don't call me crazy or say I'm in a cult cause I'm not. Kaykay's gonna be healed" "What kind of mother are you that if your son would come back you'd want to see him come back in pain" "PAIN? Do you not understand how God works? When he comes back he's not coming back in pain. God's gonna heal him." By now my dad had entered the room cause it was jus a yellin match back and forth, he was tryna calm my mom who was looking at me crazy an yelling. I saw nothing but rage. My dad looked torn between taking my mom's side or mine. He hugged me as I broke down before leaving the room with my mom and it was clear to me he had chosen her. *That's fine. This ain't new.* I continued to read my Bible, I prayed, I fasted, and I kept even closer to God. *How could she say that to me? How could she ask me what kinda mother am I? How can any mother say that to another?* Even though they were physically around me it was nothing but battles. *How was it all falling apart now when our faith was being tested?* It wasn't jus them though, I faced ridicule from friends and extended family. Only a few of my friends understood my level of faith and supported me through the process. Even friends who didn't agree with me never questioned me or made comments towards me, they supported me regardless of right or wrong.

It was my daily devotion that kept me at peace. A book by Joyce Meyers had been donated to me and I was holding on to every word.

> <u>Rooted and Grounded in God</u>
>
> Be well balanced (temperate, sober of mind), be vigilant and cautious at all times; for that enemy of yours, the devil, roams around like a lion roaring [in fierce hunger], seeking to seize upon and devour. Withstand him; be firm in faith [against his onset--rooted, established, strong, immovable and

determined], knowing that the same (identical) sufferings are appointed to your brotherhood (the whole body of Christians) throughout the world.

- *1 peter 5:8-9*

Joyce Meyers explained

To be temperate is to be self-controlled. And to be sober of mind is to be level-headed. So here you and I are told to be well-balanced, self-controlled, level-headed, rooted, established, strong, immovable and determined. According to this passage, how are we going to defeat the devil and withstand his physical and emotional onsets upon us? By being rooted and grounded in Christ. Satan may come against us with feelings, but we don't have to submit to our emotions. We can stand firmly against them even while they rage against us and even within us.

When problems arise--and they will from time to time--we are not to assume that the Lord will intervene without an invitation and take care of all our problems for us. We are to pray and ask Him to change out circumstances. Then we are to remain constant and unchanging, which will be a sign to the enemy of this impending downfall and destruction. Do you know why our constancy and fearlessness are signs to Satan that he will fail? Because he knows that the only way he can overcome a believer is through deception and intimidation. How can he threaten someone who has no fear of him? How can he deceive someone who recognizes his lies and refuses to believe them? What good does it do him to try to stir up fear and anger or depression in someone who chooses to stand firmly on the Word of God? When the devil sees his tactics are not working, he realizes he is failing and will be utterly defeated.

Joyce Meyers, *New Day, New You,* (Word Alive; 1st edition Oct. 24 2007)

I just needed to keep standing on what I believed to

be true. The process of planning this funeral was very much left up to Tara and any other friends willing to help ease the stress off of my family. A lot of work was being done behind the scenes in support of us. I had churches praying, a Go Fund me page started, and Tara helped find a funeral home that would work with my social assistance. Even the Remix Project had stepped up to donate and support me during this time period. The outpouring of love was amazing. I never understood how many people were touched by our story up until that point. Even in my stance with resurrection, the support from strangers was growing. Faith was being challenged and it was unbelievable to see how many people's faith had risen with me at such a crucial time.

The funeral was planned for the week later. My parents took care of looking for a church that had a reception area as well and found a newly renovated building in the west end. To rent the church for the funeral was $1000. *Apparently I was gettin a $500 discount. Fo real? $1000 for a church?* I didn't have money like that laying around. I thought I would of had more pull because I was surrounded by pastors but no such luck. I didn't have much time to search for other options. The $1000 was supposed to include a kitchen but what was provided was a kitchenette barely able to accommodate all our needs.

August 20, 2014
submitting to God has given me such a peace during this time, thank you to everyone who reached out. I am standing on God's promises, living by faith, expecting the change and humbled that God loves me and is working through me to bless others.

Even though I believed Kaykay was coming back I followed my parents to the funeral home in order to pick out the casket. Even picking a casket was a hassle. My mother argued that she wanted to buy something fancy but I did not have the luxury of additional money to spend. All that was available to me was the caskets that welfare provided. It didn't matter to me as long as the casket was white. I don't like making such a big deal about death. *It's jus a box, why do I need to spend so much extra money? I'm not in the mood for arguing*. After arguing over the casket, next was his outfit. *Why everything gotta be a fight? This shit is tired and exhausting. Can I just have my own opinion?* I wanted Kaykay to lay in something that made him happy. I opted to put him in a cars pajama with slippers and his cars pillow. My mother wanted him in a suit.

Tara had a brilliant idea to decorate the white coffin with cars stickers which made the experience very personal. I needed that, I needed to feel like things had not changed that much even though they were very different. Once we went through all the details it was time for me to sign the papers. It was an outer body experience. It was as if I was standing outside my body watching my hand sign my signature for the casket.

I had T and some otha friends come over to help keep me company. Even when I was surrounded by family I still needed friends to keep me grounded.

August 20, 2014 ·
Come expecting a miracle, get ready because God is ready to move and open many hearts,

August 21, 2014 ·
Kay means happy and rejoicing
Shaun means gift from God
Antwoine means highly praiseworthy
Isaiah means God's helper
Bennett means little blessed one
I miss my baby...he's coming home soon
PSALM 6:4 (AMP)
Return, O LORD, rescue my soul; Save me because of Your [unfailing] steadfast love and mercy.
PSALM 119:113 (AMP)
I hate those who are double-minded, But I love and treasure Your law.
PROVERBS 10:12 (AMP)
Hatred stirs up strife, But love covers and overwhelms all

transgressions [forgiving and overlooking another's faults].

I gathered with a few people the night before the funeral in preparation for the resurrection service. Out of all the pastors around me I decided to ask my current pastor if he would perform the ceremony. I had also asked him if he was on board with me praying for resurrection to which he said yes. He let me know that since it was last minute there would be a fee of $250 but he was gonna raise the funds in church to help offset the cost. *Like I knew he was gonna die? What's last minute mean? Anyway, all I heard him say was the cost was gonna be taken care of.* We sat discussing expectations and how the service was gonna go. He kept asking me "If he doesn't come back are you gonna be ok?" "Ye, I'll be ok" *I'm not crazy. I'm not gonna lose my mind. God's got me.* As I sat there tryna stay focus I hear God say, "Well done". He was proud of my stance and my ability to stand firm. By now I had been water fasting for 7 days and I felt as strong as ever...mentally and physically. Now I was just ready for my son to come home. I couldn't inspire anyone if I didn't stand fearlessly against everyone.

I had an outpour of facebook messages that were beautifully encouraging to read:

> "Hi there, I don't know you, but I've been following you and your son's story for a while now. I have to tell you that you both have touched my heart immensely. The faith of yourself and your son is just mind blowing. Such an inspiration. I'm believing with you and praying reverently that God will perform a miracle this weekend. I'm expecting it! Miracles, signs and wonders. That because of this souls will come to Christ. To God be the glory. God Bless you my sister in Christ."
>
> "THANK YOU for allowing me into your personal space. Your son has truly touched me. There was a moment in my life that I gave up hope & could barely force a smile. Seeing your son...even yourself.... smiling at a time like this.... I will carry

this moment forever as a source of strength if ever I feel defeated. Your family will remain in my prayers. Such a beautiful spirit you are. Thank you again!"

August 23, 2014 ·
I lost my best friend today...8 years we spent together. Love you with all my heart, I'm gonna try and make you proud. I'm happy you're chilling with Jesus. No more suffering... rest well baby, till we meet R.I.P to the sweetest little boy ever Kayshaun. May your soul rest in eternal peace. Xox

As the service is going I'm jus sitting and smiling and trusting. I could barely hear the pastor speaking but I tried to stay focused. Then he makes an announcement for only the family to come up and say goodbye. *Only family? What's that mean, we ain't discuss that. Does he even know me?* The casket is closing. *Why are they closing the casket? He hasn't gotten up yet. It can't be over. No, No, NO, NO, NO, NO, WHAT ARE YOU DOING!? DON'T CLOSE THE CASKET. He didn't get up. He didn't get up.* I didn't know what to do but I didn't wanna be there, I couldn't watch them take him away so I ran out of the sanctuary. *He was supposed to get up. What went wrong? I believed with all my heart, I fasted, I did everything I was supposed to and he did not get up.* My mind went blank. Jus silence. T ran after me and brought me to her van to sit. I got in but all I could do was stare at the ground. I saw shadows of people who came to the passenger window but I couldn't find the words to say or even the energy to lift my head in their direction. Tears started fallin and I didn't even move to wipe them away. I let them fall as I continued to stare blankly, my mind was the quietest it had ever been. Not. One. Thought. I felt the car move and I think she said she's driving me to the cemetery but I couldn't move. The drive felt long and I didn't know where she was going but then the car stopped and I saw green. I still couldn't move. So, I didn't. I sat in the car. I looked up once and saw blue. *I think that's the sky.*

August 24, 2014 ·
Look what my son did for me today...Love him

I find Joy in the small things. I smile at the most beautiful things. I'm at peace with the way things are. I woke up and decided to go to church. I had missed most of it but there was bbq happening afterwards and I needed fresh air. While I was there a woman from the church approached me. She had been following my posts on facebook and was standing with me in my quest for resurrection. She said what my stance did was challenge non-christians and complacent Christians to believe in a greater God. Whether Kaykay came back or not, all our faith had been given a face lift. Since he did not come back she was searching for her own answers and God had given her an explanation. Her response to me was "In life God gives us the choice of free will. As I was standing next to Kaykay's grave I saw a clear vision of Jesus telling Kaykay it was ok to go back and trying to nudge him to come back, but Kaykay kept shaking his head no. I also saw him running free and happy."

That was honestly the most comforting thing I could have heard in that moment. At just 8 years of age it would seem like Kaykay had truly fulfilled his purpose. He came at a time when I was headed down a destructive past and he literally saved my life and got me to focus on a future. I lived for him essentially. Everything I did was for him. The amount of times I contemplated suicide over the years but never made any attempts was cause I had a child to live for. I wasn't even tryna do church until he got sick. His untimely sickness was the only thing that brought me back to God. It also helped to begin to mend strained relationships in my life. It got me to see life and God from a different perspective.

In his passing I also understood that Kaykay was now so much better. As much as I selfishly wanted Kaykay to stay, I wasn't born into a disability. I had no clue what it felt like or what effect it had on him. I also suspected that the reason Kaykay loved race cars and anything fast was because DMD had him trapped and moving at a slower pace than he wanted. Race cars gave him the freedom he didn't have while being in his body. He taught me so much about being grateful for the smallest things. I knew what awaited me in heaven, I would continue to do my best to get there. My greatest accomplishment was teaching Kaykay who God was and ensuring he made it to heaven. The explanation given to me provided much needed peace. As long as Kaykay was happy that's all I could ever ask for.

August 24 2014 11:22pm
Cola
Do you mind if I have your number? I jus wanna keep in touch, no harassment ting. I'm doing better, I know kaykay is truly happy
Kendrick
Yes he is. My phones down but as soon as it's back up I'll msg u it
Cola
Ok no problem. I'll respect if you don't want to either. Jus wanna make sure you are ok going through this, it's still the loss of a child and I get that.
Kendrick
I will definitely give it to you
Cola
Ok, lemme ask you, why didn't you come to the viewing or funeral? Or were you there and I didn't see you?
Thank you by the way, you gave me a beautiful son
Kendrick
I'm so sorry how everything went from the start
Cola
I forgive you, I forgave you a long time ago. Nothing but love for you

He stopped talking to me right after this. Even when I sent him messages periodically he ignored them. I mean I get it, it was hard. I guess for me I would have preferred he told me straight up he didn't want to give me his number or didn't want me to contact him. I would have respected that more than thinking we could bond through this only to be left dealing with things alone once again.

Poetic Interlude

To my sons father
The love I have for my son cannot compare to the hate that sometimes I wish I had for you
Yet an still I don't hate you
Never did
Never will
Willingly I supplied you with my time
Blinded by the sweet words an intimacy
In time I was able to see that your attraction to me was only inside the parameters you deemed comfortable
Unconditional love superficially placed
Something bout a thick chic with a cute face
Too thick
For anything more than a sexual taste
Laced with the poison of rejection
I declined your erections
The direction of my decisions caused us to go our separate ways
8 month phone call
Calling it a mistake
Calling it like it never happened
Calling me a hoe
Telling me that no you weren't interested in raising a kid
You 19 left me 16
Disgraced
Pregnant
But blessed
The best gift of life came from a man who can't stand me
To my sons father
Your failed attempts to break me have made me stronger
But I wish you knew for a second what it's like raising a child with a disability
I wish you were in the office with me when doctors said our

child would never walk
I wish you felt your heart stop when you heard 18 was the age you would bury your child
Seems wild
Maybe if our child had a different mother
You would have made another attempt at being the father he needed
My heart bleeded knowing the first time meeting my 6 year old child conceded he was yours
Your potential to be a magnificent father was strangled by your inability to grow up
I gave up fighting you when I understood your mentality had you enslaved
I wish you desired to save our child
I wish you knew him like he knew you
Like he knew your name
Like he knew your face
Even though you never called
I never showed him any trace of anger hurt or hate
I respected you as the donor you proved to be
See
There's no gage or merit for good parenting
We were both simple kids trying a ting
Trying to wing myself through the stereotypes of this life
Do you know how many nights it came close to the end
When sleeping in hospital beds became a regular trend
To my sons father
I forgive you
I forgive you
I'm sorry please forgive me
I forgive you
More than anything sometimes I wish I could mourn his death with you
You let me go through everything as a single parent for 8 years
Tears flow over the moments I had but you never got
Not even his last moments convinced you to show up to his funeral
I want you to know
That I wanted you there

It would have been the final moment we shared
I wish you cared
Your silence on the matter brings this chapter to a close
I wish you that deep penetrating peace that only God knows
This journey has timeless lessons that release when experience shows
Forgiveness is attainable
If constant love and understanding
Flow

Poetic Interlude

A mother's love is greater than any ocean that flows
Deeper than any addiction that knows how to hold on without letting go
Slowly holding that fragile human being that was just created
Crying tears of blessings mixed with emotions of joy and fear
Will I be a good enough role model throughout the years?
The fear of motherhood so often
Ignored
The journey of love so readily restored
Mere seconds pass feeling like an eternity of gratitude tinged with the attitude of acceptance
Confidently repeating 'I will always love you faithful and true' 'I will always love and protect the truest of you '
I gave birth to the best piece of me
Releasing great potential God trusted me to be
the naturer of greatness
The earthly problem solver
The all around doctor
Providing stability not fragility
A Mother and a child have the ability to
grow together
Laugh together

Cry together
Try together
this journey of motherhood was a blessing to me
Taught me many lessons that only experiences held key
a mother's love runs free yet never ceases
to be
Deeper than a grave
Love always
Stay free

> August 24, 2014 ·
> Regardless of what people say, I stood in faith believing in a miracle and there's nothing wrong or unhealthy about it. At the end of the day, I know God is proud of me cause I was obedient to what HE told me. I believe kaykay is having so much fun in heaven with Jesus he just didn't wanna come back and who can blame him, its the first time he is truly free and as a mother that's all I could ever want for him. And I know Jesus is taking care of him.

People were talking about me. People were saying I was crazy. People were saying I was in denial. People were saying I was ill. People were saying I was in a cult. *I dare anyone to switch places with me. How can they ridicule me like this?* I stood for what I believed and was being ridiculed for it. No one else would have even half an ounce of courage to stand for what they believed in the face of persecution. *Why come to the funeral to pass judgments?* I know what I heard and I know that God said He was proud of me and I would do everything all over again. Even with the same outcome, I have no regrets because at least I stood for something...*what do you stand for?*

> August 25, 2014 ·
> I don't exactly know who came on Saturday but I want to thank everyone who came out even if i didn't see you personally. Understandably the reality of the situation hit me and I wasn't in the frame of mind to greet people.

> Everyone deals with situations differently. Nevertheless thank you for all the support much love

If he came back, great, if he didn't...ok. Either way I planned to be ok but I wasn't mentally available that day. People were telling me they were there and I couldn't remember half of them. I was so gone I didn't want that to be my last memory of him to be at the grave. Think positive. Always. The outpour of love and support was like any other though. People really seemed touched by the journey.

I got so so many messages from people I had never met, people heard about what I was going through, heard about how Kaykay touched so many lives. People reached out to me to express their condolences, their love, their empathy and their own stories.

> August 30, 2014 ·
> I love you baby, always and forever my best friend, really missing you today. But I'm happy you're happy and free Lord thank you for the strength today

During the process of Kaykay being sick I had gotten many prayers and even asked people anointed as prophets to pray for him, and they all told me he was going to be fine. In actual fact, he was fine cause he was in heaven but one prophet in particular had said specific things that Kaykay would have completed. I had gotten back in touch with her in search of an explanation. The first thing she said to me was that God gives free will of choice. The second thing she said was that the things she had prophesied were all in God's plan and design for Kaykay. As much as God has a plan for every single one of us, sometimes our plans can be snatched from us if we aren't careful. When things are unexplainable I looked to God for answers and here he was explaining it. The main outcome again was freedom of choice. Kaykay chose to stay and I had to respect his decision and do my best to work hard so that I could eventually join him.

Speaking of working hard, the drama and the stress

of the funeral was way too much to handle. Aaliyah took me to Niagara for an amazing time away and my next good friend opted to help me escape by planning a trip to Bermuda. Her dad lived down there and was able to accommodate us for a week's stay. She had stayed by my side during the entire process and I couldn't think of a better time to escape.

September 2, 2014 ·
Going to Bermuda this week....can't wait!

September 2, 2014 ·
Today has been a interestingly difficult day for me personally and I feel my heart bleeding for the children of my son's class who returned to school for the first day only to find out that my son would no longer join them. There was a lot of crying and shock and I can only pray for God to give the children peace as they go through this school year.

I had gotten messages from parents who were just beside themselves. They had no clue how to even have the conversation with their child that Kaykay wasn't returning to school. I didn't envy them at all, it was a difficult time for everyone. His school was a true blessing though. Kaykay had touched so many hearts at that school. His teacher and principal informed me that they were working on planting a tree in his honor at the school. This way he would always be remembered.

September 3, 2014 ·
Praise break. Thank you Lord for what you are bringing me through. Too often while we go through the storm we forget to thank you, it's not enough to jus think about it. Gotta start living a life by prayer, faith and praise. So today I will consciously praise you for the battle that is already won. I LOVE JESUS. #justincaseyalldidntgetthememo

Poetic Interlude

Identity

He changed me
now, I can never go back
February 2014
The doctors told me, my child had 3 days to live
He changed me
Gave me that peace that superseded all other emotions and rationalities
The Doctors had given up
Leaving me an empty shell in the room
With thoughts of nothing but doom
My birthday present was the decision to sign my baby's dnr
Do not resuscitate
Do not resuscitate
No resuscitation
Eliminating the hesitation
My anticipation and determination
Speak louder than my irritation
Do everything you can to save my son
He's lived passed the weekend predictions of death
I have no words left
No tears left
Realizing I was left with only two choices
Either I die or I surrender
He changed me
I've always grown up with an understanding of faith and of Him
But I've done too many things in my life to cry out and expect His help to win
I lived a life loving nothing but sin
Thin timeline caused my mind to see life is different
Differently is the only explanation for the love I have for my son who saved me
Me
Turned into we

But I was ready to lay my life down if I could see my baby grow
There's nothing more desperate than crying out help me
Help me save him
To my father who's always listening
Heal him and let him live
My only reason to live has been him
Don't take him away
I'll do whatever it takes
I surrender
Please
He changed me
The minute I gave up fighting
The minute I asked for forgiveness
He changed me
And it most definitely has not been easy
I went from wanting to die if my son left
To a person strong enough to hold him as he took his last breath
Reminiscing on his last 7 months
I exhaled the last pieces to my heart knowing God's been working hard to build it back through Love
He changed me
Jesus changed me
My faith changed me
My son changed me
And even when the hard days come
Coming from where I'm from
The day he changed me
Is the day I stopped holding my breath
With nothing left
I can never go back

CHAPTER SIXTY-NINE

Loss & Love

Owe nothing to anyone except to *love* and seek the best for one another; for he who [unselfishly] loves his neighbor has fulfilled the [essence of the] law [relating to one's fellowman].
ROMANS 13:8

September 2, 2014 ·
30 days to find a new home...this should be fun. Lord give me strength

Before I could even leave shit was already going wrong. I was receiving the family size allowance from welfare which paid my rent each month. The first of the month came and the amount I received was significantly less, so I call in tryna figure out what happened. When I spoke to a worker I was informed a glitch had switched my file from family size making $1200 a month to single size making $750 a month. My rent alone was $1175. With less than two weeks of Kaykay gone, without any time to grieve, I was essentially being put out on the streets. That's what it felt like, I didn't get a chance to breathe, to spend time packing his clothes, to even sit on the brand-new bed I bought him. In an instant my whole life felt like it came to an end. Everything that we spent the last 2 years building together was done. I now had to beg my landlord to at least let me out of my lease early. All these changes really had me thinking deep. *What's the lesson here?*

Life made me realize the importance of forgiveness and letting go - letting go quickly. Many of the people I was upset with hadn't even reached out to me when Kaykay passed. I put so much energy into being upset with people who no longer mattered.... So, I wrote them letters to release them from my pain.

To: Té

It has taken me awhile to write this letter because I'm still healing from the situation. I didn't think that meeting you over a year ago would have ended the way it did. I've tried multiple times to make sense of it all without success I guess some things are not meant to understand. It's been a struggle to forgive you I won't lie because I opened up my life, my sons life, and my house to a friend and I feel I was dealt a crappy hand in the end. My pain is not because you decided not to be friends, but in the manner you went about doing it. I would of understood, and ironically Kaykay got sick and I wouldn't have been able to be a part of the business anyway. I value my friendships and they are what cut me the deepest when they end in such an incomplete manner. Especially for the fact that there's a constant reminder on my credit card of the chance I took in life. Anyway, this email is not meant to be an attack, I am working towards forgiving you during this new change in my life and I don't want to carry any resentment forward with me. I pray that you can forgive me to for any wrong doings or hurt I may have caused.

I wish you the best in the future,

God bless you,

Cola

No response.

To: Tish,

It's taken a lot of contemplating whether or not to message you since the last time we spoke it ended on not so good terms. Not sure if you remember, but you called me morbidly obese and told me to use my money to pay for a trainer. It's still etched in my brain cause for the longest time I couldn't understand how someone could be so brutally insensitive. Over the past few months I've learned that I need to forgive you because I can no longer let your words control my mind and my action. My health is my priority but not because someone made me feel insecure to the point of self hatred, but because my life has taken a different turn and my health is part of God's plan for self healing. I also remember that you accused me of being a neglectful mother because I didn't raise Kaykay in a similar way to what you thought was good parenting. Now that he has passed and gone to chill with God I can honestly say that I gave him the best life I could have and I'm very

proud of the person and mother I allowed myself to become. He loved me very much and he knew and understood that I loved him very much. Up until the day he passed he always kept a smile because he wanted to shield me from seeing him in any pain. I hate that it took losing my son to understand the great parenting job that I did. He made it to heaven, and in this world that's a great accomplishment. I never knew how to approach you before because I always felt like I never had much of a voice around you, but I think this is a part of my journey towards forgiveness, letting go and letting God. As I type this I have already begun my healing, I thank you for the support you did provide over the years and I pray you will forgive me for any wrongdoings I may have caused. At the end of the day, we are all God's children working towards a purpose.
Wish you all the best,
Cola

Tish replied
To: Cola,
Thank you for your message. It deeply saddened me when I heard about Kay Kay's passing. I appreciate your forgiveness for what you feel was insensitive. However, I decided to pull away from you because I realized that my frustrations were causing me to say things that were truthful. After years of trying to support you and Kaykay through various challenges I had reached my limit. I guess we only remember what hurts us the most. I remember you telling me that buying fresh vegetables and paying for naturopathic treatments were too expensive and then asking you to calculate the price of two trips to New York City within a couple of months which totalled $1000.00 . I remember supporting you when you were paying for a trainer for you and Kay Kay when others thought it was a waste of time. I don't want to rehash all of our arguments and disagreements but please understand that when people love you, they cannot sit aside during matters of life and death. I do not regret what I said but how I said it. I am a dreamer when need be but I am also a realist. I have buried

my mother and understand the importance of prioritizing health and peace of mind but living in truth. I think you are a smart, talented good-hearted woman and I wish you all the best in your personal growth.

It didn't feel like much of a resolution. In the end I had to agree to disagree...I guess

To: Leo

It's been awhile. I've been thinking greatly of how I haven't heard from you since I told you you no longer had to repay me. Can't lie it bothered me, but I hope it alleviated any guilt you were holding on to. My son recently passed and has given me a new outlook on life. I forgive you for all the times you lied about money, and for taking such a large sum of money and not returning it. I hope you can forgive me for any wrong doings or stress I may have caused, or any disrespect. I wish you all the best in your life. I felt like I was always holding on and waiting for you to message me to ask how I was doing, but it doesn't even bother me anymore, we are all humans and we are all just tryna make it in this life.

Enjoy you day,
God bless
Cola

To: Cola,

I feel horrible to here now for the first time that your son passed , I wish I had the right words for you right now, I feel your outlook that we are all humans and I know there much greatness still to come for both of us in our lives n I keep my hand and heart open to you,

Real Love Bless

That lifted a weight from my heart. Even if I didn't get responses or even responses I wanted, it was a relief to let go. As liberating as that was, I was beyond exhausted and needed to leave everything behind. At first, I felt guilty for wanting to take a trip especially when money was so tight, but then I just couldn't be in a city where the earth had swallowed up my baby. I couldn't breathe the air. I couldn't smile at the sun. I only let the rainbows through.

Bermuda couldn't have come at a better time. I had

never been but I was hella excited. On the day of departure after we had said bye and got alllll excited we arrived at the airport only to realize that the tickets weren't booked correctly. Essentially, we missed the departure flight. After all the anticipation none of us were willing to accept the defeat and we stood with the attendant trying to figure out another way to get us to Bermuda. There was a flight the following day to Bermuda and there jus happened to be a sale on the flights, we got them for even cheaper. Praise God! Now we had to figure out where we were going to stay. Since my girl worked with the airport she received discounts on hotels. Apparently visa debits aren't acceptable payments for hotels. *Who knew?* I woulda had money on my credit card but I had just used the last of what was on it to book the tickets with the airline. We were ultimately stranded at the airport.

On a whim of faith I decided to try a ting by calling my credit card company, Capital One, and asking for a temporary increase in order to pay for the hotel. *I know they don't normally do this, but God can you make an exception please?* The first person I spoke to said they couldn't help me. *God please please.* "Can I speak to your manager please?" Once the manager came on the phone I explained my situation and held my breath as she put me on hold. *God, I know you are capable of all things, I'm asking for a small miracle please.* "Hello? Ms Bennett?" "Yes, I'm here" "Ok I jus spoke to someone higher up than me and they advised me that we aren't able to do limit increases like this." *Damn ok.* "But what we will do is we will put a credit on your account for the amount that you need." "What?? Really? Thank you, thank you, thank you, wait how do I pay it back?" "Oh, you don't need to pay it back" "No way!!!" Tears flood my eyes as I am overwhelmed by God's favor. *Thank you, God, Thank you God, Thank you God!!* Mind blown. Even my girl couldn't understand it. It made no sense to her. "How?" "That's jus how God works" With everything sorted out we booked our room, chilled out and anticipated our new travel.

Bermuda was hella expensive. Cheap to fly to but hella expensive. Thank goodness we didn't have to pay for a place to stay. The good thing was it was a beautiful place to travel to. It reminded me of Jamaica. As I took the time to enjoy the beautiful island before me I understood how blessed I was despite everything going on. Everyone was so nice and accommodating. My girl's dad owned a salon and beauty store which was great because I was desperately seeking a change.

> September 10, 2014 ·
> Jus got my hair highlighted...New beginnings. Having fun but missing my baby everyday cause I know he would love it out here. #heartbrokenbutGodismendingit

I was no longer the same person. I felt like my identity died when Kaykay was buried. *Who am I? I've always been Kaykay's mom and now he is not here. Where does this leave me? I have no home to go back to, no money and no child. What is the point?* If Bermuda wasn't so expensive I probably would never go back home. I was trying to enjoy my trip but with each day that passed I dreaded the reality of going home to nothing. When we weren't on a beach or traveling somewhere, my girl was on the phone with her man so in my downtime I talked to Romeo. He was devastated. It was hitting him pretty hard. He felt guilty that we never got to meet, that our kids never got to play together. It was just rough all around. His kids were taking it hard too cause they missed out on having another brother around. That made my heart hurt. There was nothing I could do to fix things for them. It was at least comforting to know someone else understood my pain. Someone I could open up to cause we had the same vision and expectations for Kaykay that were now neva gonna be a reality. I listened as he broke down. I said "At least Kaykay knew who you were and loved you very much". From birth to death this man was always there for Kaykay. I could want nothing more from a father than the example he showed. It was something I couldn't share with Kendrick. I had offered Kendrick's family a chance to go half with me in paying for the headstone but they weren't able to, so Romeo stepped up and offered. It was so crazy to me how this man had paid for Kaykay's birth certificate and was now helping me with the head stone. *Dats real, I never thought I'd have to do this, but now that I was I'm glad I had support.* It felt so unreal but I was grateful. I requested a car and an angel be put on either side of the inscription which read

Kayshaun Antwoine Isaiah Bennett

I am speed. Faster than Fast, Quicker than Quick. I am Kaykay.

It was his favorite quote from the Disney movie Cars. I found a lot of peace on that island. I tried to use the feeling from the sun rays to block out any worries but when the nights came the worries came back. Seriously *where was I gonna live?* I didn't feel comfortable moving to my parents and I had gotten a few offers from friends but I had to figure out which offer was going to be the best for me. On the trip we discussed next steps and housing and she had offered me a room at her place, but I was hesitant. We were so different and I didn't know what space I was in plus I didn't want it to completely destroy our friendship. It was a really generous offer. Best offer I had gotten since she was willing to move her daughter to her room to give me my own room. In the end I decided to move in and prayed our friendship would survive. Plus, it was only temporary, I just needed to figure life out without expectations.

Once we returned from the amazing trip the work began. I had two weeks to pack up my entire apartment and figure out where everything was going. I couldn't take most things with me and needed to get a storage locker. I couldn't even think of Kaykay's stuff. I kept his cars and a few other items, everything else either went to storage or was donated. *My heart feels so broken.* Iuno if it was a blessing or a curse that I didn't get much time to mourn over his stuff. With only $750 coming in I could only afford the smallest locker available and had to get creative with how things were to be packed in. Those two weeks were a complete blur but at least I had help.

September 25, 2014 ·
i miss you, the reality of having to move is near

September 25, 2014 · Oxtail and rice is my comfort food...

October 1st I moved in. I wasn't required to pay any rent but I didn't wanna jus stay for free, so I offered her $250 a month as a thank you. I wish I coulda done more but I was strapped. Between storage fees, phone bills, past due bills, and food, life things always felt hectic. With a new place to stay things were starting to feel more stable. I moved from downtown to uptown. From streetcars and 24-hour access to bus life. I didn't know how much I missed having a car until I moved uptown. Even still at the moment I had no plans to do anything but spend time relaxing and reflecting.

The chaos surrounding Kaykay's passing died down. As time went on, people checked in on me less and less. They seemingly went back to their lives while mine had been completely disrupted. *Where did everyone go?* It felt almost all at once that everything stopped. Most people didn't know what to say to me so they opted to say nothing at all. *Like silence is what I need right now. This only makes me feel more like a freak cause I can't hold decent conversations. I'd rather you spent time with me watching a movie or listening to music than completely avoiding me. It's excruciatingly painful having people avoid me cause they don't know what to say.* Or I would get people who would ask, "How many children did you have...just the one? Oh sorry, well at least you can have more." *That hurts. Kaykay is not replaceable.* Or I'd get people who would say "What are doing with your life now? Are you gonna get a job?" *Actually, the last 11 years of my life have been exhausting, I'd really like to do shit all and rest.* Or "Be strong, he's in a better place." *With Jesus? Ye I get that, but I want him here.* Or "What do you need?" *My child. All I need is my child. If you're asking how you can help, I don't know. My life has been turned upside down, it would be better if you ask me something like Are you eating? Taking care of yourself? Yes and no questions are all I can handle.* Or "God doesn't give you more than you can handle." *Really? This was always my fav. I get that people don't know my life but after 4 rapes, being molested by my aunt's boyfriend, being a teen mom and then my son dying, Iuno what else God was gonna bring my way that He thought I "could handle". How bout sometimes in life shitty things happen to good people. No explanation, jus truth. Look at JOB from the bible. He was soooo loved by God an yet he lost everything. Even still he was faithful.* People just didn't get it and the sincerity of the tone made it even harder for me to get upset. It was better for me to ignore people thus eliminating frustration and awkwardness.

What I did wanna do was write through the pain and go to the gym. This is all I wanted. I even signed up for the gym and had started going. That lasted about a week. My girl had jus switched her shifts at work, from day to the night shift and needed me to watch her child. *How do I say no when she's letting me stay here? I love her, and I love my goddaughter, but I really don't wanna be taking care of no kids right now.* I had tried a few nights to help her out but it was just too much for me. I couldn't handle any responsibilities. *Lord please help me.* I wasn't sure if it was prayer or jus luck but when I logged onto facebook I saw a posting for a job while scrolling through. *I didn't want to do anything but pressure from others and from myself made me need it.* I didn't think much would happen but I sent in my application. I hadn't had a real job since my first year in university where I worked for a Scotiabank call center and was nervous whether or not I'd be able to handle this job. As my girl was also looking for an additional job she also put in her resume. I had completely forgotten that my resume said I was bilingual since I barely used my French, so I was really surprised when I got a call for the position of French Customer Service Agent. I said to the woman on the phone "I speak French yes, but it's been awhile, I don't even know if I would qualify." "Well how bout this, before you turn the job down just come in for an interview, if your French isn't strong enough then we will hire you as an English agent". That sounded fair to me. I didn't even know what company I had applied for. All I knew was I was going to this agency and they were gonna send me somewhere...if I qualified. I was nervous as hell. *This is too soon. You need to rest, relax, go to the gym, not pick up new jobs. Just try, it might all work out for you.* I walked into the interview nervous and walked out with my first job! *Just Breathe.*

Things were moving too fast, I needed to reconnect with my therapist before they got worse. I felt like I was bout to spiral. I was riddled with guilt. I missed Kaykay. In my appointment with her, I explained to her that I wasn't in my own environment. North York was jus so different without a car. Waiting for buses was frustrating. Even though I was extremely grateful I felt horrible about not wanting to babysit. My girl was helping me out and I should have been able to do the same but I felt trapped and cause I didn't know how to handle situations appropriately, I ran away from them. My therapist's advice? "Be careful, taking care of a child, especially one that is not yours so soon after you lost your own child, it could be very triggering for you. Your friend should understand that." But I wasn't sure she would.

I was nervous as hell, things were happening so quickly, it was just over 2 months since Kaykay died and I didn't recognize my own life. I was a temp agent for a new campaign with Capital One. I felt this immense pressure from the company to exceed and be exceptional or risk losing the job. I was a French agent and my brain was struggling to remember all the French words I was taught. I didn't speak it as fluently as my coworkers. After my first day of training I had my first panic attack. I called Romeo on my bus ride home struggling to breathe. Over and over he repeated "You're doing great, look how far you've come, keep trusting God. Breathe baby breathe. You're gonna be ok". My chest was tight, I wanted to run and hide an just never go back. He played a song for me. I'll Trust You by James Fortune. As I listened my spirit was immediately calmed. He never got off the phone until I was safe and asleep in my room.

Even though I can't see
And i can't feel your touch
I will trust you lord
How I love you so much

Though my nights may seem long
And I feel so alone
Lord my trust is in you
I surrender to you

So many painful thoughts
Travel through my mind
And I wonder how
I will make it through this time

But i trust you
Lord it's not easy
Sometimes the pain in my life
Makes you seem far away
But i'll trust you
I need to know you're here
Through the tears and the pain
Through the heartache and rain

I'll trust you

The first time I answered a call from a real customer after the training I had another panic attack. As soon as I ended the call I ran off the phone. My manager found me sobbing in the hallway and brought me into a room. I was struggling to catch my breath but once I could breathe a bit better I explained to them what happened "I lost my son in August but I didn't wanna say anything cause I didn't want you guys to think I couldn't do the job" The managers were visibly shocked and concerned. I had to call my girl to come get me at work. Everyone wanted me to go to the hospital but I just wanted to go home and sleep. I didn't know why these attacks were coming or what set them off, I jus knew once I slept I calmed down. It was good having the truth finally out. Felt like a weight lifted from me. The job came with perks, I got paid weekly and it got me out of the house and socializing. For the first time in years I was able to buy myself things. As long as Kaykay had what he needed I was good but now I was able to shop for my own needs. The bad news was that it was already causing a divide at the house. Since my training started at 7:30am I had to leave from 6:30am which meant I could no longer babysit for her. Finding night time babysitters was so much harder than finding daytime babysitters and it left her in a jam. *I feel so bad, it's my goddaughter, it's my job to help.* She said, "I hate your new job" I said "Ye I know, sorry I can't help out more but once I get a bit more stable I think I'll be able to give you some more money monthly." That's all I could say in the moment. I jus needed to ease the tension. We sat quietly the rest of the way as we drove to do grocery shopping. The more uncomfortable things felt at the house the more overtime I worked and tried to focus on my own things.

November 19, 2014 ·
Solo book launch, then....baptism! True

Tara had stayed very close to me since the passing of Kaykay. Today the F-you project was launching their second book and had invited me to the event. It was a collective of individuals sharing their experiences and the subject of this book was Grief, Loss and acceptance. *Crazy timing God.* They had dedicated the book to Kaykay and even put his picture in it. It was the most amazing and most generous thing anyone could have done for me and I couldn't have been more grateful and honored to attend the launch. I just had one problem. The launch was on the same day as baptism. This was gonna be my 4th attempt at baptism. There was that time I was a teenager and had been banned from baptism because I was pregnant and then once when I was a teen mother. I had tried once this summer between hospital visits but the pastor wanted to do a group baptism and I was the only one who signed up. I had pretty much given up but they finally said they were ready in the late fall. *Something don't feel right.* Even though I initially said yes, for whatever reason I now felt rushed. *I had been waiting forever to be baptized but my gut was saying wait.* The night before,I texted both my pastor and assistant pastor "Hey, I'm not gonna get baptized tomorrow. I don't feel well prepared." My assistant pastor called me almost immediately "Don't let the devil win, you need to push past the feeling and still continue with the baptism." We talked some more until finally I said "Ok, I'll think about it" "Ok I know I'll see you there tomorrow." I thought I would get a similar response from my pastor, but his only response was "The only thing that should stop you from getting baptized is if you were on your period". Ye...not as encouraging as I was hoping for. I then texted them both the followin morning "I'm not coming today". My reasonings for missing the baptism were simple, I wasn't made aware until the week prior to and leading up to the day of the baptism I had received no instruction on what the next steps were. My spirit felt uneasy and speaking to my grandma validated how I felt. She was not having it. "Tell dem sey, yu nuh readi cause dem neva tell yu what to do or how to prepare" *Maybe I just wasn't meant to be baptized.*

I basically went to work, came home, went to the gym, talked with Romeo on the phone, slept and did it all over again. I cried at night when no one but God or Romeo would hear me. I stayed in my room when I wasn't at work. It was easier to cope alone. I tried when I could to spend time with my girl but she was also busy. Our schedules became increasingly challenging. Plus, after living on my own for so long I now had to adapt to living with people which wasn't as easy as I thought. *Does ketchup go in the fridge or in the cupboard?* What made things worse was that we were complete opposites. I was messy and she was a neat freak. She always had comments about the way I cleaned or didn't clean. Regardless of what I did, it had to be done a specific way or it was wrong. It caused a lot of headaches tryna live up to the expectations. By December we were already barely talking and things didn't seem like they were gonna get any better. *This is what I was trying to avoid. Damn, what now?*

I got a text message from her asking if it was possible for me to start paying $450 a month asap. *Damn this was unexpected. Where is this coming from? Why now, why so fast?* I wasn't sure how to respond to this new request without sounding mean or ungrateful. I had only been working for about a month and that increase was a big jump from $250. We were both stuck in a tight situation. All I responded with was 'I'll have to get back to you'. *What do I say to that? Why $450, where did that number come from?* $450 was a stretch but I was going to see if I could pick up more shifts to make up the difference. However, the more I worked the more exhausted I was and the less I was home. On a rare occasion we were both in the kitchen making food and I said "Man I'm so tired. This job is a lot." She responds, "Well you had the opportunity to stay home and you chose to work so you gotta suck it up" Well *damn excuse me for saying anything. Well, now I know I can't say nun around you.* It sounded more bitter than encouraging. *Screw my life.* Since being saved I was cutting back on swearing. I was tryna be different but felt the same. I was better off jus staying in the room. *I didn't ask for this, life jus handed it to me.*

The one good thing I seemed to have going on was the tree that Kaykay's school wanted to plant for him. I was honoured to attend the beautiful ceremony. The kids in his class made a song for him and presented flowers. It couldn't have been a more perfect moment. It gave me another level of peace. I never felt an urge to go to the cemetery and with this tree planted, I never had to. The cemetery represented death while his tree was a symbol of life and love.

Even with the new job I was struggling to meet the basics in life - food and shelter. It was quite stressful. The small things seemed huge and unmanageable. My girl and I used to do grocery shopping together. She had a car so we could buy more things. But as we spoke less and less, we bought less and less. Without a car I was left to buy only what I could carry home which wasn't much. This meant most of my money was spent on fast food. As quick as I made money it went towards survival. Romeo had become extremely frustrated with my situation and found an online grocery delivery. He ordered the groceries and had it delivered to the house for me. *I wish I could take better care of myself.*

January had rolled around, with everything going on between work and home I was so exhausted that I had completely forgotten to message my girl back about the rent increase. I typically gave her money on the first of the month so I messaged her saying I wasn't able to do $450 but I was able to do $350 for that month. *I barely even had the $350 but I mean I shoulda gotten back to her sooner and I didn't which is all my fault but hopefully she'll see I'm still trying.* In my absence to get back to her she assumed I was ok with paying the $450 so she had budgeted for the money and was now coming up short. "Why can't you pay the $450? I made a budget around that and now I don't have that money" We went from barely talking to not talking at all so I stayed at work more. Luckily the panic attacks had stopped and I had become obsessed with work even though I hated being on the phones.

I hated being at the house and I hated being at work. Then out of nowhere I had another panic attack. I was bawling uncontrollably, my chest was hurting, I couldn't even bus it home because of the pain. Romeo called me a cab home. I was back to work the next day but I was ready to quit. So here I am about to quit my first job because the stress is too much and I get called into a room by two of my superiors. They said, "You have the ability to learn quick and to work efficiently so we wanna offer you a position in the back-office department" "Meaning I won't have to be on the phones anymore?" "Exactly". *God...dats you? You see me! You delivered me into greatness.* I didn't even care what it was, as long as I was off the phone and had more freedom I was down. The phone system was too restricting for me and made me feel controlled all the time. My team leader in my new position had the same birthday as Kaykay. It felt like I was meant to be there. *Jus as I was about to give up, God moved me forward.*

Every once in a while my girl would cook, and when she did she would leave some for me for when I came home from work, but this time I came home to find her and a few other people eating and no food left for me. *Did she do this intentionally? Or was there really no food left? Really? Dats wassup? I'm ova dis. I'm soooo ova dis.* I left the house and started walking. I had no clue where I was walking to but I needed to be away from people. I texted Romeo tellin him what happened and he called me and tried to convince me to go back. Snow was falling heavily as my tears flowed but I didn't care. I wasn't going back there. For what? My life was jus stupid. *You think I like depending on people? I was FINE. I had an apartment.* I had pictured things being so different. As much as I was hesitant I thought maybe jus maybe things would have worked out. Now here I stood by myself in the snow with no one but Romeo to give a damn about me. I walked around for an hour tryna clear my mind enough to figure out what I wanted to eat. I was hungry and tired but I didn't know what to do with myself. Romeo was still on the phone beggin me to find anything to eat so I could get back to the apartment. He hated the thought of me walking around by myself disoriented. Between mumbling and crying I must have sounded like I lost my mind. I wanted to go home but felt so unwelcomed. I didn't feel emotionally safe there. I finally found a Mr. Sub, got my sandwich, walked back and spent the rest of the night crying myself to sleep with Romeo.

I was becoming increasingly irritated. I was waiting for the bus to go to the gym and it took longer than usual to come. When it finally did arrive and dropped me at my destination I was so irritated I couldn't even work out. As soon as I got to the gym I left but instead of taking the bus I decided to walk the 20 mins back. The minute I began to walk it started to rain. *Of course it would rain.* I looked up to the sky and said, "God can you please hold the rain up long enough for me to walk home?" Mins later the rain stopped. *Thanks God. At least I know he still hears me. I wish I had a car. I wish Kaykay was still here and I wish my life never changed.* As I walked back I walked over the bridge at don mills and york mills, I leaned over to see what was down there while I contemplated. *How much do you think it would hurt if you jumped? Would you just roll down? Or.... would it be instant? Do you think it would hurt more than losing Kaykay? Do you think it would numb some of this pain? Look at me, I have no home. No place to go. Nobody wants me. You're afraid of heights remember...oh ye! Damn new plan.* I looked at the cars speeding down the road. *What if you jus step out? Would the cars stop in time? Would it take the pain away? Would it? Would it be better this way? Whose gonna miss you? You need to be with Kaykay. Ye but if you commit suicide then you can't go to heaven. Kaykay's in heaven, you'd essentially die and still not get to see him. God...Why can't you jus kill me so I can be with him? It's not suicide if you do it. Don't even waste your time. By the time you even try to step out your phone is gonna ring and it's gonna be somebody checkin in on you. God has this annoying habit of tryna save your life.* It was tru though. Whenever I would think of or contemplate suicide God would have someone call me or check up on me to distract me from doing it. *I can't even die properly, I'm so worthless.* I knew people would be upset but I really didn't care much. It wasn't about them and all people ever did was offer up some kind of counterproductive encouragement. Like "It's going to get better." *Great, thanks for that.* I gave up and kept walking home. The minute I entered the building the rain started to fall again.

That night my goddaughter kept knocking on my door and saying, "Aunty you ok?" She couldn't see that I was crying but I always responded, "I'm good baby girl, thank you for checking". *My heart was comforted knowing that she cared.* My behaviour was causing Romeo to be stressed. He felt so helpless. No matta what, I lived in this dark hole that he couldn't pull me out of as much as he tried. I told him about my night. I told him about the bridge. It broke him, I could tell. He got really quiet. Then he said, "If you ever killed yourself I would be forced to kill myself too." "Why would you do that? You have a life to live" "Ye but I'm not living it without you, so if you kill yourself then you're killin me too" *Well shit, why you gotta say that. I can't be responsible for nobody killin themselves.* "Fine, I won't kill myself." Every night he slept on the phone with me just to make sure I was ok.

The very next morning while I was at work my dad called bright an early. *He never calls this early, wassup?* "Hey dad" "Hey what are you up to?" "Nothing just at work" "Oh ok, what were you doing last night" "Nothing why" "Cause I saw you walking over the bridge" *What the hell? What was he doing over here though? He's never in this area.* "Oh, I was just walking home from the gym" "Oh ok everything's good?" "Yep I'm good dad, I'm bout to start work so I'll talk to you later" *See I knew it, I knew it God, you always have somebody checking on me. Damn ok I got it, I got the message, I won't try no more.* I came home to a bouquet of flowers waiting for me from Romeo. He was doing his best to keep my spirit up and mind distracted.

I missed my dad but we had barely spoken, especially not about Kaykay's death. Many things were left unsaid as the months passed but I had remembered living at home and found a new appreciation for it. As naggin as my mother was and as much as we didn't get along, I felt like it was still betta than where I was living. I had survived it once and could do it again. I had gone to my parents' house a few times on the weekend since moving in with my girl and things seemed manageable. It got me contemplating if I should move back, I even talked to them about it. They seemed open to the idea of helping me out. It had been 6 years since I left home, last time I lived there Kaykay was so little but I was open to a change. *But how am I gonna get to work from there? Bus? Bruh I might as well quit. I mean it's not impossible but it's hella annoying, Imma need a car for sure.* It's Courtice though, how do I live in a suburb without a car if I'm already struggling in Toronto? We discussed me moving back and how I would get to work, they didn't want me to lose my job so they offered to help me financially with a car. *All you gotta figure out is the monthly amount for insurance and gas. This money that I'm paying for rent I could put towards that. But you know how things were with you and mom before and how she called you crazy.* My mother an I have a better relationship when we live apart. *That's tru!* I didn't know what to do. I also didn't wanna abandon my girl cause at the end of the day she still needed my help financially. Things would be different if I knew my job was stable. My contract was only supposed to be till December, now it was extended to March but there was no guarantee. I was trying to save up money to get back on my feet.

At this point the only time we communicated was when I got a text with a request for another rent increase. Since the $450 didn't work she asked for $400 rather than $350, each time I said I couldn't afford extra. One of the rare times we were home together we decided to have a face to face conversation. "I'm sorry I can't afford more than $250" "What do you spend your money on?" *Did she really jus ask me that? Wait, was that a real question? Naw she can't be serious. Yo I can't even deal with this shit right now.* "Bills, I got bills due, storage fees, a lot of different things I'm tryna pay for" *How does she know whether or not I can afford more rent?*

A week later I sent her a text. "I'm moving out by March 1st. I'm going back to my mom's house." *I wish I had known all this before I paid for storage and moving fees. It's gonna be such a hassle to move again. This leaves me practically no time to find a car.* I thought I was losing my mind every time I would come home and find my stuff packed and put by the door. At first it was my blender and cooking utensils, but then it was my keyboard. *This would be cool if she actually offered to help me pack but instead she packed when I wasn't home. It felt passive aggressive.*

The day arrived for the move and while scrolling through instagram I saw this post that just summed up everything I was feeling, so I reposted the quote.

<u>Today is Moving Day...</u>
I prophetically declare the storms and struggle are over for you, you are shifting into your destiny. What had you hostage yesterday won't have any hold on you today. You are about to hear a sound of deliverance and freedom. Joy is entering your new home and sadness is being left behind. Your latter will be greater.
#physicallymovingtoday #thechapterofJob #itallworksoutforjobafter42chapters #Godgavehimdouble #missingmyson #hangingontoGodspromiseswithathinthread

About 10 mins later I received a screenshot of my exact post in a blank email. *Why would she email this to me? She's right in the next room.* I zoomed into the screenshot and noticed she was on the phone when she sent it. *Wait, she's on the phone talkin to someone? Wooooow really? So, she's on the phone chattin bout me. So that means this email wasn't meant for me at all. That's really how we gon do this? Guess that means she ain't gon help me move? I bet once people show up she gon act like she was tryna help me the whole time. Pfft. Friends, right? The otha stuff was whatever but this? She jus sealed the deal with this.* This was hurtful. I was grateful she took me in when she did, but things fell apart so fast. *Could we ever go back to how things were before I moved in? Would I ever be stable?* Even though I moved back home I was afraid to settle in since it didn't feel like my home anymore. *I gotta be ready to leave in case it doesn't work out. Never get comfortable with shit that aint yours.*

CHAPTER SEVENTY

Restoration

Above all, have fervent and unfailing love for one another, because love covers a multitude of sins [it overlooks unkindness and unselfishly seeks the best for others].
1 PETER 4:8

Now that I was home I needed to get my car. I was just hired for a full-time position which meant that I could afford monthly payments. The same job I never thought I'd be able to work was now my full-time employment, and I had health benefits for the first time in forever. With the money I got from my parents we decided to try looking for a car at a dealership. At this point I wasn't even picky with what type of car it was. My only request was that it was blue, in honour of Kaykay. The dealership happened to have gotten in three slightly used 2013 Sonatas and were able to offer them for a discounted price. By the time we had walked in they only had one car left. One family had just left stating they would think about it but as long as it was blue, I knew it would be mine. I always look for signs from God regarding His choices for me. Out of all 3 cars brought in two were grey and the last one left was BLUE! Even though I saw the car I didn't need to. I knew it would be mine. I was worried about the financing since it was way higher than the money I had, but I told God "If you allow me to have the car, I will only play gospel music or music that edifies you in it." A week later I drove off the lot with the car. *Thank you Father!!*

Even though church played a huge role in my life I still wasn't thrilled about my parents' church. Although the original pastor had long passed away, it was the same church that had pushed me out and I was in no rush to be back. A month after I moved back home a new pastor had moved from Guyana to become the new lead pastor. My curiosity drew me in to check out his preaching. I'm glad I did. It was so different than what I was used to. For starters, he didn't yell. His messages were genuine and impactful. His energy and spirit were caring and supportive. It was such a relief and he drew me in instantly with his infectious smile. His family seemed just as dope. His oldest son had the same birthday as Kaykay, he was now the second person I met with the same birthday in such a short period. His youngest had such a vibrant spirit and his wife was a beautiful musician that encouraged me to get involved in singing again. *They want me to sing? That's different. I hadn't sung since gospel choir in University.* The most amazing thing was when I was asked to do a sit down meeting with the pastor. He asked me "How can I help you?" I told him that I hadn't been baptized yet. "Even if it's just you, you will be baptized, and I want to do it before Kaykay's one-year anniversary" *Even if it's just me? I'm that important? This reminds me of the parable of the shepherd who left his flock of ninety-nine to find the one lost sheep. God you got me.* I didn't even need to think about it. It just felt right. My spirit was calm and I felt like God was mending my heart. *Of all places to be baptized... the same church that pushed me out. It was all coming full circle.*

God had already restored a few things for me, even my relationship with my mother and sister had completely changed. I found myself working behind the scenes to forgive them for any pain that had been caused over the years. We had started a diet as a family that was working well except for the fact that my mother complained the whole time. She was tellin people how I threw out the majority of the things she ate; *they were all processed food but ok.* Regardless we got through it. Then there was this big blow up when I had started moving my things into the house out of storage. It was my mom's suggestion but once things started to change around the house she got extremely upset and I overheard her telling people how I was taking over the house. *Ye but you told me to put my stuff here...if you didn't want me here why did you say ok? I don't want to be there. I want Kaykay and my life back.* As I was working on forgiving my family, all these other situations were coming up but I was determined to get through them. No matta how hurt I was I would say "Lord don't let my heart be numb, please help me to forgive. Let me see the joy in my mother" There were moments when we could just laugh and it felt ok. It was always a rollercoaster ride. Things were going good. I was on the up and up. I was doing really well in my new position. I was beating my own personal records.

I couldn't have been happier but as I got closer to Kaykay's one year I felt myself becoming more distracted at work. I couldn't think straight some days. I would stare outside the window and wished I was anywhere but there. I spent time in the bathroom crying. I went to therapy asking her for help. I spent my days trying to look normal but the more normal I tried to look the more my days fell apart. I wanted to quit but I had jus bought a new car and knew I couldn't do that to my parents. They had co-signed to help me get the car and I couldn't jus not make payments. *I coulda said no to the promotion. I coulda said I was moving away. I didn't have to push to get the car. Now I'm trapped. What am I gonna do? I can't quiet the noise. I can't think. I can't....it hurts.* My heart rate was up, my chest was hurting all the time and it felt like I couldn't breathe. I went to my doctor for help. "I need to get some time off work. I can't focus, I can't think, I don't feel like myself" "There's no such thing as time off work, it's called a vacation". Defeated, I went back to work and started looking for my own answers. I found information on the different types of absences I could take from work. I found out I could take a leave of absence if it was caused by a disability. I went back to my doctor, this time I had to cry cause if I didn't cry, I didn't think he was taking me serious. "I NEEED Your help. I can't do this. I don't know what's wrong with my body, I can get a leave of absence from work but I would need you to sign my papers" "There's a fee attached for me to fill out the forms" "That's fine, why does my chest hurt? Why is my heart rate up?" "It's anxiety" *What's anxiety? Whateva you gotta do, jus fill out my forms please.* By July I had crashed. I couldn't function. My mind was always in pain, my chest always hurting, I was always crying or sleeping. Nothing felt normal. I didn't feel like myself and I felt like I had to fight for the help I needed.

Thanks to my benefits I qualified for a paid leave of absence under short term disability. *Wow so this is what it had come to. As long as it gives me time to breathe and focus on planning for Kaykay's one-year I'll be ok. How will I explain to my parents why I'm home from work?* I wasn't used to talking to them about issues in my life but I couldn't jus hide the fact that I'd be home every day. "I need a break from work so I'm going to be home for the next few weeks" My mom says, "What about your bills?" *What about my bills? That's what you have to say? What about me? What about the fact that I can't cope...no? This is exactly why I don't say anything.* "What about my bills?" *I'm annoyed.* "How are you going to pay them?" "They're gonna get paid" "Ye because your dad and I tried to help you out and you can't just not pay cause that puts a strain on us" *Thank you for your support. This is why I never ask for help. Why can't I just have white parents? They seem so much more supportive of their kids.*

My Pastor stuck to his promise. Right before Kaykay's one-year anniversary I was baptized. I felt like I was right where I needed to be. *God restored my faith in church and helped me overcome my pain and forgive.* For the one-year anniversary I was surrounded by love and friends and beautiful memories.

Poetic Interlude

I told God that if kaykay left I'd go with him.
After 8 years I can't imagine a life of 365 without him by my side.
Guess I lied cause I'm still here.
Year one survived, thriving only by grace and mercy
I cried mercy as I lost my apartment, my finances, my son, my everything
Thinking of the identity of a woman I no longer knew
Thinking of my life as a mother that seemed to good to be true

Truth is I feel like the last 8 years have been a dream
Dreaming of a life with an angel that always smiled
I smile through the pain like he did
I smile through the rain like he did
Keeping sane in God's lane like he did
52 weeks and I keep reminding myself that he's happy
Happiness is all I ever wanted
Haunted by the disrespect of a disease
I've fallen to my knees committing to keep my sight on God, trusting his lead cause my new journey is starting from a seed
I would call year one a success, new job, new car, returned home, I'm blessed
Stretched thin but mentally resting through the testings of life
I told God that if kaykay left I'd go with him.
After 9 years I couldn't imagine a life of 12 months without him by my side.
Guess I lied
But since God never leaves my side I chose to live and enjoy the ride to my destiny
Destined to be free
Till we meet again
Adieu

JOB 39:12

"Will you have faith and depend on him to return your grain and gather it from your threshing floor?

Short term disability was over so quickly. My doctor asked me "How are you feeling" "Better" "Ok great, so I'll put you back to work then" *Damn if I knew that's what that question meant I woulda said I'm still struggling. I felt better but not good enough to go back to work.* Nonetheless, by the time September came I was back to work. September was a hard month for me. I forgot what grade Kaykay would be in and had a complete meltdown. *I'm his mother, how could I forget something so important? What kinda mother am I?* I started therapy back up to help me cope. One of the first things my therapist asked was what type of support I had at home.

She knew of my experience with my parents during Kaykay's death and wanted to ensure I wasn't trying to cope alone. My mother had a very different way of expressing that she cared. *What was my support?* I never felt safe enough to open up to my family about my struggles. I even hid the fact that I was seeing a therapist. While I tried to manage the mental pain, the physical pain started. By October I started having weekly gallstone attacks. I was missing at least one day a week from work. I hadn't had a gallstone attack in years but it very much felt like my body was shutting down. I would get sharp pains that caused a dead stop. My stomach was bloated and all I could do was sit and wait for the pain to pass. I started to realize that my gallstone attacks were brought on by stress. As much as I tried to calm my mind it was constantly running a mile a minute and that was puttin pressure on my body. My body was attacking in every way, my resting heart rate was unusually high. Once I was home from work I would pass out for hours at a time. I couldn't think straight. Nothing made sense. I was medically diagnosed with depression in October but I couldn't understand its effects on my body. I thought those were mental things not physical.

Obviously, I wasn't doing well here in Canada, so I convinced my parents that we should go to Jamaica for Christmas. I couldn't wait to get away. If I was gonna be sad during the holidays I wanted to be sad with a drink in hand so that I could drain my tears in alcohol. The gallstone attacks weren't getting better. I was forced to go back on short term disability because of how often I was sick. My gallstone attacks made my stomach feel extremely bloated to the point it interfered with my breathin sometimes. Sometimes the continuous sharp pains affected my sleep. I decided to start a new diet to see if that would help while I waited to see the specialist. After many doctor visits I was diagnosed with sleep apnea and they decided to do surgery to have my gallbladder removed. *Problem solved...can Jamaica come already? I was ready to get the hell up outta there.*

We were staying with my dad's family for Christmas which was a beautiful change. We normally spent time with my mom's family so it was good to finally get to meet new family members. At Christmas Eve we went to Grand Market in Spanish town. Stuff my dad did when he was younger we were now getting a chance to do. Grand Market was basically a series of malls and markets that stayed open late during Christmas, even until morning and people could walk around and shop. I enjoyed that system a lot better than the way we did things in Canada. Christmas day was spent with about twenty new cousins that I got to meet. I always worried about meeting new family because their first comment was usually about my weight, but this time around no one said anything and Christmas in Jamaica was a success. Even though we stayed with family we took one day to travel to a resort in Runaway Bay. My favorite part of resorts are the free drinks that come with an all-inclusive day pass.

Everything was going well until I was in the water. The sun was bright and the waves so beautiful. I walked a little bit away from my sister and cousin and just stood in the water. It looked so peaceful. I started dreaming of floating away. Putting my body in the water and just becoming one with the waves. I dreamt of seeing Kaykay, I dreamt of God taking away the pain. It felt so real. As I battled with my decision, I drowned out all sounds behind me and stared at the beauty of the sun. I walked further out, unafraid of slipping away. I just kept walking, talking to Kaykay and God. I touched the water with my hand. It looked so clear, so unalarming. I was just at peace in the water and wanted to float away. My mind drifted in and out. *If you do drift away you'll ruin the trip for everyone else.* Then I heard the voice of my sister. "Cola...Cola... are you ok?" I snapped back to consciousness "I'm good" I stood still. *That was close. Closer than any other time. She's watching you now. Betta jus leave it alone.* I left the water and spent the rest of the time gettin drunk at the bar. *What better way to forget everything?*

The next morning we had to pack up for departure later that night. I didn't wanna leave. I didn't wanna go back but I had a job and stupid car payments. We were also packing up food to take back with us. I was standing with my dad in the kitchen as he was pulling things out of the freezer and checking them one by one. As he was opening a plastic bag to check the contents it fell from his hand and dropped on my foot. *AHSDAHJLFNSDFLBJDSAFHS.* The pain was instant. I couldn't even scream out loud but everything inside me was freaking out.

My foot was instantly swollen and I could barely walk. The pain was bad. Real bad. My mom and sister examined my foot to see if it was broken but couldn't really tell. With barely any feeling in my foot I limped my way through the Jamaican airport and boarded the plane. As much as I didn't wanna go back before, now more than eva I needed that free health care. *Ain't nobody like Jamaican hospitals.*

We landed right into Toronto's first snowstorm of the season and it was bad. None of my shoes could fit my foot so I was forced to wear slippers in the snow storm. I could barely walk in normal conditions and now I had to deal with this as well. We drove straight to the Oshawa hospital. After waiting for a few hours and getting x rays the results were in. I had fractured the tip of my second toe. My big toe, even though it was purple, was not broken and the rest of the toes were swollen cause they had also been hit by the object. The doctors asked, "What was it that fell on your toe that caused all this damage?" I responded, "Frozen turkey neck." *Only me...I swear...this shit happens to only me.*

Poetic Interlude

The day I died was august 23 2014
That's the day my heart stopped beating
An my mind went into a state of shock
Shocking me into a continuous feeling of numbness
I don't remember my son's funeral
Couldn't even tell you who came
I sat in the car as they lowered his body
Knowing I would never hear him call my name
Im tormented by the promises I made but did not fulfill

White keys
Black notes
I delayed teaching and sharing my greatest gift with my son
Thinking I had enough time since he was still young
I hear the haunting sounds of procrastination playing gracefully to the tune of Chopin
I've tried to start teaching
But the weights of guilt and regret
Entangle my fingers that contain
The melodic coloring of my heart is
Black and blue swirls creating a calming peace like waves
I gave life my everything
In return I stand alone
I once stood in the ocean begging the ripples to pull me away
Changed my mind at the thought of ruining ppls day
It's like standing on the train tracks unable to move as the train lights illuminate my face and I prepare for impact
It's like standing at the end of a gun begging life to pull the trigger
It's like being held down underwater
Not even fighting to come up for air
I've learned they call this symptoms of trauma
Isolation is comforting
I try confronting the root of the pain
But my brain conveniently navigates and journeys between memory lane and
Concentration
Shorting out everything in between
My brain feels disconnected from my body
I don't know what day it is
I get anxiety at the thought of leaving my house
I smile one minute then cry the next
Barely getting enough rest
I can't remember if I had something to eat
I'm no longer hungry
I eat for survival
All I want to do is go to sleep

But all the noises wont let me think
Let me think
I wish a drink could ease the pain
I waste time trying to keep sane
Trying to read the words on the page
But nothing makes sense
There's an eerie silence as I try to connect what my eyes see from the vocabulary to the meaning
My heart starts beating out of my chest
My head is still a mess
No activity
Limited signs of life
My minds been sliced
Between the woman I used to be
An the one that's taken over me
Too many unfamiliar traits
Uninvited emotions
Deafening mistakes
Definitely hate to love this being who hates being in this life with no direction
Inject me with life
So I can see my own potential
Running through my veins
Drain the stain of incomplete
Cause I am complete in God
He sees my every move
Saw me contemplating between the fall off a bridge or the hit of a car
Contemplating if the physical pain would mask the stain of my heart
He holds me while it feels like im spiraling down
Sends people my way to ensure I don't drown
His value in me I could never explain
Trusting his love and his faith to sustain
An break the chains of disdain

CHAPTER SEVENTY-ONE

Constant

So be very careful and watchful of yourselves to love the LORD your God. JOSHUA 23:11

Kaykay was my whole life and I didn't know how to cope without him. I absolutely hated myself without him. He was my reason to stay alive. I didn't live for myself. Since fracturing the tip of my toe I had nothing but time to sit and think. My toe hurt like hell. I would wake up in the night with shooting pains up and down my legs. I could barely walk and was confined to either my bed or a chair. What a way to begin the new year. Since I was home I spent a lot more time on the phone with Romeo. He did what he could to support me but his lack of understanding of depression left me in a spiral. Too many changes were happening too quickly. I couldn't cope. I returned to work for the last two weeks in January but the office was riddled with sickness and I developed bronchitis and was right back off work. I couldn't keep up. The only thing that resembled my past was Romeo, everything else was different. My friendships were even different. The grief had divided many of my friendships. I needed consistency and most people didn't know how to provide that. Even my relationship with God was slightly changing. Before I would run to God I would be on the phone with Romeo. He replaced everything. I needed him like I needed air. I loved God, but I sometimes needed a response right away. He masked the pain, heard all the tears and encouraged me to keep going. I know it was draining on him but I needed something to stay constant without changing.

When I look back at the relationship I had with Romeo I understood the reasons we had never met over the years. I would often say to him that we were too close. We depended on each other too much. We were too caught up in each other. It was a very toxic relationship and had we met we would have destroyed each other. God saved us from breaking. We both had tough pasts and were two injured souls addicted to making it work. Instead of leaning on God for answers we turned to each other. We were jealous of each other, we were obsessed with each other, we were both hot tempered, couldn't see anything but ourselves. In essence that's all we did, we worshipped each other. If it wasn't apparent then it was very clear now. I knew I should let go but I couldn't. *I can't lose him like I lost Kaykay.*

I went on a church retreat in Rochester New York the weekend of Romeo's birthday and it was the first time we were forced to be apart for a whole weekend. The night I returned I called him to share with him everything I had learned. He had been doing work while I was away and was extremely excited to share his news. Romeo wasn't one to talk a lot but this night he was talking my ear off. He had asked me to play him this song called My God is Awesome - the remix version.

My God is awesome
He can move mountains
Keep me in the valley
Hide me from the rain
My God is awesome
Heals me when I'm broken
Strength where I've been weakened
Forever he will reign

The two of us sat and listened until I fell asleep. I woke up to a text message from Romeo saying "Baby God has delivered me, but this means we can no longer talk. I want you to keep working on yourself and do everything you need to do to keep moving forward." *Damn. Ok. I mean at least he was delivered. At least he's happy. Imma miss him but if God has called him then I'm jus happy he listened. I'll get through this. I always do.*

Poetic Interlude

When can I breathe again
When can I enjoy the sun rays bouncing
The melodic tunes in tune with my heart
The rhythms of familiar laughter
That pull
That pull to start
Living
When will I breathe again
When will this crushing depressing cloud be a distant vapour
That my maker tears back and hand claps out of existence
I wanted to be out of existence
I wanted to be a free spirit
In heaven with my son looking down on earth looking at the images of pain
My thoughts said it would be ok
Said it would be painless
N I could finally be at peace
Oh how beautiful it would be to leave this world behind on my own terms
Before things got worse
Before I lost my breathe completely
Before I lost my mind completely
But as I sailed above I felt the burning heat
I saw my feet completely crash beneath me
I was overcome with the guilt of those left behind
My thoughts are interrupted
Every
Single
Time
This was not the answer to the questions I held hidden in my heart
Even death doesn't come easy
I guess it's not meant for me

I see the lies written on the walls of my mind
But the music notes expose the truth
I am loved
I am needed
I am a beautiful being
Then that base comes
It's The heartbeat of the rhythm
That Says
Don't give up
It's not over
Keep fighting
listening to a shuffled playlist of gospel song and it's the same message of reasoning and reassurance
I started searching for answers
Praying
Believing
Searching for that missing song
Searching for my purpose and where I belong
I long to help ppl smile
But i need to find that smile within me
When should I breathe again
When is it safe?
Where is it safe?
Who will breathe with me?
I can't keep going around in circles
I want off this ride
I feel like I'm dying inside
I smile
Then cry
Laugh
Then sigh
There's a feelin inside that keeps pushing override
Overriding the darkness
Allowing small victories inside
I ate today
I prayed today
I bathed today
I feel ok today
I didn't eat today
I stayed in bed all day

662 Cola Bennett

I didn't bath today
I still feel ok today
I went to the gym today
Heard my favorite song today
Smiled at someone today
I don't feel ok today
There's a light
A bright light that keeps coming closer
I ate bad food today
Everything is going wrong today
Lord help me get through this day
I breathed today
And the next day
And the next
Jesus thank you for everyday I wake up and take my first breath of air
Let me be thankful for what seems like small victories
Just
Keep
Breathing

CHAPTER SEVENTY-TWO

Be still

"The [flightless] wings of the ostrich wave joyously; with the pinion (shackles, fetters) and plumage of love.
JOB 39:13

Let me quickly summarize the first 6 months of 2016.
January - Fractured the tip of my toe.
February - Developed Bacterial bronchitis; I was sick for the whole month, my fever would not break and I lived on antibiotics.
March - Developed Viral Bronchitis; I attempted to go back to work but I was off again. I worked a total of two weeks this whole month.
April - Surgery to remove my gallbladder. Woke up from surgery crying for Kaykay. The first thing outta my mouth when I woke up was "I want my son". It was a horrible feeling to wake up and not have him there.
May - Sick for two weeks. Went to work and caught another cold. I was just about done with myself at this point. Why me? Why am I always gettin sick? Doctors had no answers for me as to why I was always sick.
June - Went to Cuba and went on short term disability at work again. I was mentally broken.

Every time I had to ask for time off it was like the battle of my life. I had to always prove I was sick. Then I had to pay over $100 each time I needed my doctor to fill out the form. The physical was easier to prove but anytime it was mental I was battling against not jus my workplace but my doctor as well. Being depressed was tiring enough without having to fight to show how depressed I was. It's not easy being sick for a long duration. It started to play on my psyche. I had fevers for several days in a row, whenever I coughed I peed. *That's jus embarrassing.* I was a grown woman unable to control my own bodily functions. I felt so hopeless. Since Kaykay passed I had frequent nightmares of him searching for me or feeling abandoned by me. I had flashbacks of the moments when I held him as he took his last breath. I had visions of the blood that drained from his eyes as he laid on the bed in the hospital. I had visions of leaving him behind at the hospital. I had visions. I had thoughts. I had trouble with my memory. I would blank out. I felt like my mind was separating from my body. I was always tired. I went on emotional rollercoasters. I felt great one day then suicidal the next. My lows were bad. I was afraid to leave the house. I didn't wanna be around people. I would make plans then cancel all the time.

I was extremely hard on myself whenever I couldn't remember something. I didn't know who this new Cola was but I didn't like her. I went to read my bible one day and the words didn't make sense, I picked up my phone but couldn't understand simple meanings. It hurt to look. I couldn't focus and even though I slept, my mind stayed awake all night so I woke up with headaches. I was sensitive to light. I felt like I was losing my mind. It was a constant battle with myself to stay alive. I felt like I was gonna die. I would dream of crashing my car while I was driving, I no longer trusted myself. I was scared because I didn't know what was happening to me.

I left a message for my therapist trying to explain to her everything happening to me and ended the message sayin "Can you help me please? My doctor is no longer trying to help me." Even though I had been diagnosed with depression the only help they offered me was medication. I didn't want medication which meant they assumed I wasn't serious about gettin treatment or getting better. I was labeled as someone trying to abuse the system. My doctor said it was all in my head but it made no sense. The light around me was so sensitive, I didn't have any proper thoughts inside my head. I was so paranoid I was going to die. I was at the point where I just wanted to know what was wrong with me so I could treat it. After months of feeling so disconnected my therapist finally put a name to it. I had been experiencing symptoms of trauma. She handed me a paper with a list of symptoms:

Unexplained sensations including pain
Sleep and eating disturbances
Low energy
Depression and fear
Anxiety and panic
Numbness, irritability, anger
Feeling out of control
Avoidance
Distraction
Decrease in concentration
Memory lapse
Difficulty with decisions
Compulsion
Impulsive, self-destructive behavior
Dissociation
Changes in interpersonal relationships:
Isolation, avoidance, social withdrawal
Sexual disruption
Flashbacks
Nightmares

I had experienced every single one of those symptoms. *I didn't even know this existed. Why didn't I know this before? At least I know what it is now.*

I thought I could jus pray a couple times and things would go back to normal. but nothing was normal anymore. My biggest problem was the ability to smile and look like I was holding it all together. People often said to me I didn't look like a typical grieving mother. *What is typical grieving?* My doctor felt that he had helped me enough. We tried doing a gradual return to work but even that didn't work for me. Every time I was sitting in a cubicle it felt as if I was wasting my life, my purpose, my talent. The more I kept it together the harder and further I crashed. I felt trapped. I wanted to leave work to get help but I had monthly bills. *The system has been designed for me to fail. I can't win no matta what I do.* I tried using the counselors through my work benefits but it was so uncomfortable. I couldn't find the right fit and every time I tried a new counselor I had to re-explain all my trauma which essentially re-traumatized me.

I woke up one day with my heart completely broken. I missed Romeo. *Real love was being happy for him and wanting the best for him even though he wasn't with me. Real love was praying for him constantly even though I couldn't be with him.* I was bitter for a while, thinking of all the work I had put in over the years just to lose him to someone else. I wanted to message him but wanted to respect his wishes. Then I thought about emailing him cause I knew he wouldn't answer his emails right away but decided against it. The reality of two losses was enough to push me over the edge personally. Even though I personally felt like I had gone over the edge, unless I was hospitalized, in the eyes of medical professionals I was not ill enough to get time off work. After months of back and forth I desperately pleaded with my doctor to help me and even sought out programs to justify my need to be off work. After I did the work to find my own programs he finally agreed. *Why is it so hard? Why does it take so much work? Unless I cried uncontrollably I wasn't getting nowhere. I duno when I'm going back this time. I may never go back iuno. I just need time to figure things out.*

We went to Cuba as a family to celebrate my dad's birthday. Cuba felt...different. I was at peace, I could swim without bein depressed. It was bliss. I swam out far in the water and was amazed at the beauty of God's creation. It took my breath away. Seven glorious days in God's paradise was the welcomed change I needed. While in Cuba I got a chance to play at the piano bar and to sing for a couple of guests. I had a chef who made me personal pancake designs and picked flowers for me. More than I could have imagined...I was happy. I returned home on top of the moon. I hadn't felt this good in so long.

I turned my phone back on after Cuba and saw a message from Romeo saying he put money in my account to pay for the Netflix. Even though he had broken up with me for more than a year I was paying for our Netflix account and never canceled it. It was the one thing we shared together so whenever I couldn't pay, he would send the money.

Not being able to talk to Romeo was killing me. He never called for my birthday or for Mother's Day...nothing. Many nights I cried to God before passing out. Cuba was only a momentary fix, I fell right back into depression. It didn't make sense how that much negativity could hit one person, but I thought of Job and how he was rewarded because he held on through the storm. I had to believe that it was going to get better. I had to get to know this new me. This new me loved God, loved music, loved to sing and loved to write. Whenever things got to a point where all I could say was "GOD HELP" He filled my spirit with an indescribable peace that held me together. Sometimes I couldn't speak, all I could do was listen silently as the music played. Sometimes I had to sing out loud from the bottom of my soul and sometimes I had to write until I had nothing left. Little by little the new me was mentally forming. Physically I still didn't wanna get outta bed, didn't wanna bathe, I only wanted to sleep. I was giving myself permission to take baby steps. *Deep breaths. Deeeep Brreaths.*

August 6 2016 To Romeo

I miss you......

August 24 2016 To Cola

I miss you too....

Poetic Interlude

Survivor's Guilt

Nobody tells you how to survive after a piece of you has died
cause they don't know what to say
How do you tell somebody to smile through the heartbreak
How do you tell somebody to breathe through the storm
How do you tell somebody that their mind won't betray them
This guilt
This guilt was a rotten stench I couldn't wait to get rid of
Yet I accepted at the same time
Comfortably
Guilt encompassed me
Shame startled me
Disaster, disappointment and disgrace became me until it didn't stink no more
I survived
I survived
The traumas, dramas and death of my spirit
Lay broken like childhood dreams
Adolescence stolen
Yet I fought to survive
I fought to be free
My son saved me
Love kept us together
Faith pulled us further
Memories of your hugs & smooth dances
Pranced east to west
Your body begged for rest
The stillness of your air as I held you
Your last breath blew against my heart
Blue sky above
You sleep peacefully
And I wished it were me instead
But I survived

Why
Why is a question I cannot get the answer to
I don't even want the answer to tell you the truth
I just want him
My son
My life
My best friend
My identity
I want it back
Without him who am I?
With every moment of happiness
I witness the emotional change inside
It's exhausting
Being happy without him doesn't seem fair
Doesn't seem like it should be
Not with me
See We made a promise to live life to the fullest
He fulfilled his purpose and moved on past me and left me full of jealousy that he was too good for this earth
I've searched for earthly treasures
They seem to change as often as Canadian weather
Fleeting
Leaving me empty
I feel invisible in a crowd
Laughter sometimes feels way too loud
My bed is more than jus a home,
It's where I belong as I contemplate life
Why is it that colors fade as time goes on?
God, help me
God lent me my son
Let me be a part of his light
It beamed so so bright
I was blinded and forgot that he was on loan
Now he's gone home
And I want him back
A fruit of my womb
An inheritance of smiles
Lessons of gratitude
Rewarded by his attitude
I wanna be mad and rude

Yet I stay silent
I lack understanding so I'm praying for peace
I need a new lease on life if I'm gonna keep pushing
Pushing my feelings aside & inside
Cause a color collide
Giving root to a periodic pain
That hits me like waves
Rough ocean type
That bury me
Water in my nose
I cant breath
These waves seem taller than me, 5'3
I'm drowning in feelings and stages,
Trapped in emotional cages
Mentally stewing
Numbingly alive
The size of the lies I tell myself keep growin
I say I'm ok
I say don't be happy
They say Keep smiling
I think Sadness is life
You say Act normal
I say Keep it together
To get her wisdom is to breathe honesty
It's ok not to be ok
Some moments will knock me right out
Getting up before the bell is all that counts
Learning to walk on water
Is the gift God is giving me as a replacement for the sadness
Emotionally bleeding
Plagued by memories
Takin up rent for free
It's a poison I will no longer drink
If I could just push through and touch
I knocked, He opened
I cried, He listened
A witness to my pain
My father's changing the game

Breath deeply
I am no longer the same
I'm breaking up with unforgiveness and shame
Partnering with forgiveness, love, acceptance & balanced sleep
Must quench the search for my existence
I exist for a reason
I'm still living through the seasons
My reason to live is to love in spite of my situation
Despite what life continues to challenge me with
I am not only surviving
I am thriving
Unconditional love is freeing me
Freeing my mind
Forcing me to ask myself questions
Who do I have left to give to?
What is my reason to live?
Where can I be the most impactful?
Why am I so passionate?
When it's my time to go, will I be ready?
How can I live forever?
Today
I decided to live
Washed my face, walked out the door and felt taller
Today
I decided to Love again
Cause Love runs so much deeper than the grave
I am no longer a slave
To guilt

CHAPTER SEVENTY-THREE

The End To a Beautiful Beginning

He will turn many of the sons of Israel back [from sin] to [*love* and serve] the Lord their God.
LUKE 1:16

Inspiration comes in different ways. My sister's best friend and Kaykay's older god sister (she's family) had said that she wanted to sell body butters and body wash to make some money. *Oh ye, you bought all that equipment. You ain't got nun to lose. It would get you outta bed. What would you need daily to help you get outta bed? What kinda things would you like to make? I need soap to bathe, I need deodorant, and I need lotion. I know how to make body butter but how cool would it be to make a deodorant? I still remember all the stuff I learned before when I was working with Té.*

Two things happened in November. My sister, her best friend and I started a company and Romeo and I had gotten back together. *I felt like I could breathe again.* Romeo and I weren't supposed to talk but once we reconnected this time we couldn't let go. I worked harder than I had ever worked, both personally and on the business. By December my short-term disability was up and although I had come a long way, I wasn't ready to go back yet. I felt like I was jus gettin stable. I applied for long term disability and was waiting for my case manager to respond. She was a pushy know it all and I didn't like her vibe, but she was supposed to help me. It was her tone, it was very condescending. Most of our phone calls left me in tears, left me hating that I was the way I was. *Why can't I just be normal?* I always had to answer a million questions. They couldn't find my file, they needed updated records. They needed to know why I wasn't taking medication. They needed to know my whole life top to bottom and then came the advice. "You should go outside for a walk everyday" *That would be great if I actually could get out of bed to go outside.* It was like she didn't know how this mental thing worked and maybe she didn't but why was it my job to teach her? She thought I wasn't doing enough, I thought her expectations were too high. "Well you aren't as bad as some of my other caseloads. You're not really depressed. If things were that bad you would take medication" *What am I supposed to say to this? So, because I sometimes get out of bed I can't be depressed? What about the anxiety I feel every time I have to leave the house? I get up ye but I never wanna leave. Does that count for anything?* "You're not even in a therapy program" "That's cause I don't feel comfortable with most of the therapists, I just found a new therapist but I'm waiting for his availability" "You Don't Have A Program, You're Not on Medication, You're Not Trying. I'm Denying Your Claim." click. *Did this bitch jus hang up?* I got an instant headache, I felt dizzy, nauseous and I couldn't hold my head up. I just couldn't understand how someone who was supposed to help me ended up yelling at me and denying my claim. I called her boss to report it but he never got back to me. *They don't actually care. I wonder how these insurance people treat those worse than me?*

God, I don't know where you are bringing me but I trust You. Yet again my money was gone and I had no savings and no means to make any more. I couldn't apply for another job and I wasn't ready to go back yet. *Well, I guess I gotta make this business work as much as I can.* With one business partner on the way out it was left to my sis and I to take this to the next level.

Romeo and I were going through battles upon battles. Many nights I cried. I was happy with him but when we went through the valleys things felt so low. We were going on our 11th year of being off and on and I was dying to see him but he was still hesitant. Romeo was sick often and it worried me. After several visits it was determined he had a brain tumor. *Why do I keep attracting the sick ones? I promised I wouldn't leave no matta what.* We talked marriage, kids, future. We had grown so no matta how many fights we got into I was going to stay by his side.

I always told him the only way I was leaving was if he broke up with me himself which I never thought would happen until I pushed him to make a decision on marriage. *Do you wanna marry me or not? It's that simple. We've been at this thing for 11 years now.*

He chose not to move forward with me and I had to be ok with that. *Yet again, he dumps me. I should be used to this by now.* We sat on the phone in silence. "Hello?" "Hello?" *Why does it sound like a girl on the phone, yo who the hell this man has at his house now?* "Who is this?" "It's Raquel" Click.

What the hell jus happened? Raquel? That's Romeo's twin sisters name. But he's in Vancouver so how could she be there too? Lord what is going on. I got a text message from Romeo's phone "We can't talk anymore, I wish you success on your book but this is it. Bye" I had a lot of questions and no questions all at once. *What jus happened? What is going on? Who is Romeo? Is there a Romeo?*

CHAPTER SEVENTY-FOUR

Who?

We know that we have passed out of death into Life, because we *love* the brothers and sisters. He who does not *love* remains in [spiritual] death.
1 JOHN 3:14

It was a new year, January 2018 rolled around and it had been months since that night with Romeo and I was no closer to any answers to the questions I had. *Just try again. Jus ask.*

January 2018 To Romeo

Who are you?

To Cola

I've been trying to figure all of this out as well everyday I wanted to tell you but I was jus so far into it I didn't know how or where to start. I know you hate lying and I had lied so much to you. As much as I was lying there where a lot of parts that were true. Romeo's personality and how I am is true . My heart and the connection you felt with me is true . I might not been the person in the photo or that voice that you feel in love with . But mostly everything that was me was real . So because you loved the voice and the idea of Romeo I just kept it going . Every year I would do something for you to stop talking to me but we would jus end up talking. Or we would take a break and something would pull me back. I guess in a way I jus felt comfort in you . You understood me. You got me. I was fun to chill with you . You weren't using me like everyone else. You where jus Nicola. And I know deep down it wasn't fair wat I was doing. But I did. I always felt like I was supposed to be in your life. To help you with what you were going threw. Ya I probably messed it up more and I apologise for that. I honestly meant no harm from this. I didn't do this with any bad thing in mind. It jus happened and I kept it going and I was wrong for that. Every night I would dream about being Romeo and being that person for you .And making you happy. But it can't happen and I guess one day I jus had to come to that realisation that. I'm not him. I'm someone else and I have to be okay with that. God moves mountains. He showed me that I can love myself now . You have helped me with that as well. God loves me. And he loves you. Took a while for me to realise it but I did.

Well I guess it started cuz when I was 19 I've was going through a lot. I just didn't want to be me I guess. I have been raped as well and some things I have told you. I jus wanted to escape. So that day on that computer when you asked me my name. I don't knw I guess I jus panic and said Romeo don't know where that came from. We jus talk and talk for hours and I was so comfortable with you. I guess I knew it was wrong we were both getting feelings for each other. That's when I made up the story about another girl being pregnant thinking you would jus stop talking to me and that would be my way out but you didn't. And then I slip right back Into it again being Romeo. And not dealing with my own life and stress.

You then said you were pregnant and you didn't know. Then what your sperm donor did to you .And you had chlamydia and how your family treated you . And your were jus alone . And I jus felt bad to just leave you like everyone else .cuz you had nobody and I also had nobody at that time . We both needed someone and we took comfort in each other . Jus talking to and chilling with you helped me a lot . It took my mind off of things I was dealing with. I would jus numb out being me and I could be Romeo ...

You were going through a lot and I don't know why I felt like I had to be there to help. You had Kay Kay. And struggled as a single mom with him. I was mad that I couldn't be there to help cuz I was not that person I was pretending to be in the physical aspect .
My brother is not real. My lil sister is real. Jus a different name. Everything I told you about her is true. My mom is real everything about her and how she treats me is true.

Not showing me love and all that stuff. Being used by the family that's all real. My aunt my cousin all real .My dad and what's going on with him. Cheating leaving my mom the brain tumour all real. All the kids are not real only real one is papa and another son. My friends and their personalities and all their drama is real jus different names. Baby mamas not real . My twin is basically me. Hope that helps a lil. You mostly know everything that's going on in my life jus a lil mixed around.

So your book, I dunno. You should jus leave it. I don't know what to say. I don't think you should change it . In my tumour head I was really Romeo. After awhile I jus believed my lies I guess. I don't want to embarrass you at all about this. I don't want your friends to say they were right and I was jus catfishing you. It was deeper than that. I know now that my tumour had an effect on me to do this as well. So you should keep your book how it is . That's all I can get into for now I hope you understand a lil better. If any question you can ask I'll try my best. I can't think any more about this my head is hurtin. I've been praying more, reading that devotion book we used to read and living one day at a time also learning to love myself and my life. I'm working on it .

I'm sorry I wasted 11 years of your life. It really went fast . Deep down I always thought you had a feeling I was lying but you ignored it. I'm sorry for everything. You knew my heart even though I was lying to you. I really do care about you .

P.s. my fingers are hurting that is the longest I wrote In a while. Sorry it took so long . Had to get to.a certain place first before I could spit it all out.

After 11 years, I finally knew why Romeo was never available to meet me. He never existed. I don't even have any more tears for him...I mean her.

Poetic Interlude

When is love gonna stop saying sorry for all the mess it dragged me through
When is it gonna look me in my eyes and feel the full depth of the pain my heart has endured
Real eyes recognize the sun rise as the sun sets
It's beauty uncontainable that it has you mesmerized as you realize you're staring into real eyes
And your whole being is at peace
And the real lies are all put away
Love
I miss that temporary feeling
Wishing it would last longer
I see your ashes you left at the gate
Don't make me hate you for your disregard for my life
You come in
You go out
You come in
You go out
I've suffered many casualties at your hand
Love
Each time you graze me I feel a tickle in my throat and I'm forced to yell
Enough
This is all I can take
I am time kissed and baked
I am done putting my trust in a lake
Just sitting and waiting
To be a priority
Just like the sun sets and rises I want to feel your heart beat flow through my veins
Like how wisdom now knows my name
Love
I'm so sick of your games
You don't make me laugh
Anymore

Come like a pain sore
That I'm waiting to heal up
Fill me with your good side
Gimme that good ride
Side to side
God's pushing override
Exhilarating
Debilitating
Love
Me
I love me
Let's start here and build again

CHAPTER SEVENTY-FIVE

Memories

My memory has me cautious of love and all that it has to offer. It's a process fo sure. My memories remind me that family doesn't have to be blood. Despite the negative moments, my memories don't hold no regret. They hold thoughts of laughter and joy. Since Kaykay is no longer on this earth, he's been moved to my memories, a part of me that is more of feeling than a thought . I don't remember how to love or be loved so that's something imma have to learn from scratch, but it's worth it if it will be the key to unlocking my freedom. A verse in the bible, 1 John 4 says: "There is no fear in love. But perfect love drives out fear, because fear has to do with punishment." Whenever the fear of love or the fear to love comes up, I remind myself of this verse. To me, to be afraid of love is to be afraid to live. It doesn't seem worth it to never love again. I think about my first boyfriend and how he loved me despite our argument. Why did such a small thing break us apart? Why wasn't love strong enough to keep together? Then I think of Romeo and how that all turned out to be a lie, I have too many memories of a life that was all imaginary. But how could my mind tell the difference between real and fake? So many memories from too many years to sort through. Despite everything, something inside me told me that I would be fine. No meds. Jus time to sort through all these memories and to let go of the ones that no longer served me. I needed time to breathe. I needed time to heal. I jus didn't know what this process was gonna look like, and that's what made me nervous. Could I sustain the mental battles to come?

Poetic Interlude

I had a conversation with my heart
I wanted to know when the first break was
Was it the rape, rejection or molestation that set in
Maybe it was the abandonment that had
Blue clouds painted like an ombre fades to black
I feel jacked up that dating is not in my vocabulary
Carry me off into the sunsets?
Naw I don't do that princess shit
Marry me off like juliet
I'd rather wake up than die like romeo
Loow mi tho
Cause it's a process
Less the dramatics
I truly am a love fanatic
My love lives in the attic
I'm mindful
That the tempo of love
Matches the rhythms of my feet
Meet me at the altar
We chanting freedom freedom freedom without falter
Love me till I fall back without fear
Rear view mirror of that dumb love
Begging for some love
Getting that tough love
Loving that clean love
Wanna be seen love
No longer a dream love
Don't want nobody mean love
Craving that Jesus love
Undeserving but serving a greater purpose
It's so worth it to give in
To love you despite your sin
Unlocking your false truths
Dispelling all lies
When I look into your eyes I fall deep into comfort

Ye there's some hurt but, its healing
I'm feelin like success is ours for the making
Taking vows of honesty and gratitude
Love me rude
Tickle me with your time
Awaken my taste buds with your words
Unlock my mind and drain my heart
Life's issues flow while its sustained by purity
When you're with me I am protected
I neglect inner voices that say this isn't real
Steal away my insecurity as I build up my confidence
Gone are dense moments
Tense comments that offend, twist and miscue beautiful loyalty and my hearts message that I love you
Sue me if I don't do what I'm making a promise to do
Dear husband,
this my love letter to you

CHAPTER SEVENTY-SIX

Healing

For the LORD is [absolutely] righteous, He loves righteousness (virtue, morality, justice); The upright shall see His face.
PSALM 11:7

My journey has brought me through so many situations that should have broken me. By definition, I should be dead. To be honest sometimes it feels like my head is split and I'm trying to keep it together. The trauma of everything has been weighing on me more heavily then I care to admit. Cause to admit it means to admit that I am suffering from mental illness. Ever since Kaykay passed my memory has been affected. Both long term and short term. It feels so different to be in this space. It's like I was in a car accident with life changing brain injuries, but my brain hurts and I get so frustrated that I can't remember things as easily. I used to be great at remembering but that woman no longer exists apparently. It's an adjustment that I am not ready for. How do I get back to who I was? Or is this my new norm? All I have is a desire to do great things and impact nations and speak and share my love for God and my love for life and for all it has handed me...the good and the bad. Who am I that God has saved me? The hits keep coming but I am unable to stay down. My head hurts often cause I get so overwhelmed, but I keep smiling cause that's what my son taught me. I don't know how not to smile cause it comes from a place of gratitude more than a place of hiding. In my continued quest for healing I read the bible more, I sang more, I wrote more, I listened to music more, I went outside more, I focused on building my business and I made a conscious decision to isolate myself from any negativity. This included any friend or family member that made me feel less than. I began to understand that just because they were family it did not mean I was forced to subject myself to the negative environment. My mind is so precious and fragile, to give it away carelessly to those around me looking to intentionally or unintentionally drain my energy was toxic. The more I sought after God the more He poured into me and the more I saw my value and understood my worth. You know what I jus realized? I keep telling myself that I don't know who I am and that I don't love myself, but it's all lies. On this new journey I have learned to understand my own love and my own needs. Even the small changes and decisions to keep myself away from bad energy is a conscious decision to continue puttin myself first. Love, love is always the key. When I put love first more love was poured into my life. God gave me an extended family that poured out constant love and support. A family I can travel with, eat with, smile with and build with. At the same time when I made forgiveness a priority I found it easier to forgive.

I had spoken to Renee a.k.a Romeo only a handful of times since she revealed who she truly was. I had some questions but also thought things were betta left unsaid. It took a lot for me to forgive myself for being so foolish and ignoring all the warning signs. Every time I tried to think about it I would get a headache and slowly I stopped remembering certain details. It was weird talkin to her on the phone cause I could still hear his voice. I asked if she used a device to make her voice deep, she said no. I asked her who the picture was, she said a friend of hers who was married with kids. It was a lot but strangely as much as all of this was done to me I was trying to put myself in her shoes to understand her side of it all. My flesh wanted to be mad but the God in me was workin on me. I was driving to Toronto one day and her name popped into my head, my heart had started hurting but I was smiling and all I could think of was ok God ok, I won't hate her. I brushed it off and about two weeks later I was at an event and there she was. In the flesh. It's crazy how our minds work cause from the time she confessed that she was Romeo my mind instantly brought me back to a time when "his cousin" had showed up at my apartment to conduct some survey for work. Then a couple weeks ago I had convinced her to go on skype to confirm the image I had already seen in my mind. It was like a knowing, all of a sudden from the day at my apartment to the screen on skype to here in person my mind knew exactly who she was. I had always been better remembering faces than names. So here and now, in this moment, she had showed up to an event I was at. *I had casually mentioned this event but I didn't expect her to come.* My mind was completely tripping out and because of the space I was in I couldn't even make a scene. I had to act as normal as possible. The craziest thing to me was that as I looked at her, I couldn't feel one ounce of hurt, anger, hatred, rage or jealousy, nothing but peace. I knew God had healed me. Who else but God could have given me complete peace in a situation such as this?

Forgiveness happens at different levels. It's similar to the way that people ask families of murdered loved ones how they can ever forgive. What I learned in the moment was that the forgiveness wasn't for her... it was for me. It was for my own peace, my own mental state, my own freedom from the bondage of hatred. I couldn't do it alone though, I needed God to begin the work of healin in me. I didn't have the capacity to forgive on my own just like I had no capacity to hate. Not the men who raped me, not the people who doubted me, not my aunt's boyfriend who molested me, not the cops who didn't protect me, not the men who stole from me, not my family who ridiculed me, not the friends who abandoned me, not for my own foolish mistakes and especially not for my son's death. I could no longer hate. I needed to live in love always. I went from being a Casualty Of Love's Apologies to living Confidently Open, Loving Always. Welcome to C.O.L.A's story, this is just the beginning.

Poetic Interlude

What do you wanna be when yu grow up?
That's the question they always ask me but they ask me with the assumption that growin up is what I wanted to do.
What about jus living
What about living care free
What about living care free as a child
Without worry
Without doubt
Without false certainty
Of Hopes and dreams that may never materialize
The lies lie in the disguise that we overcome as children
I believe at age 9 I wanted to be a piano teacher
Classically trained
Indulged in the beauty of Chopin studying the technicalities of liszt
Romanced by the notes of rachmaninoff
But I got pregnant at 16 and the dream gave birth to a new vision
When I grow up, I wanna be the best mother I can be
Now there's all this pressure on me and my reality is stuffed into stereotypes that I didn't want
Placed by ppl who dont know me
They attempt to lay guilt
Manipulating the truth that not everyone has it all figured out
That's what God is for
An yet they keep staring
Tearing me apart with their uninvited opinions
That I'm choosing to walk away from
I love that I don't have all the answers
At least not the answers that would be deemed acceptable
Accept that I am only able more like capable of being who God has chosen me to be
Like destiny already met fate and have collaborated to throw me a surprise when I finally arrive alive to my years of adolescents

This nonsense
This craze
This phase of becoming older is not gifted to everyone
I met a young boy
He was cheerful, buoyant, wise
Had a fascination with cars and when asked the same question,
What do you wanna be when you grow up
Without hesitation he gleefully said a race car driver
His dream far bigger than his ability but his possibilities were endless
Until the end came and although he was years above wise
His eyes did not see past 8
Did not meet at the gate of teens much less adolescence
This boy was my son
My son taught me to love everyday and see it filled with potential
Consequential understanding that its more of a blessing than a right of passage to grow older
Soldiers of gratefulness for the life I've gotten to live
The great
the challenging
and the beautiful growth that endured
So now when you ask me what do I wanna be when I grow up
I will simply answer
Alive
Living by purpose

CHAPTER SEVENTY-SEVEN

Live

I choose to live happy
I choose to live healthy
I choose to live whole
I choose to live full of life
I choose to live joyful
I choose to live in peace
I choose to live with patience
I choose to live in trust
I choose to live without judgement
I choose to live in abstinence
I choose to live without depression
I choose to live without anxiety
I choose to live without stress
I choose to live transparently
I choose to live fearlessly
I choose to live boldly
I choose to live impactfully
I choose to live free
Matthew 22: 34 Now when the Pharisees heard that He had
silenced (muzzled) the Sadducees, they gathered together.
35 One of them, a lawyer [an expert in Mosaic Law], asked
Jesus a question, to test Him: 36 "Teacher, which is the
greatest commandment in the Law?" 37 And Jesus replied
to him, " 'You shall love the Lord your God with all your
heart, and with all your soul, and with all your mind.' **38
This is the first and greatest commandment. 39 The
second is like it,** 'You shall love your neighbor as yourself
[that is, unselfishly seek the best or higher good for others].'
40 **The whole Law and the** [writings of the] **Prophets
depend on these two commandments."**

I choose to live lovingly.

Choose Love.

EPILOGUE

Mom & Dad

To my parents,

Thank you for the life you've blessed me with. It is not always easy to give your all when you yourself have your own growing to do. I understand that you have done the best you can at raising me. We have had our differences along the way but you have always remained as supportive as you could. As I grow and start to really understand human behaviour I realize that at times my expectations of you were higher than they should have been. Because you carried the title of Mom and Dad it basically gave you the title of super human. I now understand how unfair a title it was to have given you cause we are all flawed human beings running the same race. My perspective and tales of how the past has been has no bearing on the type of future that we could have. Understand that I love you both. I apologize for anything that I have done to hurt you, and I forgive you for any challenges that have endured. I forgive myself for the expectations and limitations I have placed on you both as you were building and growing.

I believe in life we are tested and the greatest test of all is unconditional love. How does a person love past disappointment? Learning to let go is what I've learnt. There came a time when I had to grow despite my circumstances and disappointments. There was a time when I had to choose love despite my feelings. It's a powerful thing to have the choice to be free and the choice to love. Freedom is mental and spiritual because I can be free mentally even when I can't be free physically. As long as I am in control of my mind I will always have freedom. I say that to say that this story is of what my life used to be. I accept the past and the choices I have made as I move on to the future. I am grateful for all you have done for me. All the times you have come to my rescue and everything you have done for Kaykay.

Let us take this time to heal from the past and move forward in love as God continues to bless us.
Your daughter,
Nicola

Kaykay

Dear baby boy,

I love you. I miss you every day. It's taken me a while to accept what has happened. Well that's not true, I tried to accept it from the day of your funeral but sometimes it feels like you were a dream that I just woke up from. Sometimes when I think of you, I cry, cause I miss your hugs but I am extremely grateful for the life you allowed me to have with you. You were such an old soul, it felt like I was raising myself at times. It's been hard letting go cause I feel like if I let go I'll forget you and I never want to forget you. You were my first love. I got mad at myself the other day because I forgot what grade you would have been in. For the life of me my mind could not remember and my mind was saying *how dare you forget.* I have since had to put my mind on a time-out because I understand that whether or not I remember your age or your grade, our bond and our life will always be the most beautiful memories of moments and there's nothing that can erase that. Even if I cannot remember the exact details, the feelings, the laughter, the joy, the peace all of those memories still remain intact. I often say your quotes just so I can laugh all over again. I have your teddy bear that has your voice recorded and I play it from time to time to remind myself how meek and exciting your voice was.

I accept that there was nothing else I could have done to save you. I accept the fact that you were never mine to begin with. I accept the fact that you knew without a doubt that I loved you. You were always such a big part of me and now I carry on your legacy so people will know and understand your spirit. I know you have and will continue to heal so many people. Baby boy at just 8 years old you have impacted the world. You have served your purpose. I now see myself as a messenger to continue spreading your life, your gifts and your value with everyone I meet. You asked me if you were still famous. Please believe me, I will make sure your story is heard by everyone who needs a word of encouragement.

I vow now to cry tears of joy as I let go of the image I had of you and embrace the spirit of who you are. Freedom is a choice and I am so happy you are free from the bondages.

Till I see you again in heaven,
Mommy

ABOUT THE AUTHOR

Cola is a proud mother, entrepreneur and multidisciplinary artist from Toronto who developed a love for writing, poetry and the arts while completing her BFA in classical piano at York University. She has been involved in various community arts projects including the AMY Project, Remix Project, Forgiveness Project (F-You) and the Tarragon Young Playwrights Unit. She loves to blend her love of classical piano and spoken word to inspire healing and restoration. Whether it be with students at university or inmates in local jails, the power of her testimony has impacted lives . When she's not writing she's busy formulating and running a wellness brand with her sister. called Unforgivingly Pur. to find out more check out www.unforgivinglypur.com.